THE NAZI HOLOCAUST

THE NAZI HOLOCAUST

Historical Articles on the Destruction of European Jews

Edited by Michael R. Marrus

Series ISBN 0–88736–266–4

1. Perspectives on the Holocaust
   ISBN 0–88736–252–4

2. The Origins of the Holocaust
   ISBN 0–88736–253–2

3. The "Final Solution": The Implementation of Mass Murder
   ISBN 0–88736–255–9 vol. 1
   ISBN 0–88736–256–7 vol. 2

4. The "Final Solution" Outside Germany
   ISBN 0–88736–257–5 vol. 1
   ISBN 0–88736–258–3 vol. 2

5. Public Opinion and Relations to the Jews in Nazi Europe
   ISBN 0–88736–259–1 vol. 1
   ISBN 0–88736–254–0 vol. 2

6. The Victims of the Holocaust
   ISBN 0–88736–260–5 vol. 1
   ISBN 0–88736–261–3 vol. 2

7. Jewish Resistance to the Holocaust
   ISBN 0–88736–262–1

8. Bystanders to the Holocaust
   ISBN 0–88736–263–X vol. 1
   ISBN 0–88736–264–8 vol. 2
   ISBN 0–88736–268–0 vol. 3

9. The End of the Holocaust
   ISBN 0–88736–265–6

THE NAZI HOLOCAUST

Historical Articles on the Destruction of European Jews

---

1. Perspectives on the Holocaust

Edited with an Introduction by

Michael R. Marrus
University of Toronto

Meckler
Westport • London

Publisher's Note

The articles and chapters which comprise this collection originally appeared in a wide variety of publications and are reproduced here in facsimile from the highest quality offprints and photocopies available. The reader will notice some occasional marginal shading and text-curl common to photocopying from tightly bound volumes. Every attempt has been made to correct or minimize this effect.

The publisher wishes to acknowledge all the individuals and institutions that provided permission to reprint from their publications. Special thanks are due to the Yad Vashem Institute, Jerusalem, the YIVO Institute for Jewish Research, New York, and the Leo Baeck Institute, New York, for their untiring assistance in providing materials from their publications and collections for use in this series.

Library of Congress Cataloging-in-Publication Data

Perspectives on the Holocaust / edited by Michael R. Marrus.
p. cm. — (The Nazi Holocaust ; v. 1)
Includes index.
ISBN 0-88736-252-4 (alk. paper) : $
1. Holocaust, Jewish (1939–1945) — Historiography. I. Marrus, Michael Robert. II. Series.
D804.3.N39 vol. 1
940.53'18 s—dc20
[940.53'18] 89-12244
CIP

British Library Cataloging in Publication Data

Perspectives on the Holocaust. – (The Nazi Holocaust; v.1).
1. Jews, Genocide, 1939–1945
I. Marrus, Michael R. (Michael Robert) II. Series
940.53'15'03924

ISBN 0-88736-252-4
ISBN 0-88736-266-4 set

Meckler Corporation, 11 Ferry Lane West, Westport, CT 06880.
Meckler Ltd., Grosvenor Gardens House, Grosvenor Gardens, London SW1W 0BS, U.K.

Printed on acid free paper.
Printed in the United States of America.

Contents

Part One: The Holocaust in History

Part Two: Historical Writing on the Holocaust

Series Preface

The Holocaust, the murder of close to six million Jews by the Nazis during the Second World War, stands as a dreadful monument to mankind's inhumanity to man. As such, it will continue to be pondered for as long as people care about the past and seek to use it as a guide to the present. In the last two decades, historical investigation of this massacre has been unusually productive, both in the sense of extending our understanding of what happened and in integrating the Holocaust into the general stream of historical consciousness. This series, a collection of English-language historical articles on the Holocaust reproduced in facsimile form, is intended to sample the rich variety of this literature, with particular emphasis on the most recent currents of historical scholarship.

However assessed, historians acknowledge a special aura about the Nazis' massacre of European Jewry, that has generally come to be recognized as one of the watershed events of recorded history. What was singular about this catastrophe was not only the gigantic scale of the killing, but also the systematic, machine-like effort to murder an *entire* people — including every available Jew — simply for the crime of being Jewish. In theory, no one was to escape — neither the old, nor the infirm, nor even tiny infants. Nothing quite like this had happened before, at least in modern times. By any standard, therefore, the Holocaust stands out.

While Jews had known periodic violence in their past, it seems in retrospect that the rise of radical anti-Jewish ideology, centered on race, set the stage for eventual mass murder. As well, Europeans became inured to death on a mass scale during the colossal bloodletting of the First World War. That conflict provided cover for the slaughter of many hundreds of thousands of Armenians in Turkey, a massacre that Hitler himself seems to have thought a precursor of what he would do in the conquest of the German *Lebensraum*, or living space, in conquered Europe. Still, the extermination of every living person on the basis of who they *were*, was something new. For both perpetrators and victims, therefore, decisions taken for what the Nazis called the "Final Solution" began a voyage into the unknown. As the Israeli historian Jacob Katz puts it: "This was an absolute *novum*, unassimilable in any vocabulary at the disposal of the generation that experienced it."

For more than a decade after the war, writing on the Holocaust may be seen in general as part of the process of mourning for the victims — dominated by the urge to bear witness to what had occurred, to commemorate those who had been murdered, and to convey a warning to those who had escaped. Given the horror and the unprecedented character of these events, it is not surprising that it has taken writers some time to present a coherent, balanced assessment.

The early 1960s were a turning point. The appearance of Raul Hilberg's monumental work, *The Destruction of the European Jews*, and the trial of Adolf Eichmann in Jerusalem in 1961 stimulated debate and investigation. From Israel, the important periodical published by the Yad Vashem Institute [Holocaust Martyrs' and Heroes' Remembrance Authority], *Yad Vashem Studies*, made serious research available to scholars in English. German and American scholars set to work. Numerous academic conferences and publications in the following decade, sometimes utilizing evidence from trials of war criminals then underway, extended knowledge considerably.

As a result, we now have an immense volume of historical writing, a significant sample of which is presented in this series. A glance at the topics covered underscores the vast scale of this history. Investigators have traced the Nazi persecution of the Jews before the implementation of the "Final Solution," showing links both to Nazi ideology and antisemitic tradition. They have indicated how the Germans coordinated their anti-Jewish activities on a European-wide scale in the wake of their territorial conquests, drawing upon their own bureaucracy and those of their allies, enlisting collaborators and various helpers in defeated countries. They have also devoted attention to the victims — whether in East European ghettos or forests, in Central or Western Europe, or in the various concentration and death camps run by the *SS*. Finally, they have also written extensively on the bystanders — the countries arrayed against the Hitlerian Reich, neutrals, various Christian denominations, and the Jews outside Nazi-dominated Europe.

The volumes in this series permit the reader to sample the rich array of scholarship on the history of the Holocaust, and to assess some of the conflicting interpretations. They also testify to a deeper, more sophisticated, and more balanced appreciation than was possible in the immediate wake of these horrifying events. The literature offered here can be studied as historiography — scholars addressing problems of historical interpretation — or, on the deepest level, as a grappling with the most familiar but intractable of questions: How was such a thing possible?

* * *

I want to express my warm appreciation to all those who helped me in the preparation of these volumes. My principal debt, of course, is to the scholars whose work is represented in these pages. To them, and to the publications in which their essays first appeared, I am grateful not only for permission to reproduce their articles but also for their forbearance in dealing with a necessarily remote editor. I appreciate as well the assistance of the following, who commented on lists of articles that I assembled, helping to make this project an educational experience not only for my readers but also for myself: Yehuda Bauer, Rudolph Binion, Christopher Browning, Saul Friedländer, Henry Friedlander, Raul Hilberg, Jacques Kornberg, Walter Laqueur, Franklin Littell, Hubert Locke, Zeev Mankowitz, Sybil Milton, George Mosse, and David Wyman. To be sure, I have sometimes been an obstreperous student, and I have not always accepted the advice that has been kindly proffered. I am alone responsible for the choices here, and for the lacunae that undoubtedly exist. Special thanks go to Ralph Carlson, who persuaded me to undertake this project and who took charge of many technical aspects of it. Thanks also to Anthony Abbott of Meckler Corporation who saw the work through to completion. Finally, as so often in the past, I record my lasting debt to my wife, Carol Randi Marrus, without whom I would have been engulfed by this and other projects.

Toronto, July 1989

Michael R. Marrus

Introduction

How should historians address the Holocaust? Few of those who have written about the massacre of European Jewry have not at one time or another worried about the proper mode of analysis, the appropriate questions to ask, or the kinds of evidence to employ. The essays in this first section introduce those that follow by engaging these important issues.

What is immediately evident is the variety of approaches. Several writers have set their course by historical precedent — examining the ways in which this particular instance of mass murder was similar to and differed from others that had gone before. Virtually all writers would agree that the Nazi-organized murder of European Jews was an awesome landmark in human history — a break with previous massacres defined less by the magnitude of the slaughter than by the systematic and machine-like process of killing. To most historians, however, seeing the Holocaust in this way does not involve its separation from history; they seek, rather, to chart its place in the experience of mankind and to try to understand it as they would understand other episodes in times past.

Some of these articles explore the philosophical or political underpinnings of various interpretations. Others assess the emerging consciousness of a subject that required investigation and the evolution of various methodological approaches to it. Finally, several articles discuss particular national schools, notably those in Germany, the United States, and the Soviet Union. Among the questions of particular interest is the way in which contemporary political agendas help define how historians write about the Holocaust. The *Historikerstreit* — a current quarrel among historians in the German Federal Republic over how to interpret the history of the Third Reich and which returns incessantly to the Holocaust — is but one of many disputes that periodically rage over the subject.

This first section presents various points of departure for the historical study of the Holocaust in order to orient the reader to the analyses that follow. Taken together, these articles are a reminder that Holocaust history is at an early stage of its development, is conditioned by climates of opinion in which historians work, and is making considerable progress in its quest for historical understanding.

Part One
The Holocaust in History

EUROPEAN JEWRY BEFORE AND AFTER HITLER *

by

SALO W. BARON

As a historian, not an eyewitness or a jurist, I shall concern myself with the historical situation of the Jewish people before, during, and after the Nazi onslaught — the greatest catastrophe in Jewish history, which has known many catastrophes.

A historian dealing with more or less contemporary problems confronts two major difficulties. The first is that historical perspective usually can be attained only after the passage of time. The second is that much relevant material is hidden away in archives and private collections, which are usually not open for inspection until several decades have passed. In this instance, however, the difficulties have been reduced. The world has been moving so fast since the end of World War II, and the situation of 1961 so little resembles that of the 1930s, that one may consider the events of a quarter of a century ago as belonging almost to a bygone historic era, which the scholarly investigator can view with a modicum of detachment. In fact, a new generation has been growing up which "knew not Hitler." For its part, the older generation is often eager to forget the nightmare of the Nazi era. Hence that period has receded in the consciousness of man as if it had occurred long ago.

* *This article is based on a memorandum that Professor Baron prepared for himself when he was invited to testify at the Eichmann trial, in April 1961, on the Jewish communities destroyed by the Nazis. The Appendix contains an extract from the official transcript of this testimony.*

Furthermore, the amount of evidence available is quite extraordinary. The capture of many German archives by the Allied armies has opened up an enormous amount of information, of a kind not usually accessible until the passage of several decades. Many protagonists in the drama, moreover, have been extraordinarily articulate. Diaries, memoirs, and biographical records are so numerous that huge bibliographies would have to be compiled merely to list them. With respect to the Jewish tragedy alone, the more significant publications are abundant enough for Jacob Robinson and the late Philip Friedman to have initiated a lengthy series of specialized bibliographical guides, some of which are yet to appear. It is possible, therefore, to attempt within this brief compass a concise evaluation of the broad transformations in the life of European Jewry brought about by the twelve years of the Nazi regime, first in Germany and later in the other German-occupied areas.

European Jewry in the 1930s

The general impression created by the Jewish people in Europe just before the Nazi era was one of extraordinary resourcefulness and vitality in the midst of a great world crisis and an equally severe crisis in Jewish life. The period between the First and Second World Wars in Europe generally resembled a prolonged armistice rather than genuine peace. The breakup of the established order; the rise of new states; the spread of Communist propaganda and the various Fascist and statist experiments in government; inflation, followed in 1929 by the Great Depression; the accelerating drive towards autarchy; the closing of frontiers to free migration; and, not least, the accompanying extremist doctrines in scholarship, letters, and the arts — all helped to keep Europe in a state of permanent tension. In Jewish life, the collapse of the oppressive Tsarist empire, the international guarantees for both equality of rights and minority rights in most of the newly arisen states, and the Palestine Mandate had inspired hopes that contrasted sharply with the reality of ill-treatment in most of the territories of mass Jewish settlement, from the Baltic to the Aegean.

Such far-reaching transformations called for great ingenuity and a pioneering spirit. With courage and perseverence the Jewish people tried to adjust to the new situation not merely passively, but independently and creatively. Accustomed through the long history of their dispersion to such creative readjustments, they were able to develop during the interwar period certain new forms of communal and cultural living which fructified Jewish life throughout the world, contributed significantly to human civilization, and held out great promise for the future. All this was cut short by the Nazi attack, unprecedented in scope, geographic extension, and murderous intensity.

Demographic Changes

Some of the challenges and creative readjustments of the interwar period arose out of the increasing urbanization, even metropolitanization, of the Jewish people. The Jews had long been urban. In Eastern Europe, especially, the *shtetl,* the small town, often had a Jewish majority. Subsequently many of these small-town Jews moved into the bigger cities of their own countries — like many Christians — and others emigrated to the rapidly growing European centers of London, Paris, and Berlin. Still others went overseas, particularly to New York, Chicago, and Buenos Aires.

By the early 1930s the metropolitanization of the Jewish people had progressed so far that fully a quarter lived in cities with more than a million population and another quarter in cities with 100,000 to 1,000,000 inhabitants. Some 12 per cent of all world Jewry lived in New York alone, their overwhelming majority having arrived from Eastern Europe in the preceding half century. This transformation was equally pronounced within the Soviet Union, where the two capitals of Moscow and Leningrad, lying outside the former Pale of Settlement, opened their gates to the Jews after the revolution. In 20 years their

Jewish population increased from 2,000 and 3,000, respectively, to 400,000 and 250,000. Warsaw and Budapest had also become cities with populations exceeding a million, with almost 600,000 Jews between them. It was in the great cities of Europe and America that the major decisions were made about the economic and political destinies of the world's leading nations and that most of the artistic, literary, and scientific movements originated. The Jews played their part.

Metropolitanization had its negative consequences, especially a sharp drop in population growth. Sociologists of the interwar period observed that these great concentrations of humanity as a rule did not reproduce themselves naturally, but had to replenish themselves from the constant stream of immigrants from their own and other countries. Some historical studies have shown that even earlier, between 1550 and 1750, several German cities had averaged only 80 to 90 birth for every 100 deaths. The other factors in the declining birth rate among the Western nations — the emancipation of women, the growing predilection for comforts, increasingly effective methods of birth control, and the like — had the stronger impact on the Jewish masses as so much larger a proportion of their population lived in the great cities. In Germany where we have relatively reliable population statistics, it was shown that between 1911 and 1924 Jewish mortality had exceeded natality by 18,252 in Prussia alone, whereas the general Prussian population had had a surplus of birth of 3,019,000. Between 1925 and 1928 Prussian Jewry lost 5,100 through such natural causes, while the general population grew by 1,180,000. These conditions were further aggravated by the growing number of mixed marriages, with their doubly negative effect upon Jewish population growth — their generally small fertility, and the fact that most children of such marriages were raised in the Christian faith. By 1930 the sociologist Ernst Kahn had calculated that if German Jews were to preserve their existing numbers, their families would have to average seven children, a wholly utopian expectation. To a lesser extent these factors operated also in other western lands and began affecting even the mass concentrations of Jews in Eastern Europe. The first Soviet census, in 1926, revealed that the previously extremely fertile Russian Jews now had one of the lowest birth rates of the major Soviet nationalities.

All this was in sharp contrast to the evolution of the Jewish people in the previous two or three centuries. Although this was the period of the greatest expansion of the European population, the Jewish people had expanded even more rapidly than its neighbors. From the mid-19th century to 1930 the ratio of Jews to the total European population had increased from approximately 1.5 per cent to 2 per cent. At the same time, European Jews had sent out disproportionately numerous emigrants to other continents, particularly the Americas. For this growth a decisive factor was the much lower mortality of Jewish children, particularly in the great reservoir of Jewish life from the Baltic to the Aegean. For one example, it was found that in 1929 and 1930 child mortality among the Catholics of the city of Vilna amounted to 243 per 1,000 births during the first year and to 370 during the first five years of life, while among the Jews of Vilna the corresponding figures were 106 and 198. Even during the interwar period the Jewish population of the world, and particularly of East-Central Europe, was still increasing rapidly. According to the estimates of the statistician Jacob Lestschinsky, the average annual increase of world Jewry during the 1920s was 140,000. It declined to 120,000 in the 1930s, a decade of crisis, hardship, and imminent peril.

This was a time when there was such a general drop in the growth of all western nations that sociologists freely predicted that, within a few decades, the West European and North American peoples would actually begin to decline in numbers. Had not France already had a stationary population for several decades?

Those predictions have not come true; indeed, there has been a "population explosion" all over the world, and France herself has grown substantially. It stands to reason, therefore, that the Jewish people, too, which, in the face of tremendous adversities, had been able to grow in numbers for many generations, would likewise have been able to resume its upward progression. (In Israel, for example, the Jews have continued to grow in numbers.) As in earlier centuries, the Jews maintained their high standards of family life, which succeeded in overcoming even some of the corroding influences of modern civilization. Now that the very metropolises of Europe have resumed their biological growth, Jews would the more fully have shared in the reversal of the interwar downward trend, as urban living had become almost second nature to most of them. In short, one of the most ancient of peoples has revealed throughout the modern period an extraordinarily youthful resilience and recuperative power. These would have led to a substantial increase in its numbers, had it not been for the Nazi catastrophe.

It was between the Atlantic and Moscow that the overwhelming majority of the approximately 9,800,000 European Jews were concentrated in the mid-1930s. Among the most important countries of Jewish settlement were Poland, which, together with Danzig, had a Jewish population of approximately 3,040,000 in 1931; the Soviet Union, which by 1932 was likewise reaching a total of some 3,000,000 Jews; Germany, whose 1933 census showing 499,682 Jews had to be increased by the 3,117 in the Saar in 1935; Austria, with 191,480 in 1934; Hungary, with 444,567 in 1930; Rumania, with 728,115 in 1930; Czechoslovakia, with 356,830 in 1930; France, with 320,000, in 1939; Holland, with 156,817 in 1933, and Lithuania, which as early as 1923 had counted 155,125 Jews. There were several other countries whose Jewish populations, though each less than 100,000, played a considerable role in the economy and culture. Because of the slight divergence in the dates here given, these figures are not absolutely comparable; nevertheless, because of the restricted migration at that time, they give a fairly adequate picture.

The emigration of Jews overseas, which had played such a tremendous role in the preceding decades, had dwindled to a minimum during the early 1930s as a result of the legislative enactments and administrative practices in the United States and elsewhere. Nevertheless, those overseas communities could still be considered to all intents and purposes as demographic extensions of East-Central European Jewry. Less than a generation had passed since one of the most astounding mass migrations of modern times. In only 24 years, from 1890 to 1914, 30 per cent of all European Jewry had moved to other continents. The impressive biological, communal, and cultural expansion of the Jews of the Tsarist empire, Austria-Hungary, Rumania, and Germany established the great new Jewish centers of population in the United States, Canada, Argentina, and South Africa, and laid the foundations for the Palestinian and Israeli *Yishuv*. At the same time, the European communities succeeded in maintaining and even increasing their population, in absolute figures. Despite the restrictions upon migration in the interwar period, the intimate relationships between the European mother communities and these overseas offshoots resulted in a basic religious, cultural and communal unity. A study of the Jewish *landsmanschaften* in New York, published in 1938, revealed no fewer than 3,000 such organizations, each of which still maintained, wherever possible, close ties with its mother community. Some of these American organizations actually had a larger membership than the entire Jewish population which had remained behind.

Economic Trends

The rapid dislocations within European Jewry, combined with economic transformations throughout the world, had tremendous effects on the economic status and pursuits of the Jews. In the preceding decades modern capitalism had become established in Eastern Europe, many old patterns of occupational life underwent severe, often painful, readjustments. These changes were accelerated by the Bolshevik Revolution, which directly affected about three million Jews, most of whom were at an early stage of the capitalist evolution. Various ideologies, socialist as well as middle-class, had long demanded a thoroughgoing reordering of the Jewish occupational structure, thus intensifying the challenge from within and without. Once again it was a testimony to the basic vitality and creativity of European Jews in the interwar period that, instead of passively submitting to these enormous pressures, they took an active part in rethinking and reshaping their economic realities.

Of course, capitalism itself was under sharp attack, with Jewish intellectuals among its sharpest critics. Yet no reasonable student of history ventured to deny its tremendous accomplishments in transforming western civilization from feudal backwardness into modern abundance. The creative role of European Jewry in this transformation, first in Western, then in Central, and finally in Eastern Europe, was universally acknowledged by friend and foe alike even in the 1930s. To be sure, the evaluation of that role was subject to bias, both pro- and anti-capitalist, pro- and anti-Jewish. But the fact that, upon being allowed to emerge from behind the medieval ghetto walls, Jews had contributed greatly to the new forms of mass production, mass distribution, international exchange, and finance could not be denied by any but the most obscurantist Jew-baiters.

Intrigued by the observation that Spain and Portugal, the leading economic powers in the late Middle Ages, had declined, while Holland, England, and France put themselves in the economic vanguard, as early as the 18th century many analysts attributed those changes in part to the expulsion of the Jews from the Iberian peninsula and their readmission to the other West European countries. In the 20th century Werner Sombart, the leading German student of the rise of modern capitalism — not particularly friendly to the Jews or to capitalism — exclaimed with his usual abandon: "Israel passes over Europe like the sun: at its coming new life bursts forth; at its going all fall into decay." Discarding such exaggerations, one may understand why 17th-century Amsterdam, rapidly growing by the admission of Jewish refugees from the Iberian peninsula and war-torn Germany and Poland, so greatly helped Holland to become the great center of international trade and the leading money market in the western world. To displace this "New Jerusalem," London made strenuous efforts to attract Jewish capitalists. As early as 1697, when the entire Jewish status in England was under debate, some 10 per cent of the seats on the Stock Exchange were reserved for Jewish brokers. From that time on Jewish bankers, businessmen, and their professional advisers played a significant part in all western capitalist countries.

In the great era of railroad building in the 19th and early 20th centuries, Jewish bankers like the Péreires and Bishcofsheims in France and Belgium, the Rothschilds in Austria, and the Poliakoffs in Russia were highly instrumental in spreading the network of transportation so essential to production and distribution. Even in far-off America it was an emigrant from Frankfurt, Jacob Schiff, under whose leadership the banking firm of Kuhn, Loeb and Company helped between 1881 and 1920 to launch loans exceeding a billion dollars for the Pennsylvania Railroad, still the largest American railway system. While less active in the heavy industries producing coal, oil, and iron, Jewish businessmen played a part in developing the Baku, Galician, and Rumanian oil fields, the coal and iron works in the Moravian basin, and the like. But their main interest was in such time-honored industries as gold and silver smithery, the production and cutting of diamonds, and particularly the lighter industries of textiles, clothing, and food processing, and eventually modern mass communications.

Perhaps the most basic transformation was the entry of Jews into the professions, from which they had long been barred by medieval legislation. While medicine was practised with distinction by many Jews in all periods, the legal profession was opened to them only with the modern emancipatory movements. The number of Jewish lawyers and doctors increased so greatly that in many East European cities they were the majority in their professions. So many Jewish students sought admission to schools of higher learning that Tsarist Russia enforced a *numerus clausus* on their admission. Interwar Poland did the same, reducing the percentage of Jews attending universities and colleges from 24.6 in 1921-22 to 16.9 twelve years later. Nevertheless, even in 1933 the ratio of Jews in universities and professional schools was still the highest in the Polish population. At one time both Czechoslovakia and Fascist Italy deliberately attracted Jewish students from Poland and Rumania. Swiss, French, Belgian, and other universities also received East European Jewish students — besides, of course, native Jews. In Italy a study published in 1931 showed that a quarter of all Jewish men 20 years old and over had studied or were studying at schools of higher learning.

Although there was a world-wide expansion of the professions, and Jews were by no means alone in seeking entry, in such times of distress as the depression of the 1930s Jewish "domination" of this or that profession became a ready target for anti-Semitic attack. The fact that Jews were something like 13 per cent of all Prussian attorneys — not of the judiciary — while only 1 per cent of the population, could be used to good advantage by agitators appealing to the "superfluous generation" of German students and intellectuals. It did not matter that the presence of a large body of Jews in the professions was the result of free choice, not conspiracy, and that they made a significant contribution to the general welfare.

Many Jews, affected by their enemies' deprecation, believed that the "lopsided" concentration of Jews in trade, the professions, and light industry was unhealthy, both for themselves and for society as a whole. The trend throughout the world was that of an accelerating transfer of population from the country to the city and from agriculture and manual labor to white-collar occupations. Going against that trend, the Jews made strenuous efforts to return to the soil and to enter industry.

EUROPEAN JEWRY BEFORE AND AFTER HITLER

At a time when millions of farmers were knocking at the gates of cities and factories, Jews—aided and encouraged by some governments, including that of the hostile Nicholas I in Russia—undertook major efforts at colonization on land. In the Soviet Union such efforts were fairly successful. Within a decade after the revolution the Jewish farming population included 33,357 families, or some 165,000 persons, living in special Jewish colonies, besides 32,800 families in other regions. In the aggregate, the Jewish farmers amounted to some 10 per cent of Russian Jewry, already rivaling in size the steadily declining merchant group. In Carpatho-Ruthenia nearly 28 per cent of the Jews were farmers. Equally noteworthy achievements were registered by Jews from Eastern Europe in the United States, in Argentina, and most far-reachingly in Palestine before and after the rise of the State of Israel, where the saga of the *halutzim* has filled some of the most memorable pages in 20th-century history.

Jews also entered the modern industrial working class in large numbers. There had always been many Jewish artisans. Despite immemorial guild restrictions, the Jews of Poland, Lithuania, and neighboring countries were able to maintain a large artisan class, which sometimes reached one-third of their population. But industrialization was the doom of handicrafts, converting most artisans into factory workers. Jewish communal leaders often tried to channel Jewish craftsmen into industrial labor, as well as to ease the passage. They were particularly successful in the countries of immigration, such as the United States, England, and France, where the new arrivals had to make a fresh start and where most could find employment only in factories. In the older countries, on the other hand, Jewish workers and would-be workers often were discriminated against by other workers. Wherever there were enough Jewish workers, they preferred to organize labor unions of their own. They cooperated with the other unions, although they often suffered the hostility both of their fellow workers and of the state authorities. (An incident during the May Day celebration of 1923 in

Lodz was characteristic: the Polish, German, and Jewish workers marched separately and, when the latter were attacked by the police, the two other groups looked on passively.) At the same time, many Jewish intellectuals became active as organizers of general labor unions and as spokesmen for socialist ideologies. Thus, from the so-called people of bankers and traders, frequently denounced by such socialist thinkers as Karl Marx or Charles Fourier, whose disciple Alphonse Toussenel circulated in the 1840s a typical anti-Semitic tirade against "the Jews, kings of our period," there emerged labor leaders and socialists, such as Ferdinand Lassalle, Eduard Bernstein, Leon Trotsky, and, in the United States, Samuel Gompers, an immigrant from Europe.

It was not then generally foreseen that technological progress would so speedily shrink the relative and even the absolute size of manual labor and swell the service industries and white-collar classes. A study conducted under the auspices of President Hoover in the United States in the 1920s had shown the continued decline, decade after decade, of manual labor in the United States. Today 9 per cent of the American population grows enough not only to supply the needs of the American people, and to help feed millions throughout the world, but also to create the enormous agricultural surpluses which have been plaguing successive American administrations for decades. In the early 1930s the 10 per cent of Jews who were farmers in the Soviet Union constituted but a small fraction of Russia's huge peasantry; since then, more and more of the farmers of Russia, the Ukraine, and other Soviet republics have become workers, technicians, and engineers. In Germany, too, between 1907 and 1925 the number of manual workers had declined by 4 per cent, while that of white-collar employees increased by 50 per cent. (In fact, it was by appealing to the white-collar workers, long neglected by socialist theorists, that Fascism in Italy and Nazism in Germany made their greatest strides.) Not surprisingly, therefore, the conversion of Jewish craftsmen into factory workers or of Jewish city dwellers into farmers was not fully successful. But even the partial success was impressive evidence of a people facing the challenges of a new age with courage and vigor.

Viewed from a historical perspective, the enormous economic difficulties confronting the Jews in the interwar period appear to have been the temporary accompaniment of profound historical transformation. In the long run the Jewish vocational distribution, so different then, merely foreshadowed the major trends of our technological era. The sharp contrast in occupation between the Jews and their neighbors has been gradually disappearing, not so much because the Jews have changed as because the Western world has become increasingly "Jewish" in its economic structure.

Emancipation

Jewish Emancipation is usually considered to date back to the American and French Revolutions. That is only partially true. Emancipatory trends are both older and newer than those dramatic 18th-century events. I have long believed that Jewish political and legal emancipation cannot be fully understood apart from economic and cultural emancipation, whose contours had already been decisively shaped a century or two before the revolutionary era. On the other hand, it required protracted struggles throughout the 19th and early 20th centuries before legal equality was promulgated on paper in most other European lands. What is more, the constant migratory movements, Jewish interdependence, and external hostility meant that emancipation in one country remained incomplete if Jews were not emancipated in other countries as well. A mere 50 years ago nearly half of world Jewry resided in Tsarist Russia, whose policies were sharply discriminatory. If we add the Jewish populations of Rumania, the Ottoman empire (where the Young Turks revolution of 1909 had only begun to transform the deeply-rooted medieval Islamic institutions), North Africa, the Yemen, and similar countries, we find that two-thirds of world Jewry then lacked even the prerequisites of formal equality.

In the very countries of Emancipation, such as the United States and France, where equality had formally reigned supreme for more than a century, shortly before the First World War most Jews were recent immigrants from Russia, Rumania, and the Ottoman empire, who had not changed overnight by moving from a country of inequality to one of Emancipation. It was, therefore, only after the Russian revolution of 1917 and the peace treaties of 1919 with Poland, Rumania, the Baltic states, and others that the Jewish people seemed to emerge for the first time into an era of freedom and equality. At least on paper, Jews were guaranteed equal treatment in all the constitutions of the newly arisen or enlarged states in Europe and the Near East, and a genuine emancipation on a world-wide scale seemed to be a realistic expectation.

Jewish leaders, realizing that a minority needed additional safeguards for the maintenance of its identity, were concerned also with the supplementation of equality by minority rights. It was a major Jewish achievement that the peace conference of 1919 promulgated for the first time the principle of minority rights as an instrument of internal peace in some multinational states — an idea whose merit has not been canceled by the neglect or violations arising out of the sharp nationalist conflicts of the interwar period. Though the Jews were specifically mentioned only in the treaties with Poland and Turkey, the new international safeguards were intended to benefit the Jewries of all the new or newly enlarged countries from the Baltic to the Aegean. Czechoslovakia and Estonia most fully lived up to those guarantees. The other countries, particularly Poland and Rumania, from the outset sabotaged not only minority rights — whose international safeguarding they considered, with some justification, as an invidious infringement of their sovereignty — but also the very equality of their Jewish citizens. Nonetheless, the Jews persisted in their struggle for genuine equality and minority rights in those countries as well. Looking back at the progress made during the preceding century, Jewish leadership must have felt justified in expecting victory of the egalitarian principle.

It is now three years since I had the honor to address an audience at the Hebrew University in Jerusalem on "Newer Approaches to Jewish Emancipation." In that lecture, subsequently published in UNESCO's *Diogène* (in French) and *Diogenes* (in English), I tried to make clear that Jewish emancipation was an even greater necessity for the modern state than it was for the Jews, and that even if Jewry had been unanimous in rejecting it — there were indeed some Jewish circles which preferred the accustomed ways of the ghetto to the new forms of integration into the western nations — the modern state would have had to force its Jewish subjects to accept equality. In fact, however, a growing majority of Jews not only accepted Emancipation but was prepared to fight hard for it, on general principles as well as on utilitarian grounds.

At the beginning of this century, in the dark era of the Kishinev pogroms and Pobedonostsev's reactionary regime, it nevertheless appeared to most observers in Russia and abroad that the universal acceptance of Jewish equality was only a matter of time. Count Vladimir Nicholaevich Lamsdorf, Russia's minister of foreign affairs, was desperate when he tried to persuade the Tsar that the revolution of 1905 had been directed by the forces of world Jewry, led by the Alliance Israélite Universelle, "which possesses gigantic pecuniary means, disposes of an enormous membership, and is supported by Masonic lodges of every description." On the basis of this obvious canard the minister suggested to Nicholas II a confidential exchange of views with William II of Germany and the Pope in order to organize united action against this alleged foe of both Christianity and the monarchical order. Notions of that kind also animated the authors of the *Protocols of the Elders of Zion,* which after the First World War attained a sinister notoriety and influence. But the progress of Emancipation seemed irresistible. Every liberal, whether a Jew or not, firmly believed that the progress of civilization would almost automatically overcome the vestiges of medieval obscurantism and establish Jewish equality everywhere.

In this respect the developments in Germany represented a decisive turn. In general, Germany served throughout the 19th and early 20th centuries as a sort of public forum for a discussion of "the Jewish question." Unfortunately, anti-Semitism had representatives among the German social and intellectual elite, from Jakob Friedrich Fries and Christian Friedrich Rühs in 1816 to Richard Wagner, Heinrich Treitschke, Paul de Lagarde, and Houston Stewart Chamberlain at the end of the century. Their respectability was a cover for the hoodlum kind of Jew-baiting which spread among the masses. However, so long as the movement remained limited to literary outpourings and, at worst, led to the formation of small parliamentary minorities, it could still be shrugged off as an echo of past ages which might slightly retard, but never wholly impede, the invincible march towards progress and equality. As the Nazi movement gradually achieved political power, however, its program of revoking Emancipation not only became a serious menace to German Jewry as such, but also set a far-reaching example for all anti-emancipatory forces throughout the world.

Jews tried to meet the challenge as best as they could, but from the outset they could do relatively little to combat it. Anti-Semitism has long been recognized as being essentially a disease of Gentile nations, generated by a disequilibrium of social forces wholly beyond the control of the Jewish communities. Only a strong resistance by the non-Jewish body politic could effectively eliminate it. In a few cases, when society at large recognized the dangers inherent in the spread of this virulent infection, it did take the necessary measures. Edouard Drumont's *La France juive,* whose appearance in some hundred French editions and many translations shortly after its publication in 1886 attested to its enormous popularity, and the ensuing Dreyfus case speedily taught such progressive Frenchmen as Emile Zola and Georges Clemenceau that their own future and that of the Third Republic were at stake. They succeeded, therefore, in rallying progressive France around their standard and staving off the attack. Nothing of the sort happened in Germany, where the liberal and socialist forces were deeply divided and where the Communist party actually collaborated with the Nazis in the overthrow of the Weimar Republic. But Jews did much to warn their neighbors of the menace of anti-Semitism to the Christians themselves. It was they who marshalled the evidence to demonstrate the falsehoods of the anti-Semitic accusations — a hopeless task, indeed, since falsehoods can always readily be replaced by other falsehoods, whereas the truth can only be one and the same. Many liberals, Jews and non-Jews, failed to realize the demonic strength of the irrational forces which were about to set Europe on fire.

Some German Jews, ably assisted by East European Jewish thinkers, now began to think seriously about the restoration of their people to its ancestral homeland as one answer to the problem of Jewish life in the dispersion. The Zionist movement became the most potent force in Jewish life during the interwar period. Its rise has sometimes been attributed by unfriendly observers to the Jews' reaction to modern anti-Semitism and their despairing conviction that "the Jewish problem" could never be solved satisfactorily by emancipation. Undeniably, such a reaction was an important factor. At the same time, Zionism was also nurtured by the ancient yet vigorous messianic hope. With the secularization of modern life generally, this old religious expectation necessarily assumed among the Jews the guise of a secular national movement. The concentration of the Jewish masses in Eastern and Central Europe, their continued use of Yiddish, the persistence of their traditional folkways — all furnished a realistic background for a national revival that was bound to come, whether or not there was hostility on the outside. It was, indeed, shortly before and after the First World

SALO W. BARON

War that almost all the shades of Zionist ideology received their more or less definitive formulations in Eastern and Central Europe and led to the formation of the various Zionist parties still dominating the public life of Israel today.

Jewish political thinking was also expressed in other movements. In Simon Dubnow's and Hayyim Zhitlowsky's diaspora nationalism an effort was made to establish Jewish national minority rights on a permanent basis within the countries of the dispersion. That expectation may have been foredoomed from its very beginning, but it came to a definite end only with the Nazi New Order. Ultimately, Dubnow himself fell victim to the Nazi conquerors of Riga, joining the millions of other victims of the great holocaust.

Among the socialist responses, that of the Russian Jewish Bund was particularly significant, since in 1897 it led to the formation of the first Jewish socialist party, whose influence on Russian socialism generally may be deduced from the fact that in 1905 it had 30,000 members, and the great Russian party had 50,000. So strong, indeed, were the national and Zionist feelings of Russian Jewry that, although before the First World War Lenin had repeatedly tried to deny the existence of a separate Jewish nationality, upon coming to power he speedily included the Jews among the national minorities whose cultural self-determination was to be safeguarded by the new Soviet regime. Nor were there lacking even in Eastern Europe intellectual spokesmen for Jewish assimilation. While some of them simply sought to escape the oppressive conditions of minority existence, others tried on more idealistic grounds to find new creative responses to the challenge of Emancipation, whether already achieved or yet to be attained.

Jews were not concerned with internal Jewish politics only. In Eastern and Western Europe there were many outstanding Jews in the general political life. In Léon Blum's premiership France fought her last, losing battle for national unity in the face of the German menace. Luigi Luzzatti had thrice been Italian prime minister, and his administrations belong to the happiest periods of Italy before the First World War. In Germany, where ever since the 1840s Jewish leaders participated in almost all significant political movements — Julius Friedrich Stahl, a Jew converted to Christianity, was often considered the chief intellectual leader of the Conservative party itself, which long fought Jewish Emancipation — the greatest statesman of the interwar era, Walther Rathenau, fell victim to Nazi terrorists.

In fact, all the services rendered by the Jews to the German cause, both nationally and internationally, failed to silence the reiterated accusation of lack of Jewish patriotism. To answer the anti-Semitic attacks, the German Jewish war veterans succeeded in listing by name no fewer than 10,623 Jewish soldiers who had given their lives for Germany during the First World War. There must have been more than 1,000 other victims who were not so listed, either because they came from territories subsequently lost to Germany by the peace treaties or because they could not be identified as Jews. Clearly, their ratio to the Jewish population far exceeded the total German ratio of the war-dead. In sum, in Germany, as in all the other countries of Emancipation, where the Jews were treated as equal citizens, they did their share — and more. What Sir Stuart Samuel had said in his report about the Polish Jews, after the First World War, had a melancholy application to many other countries as well: "The Jewish soldiers in Poland do their duty to their country in the certainty that their country will not do its duty by them."

Community Life

Emancipation and equality made great communal adjustment necessary. From ancient times the Jewish community had enjoyed much self-determination, not only in strictly religious matters but also in education, social welfare, and the administration of justice. Under Emancipation some of these prerogatives, originally supported by the European states themselves, had to be curtailed. The Jewish judiciary, in particular, lost much of its authority over the Jews in civil and criminal law, retaining jurisdiction mainly in religious and family affairs. Nevertheless, in Eastern and Central Europe many Jews continued, voluntarily, to submit their civil litigations to rabbinic courts, judging on the basis of Jewish law. Even in the 20th century legal problems were intensively studied by thousands of students of rabbinics both for theoretical reasons and for their practical application. Education, too, had to be shared now with the general school systems maintained by states and municipalities. However, as we shall see, the Jewish communities often maintained a ramified school system of their own, in supplementation to, or in substitution for, the public schools of the country. In social welfare, which until the modern development of the welfare state had always borne a predominantly denominational character, the Jewish communities strove, often with signal success, to take care of their own poor.

The Jewish communities revealed a remarkable adaptability to changing conditions. In France the reorganization of all Jewish communal life through the so-called consistorial system of the Napoleonic age was successfully maintained, with the necessary modifications, under the Napoleonic dictatorship, the Restoration, the Second Empire, and the Third Republic, despite the intimate relationships between the Jewish communal structure and the changing governmental controls. (Through most of that period the government actually defrayed a major part of the salaries of rabbis and other religious functionaries.) This structure was maintained on a voluntary basis after the separation of state and church in 1906. In the absence of governmental intervention, Jewish creativeness, especially during the interwar period, expressed itself in the formation of many new congregations, charitable associations, and cultural groupings, spontaneously organized by diverse immigrant groups. This rich and multicolored Jewish communal organization maintained a host of institutions serving the various needs of French Jewry and of Jews beyond the borders. On the other hand,

Italian Jewry, which during the liberal era of united Italy from 1871 to the rise of the Fascist regime had experienced a certain degeneration and disorganization of communities rich in traditions hundreds of years old — if not, as in Rome, two thousand years old — succeeded in regaining some unity and central guidance in the interwar period. In 1929 Benito Mussolini and the pope concluded the Lateran treaty, whereby the Catholic church was reestablished as Italy's dominant religion; in 1931 Jews secured from the dictator a new communal law reorganizing the Jewish communal life of the entire country under the leadership of a centralized *Unione.* Whether in Italy or in France, such central organization did not interfere with the autonomous workings of the individual communal groups, including the numerous voluntary associations. The balance reflected the age-old compromise between centralized controls and local self-government, in force ever since the Babylonian Exile and the Greco-Roman dispersion. The same unity within diversity was achieved also in Belgium, where the consistorial system along French lines had persisted throughout the interwar period, and in Holland, where since 1816 the Ashkenazi and Sephardi communities had central organizations in their "church associations." In particular, Amsterdam, that famous center of Jewish learning, had had a proliferation of Jewish voluntary associations as early as the 18th century. A characteristic will of an Amsterdam Jewish philanthropist, in the early years of the 19th century, provided bequests for over 200 charitable and educational societies.

Even more vigorous was Jewish community life in Germany and in the successor states of the Hapsburg empire. Although Prussia's community law of 1876 permitted the Jews to leave their community "for religious scruples," thus enabling some ultra-Orthodox Jews to form their independent congregations and others to leave the Jewish community altogether without joining another faith, the vast majority of Jews adhered to the traditional community, which was endowed by public law with the right of taxation for the support of its varied activities. In 1922 the Prussian communities organized a *Landesverband* to give these communal efforts a central direction, without interfering with the autonomy of the local groups. Similar *Landesverbände* were established in Bavaria and other states, while Baden and Württemberg had had such centralized guidance since the beginning of the 19th century. In the Austro-Hungarian empire, on the other hand, the diversity of its Jewries prevented the establishment of centralized authority, but the law of 1891 renewed, on a modern basis, the old public-law recognition of Jewish communal autonomy and taxing powers. Here, too, many secularized Jews had a choice of leaving the community without converting to another faith, but, in contrast to Prussia, they had to declare publicly their secession on the ground that they were *konfessionslos* (professing no religion). In fact, the number of such professedly irreligious Jews was rather limited, the majority respecting the authority of their elected leaders in religious and cultural affairs. In interwar Austria the numerical preponderance of Viennese Jewry was so pronounced (in 1934, 176,000 of the 191,480 Austrian Jews lived in the capital) that the Viennese rabbis and lay leaders had *de facto* leadership over all Austrian Jewry, without formal authority. In Hungary, where 46 per cent of the Jewish population resided in Budapest, the struggle between Reform and Orthodoxy had led in the 19th century to a separation between Orthodox and liberal communities. A group of united or so-called *status quo* communities bridged the gap, and gained formal recognition from the Hungarian government in 1929. From 1928 on, rabbis of both the Orthodox and liberal wings sat in the upper chamber of the Hungarian parliament as representatives of the Jewish community. Czechoslovakia had a more diversified structure, with Bohemia, Moravia, and Silesia largely following the Austrian pattern, while Slovakia and Carpatho-Ruthenia, besides maintaining the communal structure inherited from prewar Hungary, differed from the others in mores, speech, and intensity of Orthodoxy. This diversity stimulated rather than hindered Jewish creativeness.

EUROPEAN JEWRY BEFORE AND AFTER HITLER

That creativeness was richest in interwar Poland and Lithuania. In Poland, although the government of the new republic effectively sabotaged some of the minority safeguards of the 1919 peace treaty, the Jewish communities before and after the community law of 1931 enjoyed a great measure of autonomy. Of course, there were important organizational differences between the provinces formerly under Austrian or Prussian domination and those formerly under Russian rule. In the former, Emancipation had been achieved decades before the First World War, and the Jewish community had a more circumscribed status. In the latter, to be sure, the Tsar had abolished the *Kahal* in 1844, but a partly voluntary communal structure was quite vigorous. The size of the Jewish population and the fact that in most Polish cities the Jews were a substantial minority, if not an outright majority, made communal autonomy doubly meaningful. Its extension into many secular cultural domains was often imposed by the will of the Jewish population against considerable governmental resistance. In fact, Orthodoxy, forming only one of many parties, was not even in control of most communities. Despite full governmental support for Orthodoxy, which also found expression in the community law of 1931, the electorate often preferred leadership from the more secular Zionist and socialist parties. In the elections of 1936 many communal boards actually included members of the Socialist Bund as the largest party. Communal elections were taken with the utmost seriousness, being regarded as not less important than the parliamentary elections, in which a strong Jewish representation carried on the constant uphill struggle for Jewish rights. In Lithuania, where the assimilatory pressures of the relatively young nationalism were far less intense, Jewish communal self-government was even more extensive. Of the 19,500 Jews in the Lithuanian school population in 1930, 16,000 were in all-Jewish schools. Lithuania also had for some time a special ministry of Jewish affairs. To a lesser extent that was true of Latvia and Estonia as well.

Quite different were the conditions in the Soviet communities. On the one hand, the Communist ideology proved in many ways hostile to all traditional foundations of Jewish communal life: religion, the Hebraic heritage, and the messianic-Zionist hope. Together with other religions, Judaism was condemned as an opiate for the people and Jewish members of the atheistic societies actively sought to uproot all religious traditions among Jews. Hebrew was denounced as the language of religion and the bourgeoisie, while the Zionist movement was outlawed as a "tool of British imperialism." The leaders of the so-called *Yevsektsia* (the Jewish section of the Commissariat for Nationalities) were particularly ardent exponents of these anti-traditionalist views. On the other hand, the recognition of the Jews as one of the national minorities led to the raising of Yiddish to the status of the national language of that minority. In accordance with the nationality law of November 15, 1917, Jewish soviets were organized in localities where Jews formed the majority and Yiddish was used as an official language in judicial and administrative proceedings, especially in the Ukraine and White Russia. In 1930 there were 130 Ukrainian soviets using Yiddish as their main language, 23 such soviets in White Russia, and 14 in the Crimea. Farsighted observers, to be sure, even then realized the fragility of the Jewish communal structure, deprived of the age-old moorings of religion and Hebraism. They also suspected that what Lenin had written in 1903 still represented the true thinking of the Russian Communist party and that his concession in 1917 was only expediency. In his attack on the Bund, Lenin had written in 1903 that the idea of a Jewish nationality

> "has an evidently reactionary character not only in the form advocated by its consistent champions, the Zionists, but also in that of the Bundists, who try to combine it with social democracy. This idea runs counter to the interests of the Jewish proletariat inasmuch as it creates, directly and indirectly, an attitude hostile to assimilation, a ghetto philosophy."

Moreover, Lenin and particularly Stalin made it clear that minority rights for nationalities were meant to be merely a temporary measure, ultimately leading to "fusing them into one common culture with one common tongue." However, the permissiveness of the 1920s and even the 1930s led to a powerful upsurge of Jewish communal and cultural creativity, which was exploited for propaganda abroad.

In Rumania no effort was made to honor the international treaties concerning the minority rights of Jews. The growth of Rumanian nationalism and anti-Semitism led to numerous interventions by the authorities in Jewish communal and particularly educational affairs, which might have adversely affected Jewish cultural self-determination. For this reason no sustained effort was made to unify the diverse communal structures in the various provinces. Old Rumania still carried on with a Jewish community formed before 1918, in a period of total discrimination and the treatment of the Jews as aliens. At the same time Bessarabia, Bukovina, and Transylvania maintained the communal organizations inherited from the Russian, Austrian, and Hungarian denominations, respectively. All this impeded, but did not interrupt, the continued evolution of Jewish religious and cultural life in the country. A similar diversity existed in Yugoslavia between the provinces taken over from Hungary and Austria and those included in the old kingdom of Serbia. Like neighboring Bulgaria and Greece, Serbia had inherited from the old Ottoman empire a strong Jewish communal structure based upon the *millet* system, which allowed a large amount of self-determination to all non-Muslem minorities. Most of the communities in these three Balkan countries were relatively small and of limited influence. The major exception was the community of Salonika, which carried on its immemorial traditions from ancient Thessalonika. Although the Jewish community of Salonika had lost much of its pre-First World War population, it still embraced nearly three-quarters of all Greek Jewry and lived an intensely Jewish life. Its economic stratification was illustrated by the presence of a large number of Jewish longshoremen, which caused the important harbor of the city to be idle on the Sabbath. The vigorous religious and cultural life of the community, inherited from the Turkish era, made itself felt not only within the confines of Greece but all over the Sephardi world.

It would take us too far afield to discuss the variegated functions of these communal groups in any detail. The communities and their subdivisions took care of the religious needs of their constituents. They maintained synagogues, large and small, to accommodate as few as ten and as many as thousands of adult male worshippers. Since traditionally Jewish law did not consider the synagogue building but rather the congregation as essential, any ten Jews meeting almost anywhere, even in a cave or an open field, were able to worship as effectively as those assembled in a monumental edifice. This made it possible for even the smallest community or movement in Jewry, meeting if necessary in a private home, to perform religious services wholly on a par with those of the most elaborate synagogues. Of course, wherever possible communities lavished of their bounty on building and decorating magnificent structures, within the limitations of the anti-imagery injunctions of biblical law. But the beautiful baroque structure of Leghorn or the magnificent Sephardi synagogue in Amsterdam were no more cherished than the small Rashi Chapel of Worms, which, though not authentically going back to the times of the great 11th-century Bible commentator, was an important medieval monument of Jewish religious architecture. So was the *Altneuschul* in Prague, with its many memories of medieval Jewish life and with legends reaching back to pre-Christian antiquity. Similarly, the relatively small and inconspicuous wooden synagogues in certain Polish cities have long been recognized as genuine expression of a peculiarly Jewish architectural style, which added a significant chapter to the history of art. On the other hand, it was possible for the various hasidic groups, following their diverse leaders, to establish small conventicles of their own which, whether in their original East-Central European habitat or in their countries of immigration in Western Europe and the New World, readily developed into congregations of their own kind. But even this inherent diversity of rituals, rather than interfering with the basic unity of Jewish worship, merely kept the gate open to the creativity of poets, cantors, and preachers, which greatly enriched Jewish life.

From time immemorial these sacred structures stood under the protection of public life. Even in the pagan Roman empire any attack on a synagogue was considered as sacrilege. When, after the rise of Christianity to a dominant position in the Roman empire, some frenzied mobs tried to convert synagogues into churches, as a rule the emperors punished the evildoers, demanded restoration of the synagogues or, if it was too late, full compensation. One such incident led to the great controversy between Emperor Theodosius, himself rather unfriendly to the Jews, and St. Ambrose of Milan — one of the earliest recorded conflicts between state and church. Protection of Jewish houses of worship, indeed, was enjoined by canon and civil law and reiterated by popes, emperors, and kings throughout the Christian Middle Ages and early modern times. It was left to the Nazis during the *Kristallnacht* of November 9-10, 1938, to stage a wholesale destruction of synagogues as part of a well-thought-out "spontaneous" reaction of the German people. Two days later the infamous Reinhardt Heydrich rejoiced that in that night 101 synagogues had been destroyed and 76 others severely damaged, to the eternal "glory" of the Nazi party.

Similar vandalism affected the other major religious institution, the cemetery. For reasons which are perhaps not too difficult to explain, sadists of all ages often vented their spleen on the graves of deceased "enemies." In their so-called constitutions in favor of Roman Jewry, the popes found it necessary generation after generation to repeat their injunction against the violation of Jewish tombs. Secular legislation often followed suit, although many malefactors still found it possible to wreak vengeance on dead Jews, if they could not injure the living.

Not surprisingly, during the interwar period hoodlums often attacked Jewish cemeteries in Germany and other countries. The Jewish communities tried to stave off such attacks, repaired the damages, and generally kept their "houses of eternity" in good order. This communal function was all the more important in the 20th century, as many Jews who otherwise maintained few contacts with the Jewish community nevertheless sought their resting place in a Jewish burial ground. Incidentally, cemeteries could also serve as vehicles of social justice. Not only were the egalitarian forms of burial apt to level some class distinctions, but also cemetery administrations were often able to tax wealthy but uncharitable members above the average, thus somewhat equalizing the philanthropic and welfare burdens of their constituents.

Welfare activities were for the most part carried on by charitable associations acting under the supervision of the community at large. With the aid of philanthropically-minded individuals the community, directly or through its subdivisions, was able to establish a far-flung net of hospitals, orphanages, and homes for the aged; extend relief to the poor, in kind or money; take care of victims of fires and similar disasters; help the poor to educate their children or marry off their daughters, and create loan banks and otherwise help artisans and shopkeepers to embark upon new ventures or to weather a temporary emergency. Polish Jewry alone maintained 826 free-loan banks, with a capital of more than $2,000,000. The extent and ramifications of these activities were so great that hardly ever did a Jew die from actual starvation or lack of all medical care — though even in times of peace in the 20th century, famine and untreated disease still caused death in Europe. Jewish hospitals also helped to offset discrimination against Jewish physicians in general hospitals. They often also served as centers of medical research, the fruits of which accrued to the benefit of the world at large. Even where the separation between Jews and Gentiles had been traditionally very stringent, these hospitals and other

Jewish charitable institutions often helped Christians. On the whole, despite the growth of social consciousness and governmental welfare programs, the Jewish philanthropies still performed a major function in the interwar period and added another justification to the traditional claim of the Jewish people of being *rahamanim benei rahamanim,* merciful sons of merciful sires.

Intellectual Life

Among the most important communal activities was Jewish education. The Jewish people had an age-old insistence upon learning as a great virtue in itself and a vital fulfillment of man's mission on earth. With pride the Jews remembered that they were the first to introduce publicly supported schools for the entire male population from the age of six or seven. This great educational reform had been introduced in the first century, at a time when even the great Greco-Roman civilization was offering instruction only to a select few. It thus anticipated the modern public school by 17 centuries. Ever since, Jews cultivated the teaching of the youth as a major obligation of both the family and the community, while insisting also upon adult education to the end of one's life.

True to these traditions, interwar European Jewry maintained an elaborate school system and also provided extensive opportunities for self-instruction and adult education. It is truly remarkable with what creative élan the Jews of the newly independent Poland threw themselves into the task of building a novel system of education, corresponding to the different ideologies represented within the Jewish community. The Polish government, which sufficiently respected other minority rights to subsidize an extensive network of Ukrainian and German schools, evaded its responsibilities toward the independent Jewish school system, but the Jewish community was ready to expend its own money and effort. A large majority of the Orthodox population sent their children to the thousands of traditional *hadarim,* which either provided full-time instruction or gave supplementary Jewish education to the children attending the Polish public schools. In the 1930s 18,000 Jewish youth attended *yeshivot,* some of which were secondary schools up to college level. Besides these traditional schools were two major school systems, with Yiddish and Hebrew as languages of instruction. The Central Yiddish School Organization, the so-called CIShO, founded in 1921, drew its main support from the Bund and the Left Po'alei-Zion. Offering instruction in Yiddish, though using Polish for Polish history and geography, the CIShO schools had a secular curriculum with a predominantly socialist ideology. A statistical account for 1934-35, though incomplete, furnishes an idea of the size and extent of that system. The 86 schools listed gave instruction to 9,936 children, predominantly in the formerly Russian areas — 45 of those schools, with 4,730 pupils, being concentrated in the two provinces of Bialystok and Vilna alone. On the other hand, the central organization of Hebrew schools, called *Tarbut,* offered modern Hebrew instruction permeated with the Zionist ideology. In 1938 it had 70 school buildings and maintained 75 nurseries, 104 elementary schools, and 9 high schools, with an enrolment of 42,241 pupils and a staff of 1,350 teachers. Here again, most of those schools were in the eastern provinces of Bialystok, Vilna, Novogrodek, and Volhynia. (Polish culture attracted many more Jews in the ethnically Polish area of the old Kingdom of Poland and in Galicia than in the ethnically mixed eastern provinces, where the majority was Bielorussian or Ukrainian.) In all, it was estimated in 1934-37 that private Jewish schools had an enrolment of 81,895 in primary grades, 14,514 on the high-school level, and 7,821 in vocational institutions. Thus, while only 19.2 per cent of the Jewish primary-school population attended private Jewish schools, the rest going to public schools, the ratio rose to 50 per cent for high schools and 60 per cent for vocational schools. Some of the public schools maintained by the government, the so-called Sabbath schools, were set aside for Jewish children. These offered the regular public-school program but observed Saturday as the day of rest. There were also Jewish schools of higher learning, both of the yeshivah and the modern seminary types, particularly the rabbinical and teachers' seminary in Warsaw. The Yiddish Scientific Institute-YIVO in Vilna, though also a training institution, was preeminently a research institute. At the same time, of course, Jews attended general universities and other schools of higher learning. Despite discouragement by the authorities and an often hostile reaction by fellow students, 5,682 Jewish students attended Polish universities in 1936-37, many other young Jewish men and women attending universities abroad. In short, interwar Poland reveals an intensity of Jewish educational effort which, in the absence of support by public taxation, was almost unparalleled in Europe's educational history.

Even more intensive was Jewish education in Lithuania, where fewer than 12 per cent of Jewish students attended non-Jewish institutions paralleled by Jewish schools. In 1938 there were 107 Jewish primary schools with 13,856 pupils and 14 Jewish high schools with about 3,000. Most of these Jewish schools, predominantly of the *Tarbut* type, received governmental subsidies. In neighboring Latvia, too, 85.5 per cent of Jewish schoolchildren attended Jewish schools in 1935-36, though the proportion was somewhat lower on the secondary-school level. As in other countries, the Jewish school system was divided between the Orthodox, Zionist, and Yiddishist groups ,only the Orthodox being able to maintain two *yeshivot* giving instruction beyond high-school age.

It was in the Soviet Union, of course, that the secularization of the Jewish school was most pronounced. Among the tremendous adjustments enforced by the revolution was a complete transformation of the Jewish educational structure, the old *hadarim, yeshivot,* and Zionist schools being replaced by a Yiddish school system extending from the primary grades to scientific institutes and sectors at the universities. With the temporary aid of the government, Yiddish teachers, writers, and communal workers established schools in the Ukraine and White Russia which, within a decade, accommodated some 100,000 Jewish pupils. True, the Jewish content of these school programs was rather meager. After eliminating the Bible, Talmud, Hebrew literature, and most of Jewish history, all that remained was a bit of modern Yiddish literature and the history of a few decades. It made little difference whether the Communist Manifesto and Lenin's speeches were taught in Yiddish or in Russian. Like other schools of the totalitarian regime, these too were instruments for indoctrinating the youth. Nevertheless, an element of Jewish culture was retained which, under favorable conditions, might have developed a new approach to Jewish life, both in scholarship and in art. Unfortunately, here, as in Poland, the repercussions of the Nazi propaganda in the 1930s put an end to whatever auspicious beginnings had been made in the first 15 years after the Revolution.

Totally different was the development of Jewish schools in the older countries of Emancipation. In France, Belgium, and the Netherlands the large majority of Jewish schoolchildren attended general schools, both public and private. There were some special Jewish schools, serving immigrant families mostly. In 1939 France had 3 elementary Jewish day schools, 1 high school, 2 vocational boarding schools, 2 Talmud Torahs, 16 *hadarim,* and a number of part-time schools, some maintained by the Central Consistory. On a higher level there were some *yeshivot,* two teachers' seminaries, and the Ecole Rabbinique. The latter's antecedents went back to 1704, but it had been reorganized in Metz in 1829 and again in Paris in 1859. Simultaneously the Alliance Israélite Universelle made a valiant effort to spread Jewish, together with French, education through many countries of the Near East and North Africa. In 1931 it maintained 27 schools in the Balkans alone, with a school population of over 10,000.

Germany, Austria, and Hungary offered more intensive Jewish education. Among the day schools in Germany the Jewish Free School in

Berlin, the Philanthropin in Frankfort on the Main, and the Talmud Torah in Hamburg dated back to the late 18th or early 19th century. In 1926-27, despite continuous attrition, 96 Jewish day schools still operated in Prussia, 25 in Bavaria, and 3 in Württemberg. In 1931, in Germany, 8,000 pupils attended 149 Jewish elementary schools and 2,000 attended 12 Jewish high schools, the two school systems employing 600 teachers — despite the tremendous attraction of the general school, and more broadly of German culture, for almost two centuries. In Austria the Viennese Chajes Realgymnasium, founded in 1919, had an international reputation. Several high schools in Budapest likewise offered excellent training to Jewish boys and girls, one of them being attached to the Francis Joseph Central Rabbinical Seminary, founded in 1867. This institution and its sister schools in Breslau (1854), in Berlin (the Hochschule für die Wissenschaft des Judentums, 1870, and the Rabbinerseminar, 1873), and Vienna (Israelitisch-Theologische Lehranstalt, 1893) were leading centers of modern Jewish scholarship, the *Wissenschaft des Judentums.* Between the two wars they provided rabbis and teachers not only for the Central European schools but also for the rest of Europe and many countries overseas. There also were several excellent teachers' seminaries, including the Jüdisches Pädagogium in Vienna, whose alumni served in schools all over the world.

It goes without saying that Jews also participated actively both as teachers and as students in general education. Anti-Semites often denounced the alleged Jewish domination of the German schools of higher learning. According to an early Nazi writer, Rudolf Jung, there were 937 Jews among the 3,140 teachers in the German institutions of higher learning in 1914. This figure seems to be exaggerated, but there is no question that the ratio of Jews in the academic professions rose in the liberal Weimar Republic. In Austria, Czechoslovakia, and Hungary, too, the number of Jewish professors was constantly on the rise, despite sharp discrimination against them by most universities and state authorities. Ignaz Goldhizer, perhaps the greatest western student of

Islamic history and thought, was forced to earn his living as a secretary of the Jewish community of Budapest because he was long refused an appointment to the university. After the First World War, to be sure, he had achieved a world-wide reputation and his presence on the faculty conferred much lustre on the University of Budapest. Where discrimination was almost wholly absent, as in interwar France and Italy, the ratio of Jewish professors was high.

Besides their schools, the Jewish communities often maintained major repositories for the cultural treasures accumulated over the centuries. Almost all well-organized Jewish communities had archives of their own, which were often many decades, and sometimes centuries, old. Among the most renowned Jewish archival collections were those of Rome, Mantua, Amsterdam, Frankfort, Berlin, Hamburg, and Vienna. To assure the preservation of documents of Jewish interest in Germany, particularly in smaller communities, the Gesamtarchiv der deutschen Juden, founded in Berlin in 1905, assembled them in its own building and regularly reported accessions of its *Mitteilungen,* of which six volumes appeared between 1909 and 1926. No such central organization operated in other countries, but YIVO in Vilna and other organizations made consistent efforts to keep alive the testimony of the Jewish past. Several Jewish communities and institutions maintained splendid libraries and museums in which were housed significant collections of Hebraica and Judaica, including manuscripts and incunabula. Among the most renowned Jewish libraries were those of the five German, Austrian, and Hungarian seminaries, the Alliance in Paris, the Bibliotheca Montezinos in Amsterdam, the Tlomackie Street Library in Warsaw, the Straszun and YIVO libraries in Vilna, and several communal libraries in Russia, which were incorporated into major Soviet state libraries. Numerous private libraries likewise achieved great distinction, such as those of David Kaufmann, which ultimately found its way into the library of the Budapest Academy of Science, of Baron Günzberg, which was taken over by the Lenin Library in

Moscow, and of David Simonsen, which became part of the National Library of Copenhagen. Many lesser communities maintained libraries of their own, some of a specialized character, like the Medem Farband's Yiddish collection in Paris. In addition, almost every larger synagogue and academy of learning had a library, sometimes of considerable size and distinction. They had also often assembled over the generations precious Torah scrolls and their accoutrements together with other objects, exemplars of Jewish art. Special museums, too, existed in major communities like Berlin, Frankfort, and Vienna. For some of the other communities, like Worms, it was a matter of pride to maintain a museum and archive which included such precious items as a two-volume *Mahzor* of 1272, imperial privileges dating from 1551 on, and many ceremonial objects of the 16th and 17th centuries. The *Tentative List of Jewish Cultural Treasures in Axis-Occupied Countries,* prepared under my direction by Dr. Hannah Arendt and associates and published by the Commission on European Jewish Cultural Reconstruction in New York in 1946, was able to list no fewer than 430 such institutions which had existed in the European countries before the Nazi occupation. Of course, there were also significant collections of Jewish books, documents, and art objects in general libraries, archives, and museums, many of which had come there from private Jewish collectors. No fewer than 274 important general repositories were likewise recorded in the *Tentative List.* Partly on the basis of that inventory, the Allied occupation forces in Germany were able to recover more than a million Jewish books of identifiable origin and nearly 500,000 volumes whose ownership could not be identified. Their distribution helped to enrich the cultural treasures of Israel and of many of the younger communities in the dispersion.

An astonishing number of Jewish periodicals appeared in Europe before the Nazi occupation. Even the small Jewish reading public in France had at its disposal 96 Jewish journals, including 2 Yiddish dailies and 6 French, 5 Yiddish, and 1 Russian weekly. The Netherlands had 21 Jewish periodicals, Austria 19, Hungary 21, Rumania 54, and Lithuania 15. Germany's 113 publications included 33 official *Gemeindeblätter,* issued by Jewish communities. Poland produced the astounding total of 30 Yiddish and 5 Polish dailies, besides 132 weeklies, 4 of them in Hebrew. There were also 224 fortnightlies, quarterlies, and the like. In all, the list of Jewish periodicals in Axis-occupied countries includes 854 items. Of course, some of these were merely ephemeral publications or otherwise little worthy of note. But some possessed great journalistic, scholarly, or literary value, and their influence extended far beyond the borders of their countries. Dailies like *Hajnt* and *Nasz Przeglad* in Warsaw and *Chwila* in Lvov, a weekly like *Die jüdische Rundschau* in Berlin, and literary and scholarly journals such as the *Monatsschrift für Geschichte und Wissenschaft des Judentums,* published in Breslau from 1851 to 1939, the *Revue des études juives,* established in 1881 in Paris, *Magyar Zsidó Szemle* in Budapest, *YIVO Bleter* and *Ha-Tekufah* in Poland, had international importance. So had some journals devoted largely to the history and culture of particular countries, such as the yearbook published by the Czechoslovak Jewish Historical Society, the *Zeitschrift für die Geschichte der Juden in Deutschland,* the *Rassegna mensile di Israel* in Italy, and the *Tsaytshrift* in Minsk. Nor was there a lack of specialized journals for art, social welfare, crafts, and trades. Jewish journalism, starting with 17th-century Amsterdam and including such weeklies as the *Allgemeine Zeitung des Judentums,* which was founded in Berlin in 1837 and continued for nearly a century, was a potent expression of the various cultural, social, and political movements within European Jewry. Even Greece had two Ladino dailies and one Ladino yearbook, as well as a Greek monthly, all attesting to the renaissance of the Sephardi world in the Balkans and its creative response to the impact of westernization on the Near Eastern Jewries.

Even more significant, in many ways, was the constant stream of books and pamphlets in Hebrew, Yiddish, Ladino, and nearly all local languages, produced by Jews (and some non-Jews) and relating to Jewish subjects. In no other domain can one so readily see the vitality of the European Jewish communities before the Catastrophe. Even in the Soviet Union, where the revolution enforced a nearly total break with the past, Yiddish books on all sorts of political, historical, and scholarly subjects, as well as belles-lettres, poured out of the government-owned presses. I vividly remember the pride with which the vice-president of the White Russian Academy of Science announced to me in 1937 that his Academy was publishing a Yiddish scholarly book at an average rate of one a week.

When a short time thereafter I prepared a *Bibliography of Jewish Social Studies, 1938-1939,* I did not realize that those two years were to mark an end of the European epoch in Jewish history. I was able to list more than 5,000 publications of permanent interest during those two years. Unfortunately, too much space had to be assigned to anti-Semitic outpourings in Germany and elsewhere, as well as to a considerable number of apologias written in defense of Jews and Judaism by both Jews and Christians. However, the overwhelming majority of the publications were devoted to the cultivation of traditional Jewish learning, modern Jewish scholarship, contemporary Jewish affairs, and critical analyses of Yiddish and Hebrew letters. I was amazed by the intensity which East and Central European Jewry gave to the production of "old-fashioned" responsa, homilies, ethical writings, and kabbalistic, hasidic, and other works of *halakhah* and *aggadah.* It is no exaggeration to say that Polish Jewry alone produced in those two years more works of this traditional kind of Jewish scholarship than in any decade of the 17th or 18th century, the heyday of rabbinic learning. Many of these multi-volumed folio works had a sufficiently broad market to appear within a few years in third and fourth editions. Among them were works of outstanding scholarship, which, if written several hundred years earlier, would have earned for their authors distinguished places in the history of Jewish letters. As it was, they still appealed greatly to an enthusiastic following of millions of Jews not only in their home countries but also in Palestine, America, and elsewhere. Together with educational work of the leading *yeshivot* in Lithuania, Poland, and Hungary, this literary output held out great promise for the continued flowering of rabbinic learning in Eastern and Central Europe and in its offshoots in other lands.

At the same time, European Jewry produced significant modern Hebrew and Yiddish literary studies and works in the various disciplines of the *Wissenschaft des Judentums.* Great poets, like Hayyim Nahman Bialik and Saul Tchernikhovsky in Hebrew, and David Pinski, Abraham Reisen, and Shalom Asch in Yiddish, may have been forced out of their native habitat; they had to transplant themselves at a mature age to Palestine, the United States, or other countries. But they had gifted disciples in both languages who carried on their work in Poland and the adjacent lands.

Apart from creative writing, much effort was devoted to the reconstruction of the Jewish past. Outstanding historians like Simon Dubnow, Majer Balaban, Ignaz Schiper, Philip Friedman, and Emmanuel Ringelblum, writing predominantly in Russian and Polish but also in Yiddish and Hebrew, were joined by such western students of Jewish history as Eugen Täubler, Ismar Elbogen, Umberto Cassuto, Isaiah Sonne, and Ludwig Blau (a reasonably full list of names would occupy more space than can be allotted here), whose works originally appeared in German, Italian, or some other western language. The Berlin Academy's training of young scholars for the future was alone immensely productive. A few of its young research fellows, who subsequently became outstanding scholars were Hanoch Albeck, Isaac Fritz Baer, Gershom Scholem, Selma Stern, and Leo Strauss. There were, of course, many other institutions of learning, particularly the seminaries, which gave their faculty members a chance to devote their lives to the scholarly investigation of Jewish life and letters in the past and the present. Apart from training a multitude of rabbis and teachers, the seminaries also gave them sufficient scholarly training for a career at a university or a Jewish school of higher learning. Taken as a whole, the preoccupation of European Jewry with Jewish scholarship, arts, and letters exceeded in intensity that of any earlier modern generation.

All this did not keep Jews from contributing significantly to the science, literature, and art of the nations. Polish Jewry had been separated for centuries from Polish culture, yet Julian Tuwim and Antoni Slonimski belonged to the leading Polish poets of their generation. Jewish writers in Germany and Austria, such as Franz Kafka, Max Brod, Franz Werfel, Arthur Schnitzler, Richard Beer Hoffmann, Stefan Zweig, and Jacob Wasserman achieved international reputations. Catulle Mendès, Henry Bernstein, and André Spire were some of the important Jewish authors in 20th-century France. Soviet Jewry produced in Isaac Babel and Boris Pasternak, two of the leading Russian writers of our time. In music the names are too many to list, and it is enough to mention the great composers Arnold Schönberg, Darius Milhaud, and Ernest Bloch. Painters include Max Liebermann, Lesser Ury, Soutine, Modigliani, Kisling, and Chagall; sculptors, Henryk (Enrico) Glicenstein, and architects, Erich Mendelsohn and Julius Flegenheimer. What the generally anti-Jewish *Novoye Vremya* wrote in Tsarist days about the painter Isaac Levitan could be applied as well to some Jewish artists in other lands: "This full-blooded Jew knew, as no other man, how to make us understand and love our plain and homely country scenes."

Among scientists and scholars there are no greater names than those of Albert Einstein and Sigmund Freud. Distinguished philosophers included Hermann Cohen, Emile Durkheim, Lucien Lévy-Bruhl, Ernst Cassirer, and Martin Buber. Many East European Jews would have achieved an international reputation if they had lived and worked in the west. Certainly, Emile Meyerson would not have been the renowned philosopher that he was if he had remained in his native Lublin. Some of the great Jewish thinkers and scholars, to be sure, found their way to the baptismal font, but, for one example, Henri Bergson, the son of a Warsaw Jew who toward the end of his life felt the strong attraction of Catholic mysticism, refused to be converted because, as he expressed it in his will of 1937, he had "seen in preparation for so many years this formidable wave of anti-Semitism which will soon overthrow the world. I wanted to remain among those who tomorrow will be the persecuted ones." While few of these thinkers immersed themselves in the Jewish tradition, Franz Rosenzweig, like Buber, not only drew much of his inspiration from Jewish sources, but also blazed new paths in Jewish philosophy and theology. To list the names of other eminent Jewish scientists and scholars, particularly in medicine and law, would require too much space. Before Hitler's rise to power Austro-German Jewry alone furnished the majority of the 17 Jewish Nobel Prize winners in 1907-30.

A mere enumeration of names, however distinguished, cannot begin to convey the richness and variety of these extraordinary minds and personalities. One had to have the good fortune of being befriended, as I was, by the great poet Bialik to feel the impact of his genius, which expressed itself not only in a series of immortal poems, but also in an endless outpouring of words of wisdom in any private conversation, however casual. It is a pity that only toward the end of his life did some disciples make an effort to record some of these for posterity. One had to know Chaim Weizmann well before one could assess the extraordinary combination of shrewdness and humor, statesmanlike realism and prophetic vision, of the man whom David Lloyd George styled the new Nehemiah of the Jewish people. Only close acquaintance could resolve in one's mind the apparent paradox of Albert Einstein — supreme mathematical genius together with unworldliness and an almost childlike humanity. Nor should we forget the multitude of anonymous saints, heroic in charity and self-sacrifice. The interwar generation seems to have produced more than the legendary thirty-six nameless righteous men, whose undetected and redemptive presence is said to sustain the world.

Of course, the Jewish people also had its sinners and idiots, thieves and lunatics. But on balance, future historians are likely to call the first third of the 20th century the golden age of Ashkenazi Jewry in Europe, just as they will see in it the beginning of a modern Sephardi renaissance.

The notable achievements by Jews provoked envy and resentment among unfriendly non-Jews, while at times filling some Jews with excessive pride. The reason for the ability of Jews to make such contributions is not difficult to ascertain. To the historian, the explanation is to be sought in the long history of the Jewish people and its position in contemporary society. As a permanent minority for some two thousand years, Jews were forced to seek the kinds of openings that were available to newcomers. As a rule, wherever they settled they found they were forced to look for new opportunities. When they found and used such opportunities, they were working for both their own belefit and that of society as a whole. I have long believed that much of Jewish history ought to be rewritten in terms of the pioneering services which the Jews were forced to render by the particular circumstances of their history. Moreover, the Jews have always cherished learning above all other values. Even with respect to religious commandments, the ancient rabbis asserted that the study of Torah outweighed them all. Maimonides, the great philosopher, jurist, and physician, had advised the Jews to devote only three hours a day to earning a living, if at all possible, and at least nine hours more to the study of Jewish law. These counsels sank so deep into the mind of the people that most Jewish women through the ages dreamed of their sons becoming distinguished rabbis and scholars. With the modern secularization of life, those ambitions were directed to the arts and sciences. Finally, and ironically, the very anti-Semites who complained of Jewish overrepresentation in intellectual life, actually contributed to it. Precisely because discrimination against Jewish students, artists, and writers was so widely prevalent, they were forced to work doubly hard and often to do better than their neighbors if they wished to find a place in the sun. In short, it was no biological predisposition, but rather an unusual concatenation of historic circumstances which accounted for this extraordinary intellectual and artistic fecundity of 20th-century European Jewry.

Under the Nazi Heel

It was in recognition of the cultural importance of the Jews that the Nazis almost immediately after achieving power sought to combat them intellectually. Quite early they established a special Jewish-research division in their Reichsinstitut für Geschichte des neuen Deutschlands in Munich. This was followed by the Institut zur Erforschung der Judenfrage in Frankfort, the directorship of which was entrusted to the leading ideologist of the Nazi movement, Alfred Rosenberg. The Institut worked hard to assemble a library of Judaica and Hebraica which could be used for attacking the Jewish people and its religion. After confiscating many German and French collections, including the Rothschild archives and the library of the Alliance Israélite Universelle, the Frankfort institution brought together by 1941 some 350,000 volumes which could serve to support whatever distortions of the Jewish past were dictated by the Nazi ideology. Even the vulgar anti-Semite Julius Streicher, who needed no "scholarly" evidence for his pornographic attacks on the Jews, assembled a substantial collection of Hebraica, most of which is now in New York, on which he employed a number of so-called experts to find passages usable in his anti-Jewish propaganda. With the spread of the New Order, the Germans saw to it that similar institutes for the study of "the Jewish question" were also established in Paris, where it was affiliated with the Department of Jewish Affairs, and in Lodz. The Institut für deutsche Ostarbeit, founded in Cracow in 1940, likewise concerned itself with Jewish matters, as did a special professorship in Jewish history and languages attached to the newly established University of Poznan in 1941. Under Nazi prompting, Italy made available in 1942 research facilities for the study of race and Jewish matters at the universities of Florence, Bologna, Milan, and Trieste.

Otherwise, anti-intellectualism dominated Nazi ideology and greatly contributed to the sudden decline of the great German universities and research oganizations. Typical of the new approach was the exclamation of Rudolph Tomaschek, director of the Institute of Physics in Dresden: "Modern physics is an instrument of Jewry for the destruction of Nordic science." Anti-intellectualism served domestically to undermine opposition to the Nazi regime, and externally, especially later in connection with the conquered territories, to suppress the native intelligentsias and thus make the masses more amenable to Nazi despotism. With the Jews too, Nazism first sought to undermine their cultural strength. The platform originally adopted by the Nazi party in 1920, within half a year after Adolf Hitler had assumed leadership, emphasized the denial of German citizenship to Jews. Yet when Hitler was appointed as chancellor of Germany on January 30, 1933, the Nazis took their time about the removal of the Jews' citizenship, starting with discrimination against Jewish civil servants, teachers, and lawyers. These early decrees of April 7, 1933, were followed two weeks later by the exclusion of Jewish physicians from panel practice and by a *numerus clausus* in German schools. Even the decrees of July 14 and 26, 1933, merely laid the basis for revoking the naturalization of East European Jews. It was not until the Nuremberg laws of September 15, 1935, that the German Jews, too, were deprived of their citizenship and made into mere subjects of the Reich. At the same time was enacted the law "for the protection of German blood and honor," which made of intermarriage and of extramarital sex relations between "Aryans" and "non-Aryans" a criminal offense.

This early Nazi legislation revealed the general procedures which

Hitler and his associates were to use so successfully against Jews and other "enemies." Implicit in all the laws was the rationalization that the Nazis were only restoring the conditions of the pre-Emancipation era. It could be argued that just as medieval Jewry was segregated from the German people, enjoyed no political rights, and suffered considerable disabilities, and yet managed to thrive culturally and religiously, so would Nazi legislation only renew the same situation in modern conditions. All that the German government intended to do, the semi-official commentators said, was to bring about a state of affairs in which "it will henceforth and for future times be impossible for Jews to mix with the German people and to meddle in the political, economic, and cultural management of the Reich."

Even progressive people in and outside German were often deceived, and throughout the 1930s one frequently heard that the Nazis wished to turn the clock back to the "dark" Middle Ages. Such assertions maligned the Middle Ages, which tried to establish the reign of morality and order. The medieval system certainly had many shortcomings and was guilty of many injustices, particularly against the Jewish minority. But there is a fundamental difference between the medieval corporate society — consisting of a variety of corporate groups enjoying a diversity of rights and subjected to a gradation of duties, with the Jews being but one of many such corporate entities — and the Nazi legislation, which singled out one minority, of one per cent, and put it outside the frame of an otherwise uniform society. At least in theory, all Germans were equal citizens of the Reich; only "non-Aryans" were singled out as a separate caste enjoying no rights of citizenship. Writing in November 1935 in the *Independent Journal of Columbia University*, I warned that "a mere perusal of the basic privileges of medieval Jewry (enacted by Henry IV, Frederick I, Frederick II, etc.) and of the recent Nazi laws reveals the difference between a primarily positive and constructive and a purely negative type of legislation."

The unprecedented character of Nazi racial anti-Semitism could not be camouflaged by references to the Middle Ages. Anti-Jewish sentiments and deeds accompanied the Jewish people throughout the history of its dispersion, but few new arguments were added in modern times to the denunciations of Jews and Judaism by the anti-Semites of the Greco-Roman world — though with the modern secularization of life and the widespread acceptance of the doctrine of liberty of conscience, accusations against the Jews shifted from religion to the secular spheres of economics and politics. But the great innovation of racial anti-Semitism was its biological basis. In previous ages it was possible for a Jew, as well as a heretic or a witch, to escape persecution by some act of penance; for a Jew, by conversion to Christianity. While thousands of Jews throughout the ages resisted that avenue of escape and often preferred a martyr's death, conversion remained open at least to the weaker or the less conscientious. Racial anti-Semitism, with its pseudoscientific theories of racial purity, made of Jewish descent a matter of immutable nature, transcending the volition of any man or group of men.

Better concealed was the Nazi desire to uproot the Jewish religion. Although from the beginning Hitler and his followers heaped abuse upon many Jewish doctrines and rituals and even tried to revive the blood libel, they pretended that theirs was not a religious persecution. This pretense appeared necessary because both Hitler and Mussolini recognized that in a struggle with deep religious convictions the state could not win. As late as 1934 Mussolini wrote that the whole history of western civilization "from Diocletian to Bismarck teaches us that, whenever there is a conflict between the state and a religion, it is always the state that loses the battle." In *Mein Kampf* Hitler also contended that "the political leader will always consider inviolable the religious teachings and institutions of his people." On the other hand, he admitted that Nazism was not merely a political party, but also a conception of life (*Weltanschauung*) which could never compromise but of necessity had to proclaim its own infallibility. The professed avoidance of conflicts with religion, including Judaism, was therefore merely another ruse, which misled a great many observers. Pope Pius XI felt it necessary to state in his Christmas message to the College of Cardinals in 1937:

> "In Germany there is indeed a real religious persecution. It is said, and it has been said for some time past, that this is not true. We know, on the contrary, that there is a terrible persecution; only a few times previously has there been a persecution so terrible, so fearful, so grievous, and so lamentable in its far-reaching consequences."

While hundreds of Catholic priests and Protestant pastors were sent to concentration camps, the excuse always given was that they were being punished for some violation of the laws of exchange, moral turpitude, and the like. Secretly, however, the movement to establish a national German religion harking back to German paganism, or at least a specific German reformulation of Christianity with the elimination of the Old Testament and other Judaic elements, were semi-officially encouraged. The Reich Minister for Church Affairs declared, in that very year 1937: "There has now arisen a new authority as to what Christ and Christianity really is. This new authority is Adolf Hitler."

Pervasive national enthusiasm, lying propaganda, and violent suppression of all opposing points of view combined to silence most opposition, even within the churches. A few courageous Catholic and Protestant clergymen protested the religious persecution and the glorification of pagan mythology. While the once great universities, labor unions, and press speedily surrendered to the Nazis, the churches succeeded in retaining their identity and producing a number of men and women who bore witness to their faith. But these were exceptions to the rule; the majority of the faithful yielded abjectly to the ideology of their new masters. The persecution of the Jews, in particular, aroused little opposition by professing Christians — including Catholics, even after 1937, when the Pope issued the famous encyclical, *Mit brennender Sorge,* in which he sharply condemned German racialism. Genocide against the Jewish people could hardly be distinguished from the suppression of the Jewish religion, as Judaism is unthinkable without Jews. Yet it was many years before the German churches realized that the persecution of Jews and Judaism was only a prelude to the unlimited supremacy of the totalitarian state and party in spiritual matters too.

The Nazis' "mad attempt," to quote that papal encyclical, "of trying to confine within the boundaries of a single people, within the narrow blood stream of a single race, God, the Creator of the World, the King and Lawgiver of all peoples, before Whose greatness all peoples are as small as a drop in a bucket," necessarily led to unbridled terror. First came the boycott of April 1, 1933; then increasingly numerous riots by students and other unruly mobs against Jews, and still later the mass attack of the *Kristallnacht* of November 9-10, 1938. That wholesale destruction of synagogues and Jewish businesses was compounded by a fine of a billion marks imposed upon all German Jewry and by the dispatch of 20,000 leading Jews to concentration camps. Once again all could see, although many still refused to see, how different was Nazi anti-Semitism from medieval Jew-baiting.

Throughout the Middle Ages, not only the Muslim but also the Christian states usually tried to maintain public order. Emperors and princes, bishops and municipal authorities usually tried to stave off mob attack upon their Jewish subjects. Whenever a state ceased to tolerate Jews, it issued a decree of expulsion, thereby revoking the formal toleration of the Jewish faith in its domain. There is no evidence of any important medieval ruler engineering riots against his Jewish subjects. With the Nazis, however, nearly every attack on the Jews was planned in advance by the authorities, especially the S.S. and executed by government and party officials. Of course, much room was still left to the individual initiative of official underlings, lesser party members, and the general public. Sadists of all kinds felt free to gratify their impulses at the expense of helpless Jewish victims. But the direction remained firmly in the hands of the authorities, even the generals of the army often being powerless to stem excesses that actually interfered with the prosecution of the war. The *Kristallnacht* was a curtain raiser for the ever more bloodthirsty drive of the Nazis toward the "final solution of the Jewish question."

This is not the place to recount in detail the tragic history of the gradual evolution of the Nazi program from the expulsion of the Jews from Europe, after the confiscation of most of their property, to their ultimate murder. So long as world opinion still carried considerable weight, Achim Gercke, the race expert in the Reich Ministry of the Interior, well expressed the Nazi line: "In short, there can and shall be only one sort of governmental regulation — an orderly exit of the Jews, their emigration." All sorts of schemes were aired, including, after the conquest of France in 1940, the transplantation of millions of Jews to the distant island of Madagascar, then a French colony. Taking a clue from schemes discussed earlier in Poland, the Nazis thought, or pretended to think, that such a mass expulsion would help them establish, at least in Europe, a completely *judenrein* New Order.

During the 1930s genocide was not publicly discussed; it was at most whispered in the inner circle, with no written records left behind. A major deterrent against the public proclamation of such a program was the fact that anti-Semitism served as an excellent instrument of Nazi foreign policy in preparing for a war of conquest. By stimulating anti-Jewish feeling among Germany's neighbors — and such feelings were always latent in most of Western and quite overt in Eastern Europe — and by combining attacks on the Jews with attacks on Bolshevism through the myth of the Jewish responsibility for the Communist revolution, the Nazi propagandists succeeded in undermining the unity of nations that were themselves to be victims of Nazi aggression. Even in France, Germany's so-called hereditary enemy, important rightist factions arose which were prepared to compromise with the Third Reich. In 1938 the French writer Thierry Maulnier, justifying France's abject surrender in Munich, asserted that the parties of the right "had the impression that in case of war not only would the disaster be immense, not only was defeat and devastation of France possible, but also a German defeat would mean the crumbling of the authoritarian systems which constitute the main rampart against the Communist revolution, and perhaps the immediate Bolshevization of Europe." Those rightist movements were ready even to surrender French sovereignty in exchange for preserving class prerogatives. A humanitarian defense of Jewish victims of Nazi persecution, when combined with a sharp opposition to the Third Reich, was often denounced by pro-fascist elements as a betrayal of French patriotism. Such was the irony of the situation even in Western Europe, at least until it was occupied by the Nazi armies and the population came face to face with the Nazi terror.

In Eastern Europe, on the other hand, little Nazi encouragement was required to spread the flames of anti-Jewish feeling and action. Poland, temporarily reassured in 1934 by a treaty of amity with Germany, could more freely indulge in anti-Jewish legislative and popular excesses. Even murders of Jews, which in the territories of ethnographic Poland had always been held to a relative minimum, now multiplied. It is estimated that during the 1930s, riots, such as those of Kielce and Przytyk, and student disturbances at universities cost 500 Jews their lives. But these were mere skirmishes preliminary to the wholesale slaughter which was to follow. In Rumania and Hungary, too, such organizations as the Rumanian Iron Cross long agitated against the Jews. After the outbreak of the war it was quite an achievement for Premiers Ion Antonescu and Nicholas von Kallay to persuade the Germans that they, rather than the uncontrolled extremists, would be useful allies. But the rabid anti-Semites felt free to attack Jews, certain of the protection of the German overlords.

In general, the first two years of war saw the Germans much too preoccupied with conquest and with reorganizing the administration of the conquered territories to proceed to the ultimate stages of the "final solution." There also were great differences between individual countries. While Austria, the Sudeten, and the western part of Poland were directly incorporated into the Third Reich, most of the other territories remained nominally independent. In Austria, immediately after the occupation by the German troops on March 12, 1938, Arthur Seyss-Inquart voluntarily surrendered Austrian independence. The country was reorganized as the Ostmark, and Jews were forced to emigrate more rapidly than in Germany itself. In fact, Austria was used as a model for the acceleration of the forced departure of Jews from the rest of the Reich — which, according to the law of November 21, 1938, following the Munich agreement of September 30, 1938, included also the Sudeten — and, after March 1939, from Czechoslovakia. Here Bohemia, Moravia, and Silesia were reorganized as a German "protectorate" on April 5, 1939, with Baron Constantin von Neurath as protector. Slovakia proclaimed itself an independent republic on July 21, 1939. In September 1941 von Neurath was succeeded as protector by the ruthless Heydrich, assassinated on June 4, 1942. This change in regime symbolized the end of the transition that had begun with the occupation of Poland in September 1939. While the Polish provinces east of the San-Bug-Narev line were incorporated into the Soviet Union (September 17), western Poland was reorganized as a German "General-Gouvernment," except for the territories which before 1914 had belonged to Germany and which, together with Lodz and other areas, now reverted to German suzerainty (October 19, 1939).

Differences persisted also among the Scandinavian countries after their invasion in April 1940. Denmark, which had offered no resistance, was treated with greater moderation (toward the Jews too, temporarily) than Norway, despite the transfer of power in Norway on April 10, 1940, to the local Nazi Vidkun Quisling, whose party had received 2 per cent of the popular vote in the previous election. Then in May, followed the speedy conquest of Holland, Belgium, Luxembourg, and France. Holland — whose Queen Wilhelmina was soon joined in England by the Norwegian King Haakon, both being leaders of their governments-in-exile — was governed with increasing ruthlessless by Seyss-Inquart, appointed to office on May 30, 1940. Luxembourg was ultimately incorporated directly into the Reich, on August 30, 1942. After the surrender of King Leopold to the Germans on May 28, 1940, Belgium retained a measure of independence, but it was nonetheless effectively ruled by General Alexander von Falkenhausen, who also administered the affairs of northern France. For a while, much of the rest of France was allowed to go on as a semi-independent country under the Vichy regime of Marshal Philippe Pétain and Pierre Laval. There was an obvious difference in the treatment of Jews between the two parts of France. Similarly, conditions differed between the parts of Yugoslavia and Greece which the German authorities administered directly after their conquest in April 1941 and those parts assigned to Italy or Bulgaria or, as in Croatia, run by a sattelite regime. Direct Nazi rule was always worse.

Soon thereafter came the turn of Russian Jewry. In the campaign that began on June 22, 1941, the German armies had made such rapid progress that by July 17 the major Russia territories in the west, including those taken over by the Soviets from Poland in September 1939 as a result of the Stalin-Hitler pact a month earlier, could be handed over to Alfred Rosenberg as minister for those occupied territories. Under him operated a special Reichskommissariat Ostland, which embraced the Baltic states and the former northeastern provinces of Poland under Heinrich Lohse, and another for the Ukraine, which included Podolia and Volhynia and was entrusted to Erich Koch. These underlings outdid even the Nazi ideologist Rosenberg in savage maltreatment of the Slavic as well as Jewish populations.

Paradoxically, some Jews were saved by the fact that Italy (in May 1940), Bulgaria, Rumania, and Hungary (in April and June 1941) had joined Germany as allies, rather than opposing her as enemies. As allies they retained a measure of domestic autonomy, although in military affairs they increasingly became subordinate. It is true that upon joining the Axis, Mussolini reversed his earlier friendly attitude toward the Jews and adopted Hitler's racial policies — so much so, according to his son-in-law, Count Galeazzo Ciano, that in 1941 he expressed amazement that the Nazis had not yet abolished Christmas, which in his eyes commemorated "the birth of a Jew who gave the world debilitating and devitalizing theories, and who especially contrived to trick Italy through the disintegrating power of the popes." Yet Mussolini did not succeed in stilling racial anti-Semitism in the masses of the Italian people, nor were his officials either as terroristic or as efficient as their German counterparts. Consequently, the greatest sufferings of Italian Jewry came during the relatively short period of direct German domination after Mussolini's dismissal by the King on July 25, 1943, and even then large parts of the Italian population helped to save many Jews from the Nazis. Similarly, the Bulgarian people, following the lead of their government, helped stave off the most brutal Nazi attacks on the Jews. In Rumania, however, as in Poland and the Ukraine, much of the population was ready to collaborate in the murder of Jews. Only a certain lack of bureaucratic efficiency and a corruption even greater than the Gestapo's helped the Jews. In Hungary, finally, the Horthy regime tried to steer a middle course even during the war, and the murder of most Hungarian Jews came about only after the Germans occupied the country, on March 19, 1944. Although no longer inhibited from murdering Jews by a concern with public opinion outside the areas occupied by their armies, some Nazis spared Jewish lives for ransom, while others wanted the Reich to benefit from the employment of Jewish workers, particularly those with special skills.

In retrospect, many scholars have expressed amazement at the tremendous waste of manpower and human talents by the Nazi war machine at a time when the exigencies of the war required the utilization of every available resource. Yet the generals, who realized this source of weakness, readily yielded to Hitler's orders, at least so long as the armies were victorious. Only belatedly were conspiracies hatched to kill the Führer and replace him by a more moderate leader. At the same time, the main authors of the "final solution" realized that many of their compatriots and allies would have recoiled if they had known the extent and manner of the genocide in which their nations were engaged. The Nazis therefore went about their work of destruction with as much secrecy as their terroristic methods would allow, used soft words for their most brutal deeds, destroyed many records, and exercised a rigorous censorship. That policy is well illustrated by Heinrich Himmler's address to the S.S. generals in Poznan. Delivered on October 10, 1943, when it must have been clear even to them that the tide had turned against the Reich, the speech included a reference to a "very grave" matter: "Among ourselves it should be mentioned quite frankly, and yet we will never speak of it publicly... I mean... the extirpation of the Jewish race... This is a page of glory in our history which has never been written and is never to be written." Nevertheless, enough indications of what was going on reached the German people and even some Allied leaders. Only future historians will be in a position to explain the reasons for the relatively passive reaction of the majority of both the German and the other nations.

Effects of the Catastrophe

Among the Jewish *morituri* there were not lacking voices questioning not only the justice of the nations but even the divine order which tolerated such evil. Job's old challenge was now repeated, with many variations, by some of the most pious and dedicated souls. For one example, a hasidic leader, Kalonymus Kalmish Shapiro, once asked: "How can the universe remain standing and not turn into primordial chaos?" (There is a talmudic legend that when the Ten Martyrs were put to death, in the days of Hadrian, the angels asked whether that was the reward for devotion to Torah; whereupon a divine voice proclaimed that if anything like it happened again, the world would be turned into water.) The rabbi continued: "And now innocent children, pure as the angels, as well as great and holy men in Israel, are being killed and slaughtered only because they are Jews... and the world's space is filled with their heart-rending shouts: 'Save us, save us!' They, too, cry, 'Is this the reward for devotion to Torah?' Yet the universe is not destroyed but remains intact, as if nothing happened." Nonetheless, the same rabbi, in the dark years of 1941 and 1942, continued Sabbath after Sabbath to preach to his ever-dwindling congregation, trying to explain to it the hidden meaning of its suffering and consoling it with the inscrutability of the Lord's ways. He continued until he was carried away to the concentration camp where he was cremated in September 1943. Such acts of passive heroism were fully in accord with the age-old traditions of the Jewish people, which ever since the Maccabees extolled religious martyrdom. Others preferred more active resistance. Many Jews in Poland, White Russia, and the Ukraine, as well as the West, joined the partisan units fighting the invaders. The uprising of the Warsaw Ghetto fighters will forever remain a glorious chapter in the Jewish resistance to barbarism and injustice. There were smaller uprisings in other communities as well. Even in the West, the relatively few Jews tried to carry on in the best way they could. A story was current in postwar Brussels that two Polish Jewish refugee brothers decided to use the period of the Nazi occupation to translate the Talmud into Yiddish. They divided their tasks so that one brother permanently remained in an attic working on the translation, while the other clandestinely ventured out into the open to earn a little food for them both. I still recall the strong impression it made on me when, soon after the war, the late Maurice Liber told me how he and his colleagues of the French Ecole Rabbinique had tried to keep Jewish learning alive, underground, during the occupation. As late as 1943 they were still awarding rabbinical degrees to pupils they had been training under the most arduous and dangerous conditions. All of this was a testimony to the Jewish spirit.

Nevertheless, for the first time in many centuries, a Jewish generation was growing up without Jewish or general elementary schooling, and the educational careers of young people of high-school and college age were interrupted, often permanently. For the few survivors, what they had lived through made readjustment extremely improbable. But the power of the spirit was so great that the heritage of the Nazi-enclosed ghettos remained to furnish new spiritual sustenance to the survivors and, beyond them, to Jews in other lands. The songs of the ghetto, a diary such as that left behind by Emmanuel Ringelblum, and the living messages conveyed after the war by the outstanding theologian Leo Baeck, after his emergence from the concentration camp in Theresienstadt, all added a new and significant chapter to the spiritual history of their people.

However, the physical destruction of Jewish lives and property was overwhelming. According to the survey prepared by the Central Jewish Committee in Poland on August 15, 1945, there were altogether 73,955 Jews left in that country, including some 13,000 serving in the Polish army and 5,446 recorded in 10 camps in Germany and Austria. This tiny remnant of more than 3,300,000 Jews (in the somewhat larger area of prewar Poland) was distributed over 224 Polish localities, leaving the large majority of the former 2,000 communities devoid of any Jewish population. Germany and Austria likewise had lost the vast majority of their Jews; the small remnant of some 15,000 living in Germany outside the Displaced Persons' camps consisted largely of those who had escaped deportation and death because they had intermarried and had long lost contact with the Jewish community. The Nazi murder program had most severely affected the children. In Bohemia, Moravia, and Silesia, for instance, where, according to the census of 1930, there had lived 117,551 Jews, only 14,489 were registered in October 1945, including only 1,179 children under 15 — an abnormally low ratio of

8.6 per cent. There was a low ratio of Jewish children even in countries like Rumania and Hungary, with their relatively large percentage of adult survivors. According to the Jewish health organization OSE, at the end of 1946 there were altogether 130,000 Jewish children in continental Europe outside the Soviet Union, although, like their elders, some children had been saved by escaping in the interior of the Soviet Union and had subsequently returned to their home countries.

It is difficult to be precise about the total Jewish losses in Europe, since the Germans wiped out not only the people but also the documents on which reasonably correct calculations might have been based. Most statistical estimates converge around a total of six million Jews killed, a figure cited at the trial of the major war criminals at Nuremberg. Gregory Frumkin, who for years edited the *Statistical Year Book* of the League of Nations, writes in his *Population Changes in Europe Since 1939* that the total figure of Jewish dead in all places that had been occupied by the Germans might easily be between six and seven million. The Anglo-American Committee of Inquiry on Palestine in 1946 estimated the loss of Jewish population in Europe between 1939 and 1946 at over 5,700,000. Consequently, the figure of six million that is usually cited is probably close to the actuality.

This enormous loss augured badly for the future of the Jewish community, even though the biological strength of European Jewry had not been entirely broken. The people's regenerative power was shown by the relatively few survivors in the D.P. camps, whose birth rate was among the highest in Europe. But the children born in those exceptional conditions still are only adolescents today. Together with their elders, they were sooner or later evacuated, for the most part to Israel, and they could not contribute to the reconstruction of the communities from which their parents had come and which they themselves had never seen.

The tragedy was greatest where Jewish communal and cultural life had flourished most — in Poland, Germany, and the bordering countries. Gone were the cultural treasures painfully accumulated over many centuries. The 3,000 *kehillot* with their age-old institutions had vanished, and their place was taken, at best, by some new tentative bodies, making valiant but often futile efforts to start afresh. The great schools of higher learning, the newspapers and magazines, the book publishers, and artistic centers had been stamped out, with no possibility of even a semblance of replacement. Even more than might be indicated by the enormous percentage of Jews who perished during the Catastrophe, their intellectual elite was so depleted that the few struggling remnants were deprived of their traditional rabbinic, literary, scholarly, and informed lay leaders.

The sharp decline is doubly pronounced when compared even with the fate of nations defeated in the war. Germany herself had suffered much retribution. At the time of its surrender many of its cities lay in ruins, certain regions were depopulated, and most of the others suffered from hunger and want. Japan had her Hiroshima and Nagasaki. Nevertheless, today, 16 years after the war, the population of divided Germany has increased substantially and that of Japan is about a third larger than twenty years ago. By contrast, world Jewry still numbers only some 12,000,000, as against the 16,500,000 or more living in 1939.

The extent of the decline becomes manifest when one realizes that, in the 22 years since 1939, the Jewish people should have *increased* by more than 2,500,000, if we assume a continuation of the average growth in the 1930s, namely, 120,000 per annum. If the Jews had participated in the general population growth of the 1940s and 1950s, the average might well have exceeded even the annual growth of the 1920s, 140,000. If that had been so, the world Jewish population now would have reached or exceeded 20,000,000. What is more, the Jewish communities in formerly Nazi-occupied Europe still are crippled, qualitatively even more than quantitatively. That great reservoir of Jewish population and of cultural and religious leadership has dried up, leaving the rest of Jewry, particularly the segments residing in Israel, the New World, and the British Commonwealth, bereaved.

One's imagination is staggered if one considers what might have happened, if during the Franco-German War of 1871 a Hitler, rather than a Bismarck, had guided Germany. If that Hitler of seven decades earlier had succeeded in overrunning the same countries that were overrun between 1939 and 1945, and if he had had the same program of murdering the Jews from the Atlantic to the Russian Pale of Settlement, the genocide of the Jewish people would have been almost total. There would have been no Israel today, and the other present-day largest concentrations of the Jewish people — in the New World, the Soviet Union, and the British Commonwealth — would have consisted, at best, of small, struggling communities.

Through the disappearance of the Jewish communities the European continent has been deprived of an industrious and enterprising population that contributed significantly to economic and cultural progress. Moreover, the Nazis' genocide left behind a permanent precedent and menace for all mankind.

It is true that even in 1942 an Archbishop Jules Saliège of Toulouse dared to circulate a pastoral letter to his diocese which included the following touching statements:

> "Pray for France, our Lady. In our diocese scenes of horror have taken place in the camps of Noé and Récébédou. Jews are men. Jews are women. Not everything is permissible against them, against these men and women, against these fathers and mothers of families. They form part of the human race. They are our brethren like many others. A Christian cannot forget that. France, beloved Motherland, France who carries in the conscience of all her children the tradition of respect for the human person, chivalrous and generous France, I have no doubt you are not responsible for this terror."

Many other saintly and self-sacrificial Christians who saved Jewish neighbors in the face of extreme danger to themselves are mentioned in Philip Friedman's eloquent *My Brother's Keepers.* Unfortunately, however, men like those were vastly outnumbered, especially in Germany and Eastern Europe, by Jew-baiters, sadists, and careerists who gladly collaborated with the Nazi murder squads.

Only belatedly, after the war, was the conscience of mankind aroused by the Nazi murder camps. Men began to realize that such wholesale slaughter of the members of one people can serve as a ready precedent for the murder of any group disliked, for whatever reason, by another group in power. The Nazi doctrine of a Master Race remains a threat for all future times.

Yes, despite these warnings, all too numerous voices are still heard in many countries against the anti-genocide convention proclaimed as a major principle of international law by the United Nations. The genocide committed by the Nazis on European Jewry has been readily forgotten by many non-Jews and even by some Jews who were not personally affected. It is time that the public, as well as its intellectual leaders, understand the danger to human life, to culture, to political decency, and to religion.

APPENDIX

(From the record of the trial of Adolf Eichmann, Jerusalem, April 24, 1961)

DEFENSE ATTORNEY (Robert Servatius): Professor, you have described the history of the Jewish people in the last 150 years and you have touched on the persecution visited upon them since antiquity. Finally you said that the question has been raised of the reason for all this, for these persecutions, in return for all the good that the Jews did. As a professor of history, can you explain the causes of that negative attitude, which has existed for so many hundreds of years, and of that war against the Jewish people?

WITNESS (Salo W. Baron): Your Honors, many theories have been advanced about the origin and development of anti-Semitism. Usually the most conspicuous element has been hatred of the Jewish religion. Judaism was different from the other religions and the Jews were simply hated as infidels, heretics, men who did not believe in what the majority believed, whether that majority was Christian or Muslim or anything else. In the modern period, this changed somewhat as it was increasingly felt, especially as a result of the Thirty Years' War between Protestants and Catholics, that it was impossible to prolong a state of affairs in which a religious majority could impose its religion on the minority. Therefore, religious freedom became a basic principle, at least in the West — Europe, America, etc. In place of the old religious hatred there rose another kind of hatred of the Jews — which is sometimes called the dislike of the unlike. For this, various rationalizations were found, such as that the Jews had too much economic power, that they were usurers, that they tried to dominate intellectual life, and the like. In all this there is one common element: hatred arises only because of the difference between majority and minority. The purpose of the rationalization is to justify the hatred somehow.

Sometimes the hatred was expressed in bloodshed, but in the modern age that had disappeared almost completely. Only in Eastern Europe were Jews still attacked physically — in the Ukraine, in White Russia. It was possible to say that that phase was on the point of disappearing, that the difference between Jews and Christians, or believers in any other religion, would persist, that there might be conflict, but that it would not lead to bloodshed. So people believed. I may say as a historian that when small-scale pogroms broke out in Russia in 1881, the whole world was shocked; nothing like it had happened for a century and people thought that anti-Semitic bloodshed had died out. Yet all that was trivial in comparison with what happened in the 1940s. What happened then has no precedent in Jewish history.

I can conclude by saying that although there has been immemorial anti-Semitism and opposition to the Jewish people, whether in the Greek world, or in the Persian world — witness the Book of Esther — or in the Christian and Muslim world of the Middle Ages, it is well to remember that there was practically no violence accompanied by bloodshed under the Persians or under the Greeks. There were minor outbreaks in the days of Philo of Alexandria. There were no pogroms under the Muslims.

PRESIDING JUDGE (Moses Landau): The question was, what are the motives for anti-Semitism?

A.: The answer is, dislike of the unlike. There was economic jealousy — people who did not like their competitors, in the crafts or in commerce. In addition, there were special reasons of every kind. But the basic difference — and this is what I want to emphasize — was that hatred of Jews does not necessarily cause bloodshed and violence, whereas in this case that tragic thing did happen.

DEFENSE ATTORNEY: Do you not think that nonrational factors, beyond human understanding, are responsible for the fate of the Jewish people?

A.: To some extent we enter here into the realm of theology and philosophy. That question is almost beyond human reason. I am a historian, and as such I must seek comprehensible reasons for any historical development. Nevertheless, it seems to me that it cannot be denied that religious difference alone is not enough to understand most of the hatred of the Jews. Even the Jewish saints and sages believed that the exile was basically beyond human understanding, that it was God's punishment for the sins of the ancient Jews in their land. Theologically all that may be so, but it cannot absolve any man or group of men who deliberately, voluntarily, willfully make themselves the instrument for punishing the Jewish people.

Q.: Professor, I do not wish to raise a philosophical question but only a historical question, a question of philosophy of history. Hegel and Spengler, for instance, say that there is a spirit in history which drives forward through necessity, without the cooperation of human beings — Hegel calls it spirit, and Spengler calls it culture. Should we not see here a similar phenomenon, working through necessity, without being influenced by any particular person?

A.: Your Honors, here we enter into profound questions of philosophy of history. I am not a historical determinist. Hegel and Spengler may be called idealistic determinists. Though they are sometimes right, I have never felt that their approach was correct. According to my opinion, history develops by reason of causes and changes within society, many of which are unpredictable. Accident is very important. Personality is very important. Together all these things create history. Of course, there are also basic movements and there is tradition. All these things develop simultaneously. History does not hop on one foot, but marches on a hundred feet. Each foot is part of the historical process. As far as our question is concerned, I am sure that even the determinists, those who believe that everything that happens in history happens necessarily — like Hegel, for example — would nevertheless agree with our sages that while everything may be determined in advance by God, or by other deterministic forces, nevertheless there is free will. That is to say, every individual must decide how he will act, and he is responsible for his deeds. Even the uncompromising religious predestinarianism of a Calvin cannot justify any man in sinning or committing a crime. If he commits a crime, he is accountable not only to God but also to man.

Q.: Whether man has free will is a religious question, but I would like to bring the discussion back to the historical school in jurisprudence [*historische Rechtsschule*]. Does that school not teach that political leaders often do not achieve what they wish, but the very opposite? For instance, an attempt was made to destroy the Jewish people and instead a flourishing state arose. What do you think of that doctrine?

A.: The consequence of what men do is not always what they intend. That is well known, and we see it every day. As for the historical school in jurisprudence, I have always been a disciple of Savigny and Einhorn and have believed that they were essentially right in saying that even historical jurisprudence is only the result of the forces of tradition, perhaps centuries old. I go farther. I myself once tried to show how greatly social forces influence the development of religion, and *vice versa.* My book, *A Social and Religious History of the Jews,* was based on a series of lectures called "Interrelations of the Social and Religious History of the Jews." I believe that society influences religion and religion influences society; and so it is with law. Without doubt, there are forces independent of men's will. But despite everything that has been said thus far, and however much we may admit that history sometimes acts in an autonomous fashion — i.e., that it does not act according to the will of men — nevertheless, in my opinion, every man and every group of men are responsible for what they do and cannot plead that they are only carrying out what history demands of them. Otherwise everyone would be able to interpret the demand of history in his own way, and there would be chaos.

Q.: You must certainly know that Hitler often relied on Providence, but nevertheless failed. If even a political leader could not do anything against the current of history, must we not regard what an ordinary man does as insignificant?

A.: That is not a historical but a legal question. As to how much an individual who is not a leader is also responsible in a historical sense, there is no doubt that sometimes unimportant people influence the course of history much more than their lowliness might suggest. There is also the kind of accident that I have mentioned. We do not know what the history of Europe would have been if on the day of the Battle of Waterloo Napoleon had not had a headache. There are accidents like that, chance occurrences in the lives of individuals, that have a great influence on history. But I do not see any relation between philosophy of history and the question of a man's personal responsibility, whether he be a leader or a completely unimportant person. Personal responsibility for basic morality, for good or evil, has nothing whatever to do with historical questions, but with religious or moral question in the mortal life of man, in society and in religion.

PRESIDING JUSTICE: That is clear, but I do not see why you call it a legal question.

A.: We were talking about whether there is a difference between a leader and an unimportant person. Is the unimportant person responsible?

PRESIDING JUSTICE: Perhaps we had better leave that to the jurists.

JUDGE BENJAMIN HA-LEVI: Perhaps Professor Baron can tell us something about the so-called *Protocols of the Elders of Zion.*

A.: The *Protocols of the Elders of Zion,* essentially, were compiled before the First World War. They were compiled from several sources, life Hermann Goedsche and Father Sergius Nilus in Russia. They were essentially part of an anti-Semitic movement in Russia, and it is perhaps worth mentioning that the Russian Tsar personally, out of his private fortune, spent money to support anti-Semitic propaganda at the beginning of this century. That became known after the Tsarist archives were opened in 1917. The purpose of all this propaganda was to show that the Jews were trying to conquer the world and that they had a highly secret organization that met from time to time to plan that conquest. Only after World War I was this book translated into many languages and widely circulated, as a weapon to destroy the Jewish people. That was one of the most conspicuous examples of the use of a complete lie, a lie without a grain of truth in it, to advance the victory of anti-Semitism. A Columbia University scholar, John Shelton Curtiss, wrote a book, *An Appraisal of the Protocols of Zion,* published in 1942, which in my opinion is the best analysis of the history of that legend. The *Protocols* were used especially in Germany, where it was reprinted in several editions, and Alfred Rosenberg wrote a kind of commentary on it.

Q.: Since the Nazis insisted that the Protocols were authentic, I would like to know whether all serious historians — not only Jews, who are interested parties, but also all other historians — agree that it is a forgery and completely untrue.

A.: To the best of my knowledge, not one serious historian today will deny that the book is a forgery. Curtiss himself is not a Jew and he wrote his book under the supervision of some of the greatest historians in America: Carlton J. Hayes, Allan Nevins (both later presidents of the American Historical Association), and others. He offered a final and conclusive proof that there is not the slightest grain of truth in all those forgeries.

Q.: You know that Hitler, in *Mein Kampf,* emphasized the importance of the *Protocols.* He says that the very fact of the Jewish denial proves the truth of the document.

A.: That can be said about many things.

Q.: In the Nazi period many believed it. It had an evil influence.

A.: It had an evil influence throughout the world. In the United States, Henry Ford himself published it in the *Dearborn Independent.* But when he was challenged, he admitted that he had made a mistake, that the *Protocols* were a forgery. In Germany, too, there were many who proved that it was a forgery, but those who did not wish to hear remained deaf.

CONCERNING AUTHENTIC AND UNAUTHENTIC RESPONSES TO THE HOLOCAUST

EMIL L. FACKENHEIM
The Hebrew University of Jerusalem

Abstract — Whereas it is impossible to find meaning in the Holocaust, it is imperative to find authentic responses to the event. The article grapples with the dilemmas attached to defining authentic and unauthentic responses to the Holocaust, and addresses criteria for distinction of such responses. Unique and universal are inadequate in that they either diminish the Holocaust to a passing episode or dilute it into another example of man's inhumanity to man. Philosophical reflection on the Holocaust must somehow unite the persistence of history with the transmutation of history as evident in the event. Responses from four concerned groups are examined: those of scholars, of Germans, of Christians and of Jews. In each case, criteria for authenticity are sought and applied.

Our topic presents formidable dilemmas. To begin with, how dare we respond to the Holocaust *authentically,* that is, face the Fire and risk being devoured? And how dare we respond *unauthentically*, that is, treat the perpetrators, onlookers or victims as if they had not been what they were — or had not been at all?

Further, how dare we *categorize* responses as *either* authentic *or* unauthentic, when even in normal circumstances 'the heart is deceitful above all things and exceeding weak' (Jeremiah 17:9).[1] As surely as there is no man who lives and sins not, even the greatest of saints could not respond to *this* event with absolute authenticity, while responses suggesting utter unauthenticity may well cover an unspeakable anguish.[2] Yet, to refrain from all acts of judgement would be to lapse into pious irresponsibility.

Third, how dare we lay down *criteria of distinction?* The enormity of the event must open chasms between those involved — Germans, Christians, Jews — chasms which cannot be bridged by means of mere scholarly detachment, let alone be transcended altogether in a philosophical speculation pretending to rise wholly above the event (and evading entry into the abyss). Yet, without at least elements of transcending criteria the aim of this essay is in principle unachievable. Writing from the standpoint of a Jewish involvement in the event (albeit not without philosophical aspirations), I could then express neither comprehension nor judgement concerning persons of a German or Christian involvement. Moreover, there being no one single Jewish standpoint, the topic would fragment itself still further, the more so the closer we came to the event. Scholarship and philosophy would reflect all such fragmentation precisely to the degree to which they achieved the necessary dialectic between detachment (or transcendence) and involvement. However, although the Holocaust Kingdom has, like Satan, fragmented the Creation, we are bidden to make every effort at repair.

---

*This paper was delivered at a seminal conference on the Holocaust, which met in New York in 1975 and was organized by the Institute for Contemporary Jewry of the Hebrew University in Jerusalem.

EMIL L. FACKENHEIM

To find a meaning in the Holocaust will forever be impossible, but to find authentic responses is an imperative which brooks no compromise.[3] The nature of the dilemmas involved make this task at once profound, formidable and perilous.

Texts

We therefore do well to begin modestly, by considering some texts which report responses of the victims themselves. Our texts will share these characteristics:

(i) they accurately report Nazi crimes;
(ii) they accurately report Jewish responses whose authenticity is beyond dispute;
(iii) the events concerned occurred early in World War II, that is, before the crimes reached a degree of monstrosity which may have rendered them (and hence the responses of the victims) forever beyond adequate comprehension and judgement;
(iv) most important of all, those responses may help to guide our own search for authenticity a generation after.

The first text is as follows:

> In September 1939 the wicked ones came to Bendin, surrounded the Jewish quarter and the synagogue in it, and set fire to the synagogue and the houses adjacent to it. Every Jew who left his house was shot by them on the spot.
>
> Yet even as the flames engulfed the synagogue, several Jews rushed into it, led by a certain Schlesinger, his son and his son-in-law. They fought their way through to the Holy Ark, . . . and each succeeded in rescuing two Torah scrolls, one in each arm.
>
> But as they approached the door of the burning synagogue, they were all shot by the wicked ones and died as martyrs.

Being much longer, the second text may be summarized as follows:

> In the town of Piotrkov a car full of Nazi officers arrived one day, headed straight for the synagogue, dragged out some thirty Torah scrolls, and dumped them into an open lot, leaving guards on twenty-four hour duty lest some Jews 'steal' them. After some days of this a certain Bundist named Abraham Weisshuf was unable to stand this sight any further. So he rallied some other Bundists and, one by one, they sneaked in and carried off the Torah scrolls, hid them in the cemetery, and neither the scrolls nor the Bundists were ever discovered.

Yet this chronicle ends by telling us that all those involved in the incident were eventually murdered at Auschwitz.

The following, with some omissions, is the third and last text:

> In Radzimin there lived a Hasid by the name of Rabbi Yitzhak Meir Kaminer. . . . [There follows a complicated account of typical Nazi ways of singling out a helpless Jew for humiliation and torture.] Then they forced him to dress in his Streimel, Tallith and T'fillin, took him to the town square, stood him against the Christian cross, and ordered him to kiss it. When Kaminer refused to obey them, one of the policemen threatened they would not simply shoot him but rather beat him to death. Kaminer remained unmoved. Then they fell upon him like wild beasts, and beat him senseless until they thought he was dead.
>
> After the policemen were through with him and had left, several Jews ran toward Kaminer who was lying on the ground, and lo, he was still barely alive. They carried him to his apartment, rushed for a doctor, and he managed to bring him back to life.[4]

We are in danger today, as were all those involved then, of letting Nazi monstrosities dissolve themselves into banalities. At such an effect the perpetrators consciously aimed, by means of a system of infinite repetition and steady escalation, until finally, in the

Holocaust Kingdom, horror became ordinary and any sign of common decency miraculous. In our texts, this danger is averted by the Jewish responses, which let the crimes stand out in all their nakedness.

These responses all show a heroism and strength of heart which are almost beyond belief. Without hesitation, Schlesinger and his assistants and Rabbi Kaminer all showed the heroism known in Jewish tradition as *Kiddush ha-Shem* (sanctification of the divine Name). Their martyrdom is equal to any in a holy, millennial tradition. Moreover, lest we lapse into glib fideism, we must stress that in the Piotrkov case *Kiddush ha-Shem* in the 'pious' sense does not apply, since Bundists were not known for their piety. What made the Weisshuf group risk their lives for what to them must have been mere scrolls of parchment? We can offer only some 'secularist' answer like 'the honour of the Jewish people and its Book'.

Then how is it that such heroism and strength of heart — religious or secular — did not move *even one* of the tormentors and murderers? The chronicler does not specify what kind of 'wicked ones', 'policemen' or 'Germans' did the torturing and the murdering. Yet, might not even an SS squad — after all, members of the human species — have been moved to lower their rifles when Schlesinger and the others emerged from the flames? Or, if 'follow orders' and shoot they must, might they not at least have shown admiration or pain?

They are not reported to have done any of these things. They failed to recognize Jews as human even when they were superhuman. For Jews were to them not part of an inferior yet still human 'race', but rather 'vermin'; and one does not admire vermin, but simply 'exterminates' it. Heroism shown by Jews was not heroism but just an additional nuisance to the exterminators. Resistance from Jews was not resistance but rather an outbreak of the plague, Thus, with grim logic, the successful resistance of the Weisshuf group made no difference this side of eternity: in the end, they were all murdered indiscriminately, that is for who they *were*, not for what they *had done*.

And yet, why the Nazi fascination with synagogues, Torah scrolls, prayer shawls and phylacteries — all of them products of Jewish belief, will and deed? Why the ceaseless, limitless efforts to degrade *both* Jews *and* Judaism? Vermin cannot be degraded, and people are degraded for what they believe in or stand for, not for who they are. Why the climactic demand that Rabbi Kaminer kiss the cross?

Doubtless, obedience on his part would have been greeted with the same torments as was his refusal. Here the difference becomes manifest between Nazi and Christian antisemitism. Yet the one, although non-Christian and even anti-Christian, was also heir to many centuries of the other, and it is the conjunction of these two elements that constitutes the uniqueness and mystery of Nazi antisemitism. Other forms of religious hatred may show analogies with Christian antisemitism, and there are many varieties of racism. But there is *no parallel* anywhere for that hatred which singled out the Jewish people and its faith, which sought death and degradation in like measure and reached its climax at Auschwitz. And since this unique enthusiasm for 'non-Aryan' degradation and death had no corresponding enthusiasm for 'Aryan' exaltation and life,[5] *the Holocaust Kingdom was the innermost essence of the entire Nazi system.*

Categories

The above reactions to our texts have already led to a basic problem: in considering the Holocaust, the basic categories of the unique and the universal seem to fail us. If we regard the event as simply unique, this cuts it off from preceding and succeeding history, but if as simply universal, this makes it merely another example of some such species as 'persecution', 'racism', 'antisemitism' or 'genocide'.

Treating the Holocaust as simply unique leads to unauthentic responses on all sides. For Germans, it then becomes a single aberration in an otherwise respectable history, which latter may therefore be simply resumed. For Christians, it becomes a foreign episode: since Nazi antisemitism was evidently anti-Christian, it can apparently have no relation to Christian antisemitism (and so the active or passive support of many Christians for Nazism calls for critical reflection, not on Christianity, but at most on 'Christendom'). For a Jew, to be sure, the groundless murder of one-third of his people in the 'enlightened' modern world remains a trauma; yet if he treats it as utterly unique, he makes it into an episodic catastrophe, as it were, an event which need change nothing in his stance, whether religious or secular, and which is, moreover, destined to fade from memory.

Scholarly responses, lastly, cannot be authentic without (as we have said) entry into the abyss as well as detachment. But viewing the event as simply unique will fragment the scholarly community into two groups without essential communication. A handful will painstakingly gather fact upon horrifying fact; but such facts will be unintelligible both in themselves and within the wider panorama of history, since the unique is by nature unintelligible. And since the task of the scholar is understanding as well as fact-gathering the rest of the scholarly community will bury the findings of these colleagues of theirs in footnotes, if it does not ignore them altogether as mere curiosities, abnormalities, and in any case as 'unessential'.

Such are the perils of unauthenticity which arise when the Holocaust is viewed as simply unique, that is, as disconnected from history before and after. Unauthenticity must also follow from the more fashionable error of seeing in the Holocaust merely the universal, of making it merely a case of the species 'persecution-in-general', 'racism-in-general' or the like. For then all of us — Germans, Christians, Jews, the world — will be morally obliged to transform all 'fruitless' brooding upon that particular past into universal future action: against racism in South Africa, hunger in India, oppression and hatred everywhere. These are authentic responses in themselves, but unauthentic insofar as they flee from the *unique* past. Scholars will be intellectually obliged to explain the apparent uniqueness of the Holocaust as mere appearance. Philosophers will use the Holocaust as an occasion to ponder man's inhumanity to man. In such august company, any Jew haunted by the starkly unique memory of the 'holy ones' of Maidanek and Bergen-Belsen will quietly steal away.

'Uniqueness' and 'universality', then, are inadequate categories, preordaining unauthentic responses to the Holocaust. The hermeneutical concepts we need, however, are implied by Raul Hilberg's thoughtful and thought-provoking remark:

> The missionaries of Christianity had said in effect: You have no right to live among us as Jews. The secular rulers who followed had proclaimed: You have no right to live among us. The German Nazis at last decreed: You have no right to live.[6]

This statement *unites* the universal and the unique through the medium of *history;* thus, a corresponding philosophical explication must somehow unite an aspect of *persistence* in history with an aspect of *transmutation* of history. Since transmutation represents a qualitative leap, it is indeed unique; but since it is transmutation of a persistent feature (in itself a universal element), the leap does not appear from nowhere, but rather has historical antecendents without which it would not have been possible — and historical consequences with which we must live.

RESPONSES TO THE HOLOCAUST

Even by itself, however, the degree of persistence seems, though inescapable, almost incomprehensible. Hilberg lists chilling similarities between mediaeval Christian and modern Nazi anti-Jewish legislation,[7] and one may similarly compare (as we shall) Patristic and Lutheran anti-Jewish diatribes with Nazi hate literature. Such a stubborn persistence through the centuries can be grasped only partly in terms of a *mere* 'tradition', whether conscious or semi-conscious. The Nuremberg laws were not simply a *'product'* of mediaeval tradition, but rather *fell back* on that tradition. Julius Streicher's murderous Jew-hatred was not kindled by Luther's venomous diatribes, but rather *took recourse* to them in order to reinforce, justify and propagandize what needed no kindling by the father of the Reformation.[8]

To comprehend the survival of this phenomenon, through long stretches of time in which it seemed to have lost its strength (if not disappeared altogether), we seem to have only the imagery of a subterranean survival, like that of an evil beast which, apparently safely dead and buried, was in fact only asleep.[9] And even this imagery leaves unanswered questions such as: what feeds such a beast while it is asleep? What awakens it to renewed frenzy? And what — if anything — can be done to destroy it forever? These questions raise deep theoretical and moral problems concerning history as a whole. They also have a terrible urgency at a time of world-wide resurrection of Jew-hatred, thinly disguised as 'anti-Zionism', one generation after Auschwitz.

If even the aspect of persistence of antisemitism through the ages gives rise to deep questions, then, combined with the aspect of transmutation, it boggles the mind. The professional historian can adduce facts 'leading to' the expulsion of the Jews from mediaeval countries, and ones 'leading to' the Holocaust itself. Yet there is a vast and qualitative leap from possibility or even likelihood to *actuality.* Historical explanations of such a leap never answer 'Why was this necessary?' but at most only 'How was this possible?' In order for it to become actual, *somebody had to do it;* in doing it he took a qualitative leap and thereby transmuted future history. What once belonged to the realm of barely thinkable possibility is now all-too-thinkable, for it has once been actual. At least until some future generation should muster the knowledge and the strength to *reverse the whole process,* an escalation has occurred which is like a dark cloud that will not go away.

The Nazis themselves recognized the enormity of the leap by the secrecy with which they undertook the genocide of the Jewish people. By contrast, in their prior policy of mass expulsion of the Jews they had felt no need for secrecy, because there were precedents ranging from mediaeval Spain and England to modern Czarist Russia. And history grimly bore them out. Mankind may have considered such behaviour as contrary to modern enlightenment but, after all, not as without precedent, and hence not calling even for truly *radical* outrage, to say nothing of actions. One likes to think that things would have been otherwise had the events of Treblinka and Auschwitz occurred in the limelight of world-wide publicity.

Raul Hilberg has remarked that, unlike the mediaeval expulsions, the Holocaust 'has not yet been absorbed as an historical event'.[10] One feels a terrible uneasiness when considering the ways in which such absorption can occur. As early as 1945, Abba Kovner had absorbed the event in one way when he wrote:

> We feel with our whole being the sound of the coming *sword.* A sword which lies in wait in all corners of Europe . . .. This new sword was born in the fields of Maidanek, Ponary, Treblinka, where millions of people of varied nationalities saw *how it is done.* How easily. How simply. With how much composure. This new sword in liberated Europe where the guilt of the millions of those implicated in murder which ought to change their consciousness is not yet felt: *for it is permitted,*

> *for it pays off.* I know — and no political judgement, however intelligent, will change my conviction that the next war is not far away . . . . I also know, no matter who starts this war and what its character, the flag of this war will be *our neck*, the neck of us all.[11]

Made under the immediate impact of the horror, Kovner's predictions have thus far mercifully not come true.[12] (Though twenty-five years of Arab Nazi-inspired hate propaganda might not be dismissed so lightly by the world as 'mere words' if any people other than Jews were its target — and it has been 'harmless' thanks not to the conscience of mankind but to the Israeli army.) Not mistaken was the insight that, through the Nazi Holocaust, all history is transmuted. A previously inconceivable dimension of evil has been made conceivable, made part of our human world. A beast of unprecedented monstrosity slumbers underground. No response to the Holocaust can be authentic without first recognizing this fact and then asking, with desperate seriousness, what can be done to slay the beast, or at least to render it harmless for all future time.

Scholarly responses

Having established, at least in outline, some concepts for judging authenticity, let us pursue the implications of these concepts for all involved, whether scholars or individual Germans, Christians or Jews. We shall begin with the responses of some scholars, of ones who have not lightly ignored the terrible issue but rather conscientiously sought to grapple with it. Yet even they will be seen ultimately to have failed to come to terms with this issue. This does not mean, however, that the fault is theirs.

'What caused the Nazis to seek the extermination of the Jewish people?' Erich Goldhagen thus opens an essay[13] which, never losing sight of this question, brings out the whole Nazi hatred of the Jewish people. First, antisemitism was not a cynical tool for Nazism, but rather the core of its 'philosophy'. Second, that core was beyond refutation, since Jews were viewed as conspirators whose virtuous actions, too, could only disguise viciousness. Third, this viciousness was innate; thus, despite being considered 'criminal' as though it were imputable, it was at the same time viewed as a 'bacillus', as something which is not imputable and for which no punishment — including capital punishment — but only 'extermination' could be the cure. Liberal, Marxist and many other historians may find it impossible to believe that 'sane men could . . . possibly have believed such monstrous drivel'.[14] Goldhagen's essay has the merit of recognizing that the Nazis *did* believe it.

It also recognizes that even this Nazi 'philosophy' cannot account for the 'venomous hatred that breathed through Nazi writings and speeches concerning the Jews'. The Jew was the 'dreaded, dark, Satanic enemy'. A single Jew alive threatened death to those near him; every Jew dead was a step toward salvation. In some cases Nazis would wear gloves when dealing with Jews; in others, cups from which Jewish slave labourers had drunk would be ordered destroyed. Hitler had a moment of truth when he told an interviewer in 1938 that 'he had only one idea for export . . . not National Socialism . . . but . . . antisemitism'. So much more deep-rooted was this hatred than any mere Nazi 'idea' or 'philosophy', that Goebbels could say in May 1943 (!): In this war the Jews alone have shed no blood nor performed any work; they have only profited from it.[15]

Yet while Goldhagen states and develops his question admirably, his answer is feeble and anti-climactic. Even if a Nazi work of 1944 argues that the murder of the Jewish 'race of criminals' is an act of justice, this 'argument' does not explain Nazi hatred but only reflects it. Doubtless, when Hitler in 1942 described extermination as a 'reasonable solution' of 'the Jewish question', and as an application of the biblical 'an eye for an eye, a tooth for tooth', this self-styled 'scientific insight' was a 'hallucinatory vision'; however, to call it such does not answer the question but only restates it. The author sums up his explanation that the Nazi leaders were possessed by a primitive mago-mythical outlook. While one part of the German mind cultivated reason and pursued science with undiminished vigour, the other part sank into primitive magic.[16] This, besides insulting all magic, myth and primitivism as such, simply fails to account for the scandalous uniqueness of *Nazi* 'magic', 'myth' and 'primitivism', and for their equally scandalous concentration, not on a mythical figure, but on the actual Jewish people.

The essay, not surprisingly, also lapses into basic inconsistency. Throughout the author rightly insists that for the Nazis antisemitism was no mere Machiavellian means, but rather an ultimate end, perhaps the only ultimate end. Yet he also cites with approval the contrary view — implying that the Jews were merely a scapegoat — once supposedly voiced by Hitler according to a dubious authority: 'If the Jew did not exist, we should invent him.'[17]

Karl Dietrich Bracher's *The German Dictatorship,*[18] relentless both in its fidelity to the facts and in its drive to explain them, time and again explodes simplistic theories and apologetic myths. In refutation of the view that Nazism somehow falls outside German and European history, the work deals extensively with Germany and Nazism before 1933 and concludes (in 1970) that Nazism is not yet dead.

Perhaps most persuasive is Bracher's account of Nazi Germany as a dual system. One system — the inner core — revealed itself ultimately as the SS State. The other was the traditional German system: civil service, army, educational and clerical establishments, and the like. This latter system was increasingly penetrated, manipulated and perverted by the former. Although remaining distinct and occasionally opposed to the first system, its often active cooperation enabled the SS system to do what it could never have accomplished by itself. It thus follows — despite protestations to the contrary unceasing to this day — that the traditional German system must assume its share of responsibility and guilt.

Bracher's persuasiveness abruptly disappears when he reaches two cataclysmic events: the Nazi invasion of Russia and the Holocaust. The author himself connects these two events as manifesting a 'contradiction inherent in totalitarian ideas and . . . politics' and as having 'proved highly detrimental . . . to the conduct of the war and to the new Order'.[19] He falters, not in his narrative, but in interspersing it with 'explanations' which do not explain. Thus, when contrasted with his account of the Nazi attack on Russia in all its absurdity (which produced the very two-front war that Hitler had sought at all costs to avoid), Bracher's explanation of what Hitler himself called 'the most difficult decision of his life'[20] sounds almost ludicrous: that it was 'an attempt to seek a way out of the war'.[21]

This juxtaposition of relentlessly faithful narrative and feeble explanation is still more striking in Bracher's treatment of the Holocaust. The narrative, 'terrible in its authority', spares us nothing: the murder for murder's sake, the unrelenting murder machine, the even active involvement of the German armed forces, Himmler's unbelievable speech about the SS 'decency' manifested in the murder camps as 'a never to be written glorious page' in German history.[22]

As before, Bracher falters when he yields — however rarely and cautiously — to the temptation to give explanations which do not explain. Early in his work he rightly characterizes 'antisemitism and race mania' as 'probably the only "genuine" fanatically held and realized conviction of [Hitler's] . . . entire life' and observes that this 'fanatical hatred of the Jews defies all rational explanation'; nor does he evade 'the fact that an entire nation followed [Hitler] . . . and furnished a legion of executioners'.[23] Even here, however — in discussing only Nazi antisemitism and not yet the Holocaust — Bracher's 'explanation' is 'rational' enough, but not an explanation:

> We are confronted not merely with the inexplicable dynamics of one man, but with a terrible disease of modern nationalism, whose desire for exclusivity and war against everything 'alien' constitutes one of the root causes of antisemitism.[24]

Here we have no answer but, properly considered, merely a restatement of the question. Just what is a 'nationalism' which is totally and exclusively negative? Just what *is* its dynamics when it refuses to deviate from Jews as the object of hate? And what is explained by the metaphor 'disease'?

The full authenticity of Bracher's scholarly response reappears when he does not flinch from relating the horrors of the Holocaust itself. Even then, however, the narrative is marred by terms such as 'obsession', 'biologistic insanity' and 'disease'. One asks: are such terms intended to have explanatory force? If so, they trivialize the unthinkable in an attempt to render it intelligible. If not, an appearance of intelligibility is given when in fact nothing is being explained. In either case, we are faced with lapses in a work of otherwise outstanding authenticity. These lapses suggest that, faced with the Holocaust, even the best of scholarship — whose task, after all, is to explain as well as to relate — cannot but fall short of its task.

This overall conclusion is reinforced by two other scholarly efforts which, though less comprehensive than Bracher's, are focused on our central questions. One is an essay by Andreas Hillgruber[25] which confines itself (presumably not by accident) to the very two aspects of the Nazi programme on which Bracher comes to grief — the *Drang nach Osten* and the 'Final Solution'. The other, a masterpiece of popularization by Werner Jochmann and Bernd Wellessen,[26] is a skilful juxtaposition of explanatory narrative with documentation in which, time and again, the documents overwhelm all the 'explanations'.

Hillgruber's essay begins with a powerful attack on the frequent view of Nazism as a 'nihilistic' revolution devoid of all principles, such that 'Nazism, as it were, falls outside German and European history' and any Nazi recourse to German tradition was a mere tactical device of the 'demonic' Hitler in his search for total power. Hillgruber argues, besides the illegitimacy of blaming everything on the 'demonism' of one individual, that this particular individual, however 'nihilistic' otherwise, *stood for something,* for ideas of which necessary preconditions *already existed in pre-Nazi Germany.* Among these were radical universal antisemitism and the *Lebensraum* idea. The 'indissoluble synthesis' of these two elements was the essence of Nazi ideology, and only this synthesis makes the transformation of mere ideology into unspeakable practice intelligible at all.[27]

Hillgruber divides pre-'racist' antisemitism into liberal, socialist and conservative variants, according as it blamed Jews for their 'separatism', 'mammonism' or 'revolutionary' inclinations respectively. He then shows how 'racist' antisemitism, far from emerging *ex nihilo,* in fact 'preserves all these accusations and prejudices' and only makes them into expressions of a Jewish essence which is held to be immutable. It consequently repudiates all and every Jewish emancipation and assimilation. Faced with the problem of holding together accusations and prejudices which are clearly incompatible, racist antisemitism 'solves' this problem through hypothesizing a supposed Jewish world conspiracy in which communism and capitalism, assimilationist universalism and separatist particularism, are all mere guises in a plot to rule the world.

Thus it could appear — decades prior to Nazism! — that the most rabid form of 'nationalist' antisemitism was simply an act of self-defence. And once the 'Jewish' and the 'Bolshevist' 'mortal enemies' had been identified in the Nazi mind, abstractly ideological elements became sufficiently concrete and specific to motivate overt action which would otherwise remain wholly inexplicable: the *Lebensraum* idea concretized itself in the *Drang nach Osten*, and the 'fight against the Jewish enemy' became Auschwitz and Maidanek.[28]

The synthesis Hillgruber ascribes to the Nazi mind may well be a fact and go far toward explaining, at last, the Nazi attack on Russia.[29] But does it suffice to explain Auschwitz? And did the synthesis, if ever a fact, remain indissoluble?

One may well grant that theory explains theory: the theory of the 'moral Jewish–Bolshevist enemy' may well have led to the *theory* that both unprecedented barbarism in the war on Russia and the 'extermination' of East European Jewry were necessities. Moreover, in a manner recalling Bracher's two systems, such 'theory' may explain *execution* to a degree, for example, the ultimate collapse of the fictional separation between 'military warfare' and SS activities in the occupied eastern territories, after which the two became an 'indissoluble whole'. Yet while military complicity explains how the SS could do what they wanted to do, the fact of military complicity in actions *such as these* remains *itself* to be explained. Reference to 'military honour' respecting orders supporting and covering SS bestialities only serves to heighten the mystery.

To be sure, Hillgruber can insist that the age-old Prussian 'tension' between 'the ethics of an officer' and 'the duty of obedience' had shrivelled into blind obedience, and that this fatal development had been made possible by a 'loss of moral and religious substance'.[30] However, explanations such as these are grotesquely inadequate if not indeed circular. As for Himmler's reference to the 'decency' shown and preserved by the SS mass-murderers of Jewish men, women and children, it takes the historian beyond even ideological intelligibility, into a realm where there is only shuddering.

Hillgruber admits as much when he concedes that even after Hitler's synthesis between 'eastern empire' and 'Final Solution' had collapsed, the Final Solution was pursued as relentlessly as ever.[31] There no longer remained *any* exaltation of the 'Aryan', however desperate, but only a groundless, inexplicable, yet implacable hatred of the 'non-Aryan' — the Jew. Thus, the essay creditably ends by stressing the necessity, and yet the utter impossibility, of judging 'even the approximate adequacy the monstrosity of the event and its perpetrators and accomplices, to say nothing of doing justice to the millions of its victims'.[32]

Turning now briefly to the popular book by Jochmann and Nellessen, we find as a typical example the following:

> In developing his hierarchical views of domination, Hitler begins with the view that the value of human beings has degrees. At the top are those . . . destined to be leaders, composed of those who have proven themselves stronger in struggle, accept all orders without thought, and know how to carry them out ruthlessly. The fact that they carry out Hitler's orders without question is by no means based only on a brutal power instinct . . . but has its ultimate basis in an absolute faith . . . in the *Führer* and his historical mission. *This explains, to give but one example, that SS commandos carry out murderous actions of extermination against Jews and alien nationals,* with the consciousness of serving the *Führer* and his historical mission, hence, as they understood it, a good cause.[33] [emphasis added]

The document meant to corroborate the second half of the above passage is this excerpt from the notorious speech of Himmler already alluded to above:

'The Jewish people must be exterminated', say all party comrades, 'obviously; our party programme contains exclusion of the Jews, extermination, and we'll do it.' And then they all come, those honest eighty million Germans, and each and every one has his one decent Jew. Obviously, the other Jews are all swine, but this one is first class. Of all who talk like this not a single one has looked on, has endured it. Most of you, in contrast, will know what it means when a hundred corpses lie there together, five hundred, a thousand. To have endured *this* and — apart from a few exceptions of human weakness — to have remained decent, this is what has made us hard. This is a glorious page in our history which has never been written and will never be written.[34]

Jochmann and Nellessen are doubtless correct when they assert that this speech to the SS élite, and the actions to which it refers, are *connected* with 'ideas' such as the mission of Hitler. But does talk of an 'absolute faith' or a 'mission' — does anything on earth, in heaven, in hell — *explain* the unutterably grisly sentiments and actions recorded in this speech? What beyond the fact that they were actual extorts our admission that such sentiments and actions *must* have been possible? All attempts to show *how* they were possible, much less what could have made them necessary, have failed; all explanations proferred are in the end circular or tautological. Such are the intellectual perplexities defying the honest historian who now attempts to 'absorb' the Nazi Holocaust 'as an historical event'.

Schlesinger, Weisshuf and Rabbi Kaminer all lacked the benefit of our historical hindsight. They could not better understand the groundless and merciless hatred against them than does the social scientist or historian a generation after. This did not prevent them either from recognizing the absolute evil clearly and without illusion, or from opposing it fearlessly and without compromise. Their testimony is an outcry against any scholar who would either ignore that evil or explain it away.

German responses

On the wall of the Nuremberg municipality there was inscribed, long before the Nazis, the following legend: 'Never trust a fox on the heath, or a Jew when he swears on oath!'[35] Despite modern enlightenment and Jewish emancipation, it was never removed. This fact poignantly illustrates the need to consider the German antecedents of Nazism. And yet: as such it tells us little. A Catholic church facing the Roman Ghetto bears a similar legend of hate. France had its Dreyfus affair. Perhaps there are many countries in which the Holocaust *could* have happened. In Germany alone, it *did* happen. Today's world includes victims, accomplices, bystanders, and all their heirs. *The Germans* must live with a past which includes *the unspeakable crime itself.*

After four decades of debate, some preliminary questions can be disposed of quickly. Thus, 'individual or collective guilt?' has clearly proved a false question when, on the one hand, a whole generation of Germans has arisen that did not know Hitler, and, on the other, the plea of 'only following orders' has shown itself to be a mendacious excuse bespeaking an unrepentant Nazi or crypto-Nazi mind. One can neither absolve those who 'only followed orders', nor consider the obviously innocent guilty by association or inheritance.

To pass from guilt to repentance, the innocent also obviously have nothing for which to repent. For the guilty — in whatever degree — repentance must in principle be possible; yet is it, in *this* case, possible in practice? Here we turn from easy abstract issues to a concrete question of great intractability. Can one repent for one's complicity in a crime without understanding it, and can *anyone* claim to have understood this crime? Perhaps it is no accident that Germans often feel the less guilty the guiltier they are, and are more profoundly wracked by a sense of guilt the greater their innocence. One can imagine the German people torn apart into two groups: one even descending to masochistic self-flagellation as it attempts to atone vicariously for sins it did not commit, the other moved to Nazi humour at the sight of those fellow-Germans, whose behaviour only hardens its own impenitence.

We move to obscurer realms still when we turn from repentance to the question of forgiveness. That genuine repentance always merits forgiveness is said to be the Christian view, and sometimes to be the Jewish view as well. When the Holocaust is involved, however, such a summary answer reflects an unauthentic sentimentality which does not wish, or is unable to face up to the crime.[36] Who, one may ask, is to forgive? How can a Christian forgive the mass-murder of Jews when (in a special sense to be considered below) he is himself implicated in the crime? How can a Jew forgive a crime directed not against himself alone, but against his whole people? Indeed, it may be questioned whether even God Himself can forgive *this* crime.[37] An authentically repentent ex-SS man must live bravely *without the assurance of forgiveness;* indeed, he will sternly insist that, in this case, grace would be cheap.

The above considerations, however important, are only preliminary; for if guilt, innocence, repentance and forgiveness were the essence of the German problem, that problem would pass away with the Hitler generation. What will not die, however, is the issue of German *historical responsibility.* A young German, innocent of the crime itself, has only one way of repudiating such responsibility: by repudiating German history at the same time, i.e. by emigration. To participate in German history, and yet to deny any responsibility issuing from the Holocaust, is to pretend that 'Nazism, as it were, falls outside German and European history' — a view which has already been revealed as the core of unauthentic scholarship. Since it is German scholars who have exposed this view as spurious, the German people are not in principle incapable of assuming the historical responsibility for the Holocaust, however vast the task may be of discharging it.

Evidence is lacking, however, of a widespread German willingness to accept this responsibility. For instance, a revisionist history of Nazism by Werner Maser and Heinz Höhne, serialized in *Der Spiegel,* claims that until 1938 or 1939 Hitler confined himself to such decent conservative objectives as the 'correction' of the 'for Germany unfavourable results of World War I'. His 'friends and supporters' were 'horrified' by Hitler's 'new course'. Göring bellowed that the great pogrom of 1938 was 'the last infamy' for which he would cover up (but three months later decreed the confiscation of all Jewish gold and jewelry!). Gestapo chief Werner Best viewed the march into Prague as an act of 'illegitimate imperialism' (but later became the Nazi ruler of Denmark!). Hitler's 'radical change' has remained a 'mystery to this day'.[38] Only one page subsequently describes the Holocaust (stating the facts accurately enough), whose 'explanation' is that Himmler and his henchmen stayed faithful to their *Führer,* although he was by then — according to a lengthy account complete with doctors' testimonies — a sick and prematurely aged man. In short, only one man was responsible — and he was ill.[39]

It is difficult to conceive of a more revolting whitewash. Still, it is Maser and Höhne, not such scholars as Bracher Hillgruber or Jochmann, that are serialized in a German mass magazine which is anything but a Nazi rag.[40]

Even if Nazism *were* incidental to German history — as it is all-too-human for Germans to pretend — the German people would be burdened with historical responsibility for it. For the murdered European Jews are not of the past alone; they are, as it were, the presence of an absence. The German people must *live with* this presence, and no one else (perhaps least of all Jews) can show them how this is possible. Others can at most warn them that to *ignore* this presence would be to murder the memory of those already murdered.

However, the view that Nazism is no essential part of German history is indeed a falsehood, to embrace which is to invite disaster. For the right, it is to risk falling back on the traditional pre-Nazi German virtues of patriotism and military honour, as if these were not compromised by their implication in the crimes of Nazism. For the left, it is to risk indulging in the time-honoured leftist move of wiping the past off the map — a move which, always impossible, has a demonic potential when the past includes the Holocaust. Through such unauthentic responses, both German right and left may lapse into antisemitism; and antisemitism, intolerable anywhere since the Holocaust, is obscene when it is German.

The core of all *authentic* German responses is to attempt to undo for all future German history what one generation of Germans has done. The past itself cannot be undone. What we must hope is that the future can be liberated from contamination by the past, for this is a moral and spiritual necessity.

Forgetfulness is no way to achieve that end. A Jewish scholar writes as follows:

> A young German recently wrote to me expressing the hope that Jews, when thinking of Germany, might keep in mind the words of Isaiah: 'Remember ye not the former things, neither consider the things of old.' I do not know whether the messianic age will bestow forgetfulness upon the Jews. It is a delicate point of theology. But for us, who must live without illusions in an age without a Messiah, such a hope entails the impossible. However sublime it might be to forget, we cannot. Only by remembering a past that we will never completely master can we generate new hope in the resumption of communication between Germans and Jews, and in the reconciliation of those who have been separated.[41]

Christian responses

If 'racist' antisemitism is an escalation of the 'liberal', 'socialist' and 'conservative' variants, where do these latter have their ultimate origin? We reply: in the words of 'the missionaries of Christianity'. The Holocaust imposes a historical responsibility upon Christians too, though one distinct from responsibility for the doing of the deed. *As Christians,* indeed, they could not have done it. Yet it is Christians who created its ultimate, if remote, *possibility.*

This assertion is keenly rejected by Christian apologists, maximally by those who consider antisemitism a pre-Christian phenomenon which entered Christianity only, as it were, by accident. However, whereas the ancients viewed Jews as 'enemies of mankind', Christians viewed them as enemies of God Himself. Hellenism had desired an end to Jewish 'separatism'; Christianity desired the end of Jewish existence. The pagan Roman Empire had made Jews into citizens;[42] as soon as it became 'holy', it robbed Jews of this right: 'The Church and the Christian state, concilium decisions and imperial laws, henceforth worked hand in hand to persecute the Jews.'[43] Christian antisemitism so obviously escalated its pagan antecedent that two assertions can safely be made. First, the modern 'secular' variants of antisemitism are further developments of the mediaeval Christian form and not (as they sometimes pretend) a resurrection of ancient pagan antisemitism. Second, the latter would long have been dead had Christian antisemitism not arisen.

In retreat from their maximal posture, Christian apologists distinguish between Christianity and 'Christendom'. As a religion of love, Christianity is necessarily opposed to all forms of hate; thus, hatred of Jews may appear within a 'Christendom' coeval with Christianity, but has otherwise no connection. Yet, why did antisemitism appear so regularly in times and places 'nominally' Christian, and why was Christian love mostly so feeble in one particular — opposing the Jew-hatred of 'nominal' Christians? There is at least this connection between Christianity and the antisemitism of 'Christendom': that such a hatred, while opposed to Christianity, is at the same time a perversion *peculiar* to Christianity. For this, therefore, Christianity must assume *some kind* of responsibility.

That this conclusion is unpalatable is illustrated by the widespread and possibly growing myth that no Christian was a Nazi. Unfortunately, the truth is otherwise. Using a tradition harking back to the 1880s and even to the Wars of Liberation, Nazi antisemitism spoke more often and loudly in the name of 'positive Christianity' than in that of pagan Teutonism. Its following amongst German Protestants and Catholics alike was vast. Nor is antisemitism dead even now within either denomination.

But the retreat from apologetic unauthenticity is not complete until contemporary Christian thought faces up to the antisemitism of even the true anti-Nazi Christians. We rightly revere the heroism of that small minority of Christians in Nazi Germany who bore witness against Nazism at the risk of death and sometimes continued into martyrdom. All the same, the Catholic bishops who protested — successfully! — against the Nazi murder of their incurably ill fellow-human beings, failed to protest against that of their Jewish fellow-human beings. Their Protestant counterparts confined their defence of 'non-Aryans' to the safely converted. Not until far too late did a Niemöller or a Bonhoeffer discover the martyred Jewish people as their brethren,[44] and perhaps even then more despite than because of their own theology.[45]

Doubt on this last point is virtually removed by a post-war German Christian declaration of guilt which, though very probably inspired by the Holocaust, made no mention of the Jews. Even this declaration had to be defended in Germany in the seventies.[46] It is the antisemitism of its saints, not merely of its sinners, that Christianity must face, if it seeks an authentic response to the Holocaust.

For Christian antisemitism cannot be treated as a single unfortunate accident, i.e. as the canonization of first century Jewish–Christian animosities in the New Testament. The *merely* accidental can always be somehow overcome, even if it has been canonized; indeed, every scriptural religion has been both forced and able to cope with unpalatable elements in its sacred writings. No accident, but something essential was at work if, for centuries after the New Testament period, a whole literature — the *Adversus Judaeos* writings of the Church Fathers — could arise which contains nothing but venomous hatred of the Jewish people, and if this same hatred was resurrected yet again in the writings of the father of Protestantism. One can neither deny Luther's spiritual greatness, nor make little of his savage antisemitism. Nor can one separate St. Chrysostom, the vile Jew-hater, from St. Chrysostom, the 'preacher of the golden mouth'. Nor again can one pretend that St. Chrysostom stood alone, since he was merely the most extreme among giants of the church who included the great St. Augustine.

It is a principle of the *Adversus Judaeos* literature that Jews either are miserable or ought to be made so. Christians, if persecuted, are witnesses beloved of God. Jews, if persecuted, are sinners who suffer the divine wrath. Christians, if happy and successful, are recipients of divine Grace. Jews, if happy and successful, are self-seeking hunters after wealth and power, engaged in anti-divine scheming or showing anti-Christian impertinence.

This leads us to three general characteristics of this Jew-hatred. First, it is impervious to all empirical evidence: it makes charges which, in their very incoherence, form a closed system permitting no escape. Second, it is aroused not by what Jews do, but by who they are: a people which, in insisting on surviving, *ipso facto* rejects the Christian redeemer. Third, this hatred is forever tempted to pass from the sphere of theory into that of action, and to become a self-fulfilling prophecy. These elements of Jew-hatred, spelled out in the *Adversus Judaeos* literature, must also be regarded as latent, however mildly and unobtrusively, in every form of Christian theology which maintains that Jews are either a 'has been' or 'never was'.

The *Adversus Judaeos* literature goes a fatal step further, becoming in germ the Nazi view, when it maintains both that Jewish 'wickedness' is imputable (as though it were corrigible, at least by the act of conversion) and at the same time that it is innate (and thus absolutely incorrigible). Not Abraham but Cain is the father of the Jewry, which makes them a nation of murderers. Not Sarah but Hagar is their mother, which destines them to eternal servitude. Consequently, even the apparent virtues of the Jews are vices, and their very faithfulness is perverse. Jews act perversely *both* when they obey the Law *and* when they disobey it. They deserve blame *both* for 'legalistically' observing the sabbath *and* for giving to God only one day out of seven. In short, of all the nations only this one is wholly and utterly beyond redemption.

If one asks how this totally unChristian doctrine, venting its hatred upon an image of the Jew devised by itself, should have crept into the writings of Christian saints, does it suffice to cite irritation by Jewish 'stubbornness' as the essential cause? The whole *Adversus Judaeos* literature was permeated less by the desire to save the Jews than by the desire to save the Judaizing Christians from their 'clutches'. But how great was the 'danger'? And, small or great, does it suffice to explain a hatred in the hearts of saints which, permitting its victims no redemption, is *itself* without redeeming characteristics?

In its formative period, Christianity proved unable to affirm itself without the simultaneous negation of both the Jewish people and its faith. Universal love went together with this particular hatred. And so deep and close has been this demonic conjunction that Christianity has not rid itself of it decisively to this day.[47]

This inescapable conclusion supplies partial answers to questions asked earlier in this essay. What, beyond conscious tradition, accounts for the persistence of Jew-hatred over long periods of apparent decline or even total disappearance? Less fatally the lingering prejudices and resentments of the most sinful than the passivity and even enthusiasm of the most saintly. What made possible the escalation of Jew-hatred beyond limits ever intended by its originators? While the *actual* escalation belongs to none but those who did it, among the accessories before and during the fact are those who sowed the evil seed, or proved too weak and confused to destroy its unwelcome harvest when the devil came up from underground. We are told that St. Chrysostom never preached violence against the Jewish people. We need not doubt it. Indeed, we can picture the preacher of the golden mouth horrified by the mediaeval expulsions. And we can also picture him suffering martyrdom in a Nazi murder camp. This in no way affects the conclusion that he and his heirs created the ultimate, if remote, cause of the *possibility* of the Holocaust.

Christian thought can respond authentically to the Holocaust only if it understands it as nothing less than a *negative epiphany*. With every escalation of Jew-hatred since the birth of Christianity, the dark underside attached too deeply to the Christian tradition has escalated the threat to turn against and destroy its substance until finally, in the Holocaust Kingdom, the darkness overwhelmed the light.

Only Christians themselves can find their way out of this catastrophe of their faith. The goal, however, is easily defined. Re-enacting its entire history from the time of its earliest missionaries, Christianity needs systematically to eradicate the negation of the Jew and his Judaism implicit within itself, and replace it with a radical affirmation. Having contained anti-Jewishness as such an integral part, Christianity now takes an incalculable risk in repudiating it. However, it cannot shrink from that risk. After Auschwitz, Christianity can live only if it systematically affirms the Jew in his Jewishness. A Christianity which continues to seek the end of the Jew is itself at its end, fallen victim to a demonic element within itself.

A Christian in search of an authentic response may ask: where was Jesus during the Nazi Holocaust? One among the many answers is surely this — that, like Rabbi Yitzhak Meir Kaminer, Jesus would have let himself be beaten senseless by Nazi Christians rather than kiss their cross.

Jewish responses

Any authentic Jewish response to the Holocaust must begin by recognizing those who responded authentically in the midst of the catastrophe itself. Who among us 'religious' Jews would, like Schlesinger, his son and son-in-law, rush into the flames to rescue a few *Sifrei Torah,* however sacred to us? Who among us 'secularist' Jews would, like Weisshuf and his followers, risk his life for the honour of the Jewish people as represented by a few pieces of parchment? And how many Jews — religious or secularist — would keep refusing to kiss the cross as they were being beaten senseless? While the Nazis did their best to murder even the memory of martyrdom, in cases such as these they were defeated. Our part, before all else, is to confirm the victory of our martyrs and heroes by making it live for ever in reverent memory.

This memory, moreover, must extend not only to the strong, to the heroes and evident martyrs. It must also include the weak who were 'only' victims: the children, their mothers; the grown men who could not believe what was indeed unbelievable; even those who, sucked in by the evil system, believed vainly that they could save some by sacrificing others. All these are *an overwhelming revelation of innocence.*

The unique light of this revelation may elude our perception unless we muster the will to look steadily at the unique darkness of Nazi evil against which it shines. Then, however, all the 'merely passive' innocence may well blaze forth in a sacredness fully matching the active martyrdom and heroism. And of the two it is the innocence that is the more unbearable. Yet, though heaven and earth stop their ears, theirs is a cry which will never be stilled.

It has therefore well been ruled by halakhic authorities[48] that *all* Jews murdered for no reason other than their Jewishness are to be considered 'holy ones'. For us to obey this ruling, however, is to attempt the nearly impossible. The innocence of the victims shines forth as the stars in the firmament; their degradation at the hands of the torturers blackens all the heavens. The martyrdom of the heroes vanquishes this degradation; it is vanquished in turn wherever the criminals have succeeded in wiping out all record of that heroism.

Moreover, as we try to rescue for memory what fragments we can, fresh adversaries arise: hostile ones, Ideologues on right and left, heirs of Nazism all, who degrade the memory or erase the Jewishness of our holy ones even in death:[49] and friendly ones, the good people of this earth, who want us to 'forgive and forget' for our own sake and are unsure about our goodness when we cannot. Finally, there is an eternal enemy: time itself, which would have all things vanish indifferently in the river Lethe — forgotteness. Thus, like Germans and Christians, we too must live without the assurance we stand most in need of

— in our case, whether even our most desperate efforts to sanctify memory can prevail.

If desperation tinges our most authentic response to the Nazi assault on Jewish dignity, it threatens to dominate our response to the assault on Jewish life itself. Most assuredly, we are commanded to answer the Nazi celebration of Jewish death with an unwavering celebration of Jewish life. Yet not one of our ways of affirming and celebrating life will bring back the dead, or bestow life on their children who were never born. We may hear the ancient tale of *tehiyat ha-metim,* of a resurrection of the dead which is past all finite understanding. But we are forbidden to hear it more than faintly, lest it become a glib *theologumenon* and a cheap escape from our earthly tears and from our stern historical task.

Our stern historical task. We ask: where must we *believe and act differently* from Schlesinger, Weisshuf and Rabbi Kaminer? We reply: their examples fail us in no respect except where our situation has changed. *We are required to be either in Israel or dedicated Zionists.*

Auschwitz climaxed a millennial combination of Jew-hatred with Jewish powerlessness. There can be no authentic response to this climax by anyone — German, Christian, Jew, the world — which omits a determination to *end* this unholy combination; for Jews themselves, this implies the duty however reluctantly assumed, of acquiring the means of self-defence. This duty, forced upon Jewish resistance fighters in Warsaw and many other ghettos, has found an indispensable expression in the establishment of a Jewish state. The epoch-making significance of that development for Jewish and indeed world history, however, is as yet recognized but dimly even by Jews.

For it responds to the three-fold prohibition, so well formulated by Hilberg. 'You have no right to live' — the Jewish state, although it is impossible to discount a second Masada, will never permit a second Auschwitz, 'You have no right to live among us' — the Jewish state cannot end the persecution and expulsion of Jews, but through its Law of Return it gives a home to such Jews as the persecutors permit to leave. 'You have no right to live among us as Jews' — the very name of the Jewish state in effect replies to Christianity, Paul's 'new' Israel, and to its secularist successors, that the 'old' Israel is not a defunct people of a non-people, but alive.

This is a breathtakingly swift reversal of an evil, escalated over a period of two millennia, and de-escalated by a single, momentous historic act. Since it has no parallel anywhere, even Jews catch a glimpse of this act's significance only in moments of crisis, while the world's behaviour proves that it takes more than one generation to destroy a bimillennial hatred. Hence we should perhaps not be surprised that large sections of the world resist and slander the Jewish testimony incarnate in the Jewish state. Every war Israel has had to fight has been for her life — and has been denounced as aggression. For opening her doors to Jewish immigrants, for ending Jewish homelessness, she is branded a 'racist state', And the elementary right to existence itself, denied to no other state on earth, has been granted by the 'family of nations' to this nation only on terms which, once acceded to, would destroy her. So little has the world changed since the Nazi Holocaust.

But Jewish responses to the Holocaust would lapse into unauthenticity if they therefore wavered in their commitment to Zion. The Talmud observes that if the Gentiles but recognized the significance of the event, they more than the Jews, would lament the destruction of Jerusalem at the hands of the Romans. Today, if the Gentiles but understood, they, more than the Jews, would mourn Jewish death at Auschwitz and celebrate Jewish rebirth at Jerusalem. We owe our obligation not to waver not only to the Jewish future, but also to the future of the world.

RESPONSES TO THE HOLOCAUST

When speaking of Auschwitz to others we should say: 'Weep not for us! Weep for yourselves!' Let Germans weep for fathers or uncles involved in the most heinous crime in all history, and for a culture which, despite its greatness, mistook the devil for a saviour. Let Christians weep for a faith which, despite its spirit of love, encouraged hatred against the people to which it owes its own life, and for their saints flawed by this hatred. Let the world weep for its indifference and its half-heartedness. And let the tears of us all not be for yesterday only but also for tomorrow — for the consequences of the past which have yet to unfold.

But, astonishingly, we can also say to the world: 'As our weeping keeps us apart, so let rejoicing bring us together! Join our joy over Jewish rebirth in Jerusalem!' For there can be no greater blessing to any German who assumes his historical responsibility for a new German future, than a Jewish state invulnerable to all forms of post-Nazi German hatred of the Jewish people. Nor can there be a greater blessing to any Christian who now seeks to eradicate the dark underside of his faith, than a Jewish state sufficiently strong to be independent of Christian charity. Only because of the existence of the Jewish state is it now possible to imagine a time when the evil beast of Jew-hatred will, at long last, be slain.

Conclusion

Jewish tradition bids us end every discourse on a note of hope. In the uniquely grim case of the Holocaust, it is necessary to bend this rule, mixing with hope uncertainty and even foreboding. The Midrash has it that when the Egyptians pursued and the Red Sea split, the people hesitated, until Nachshon the son of Amminadav jumped into the waves.[50] Not accidentally are Israelis fond of naming their sons Nachshon, for they have learned the stern truth that there are no miracles without human action.

The Jewish people itself became a modern Nachshon when it responded to the Nazi Holocaust not with despair or escapism, but with the founding of a Jewish state. In two respects, however, this Nachshon differs from his remote original. Then only a threat, in our time catastrophe occurred. And the miracle, then preceding the human response, is today still only a hope. The modern Nachshon had no time to wait for miracles. He had only two choices. One was to die. The other was to jump into the waves, not knowing whether the sea would split and, if not, whether he would have strength enough to swim through the raging waters, if necessary, alone.

NOTES

1. Kant ventured to define non-moral and moral motivations, but considered it to be beyond human power to *identify* even a single case of unmixed motivation.

2. This writer heard of a recent Jewish wedding at which no expenses were spared. Thousands of candles lit up every part of the large hall, so that not a single a spot was dark. Except for the bride, all members of her parents' family had perished in the Holocaust.

3. I have argued previously that while a meaning cannot be found in the Holocaust, to seek a response is inescapable. See, e.g.; E. Fackenheim, *Quest for Past and Future* (Boston, 1970), pp. 17ff.

4. Shim'on Huberband, *Kiddush ha-Shem* (Tel Aviv, 1969), pp. 27, 25ff., 33ff.

5. Leo Strauss characterizes the Nazi state as the only regime ever 'which had no other clear principle than murderous hatred of the Jews, for "Aryan" had no clear meaning other than "non-Jewish"' [preface to 'Spinoza's Critique of Religion', in Judah Goldin, ed., *The Jewish Expression* (New York, 1970), p. 247].

EMIL L. FACKENHEIM

In 1944 Hitler made the following remark to his associate Walter Schellenberg (to be found in W. Jochmann and B. Nellessen, *Adolf Hitler: Personlichkeit — Ideologie — Taktik* (Paderborn, 1960), pp. 34–5]:

> In this war there can be no compromise. There is only victory or extinction. In case the German nation should fail it will perish . . . . Yes, in that case let it perish, let it croak; for the best will have fallen, and the rest should give way to those who are biologically stronger. In case the German nation fails, the end for Germany will be cruel. However, it will have deserved nothing better.

Readiness to 'let it perish' is illustrated by Hitler's bunker-order (not obeyed) to flood the Berlin subways in a futile attempt to stop the Russian army, even if thereby drowning thousands of German civilians seeking shelter from air attacks.

6. R. Hilberg, *The Destruction of the European Jews* (Chicago, 1961) pp. 3ff.

7. *Ibid.*, pp. 5–7.

8. At the Nuremberg trials Streicher pleaded that he only followed Luther's teachings. On these, see below, note 47.

9. We use this imagery *not* as a pseudo-explanation, but merely to bring out what demands an explanation. And we would in any case refuse to resort to the Jungian 'collective unconscious' which suggests (besides bogus metaphysics) a phenomenon neither generated nor destructible by *historical action.*

10. Hilberg, *The Destruction,* preface.

11. *Yalkut Moreshet,* **16** (April 1973), 36–7 (in Hebrew).

12. In private conversation with this writer, Kovner has claimed that only Stalin's death at the time of the 'doctors' plot' prevented a second Holocaust.

13. E. Goldhagen, 'Pragmatism, Function and Belief in Nazi Antisemitism', *Midstream* (December 1972), pp. 52–62.

14. *Ibid.*, p. 52.

15. *Ibid.*, pp. 54, 57.

16. *Ibid.*, pp. 60, 61.

17. *Ibid.*, p. 54. The dubious authority is Hermann Rauschning who broke with Nazism when he came to understand it as a 'revolution of nihilism'. That this latter conception, though not implausible, is ultimately not only untenable but harmful as well, has been shown most effectively by A. Hillgruber, in the essay cited in note 25.

18. K. D. Bracker, *The German Dictatorship* (New York, 1970).

19. *Ibid.*, p. 403.

20. *Ibid.*, p. 403.

21. *Ibid.*, p. 402.

22. *Ibid.*, p. 423.

23. *Ibid.*, p. 63.

24. *Ibid.*, p. 63.

25. A. Hillgruber, 'Die "Endlosung" und das Deutsche Ostimperium als Kernstuck des Rassenideologischen Programms des Nationalsozialismus', *Vierteljahrshefte für Zeitgeschichte,* **20** (1972), 133–53.

26. Jochmann and Wellessen, *Adolf Hitler.*

27. Hillgruber, 'Die "Endlosung"', pp. 133–5.

28. *Ibid.*, pp. 135–7.

29. Hillgruber demolishes the notion that Hitler's attack on Russia was an attempt to escape from a military dilemma posed by Britain's refusal to surrender (p. 139); he goes on to show that both the attack itself and subsequent German escalations of brutality require for their explanation an ever-increasingly rabid ideological 'racism'.

30. *Ibid.*, p. 149. Hillgruber shows to what extent representatives of the old officer caste such as Generals von Brauchitsch and von Manstein became implicated in the perversion of 'military honour'.

RESPONSES TO THE HOLOCAUST

31. *Ibid.*, p. 151.

32. *Ibid.*, p. 153.

33. Jochmann and Wellessen, *Adolf Hitler* pp. 31–2.

34. *Ibid.*, pp. 40–1.

35. This legend is due to none other than Martin Luther, and it was used as the title of a viciously antisemitic picture book for children by Julius Streicher; see Martin Stöhr, 'Martin Luther und die Juden', in W. D. Marsch and K. Thieme, eds., *Christen und Juden* (Mainz, 1961), p. 115.

36. Consider, among countless instances illustrating this point, the fundamentalist Canadian Christian minister who sought out Eichmann in Jerusalem, equally sure that a converted Eichmann would find salvation and that his countless unconverted Jewish victims would not. Or the famous American Liberal Protestant theologian who urged his Jewish audience to forgive the German people, but was left speechless when asked by a Jewish layman how Christians could expect Jews to forgive the murder of six million Jews, committed a single generation ago, when Christians had yet to forgive the murder of one Jew, committed two thousand years ago.

37. In one of the camps an orthodox rabbinical court is said to have put God on trial and found Him guilty.

38. Werner Maser and Heinz Höhne, 'Adolf Hitler: "Aufriss über meine Person"', 8th instalment, *Der Spiegel,* 28 May 1973, pp. 110, 111, 113, 121.

39. Maser and Höhne, 'Adolf Hitler', 9th instalment, *Der Spiegel,* 4 June 1973, pp. 126, 129ff.

40. Maser's and Höhne's more scholarly works (along with others, non-German as well as German) also evade the Holocaust instead of confronting it. See E. Fackenheim, 'The Nazi Holocaust as a Persisting Trauma for the Non-Jewish Mind', *Journal of the History of Ideas* **36** (1975), 369–76.

41. Gershom Scholem, 'Jews and Germans', in Golden, ed., *The Jewish Expression,* p. 483.

42. 'Pre-Christian Rome had no anti-Jewish policy. Rome had crushed the independent Jewish state of Judea, but the Jews *in* Rome enjoyed equality under the law. They could execute wills, enter into valid marriages with Romans, exercise the rights of guardianship, and hold office' (Hilberg, *The Destruction,* p. 1).

43. Otto Stobbe, *Die Juden in Deutschland während des Mittelalters* (Leipzig, 1902), p. 2; quoted by Hilberg, The Destruction, p. 4.

44. In 1933 Martin Niemöller wrote that whether or not German Christians found it 'appealing', the agency of the Holy Spirit made converted Jews members of the church equal to other Christians; but since the German *Volk* had 'suffered greatly through the influence of the Jewish *Volk*', to treat such Jews as equals 'required a high measure of self-denial' on the part of German Christians; thus, pastors of non-Aryan descent ought to exercise 'appropriate unobtrusiveness' lest they give 'offence' [*Die Evangelische Kirche in Deutschland und die Judenfrage* (Geneva, 1945), pp. 42–4].

Also in 1933, Dietrich Bonhoeffer wrote:

> Now the measures of the state toward Judaism in addition stand in a quite special context for the church. The church of Christ has never lost sight of the thought that the 'chosen people', who nailed the redeemer of the world to the cross, must bear the curse for its action through a long history of suffering. [*No Rusty Swords* (London, 1965), p. 226]

45. See, e.g., Franklin H. Littell, 'Christians and Jews in the Historical Process', *Judaism* **22** (1973), 267–77. Littell not only cites some of the more shocking statements of the Nazi Christians but also shows the 'meagre' (Wilhelm Niemöller) results of any search for pro-Jewish attitudes among the militant anti-Nazi Christians.

46. See A. Boyens, 'Stuttgarter Schuldbekenntnis vom 19ten Oktober 1945: Entstehung und Bedeutung', *Vierteljahrshefte für Zeitgeschichte* **19** (1971), 274–397. This article reveals that, although largely motivated by the Holocaust in their endeavour to produce the declaration of guilt, even privately such men as Pastor Asmussen spoke in 1945 of 'the sins of our people toward Poles, Danes, Frenchmen, etc.', while at the same time the great ecumenist Visser t'Hooft, seeking to

emphasize that 'no one is right before God, that all are involved in the common guilt', effectively if surely unintentionally blotted out the unique scandal of Auschwitz. The purpose of Boyens' article, moreover, is to *defend* the authors of the declaration — presumably against German claims that those authors were driven to their confession, not by their conscience, but by the occupying powers.

47. This account of the *Adversus Judaeos* literature is deeply indebted to Rosemary Ruether's *Faith and Fratricide* (New York, 1974); I wish to thank her for showing me the manuscript prior to publication.

That an inner theological tendency is responsible for the persistence of Christian Jew-hatred is corroborated by Luther's *About the Jews and Their Lies.* Luther claims: the Jews want to rule the world and already dominate many good Christians; they are arch-criminals, killers of Christ and Christendom; they are 'a plague, pestilence and pure misfortune'.

Among his 'remedies' are: burning synagogues; burning Jewish homes, since in these too Judaism is practised; confiscating Jewish religious books; prohibiting rabbis the teaching of Judaism, on pain of death; prohibiting Jewish travel; prohibiting Jewish money-lending and confiscating Jewish gold and silver. According to Martin Stöhr 'Martin Luther und die Juden' the essential cause of Luther's hatred is that his entire faith seems threatened by the mere *existence* of the Jewish people and its faith.

48. This ruling has been ascribed to Maimonides but, so far as I know, without justification.

49. Like many others in Eastern Europe, the Jewish cemetery in the East German city in which this writer's relatives are buried bears the legend 'To the Victims of Fascism'. This half-truth subserving the ideological purposes of communism victimizes the Jewish victims a second time, by blotting out their Jewishness.

50. *Mekhilta, Tractate Beshallah.*

The "Incomprehensibility" of the Holocaust: Tightening Up Some Loose Usage

DAN MAGURSHAK

AS SCHOLARSHIP CONCERNING THE DESTRUCTION of European Jewry accelerates, articulate survivors and some well-informed scholars remind the researchers that, as an event which demands serious investigation, the Holocaust may be, nonetheless, uniquely incomprehensible. Nora Levin writes:

> The Holocaust refuses to go the way of most history, not only because of the magnitude of the destruction . . . but because events surrounding it are still in a very real sense humanly incomprehensible. . . . Indeed, comprehensibility may never be possible.[1]

In the same vein Elie Wiesel asserts that "Auschwitz cannot be explained . . . " because " . . . the Holocaust transcends history." Emphasizing his point, he soberly adds, "The dead are in possession of a secret that we, the living, are neither worthy of nor capable of recovering."[2] If Holocaust scholars accept these statements about the incomprehensibility, the inexplicability, and the historical transcendence of their subject matter as true, they find themselves in the bind of secular Aquinases. Committed to complete understanding and explication of an inexplicable, they can hope only to make the darkness a little brighter. Convinced that the horror of systematic genocide must be comprehended, they must still admit that their subject, like Thomas' Trinity, is theoretically incomprehensible in principle.

As Levin and Wiesel use the notion, incomprehensibility, at the very least, means the impossibility of understanding fully and adequately the "jointly sufficient," or the necessary, conditions for the Holocaust's occurrence. It means that even after ideally exhaustive historical, psychological, and sociological analyses, the researchers would still have failed to penetrate the essence of this event. It also implies that, since control and prevention of such outrages presuppose some understanding of their essential components, a generation whose scholars remember the past may, because of its incomprehensibility, still be doomed to repeat it. Indeed, some would-be investigators might even conclude that, since a

1. Nora Levin, *The Holocaust: The Destruction of European Jewry, 1933-1945* (New York: Thomas Y. Crowell Company, 1968), p. xi.
2. Elie Wiesel, "Trivializing the Holocaust: Semi-Fact and Semi-Fiction," *The New York Times*, April 16, 1978, section 2, p. 29.

DAN MAGURSHAK *is assistant professor of philosophy at Grinnell College.*

"historically transcendent" phenomenon is inexplicable, scholarly "remembrance," except for honoring the dead, is rather fruitless.

If the Holocaust is humanly incomprehensible, then the incentive to study the phenomenon, the commitment to spreading an awareness of it beyond academic circles, and the ability to prevent a similar occurrence are seriously diminished. And, since these implications are not inconsequential for humankind's appropriation of the past in constructive self-knowledge, I intend to examine this notion of incomprehensibility to show in what legitimate sense the Holocaust may be considered incomprehensible. Distinguishing the various important meaning-variations of this term one from another, I suggest that, except in the case of "affective comprehension" and for the "theological" and religiously neutral "cosmic" ways of asking why the Holocaust occurred, the Holocaust is, in principle, as comprehensible and as amenable to disciplined study as any complex human phenomenon. And where it is incomprehensible I suggest that it is not uniquely so.

I. The Holocaust as Incomprehensible

A. "Wholistic" and Empathetic Incomprehensibility.

In standard usage, to comprehend is "to grasp with the mind, conceive fully or adequately, understand, 'take in'."[3] To call an event "incomprehensible," then, is to assert that one cannot fully or adequately understand it; in this sense, one may find modern physics incomprehensible. There is, however, an extended use of this term not unfamiliar to students of the Holocaust. After watching *Night and Fog*, listening to a survivor soberly recalling an "average" day in Auschwitz, or reading Elie Wiesel's *Night*, one is often overwhelmed as an affective, intelligent, and articulate being. Consider the following passage from *Night*:

> Not far from us, flames were leaping up from a ditch, gigantic flames. They were burning something. A lorry drew up at the pit and delivered its load — little children. Babies! Yes, I saw it with my own eyes . . . those children in the flames. (Is it surprising that I could not sleep after that? Sleep had fled from my eyes.)[4]

Having entered the kingdom of darkness through such testimony, one seems to collapse; a benumbed mind is unable to reflect as one dumbfoundedly sits in a silent unreality. A mixture of moral outrage, frustration and profound sorrow churns in the pit of one's stomach. One is unable to speak, one does not know how to respond to children burning alive for the sake of saving two fifths of a pfenning on poison gas. The occurrence is "unimaginable," "unbelievable," "incomprehensible." And even after one has analyzed such an atrocity historically, psychologically, and from other perspectives, a rereading of the account can plunge one

3. *Oxford English Dictionary* (Oxford: Clarendon Press, 1961), Vol. II, p. 741.
4. Elie Wiesel, *Night*, tr. Stella Rodway (New York: Avon Books, 1960), p. 42.

back into the same experience. Somehow, the fact of burning children is irreducible to a complete explanation.

Nonetheless, the terms used in this context do not assert that this typical Holocaust atrocity is actually beyond the bounds of human imagination, unworthy of epistemic belief, or unintelligible in principle. They simply express a sense of being completely overwhelmed, a sense which is not unique to the horror of the Holocaust either in its occurrence or in its reoccurrence after explanations of the horrifying event have been given. One can, in fact, have the same experience with beauty.

Take, for example, the comparatively trivial phenomenon of a sunset. The explanation of this occurrence is quite complete; the earth orbiting around the sun and rotating on its axis has an atmosphere of a certain composition which refracts and diffuses light rays in ways determined by the angle of incidence and other physical considerations. Even the human interest in the sun is fairly explicable; we are a diurnal species whose survival depends upon the light, heat and relative position of this star. In spite of such comprehension, however, we are still overwhelmed by a sunset and we still call it "mysterious" or "unbelievably beautiful" to express our aesthetic wonder. Such expressions do not assert that a sunset is theoretically impenetrable, since we already understand it; they simply call attention to two different human modes of encountering the phenomenon, modes (a theoretical one and an affective or aesthetic one) whose relation to one another and whose relative importance to human beings are still much debated. Analogously, an investigator can comprehend rather completely the course of political, social, and economic events which led to modern German anti-Semitism and to the adoption of a policy which exterminated the Jew like vermin. Yet, when s/he rereads the passage quoted above, s/he may still numbly ask how it could have happened. From a perspective importantly similar to that in which one experiences the majesty of a sunset, the Holocaust as a totality and in its particular atrocities may be called "incomprehensible." Such incomprehensibility, however, does not entail the conclusion that the Holocaust is theoretically incomprehensible, i.e., an impenetrable mystery which remains in principle beyond the grasp of human understanding. Like other instances of overpowering beauty or horror, it is overwhelming without necessarily being incomprehensible. One may still conceive of it adequately, understand it, "take it in."

One can also speak of the incomprehensibility of the Holocaust in a related but narrower sense when one notes the difficulty which a sympathetic non-participant might have in empathizing with survivors. As Wiesel asserts, "Only those who were there know what it was; the others will never know."[5] Levin concurs when she writes:

> Ordinary human beings simply cannot rethink themselves into such a world and ordinary ways to achieve empathy fail, for all of the recognizeable

5. Wiesel, "Trivializing the Holocaust," p. 29.

> attributes of human reaction are balked at the Nazi divide; the world of Auschwitz was, in truth, a new planet.[6]

Both writers state that even sympathetic readers are unable to identify intellectually or to experience vicariously the feelings, thoughts and attitudes of the victims. And anyone who has read Holocaust literature extensively would have no difficulty extending this claim to the experiences of the executioners and the bystanders as well. When one reads about Warsaw Christians apparently enjoying the infernal spectacle of the Ghetto's destruction on Easter Sunday, one finds it sickeningly difficult to empathize with these spectators, some of whom were more than willing to call the Nazis' attention to burning people as they leapt from the blazing buildings.[7] Nor can one easily "think oneself back" to experience the world as did Eichmann in Vienna. If the term "incomprehensible" refers to this overtaxing of one's capacity for empathy, then, perhaps, the Holocaust is incomprehensible.

Upon careful consideration, however, one sees that such incomprehensibility is again neither unique to the Holocaust nor unquestionably absolute. For example, no matter how much one reads about men in battle or steeps oneself in war films and documentaries, one still remains an observer rather than a participant if one has never been in combat. Even if one successfully empathizes with the young soldier in *All Quiet on the Western Front*, one still has not lived that experience which belongs to the veteran. Given any possible experience, one who has lived through it has, in some sense, a jump on those who have experienced it only vicariously, at least in terms of "knowing" what that experience is like. Of course Wiesel and Levin assert that one cannot even empathize with the people of the Holocaust, that a gulf exists between one's total experience and that of the survivors which makes it nearly impossible to experience even vicariously the world of gas chambers and incinerators. The same thing might be said, however, of the attempt to empathize with a combat soldier if one lacks any experience of a combat situation. At first, both kinds of experience are relatively incomprehensible; but as one begins to identify feelings, attitudes, and thoughts in one's own experience which appear analogous to those described by soldiers, inmates, or S.S. guards, one may piece together a fairly accurate sense of what it must have been like to live through some aspects of battle or some episodes of the Holocaust. For example, a person who has been subject to military induction or some other impersonal processing might well imagine what deportation might have been like. And if one is honest about one's own feelings of prejudice, one might begin to understand how such emotions, combined with the proper circumstances and ideology, could become murderous. The more

6. Levin, p. xii.
7. Alexander Donat, *The Holocaust Kingdom* (New York: Holocaust Library, 1978), pp. 152-153.

one reflects upon and analyzes the experiences in question, the more one is able to explore that "new planet" which first seemed inaccessible to "ordinary people." The difference between the experiences of a participant and a spectator is undeniable; nonetheless, the initial inability to empathize with the Holocaust people may be overcome asymptotically as one studies, reflects, and steeps oneself in the vivid testimony of that time. It is, after all, precisely one of the functions of literature and film to allow us to enter into a new world and to experience it as if we had lived through it ourselves.

B. Theoretical Incomprehensibility.

In addition to speaking about the "wholistic" and empathetic incomprehensibility of the Holocaust, one can also refer to its "cosmic" incomprehensibility.[8] That is, when one asks the theoretical question, "Why did, or how could, the Holocaust occur?" From either a theological or religiously neutral perspective, one can offer no empirically verifiable answer. As is the case with any event, one cannot fully grasp or adequately understand why God would let such an atrocity occur or why the cosmos is such that it could have happened.

Believers in Israel's God of history or in the Christian God of the resurrection have often asked how God — omnipotent, omniscient, benevolent — could let the children burn under the blue and empty sky. The event demands a rethinking of speculations about God's nature, its relationship to humankind, the plausibility of its existence, and its purpose in at least allowing, if not willing, such carnage. Whether it is proper or not, some troubled believers, in Berkowitz's words, would like " . . . to steal a glance at 'the hand' of the Almighty in order to be able to appreciate what meaning the senseless destruction of European Israel might have in the divine scheme."[9] But, given the nature of theological questions, no complete and totally satisfying answers will be forthcoming; at best, believers can hope only for disciplined speculation consistent with a certain set of theological assertions perhaps rationally supported and made within a context of a particular faith. And if theologians accept Irving Greenberg's injunction not to present any insights which would mock the reality of the burning children, they are constantly reminded of the difficulty of reconciling traditional notions of God with the technological mass murder of the chosen people.[10] In the context of traditional theistic theology, the Holocaust seems theoretically incomprehensible; as such, however, it is only another case of theological puzzlement familiar to every theologian,

8. The notion of cosmic questions, with its distinction between theological and ultimate questions, is used by Paul Edwards in his article, "Why," in the *Encyclopedia of Philosophy* (New York: Macmillan, 1967), vol. 8, pp. 296-302.

9. Eliezer Berkovits, *Faith after the Holocaust* (New York: KTAV, 1973), p. 69.

10. Irving Greenberg, "Clouds of Smoke, Pillars of Fire: Judaism, Christianity, and Modernity After the Holocaust," in *Auschwitz: Beginning of a New Era?* ed. Eva Fleischer (New York: KTAV, 1977), pp. 23, 26, and 34.

a case not unlike that of the Lisbon earthquake which dominated philosophical theology for a century. The problem of evil and the purposes of the intelligent God of theism have always taxed human comprehension.

A similar incomprehensibility appears when one asks the "ultimate" cosmic questions. Paul Edwards correctly observes that " . . . when we ask of anything, x, why it happened or why it is what it is . . . we assume that there is something or some set of conditions, other than x, in terms of which it can be explained."[11] But once one has investigated the historical, socio-economic, and psychological conditions which made the Holocaust possible, one often has a not uncommon tendency to ask why the universe could not have been such that a technologically simplified program of genocide would have been impossible. Could there not have been a universe with all of the advantages of this one but with none of its disadvantages, particularly moral evil? If confronted with a theological response to this question, the inquirer could simply ask why the God that does exist should exist, rather than another. The question is ultimate insofar as the questioner accepts no set of conditions as an adequate response; s/he simply asks why these conditions, rather than others, should obtain and, therefore, rules out, a priori, any answer to the inquiry. If this is the case, then the Holocaust is also "ultimately" incomprehensible, but no more so than any event in human or natural history. Any time one presses an inquiry to the ultimate "why," one places oneself within a realm where self-consistent speculation lacking cogency and compellingness is all that one can achieve. For some thinkers, unanswerable ultimate questions are, in some sense, the most meaningful and most important inquiries; hence, to say that the Holocaust is incomprehensible in this sense is, for them, to say that, in the way that really matters the event is, indeed, an impenetrable mystery. But this means only that the destruction of European Jewry, like any event in the cosmos, is not "ultimately" explicable.

II. The Holocaust as Comprehensible

Once one has noted that confronting the Holocaust is overwhelming, empathetically taxing, and both theologically and ultimately incomprehensible, one is free to investigate it simply as a tragic but, nonetheless, human phenomenon. One can take the general question, "Why, or how, did the Holocaust occur?" and break it down to the following concerns:

1. How was it possible for a modern state to carry out the systematic murder of a whole people for no other reason than that they were Jews?
2. How was it possible for a whole people to allow itself to be destroyed?
3. How was it possible for a world to stand by without halting this destruction?[12]

---

11. Edwards, p. 301.
12. Lucy Dawidowicz, *The War Against the Jews, 1933-1945* (New York: Bantam Books Inc., 1976), p. xxi.

And, in asking these questions, one assumes that one can discover the jointly sufficient or the necessary conditions — depending upon one's theory of explanation — which make aspects of the phenomenon intelligible. One expects that the event will yield to the analytical efforts of the various disciplines, and nothing that has been said about its incomprehensibility entails a contrary expectation. At present the Holocaust may be, in large measure, uncomprehended, but this is no way entails or even plausibly suggests that disciplined study is incapable of comprehending it. There is no good reason to deny that careful, exhaustive, historical, cultural, and psychological studies will not, at least ideally, yield a complete and coherent account which traces the course of events and the play of factors by which the atrocity came about. Like any event of similar magnitude, the mass annihilation of Jews, Gypsies, and other enemies of the Reich rests upon a complex foundation of conditions which may never be completely excavated because of time limitations, lack of information, and a dearth of investigative insights; nonetheless, the investigator aims at an ideal completeness which indicates at least the possibility that more time, more information, and new theories will gradually diminish the relative incomprehensibility of this event. One can see the plausibility of this approach in a brief summary of two analyses, one historical and the other psychological, which makes partially intelligible what some thinkers might have once relegated to the realm of impenetrable mystery.

Breaking down the first question quoted above, one can ask how anti-Semitism in modern Germany developed; more importantly, one might ask how anti-Semitism became politically acceptable. In the second chapter of *The War Against the Jews*,[13] Lucy Dawidowicz sheds a good deal of light upon the conditons which made this acceptance possible. As she explains it, the German peoples of the Nineteenth Century inherited a Christian-inspired popular and intellectual anti-Semitism which depicted Jews as foreigners — a state within a state — killers of Christ, well-poisoners, and the cause of every misfortune, whether natural, economic, or political. The forces of nationalism, *Volkist* theory, bogus racial science, and fear of modernity reinforced and built upon this foundation. The religious outcast and transmitter of plague now became politically dangerous, a threat to national unity, a defiler of the transcendental essence of the German peoples, and the capitalistic cause of the urbanism and industrialism which threatened the peasant, the small merchant, and the *Volkist* ideal of the simple life rooted in the soil of the homeland. Involved in the expanding money economy, the Jews became the scapegoat for the depression of 1873. Soon, politicians campaigned on explicit anti-Semitic platforms and, in 1887, a man named Böckel was elected to the Reichstag by a peasant constituency which agreed with his message that Jews were, by nature, alien to Germany. In 1892, the Con-

13. Ibid., pp. 29-62.

servative Party, the most prestigious party of its day, adopted an explicit anti-Semitic plank. In this account, Dawidowicz weaves the various forces and influences into a coherent narrative which allows one to comprehend how an important segment of the German voting population could live with, and support in good conscience, the apparently self-evident truth that the Jew was, and always would be, a troublemaking, alien inferior. She also helps one to understand that when such an unquestioned assumption was reinforced by intellectuals, "scientists," and politicians, an upstanding German might consider himself bound to seek a "final solution" of some sort to the "Jewish question." On the basis of this account, one can comprehend, perhaps with a shudder, how insidiously subtle and unnoticed the development of a catastrophe might be, particularly for those involved in it.

But once the murder began, how could an upstanding German participate in any of its phases? Stanley Milgram's by now classic experiments on obedience to authority contribute much to comprehending this aspect of the general question, an aspect which initially strained the understanding of both lay people and social scientists.

Milgram introduces his investigation by placing it in the following context:

> . . . from 1933 to 1945 millions of innocent people were systematically slaughtered on command. Gas chambers were built, death camps were guarded, daily quotas of corpses were produced with the same efficiency as the manufacture of appliances. These inhumane policies may have originated in the mind of a single person, but they could only have been carried out on a massive scale if a very large number of people obeyed orders.[14]

In order to find out whether or not ordinary people would act against their own moral standards in obeying the commands of one preceived as a legitimate authority, Milgram devised an experimental situation in which the subject agreed to perform a task which, s/he believed, inflicted pain upon another person whenever the latter failed to respond correctly. Milgram's findings were as follows:

> It is the extreme willingness of adults to go to almost any lengths on the command of an authority that constitutes the chief finding of the study and the fact most urgently demanding explanation. . . . [O]rdinary people, simply doing their jobs, and without any particular hostility on their part, can become agents in a terrible destructive process. Moreover, even when the destructive effects of their work become patently clear, and they are asked to carry out actions incompatible with fundamental standards of morality, relatively few people have the resources needed to resist authority.[15]

Milgram explains these phenomena in terms of antecedent conditions, the nature of the "agentic state," and the factors which bind one to

14. Stanley Milgram, *Obedience to Authority* (New York: Harper Colophon Books, 1975), p. 1.
15. Ibid., pp. 5-6.

submisive obedience. According to him, human beings manifest a tendency to obey which functions adaptively in communal life and which all types of social groups strongly reinforce. One develops a habit of obedience to authority and although one may intellectually decide not to obey a particular order in a situation like Milgram's experiment, one is "... frequently unable to transform this conviction into action."[16] One is tightly bound to the task by the recurrent nature of the action (to quit now is to admit that it was wrong to do up until now), the initial agreement with the experimenter, and anticipated embarrassment of breaking up a well-defined social situation. Furthermore, one sees the entire project with reference to one's relationship to the experimenter; wishing to perform competently, one attends to instruction, focuses almost exclusively on the authority while tuning out the victim, and endows the authority with an almost superhuman character. One also tends to accept the definition and interpretation of the situation provided by authority, e.g., that this experiment is a noble pursuit of knowledge. But, perhaps most importantly, once a person submits him/herself to authority, then a superego function shift occurs; that is,

> ... a man feels responsible *to* the authority directing him but feels no responsibility *for* the content of the actions that the authority prescribes. Morality does not disappear, but acquires a radically different focus: the subordinate person feels shame or pride depending on how adequately he has performed the actions called for by authority.[17]

Milgram's findings apply to people acting in a freely accepted situation. When conditons such as a totalitarian state, the dehumanization of the victim, and the threat of capital punishment for disobedience are added, then one comprehends even better how decent people could participate in the task of mass murder.

Neither Milgram nor Dawidowicz answers all questions about the respective problems, but such incompleteness is neither absolute nor unique; given access to all relevant information, an investigator can, at least in principle, fill in the picture up to the boundaries of the cosmic questions already discussed. Practically speaking, the Holocaust, like the French Revolution, the Second World War, or any complex human phenomenon provides the various disciplines with an almost endless field of investigation which is, nonetheless, always open to further comprehension.

III. Conclusion

The argument of this paper has not intended to minimize the overwhelming importance of the mass murder of six million Jews, five hundred thousand Gypsies, and millions of other people. It denies

16. Ibid., p. 148.
17. Ibid., pp. 145-146.

neither the awesome horror of this event nor the harsh challenge with which it confronts the contemporary generation of scholars and thoughtful laypersons. It simply clarifies the senses in which the Holocaust may be properly called incomprehensible and, thus, clears the way for the unimpeded investigation of this event. The calculated extermination of human beings, pursued for its own sake, must not be forgotten, but neither should it only be remembered; it must be critically and compassionately analyzed, explained, and comprehended. Only in this way might the fires of Auschwitz " . . . illumine otherwise dark corners of our moral landscape, making us aware of present acts of human demonry we would not otherwise see."[18] Through the study of the Holocaust, human beings can gain a brutally harsh knowledge of their capabilities and tendencies, a self-knowledge which is a necessary condition for the prevention of the actualization of their worst possibilities.

18. Robert McAfee Brown, "The Holocaust as a Problem in Moral Chioce," in *Dimensions of the Holocaust* (Evanston: Northwestern University Press, 1977), p. 62.

YEHUDA BAUER

Against Mystification: The Holocaust as a Historical Phenomenon

TO MYSTIFY: TO MAKE OBSCURE OR SECRET. THAT is how a dictionary defines the term.[1] Of late, the Holocaust has been subjected to a great deal of treatment resulting in obscurity or obfuscation. This should not really surprise us. The event is of such a tremendous magnitude that an ordinary person's mind is incapable of absorbing it. There will therefore be a natural tendency to run away from it, deny it, and, mainly, try to reduce it to shapes and sizes that we can cope with, reaching back into our own experience. This of course applies to those attempts at mystification that are not motivated by ulterior purposes. People whose political or ideological predilections are anti-Jewish will produce denials or obfuscations that are in accord with their prejudices. The line between "authentic" and "unauthentic" responses, as Emil Fackenheim termed them,[2] is sometimes rather thin. The purpose of this chapter is to try to examine some such mystifications.

The first of these arises out of the misuse of the term Holocaust, but it is not just a semantic argument. The problem posed is: What do you mean when you say Holocaust? The term, whether appropriate or not, has come to be used for the mass murder of probably around 5.8 million Jewish people in Europe under the Nazi regime.[3] This, to some of us, may sound a trite sort of statement. Is it not clear that this is what we mean by it? Well, no, not exactly. In October 1977, when the New York Board of Education discussed a curriculum on the Holocaust to be introduced into the public education of the city, letters were written to the *New York Times* indicating that the Holocaust was much wider than just the murder of the Jews. It was pointed out that Poles, Lithuanians, and others were also murdered, and after the war the Soviets engaged in wholesale destruction of, for instance, the Baltic nationalities.[4] "Holocaust" has been widely used to describe the discrimination against Blacks in the United States, against Jews in the U.S.S.R., against Arabs in Israel's occupied territories, and against any number of other victims of real or imagined injustices perpetrated all over the globe.

The term Holocaust, as Gerd Korman pointed out in an article some years ago,[5] came into use in the English language to describe what happened to European Jews only some years after the end of World War II, between 1957 and 1959. The feeling was widespread that what had happened to the Jews was in some way unique, or unprecedented or, as Roy Eckardt put it, "uniquely unique."[6] Yet here we are faced with a very real problem: if what happened to the Jews was unique, then it took place outside of history, and it becomes a mysterious event, an upside-down miracle, so to speak, an event of religious significance in the sense that it is not man-made as that term is normally understood. On the other hand, if it is not unique at all, then where are the parallels or the precedents?

In order to avoid mystification, we must therefore probe the historical backgroud. The uniqueness of the position of Jews in the Nazi world was that they had been singled out for total destruction. Not because of their views or their religion, their age or their sex, but simply because they had been born of three Jewish grandparents. In other words, for the first time in history a sentence of death had been pronounced on anyone guilty of having been born, and born of certain parents. The only way of avoiding that death sentence was not to have been born of three Jewish grandparents—a patent absurdity. This Nazi decision was based on an ideology in which the Jew was defined as the anti-race, or in other words as that mixture of characteristics that could be described, in Nazi terms, as an absolute evil. Leaning very heavily on Christian theology, but twisting it in accordance with their own ideas, the Nazis made the Jew the Satan to their Christ, who was Hitler.[7] The Jew was the personification of evil, and thus not human at all. He only appeared human, and when the Nazis had to describe what the Jew was in their eyes, they borrowed terms from the insect world that aroused feelings of disgust—cockroaches, parasites—or from the microbe world—viruses, and so on.[8] The Jew then was both a devil and a parasite. The devilish quality of the Jew expressed itself in his desire to rule the world and to destroy the healthy, Nordic races by biological and cultural corruption. Just like the medieval image of the devil, the Nazi image of the Jewish devil had very marked sexual overtones. The chief way in which the Jew corrupted the Aryan nations was through intermarriage and sexual contact generally. The blood of the Gentile was contaminated, hopelessly corrupted, by even one such contact, and this contamination was hereditary. The Jews had a world government, hiding behind their religious and other organizations, and this government was out to rule and destroy.

This picture agreed with the notorious "Protocols of the Elders of Zion," a forgery produced by the Tsarist police in 1905, purporting to describe a meeting supposedly held at the founding of the Zionist movement in 1897. There, the forgery said, the Jews had prepared their plans to control the world.[9] The Nazis complemented this picture by arguing that as the Jews were parasites and incapable of either a productive life or a permanent political structure of their own, they would, like any other parasite, destroy not only their victim, but in the end themselves as well, because they could never exist on their own.

The result of this pernicious fantasy, which was believed by many thousands of the Nazi party's ardent adherents, was that the ground was prepared for doing away with the Jews, if the occasion arose. For if the Jew was the incarnation of the Devil, or the Devil himself, or if he was the implacable enemy of the Nordic races, out to control the world, or if he was not really human but a kind of dangerous parasite, then the normal laws of human behavior did not apply to his treatment by the Nazis. The Nazis did not treat the Jews as humans because they did not see them as humans.[10]

The problem arises, what was the Nazis' attitude to other groups, to Slavs, for instance. There are any number of textbook or lay statements that the Nazis began their destruction with the Jews, and had the Nazi regime persisted for any length of time, Poles, Czechs, Russians, and others would have suffered the same fate. There is some basis in fact for this statement. It is not definitely known how many Soviet prisoners of war were killed by the Nazis through starvation and ill-treatment, but they cannot have been less than two and a half million.[11] There were many thousands of Polish intelligentsia who were murdered by the Nazis during the first year of occupation in Poland in a special "drive." Tens of thousands of other Poles were brutally murdered as resistants, real or imagined. Whole Polish villages were destroyed.[12] The Czech intelligentsia were treated only very slightly better. At Lidice, all males were indiscriminately butchered. Many thousands of Russian, Belorussian, and Ukrainian peasants were slaughtered during the German occupation.

The purposes and aims of these policies were clearly defined in a memorandum submitted by Himmler to Hitler in May 1940.[13] They were designed to denationalize the East European nations, absorb into the Germanic race those people who were of what the Nazis thought was "Nordic" blood, murder the intelligentsia, destroy all autochthonous cultural life, and turn the rest into a mass of slave laborers who would enjoy the benefits of the Nazi Kultur by building its monuments and continuing to exist under the strict but just rule of their overseers. What emerges from a detailed examination of both the theory and the practice is a policy of selective murder designed to destroy the nations as such, but keep most of their members alive to become a Helot working force for the glory of the Reich.

What shall we call this policy? We could do worse than quote the man who invented the term "genocide," Raphael Lemkin. Writing in 1943, and referring to the German policy in occupied Europe, he said:

> The practice of extermination of nations and ethnic groups as carried out by the invaders is called by the author "genocide." . . . Genocide is effected through a synchronized attack on different aspects of life of the captive peoples: in the political field (by destroying institutions of self-government and imposing a German pattern of administration, and through colonization by Germans); in the social field (by disrupting the social cohesion of the nation involved and killing or removing elements such as the intelligentsia, which provide spiritual leadership . . .); in the cultural field (by prohibiting or destroying cultural institutions and cultural activities; by substituting vocational education for education in the liberal arts, in order to prevent humanistic thinking . . .); in the economic field (by shifting the wealth to Germans . . .); in the biological field (by a policy of depopulation and by promoting procreation by Germans in the occupied countries); in the field of physical existence (by in-

troducing a starvation rationing system for non-Germans and by mass killings, mainly of Jews, Poles, Slovenes, and Russians); in the religious field (by interfering with the activities of the Church, which in many countries provides not only spiritual but also national leadership); in the field of morality (by attempts to create an atmosphere of moral debasement through promoting pornographic publications and motion pictures, and the excessive consumption of alcohol).[14]

The lengthy quote is, I think, appropriate, because this definition of the term "genocide" has been universally accepted. Clearly, what was happening to quite a number of peoples in Nazi Europe was genocide: their institutions of learning closed, their political leadership decimated, their language and national culture discarded, their churches eliminated from a free exercise of their functions, their wealth despoiled, and subjected to killings of groups and individuals as the Nazis pleased—they were victims of the crime defined, or described, by Lemkin. The difference between that and the Holocaust lies in the difference between forcible, even murderous, denationalization, and wholesale, total murder of every one of the members of a community. Contrary to legend, there never was a Nazi policy to apply the measures used against the Jews to other national communities. It was quite natural for the commander of the Polish underground Home Army, General Stefan Rowecki (Grot), to publish, on 10 November 1942, an order to his organization referring to the "extermination of the Jews" and the fear of the "Polish society, that after the termination of this action, the Germans will commence to liquidate the Poles in the same manner" ("że po zakończeniu tej akcji Niemcy zaczną w ten sposób likwidować Polaków.").[15] When the Polish rebellion of August-September 1944 collapsed and the Polish inhabitants of Warsaw were expelled from the ruined city, many Poles thought that they would now suffer the fate of the

Jews. But there was a vast difference between the subjective feeling of the threatened populace and the actual plans and policies pursued by the oppressors. The only group that was destined for wholesale murder was the Jews, for the reasons we have outlined above. From what we know of the Nazi policy towards the Gypsies, a parallel exists, but it is more apparent than real. There were Gypsy tribes that were murdered, and there were others that were protected. Individual Gypsies living among the rest of the population were not ferreted out and many even served in the Nazi army. It appears that the Nazis were ambivalent about what to do with them, but those who were murdered were the victims more of a campaign against so-called "asocials" than against the Gypsy people as such.

To sum up, there may be no difference between Holocaust and genocide for the victim of either. But there are gradations of evil, unfortunately. Holocaust was the policy of the total, sacral Nazi act of mass murder of all Jews they could lay hands on. Genocide was horrible enough, but it did not entail *total* murder if only because the subject peoples were needed as slaves. They were, indeed, "subhumans" in Nazi terminology. The Jews were not human at all.

Not to see the difference between the concepts, not to realize that the Jewish situation was unique, is to mystify history. On the other hand, to declare that there are no parallels, and that the whole phenomenon is inexplicable, is equally a mystification. The partial similarity to the Gypsies has been mentioned already. During World War I, about half of the Armenian population in Anatolia was murdered by Enver Pasha's troops. Yet at the same time, the Armenians at Istanbul, the heart of the Ottoman Empire, were not killed. The Armenian massacres are indeed the closest parallel to the Holocaust; they were motivated largely by extreme nationalism and religious fanaticism, and were not total—whereas the Nazi policy towards the Jews was motivated by a pseudoreligious and anti-Christian ideology that was based on a very deep antisemitic European tradition, and it was total and logical. The differences are as important as the parallels are.

In the post-Holocaust world there have been several genocides and several near-Holocausts already. Suffice it to mention the threatened mass murder of the pro-Indian Bihari minority in Bangladesh during the struggle for independence of that country, the horrible fate of the Kurds in contemporary Iraq, the threatened slaughter of the Christian population in Lebanon, or the fate of Sudanese Blacks, the so-called Anya-Anya, over two million of whom are said to have perished in a number of punitive expeditions organized by the central Sudanese government.

There is of course no unique event in history, beyond the trite statement that every event is nonrepeatable. Once an event has happened, it can happen again, not in precisely the same form, but in one of an infinite number of variations. Events happen because they are possible. If they were possible once, they are possible again. In that sense, the Holocaust is not unique, but a warning for the future. I prefer to use Emil Fackenheim's term "epoch-making event" for the Holocaust.[16] It is as if we viewed a forbidding landscape of dark, deadly sheer rocks and bare mountains, in whose middle there rises a huge volcano spouting forth fire and lava. The volcano becomes meaningless if viewed without the natural background from which it rises. To view the landscape without the volcano is equally a denial of reality. To view the Holocaust as just another case of man's inhumanity to man, to equate it with every and any injustice committed on this earth—and, God knows, the number is endless—to say that the Holocaust is the total of all the crimes committed by

Nazism in Europe, to do any or all of this is an inexcusable abomination based on the mystification of the event. On the other hand, to view it as totally unique is to take it out of history and out of the context of our everyday lives, and that means opening wide the gates for a possible repetition.

We should properly use the term "Holocaust" to describe the policy of total physical annihilation of a nation or a people. To date, this has happened once, to the Jews under Nazism.

Let me now very briefly deal with another form of mystification which I find most disturbing. This arises out of a recent trend in historiography which, a generation after the event, is trying to deny some of the basic facts. There are two distinctive groups of writings or actions connected with this. One of them is the neo-Nazi gutter history; the other is a well-respected, seemingly serious attempt to question accepted visions of the Nazi period.

The Nazi gutter historiography not only exists, but flourishes. A French postwar convert to Nazism, Paul Rassinier, started the fashion with his book *Le Mensonge d'Ulysse* (Paris, 1955).[17] He was not sure whether gassing installations existed at Auschwitz. It was clear, to him in any case, that the Jews invented the story about their murder. Two German Nazis, Heinz Roth and Manfred Roeder, have been writing pamphlets and booklets repeating the canard.[18] The United Nations have had read into the protocol of the General Assembly a speech by His Excellency the delegate from Saudi Arabia, Jamil Baroody, on 24 and 25 March 1976,[19] which explicitly denied that the Holocaust ever happened. Baroody quoted from Rassinier and the others. Recently, in New York, a self-styled representative of the German-American community, Georg Pape, repeated the same argument.[20] One could dismiss this as a passing *Schweinerei,* but this kind of propaganda has received considerable support from a book recently published by a professor of electrical engineering at Northwestern University,[21] who tries to prove that the Jews were not murdered—well, one million maybe died in the war, just as many millions of others did, but all the rest fled to the Soviet Union, where they were absorbed by the Communists, and the rest immigrated to the United States and Israel. The Soviets did not report this, but then you cannot rely on Communist statistics. There were no gassing installations at Auschwitz—or, rather, the installations there were designed for the disinfection of clothes because of the typhoid epidemics, but no humans were gassed. The Jews were transported to the East, just as the Germans claimed. Faced with the evidence of the Nazi murderers themselves, this Nazi book simply says they testified under pressure, or else the testimonies are forgeries.

One really should add to the gutter literature the products that come out of Eastern Europe and the Soviet Union, and that claim that the Zionists collaborated with the Nazis in killing off the Jewish masses. There are too many examples to quote from, but let me mention just a certain Jiří Bohátka, who writes for the Czech press, and who specializes in distributing this kind of poison.[22] In Poland today, the fact that the Warsaw ghetto rebellion was led by Zionists, as were the ghetto rebellions in Bialystok, Cracow, Czestochowa, Tarnow, and other places, is not mentioned at all. More than that: no mention is made of the fact that these were Jewish rebellions—in contemporary Polish literature these are said to have been resistance acts by the Polish population, believe it or not.

Why is this literature so appealing and so dangerous? Why is it copied and used by opponents of Israel, such as Dr. Mehdi of the Arab-American group, who explicitly used it in a recent communication quoted in the *New York Times?*[23] There is a basis of antisemitism pervading what we know as Western culture. For a certain time the facts of the Holocaust made antisemitism a phenomenon that was beyond the pale for civilized humans. But a generation after the event the old poison reasserts itself, especially when you consider that the facts of the Holocaust are indeed unbelievable. Why on earth should a modern technological society at war devote some of its very scarce resources to murder potential laborers whom it desperately needs in its production plants? Has anyone ever heard of a regime that simply murders whole populations for no other reason but their grandparents' religious or ethnic background? The Jews that were led into the gas chambers had no idea what was happening to them in a majority of cases. It was unprecedented, impossible, contrary to all previous experience. Why should you, thirty years after, believe it? Just because it happens to be the truth? When you combine the tradition of Jew-hatred, so brilliantly analyzed just recently again by Franklin H. Littell in his book *The Crucifixion of the Jews,*[24] with the specific problems engendered by the Holocaust, you have the foundation for contemporary anti-Jewishness. When you add to it the fact that, contrary to Christian antisemitic doctrine and contrary to Communist doctrine, the Jewish people exercised their right to self-determination and reemerged into global political history after the Holocaust, then it is not surprising that literature designed to deny the whole background of contemporary Jewish life is written and is believed. If you deny or obscure the Holocaust, in part or in whole, you have created the necessary precondition for a denial of the right of the continued existence of the Jewish people in the post-Holocaust world.

Denial of the Holocaust can be made in a more refined way than in the openly Nazi literature. Thus, for instance, the recent best seller by David Irving, *Hitler's War,*[25] does not actually deny the mass murders themselves, though it refers to them only very briefly. Irving befogs the issue in another way. He claims that it was not Nazi Germany that was solely responsible for the Second World War. He presents Hitler as a perfectly normal human being, and he denies that Hitler knew anything about the murder of the Jews prior to 1943. He de-demonizes Hitler. The same tendency can be seen in Joachim Fest's famous film, now being shown all over Western Europe, in which the question is asked: How did Hitler seduce the German people? A one-sided treatment of the Hitler phenomenon tends to make a bagatelle of the basic immorality of the regime and hides its murderous quality. Explicitly, Fest declares that his is another attempt to de-demonize Hitler.[26]

The problem with this is that one cannot get away from the demonic, or totally evil, qualities of the Nazi regime. One cannot de-demonize Hitler, because Hitler *was* a totally evil personality operating within a framework that only very evil personalities could exist in. "Evil" here stands in basic contradiction to the Ten Commandments and their social, economic, religious, philosophical, and other consequences. Once one de-demonizes Hitler, contrary to all historic evidence, one can then come up with the ultimate absurdity of denying that the dictator of the Third Reich knew anything about the way the Jews were dealt with, which is what David Irving says. By implication one then denies the main point in Hitler's whole program. But Hitler's war of conquest was ideologically a war against the Jews, as Lucy Dawidowicz rightly pointed out.[27] His attack on the Soviet Union was motivated by a struggle for *Lebensraum* of the Reich, and the real enemy was World Jewry, which, in its Bolshevik guise, was not only denying that *Lebensraum* to the Germanic peoples but was trying to establish a world rule of its own, albeit a parasitical world rule destined ultimately to self-destruction.

If you permit me to quote from Hitler's turgid prose, this will become clear: "Present-day Russia," he says,

> has received as master the Jew, who first eliminated the former upper stratum and now must prove his own state-forming power. In view of the endowment of Jewry, which after all is only destructive, it will operate here only as the historical "ferment of decomposition." . . . A gigantic land area will thus be surrendered to the most variegated fate . . . and a period of the most restless changes will begin. . . . it is good fortune for the future that this development has taken place in just this way because thereby a spell has been broken which would have prevented us from seeking the goal of German policy there where it solely and exclusively can lie: territory in the East. . . . [The Jew] tries to bring nations into a state of unrest, to divert them from their true interests, and to plunge them into reciprocal wars and in this way gradually . . . rise to mastery over them. His ultimate goal is the denationalization, the promiscuous bastardization of other peoples, the lowering of the racial level of the highest peoples as well as the domination of this racial mishmash. . . . The end of the Jewish world struggle therefore will always be a bloody Bolshevization . . . hence the result of Jewish domination is always the ruin of all culture and finally the madness of the Jew himself.

The basic aim of Hitler was always the struggle against the Jews. To befog this issue is to misunderstand the whole historical process.[28]

The historians and journalists who write in a revisionist vein are by no means agreed on the angles of their critique of the older historiography. Irving denies the Nazi war guilt. Fest simply ignores the central problems and concentrates on marginal issues. Geoffrey Barraclough, one of the greatest living historians, goes a step further.[29] To him, the whole problem of the Nazi regime is secondary. Communism is important, the Third World is central. Nazism was a regrettable, brief episode, not really worth wasting much time on. This is of course the final absurdity. You ignore the dozens of millions of dead of dozens of nations, you ignore totally the vast destruction of cultural values and heritages, you ignore completely the totalitarian structure that spawned all this and the possible paradigmatic quality of Nazism. You can then ignore the Holocaust, or brush it aside as a footnote. Nazism taught that the purpose of industry can be to produce death in specially designed death factories—so what? Nazism taught that you can combine an ancient hatred with modern technology and liquidate, or rather gassify, an ancient people lock, stock, and barrel, and nobody in the so-called free world will budge—so what? The credibility of Western civilization is called into question because, as Littell pointed out, this was done by baptized Christians in the midst of Christianity—so what? To Professor Barraclough, this is a footnote. Our problem lies in the fact that the revisionist intellectuals, from A. J. P. Taylor through Barraclough, Werner Maser, and Joachim Fest in Germany, and the many others who lately seem to be jumping onto this particular bandwagon, have created the preconditions for a rehabilitation of Nazism and have thereby paved the way for a linkup between revisionist history and neo-Nazi pseudoscientific gutter history. It is by no means certain that spreading the teaching of the Holocaust as wide and as far as possible will successfully prevent any such untoward development; but we fight, therefore we are.

There is a third type of mystification to which I want to address myself, consisting of two contradictory aspects. On the one hand, we find a well-meant and perfectly legitimate allegorization and symbolization of the events of the Holocaust, which may lead to the relegation of the Holocaust into mythology and empty universalization. And on the other hand is the supposedly "scientific," "academic" treatment of the Holocaust that turns the event into a vast sea of footnotes and rationalistic analyses, a subject matter for academic careers, doctoral theses, and suchlike, avoiding the abyss that was the Holocaust, turning the Holocaust into the subject of Holocaustology, a subbranch of history on equal footing with the study of the rise of the silk industry in France in the mercantilist era. In other words, we teach how to wipe out the Holocaust without having to shed a tear.

Let us turn to the first problem. Katzetnik (Yehiel Dinur) the great Holocaust novelist, whose works are, alas, not well known in the English-speaking world, writes books about Auschwitz. The books are written in a combination of naturalistic and symbolistic prose. But when he came to describe Auschwitz, he called it "Another Planet."[30] In his many writings and speeches, Elie Wiesel makes the point that the Holocaust was inexplicable, that the only true reaction to it would have been silence, that the problem posed by the Holocaust is man's relation to man and God, that in essence you cannot explain Auschwitz with a God and you cannot exclude God from Auschwitz. The contradictions in any approach to the problem of Auschwitz lead him to speak, but speak in pain. Not directly—except in his first novel, *The Night*—but symbolically, allegorically.

There is of course a sense in which there is absolutely no way by which one can approach the reality of Auschwitz. Not even the most trivial pain of one human can be actually felt by another human. It is only by a similar, or equivalent, experience that a person is prepared for an explanation or partial understanding of the other's experience. When, however, one approaches an event that is unprecedented, there are vast difficulties in making an understanding possible. The well-known and much-used Hassidic parable applies here: that the Ba'al Shem Tov knew the prayer that had to be said at an appointed time and an appointed place over a fire lit in the midst of a forest, a prayer that would be heard and would avert a calamity. And his disciple would know the time and the place, and how to light the fire, but he no longer knew the prayer. But that was enough, and the prayer of the heart was heard. And his disciple no longer knew the place in the forest, but there was a prayer in his heart. We who were not in that terrible forest of the Holocaust no longer have the ability fully to understand what transpired there, but we learn from the words of those who were there, though the words are but shadows. The symbols that we use are designed to make the event more understandable, more reachable. Were this not so, the Holocaust would die with the generation that went through it. The extreme insistence on the right of only the direct survivors of the Holocaust to describe it, deal with it, analyze it, and agonize about it, is in effect a death sentence on any understanding of that "epoch-making event." On the contrary, the crucial problem is how to anchor the Holocaust in the historical consciousness of the generations that follow it.

Were we to say that the Holocaust took place on another planet, we would in effect enable mankind to run away from it—what a marvelous, elegant form of escapism! It would then seem terrible, mysterious, far away, and not ours. If the problem is perceived as being primarily one of God's intervention, or of Satan's, then we do not have to bother about a historical understanding. Instead of the Nazis being responsible, an inexorable, mysterious, supernatural force caused this event. Human responsibility is removed from the scene, except in vague universalistic generalizations like "the results of prejudice," "man's inhumanity to man," and similar meaningless drivel.

The poets, the writers, the true mystics, the Katzetniks

and Wiesels and Schwarz-Barts, are as far from falling into this trap themselves as possible. They have not only experienced, they have learned and read. They know the factual background, the broad European framework, they have battled with historical and sociological analyses that certainly do not explain the deeper meanings, but without which no discoveries of such meanings appear possible.

What does one do, however, with students who come to a fifty-minute lecture about the Holocaust in general, having read two novels and one poem, who experience their emotional catharsis, and go away cleansed and purified, never to touch the subject again, not having learned a thing? The flow of words, even a flow of words about silence, hides an emptiness, a lack of realization of the here and now of the Holocaust, of its being a phenomenon not of the past but of the present. I fear we have to delve into the reality of the matter to be able to scale the emotional heights: what were the bases of Nazi Jew-hatred? What in Christian theology, in popular antisemitism, prepared the ground? Who were the murderers? What social strata did they come from? What did they think? When was the mass murder planned and how? How did the bureaucracy work that was able to sit behind their desks and direct the murder? Who built the gas chambers? What was the reaction of the victims? Sheep to the slaughter? Glorious resistance? Was there a way of rescue? What were the relations between Jew and non-Jew in the European countries occupied by the Nazis? What were the demographic, cultural, psychological consequences of the Holocaust? How did the State of Israel, into which two-thirds of the survivors immigrated, emerge just three years after the end of the mass murder? What are the effects of the Holocaust on the Jewish people, in Israel and in the Diaspora? What is the responsibility of the free world towards this event?

Such questions and many others cannot be avoided. It is only when they are faced that Katzetnik, Wiesel, Abba Kovner, Nelly Sachs, and the others become intelligble and meaningful. Without a return to the very hard and arduous task of actually knowing something about the Holocaust, the symbolic descriptions that occupy, quite legitimately, the center of the literary stage in Holocaust literature, become just another escape route for the superficial. Mass meetings with tears and emotion may be genuine; they may also be just another cheapening of the experience, or even a desecration of the memory of the victims.

The other way of mystification is that of which I myself may, heaven forbid, be guilty, and which I unwittingly may perpetuate in my students. It is the way of academization, of turning away from the abyss,[31] of escape by way of a footnote. In my own classes at the Hebrew University, I make my students go and see at least one Holocaust film during the year, lest they think they are dealing with a sterile, clean scientific enquiry. I can testify myself to the ease with which you can describe murder and then turn it into a seminar paper. There are hardly any easier ways to dehumanize the dead after their murder than by unconsciously imitating the Nazis and turning them into objects once again—this time objects of historical, sociological, or other research. To use once again Franklin Littell's terminology, the combination between Techne and Clio can indeed be deadly.

How then do we avoid mystification without destroying the mysterious quality that every historical event, and most certainly this one, possesses?

The first thing to remember is that the Holocaust was an actual occurrence in our century. It was not the product of an inexplicable fate or of a supernatural intervention, but one logical, possible outcome of European history. It was done by reasonably educated people in the midst of the most civilized continent on this earth, and, in fact, the SS, the murderers, were led by highly educated and sophisticated individuals. We must, I think, bear in mind that the ideology, the bureaucratic practice, and the psychology of the murderer have to be studied in order to advance to a better understanding of the event. The study of the victim and the bystander are of equal importance. The Jews were not passive victims: they tried to fight for their existence, without arms in most cases; they tried to survive, to escape, to run. They also tried to fight. The bystanders, both in Europe and in the non-Nazi world outside, acted and reacted, or remained passive. We must ask why and how. The story, its background, its consequences, must be told and taught. When doing that, we must be accurate and conscientious. All the footnotes must be right. All the documents must be genuine. Everything we say must be subject to the most rigorous known scientific verification processes. The responsibility we feel must try to be commensurate with the vastness of this "epoch-making event." I turn to those of you who happen to be Jewish. You are all the survivors of the Holocaust. It is only by accident that your parents, grandparents, or great-grandparents came here and did not stay there as their relatives did. You must find out who you are, where you come from, what the Jewish people lost in the gas chambers and the shooting pits. You must find out how *they* behaved and why. You are the descendants and heirs of a great civilization. Why did it happen to you? How did we face the most terrible thing any civilization has faced to date? What is the meaning of it to the Jewish people, and to others?

I turn to those of you who happen to be of non-Jewish parentage. It could have been you, or your parents. The Holocaust has created a precedent. Will it be followed? The non-Jewish governments, including that of the

United States, bear a sad share in the responsibility. You must learn so that a flicker of a chance may exist that we may avoid a repetition. Who can tell who the Jews will be next time?

We must be aware of the danger of the morass of footnoting. We must approach the Holocaust from both ends. The Jewish people were caught in a cage; they had no way out. The hopelessness of their situation, the problems they faced, their behavior in the face of death, all these cannot be relegated to our historical research alone. You cannot approach an understanding of the Holocaust without the soul-searing writings of those who were there and of those who learned from them. So we have to do both.

I would argue in favor of an alliance of the Chronicler with Job, as a way of approaching the problems of the Holocaust.

1. A. M. MacDonald, ed., *Chambers Twentieth Century Dictionary* (Totowa, N.J.: Littlefield, 1975).

2. Emil L. Fackenheim, "The Nazi Holocaust as a Persisting Trauma for the Non-Jewish Mind," *Journal of the History of Ideas* 36, no. 2 (April–May 1975): 369–76; idem, "Concerning Authentic and Unauthentic Responses to the Holocaust," lecture at "The Holocaust—A Generation After" conference, New York, March 1975 (to be published shortly).

3. Cf. Jacob Robinson's section on the Holocaust in *Encyclopaedia Judaica* (Jerusalem, 1971); cf. also Keter Publishing House Staff, *Holocaust* (Jerusalem: Israel Pocket Library, 1974), pp. 52–55. Of all the attempts to calculate the losses of the Jewish people in the Holocaust era, Robinson's seems to be the most authoritative (cf. George Wellers, "La Mythomanie Nazie," *Le Monde Juif,* no. 86 [April–June 1977]).

4. "Teaching the Holocaust," *New York Times,* 9 November 1977; letter from Paul Ronald, *New York Times,* 15 October 1977.

5. Gerd Korman, "The Holocaust in American Historical Writing," *Societas* 2 (summer, 1972):251–70.

Footnotes continued after page 447.

Was the Holocaust Predictable?

Jacob Katz

Almost anyone who lived through the period of the Holocaust, observing it from either near or far, will readily testify that information concerning the Nazi murder of the Jews, when it first came out, seemed absolutely unbelievable—impossible. In retrospect, however, as we look back on the exact sequence of events that led to the tragedy, we tend to conceive of it as the culmination of a predetermined and unavoidable march of destiny. Such a complete turnabout in our attitude to past events is hardly unique, but in the case of the Holocaust the contradiction is an especially flagrant one because the contradictory attitudes are so emphatic. The enormity of the crime being committed by the Nazis, as intelligence of it began to filter into the countries outside the occupied areas, placed it beyond belief. Yet once it became evident that the unbelievable had indeed occurred, it began to seem altogether necessary and inevitable. Now the question, often put in a self-torturing way, is, how could we have overlooked the signs that unmistakably foretold the impending tragedy?

This query reaches out to different dimensions of the past. The prehistory of Nazidom as well as the first years of Hitler's regime have been scrutinized by historians for signs indicating a readiness on the part of the Nazi movement to implement a program of destruction, or a resolve on the part of Hitler to carry out such a program in the simple, physical sense. Next, the spotlight has

---

Jacob Katz is professor of sociology at the Hebrew University of Jerusalem and the author of, among other works, *Exclusiveness and Tolerance*, *Tradition and Crisis*, and *Out of the Ghetto*. A somewhat different version of the present essay was read at an international conference on "The Holocaust—A Generation After," held in New York this March.

been turned on German anti-Semitism of the last decades of the 19th century, and its forerunners in the romantic nationalism of the early 19th century, there to detect the seeds of Nazism and its ideology of Jew-hatred. Some have gone further, attempting an analysis of the German mentality as reflected in typical representatives of the German *Geist* like Luther, Hegel, Wagner, or Nietzsche, and meaning to reveal an innate tendency toward tyranny, totalitarianism, and social intolerance. Indeed, the inquiring mind has not stopped at the German border. The teachings of the Christian churches since the Middle Ages, and Jewish-Gentile relations since antiquity, have been examined for an answer to the frightening riddle of the present. Though a connection between past history and the climax represented by the Holocaust has not always been explicitly asserted, virtually no contemporary historical, sociological, or philosophical analysis of early anti-Semitism ignores the symbolical presence of the six million dead of Auschwitz and Treblinka.

Now, remoteness in time does not of itself exclude a possible connection between two phenomena, and there can be no doubt that the history of Jewish-Gentile relations since antiquity does have a bearing on the Holocaust—in what sense, we shall explore later on. Still, the antinomy persists between the feeling of having been taken by surprise by the events of the Holocaust when they occurred and the inclination, after the fact, to reconstruct those events in such a way as to make them appear inevitable. This antinomy is often overcome by asserting that some people, at least, *had* foreseen the events in question, but their warnings went unheeded.

In 1945, when the horrors of the Holocaust were already fully known, I heard Arnold Zweig quoting what he himself had told the Zionist leader Menahem M. Ussishkin during a visit to Jerusalem in 1932, when the ascendance of Hitler seemed imminent—namely, that this would lead to the total destruction of German Jewry. Yet the book written by Arnold Zweig shortly after Hitler's rise to power, *Bilanz der deutschen Judenheit* ["The Balance Sheet of German Jewry"] attests that his real views at the time were not so clear-cut. Zweig did fear the downfall of German Jewry, and saw a danger to leftist intellectuals like himself, but he believed that a man like Martin Buber still had a chance to fight for the ideal of religious socialism in Germany, and Zweig strongly enjoined Buber to continue his work. Zweig himself left Berlin and settled in Haifa in 1934; from Palestine he commented (in the newly-published correspondence between him and Sigmund Freud) on the events in Europe, taking every setback in Hitler's advance as a sure sign of his pending downfall. In quoting what he later claimed he had said to Ussishkin, I am by no means suggesting that Zweig in 1945 was not telling the truth. What often occurs in such cases is that statements uttered under certain circumstances assume, in retrospect, a weight they were far from having carried in their original setting.

Vladimir Jabotinsky, leader of "right-wing" Zionism in the pre-State era, is often credited by his followers with having had a remarkable prescience of the catastrophe awaiting European Jewry; it is he who is said to have coined the phrase, "Liquidate the *Galut* [Diaspora] or the *Galut* will liquidate you." Indeed, rereading Jabotinsky's speeches from the years preceding World War II, one comes across sentence after sentence that sounds like an apprehension of coming doom. But what did these warnings mean in their original context? This great patriot tried to prod his audience into a more activist Zionist stance than the Jewish leadership at the time thought possible, or even contemplated. In the late 30's he urged the "evacuation" of Polish Jewry, and would not have hesitated to enlist the help of the anti-Semitic Polish government in implementing his plan. Jabotinsky pointed to the plight of German Jewry, then leaving Germany because of the pressure of anti-Jewish legislation, as evidence of the urgent necessity of his scheme, and he used phrases that seem to us to indicate foreknowledge of the Holocaust.

But what Jabotinsky actually had in mind in speaking of a worsening of the Jewish position was the aggravation of economic, social, and political measures against the Jewish community in Poland itself, not the possible conquest of Poland by the Nazis. Together with many Jewish intellectuals he shared a conviction that Nazi rule was fragile and would crumble through internal difficulties or at the first clash with a foreign power. How unaware he was of even the near future is clearly demonstrated in the very idea of "evacuation": he suggested transferring a million-and-a-half Polish Jews to Palestine over the course of the next ten years. Jabotinsky's vision, inspired though it was by a deep passion for the welfare of his people, was as limited as anyone's by the impenetrability of the future.

Analysis of these two instances confirms once again the intrinsic dichotomy between past and future: only in retrospect do statements made about the future assume the nature of prophecy. Nevertheless, instead of solving our problem, this observation only succeeds in placing it in sharper focus. Why should human reason be incapable of reaching a proper conclusion about the logic of events in advance of their culmination? Why did no one realize that European Jewry was doomed, as we today, looking back, know it to have been? Are contemporaries to be blamed? This last question hovers over many partisan deliberations concerning the period, and in fact blame has often been explicitly assigned to groups or individuals that supposedly could have foreseen events and taken appropriate steps to forestall or prevent them. Blame is also implicit in many historical works of simple narrative that cannot avoid casting pitying glances at those contemporaries who ignored the warning signals that seem so crystal-clear to the historian. But in both cases there is a failure to consider adequately the intrinsic limitations—epistemological and psychological—of historical prediction.

II

UP TO January 1933 one could know only that Hitler might come to power, one could not know that he *would*—even though, in retrospect, the historian may present the Fuehrer's accession as a chain of events following each other with the force of inevitable necessity. In November 1932, Hitler's fate still seemed to depend on the votes of millions, and indeed the elections of that month indicated a diminishing trend in his popular support. The economic crisis, one of the main factors through which Nazi propaganda appealed to adherents, had passed its peak; the number of unemployed was clearly decreasing. There were defections from the party and Hitler was having difficulty keeping it solvent and retaining his authority over the various internal groupings. That power fell into his hands nevertheless was due to the condition of the other political parties in Germany, which, split between the Left and the Right, were incapable of establishing a working majority. It was at this juncture that President Hindenburg charged Hitler with forming a coalition government together with the non-Nazi right wing, which accepted the deal out of the belief that it could keep him in check.

In retrospect Hindenburg's decision to call upon Hitler to form a government is rightly regarded by historians as one of the most fateful decisions not only in the history of Germany and of the Jewish people, but also in the history of the world community. Yet the very expression "fateful" indicates that the full significance of the step was bound up with its future consequences. Contemporaries may have felt it to be decisive but could only speculate where it might lead. Some leftist intellectuals, it is worth remembering, conspicuously represented by Jews like Leopold Schwarzschild, the editor of the influential *Tagebuch*, had long recommended that Hitler be allowed to come to power and thus be given the opportunity to fail and seal his doom. But even disregarding such fancies (typical of the too-clever intellectuals), the significance of the event could only be assessed according to what was inherent in it in its time.

This was momentous enough, to be sure. The Nazi accession to power meant the domination of Germany by a party that denied the principles on which the former government and the established order had been founded: the principles of democracy, parliamentarianism, racial tolerance, and equality before the law. Instead, the Nazi party avowed the principle of leadership, i.e., government by a self-appointed elite that owed allegiance to one man whose command was law, and this man had given indication enough of his irrational visions and his passionate hatred of his enemies, among whom the Jews bulked most largely. Even so, public declarations by even the most revolutionary parties have never been taken as actual guidelines to be used in implementing practical policies, and in this case even those who supported Hitler very often did so with the tacit assumption that although he might indeed reverse some of the trends of postwar Germany, he would relinquish his more radical ambitions and become more restrained as he assumed responsibility for the conduct of affairs of state.

III

How could people have been so foolish as not to have seen what was in store for them at the hands of Adolf Hitler? After all, he did nothing but execute what he had said he would do, in so many words, in *Mein Kampf.* The answer to this frequently asked question is not that people did not read the Fuehrer's voluminous treatise; whether they did or not, there was ample opportunity to learn his declared intentions through other channels during the propaganda years and from occasional utterances during the first years of his rule. Nor does the answer lie in the well-documented phenomenon of partial apperception or the selective acceptance of what reaches one's senses and understanding—although this does go a long way toward explaining the seemingly faulty response to received stimuli. The fact is that an essential difference exists between announcing an intention and resolving to act upon it. Nobody, including Hitler himself, could know whether he would ever have the opportunity to carry out his intentions and how far he would go. Only in retrospect does this essential difference tend to become blurred, and thereby contribute again to misjudgments of the past.

This whole complex of problems can be illuminated by an episode during Hitler's bid for power. In the winter of 1926 an exclusive club of well-to-do, conservative-minded citizens of Hamburg, the *Nationalklub*, invited Hitler to give an address on his political philosophy. Hitler was then in the first stages of reorganizing the party after the failure of the 1923 putsch, which had landed him in prison and placed him in temporary political eclipse. He was not yet free to make public speeches everywhere in Germany but had succeeded in attracting attention as a consistent opponent of the ruling parties of the country and, indeed, a radical detractor of the republic itself; in that respect he conformed to the principles avowed by the members of Hamburg's *Nationalklub*. His two-and-a-half hour speech to the club was taken down in stenogram, but remained unpublished until 1960. As Professor Werner Jochmann, who edited the text, has observed, it is a most revealing document, not only for what it shows about Hitlerite propaganda, but even more for the way in which that propaganda was received. In his speech Hitler attributed the weakness of postwar Germany exclusively to the influence of Marxism, which, he held, had undermined the former strength of the country, and the eradication of which he saw as the highest national goal, worthy of the support of his listeners. The Hamburg patricians shared with Hitler a resentment of the prevailing social-democratic order, although few if any of them could have wished to replace it with an even more radical order, of an even less aristocratic character; nevertheless a common ground was created between them, enabling the speaker to secure the future support of at least some members of his audience.

Now, Hitler's speech as it has been analyzed by Professor Jochmann clearly reveals all the radical elements of his program and points the way to its execution. Properly understood, the speech should have frightened away the conservative audience of the *Nationalklub*. Professor Jochmann, puzzled by the divergence between what the speech contained and what the audience apparently took from it, theorizes that the listeners paid attention only to what was in harmony with what they themselves felt and thought but neglected and overlooked what would have repelled them had they understood it properly. This explanation may be correct as far as it goes; the trouble with it is that it draws once again on a knowledge of events since 1926 and attributes to Hitler's words a weight absorbed, so to speak, from later history. Thus, for example, although Jews are not mentioned in the speech at all, one cannot help thinking gruesomely of Auschwitz as one reads Hitler's remarks on the Darwinian struggle between the strong and the weak, and his assertion of the natural right of the former to overpower and eliminate the latter. Yet this, from the historian's view, is an impermissible predating of notions and events. We may well recognize in the Hamburg speech the *potentiality* of Hitler's later deeds, but we must not disregard the ever-present fact of contingency, on which the realization of his intentions rested.

IV

TO DENY the possibility of foreseeing the course of events is not to imply there is no way of assessing a situation and its potential dangers in a more or less intelligent fashion. Such an appraisal has to be based on an analysis of factors at work in the present that take into account the chance of possible shifts and changes in the future. In the case of German Jewry, obviously no real agreement was reached either on a diagnosis of the situation or on a prescription for action. Contradictory recommendations were made and conflicting decisions taken by different people on the basis of their respective evaluations of the situation: to emigrate or not to emigrate, choosing instead to weather the storm until the Nazis moderated their attitude toward the Jews or fell from power; to cooperate with the regime in order to facilitate emigration and save as many Jewish possessions as possible—the line taken by the official leadership of the Jewish

Agency—or to support instead a worldwide boycott of German wares in order to hasten an economic debacle—the passionately defended position of the Revisionists. The records of the Nazi period, especially in its later phases of ghettoization and deportation, are full of even more frightful dilemmas; in extreme cases the decision to send some people to death in the hope of saving others depended upon an assessment of what was in store for all concerned.

The historian who wishes faithfully to record and judge the struggle of those involved has first of all to explain people's behavior on the basis of what they themselves knew at the time; whether a particular decision was rational, judicious, moral, must be determined by whatever yardstick the participants themselves would have been ready to submit to. Naturally, people will be found to have acted on different levels of rationality, and where moral considerations are involved, they will be found to have possessed different degrees of courage and character. But moral judgment can only be pronounced on individuals when we have fully imagined the plight they were in, and that is why any such moral judgment has to be preceded by a reconstruction of the situation as exact as the historical sources will permit. To my mind the basic fault of Hannah Arendt's *Eichmann in Jerusalem* lies in her having skipped the stage of historical reconstruction in her rush to pass judgment on the actors. Lacking a concrete conception of what happened, and exploiting the wisdom of hindsight, she assumed a stance of moral superiority to which nobody who was not tested in the situation could possibly have a claim.

The behavior of individuals is not the only object of the historian's judgment, nor is the yardstick always a moral one. Even in the most extreme situation in the ghettos it was not only individual character that determined who elected to go along passively with events as they unfolded and who joined the underground, vowing to go down fighting. Degrees and kinds of education, religiosity, social and political aspiration, made the difference between passivity and quietism on the one hand, activism and initiative on the other.

This rule applies with even greater force to earlier stages, when the depth of one's insight into the texture of the situation determined which course of action was decided upon. Here too group mentality was just as powerful a factor as individual character. There were, for example, the attempts by rightists like Max Naumann and Hans Joachim Schoeps to be accepted by the Nazis by virtue of their espousal of a Germanic *Weltanschauung*—attempts which may be dismissed today as autistic self-deception (quite apart from what they may have entailed by way of disloyalty to other Jewish groups). At the other end of the spectrum, the leftist intellectuals represented by the Frankfurt school, committed as they were to a Marxist interpretation of history, could conceive the Nazi ascendance only as an aberration of social forces, and were entirely blind to the role played by the defamation of Jews in Nazi ideology and politics. I may in this context adduce something from my own experience. In 1932, I was preparing my doctoral thesis at Frankfurt university under the guidance of Karl Mannheim, the sociologist. Mannheim did not actually belong to the Frankfurt Institute but was personally and ideologically an integral part of the group. Apprehensive lest my studies at the university be terminated because I was a Jewish foreigner, Mannheim urged me to complete my thesis and be examined for the degree before the end of the academic year. As to his own position, he remarked that the Nazis would not dare touch incumbents of full professorships. By April of the same year, when the purging of academic institutions began, Mannheim was one of the first to be thrown out. I may add, with no intention of irony, that some years later, having found refuge at the London School of Economics, Mannheim wrote his *Diagnosis of Our Time*, in which he exposed the underlying forces that led to the Nazi takeover and regime.

V

Rootedness in Jewish consciousness was certainly a help in orienting oneself to the new situation. At least it protected one from despair—the suicide rate was conspicuously high in assimilated circles that suddenly found their world in a shambles. After the first shock was overcome, the Orthodox and the Zionists, on the other hand, tried to make the best of things. German Jewry experienced a kind of cultural regeneration, a marked increase in literary and educational activity that dwindled only when continuous emigration had sapped the available forces and the Nazis put an end to even these signs of Jewish public life. The Zionist movement in particular drew many formerly indifferent Jews into its orbit, not only because it offered a way of escape to Palestine, but because its ideology came closest to offering a cogent analysis of the situation that had evolved: The exclusion of Jews from German society seemed to demonstrate unequivocally the error of assimilationist ideologies.

The congruence between the Zionist interpretation of Jewish history and the existing circumstances lasted, however, only as long as Nazi persecutions kept within the bounds of prior historical experience. The historian Yitzhak F. Baer, who left Germany for Jerusalem as early as 1930, had an opportunity to ponder from a distance the significance of what was happening in his country of origin. The result was a short book, *Galut,* written during the first two years of the Nazi regime: an in-depth analysis of the concept of Exile since early antiquity. Baer concluded his analysis by observing, "We today can read each coming day's events in ancient and dusty chronological tables, as though history were the ceaseless unrolling of a process proclaimed once and for all in the Bible." As the preeminent historian of Spanish Jewry, Baer may well have been reminded by events in Germany of the fate that had overtaken Spanish Jews five hundred years before. Such an analogy was painful, but at the same time it could also have a soothing effect: one was entering upon a prescribed course that followed an inherent pattern in Jewish history.

This, at any rate, was a possible mental response to events in the mid-30's when the forced displacement of German Jews from their position raised an apprehension of their ultimate expulsion. In the ensuing years, however, as the waves of persecution mounted and especially when the frightful information about the ghettos and death camps began to reach the outside world, it was suddenly realized that events had transcended all the old, wonted concepts deriving from historical experience. To Auschwitz and Treblinka there was no historical analogy, no philosophical or, for that matter, theological, framework in which they might be accommodated. This was an absolute *novum*, unassimilable in any vocabulary at the disposal of the generation that experienced it. And it remains so to this day, despite the tremendous effort to investigate all its aspects: the historical, the philosophical, and the theological. Whatever subsequent generations will make of it, for the generation that lived through it the Holocaust can only be characterized as a trauma, a wounding experience beyond the reach of intellectual conceptualization.

VI

GIVEN THE radically transcendent nature of the Holocaust, what significance can there be to the mere historical recording of its events, let alone attempting to lay bare their roots in the more or less remote past? What enlightenment can we possibly derive from tracing the history of anti-Semitism, or Jewish-Christian relations in past centuries, if indeed the Holocaust has to be conceived of as an absolute *novum*, unparalleled in previous generations? And what is the use of rehearsing these horrors in historical retrospect? Is it not a kind of masochism, a form of useless penitence for not having shared the fate of the victims?

The Holocaust *was* something new, unexpected even by those well acquainted with the history of Jewish sufferings in the past. The long-standing

Christian depreciation of whatever pertained to Jews and Judaism is not enough in itself to explain it. Neither is the special record of Jewish-Gentile relations in modern Germany, burdened as it was by the super-national self-esteem of the German people, and the racial defamation of Jews. All these factors, even taken together, were not necessarily destined to produce the Holocaust. Nevertheless, the fact that a later event is not the necessary result of previous ones does not mean there are no relations between them. The Holocaust, produced through unforeseen and unforeseeable historical process, absorbed into itself all these previous elements, without whose existence the later phases of the process would have been impossible.

The Holocaust marks the culmination of modern anti-Semitism, the roots of which hark back to Jewish-Gentile relations in antiquity and to the Christian defamation and persecution of the Jews in the Middle Ages. Modern anti-Semitism transplanted the negative attitude of those ages into the context of modern secularized society.

In ancient times the Jewish community outside the homeland of Palestine was one which habitually separated itself from its social surroundings, wherever these happened to be. Exclusive religious concepts and commitments acted as a barrier between Jews and their polytheistic neighbors. The Jewish community paid for this exclusiveness by drawing upon itself misconceptions about its make-up and beliefs, and inevitably, hatred. When the polytheistic world itself became indebted to Jewish tradition, "accepting" it in a Christian reinterpretation that was in turn unacceptable to Jews, mutual exclusiveness and denial assumed a singular, historically almost unparalleled character. Christians tolerated the existence of a Jewish minority among them on condition that, politically and socially, it be kept on the level of a pariah group. Jews for their part submitted outwardly to Christian governance, maintaining at the same time a kind of mental reservation about its legitimacy, and awaiting its termination—at least so far as the Jewish sojourn in foreign lands was concerned.

Jews in Christian society were allowed a precarious existence, fulfilling an economic role that was sometimes not unimportant, but never highly regarded. They were at any rate never permitted to transcend the status of strangers, and whenever their service was deemed unnecessary, or utilitarian factors became outweighed by other, notably religious, considerations, they could be dispensed with, expelled, or physically destroyed. In his perennial role as outcast, the Jew came to be depicted as an almost inhuman being; by the end of the Middle Ages, the name, Jew, had diabolical associations in every European language.

The Jew's pariah status seemed to come to an end when, in the wake of 18th-century rationalism and Enlightenment, as well as the ensuing social and political changes in European society, Jews were extricated from their peculiar position and included in the new category of citizens. With the subversion of traditional concepts of Christianity in the Enlightenment, the theological prop of Jewish exclusion also seemed to be broken. In a secularized state and society, so the prognosis went, not only would barriers to the economic, social, and political integration of Jews be removed, but all vestiges of prejudice would also evaporate in the sunlight of reason.

This prognosis, though supported by logic, was only partially fulfilled. If the index of integration was the disappearance of peculiarly Jewish choices of profession, or patterns of family and communal life, or cultural traits, the prophets of total assimilation had reason to be disappointed. For the Jewish minority, even where it had been granted formal emancipation at one stroke, as in France and Holland, remained a clearly recognizable subgroup even after the lapse of three or four generations. It distinguished itself through concentration in certain fields of economic activity, through the tendency to endogamy, through communal solidarity, and of course through religious nonconformism. Jewish social existence, in other words, still presented a problem, possibly an even more perplexing one than heretofore, when accepted theological conceptions had sufficed to explain Jewish origin and character, had justified Jewish apartness and inferior social status, and had looked forward to an ultimate Jewish conversion to Christian truth. Once the elements of this old ideology were confuted by rationalism, a new theory was needed to account for Jewish peculiarity.

Such a theory was provided by rationalism itself, and was based on an ethnological conception of history spelled out most eloquently by Voltaire. According to this theory, the conduct and fate of tribes and nations could best be understood through a study of their literary and other cultural productions. Jewish religion, and especially its literary fountainhead, the Bible, remained the clue to understanding Jewish history, but not in the traditional way of seeing the Jews as the chosen people forsaken because of their religious failure, but rather as a documentation of Jewish character. Voltaire was convinced that, by exposing the immoral, indeed the barbaric, character of biblical figures, he had found the clue to the behavior of Jews in his own time and throughout the ages. In effect he simply took over from the Christian tradition its centuries-old stereotype of the Jew, finding an explanation for it that accorded with his own philosophic outlook.

Here we come to the crucial point of transition from Christian to post-Enlightenment anti-Semitism. Jews entered the modern world under the auspices of rationalism, a doctrine positing that neither national origin nor religious affiliation should bar the way of the individual in state and society. Jews were given a chance to rehabilitate themselves, to move away from their marginal position in society and thus dispel the prejudices that clung to their image and their very name. Such rehabilitation indeed took place more or less completely in some countries. In Holland, for instance, where, as elsewhere, Jewish emancipation was regarded apprehensively and strong arguments were marshaled against it, emancipation once achieved was scarcely ever questioned; Dutch Jews were able to find their place in the social structure while retaining a good deal of their ethnic and cultural make-up. In Britain, social barriers against Jews remained strong for a long time; still, their status as legitimate citizens became firmly established in time and negative reflections on Jewish status and character, though sometimes strongly voiced, never really gained ground. In France, Austria, and Hungary, and most conspicuously in Germany, on the other hand, initial misgivings on the subject of Jewish emancipation were never wholly silenced. From the very beginning, public opinion wavered between the utopian expectation of absolute assimilation through the effacement of Jewish characteristics, and a disbelief in Jewish willingness or ability to shed real or alleged character traits. The first generations of emancipated and half-emancipated Jews were exposed to permanent scrutiny to see whether they would live up to expectations or, on the contrary, end by confirming the skeptics in their conviction of the futility of this social experiment.

AMONG opponents of Jewish emancipation the anti-Jewish sallies of a Voltaire were only one of many varied ideological arguments to be drawn upon. Voltaire's anti-Jewish remarks were themselves a sequel or by-product of his anti-Christian campaign, yet in combination the two offered a prototype for a kind of pagan anti-Semitism that made Judaism responsible even for the evils caused by Christianity. At the other end of the scale was the combination of Jew-hatred with a revived interest in Christianity itself, the attempt to salvage Christianity from the historical and rationalistic critique of the Enlightenment. All such reconstructions of Christianity as a religious *Weltanschauung* or system of morality took Judaism as a foil to demonstrate the superiority of the religion that had supplanted it. Even where Christian dogmas and traditions were denied or ignored, the inferiority of Judaism was taken for granted, and this inferiority could then be ascribed by transference to those living individuals who were attached to Judaism if only through their racial origin. Diluted Christianity thus served as one of the most fertile grounds of anti-Semitic theories; as the historian Simon Bernfeld has observed,

"Even those Christian scholars who maintain that Jesus never existed concur that the Jews crucified him."

The main arena for anti-Semitism of this kind was Protestant Germany, but it existed in Catholic countries as well. In France, the politician and journalist Edouard Drumont, the central figure of French anti-Semitism, embraced Catholicism not out of a conviction of its religious truth but rather because it was, he held, a central part of French mentality—a frame of mind to which he declared Jews incapable of conforming even if they were to convert. Thus were explicit notions of race smuggled into the discussion, giving ideological support to the assumption of a deficiency in the Jewish character that had long been implied in the theological traditions of Christianity and in popular European culture.

The main function of modern anti-Semitic theories was not to create new animosity against Jews but to impede the retreat of inherited emotions and prejudices. Yet preserved under the cover of modern ideologies, anti-Jewish bias and passions tended to become even more radical than in their original theological setting. Christian doctrine had prescribed a pariah status for the Jew but at the same time had justified and even underwritten his continued existence. Jews were spiritually contaminated but capable of regenerating themselves through conversion to Christianity. The supplanting of Christian teachings by rationalistic ideologies changed this whole perspective. Once the notion of spiritual contamination turned into a character defect, and the defect was held to be indelible, the presence of Jews in non-Jewish society could begin to appear intolerable. Indeed, the more consistent anti-Semites, like Gyozo Istóczy in Hungary, Edouard Drumont in France, and Eugen Duehring in Germany did not limit their recommendations to the restriction of Jewish rights, but spoke openly of expatriation and extermination.

Because of the similarity between the conclusions of these men and Nazi ideology they are often regarded as precursors of Nazism. The Nazis themselves acknowledged their indebtedness to anti-Semites of earlier generations, but the connection between the two phases of development is certainly not one of historical causation. In surveying the German past Nazi ideologues freely rejected trends at variance with their intentions and adopted others that seemed to fit them. For having supported the cause of Jewish emancipation, figures like Christian Wilhelm von Dohm, Wilhelm von Humboldt, and Karl August von Hardenberg were decried as un-German; Luther, Fichte, Duehring, and others were hailed as the legitimate representatives of the German spirit. The fact that such a choice had to be made shows that, rather than the past's determining the present, it was the present that made its own connection with the past by adopting figures and trends with which it felt an affinity.

Of course, between the deeds of the Nazis and those figures accepted by them as their spiritual mentors, or designated by the historian as their precursors, there lies the hiatus of time. This is true not only of remote figures like Luther, but even of political anti-Semites of the late 19th century like Duehring, whose thinking may have had a demonstrable bearing on the emergence of Nazism. Duehring, to be sure, harbored an almost morbid hatred of Jews and anything reminiscent of Judaism, and was committed to the Darwinian concept of human history. But who could say in 1880 that fifty years hence, the ideas of this lonely philosopher would be adopted as a practical program by a political party, and that this party would acquire the apparatus of a mighty state to implement those ideas? Between Duehring and Hitler there is not only the gulf of a half-century of fateful history, but also the psychological difference between the man of thought, detached from the plane of action and giving free reign to his ideas and fantasies, and the man of uninhibited will who was prepared to act on those fantasies.

VII

THE PERPLEXING interdependence of past and future can perhaps be illuminated by a mental experiment. Had France produced a French Hitler or Hungary a Hungarian one, Drumont or Istóczy might have easily assumed the role of Duehring, as precursor of catastrophe. There is nothing frivolous in imagining such a contingency. France and Hungary each had its own anti-Semitic tradition, which *could* have emerged in radicalized fashion, and though these countries did not in fact produce a Hitler, when Nazi Germany gained control of them in the war the presence of local anti-Semitism insured acquiescence, sometimes enthusiastic, in the Hitlerite program. But let us carry the mental experiment a step further. Is a Dutch Hitler imaginable? The notion seems absurd. Such a man would have had to create, *ex nihilo*, an anti-Semitic ideology and anti-Jewish impulses in the Dutch populace; the absence of these elements is documented not only in the history of Jewish-Gentile relations in Holland in the 19th century, but also in Dutch behavior toward Jews and Germans during the Nazi occupation.

Imagining fictitious events is a legitimate methodological tool for setting reality in perspective. History, however, consists of hard facts, things that occurred and, once having occurred, became irreversible. You may be convinced that a Hitler could have arisen in France or Hungary, or for that matter that his rise could have been prevented in Germany. What might have happened does not belong to history, what happened does. The Hitler period is indelibly marked in the recorded history of all the European nations, first and foremost in the history of the German people; on an altogether different plane it has also become a part of Jewish history, never to be deleted or forgotten. It is the allotted task of historians to record these events as completely as they can. They must do so not in order to be able to predict the future, but to derive from a knowledge of the past a proper diagnosis of the present.

We may define Jewry as it left the ghetto as a community in need of rehabilitation—the objective of emancipation in its broad historical meaning. Anti-Semitism, on the other hand, represented a tremendous effort to impede this process of rehabilitation. The counterblast of anti-Semitism having reached a frightful climax in the Holocaust, the question to be asked concerns the direction in which we are moving at the present time. For rehabilitation has also in the meantime taken a momentous step forward, through the act of Jewish auto-emancipation, the establishment of a Jewish state. The connection between the Holocaust, with all that it signified, and the establishment of Israel and the readiness of the majority of the Jewish people to protect it, is more than obvious. But what about the resistance to Jewish rehabilitation? Did it spend its vigor in the frightful act of the Holocaust, or is it only in a state of dormancy, ready to awaken on some future occasion?

To put the question differently, is there a lasting effect to the Holocaust? Does it operate as a permanent cathartic agent, paving the way to a final reconciliation between Judaism and its adversaries, or does it serve as a paradigm, proving that the Jew as Jew, either as an individual or as a collective, has a lower claim to existence and dignity than any other human group on earth? Indications of both tendencies could be pointed to in the history of the post-Holocaust decades. Which tendency will prevail in the long run is the fateful question hovering over our generation. The doubt implied in the question arises out of the context of past events. The answer to it is hidden in the womb of time.

Some Aspects of the Historical Significance of the Holocaust

Saul Friedländer

The Holocaust, thirty years later: three decades have increased our knowledge of the events as such, but not our understanding of them. There is no clearer perspective today, no deeper comprehension than immediately after the war. Indeed, we know that any attempt to assess the historical significance of the Holocaust means trying to explain in a rational context events which cannot be encompassed in rational categories alone, or described solely in the usual style of historical analysis.

The limitations of the historian cannot, however, quell the urge to know, and the same question returns to haunt us again and again: how was the extermination of the Jews of Europe possible? This singular question leads us ineluctably to consider its essential facets: the behaviour of the exterminators, that of the onlookers, and that of the victims. Can one identify and eventually explain the motivations behind the exterminatory drive of the Nazis? Can one account for the absence of significant countervailing forces which could have impeded the extermination, within Western society as such (the onlookers), and also among the victims themselves, the Jews? These are the vantage points chosen here.

We are confronted immediately with a preliminary issue of crucial importance to every aspect of our interpretation of the

* Saul Friedländer is Professor of Modern History at the Graduate School of International Relations, Geneva and the Hebrew Univesity of Jerusalem. The text here published is an expansion of the Second Philip M. Klutznick International Lecture on Contemporary Jewish Life and Institutions, delivered at the International Scholars Conference on 'The Holocaust — A Generation After' held in New York City on March 3 through March 6, 1975 under the auspices of the Hebrew University Institute of Contemporary Jewry's International Committee.

Holocaust: are we dealing with a phenomenon comparable to some other historical event, or are we facing something unique not only within any traditional historical context, but even within the context of Nazism itself?

If the extermination of the Jews by Nazis could be convincingly compared to other phenomena belonging to the framework of National Socialism itself, or to a category of contemporary political behaviour encompassing Nazism, or to some type of murderous outburst known in other periods of history, then our quest for understanding the Holocaust would be greatly facilitated. But, in my view, this is not the case.

As far as Nazism itself is concerned, one can say, on the basis of the documentary evidence available, that contrary to what is sometimes stated, there was never any plan for the *total* extermination of the Poles or the Russians.[1] Even the extermination of the Gypsies, who were considered less 'enemies' than 'asocial' elements, was planned only in part and after many hesitations (Gypsies could serve in the German army up to July 1942), and executed on a limited scale during a single month in 1944.[2] It is the absolutely uncompromising aspect of the exterminatory drive against the Jews, as well as the frantic extirpation of any elements actually or supposedly linked to the Jews or to Jewishness (or to the 'Jewish spirit'), that is, the identification of the Jews as absolute Evil, which, from the outset, marks the fundamental difference between the anti-Jewish action of the Nazis and their attitude towards any other group.

The absolute character of the anti-Jewish drive of the Nazis makes it impossible to integrate the extermination of the Jews not only within the general framework of Nazi persecutions, but also within the wider aspects of contemporary ideological-political behaviour such as fascism, totalitarianism, economic exploitation, and so forth.

At the beginning of his monumental study of fascism, the German historian Ernst Nolte speaks of 'a Jewish interpretation...based on the most appalling of all human experiences...[which] brings the whole weight of this experience to bear in favour of a distinction between National

On this subject see Jacob Robinson, *And the Crooked Shall be Made Straight*, New York, 1965, p. 92 ff. The notorious Thierack letter of October 13 1942 (Nuremberg Document NG-558, quoted in Raul Hilberg, *The Destruction of the European Jews*, Chicago, 1961) implies that mass killings of Poles and Russians were considered – and did take place – but says nothing about total annihilation.

Hans-Joachim Döring, *Die Zigeuner im NS Statt*, Hamburg, 1964, pp. 189 sq., 193 sq.

Socialism and Fascism'.[3] One does not have to be a Jew to discern in the general term 'fascism' a multitude of diverging phenomena, and to realize that this common denominator is of questionable value, especially when one reaches some of the core problems of the various movements included. For us, the most dubious of Nolte's points is his identification of fascism and anti-Marxism. In such a context, the persecution and extermination of the Jews becomes but the consequence of a general counter-revolutionary, counter-Marxist drive.

That the systematic destruction of a Jewry which was mostly 'liberal' and 'capitalist' should have created doubts in the minds of the Nazis, if anti-Marxism had indeed been their first and major objective, is one point. The fundamental objection to the 'fascist' explanation, however, arises from the simple fact that documentary evidence itself shows very clearly that the anti-Marxist crusade of the Nazis derived from their anti-Jewish position, and not the other way round. In recent studies of Hitler's world-view, for instance, one finds a demonstration not only of the centrality of Hitler's anti-Semitism (Nolte, by the way, was aware of this as well, but acrobatically explains the fundamental anti-Semitism as a kind of *Ersatz* anti-Marxism[4]), but also of the fact that Hitler's living-space conception was in great part influenced by his anti-Jewish drive.[5] But why not turn to the sources themselves? Martin Borman explained the relationship between anti-Marxism and anti-Semitism in the clearest way when, at the end of 1944, he stated: 'National Socialist doctrine is totally anti-Jewish, which means anti-Communist and anti-Christian; everything is linked within National Socialism and everything concurs towards the fight against Judaism'.[6] After all, Hitler's first and last political utterances were directed not against Marxism but against the Jews. This, it seems to me, should seriously put into question the 'fascist' generalization, at least insofar as the Holocaust is concerned. However, the importance of the link between Nazi anti-Semitism and anti-Marxism remains crucial, and I shall return to it later.

The 'totalitarian' generalization is no more solidly founded than is the 'fascist' one. From our viewpoint, a close comparison between Nazi Germany and Stalinist Russia, for example, according to the accepted criteria of 'totali-

[3] Ernst Nolte, *Three Faces of Fascism: Action Française, Italian Fascism, National Socialism*, New York, 1966, p. 19.

[4] *Ibid.*

[5] Eberhard Jäckel, *Hitlers Weltanschauung: Entwurf einer Herrschaft*, Tübingen, 1969; Andreas Hillgruber, 'Die "Endlösung" und das deutsche Ostimperium als Kernstück des rassenideologischen Programms des National-Sozialismus', *Vierteljahrshefte für Zeitgeschichte*, vol. 20, 1973

[6] In Adolf Hitler, *Libres Propos sur la Guerre et la Paix*, vol. 2, Paris, 1954, p. 347.

tarianism', shows clearly that the differences are greater than the similarities on almost all counts, and certainly so far as the conception of 'the enemy' is concerned.

According to the accepted understanding of totalitarianism, 'enemies' are fought and persecuted in order to galvanize energies and frighten opponents. In various totalitarian regimes 'the enemy' is a functional concept which changes with time, according to circumstances. But for National Socialism there was one 'enemy' that did not change from the very beginning to the very end of the regime: the Jews. In other totalitarian regimes the persecution of enemies is widely publicized in many of its aspects; even the fate of the inmates of Siberian camps was not kept secret by the Stalinist regime. The same held true for the executions of many so-called opponents from the very first days of the Bolshevik Revolution. The Nazis, as well, made no secret of the executions of the S.A. leaders or of other opponents to the regime, both before and during the war. But as far as the Jews were concerned, although one may say that the exploitation of the myth of a world Jewish conspiracy could serve to galvanize energies and that the early persecutions had a frightening effect on the German population, the later stages of Nazi policy - the extermination itself - cannot be included in the same context; everything possible was done to keep it secret. For the Nazis, the extermination of the Jews was a fundamental urge and a sacred mission, not a means to other objectives.

This is not to say that the Nazi action against the Jews did not utilize the extreme forms of bureaucratic manipulation and domination which are typical of totalitarian regimes and - on a more diffuse level - of modern society in general. Nor does it mean that the complete disregard for human life and for the value of the individual, so often demonstrated in our century, did not make the Nazi task easier. But these are only circumstances which facilitated the exterminatory drive: they do not explain its chief characteristic - its absolutely uncompromising nature.

Some historians seek explanations in the supposed economic function of the extermination of the Jews.[7] They forget that the persecution and extermination of European Jewry destroyed an immense labour force at the very moment when the Nazi Reich was involved in the most desperate stages of total war. Even at the height of this 'total war', less than a quarter of every Jewish transport arriving at the camps was not exterminated on the spot; it was absolutely clear that the remainder was only temporarily saved and was intended to

[7] See, for instance, O. Kraus and E. Kulka, *The Death Factory: A Document on Auschwitz*, London, 1966.

die from exhaustion.[8] It has been calculated that, from the viewpoint of the German war economy, the Final Solution brought about a loss of immense magnitude, indeed, of a magnitude which completely dwarfed any gains drawn from despoiling the victims.[9] But here again, the Nazi sources speak for themselves. When, in 1941, Reichskommissar Lohse asked Rosenberg if all the Jews of the East were to be exterminated 'without considering the economic interests, for example, the needs of the Wehrmacht for specialized workers for the armaments industry', the minister answered: 'On principle, one shall not take into account any economic consideration in the solution of this problem'.[10]

Apparently unique within both the Nazi context and that of other contemporary political-ideological frameworks, could the extermination of the Jews be compared to previous murderous outbursts in history? Some have mentioned the witch-hunts of the sixteenth and seventeenth centuries, in which thousands of women considered 'witches' were executed. But this comparison does not hold on many counts. First of all, how can one compare the scale of the persecutions: during the 'great witch-hunt' in Western and Central Europe which extended over approximately 200 years, at the most some tens of thousands of witches were killed. Horrible as these killings are, these numbers represent the executions of no more than a few days at the peak of the Final Solution. Moreover – and this is the main point – the witch's confession, although not necessarily exempting her from death, brought her and the inquisitor together to work for the salvation of the witch's soul, even if it meant death at the stake.[11] That is, within religious thought as applied to the witch, there was no unredeemable damnation: quite the contrary. For the Nazis, however, the Jew was irredeemably evil in his very being.

As for various past or contemporary attempts at genocide (the usual reference being to the massacres of the Armenians by the Turks during World War One), the difference is quite obvious: these murderous attacks stemmed always from easily identifiable ethnic or political conflicts between a majority and a minority group, and the attempted annihilation was never related to some

[8] Joseph Billig, *Les camps de concentration dans l'économie du Reich Hitlérien*, Paris, 1973, p. 66.

[9] Raul Hilberg, *The Destruction of the European Jews*, p. 645 ff.

[10] Nuremberg Document PS-3663 and PS-3666. It has been pointed out that on some occasions, economic imperatives seem to have had priority over the exterminatory imperatives. Even Hitler gave orders, on at least two occasions, to postpone the killing of a number of Jews for economic reasons. Indeed, one can mention several examples of that kind; but they remain exceptions. There is not the least documentary evidence that at any moment, except during the very last months of the war – and even then only very partially – did the exploitation of the Jews as slave labour take precedence over their extermination.

fantastic myth or to the 'inherent evil' of the group to be exterminated. The criminal dimension is certainly the same in every case of genocide, be the victims Armenians, Jews or Tutsis; the attempt at total physical eradication may sometimes be identical, but the motivations are quite different; in that sense, the Nazi exterminatory drive against the Jews remains unmistakably singular.

Finally, the Nazis were innovators even within the context of the long history of anti-Jewish persecutions. As has been pointed out, before the Nazi era Jews were subjected to conversion and to expulsion, as well as to sporadic acts of violence. But only in the case of the Nazis was the idea of systematic extermination elaborated and implemented.

Let me, at the end of these preliminary remarks, turn to a very recent interpretation which actually eliminates the specificity of the extermination of the Jews, by eliminating the historical significance of National Socialism within the context of recent German history. I refer to the stand taken by Professor Geoffrey Barraclough in a series of three articles published by the *New York Review of Books* in Fall 1972.[12] His criticism is directed essentially against what he calls the 'liberal view' of German history which, by stressing ideological, political and constitutional history at the expense of social and economic trends, has attributed, according to him, an artificial specificity to the Nazi Reich and to German history between 1933 and 1945. 'Post-liberal' historians, in Barraclough's terminology, are now setting things straight: a new periodization of contemporary German history shows the progressive structural changes which began within German society in the late seventies of the nineteenth century and which continue into the present time, thereby including the Nazi era within a general process of social and economic transformation in which its specific and outstanding characteristics are lost. 'For the younger historians', writes Barraclough, 'the central theme is not the rise of Nazism, but the incipient class conflict ... this is the thread which lends unity to the period 1879-1969 ...' Or: '... the obsessive preoccupation of the older historians with the rise of Nazism, as though it were the main content of German history since Bismarck, is bound to result in distortion. The younger historians have restored the balance ...' But what then of those facts which characterized Nazism for the 'liberal' historian? What of the particular aspects of the Nazis's ideology and criminal behaviour? Barraclough mentions 'Nazi beastliness', but he 'smooths it over' (I use the

[11] On this subject see especially Norman Cohn, *Europe's Inner Demons*, London, 1975, pp. 253-255.

[12] Geoffrey Barraclough, *New York Review of Books*, October 9 1972; November 2 1972; November 16 1972.

terms that he himself applies to the manner in which he feels 'liberal' historians deal with social dichotomies).

In his own way, Geoffrey Barraclough stumbles on the same obstacle which so blatantly invalidates the 'fascist' and the 'totalitarian' generalizations about Nazism. Both Hannah Arendt and Ernst Nolte were aware of the centrality and the specificity of the Jewish question within Nazi ideology and practice, and both nevertheless built a general theory which, instead of attempting to explain this specificity, disregarded all its main aspects. Barraclough, at the beginning of his series, agrees that 'our knowledge of what happened at Auschwitz has vastly increased, but not our understanding'; then, instead of proposing a historical framework within which the factors leading to Auschwitz could be better scrutinized, he offers us a view of history from which Auschwitz virtually disappears. It means, to put it bluntly, that to understand what happened at Auschwitz is by far less important to Barraclough than some aspects of social mobility within contemporary German society. There is no objective criterion of what is important in history; each historian interprets history according to his own values. The answer to Barraclough and to the 'post-liberal' historians is therefore a very simple one: you may choose whatever point of view you wish in order to look at the German past, but you cannot deny that your viewpoint stems from very specific values, from an explicit view of what are the important problems of that past and what are the side-issues.

From the preceding remarks it should be quite clear that for me the extermination of European Jewry cannot be subsumed under generalizing explanations, even less 'smoothed over' in the 'post-liberal' fashion. This, however, immediately raises an obvious question: if these events do not fall within general socio-political categories of analysis, and if the explanation within the wider framework of German history is not apparent, then is not the Holocaust a unique event, that is, an anomaly of history which may have the utmost significance on a theological or even philosophical level, but falls outside the scope of any historical interpretation? By trying to escape the banalization of the Holocaust through the use of inadequate generalizations or outright evasions, do we not fall into the other extreme, that of making the Holocaust an event so unique in human history that we cannot give it any signification whatsoever?

To this dilemma one may tentatively answer that the Holocaust indeed does not fall within the framework of explanatory categories of a generalizing kind, but it is nevertheless the result of cumulative historical trends which can, in part at least, be identified and explained. These trends lead us necessarily to the major questions mentioned at the outset: the behaviour of the exterminators, that of the onlookers, and that of the victims.

The behaviour of the exterminators has usually been explained in the following ways:

Some historians of modern anti-Semitism have put the main emphasis on the social and political roots of Nazi anti-Jewish policies, stressing the political exploitation of the socially-induced resentment of the Austrian and German middle classes in the second half of the nineteenth century and the beginning of the twentieth century as a fundamental explanatory framework.[13] Others accentuate the importance of the ideological roots of Nazi anti-Semitism; within this context, the Final Solution seems to be the result of the unfolding of theories, of ideas, sometimes propagated by small esoteric groups, but seeping into increasingly wider social strata.[14] Another approach deals essentially with the organization of the extermination, with its administrative and bureaucratic processes.[15]

Both the general sociological and cultural approaches are usually related to the investigation of such phenomena as the exacerbation of contemporary nationalism, the expansion of racial and neo-Darwinist thinking, as well as the cult of violence and the mood of cultural despair; this returns us to the usual explanation of fascism. The 'bureaucratic' approach alludes implicitly or explicitly to the rise of all-powerful bureaucracies in modern society, to the spread of mass phenomena, to the all-pervasive impact of modern organizations and technology, mostly in reference to mass death: we are back within the general framework of totalitarianism. A synthesis of these various approaches is possible and, in a way, Hannah Arendt's *Origins of Totalitarianism* is an effort in that direction. But in all these cases, one wonders if an additional dimension, that of the utterly irrational impulse, of some kind of insanity, is not missing.

It is precisely in order to stress the centrality of the irrational dimension that another approach has developed.[16] It tries to

[13] See for instance, among many other titles, Paul W. Massing, *Rehearsal for Destruction*, New York, 1949, as well as Peter G.J. Pulzer, *The Rise of Political Anti-Semitism in Germany and Austria*, New York, 1964.

[14] George L. Mosse's *The Crisis of German Ideology* is a good example of this approach, which also seems to be the main guiding line of Leon Poliakov's massive *Histoire de l'antisémitisme*, 3 vols., Paris, 1955 1968.

[15] Raul Hilberg's *The Destruction of the European Jews* exemplifies this line of inquiry.

[16] This approach is not new. It has been a central preoccupation of two major collective endeavours, the *Studies in Prejudice* sponsored by the American Jewish Committee after the war, and the *Studies in the Dynamics of Persecution and Extermination*, initiated in recent years by the British 'Columbus Centre'. In both cases, we have illuminating monographs; but the difficulty is in the synthesis between the inquiry into the irrational motivations of the extermination, and the other factors. For an attempt at such a synthesis, see my own book, *L'antisémitisme Nazi: Histoire d'une psychose collective*, Paris, 1971.

analyze the motivations of the Nazis and to identify the pathological origins of their exterminatory drive. It is not the killing as such that is considered pathological, but the obsession with the Jewish danger which motivated the killing, the various fantasms that initiated the uncompromising drive towards first the expulsion of the Jews, and then their extermination. This approach does not mean that the other factors are disregarded: quite the contrary; but it tries to achieve a more encompassing synthesis. It immediately raises the following questions: can one take into consideration an element of pathology in the pre-Nazi hatred of the Jews as well as in the analysis of Nazi anti-Semitism? If such is the case, what would be the link between the pre-Nazi and the Nazi type of anti-Semitism, from this particular viewpoint? The possible answers can barely be hinted at in the present framework.

It is fully accepted that once the Jew was defined as one of the major symbols of Evil within Christian society, the profound transformations of this society brought about changes in the outward characteristics of the symbol, but not in its nature itself. In a way, the Jew fulfilled the essential function of a collective counter-ideal, a means of distinguishing between Good and Evil, between Pure and Impure, between what society ought to be and what it was forbidden to be. The objective social tensions between the Jews and their environment, either because of the auto-segregation of the Jews or because of their penetration into the most sensitive fields of social competition, reinforced a situation originally induced by factors independent of anything the Jews could have done or refused to do.

In every age, each social group projected some of its fears onto the Jew; for the great majority of people these culturally and socially induced projective mechanisms manifested themselves, for the most part, in relatively mild form. For a minority, however, the attitude towards the Jew became an outlet for deep-seated emotional disturbances. The studies of Ackermann and Jahoda, of Loewenstein, of Gough, of Adorno and his group,[17] have established, each in its own way, the possible links between extreme anti-Semitism and individual pathology. I have tried, in my own work, to confirm these assumptions through inquiry into the biographies of extreme anti-Semites: their psychopathological motivations, so far as I can judge, seem demonstrated.[18]

[17] Nathan W. Ackermann and Marie Jahoda, *Antisemitism and Emotional Disorder*, New York, 1950; Rodolph Loewenstein, *Psychanalyse de l'antisémitisme*, Paris, 1952; H.G. Gough, 'Studies in Social Intolerance', *The Journal of Social Psychology*, vol. 33, 1951; Theodore W. Adorno, *et al.*, *The Authoritarian Personality*, New York, 1950.

[18] Saul Friedländer, *L'antisémitisme Nazi*, p. 27 ff.

In non-crisis periods, the obsessions of the pathological anti-Semites found little echo outside a very limited circle; but one easily notices that in times of crisis and upheaval, when existing interests, norms and certainties seem threatened or do collapse, the emotional regression experienced by vast masses of people, the weakening of rational controls, opens the widest fields of influence to the minority of the extreme anti-Semites. This was the background for the expansion of extreme anti-Semitism in post-World War One German society and the background for the impact of Hitler's own obsessions. But this very general analysis, although eventually clarifying the background for the rise of Nazi anti-Semitism, does not relate to that specific brand of Jew hatred; nor does it explain the possible relationship between the pathology and the bureaucracy, that is, between the anti-Semitic obsessions of a leading group and their implementation within the huge organizational framework of the Final Solution.

At this particular level, our starting point should be, it seems to me, a re-examination of the myth of the Jew in the Nazi world-view, and particularly in Hitler's world-view. A careful analysis of this myth may show quite distinct elements.

First of all, there was an almost metaphysical conception of the Jew which described him as a kind of cosmic principle of Evil. This view, a manifest transformation of the extreme religious trends of anti-Semitism, appears very clearly in Hitler's conversation with Eckart and in *Mein Kampf* ('if the Jew wins, his crown will be the death wreath of humanity').[19]

On another level, we find the classic racialist position pushed to its extremes: set against the culture-creating and culture-bearing races, the Jews are a culture-destroying race which, throughout the course of history, has attempted to eliminate the culture-creating efforts of the higher races, and is now aiming at world domination through racial defilement, internationalism (Marxism), democracy and pacificism.

Finally – and this may well be the most important aspect of the myth – the Nazis considered the Jew a bacillus, a source of possibly fatal infection. This bacterial level of the myth is quite different from the general racial one, and the fact that it does not enter into the explicit ideological framework does not diminish its importance: on the contrary. This is the image of the Jew that is discovered, first of all, at the level of spontaneous expressions, but also at the level of extermination practices and rituals.

[19] At this level, Nazism appears not only as a transformation of Christian anti Semitism, that is, as a mutation of Christian 'orthodoxy', but also as a modern version of Manichean heresies, or even older religious conceptions, in which a principle of Evil struggles with a principle of Good for the control of the universe.

In his analysis of the image of the Jew as parasite, Alex Bein demonstrates that in the Nazi version parasite and bacillus were quite identical, and that there was a difference between the racial view and the parasitical-bacterial one. Bein quotes Rosenberg and Schickedanz to show the differences between the view concerned with races, inferior or superior, and the conception of the Jew as an anti-race.[20] One may add an example taken from Himmler's notorious Posen speech.

In this speech, delivered on October 4 1943 on the occasion of an S.S. military group-leaders meeting, Himmler refers to the Russians in a racial context and the Jews in a bacterial one. If the racial metaphor had been carried through, Himmler would have compared the Russian inferior race and the Jewish destructive race. But Himmler brought in the microbial metaphor. He explained that Russians were like animals; thus the death of tens of thousands of Russian women working on German anti-tank trenches was of no more consequence than the death of animals, if it could save German lives; but since the Germans were not cruel to animals, they would not be unnecessarily cruel to these 'human animals' *(Menschentieren)* if need not be. On the other hand, the Jews were bacilli which had to be eradicated at all costs, and Himmler warned that this had to be undertaken in a manner in which those engaged in the eradication of the bacilli should not be infected themselves: 'We don't want, in the process of eradicating a bacillus, to be infected by that bacillus, to fall ill and die ourselves'.[21]

How then does the distinction between the three levels of the myth allow for the insertion of the pathological element into the context of Nazi extermination policies and, more precisely, how does it allow for the establishment of a link between the pathology of the limited group - and particularly that of the Führer himself - and the dedication of the bureaucratic machine to its murderous task? Blind obedience may not be enough to explain their dedication, and other aspects may have to be taken into account.

The effect of Hitler's 'charisma' in contributing to the acceptance of his own fantasies about the Jew is, certainly, a major factor. Secondly, the constant tendency of National Socialism to obliterate the distinction between the symbolic plane and that of reality[22] allowed, by definition, the interlocking of fantasies and reality assessments; this

[20] Alex Bein, 'The Jewish Parasite', *Yearbook of the Leo Baeck Institute*, London, 1964, p. 21 ff.

[21] Nuremberg Document PS 1919.

[22] This point was convincingly demonstrated by Uriel Tal in his lecture 'Pre Holocaust Structures of Political Theology and Myths in Nazi Germany', delivered at the conference on 'The Holocaust - A Generation After', New York, March 1975.

tendency would suffice in itself to explain the easy penetration of the most extreme delusions into the context of Nazi theory and practice. Finally, from a more limited viewpoint, the biological framework of racialist ideology made it easy to establish a link between the microbial conception of the Jew and the general racial one. What was considered reality at the microbial level became metaphor at the general racial one. In that way, the microbial element of the Nazi myth of the Jew gave the fundamental impetus to the relentless drive for physical exclusion first, physical extermination later; the racial ideology, the general historical and philosophical framework of which was adapted to the common views of the German middle classes of the time, served as the rationalizing framework within which instructions could be given to the vast masses of civil servants in charge of the details of the Final Solution. The fuzzy racial ideology could not have been the 'prime mover'; it was the 'transmission belt', the mediating element between the murderous pathological drive and the bureaucratic and technological organization of the extermination.

If, in order to be transmittable to the bureaucratic level, the microbial obsession of the Nazi 'true believers' required the racist rationalization, that rationalization itself was part of a wider synthesis, the other main elements of which were the neo-romantic and anti-liberal trends and the anti-Marxist stance. But some of the elements of this ideological synthesis, particularly its anti-liberal and anti-Marxist tenets, were themselves only the particular Nazi expressions of much wider currents that shaped the world view of important segments of the middle classes throughout Europe. In that sense, ideology becomes one of the links between the anti-Jewish attitudes of the Nazis and the behaviour of the onlookers, that is, Western society.

The structural link between the behaviour of the exterminators and that of the onlookers in the context of the destruction of European Jewry is obvious: the extermination of nearly six million Jews did not take more than three years to accomplish. It emerged and developed virtually unchecked, and therefore could reach such proportions in so short a time. Any important countervailing forces, be they massive attempts at hiding, constant protests and demonstrations, or violent intervention from outside occupied Europe, would have made the course of extermination much less rapid and more difficult. The absence of these countervailing forces on any significant scale – that is, the passivity of the onlookers – is what directly relates their behaviour to that of the exterminators themselves, whatever the differences in motivation and in culpability. The question again is: why?

The 'banality of evil' is certainly insufficient to explain the murderous anti-Jewish drive of the Nazis. An element of pathology has to be added to the usual attempts at explanation, as I have tried to demonstrate. But so far as the quasi-general passivity of the onlookers is concerned, the first and foremost explanation is precisely that which relies on the most banal behaviour, be it pure self-interest at the individual or group level, pseudo-ideological choices, or traditional anti-Semitism to a greater or lesser degree. However, even at this level of banality one point has to be stressed: whatever the motivations of the passivity – not to speak of the collaboration with the Nazis – it always resulted from a choice in which the Jew was less than whatever other consideration he was weighed against. This being said, the problem that confronts the historian remains: can one, beyond these simple arguments of common sense which, although correct, seem to remain on the surface of things, find more general and basic explanations for the passivity of the onlookers?

Several explanatory frameworks could contribute to our understanding of these attitudes: a general trend of indifference to mass death in modern society, mostly in the midst of war; the differential impact of spiritual (religious) leadership and state collaboration on the attitude of the masses; the various degrees of integration of Jews within the surrounding social frameworks; the cohesiveness of the societies themselves, and so forth. I should like to suggest an approach which allows one to link the attitude of the onlookers with some aspects of that of the exterminators, but which is also of some relevance to the behaviour of the victims.

I shall hardly mention Eastern and Southeastern Europe: the intensity of traditional anti-Semitism there is a sufficient answer (although many nuances are evident even there). In the West, however, the appraisal of motivations is much more complex.

I have mentioned that the anti-liberal and anti-Marxist tenets of Nazi ideology were part of a much wider current, a counter-revolutionary atmosphere that spread far beyond the 'fascist' movements and, in one way or another, touched most parts of the European middle classes during the thirties and up to the middle of the war. This very well-known ideological background has, in our context, a crucial significance which I would formulate as follows: the anti-liberal feelings vastly contributed to the total isolation of the Jew, to the elimination of whatever protection he had within Western society, to his becoming a total 'outsider' at the very moment when these same anti-liberal feelings, as well as the anti-Marxist aspirations of the middle classes helped to advance the view of the Nazi as 'insider'. The convergence of these ideological trends contributed to the passivity of the onlookers at least during the decisive period in which help could still have had a major effect, that is, up to the middle of the war. Beyond that time, when the major deportations from the West had been completed and the exterminating machine was working at full speed, it was too late. Let me try to dwell briefly on these points.

The emancipation of the Jews meant above all their acceptance within the legal framework of European states, as citizens equal before the law; but, except in rare cases, it did not mean their undifferentiated acceptance by society within those states. The rise of anti-Semitism in the West during the second half of the nineteenth century created a growing hiatus, a growing dissonance between the legal status of the Jews as citizens equal to others, and their real status within society. This hiatus was obviously compounded by the growth of the anti-rationalist, anti-liberal current just mentioned (in any case, we are dealing with different facets of the same ideological trend). The growing rejection of the legalistic and universalistic values of rational liberalism obviously implied a growing readiness to accept the annulment of the legal equality of the Jews. The distinction between the *pays légal* and the *pays réel* coined by Maurras spread far beyond the narrow limits of the *Action Française*, and it is useful in describing the gist of the situation throughout Western Europe, at least on the continent. Some historians will reply that this is a post-Holocaust view of the past and that, in reality, the 'symbiosis' between Jews and their surrounding society - in Germany for instance - was genuine until well after World War One. It would be easy to amass documents proving this 'symbiosis' to be an illusion, a Jewish illusion. It seems to me that Hannah Arendt correctly summed up the situation when, in *The Origins of Totalitarianism*, she wrote: 'Society, confronted with political, economic and legal equality for the Jews, made it quite clear that none of its classes was prepared to grant them social equality, and that only exceptions from the Jewish people would be received'.[23]

The fundamental reticence of large strata of Western society towards the Jews, compounded by the anti-liberal feelings which despised the legal framework of universalistic democracy, explains why, when the legal exclusion of the Jews once more became fact, it was accepted - even promoted (certainly not strongly opposed) - among wide groups of this same society. The most damning evidence is that the process itself, although encouraged by the Nazis beginning in 1933, was taken over almost autonomously by various other authorities and institutions. When Swiss Chief-of-Police Rothmund suggested to the Germans, in 1938, that the letter 'J' be printed on the passports of German and Austrian Jews, he was, on the face of it, creating further legal discrimination against German and Austrian Jews; but implicitly, he was

[23] Hannah Arendt, *The Origins of Totalitarianism*, New York, 1958, p. 56.

suggesting that the legal rights of Jews could be rescinded within the Western world in general.[24]

The passengers of the *St. Louis* wandering through the Atlantic Ocean, in the spring of 1939,[25] became symbols of the new Jewish situation, as later would the passengers of the *Patria* sinking in sight of the coast of Palestine.[26] It was, so it seems, French Foreign Minister Georges Bonnet who, during his conversation with Ribbentrop, at the end of 1938, mentioned the possibility of shipping thousands of Jews to Madagascar.[27] When the Vichy government promulgated its anti-Jewish laws, in 1940 and 1941, it did not take these steps under Nazi pressure, but rather on its own initiative; it was independently eliminating the gap between the *pays légal* and the *pays réel*.[28] And when Leon Bérard, Vichy's ambassador to the Vatican, inquired about the Holy See's reaction to these contemplated measures, he was encouraged to abolish a legal equality which seemed offensive to Christian society.[29] Three years earlier, the Evian Conference proved that virtually all Western countries were wary of accepting more Jews, and that the disappearance of legal protection for hundreds of thousands of Jews was contemplated with equanimity. In 1944, the Bermuda Conference *de facto* restated the same position under the cover of vague formulas, but also with the knowledge of mass extermination...

This whole process is epitomized, in my view, by the letter sent in January 1944 by Msgr. Adolf Bertram, Archbishop of Breslau, to the Reich Minister of the Interior. The German bishops had just learned that measures which heretofore had applied only to full Jews would henceforth be imposed upon Christians of mixed race *(Mischlinge)*. The Archbishop summarized the measures that had already befallen these people of mixed origin and added: 'All these measures aim

[24] For this entire question, see the report written by Professor Carl Ludwig, *La politique pratiquée par la Suisse à l'égard des réfugiés au cours des années 1933 à 1945*, Berne, 1958.

[25] See Arthur D. Morse, *While Six Million Died*, New York, 1968, p. 270 ff.

[26] The sinking of the *Patria* was a direct consequence of the British refusal to open the gates of Palestine to Jewish refugees even in the midst of the war. Later, the British government rejected a notorious proposal to exchange Hungarian Jews for trucks. To this very day, however, many aspects of British policy towards the Nazi persecution and extermination of the Jews remain shrouded in mystery. For instance, according to a German source, in 1937 Hitler proposed to the British that all the Jews of Germany be sent to Palestine; the British rejected this idea. On this particular point, see *Heeresadjutant bei Hitler 1938-1943: Aufzeichnungen des Major Engel*, herausgegeben und kommentiert von Hildegard von Kotze, Stuttgart, 1974, pp. 65, 95.

[27] For the attitudes of various governments concerning the fate of the Jews during the thirties, see Eliahu Ben-Elissar, *La diplomatie du IIIe Reich et les Juifs, 1933-1939*, Paris, 1968.

[28] Raul Hilberg, *The Destruction of the European Jews*, p. 393 ff.

[29] Saul Friedländer, *Pius XII and the Third Reich*, New York, 1966, p. 92 ff.

clearly at segregation at the end of which threatens extermination...' The German Catholics feel 'deeply hurt', continued Msgr. Bertram, 'if these fellow Christians now would have to meet a fate similar to that of Jews'.[30] I once wrote about the 'ambiguity of that sentence'.[31] But there is actually no ambiguity: the Jews who remained Jews were unprotected by any law, be it human or divine: they could be exterminated.

The attitude described here concerning the Jews takes into account neither acts of courage and devotion, public protests, nor various manifestations of solidarity, because my objective is to sketch the main lines of a very general trend. Similarly, the remarks which follow, about the attitude towards National Socialism, aim at describing a tendency and in no way attempt to analyze the various aspects of a very complex historical situation. In that sense, one may say that the attitude of important groups of Western society towards the Jews arises from the same internal crisis which explains their attitude towards Nazism.

In its propaganda as well as in its spontaneous expressions, National Socialism consistently presented itself as an outgrowth of the 'true' values of European culture; and – of more importance to us – it was perceived as such by large numbers of Europeans. The reasons for this tacit or explicit acceptance of Nazism as part of the West have been mentioned: the adherence of large segments of the European middle classes to the anti-liberal trend, and especially their absolute hostility to Marxism, that is, to 'Bolshevism'.

There is no need for an elaborate demonstration. We have, first of all, the multitude of explicit ideological justifications of the 'appeasement' policy of the thirties until the very last days before the outbreak of war. We have the tacit or explicit admiration for many characteristics of the National Socialist 'revolution', and this not only among European fascists or even within the ranks of the traditional Right. So-called liberals and even groups which could be considered as tending towards the left were not absolutely immune to such temptations.

During the war itself such attitudes became blatant in Western continental Europe. The Nazi Reich was, until the middle of the war, considered an acceptable partner by many; the 'new order' was not the aspiration of a small minority of extreme collaborationists, but rather 'collaboration' was accepted, if not

[30] Guenter Lewy, *The Catholic Church and Nazi Germany*, New York, 1964, pp. 290-293.

[31] Saul Friedländer, *Kurt Gerstein: The Ambiguity of Good*, New York, 1969, p. 148.

actively sought, by important sectors of the society in the occupied or neutral countries of Europe.[32]

As far as France is concerned, for instance, one usually distinguishes between 'state collaboration', the necessary collaboration imposed by a kind of *raison d'état,* and 'collaborationism', which was emotionally motivated.[33] I wish to suggest that 'state collaboration' disguised much 'collaborationism' that did not dare show itself, and that, moreover, among many of those who kept aloof or declared themselves favourable to a victory of the Anglo-Saxon Allies, there was, up to about 1943, a sneaking admiration for the Reich as representing the true values of Western civilization in its fight against Bolshevism.

A recent unpublished doctoral dissertation shows that after the entrance of the Soviet Union into the war, public opinion in French Switzerland was by far more animated by hatred and fear of the Soviet Union than of the Nazi Reich.[34] In the case of the Vatican, the same thesis has been more than amply demonstrated. In general, it seems that regarding European public opinion, the tide turned against the Reich only some time in 1943, when Germany's defeat became a certainty. It appears therefore that the more or less explicit revolt of an important part of the Western middle classes against the liberal tradition contributed to the isolation of the Jews, and that the same revolt, as well as extreme anti-Bolshevism, contributed to a largely tacit acceptance of many aspects of National Socialism until the middle of the war. By then, the major deportations of Western Jews had taken place. In other words, one could say that at the very moment when the Jews, losing their legal status, were becoming *total outsiders* again in their relation to Western society, that is, bereft of any protection whatsoever, in the eyes of many the Nazis – especially after they began their attack against the Soviet Union – they managed to appear as true bearers of Western values, as *real insiders,* although formal enemies. To help the outsider against the insider requires a strong motivation indeed: the Jews had no chance of being massively helped, be it for this fundamental reason alone until it was too late for a great many of them.

[32] Robert O. Paxton, *Vichy France: Old Guard and New Order, 1940 1944,* New York, 1972.

[33] For this distinction, see Stanley Hoffman, *Essais sur la France; Déclin ou renouveau,* Paris, 1974. [Cp. also (in English): idem, *Decline or Renewal; France since the 1930s,* New York, 1974].

[34] Jacques Meurant, 'La presse et l'opinion de la Suisse romande face à la guerre européenne et à ses répercussions en Suisse', unpublished doctoral dissertation, Geneva, 1974.

When one turns to the last aspect of our study, the behaviour of the victims during the Holocaust, one reaches the unwritten part of that terrible history, the one that few historians would feel able to write. There has been no attempt yet at a general outline, not even at a general conception of how to address oneself to the history of 'the life and death of the Jews of Europe in the Nazi era' - history which probably would have to start not in 1939, not even in 1933, but with the end of World War One. This, manifestly, will be the major task of historians of the Holocaust for years to come, a task made almost impossible not only because of the particular emotional strain which it entails, but even because of the scarcity of reliable documentary evidence. However, the aspect of the question which will be dealt with here is different. After having attempted to formulate some hypotheses about the behaviour of the exterminators and that of the onlookers, we have to turn to the victims and ask: did anything in the behaviour of the Jews either play into the hands of the exterminators or hamper them? Did anything in that behaviour contribute to the passivity of the onlookers?

Defined that way, the question immediately evokes the behaviour of the Jews during the war and, more specifically, that of the Jewish leadership in occupied Europe, the 'Jewish Councils'. I shall not deal with this aspect at any length, as it seems to me that by now, especially since the publication of Isaiah Trunk's study on the Jewish Councils,[35] the facts are more or less known, although the polemics about their significance go on unabated. As for the facts, one could hardly reject Raul Hilberg's comment on Trunk's study: 'It should be emphasized that the Councils were *not* the willful accomplices of the Germans. Within the German superstructure, however, they were its indispensable operatives. Even when their activities were benign, as in the case of housing refugees or promoting sanitary conditions, they could contribute to the overall purpose and ultimate goals of their German supervisors. The very institution of an orderly ghetto was, after all, an essential link in the chain of destructive steps. In building this order and preserving it, the Councils could not help serving their enemy'.[36] The point to be stressed, it seems to me, is the distinction between the objective elements of the situation and its subjective aspects, the realm of intentions and that of results. Objectively, the Jewish Councils may have facilitated the task of the Nazis in

[35] Isaiah Trunk, *Judenrat: The Jewish Councils in Eastern Europe during the Nazi Occupation*, New York, 1972.

[36] Raul Hilberg, 'The Ghetto as a Form of Government: An Analysis of Isaiah Trunk's *Judenrat*', paper presented at the Conference on the Holocaust, New York, March 1975

the majority of instances; subjectively, the intention of the Jewish leadership was obviously the very opposite of this.[37]

The attitude of the Jews of Europe between the wars is of no less importance and is no less relevant than that of the Jewish leadership during the war when one wishes to understand the Jewish element in the Holocaust. Two major questions arise immediately: how does one explain the unawareness of the majority of European Jews of the nature of the unfolding events, an unawareness which resulted in many tens of thousands of people, who probably could have left continental Europe in due time, remaining passively where they lived until it was too late? More than that: what historical interpretation can one give to a certain type of Jewish involvement in public life which, if it did little to change the views of the extreme anti-Semites, probably added some intensity to the diffuse anti-Semitism of those who were to become the onlookers?

The unawareness of European Jews during the thirties of the nature of emerging events is a fact which one cannot question today. One can argue that there is no way of foreseeing developments of so unique a character. Indeed, nobody could have foreseen the Final Solution itself; but a sense of imminent danger, of possibly catastrophic changes, could have been naturally expected from European Jews as soon as Hitler came to power. Most Jews remained unaware of the fact that the time of radical changes had come.

Recent research on the situation among German Jews makes sad reading indeed: one sees how each group was wrong in its own way, because each one was blinded by its own ideology and presuppositions.[38] The emerging trend of events was hidden by pre-formulated models. But then, the various types of mistakes can be explained by some general underlying motivations which are painfully simple.

Many German Jews - and many European Jews in general - were unable to face the fact that assimilation, 'symbiosis', had failed, that all their efforts and hopes had largely been in vain. They were not ready to critically evaluate the past and to recognize that their legal status was not identical with their real status. To abandon their illusions would have meant drawing the most painful conclusions, not only on an abstract level, but about the very nature of Jewishness itself,

[37] It is this absence of distinction between the subjective intentions of the Jewish leadership in occupied Europe and the objective results of its actions that makes Hannah Arendt's analysis of the problem unacceptable. See Hannah Arendt, *Eichmann in Jerusalem*, New York, 1963.

[38] Abraham Margalioth, 'The Political Reaction of German Jewish Organizations and Institutions to the Anti-Jewish Policy of the National Socialists, 1932-1935', unpublished doctoral dissertation, Jerusalem, 1971 (Hebrew).

and worse yet for many, about the very physical existence of the Jews in Europe. It would have entailed drawing conclusions as far as the course of daily life was concerned – conclusions which most had not the strength to draw. It would have meant severing roots which were strong and real, and trying a new course which seemed repellent to most: the course of expatriation, whatever its geographical destination.

Moreover, by seeing themselves as full-fledged members of Western society and by adopting the criteria of perceptions and evaluations of that society, the Jews had difficulty, until it was too late, in reaching conclusions concerning National Socialism that the most influential strata of Western society did not share. That the Jews of Europe reacted with vehemence to the anti-Semitic measures of the Nazis is a fact; but that, deep down, many of them were convinced, as were other Europeans, that the Nazis – members of Western civilization, after all – would 'settle down', is also a fact. After all, not a small percentage of German Jews who had emigrated in 1933 came back to Germany in 1934 and 1935...

These fundamental difficulties were compounded by two rather typical ways of apprehending their surroundings which made the Jews even more impervious to the true evolution of the situation: on the one hand, a tendency to extreme and short-range pragmatism, which turned many of them into fundamentally apolitical citizens whose major aim was to succeed in life, relatively oblivious to various shifts in the political scene or signs of approaching storms until too late. (Short-range pragmatism and the exacerbated need to achieve success as a 'guarantee' of equality and safety can account for what has not always been a high regard for legal niceties among some fringe groups within the Jewish population....) On the other hand, the trend among a minority was to try to solve their own problems by solving the general problems of humanity: the refusal to admit the specificity of the Jewish situation, the intense desire to believe that such specificity did not exist, led these Jews towards a kind of abstract theoretical thinking which, by its very nature, eliminates nuances and ambiguities and hides the complexity of social and political developments under the *a priori* smoothness of theoretical constructs. This last point immediately evokes further questions about the behaviour of this particular category of Jews. In our context, the main question may be formulated in the following way: what historical interpretation can one give to a certain type of Jewish ideological and public involvement which has probably added some intensity to the rejection of the Jews by those who were to become the onlookers during the Holocaust?

In very general terms, one may say that the strong involvement of the Jews in the rise and expansion of modern capitalism fed many of the anti-Semitic slogans of the nineteenth century, and still retained a strong impact after World War One. No less important, however, was the stereotype of the Jew as revolutionary and, in a more general way, as a detractor of established values. This second aspect played a major role in the expression of anti-Semitism after the First World War.

Take the case of Germany and Austria: the most bitter critics of the most hallowed values were Jews – Harden, Kraus, Tucholsky – critics of values, critics of the surrounding culture, critics of the misuse of the German language itself. What could have created more profound irritation within a deeply-wounded society which felt precisely that all its most sacred traditions were suddenly disintegrating? Even if they were correct *in abstracto*, these Jewish critics were painfully unaware of the morbid sensitivity of the groups that surrounded them. Franz Kafka, in a letter to Max Brod written in May 1920, rightly condemned a tendency which did bring about the greatest harm to the Jews themselves.[39] But needless to say, it was the particular involvement of Jews in the revolutionary movements of the war and the post-war period which became, in this respect, the antagonizing element of the greatest significance.

Ya'acov Talmon has recently described the intimate link between Jews and revolution through the whole of European history since the French Revolution and Jewish emancipation.[40] The reasons are quite well-known: the Jews transferred into the ideological and political realms a secularized version of the messianic ideals of Jewish religion; having rebelled against religious tradition and having left the framework of their religious and social community, the Jews who looked for other horizons never really integrated into non-Jewish society and, therefore, free of the bonds of old and unhampered by allegiances to some new traditional unit, they were more open to all the ideas of radical change than many of their non-Jewish contemporaries.

One could enumerate other reasons. The facts remain, and they were particularly visible during the critical period with which we are dealing. The involvement of an extremely high percentage of Jews in German revolutions at the end of World

[39] Franz Kafka, *Correspondence, 1902-1924*, Paris, 1965, p. 325. [Cp. also: idem, *Gesammelte Werke; Briefe 1902 1924*, Frankfurt a.M. 1958(?), p. 274].

[40] Ya'acov Talmon, 'Jews and Revolution', in *The Age of Violence*, Tel Aviv, 1974 (Hebrew). [Cp. also: idem, 'Jews Between Revolution and Counter-revolution', *Israel Among the Nations*, London, 1970].

War One, their leading part in those revolutions, became the object of endless ulterior polemics. It may well be that more often than not Jewish revolutionary leaders were well-meaning and fuzzy idealists, burning with messianic fervour but with little practical idea of how to really change society. Recent studies of the role of the Jews in German revolutions certainly give that impression;[41] but for anti-Semites and for non-Jewish society in general, such fine distinctions were irrelevant. Is it not significant that Thomas Mann, the most respected representative of contemporary German liberalism, felt the need to identify two of the most anti-liberal figures in his novels as Jews, and to portray them with particularly negative traits?[42]

The myth of the revolutionary, culture-destroying Jew who, perhaps, tried to achieve world domination, penetrated into Western consciousness with much greater strength than ever before. The relentless revolutionary drive of a tiny fraction of the Jewish people – actually of such Jews that maintained no link with their community ('non-Jewish Jews', to use Isaac Deutscher's phrase) – brought upon Jews as a whole a stigma of immeasurable potency which was to have the most dire consequences.

Here indeed we are closing the circle. In order to leave no misconceptions about my thesis, let me, at the end, restate it again: whatever the Jews did or did not do, they could not alter the fact of anti-Semitism as such, and in particular the emergence of the murderous anti-Semitism of the Nazis which was fed by an element of true insanity on the one hand, and growing social disintegration on the other, both totally independent of the Jews themselves. However, Nazi anti-Semitism did reach its full scope because there were no strong countervailing forces within European society. The absence of these forces stemmed from a view of the Jew as 'outsider', and of the Nazi as 'insider' – view which the Jews could not have radically altered; but it is not improbable that the identification of Jews with world revolution made the task of Nazi propaganda easier and reinforced the pre-existing tendency of Western society to consider the Jews undesirable elements which had to be excluded, whatever the consequences this would entail for the victims of exclusion.

[41] Werner T. Angress, 'Juden im politischen Leben der Revolutionszeit', in Werner E. Mosse (hrsgb.), *Deutsches Judentum in Krieg und Revolution, 1916-1923*, Tübingen, 1971.

[42] One might answer that Thomas Mann was not exempt from anti Semitic tendencies, but it is too facile an escape. For a balanced view of the question, see Kurt Loewenstein, 'Thomas Mann zur Jüdischen Frage', *Bulletin des Leo Baeck Instituts*, vol. 10, 1967. At any rate, the main point of my argument is that the Jewish revolutionaries added a lot of fuel to pre-existing resentment and prejudice.

But then, let us ask again: why did a fraction of the Jewish community turn with such ardour towards revolution? Because, after leaving the ghetto physically and spiritually, they did not find a non-Jewish society ready to integrate them totally, to accept them as they were, beyond the mere legal equality granted them as citizens.

There is a deadly logic in the dialectic of anti-Semitism.

Writing in 1944, Hannah Arendt analyzed the total foreignness, the loneliness of the Jew, the 'pariah tradition', as she called it; and she quoted a famous sentence from Kafka's novel *The Castle*, in which the hero, the symbol of the Jew, is told: 'You are not of the castle, you are not of the village, you are nothing at all'.[43]

The pariah tradition is not meaningful if we look at the situation of the Jews from the viewpoint of the exterminator. If she had referred to the Holocaust, Hannah Arendt should have chosen the last scene of Kafka's *The Trial*, the cold-blooded execution of a hapless, defenceless man. She could have mentioned the most ambiguous detail of that last scene: the victim sees someone looking at him at his last moment from a distant window, someone leaning from the window to see the execution, even making a movement of some kind with his hands – a movement which, from far away, might appear to be commiseration, but which the victim cannot interpret and which, at any rate, is of no help. The victim is then stabbed – 'as a dog', he thinks, – and dies.

But if we consider now, at the end of these remarks, the wider historical setting, the relationship between the Jew and that Western society in which he tried to integrate himself and from which he was rejected – that society which left him alone in his hour of greatest need – then the symbolism of *The Castle* assumes a profound significance, but one which Hannah Arendt has not mentioned: the hero of *The Castle*, the Jew, is a foreigner who believes that he has been allowed to enter the social system represented by the castle and the village. Indeed, he has been formally asked to join (is even this certain?), but when he tries to fit himself into the system he discovers that no one is really ready to accept him. He then becomes a revolutionary of sorts, trying to circumvent the traditional channels of authority, expressing his opposition to injustice as he sees it, siding with the 'pariahs' of the system (the Barnaby family). His revolutionary effort is ambiguous; and in that sense we may say that the hero of *The Castle* represents the whole Jewish situation in modern society, with

[43] Hannah Arendt, 'The Jews as Pariah: A Hidden Tradition', *Jewish Social Studies*, vol. 6, 1964, p. 115.

the drive for radical change, or a part of it, but also with the intense desire to belong to society as it is, to the majority of the community. At any rate, the more the hero of the novel, the Jew, attempts to belong and the more idolated he becomes, the lower he sinks. One can foresee his ultimate doom.

Kafka never finished the novel, but he mentioned to some friends the end which he envisaged. According to his biographer, Max Brod, Kafka planned to show the hero falling lower and lower; suddenly a message is sent from the castle: he is accepted. But the message is too late; the hero is dying or dead.

When, after the end of the war, Western society opened its arms to the Jews; when, in reaction to the discovery of the whole magnitude of the Nazi massacres, the Western anti-Semitic tradition was - temporarily at least - discarded, most of the Jews of Europe could no longer enter into that new society. But the most terrible question remains to be answered, the one question that will probably never find its answer, although for us it is the most crucial one to understand the past or foresee events to come: did the castle send the messenger because the injustice, the evil done, was recognized? Or was the messenger sent because the hero was dead?

Jews, Antisemitism, and the Origins of the Holocaust

Eugen Weber
University of California, Los Angeles

The Holocaust is not about antisemitism, but it is (and it is about) the fallout of antisemitism.[1] When one asks about the origins of the Holocaust, one really asks how an infection latent in Western Christian society for centuries could become a murderous plague just when that society had become least Christian and most orderly. And the answer to this sort of question must refer to cultural tradition.

Societies produce stereotypes (which are the height of artifice), and then consume them as commonplace (which are the height of naturalness). That is how bad faith can pass for good conscience. That is how religious distinctions and cultural stereotypes can lead to murder – which is not an unusual case in history but unusually gruesome and shocking when practiced on the scale that marks the Holocaust.

Hence the desperate attempts to understand or, more correctly, to comprehend, in the sense of taking in and rendering intelligible a phenomenon so inapprehensible by its nature. Let me say at once that understanding something (or understanding just a bit better) is simply the satisfaction of a curiosity. I do not believe that, in the popular phrase, to understand all is to forgive all. Indeed, it is one of the weaknesses of contemporary thinking to act as if one could understand all, and as if one could or should forgive all. Nor can we really understand. And social scientists are silly if they think that to explain all is to understand all. We cannot explain everything, and we understand even less.

Others have tried before us, of course. So much has been written on the subject that it is hard to say anything new – anything that is not already a platitude. A dip into even one or two representative books – say, Rudolph Loewenstein's *Christians & Jews,* or Hannah Arendt's *Origins of Totalitarianism* – will provide all the basic interpretative

[1] The term seems to have been coined by the German journalist, Wilhelm Marr, in the popular pamphlet, *The Victory of Judaism over Teutonism,* published in the wake of the German stock exchange crash of 1873. It really means antijudaism, of course; but I shall use it in its accepted sense.

themes: Jewish peculiarity and particularism; the association of Jews with the death of Christ, with usury, and with dark-mysterious-implicitly threatening forces; the ubiquity of the Jew as *other* in so many places and at so many social/economic/cultural levels; and finally the resentment against Jewish pretensions and upstartness. These are also the basic explanations that I should advance for anti-Jewish sentiment. And I shall treat them in due course.

More interesting, though, and more debatable, is another point I want to raise, one which stems from the fact that antisemitism does not necessarily imply genocide, or even mass-murder. But a desire for riddance from what is regarded as alien and potentially menacing can lead to such conclusions, as may be seen in a well-known document, whose accuracy is debatable but whose contents are revealing. In Book I of *Exodus* (I, 7-10), Joseph, under whose aegis the Jews had prospered in Egypt, dies:

> *And the children of Israel were fruitful, and increased abundantly, and multiplied, and waxed exceedingly mighty; and the land was filled with them.*
>
> *Now there arose up a new king over Egypt, which knew not Joseph.*
>
> *And he said unto his people, Behold, the people of the children of Israel are more and mightier than we:*
>
> *Come on, let us deal wisely with them; lest they multiply, and it comes to pass that, when there falleth out any war, they join also unto our enemies, and fight against us, and so get them up out of the land.*

Pharaoh, as we know, tried persecutions of all sorts and, when these did not work, he began to have all the male children killed at birth – which is the beginning of the story of Moses.

A few hundred years later the story repeats itself, and the text is even more suggestive. In the Book of *Esther* (III, 819), we find the Jews in Babylonian exile, that is, essentially in Persia:

> *And Haman said unto King Ahasuerus, There is a certain people scattered abroad, and dispersed among the people in all the provinces of thy kingdom; and their laws are diverse from all people, neither keep they the king's laws: therefore, it is not for the king's profit to suffer them.*
>
> *If it please the king, let it be written that they may be destroyed. . . .*

A rather similar decision, though more piecemeal is reported by

Tacitus for the reign of Tiberius: send the men of military age to Sardinia to fight the bandits. "If they perished as a result of the unhealthy climate, it would be no great loss. The remainder would have to leave Italy if they had not abjured their profane rites before a set date. . . ."[2]

And why all this? Why such extreme measures? The sources suggest the extent to which apparently modern arguments and criticisms were articulated hundreds of years before Christ. For one thing, the Egyptians and their friends had to find an explanation for the embarrassing events of the 12th century (whether they had occurred or not). And so in the third century BC we find the Egyptian Manethos, and also the Greek Hecateus of Abdera, accusing the Jews of contagious maladies, subversion, rebelliousness and lack of piety[3] – and these are all dangerous to the realm; but they also accuse them of *misanthropy* and *misoxeny*.[4] And here we come to the crux of the matter, especially when we read that the Jews, chased from Egypt for their lack of piety, perpetuated in Jerusalem their hatred of men/of mankind/of strangers: "This is why they instituted special laws, like never to sit at table with a foreigner and to show them no kindness."[5]

Here is one leitmotif, one major theme among many, that one runs into all the time: in the first century BC, Posidonius of Apamea thinks that "[the Jewish race] alone of all nations refused to have any social relations with the other people and considered them all as enemies."[6] More explicit is Philostratos of Lemnos, another Alexandrian Greek, writing around 200 AD:

> *For this people had long raised itself not only against Romans but against humanity in general. Men who have imagined an unsociable life, who share with their fellows neither table nor libations, neither prayer nor sacrifices, are further from us than Susa or Bactria, or even the farthest Indies.*[7]

Finally, Juvenal repeats some of these charges but makes explicit two of their implications: suspicion growing out of a sense of mysterious doings among the suspect; and resentment of a people that insists on

[2] Théodore Reinach, *Textes d'auteurs grecs et romains relatifs au judaisme* (Hildesheim, 1963), 295.

[3] *Ibid.*, 27, 14-15.

[4] *Ibid.*, 17, 30. This would be repeated by many Greek authorities on the Jews and, after them, by Romans as late as Rutilius Namatianus in the fifth century.

[5] Posidonius of Apamea, quoted in *ibid.*, 57.

[6] *Ibid.*, 176. See also Angelo Segré, "Antisemitism in Hellenistic Alexandria," *Jewish Social Studies*, VIII, 2, 1946, 127-36.

having its own way and does not participate or share in some of the essential aspects of its neighbors' lives. Juvenal accuses the Jews of spurning Roman law and revering only their own, which he says, Moses passed on "in a mysterious volume: not to show the way to the traveller who doesn't practice the same ceremonies; to point out a fountain only to the circumcised. . . ." And to spend the seventh day doing nothing, "without sharing in the duties of life."[8]

One last quotation, to show how many familiar themes had been developed 2,000 years ago: in 59 BC, Valerius Flaccus, a corrupt Roman official who had served in Palestine, was accused of having appropriated the gold that Jews all over the Empire sent for the upkeep of their temple. Flaccus hired Cicero, who was the best lawyer in town; and Cicero argued that, in confiscating the Jewish gold, Flaccus had merely opposed a barbarian superstition and an uneconomic drain on Roman resources. And here again a familiar note creeps in: Flaccus, says Cicero, in effect, *a bien mérité de la patrie,* because it takes a brave man to take on the Jews: "You know how numerous their gang, how they support each other, how powerful they are in the assemblies. . . to despise in the interest of the Republic this multitude of Jews. . . is proof of a singular strength of mind."[9]

So here we have a people (or sect) whose insistent particularism arouses strong resentments – which will be further reinforced by Christian experience and Christian tradition. And this brings me to my first component of modern anti-Jewishness: religious indoctrination.

I shall not insist on it, because it is obvious; yet it is basic.[10] By the 19th century, traditional religion was no longer a dominant component of High Culture – sometimes not even of Official Culture. But religious tradition was; and religious tradition in its most basic form shaped the mentality and conditioned the reflexes of most people – especially simple people.

One thing everybody knew was that the Jews had killed Jesus. The crime and its implications were reiterated in liturgy and catechism, generation after generation and year after year, at the very least in Easter-Week services which often included the wreaking of symbolic retribution on the Jews, either during the Tenebrae service on Maundy Thursday, or on Good Friday. Symbolically, beating "the Jews" with

[8] Satire XIV, Reinach, *Textes, 293.*

[9] Cicero, *Pro Flacco* #67, cited in *ibid.*, 238.

[10] It has been thoroughly treated in Jules Isaac, *Jésus et Israel* (Paris, 1948); Léon Poliakov, *Du Christ aux Juifs de cour* (Paris, 1955) and a host of other works. For a swift treatment, see George La Piana, "The Church and the Jews," *Historia Judaica*, XI, 2 (October, 1949), 117-44.

hammers or cudgels or fists; extinguishing them with candles; burning them in bonfires – these were practices that survived in France around 1900, and elsewhere, I suspect, longer than that.[11]

The memory of alleged Jewish "crimes" was also preserved in the legends of a number of saints whom the Jews were supposed to have martyred, like St. Hugh of Lincoln, or St. Verney in Auvergne – who had been crucified head down by local Jews – whose official or officious worship lent authority to the legends of ritual murder that kept reviving into the 20th century.[12]

In 1892-93, a French friend of the Jews, Anatole Leroy-Beaulieu, wrote a book about and against antisemitism, in which he remarks that "races conserve for a long time at the instinctual level repugnances whose cause they do not really know very well."[13] I am convinced that the firm base of visceral antisemitism in the West was laid down by this long-persistent conditioning that made suspicion and condemnation of Jews integral parts of prejudices and aversions that could be evoked almost at will. Two references to Hannah Arendt's work will illustrate this.

At one point, talking about the time of the Dreyfus Affair, she says: "There can be no doubt that in the eyes of the mob the Jews came to serve as an object lesson for all the things they detested."[14] The point is well made, but it begs the question: could that have happened without preparation? If Dreyfus had been an Armenian, or even a Turk, could the press campaign against him have achieved so much so quickly? The ground had to be prepared, and Arendt herself tells us about the preparation, though that is not her purpose in this passage: "For 30 years," she writes, "the old legends of world conspiracy had been no more than the conventional stand-by of the tabloid press and the dime novel, and the world did not easily remember that not long ago. . . ."[15] Etc. One may notice here

[11] For example, see *inter alia* Robert Jalley, *Le Folklore du Languedoc* (Paris, 1971), 151; Dieudonné Dergny, *Images, coutumes et croyances ou livre des choses curieuses* (Brionne, 1885), *I, 330-42;* Charles Beauquier, *Traditions populaires: Les Mois en Franche-Comté* (Paris, 1900), 44. In Corsica, in 1914, "Le jeudi saint, à la lecture de l'évangile de la Passion, on voit des hommes entrer en fureur quand Ponce-Pilate livre Jésus aux Juifs. Ils injurient le pusillanime procurateur de Judée; ils tapent sur les bancs à casser leurs bâtons." Albert Quantin, *La Corse* (Paris, 1914), 257. In the opening scene of his novel, *The Last of the Just,* André Schwartz-Bart has described the effect of good Friday services on the Jews of rural Poland.

[12] The Feast of St. Verney, patron of the winegrowers of Beaumont (Puy-de-Dôme) was a great annual event. See Francis Gostling, *Auvergne and its People* (New York, 1911), 25-26.

[13] Anatole Leroy-Beaulieu, *Israel chez les nations* (Paris, 1893), 16.

[14] *The Origins of Totalitarianism* (New York, 1958), 108.

[15] *Ibid.*, 94.

a rather haughty disparagement of the most widely-diffused creators and expressors of popular lore, because they are cheap and vulgar; *and* the mistaken assumption that "the world" did not easily remember, when in effect it had never forgotten.

This is the sort of protective self-delusion, which can also be found in Rudolph Loewenstein's preface to his book where this very able analyst refers to his surprise in 1940 (having completely identified himself with France for many years) "suddenly to find himself morally rejected by his adopted country because he was a Jew."[16] It is difficult to understand how an intelligent man living in the France of the 1930's could find his rejection by his adopted country *sudden*.[17] But, whatever the psychological interpretations, it is hard to miss the readiness with which potential rejection becomes actual. Which makes antisemitism an excellent recruiting agent.

Hannah Arendt perceives a "grand strategy of using antisemitism as an instrument of Catholicism."[18] This is very debatable – and the more so because the idea was first mooted by the anticlericals, notably in a famous open letter of Emile Zola (January, 1898), where he argues that antisemitism was the Church's handle for rechristianizing the masses. The Catholics, said Zola, were trying to regain popular support by founding workers' clubs and organizing pilgrimages, but belief would not return. It was only when they started to appeal to antisemitism that they began to win back the masses. The People, says Zola, still do not believe, *"but is it not the beginning of belief to make them want to burn the Jews?"*[19]

This brings me very conveniently to my second argument, because the idea that, while antisemitism may be beside the point, it can be put to use – an idea which Zola attributed to the Catholics – was also explicitly shared by the Socialists. It was a Socialist who condemned antisemitism as the socialism of fools. But plenty of socialists also believed that it could be useful in winning them a hearing, in introducing the politically illiterate to integral Socialism. One of the great figures of the French Left

[16] *Christians and Jews* (New York, 1951), 11.

[17] This may have been due to "the philosemitism of the liberals" of the circle in which he moved. (Arendt, *Origins, 335)*. Lucien Rebatet exaggerates when he claims that in the four or five years before the war "Paris était antisémite a 80% de sa population capable d'une idée," but he cannot have exaggerated much and Arendt, *loc. cit.*, seems to confirm it. As Rebatet says, simplistic antisemitism was much more widespread "dans la petite bourgeoisie, dans les couches populaires que chez les intellectuels." *Cahiers de l'Herne*, Special number on Céline (Paris, 1963), 44.

[18] *Origins*, 116-17.

[19] Emile Zola, "Lettre à la France," January 6, 1898, in René Rémond, *L'Histoire de l'anticléricalisme* (Paris, 1976), 206.

(Augustin Hamon) said this quite explicitly in an interview of 1898: "With the petty bourgeois especially, anti-Judaism is the road to Socialism. . .the stage through which the petty bourgeois passes before becoming a Socialist."[20] But for the Left as for the Catholics, anti-Jewishness was far more than just a recruiting device: the utilitarian argument itself probably the rationalization of more profound sentiments.

Until a few years ago, to talk about an antisemitism of the Left seemed like a contradiction in terms. By now we know much about the equation of moneypower, banking, capitalism and usury, with Jews; and how this notion was symbolically incarnated in the Rothchilds. The fact is that, in France at least, most of the great anti-Jewish works (great in size and impact, of course, not in their contents, which are largely a farrago of nonsense!) came from the Left: Fourier, Proudhon; and, in a major key, Toussenel, Chirac; even, in some ways, Drumont. Which is understandable if you remember that, through most of the 19th century, the historic Left was *against* what we used to call progress, i.e., the development of capital and industry.

The Left probably remained the most audible source of attacks on Jews until the 1890's, with frequent antisemitic articles in officious publications like the *Revue socialiste,* where the use of terms like "parasites" and "microbes" was nothing exceptional.[21] In 1894, *Le Chambard socialiste* (March 24) still called the Jews *youpins*. The popular rebellion against the hardships of the modern world found in the Jew a convenient symbol. But I would argue that the economic component of antisemitism is not crucial in itself: – only as alimented by, and alimenting, basic cultural tensions and (again) cultural stereotypes.

For example, one cannot help being struck by the epidermic nature of prejudices that came out even in the opponents of antisemitism, like Anatole France, or Marx's son-in-law Paul Lafargue who, when he attacked Drumont, could not find anything better to call him than a "dirty Jew"![22] Jean Jaurés himself allowed himself derogatory remarks about

[20]François Bournand, *Les Juifs et nos contemporains* (Paris, 1898), 215.

[21]For more detailed treatment of all this see Edmund Silberner's numerous writings, notably, "French Socialism and the Jewish Question, 1865-1914," *Historia Judaica*, XVI, 1 (1954), 3-38 and, more recently, Zeev Sternhell, *La Droite révolutionnaire, 1885-1914* (Paris, 1978).

[22]Silberner, *op.cit.*, 21-24. Some socialists, like Réne Viviani who once remarked that "antisemitism is the best form of social struggle," had picked up their antisemitism in Algeria, which was a hothouse of anti-Jewish feeling. See *Journal Officiel, Chambre des députés, Débats* (February 21, 1895), 592-93. For the influence of Algerian antisemitism on metropolitan socialists see Charles Robert Ageron, *Les Algériens musulmans et la France* (Paris, 1968), 1, 583.

la juiverie, notably about the Jewish race "subtle, concentrated, always devoured by the fever of gain. . . ."[23] And if one reads Marx's notorious essays on the Jewish question (of which the second is the only really hostile one) one will find that their interest does not lie in their anti-Jewish statements, but in the fact that Marx, like his contemporaries, identified the Jew with "gross and unrelieved commercialism" – with "huckstering" and money-grubbing.[24]

If Marx is considered a hostile witness, let us take a more acceptable figure: Bernard Lazare, himself a sephardic Jew from Nîmes, and one of the heroes of the Dreyfus Affair, contrasts *israélites de France* and *juifs* (of whatever race) and describes the latter as "dominated by the single preoccupation of rapidly making a fortune. . . by fraud, lying and trickery." If only antisemites would become specifically *anti-Juifs,* he says, a lot of israelites could join them. As the for French israelites, they should leave the Alliance Israélite Universelle, and work to stop "the continual immigration of these predatory, rude, and dirty Tartars (East European Jews) who come to feed upon a land that is not theirs."[25] Lazare changed his mind about these things, but his first position is revealing. Nor was Lazare's view an isolated one, because as late as the winter of 1898-99, when the leading antisemitic paper in France, *La Libre Parole,* launched its notorious subscription to build a monument to Colonel Henry (the man who forged the papers incriminating Dreyfus), quite a few Jews sent contributions, including one who described himself as *"un israélite dégoûté des juifs."*[26]

Whatever one may think about Lazare's description of these "rude and dirty" aliens, it is a fairly mild reflection of a widespread reaction to people who looked, spoke, acted, very different – in consequence easy to perceive as ugly, grubby, unmannered – essentially uncivilized because essentially different. Even a friend like Leroy-Beaulieu had to admit that "It is true that the race is neither strong nor handsome. . . ."

[23] For Jaurès, see Ageron, *loc. cit.;* Stephen Wilson, *Wiener Bulletin,* 1972, No. 3/4, 34; also *Dépêche de Toulouse,* May 1, May 8, 1895.

[24] See, for example, in Robert Tucker (ed.), *The Marx-Engels Reader* (New York, 1972), 46-51.

[25] Bernard Lazare, *Entretiens politiques et littéraires* (Paris, 1890) I, 177, 179, 232 and *passim.*

[26] P. Quillard, *Le Monument Henry* (Paris, 1899), 476. For Charles Péguy, writing in 1900, three quarters of the Jewish upper bourgeoisie, half of the Jewish middle class, a third of petty bourgeois Jews are antisemitic. *Oeuvres en prose, 1898-1908,* 290. This appears confirmed when Arthur Meyer, *Ce que mes yeux ont vu* (Paris, 1910), 124, 134, expresses his admiration for Drumont and insists that nowadays "one can, one must be antisemitic." For this and more see Stephen Wilson, "Antisemitism and the Jewish Response in France during the Dreyfus Affair," *European Studies Review,* 6 (1976), 237.

And he repeats: "The race is not handsome," before he goes on to quote a young Russian woman: "They are so ugly that they deserve all their troubles."[27] Leroy-Beaulieu attributes Jewish unpopularity with "so many women" to their ugliness. But the remark, insofar as it is significant or revealing, does not necessarily apply to women alone. Karl Marx once described a boring woman he met during a visit to Germany as "the ugliest creature I ever saw in my life, a nastily Jewish physiognomy."[28]

In this context it is useful to remember that Jewish emancipation itself carried very equivocal implications; that its advocates had seen emancipation in terms of assimilation – a contractual demand for fusion in exchange for freedom. This vision had been inspired, it is true, by belief in the rights of man; but the rights of man not so much to *be* what he will, but to *become:* secularized, homogenized, "civilized," like his fellow-citizens.

To the extent that Jews refused the implications of this tacit understanding; to the extent that they hesitated or tarried; to the extent that unassimilated Jews tarred the assimilated with the brush of their difference (their "ugliness"), the promises of emancipation itself turned into a new source of resentment and criticism – and even into the source of a certain liberal antisemitism.

We are talking of an age and of societies that are culturally imperalistic, for which cultural integration and homogenization are basic principle and active practice. And here are the Jews – who, on one hand, take some time to assimilate and, on the other, are continually irrigated by fresh streams of immigrants whose presence and whose strangeness help to stress their difference-by-association.

And so another factor of irritation is the insistent persistence of cultural difference, of Jewish particularism, or apparent particularism willy-nilly, whose results, again, are well-reflected when Leroy-Beaulieu has to admit and to justify the incomplete integration and assimilation of the Jews. The change from Jew to Frenchman or Englishman, he says, "has been too sudden to be complete." They have sometimes for us "something that jars/something discordant" – "a look, a word, a gesture, suddenly bares the old Jewish base. . . . Scratch an israelite, one of my friends said to me, and you will find the ghetto Jew. That is not always true. What we take for the Jew is often only the stranger . . . . What one does feel coming through in the civilized israelite, is not so much the Jew as the parvenu. . . . Parvenus! Most of the Jews we know are certainly that. . . ." And he lists their characteris-

[27]*Israel chez les nations,* 175-76.

[28]Quoted by Hugh Lloyd-Jones, "The Books that Marx Read," *Times Literary Supplement,* February 4, 1977, 119.

tics: pretentious, conceited, vain, lacking distinction or elegance or tact, revealing bad taste, bad manners, bad breeding, their excessive ways, their tendency to be either overfamiliar or overdiffident, the trouble they have in showing the measure of men of the world. . . .[29]

The justice of such charges is quite irrelevant; the fact that they reflect the perceptions of a friend and defender is not. But this aspect of the Jew – which Leroy-Beaulieu cites as a venial drawback, only to explain it as a passing phase – brings tremendous grist to the mill of the antisemites. Hence my third point, best introduced with another quotation from Hannah Arendt: "The antisemite tends to see in the Jewish parvenu an upstart pariah."[30] The upstart pariah is at the center of many a hostile paroxysm and, given the guilt-by-association syndrome, all Jews who act as if they think themselves the equals of their fellows may be so considered.

Here is another opportunity to articulate griefs founded in feelings that remain inarticulate. Jewish emancipation creates passional problems not very different from those aroused by the legal emancipation of the Blacks, which was roughly contemporary. Here are people who (until Louis XVI abolished the practice), paid the same tolls on entering towns as those charged on cattle.[31] This group, so traditionally and so obviously inferior, is declared equal to all. What is worse, its members declare themselves to be equal and act as if they believed it. Indignation at such pretensions made North Africa (where Jews had been a particularly despised and disadvantaged community) a hothouse of antisemitism, both French and Muslim. It also contributed to European antisemitism – whether at the benign level one can find in Leroy-Beaulieu, or at the bumbling redneck level, or at increasingly explicit levels – a fund of more or less articulate indignation, also very available, also very easy to exploit.[32]

[29]*Israel chez les nations*, 253-54.

[30]*Origins*, 118. Compare with the remarks of E.F. Gautier, *Un siècle de colonisation* (Paris, 1930) on the "exemple quotidien et contagieux du mépris musulman pour le Juif!" On top of which Algerian Jews are "natives". Ageron, *Les Algériens musulmans*, 589, also speaks of their "nativeness" *(indigénat)*, which prevented the *colons* from accepting them as equals, and refers to "the atavistic contempt of the Muslims. . . which surrounded them with a sort of blemish, constantly renewed."

[31]Leroy-Beaulieu, *Israel chez les nations*, 31, makes much of this. See Joseph Lémann, *L'Entrée des israélites dans la société française* (Paris, 1886), ch. 1.

[32]Thus Alsatians (and Lorrainers), who despised Jews as much as Algerians did, settled heavily behind the Gare de l'Est, around La Villette where in the 1880's and thereafter Parisian antisemites recruited their toughest supporters. Emile Durkheim, born at Epinal in 1858, could testify that in 1870 it was the Jews who were blamed for the defeat, just as in 1848 Alsace they suffered from the Revolution. See his contribution to Henri Dagan, *Enquête sur l'antisémitisme* (Paris, 1899), 60.

Were one trying to be exhaustive, one would have to include every personal maladjustment which could find expression in some anti-Jewish rationalization. That is not my purpose. But I would add that antisemitism proved useful not just for diverting social tensions, but for arguing the case of national unity against the divisions and dissensions that could be declared artificial and attributed only to Jews or to their influence. To those who wanted to avoid or play down class issues and antagonisms, antisemitism could be useful, because it translated economic resentments and revendications from a class to a national or racial context. Other national groups beside the Jews could provide scapegoats for economic distress and social crisis, but Jews were the most widely available and traditionally-designated villains of the piece.

So, in this context, anti-Jewishness was not merely the identification of a scapegoat, but a rallying-cry in the precise sense of the term: the assertion of unity and community, in terms of an appeal to common stereotypes and, hence, at least by implication, to common interests more powerful than any divisive factor.

Here we have an out group whose inferiority and whose noxiousness have become a cultural commonplace; and whose cultural difference, constantly reaffirmed by themselves and by their critics, is a constant irritant, a constant reconfirmation and reinforcement of prejudice, and an invitation to further rejections. Any deliberate campaign – whether motivated by concrete resentments or private paranoia – could build on prejudice, could make the latent manifest or, at least, could expect to be greeted with understanding. There was nothing extraordinary in the fact that Jews should provide an object of prejudice and persecution, whether continuous or sporadic, according to circumstances and to the interests a given situation suggests. What is extraordinary is that they managed to survive so long.

There is not even anything illogical about taking such attitudes to one possible conclusion, which is the elimination or extermination of the rejected out-group. Especially when the Christian Church, which needed their presence, was losing its grip![33] The Old Testament provides precedents; and so does History.[34] The only thing about such precedents is that the means of execution available in pre-modern times (whether to

[33] While trying to hold on, meanwhile, the Catholic Church sponsored a lively revival of anti-Jewish phantasies brought up to date..See Pierre Sorlin, *La Croix et les Juifs* (Paris, 1967), and Pierre Pierrad, *Juifs et catholiques français* (Paris, 1970). Catholic publications supported Drumont and spread the wildest antisemitic accusations. Antisemitic literature was widely used in Catholic Schools.

[34] In 1898, Jules Guérin's Ligue Antisémitique advocated a "Saint-Barthélémy des juifs" and invited the French to imitate those Galicians who had burnt a Jewish family alive. Wilson, *Wiener Bulletin* (quoted note 22), 35.

Pharaoh, or to Louis XIV, or to the Young Turks) were imperfect. And the execution of almost any scheme tended to be piecemeal and incomplete at best!

On the other hand, pre-modern societies, living on the margin of subsistence, offered great incidental opportunities for the destruction of rejected individuals or groups; because any such who were placed "without the law" tended to be removed from access to food, to shelter, to the means of keeping alive. Mortality rates were already very high. They were vastly higher for the outlaws. Which meant that the mere decision to destroy, however inefficiently executed, tended to have self-fulfilling effects.

Modern society, by contrast, could be far more exhaustive and efficient. Its dominant values operated against the destruction of human groups, at least in times of peace. But when such moral prohibitions were suspended, destruction could be surpassingly thorough. It also had to *be* more thorough, because the modern policed state had mitigated the operation of natural processes of selection and destruction. No modern society could accept the kind of disorder that its predecessors took for granted, and that permitted these "natural laws" to operate. Nor would modern sensibilities accept it. Even if it had been possible, the social hygiene of the modern policed state could not tolerate great numbers of people starving in public places, dying in ditches, bleeding on somebody's threshold, corpses cluttering up the sidewalks or the highways, the impediments to shopping and traffic, the possibilities of infection and disorder, or even, simply of violence as private enterprise.

If an out-group had to be eliminated, the *ad hoc* possibilities of earlier times, occasions built-into the pre-modern economy but also into the nature of pre-modern society and state, were excluded. Social hygiene prescribed something more orderly, and something that could proceed without contaminating the regularities of policed society. Natural forces could no longer be trusted to operate "naturally": first, because they no longer did; but also because if they did they would be far more destructive of the social fabric than in the earlier, looser context of the pre-modern state.

So there is a logic to concentration camps and to extermination camps. If extermination is going to take place, it has to take place in isolated centers. This was not a consideration in more bucolic days.

One can see this clearly if one compares other great massacres of the 20th century with that of the European Jew. All but this last have taken place in backward, undeveloped societies. In India, in Bangladesh, in various parts of Africa, hundreds of thousands of people at a time have been massacred by traditional means; or simply driven out by the millions. Patchy but impressive examples of what artisanal methods can achieve when the preservation of social order is not a high priority. The best illustration of my point, however, is to be found in what happened to the Turkish Armenians in 1915.

It is a good illustration because Christians living in Turkey were also a subject, inferior race, and traditionally designated as dogs.[35] The reformed state of the Young Turks had declared Christians and Jews to be equal citizens with Muslims. But the nationalist passion for Turkification also demanded the extinction of separate communities, including the Arabs, but especially when, as in the case of certain Christian communities, these existed as distinct colonies and cultures.

The war of 1914 provided opportunities for extreme action that would have been difficult in times of peace; and the geographical situation of the Armenians on the Russian border designated them for this sort of action. Precisely what the Turkish Government, the Turkish authorities, wanted to do to the Armenians remains the subject of debate. What they did is less debatable. The men were disarmed, and then butchered. U.S. Ambassador Henry Morgenthau, tells how at Ankara all Armenian men between 15 and 70 years of age were sent off on the Cesarea Road, bound in groups of four and massacred by a mob of Turkish peasants "in a secluded valley" where "their bodies, horribly mutilated, were left" to be "devoured by wild beasts."[36] The young and the old and the women were deported, mostly on foot and mostly to various desert places. Morgenthau reports that out of one such convoy of about 18,000 souls only about 150 women and children reached Aleppo. Fridhof Nansen makes this 350, but he tells us about another convoy from Erzerum which had 11 survivors out of 19,000.[37]

The description of what happened to the convoys is very repetitive; a few extracts taken from German and American witnesses, mostly missionaries, will convey the gist. Here is one American in 1916: the deportees were driven to die by the roadside, left to bleed to death, or to commit suicide, many women and children were raped, many others were sold cheap or given away to peasants. Arnold Toynbee and others mention that hundreds of thousands died of hunger, thirst, exposure; or, if turning from the road, were shot or speared, hunted down by Kurds and

[35] Compare this with certain explanations of Algerian antisemitism. Agéron, *Les Algériens musulmans*, 589, explains that Algerian Jews, long isolated in their *mellahs*, lived in narrowly endogamic communities and were recognized as a Jewish "nation," governed by its own law.

[36] *An Anthology of Historical Writings on the Armenian Massacres of 1915* Beirut, 1971), 118.

[37] *Ibid.*, 126, 194.

Turkish peasants.[38] After the American, here is a German eye-witness writing about the deportees driven into the great limestone deserts of Asia Minor, into the wilderness and semi-tropical marshes of Mesopotamia, barefoot, part-naked, starved: new-borns buried in dungheaps, severed heads rolling about the roads (and there are photographs that can compare with concentration camp ones!), "fields strewed with swollen blackened corpses, infecting the air with their odors, lying about desecrated, naked. . . ," and about those who were driven into the Euphrates bound back to back. . . .[39]

As in the India of my day (1946-47), river-crossings were favorite places for massacres. One report says: "In a loop of the river, near Erzinghan. . .the thousands of dead bodies created such a barrage that the Euphrates changed its course for about 100 yards."[40] And everybody notes the intolerable mess along the routes: dead, dying, sick people spreading epidemics around them, bodies unburied or only halfburied with vultures and dogs tearing at them, occasional corpses thrown in wells, and so on. I am not trying to insist on the horrors, but on what would seem to us the disturbance involved, and to show how much can be done just by encouraging private enterprise when the circumstances are right. But one has to notice, too, that these haphazard methods missed a lot of people. Thus, Toynbee estimates that there were about 1.8 million Armenians in Turkey when the war broke out and that about equal numbers "seem to have escaped, to have perished, and to have survived deportation in 1915."[41] That is scarcely thorough. And even this limited success depends on high tolerance for disorder, and the availability of large waste spaces.

It is hard to tell how much of this was deliberate and how much just to be expected in the semi-primitive Turkish context aggravated by the wartime breakdown of almost everything. But one can see that it could be quite destructive in its way.[42] One can also see that it could never have been tolerated in a Western country – especially in that model of the policed state which was Germany!

[38] Herbert Adams Gibbons, *The Blackest Page in Modern History* (New York, 1916), 15-17; Arnold Toynbee, *Armenian Atrocities* (New York, 1917), 22.

[39] *The Turkish Armenocide: An Open Letter to President Wilson*, by Armin T. Wegener (reprinted *AHRA*, 1965), 76.

[40] *Anthology*, *op. cit.*, 123.

[41] *Ibid.*, 70. For many details, see the British White Book, *The Treatment of Armenians in the Ottoman Empire, 1915-16*, edited by Viscount Bryce (London, 1916); and, further, Henry Morgenthau, *Secrets of the Bosphorus* (London, 1918), chs. 23-27.

[42] Note that the Turkish persecution of Armenians sacrificed even military interests and the efficient pursuit of war to the superior aim of their destruction: blocked roads, spreading typhus, loss of rare skilled personnel – doctors, government and railroad officials, bank

I conclude that if you determine to eliminate an out-group today, the logic of that determination suggests that this be done in isolation; and the technological and administrative means at your disposal are bound to make the process itself very efficient. Platitudes perhaps, but platitudes to which a lot of Armenians probably owe their lives.

One last consideration arises: before the Jews could be isolated and exterminated, they had to be divested of the human qualities with which emancipation and liberalism had endowed them like other members of modern societies. There were certain things one could do to people in the old world, and that people did to each other all the time before didactic civilization put its mark on us, that one could no longer do after the 19th century had humanized and sensitized our sensibilities. There were certain things Turks could do to Armenians that Europeans could not *normally* regard except as crimes. So there were things one could not do to Jews, and murder was certainly one of these. The rights of man, however diffuse the concept, were also the rights of Jews, as long as Jews were recognized as men and women. This is where the logic of the situation demanded that the Jew be dehumanized. And the didactic and exemplary process of isolation and dehumanization was able to draw on the whole treasury of prejudice and resentment that has been chronicled.

But then, if the Jew was less than human – and harmfully so, of course: a microbe or a parasite – it was not enough to expel him from society, from this country or that. One had to rid the world of him. The logical conclusion of his dehumanization was his extermination. The rest is history. And, to the extent that it has become a part of history, it suggests that the humanization and sensibilization of man may have been a transitory phase: the generalization of particular and limited experiences treated as irreversible by people who took the exception for the norm.

The question remains, and it continues to obsess or fascinate our time: how could an apparently civilized society, an ordered modern society, produce and condone the mass murders that we describe as genocide? I believe that this is a false question. If an earthquake leveled a city and killed most of its inhabitants, we would say: "How could this happen?" Scientists could answer our question in terms of general laws and particular conditions, but that would not satisfy us; because our

clerks, drivers, artisans, even army effectives, were sacrificed to a higher passion. The German Ambassador commented: "It looks as if the Turkish government wants to lose the war!" Johannes Lepsius, "The Armenian Question," *Muslim World* (London), X, 1920, 350. Morgenthau, *Secrets of the Bosphorus*, 223, quotes Talaat Pasha: "We care nothing about the commercial loss."

words are really an expression of shock and horror at the very notion of such destruction – and of destruction on such a scale!

The fact is that the question of Jewish genocide can also be answered in matter-of-fact terms, too banal to satisfy. Tragedies on this scale seem to defy the trivialization that explanations inflict upon them; and almost reject the attempt to explain as a sort of insult. That may be right, because explanation is sometimes advanced as an exorcism (and that is an evasion!), or as an excuse (and that is inexcusable!). But explanation is also advanced at times as if it could help to prevent similar tragedies in the future. And it may be a last question one might wish to consider – whether that is not a form of naïveté.

———o———

Quand on se renseigne sur les origines de l'Holocauste, on se demande, en fait, comment une infection à l'état latent, qui dura des siècles dans la société chrétienne européenne, a pu devenir un fléau meurtrier au moment où cette société était devenue moins chrétienne et plus méthodique. La réponse se trouve en partie dans la tradition culturelle. Les sociétés produisent des stéréotypes et ensuite elles les intériorisent. Les thèmes interprétatifs de base sont bien connus: la particularité et le particularisme juifs; l'association de ces derniers avec la mort du Christ, avec l'usure, et avec les forces mystérieuses menaçantes; l'ubiquité du juif en tant qu'*autre*, en tant d' endroits et à tant de niveaux: social, économique et culturel; et le ressentiment contre les prétentions et les attitudes des juifs nouveaux riches. On peut trouver ces thèmes dans la pensée européenne depuis toujours.

A différentes époques l'antisémitisme était utile à ceux qui essayaient de forger une unité entre groupes d'une communauté divisée. Il peut paraître surprenant que l'antisémitisme maintint ses pouvoirs, même quand la chrétienté diminua. L'identification traditionnelle des juifs comme étant un "groupe à part" continua après leur émancipation des vieilles contraintes et leur don des qualités humaines par libéralisme. En effet, l'antisémitisme atteint une méchanceté nouvelle à cause de besoin, après l'émancipation, de priver les juifs de l'égalité et de l'humanité dont le libéralisme les avait dotés.

La plupart des sociétés ont eu des souffre-douleur, des individus et des groupes tenus "a l'écart des lois" de la communauté et privés de nourriture d'abris et de toutes les ressources qui semblaient essentielles à cette communauté. Souvent, le traitement de ces groupes "non admis" a été extrémement brutal et a amené un grand nombre de morts. Cependant, dans les sociétés traditionnelles qui arrivaient à peine à vivre, la destruction des individus et des groupes rejetés a été plus ou moins fortuite. Les sociétés traditionnelles sont trop désordonnées pour permettre une répression prolongée et sévère.

Par comparaison, les sociétés modernes sont beaucoup plus efficaces. Quand elles reconnaissent un ennemi, elles font tout pour l'éliminer. Aucune société moderne n'accepterait le genre de confusion qui, au préalable, était considéré comme tout naturel. L'hygiène sociale des états modernes gouvernés par la police ne tolérerait pas un grand nombre de gens assassinés ou mourant de faim publiquement. C'est ce qui explique la création des camps de concentration et d'extermination, la particulière cruauté des temps modernes et l'Holocauste.

On the Study of the Holocaust and Genocide

URIEL TAL

A. *The Term "Genocide"*

It was in 1943, at the height of the war, that Raphael Lemkin coined the term "genocide" to describe the mass extermination of Jews in Europe under the Nazi regime.[1] In his biographical essay "My Battle with Half the World," Lemkin, former Adviser on Foreign Affairs to the U.S. War Department, said that it was the study of the persecutions of the Jews in ancient, medieval, modern and contemporary times that made him aware of the universal scope and significance of acts of extermination perpetrated against:

> ... National, racial and religious minorities... I began to understand that it was not a matter of the Jews, of Arabs, or Catholics, Protestants and Buddhists separately, but of all peoples, religions, and nationalities... the pogroms under the Tzar, and the destruction of... Armenians in 1915, and... the destruction of... six million Jews by Hitler...[2]

1 Raphael Lemkin, *Axis Rule in Occupied Europe,* Carnegie Endowment for International Peace, Washington, D.C., 1944, pp. 79–95.

2 *Idem,* "My Battle with Half the World," *Chicago Jewish Forum,* No. 2, Winter 1952, p. 98 ff.; *idem,* "Genocide: A New International Crime," *Revue Internationale de Droit Penal,* No. 10, 1946, p. 361 ff.

And further:

> ...There are basic phases of life in a human group; physical existence, biological continuity (through procreation) and spiritual or cultural expression. Accordingly, the attacks on these three basic phases of the life of a human group can be qualified as physical, biological or cultural genocide. It is considered a criminal act to cause death to members of the above-mentioned group directly, or indirectly, to sterilize through compulsion, to steal children, or to break up families... by destroying spiritual leadership and institutions, forces of spiritual cohesion within a group are removed and the group starts to disintegrate... Religion can be destroyed within a group even if its members continue to exist physically.[3]

Ever since, the term "genocide" has been applied to destructive policies and mass atrocities committed against a growing number of peoples, against the Gypsies under the Third Reich;[4] against the Baltic peoples during and after World War II;[5] against the

[3] Raphael Lemkin, "Genocide as a Crime under International Law," *UN Bulletin*, Vol. IV, No. 2, January 15, 1948, p. 71, quoted in *Law Reports of Trials of War Criminals*, Selected and Prepared by the UN War Crimes Commission, Vol. XIII, H.M. Stationery Office, London, 1949, p. 40.

[4] Donald Kenrick and Grattan Puxon, *The Destiny of Europe's Gypsies*, The Columbus Center Series, Basic Books Inc., New York, 1972, (esp. Part Two, pp. 59–184); Grattan Puxon, *Rom: Europe's Gypsies*, Minority Rights Group, Report No. 14, London, 1973; Hans-Joachim Döring, *Die Zigeuner im NS-Staat*, Kriminologische Schriftenreihe, Vol. XII, Hamburg, 1964; *idem*, "Die Motive der Zigeuner-Deportation vom Mai 1940," *Vierteljahreshefte für Zeitgeschichte*, No. 4, Stuttgart, 1959, pp. 418–428; Selma Steinmetz, *Österreichs Zigeuner im NS-Staat*, Monographien zur Zeitgeschichte, Europa-Verlag, Wien, Frankfurt a/M, Zürich 1966. Also see one of the earliest reports "Hitler and the Gypsies—the Fate of Europe's Oldest Aryans," by Dora E. Yates, Secretary of the Gypsy Lore Society in London, *Commentary*, November 1949, pp. 455–459; Joseph B. Schechtman, "The Gypsy Problem," *Midstream*, November 1966, pp. 52–60; Derek A. Tiler, "From Nomads to Nation," *ibid.*, August 1968, pp. 61–70.

[5] Aleksander Kaelas, *Human Rights and Genocide in the Baltic States*,

Ibo people during the Nigerian Civil War of the 1960's; against the Bengals in Bangladesh's struggle in 1971; against the aborigines in Australia;[6] in the struggle between ethnic groups in Burundi in 1972;[7] against the Indians in Paraguay;[8] against Indians in Brazil;[9] against traditional society and religion in Tibet;;[10] against the Kurds in Iraq[11] etc. etc. In several studies

Estonian Information Center, Stockholm, 1950; *The Violations of Human Rights in Soviet Occupied Lithuania*, Lithuanian American Community, Inc., A Report for 1971, 1972, 1973, Delran, New Jersey; K. Pelėkis, *Genocide—Lithuania's Threefold Tragedy*, edited by J. Rumsaitis, Venta, Germany, 1949; *Appeal to the U.N. on Genocide*, Lithuanian Foreign Service, 1951, p. 80.

6 C.D. Rowley, *The Destruction of Aboriginal Society: Aboriginal Policy and Practice*, Vol. I, Aborigines in Australian Society No. 4, a series sponsored by the Social Sciences Research Council of Australia, Australian University Press, Canberra, 1970.

7 René Lemarchend and David Martin, *Selective Genocide in Burundi*, Minority Rights Group, Report No. 20, London, 1974; *idem*, "Ethnic Genocide," *Society*, Vol. XII, January/February 1975, pp. 50–60; Roger Morris, "The US and Burundi—Genocide etc.," *The Progressive*, April 1974; Roger Morris *et al.*, "The U.S. and Burundi in 1972," *Foreign Service Journal*, Vol. 50, No. 11, November 1973, p. 8 ff.; *ibid.*, p. 31, Thomas R. Hughes of the Carnegie Endowment for International Peace and also "State Department Reply," p. 15, 29 ff. Also see the shortened version of a study on US policy and the Burundi situation, sponsored by the Carnegie Endowment for Peace under the directorship of Roger Morris, in *Africa Report*, July–August 1973, pp. 32–39.

8 Mark Münzel, *The Aché Indians: Genocide in Paraguay IWGIA*, Document Series No. 11, Copenhagen, 1973; Richard Arens, *Genocide in Paraguay*, Temple University Press, Philadelphia, 1976; *idem*, "A Violation of Human Rights in Paraguay," *Congressional Record—Senate*, March 24, 1976, S 4114.

9 Norman Lewis, "Brazil's Dead Indians: The Killing of an Unwanted Race," *Atlas*, Colorado, January 1970, pp. 28–29; "The Killing of a Colombian Indian Tribe," *ibid.*, January 1971, pp. 47–48.

10 Gilbert Rodney, *Genocide in Tibet—A Study in Communist Aggression*, American Asian Educational Exchange, Inc., New York, 1959; Richard L. Walker, "The Human Cost of Communism in

or essays additional terms have been coined such as "Armenocide"—the term "genocide" is of course used more frequently[12]—or "aristocide," extermination of intellectual and political leadership under both Nazi and Soviet Russian regimes.[13]

Works touching on genocide differ in their aims, methods and forms, and range from collections of primary sources, historical and sociopolitical analyses, minutes of scientific conferences, studies in collective psychopathology,[14] and minutes of sessions

China," *Senate Internal Security Subcommittee,* 92nd Congress, 1st Session, 1971, p. 13 ff.

11 Roger N. Baldwin, Honorary President of the International League for Human Rights, *Statement to the Members of the United Nations Committee on the Elimination of Racial Discrimination,* New York, January 14, 1977; *On the Kurdish Question at the United Nations,* published by the Information Department of the Kurdistan Democratic Party, No. 2, New York, 1974 and Exhibit G (also exhibits E, F, H, K).

12 *The Memoirs of Naim Bey*—Turkish Official Documents Relating to the Deportations and Massacres of Armenians, compiled by Aram Andonian with an introduction by Viscount Gladstone, Armenian Historical Research Association, reproduced 1964, (1st ed. England, 1920). See "Two Memoranda on Subject of 60th Anniversary of the Turkish Massacre of the Armenians," *Armenian Review,* Vol. XXVIII, No. 1, Boston, 1975, p. 75 ff. Vakan N. Dadrian in his seminal research on genocide established structures of functional analysis for the comparative study of historical cases, such as the mass annihilation of Armenians and Jews, cf. "Some Determinants of Genocidal Violence in the Intergroup Conflicts—With Particular Reference to the Armenian and Jewish Cases," *Sociologus,* Vol. XXVI, No. 2, New Series 1976, Berlin, pp. 129–149; *idem,* "The Common Features of the Armenian and Jewish Cases of Genocide—A Comparative Victimological Perspective," *Victimology—A New Focus,* Israel Drapkin and Emilio Viano, eds., Vol. IV, Lexington Books, Lexington, Toronto, London, 1975, pp. 99–119.

13 Nathanel Weyl, "Aristocide under Fuehrers and Commissars," *Modern Age,* Vol. 19, No. 3, Summer 1975, pp. 285–294.

14 Anthony Storr, *Human Destructiveness,* The Columbus Center Series, Basic Books, Inc., New York, 1972.

HOLOCAUST AND GENOCIDE

of congressional committees,[15] to surveys, travellers' reports, journalistic reports and writings with political and polemic intent both explicit and/or implicit. Many of the writings on genocide refer, in different ways and for different purposes, to several of the major documents on human rights adopted by the United Nations, primarily to the following two: (1) *The Universal Declaration of Human Rights* to the General Assembly of the U.N. in Paris on December 10, 1948, whose preamble states: "... recognition of the inherent dignity and of the equal and inalienable rights of all members of the human family is the foundation of freedom, justice and peace in the world" and "... disregard and contempt for human rights have resulted in barbarous acts which have outraged the conscience of mankind ..." and (2) *The United Nations Genocide Convention*, adopted by the General Assembly on December 9, 1948. The Genocide Convention was a result of World War II, and in particular an answer to the International Military Tribunal at Nuremberg which considered the mass murder of the Jews of Europe as being beyond its jurisdiction.[16]

15 "Armenian Massacre—1915–1918 and Holocaust that Struck European Jews 1930s–1940s," pp. 4–137, U.S. Congress House, Committee on International Relations, *Hearings Before Subcommittee on Future Foreign Policy Research and Development*, H.R. 94th Cong., 2nd Sess., May 11, August 30, 1976; U.S. Congress, Senate, "The Ad Hoc Committee on the Human Rights and Genocide Treaties," *Congressional Record*, Vol. 116, June 10, 1970, p. 58720; "The Genocide Convention," *Congressional Record*, Vol. 119, No. 49, March 29, 1973; Subcommittee on the Genocide Convention, Foreign Relations Committee, April 27, 1970, S 6260; Subcommittee on the Genocide Convention, *Statement of Hon. Arthur J. Goldberg on Behalf of Ad Hoc Committee on Human Rights and Genocide Treaties*, Senate Foreign Relations Committee, March 10, 1971 and May 29, 1977.

16 American Bar Association—Section of Individual Rights and Responsibilities, Recommendation, adopted August 13, 1966, MS p. 3 ff.; Jacob Robinson, "The IMT and the Holocaust," *Israel Law Review*, Vol. VII, No. 1, Jerusalem, 1962, pp. 1–13; Yoram Dinstein, "Inter-

URIEL TAL

Following the General Assembly Resolution of December 11, 1946, that declared genocide an international crime, the "Convention on the Prevention and Punishment of the Crime of Genocide" states that genocide means any of the following acts committed with intent to destroy, in whole or in part, a national, ethnic, racial or religious group, such as: (a) killing members of the group; (b) causing serious bodily or mental harm to members of the group; (c) deliberately inflicting on the group conditions of life calculated to bring about its physical destruction in whole or part; (d) imposing measures intended to prevent births within the group; and (e) forcibly transferring children of the group to another group.

Acts of violence listed in paragraphs a) to e) of article III of the U.N. Convention of December 1948 and defined there as crime are mainly physical in nature, such as killing people as members of a human group, creating conditions leading to the extermination of people as members of a human group, in whole or in part. In addition, these paragraphs include acts of violence of the character of biological genocide, such as creating conditions designed to prevent reproduction, that is, the biological survival of a specific human group.

As already noted by Pieter N. Drost,[17] the acts of violence included in the definition of genocide do not exhaust the list of crimes by means of which the annihilation of a human group can be accomplished. Such annihilation can also be achieved through mass deportations, arrests, imprisonments, incarcerations and hard labor, or through organized terror, torture, and other

national Criminal Law," *Israel Yearbook on Human Rights,* Vol. V, Tel Aviv, 1975, p. 59 ff.

17 UN Economic and Social Council, Commission on Human Rights, Sub-Commission on Prevention of Discrimination and Protection of Minorities, Twenty-Sixth Session, *Study of the Question of the Prevention and Punishment of the Crime of Genocide,* Progress Report by Mr. Nicodème Ruhashyankiko, Special Rapporteur, June 25, 1973 (hereafter—*Study 1973*), p. 25.

forms of inhuman treatment. This conception of the notion of genocide is similar to the position adopted as early as 1947 by the U.S. Military Tribunal at Nuremberg in its trials of *Ministerialdirektor* Josef Altstötter and other judges, law officers and officials of the Ministry of Justice in the Nazi government. The Tribunal defined the crimes of the accused as genocide and thus a crime against humanity, according to what was stipulated in Allied Control Council Law No. 10, enacted by the four occupying powers and applied by the Nuremberg military tribunals and some German courts during the occupation. Accordingly genocide is defined as acts and also intentions or plans "... involving the commission of atrocities and offenses, including but not limited to murder, extermination, deportation, illegal imprisonment, torture, persecution on political, racial and religious grounds..."[18]

Additional complementary definitions of the concept of genocide are contained in studies, surveys, official reports and substantial petitions submitted to international institutions. These sources, among them testimony on communist oppression, include within the notion of genocide also acts like the forced deportation of scholars, of priests or of children and minors; the breaking up of families and prohibition of marriages between certain categories of citizens; shootings, torture, slavery, starvation, inhuman working conditions and standards of living; enforced collectivization of farms and lack of freedom of residence or choice of employment; extermination of culture, traditions or religion.

[18] UN Economic and Social Council, Commission on Human Rights, Sub-Commission on Prevention of Discrimination and Protection of Minorities, Twenty-Eighth Session, *Study of the Question of the Prevention and Punishment of the Crime of Genocide,* Progress Report by Mr. Nicodème Ruhashyankiko, Special Rapporteur, June 25, 1975 (hereafter—*Study 1975*), p. 3. On the definition of genocide in the context of crimes against humanity cf. *Law Reports of Trials of War Criminals,* selected and prepared by the UN War Crimes Commission, Vol. VI, H.M. Stationery Office, London, 1948, pp. 1–110 (*ibid.,* footnotes 3, 4, 5).

URIEL TAL

Definitions of this kind expand the notion of genocide beyond the five paragraphs of the Genocide Convention, and indeed numerous investigations and discussions in international bodies have dealt with the question of extending the connotation of genocide, to include among others the following aspects: the persecution of children, cultural genocide, and the definition of various groups, such as ethnic, racial or political groups to which the term genocide may be applied. With regard to the persecution of children, the draft convention prepared by the U.N. Secretary-General still includes the paragraph covering "forcibly transferring children of the group to another group" in the idea of actual genocide, the rationale being, among other things, that "... the separation of children from their parents results in forcing upon the former at an impressionable and receptive age a culture and mentality different from their parents. This process tends to bring about the disappearance of the group as a cultural unit..."[19]

After consideration, however, this paragraph on the forced transfer of children from one group to another was incorporated into article II as subparagraph e. The explanation was that the forced transfer of children from one group to another has serious physical and biological consequences and thus imperils the survival of a human group; it is thus in itself genocide, and not necessarily, or not exclusively, cultural genocide, the transfer of children from their original group to an alien one being construed as an act resembling compulsory measures to prevent reproduction, or in other words, to prevent the biological survival of a human group.

The term cultural genocide too is an extension of the original idea of genocide, and was not included in the 1948 Convention. However, in the draft convention prepared by the Secretary-General the types of acts constituting cultural genocide were enumerated as follows: a) forced transfer of children to another

[19] *Study 1973*, p. 24.

human group; b) forced and systematic exile of individuals representing the culture of a group; c) prohibition of the use of the national language even in private intercourse; d) systematic destruction of books printed in the national language or religious works or prohibition of new publications; e) systematic destruction of historical or religious monuments or their diversion to alien uses; f) destruction or dispersion of documents and objects of historical, artistic, or religious value and objects used in religious worship.[20]

Article III of the draft of the Ad Hoc Committee on Genocide which prepared the 1948 Convention, included the statement that "... genocide means any deliberate act committed with intent to destroy the language, religion or culture of a national, racial or religious group on grounds of national or racial origin or religious belief..."[21] Those on the Ad Hoc Committee who supported the inclusion of "cultural genocide" in the Convention, emphasized that there were two ways of suppressing a human group, the first by causing its members to disappear, and the second by abolishing their specific traits, without making any attempts on the lives of the members of the group. Those who opposed the inclusion of "cultural genocide" emphasized that there was a considerable difference between physical and cultural genocide, and that it was specifically physical genocide which presented those exceptionally horrifying characteristics which had shaken the conscience of mankind. They also pointed to the difficulty of fixing the limits of cultural genocide, which impinged upon the violation of human rights and the rights of minorities.[22]

The Convention did not include article III of the draft of the Ad Hoc Committee dealing with "cultural genocide." The main arguments given for the exclusion were that "cultural genocide"

20 *Ibid.*; Nehemia Robinson, *The Genocide Convention—A Commentary,* Institute of Jewish Affairs, World Jewish Congress, New York, 1960 (hereafter—*N. Robinson*), p. 64.

21 *Study 1975,* p. 71.

22 *Ibid.*

was too indefinite a concept; that the difference between mass murder and the destruction of cultural facilities or even creative works, was too great; that cultural genocide legitimately falls within the sphere of the protection of minorities. Also, it was claimed, a state may have legitimate reasons to follow a policy of assimilation by lawful means in order to create a certain degree of national and cultural homogeneity. But in practice it would be difficult to outline the precise limit between these acts of state sovereignty and cultural genocide.[23] The omission of the article on cultural genocide has been considered by numerous commentators and scholars to be a contradiction to the spirit of the General Assembly's Resolution of December 1946 which explicitly spoke of cultural values lost as a result of acts of genocide.

The difference of opinion regarding the nature of cultural genocide still exists. Throughout the 1970's, various government and international and scientific institutions have declared themselves in favor of the inclusion of cultural genocide in the 1948 Convention, among them the governments of countries such as Austria, Ecuador, Israel, Oman, Rumania and Finland.[24] The

23 *Ibid.*, p. 73; Irving L. Horowitz, *Genocide—State Power and Mass Murder,* Transaction Books, New Jersey, 1976. "Issues in Contemporary Civilization," p. 37, suggests to make a "crucial distinction" between genocide and various forms of coercion, i.e. "between the physical and cultural liquidation of peoples in contrast to mind-bending the will of peoples." A similar qualitative difference between forms of persecution and actual physical mass extermination has been made recently by Yisrael Gutman, "Martyrdom and Sacredness of Life," in *Yalkut Moreshet,* No. 24, October 1977, p. 11 (Hebrew).

24 *Ibid.*, pp. 74–75. As to the ratification of the Convention by the US see American Bar Association, *Report by the Section of Individual Rights and Responsibilities,* adopted by the Council of the Section on October 17, 1969; Also cf. American Bar Association, *Report and Recommendations* of the Standing Committee on World Order Through Law on the Genocide Convention, January 1970; also see the "Remarks of Senator Proxmire Before the Special Foreign Relations Subcommittee on the Genocide Convention," in *Congressional*

Vatican's declaration of September 18, 1972 is of special interest: "Information and Views to the Commission of Human Rights" stated as follows:

> ...Genocide is also a crime against the rights and dignity of a people. Each people has its own heritage...It is a people's cultural heritage that is the expression of that people...with its traditional language, customs, beliefs, art, laws, social patterns, and ways of looking at reality...All the individuals and social groups that make up a given people should be able to attain full cultural development in accord with their tradition. They should not be held back, nor have other cultures imposed on them...In view of the above-stated principles, serious consideration should be given to the matter of those acts which might be called 'cultural genocide' or 'ecocide.'[25]

The inclusion of the terms "ethnic" or "racial" in the notion of genocide is part of the overall question of the nature of the human group to which the notion of genocide may be applied. According to the Genocide Convention, the term is applicable to a number of people constituting a group, and not to individuals. The draft of the Ad Hoc Committee noted explicitly that the act of extermination is termed genocide if it is designed or carried out "...on the grounds of the national or racial origin, religious beliefs or political opinion of its (the group's) members..."[26] At the same time, and this is also the opinion held by investigators of crimes of violence such as Herbert Jäger,[27]

Record, Senate, April 27, 1970, S 6260/1; and "The Ad Hoc Committee on the Human Rights and Genocide Treaties," in *Congressional Record,* Senate, June 10, 1970, S 8720.

25 *Study 1975,* p. 74. On aspects of the historical-theological context of the changing attitudes of the Church cf. Uriel Tal, *Patterns in the Contemporary Jewish-Christian Dialogue,* The Institute of Contemporary Jewry, The Hebrew University, Jerusalem, 1969, pp. 12–19 (Hebrew); *idem,* "Historical Roots and Cognitive Forms," *Concilium —Theology in the Age of Renewal,* New Series, Vols. 7/8, No. 10, London, September/October 1974, p. 175 ff.

26 N. Robinson, *op. cit.,* p. 60.

27 Herbert Jäger, *Verbrechen unter totalitärer Herrschaft—Studien zur*

killing entire groups or part of them carried out in the course of war does not necessarily constitute genocide. According to the Genocide Convention an act of annihilation is termed genocide even if it is not directed at or carried out on an entire group; the concept of genocide can apply also to the intention of exterminating parts of a group, because of their belonging to it. This was clearly worded in the report of 1973 by the *Special Rapporteur*: "... a group of individuals identifiable by racial or national features because they constituted distinct, clearly determinable communities..."[28] The term "political groups" was deleted from the Genocide Convention although in the bodies that prepared it, among them the Sixth Committee in its deliberations of August 15, 1948, there was a desire to retain "political groups" within the overall definition of genocide.[29] The reasons against the inclusion of the notion of "political groups" were primarily political, deriving from the fear that its inclusion would afford an opening for international bodies to intervene in what was termed the internal political life of individual countries. Another justification for the non-inclusion of "political groups" in the concept of genocide was that political groups are not permanent communities and are not therefore homogeneous in character, and in any case are not clearly defineable. Countering these arguments it was noted that the extermination of a political group should properly be included in the concept of genocide because these groups resemble religious groups in that they focus around a particular value system.[30] In the same spirit, the International

nationalsozialistischen Gewaltkriminalität, Walter Verlag, Olten & Freiburg i.Br., 1976, (hereafter—Jäger), Part IV "Krieg und Genozid," p. 331 ff.

28 *Official Records of the General Assembly of the UN, 3rd Session, Part I,* Sixth Committee, meetings 4, 66, 74, also quoted in *Study 1973,* p. 16.

29 N. Robinson, *op. cit.,* p. 59.

30 *Study 1973,* p. 22.

Commission of Jurists declared a few years ago that "...the definition of genocide should be extended to include acts done with the intent to destroy in whole or in part a political group as such, as well as national, ethnic, racial or religious groups. The massacre of unarmed political opponents is just as criminal as the massacre of these other groups, and should be recognized as such..."[31]

Bowing to objections to the inclusion of "political groups" in the list of groups meriting protection against genocide, the Sixth Committee added the category of "ethnical."[32] However that term, like the term "racial," turned out to be very complex and to have many and varied meanings. Research on the manifestations of "ethnocide," especially as it has developed in recent years,[33] considers ethnicity one of the basic, primary factors in every civilization, in ancient as well as modern times. It is due to ethnicity that national or social groups maintain their cultural uniqueness.[34] In this view, the term "ethnical" is close to the term "racial," and in fact as early as 1950, in discussions in U.N. bodies on the definition of "minorities," members felt that the word "ethnic" relates to all the biological, cultural and historical characteristics of a group, while the word "racial" relates only to hereditary and physical characteristics. In that connection, it was argued that in the 1948 Genocide Convention the term

31 *Ibid.*

32 N. Robinson, *op. cit.*, p. 59; Pierre L. van den Berghe, *Race and Ethnicity*—Essays in Comparative Sociology, Basic Books, New York, 1970.

33 Robert Jaulin, *La decivilization—politique et pratique de l'ethnocide*, Edition Complexe, Bruxelles, 1974.

34 The fundamental study by Salo W. Baron, *Modern Nationalism and Religion*, Meridian, New York and JPS, Philadelphia, 1960, chapters I, IV, V, VII. Contemporary theology has become aware of the renewed significance of the ethnic-cultural factor, cf. "De Ecclesia in Mundo Huius Temporis," in *The Documents of Vatican II*, Walter Abbott, M.S.J. ed., Guild Press, New York, 1966, p. 199 ff.

URIEL TAL

"ethnic" was used to qualify the cultural, physical and historical characteristics of a group.[35]

Some anthropologists and social scientists tend to draw a distinction between the terms "race" and "ethnic" by pointing out that "race" indicates "a group of persons with certain physical characteristics which are hereditary and transmissible," while "... ethnic groups are descent groups differentiated by language, culture, style, national origin, kinship ties and religious belief..."[36] The 1950 statement of UNESCO adds a significant aspect by emphasizing that those hereditary factors "... fluctuate and often disappear in the course of time ... the cultural traits of such groups have not demonstrated genetic connection with racial traits. Because serious errors of this kind are habitually committed when the term 'race' is used in popular parlance, it would be better when speaking of human races to drop the term 'race' altogether and speak of ethnic groups..."[37]

The formal, seemingly technical definitions of the terms "ethnic" and "racial" and their applicability to the notion of genocide may prepare the ground for a keener moral perception. However, this sharper perception has not yet put an end to policies of discrimination and genocide and has remained confined to the declarations of intellectuals and international institutions. Examples are the series of resolutions by ecumenical organizations even before World War II, but mainly after, in reaction to present-day racial discrimination and genocidal policies, or the 1953 conclusion of UNESCO on the race concept, etc.[38] The theories all stress that the use of terms referring to biological heredity for defining the nature of human groups is wrong from the point of view both of the facts and of social morality. Physical

35 *Study 1973*, pp. 19–20.

36 *Ibid.*

37 *Ibid.*

38 Klaus Martin Beckmann, ed., *Die Kirche und die Rassenfrage*, Kreuz-Verlag, Stuttgart, Berlin, 1967, p. 11 ff.; Part II "Dokumente," p. 76 ff.

and medical conditions, education, and the cultural life style—and not biological determination—are the elements that should be protected by treaties against genocide. Living conditions in which man can develop his physical, intellectual and moral potential; in which man can be responsible for himself, his desires, his acts and their consequences; living conditions in which man can maintain autonomy, that is moral freedom, while remaining true to himself and his historic, ethnic or religious heritage—those are the elements requiring protection against genocidal policies.

The conclusions in the area of social morality, though not yet translated into the language of political action, indicate an additional dimension for the definition of genocide—the dimension of time. Ever since the term genocide was coined, acts of persecution, expulsion, religious pressure or group extermination perpetrated even before the twentieth century are now classified as genocide. The preamble of the 1948 U.N. Convention has stated among other things "...at all periods of history genocide has inflicted great losses on humanity... while the concept of genocide is a recent one, the acts which it covers are as old as the history of mankind itself... where national, ethnic, racial or religious groups were destroyed."[39]

The term genocide or religious genocide is used when dealing with historical phenomena such as the persecution of Christians by Roman emperors, atrocities against Jews who refused baptism by the Crusaders in 1096 and afterwards, the destruction of religious sects such as the Albigenses in 1209–1220 or the burning of heretics in the Middle Ages. In recent years the term genocide has been used also in studies on the history of Indians and Indian civilization in North and South America and the Caribbean Islands. The fate that befell the Arawak Indians according to primary source materials such as the letters and journals of Columbus or the historiography of the massacres of the West

[39] *Study 1973*, p. 4.

URIEL TAL

Indies by Father Bartolome de Las Casas have been termed genocide.[40]

One may on the other hand argue that genocide is a phenomenon typical of modern motivations and techniques, especially those of the twentieth century; hence it differs from the destructive treatment of captives or conquered peoples, massacres or mass murders of previous times, such as the often cited example of Genghis Khan, even though they too have resulted in the extermination or disappearance of entire groups. Genocide in the modern era is being perpetrated after, and in spite of the emergence of critical rational thought, Enlightenment, the French Revolution, the utopias of freedom, equality and peace, despite, or because of, modern technology and amidst a civilization rooted in the ideas of human ethical autonomy, of man's inalienable right to self-government, self-knowledge, freedom of oppression, freedom from want and freedom from existential alienation. This becomes even more accentuated in recent trends in the study of modernization. Accordingly, the spread of European civilization connected with colonialism, missions, and with the uprooting process of industrialization also caused cultural and ecological changes that, intentionally or not, helped to liquidate traditional forms of society, religion and culture.[41]

Recent trends, not only in historiography, lean towards these versions of indirect genocide. Contemporary religious thought is wrestling with the interrelationship of historical phenomena of genocidal implications, historical traditions of

40 The interesting, though impressionistic essay "Christliches Vorspiel," in *Das Jahrhundert der Barbarei,* Karlheinz Deschner, ed., Verlag Kurt Desch, *München,* 1966, pp. 7–42.

41 Wilbur R. Jacobs, "The Tip of an Iceberg: Pre-Columbian Indian Demography and Some Implications for Revisionism," *William and Mary Quarterly,* Series 3, Vol. 31, No. 1, Williamsburg, Virginia, January 1974, p. 123 ff.; Martin Calvin, "The European Impact on a North-eastern Algonquin Tribe: An Ecological Interpretation," *ibid.,* pp. 3–26.

missionaries and colonialism, and the current awakening of the Third World.

Now, after the Second Vatican Council, even the language used in theological thought as well as in actual Church affairs is undergoing changes. Concepts that were essential to missionaries regarding the "falseness" of "pagan culture," "darkness," "depravity," "blindness" of the indigene whose religion, culture and life-style had to be converted and westernized, are often changed. Circles in the Church feel to an increasing extent that one of the results of the Church's mission work in the past has been to aid in the obliteration of "primitive" cultures, an effect that nowadays is critically called "cultural" or "ethnic" genocide.[42] Theologians such as Jules Isaac and James Parkes pointed out the dialectic interrelationship of traditional Christian anti-Judaism and modern anti-Semitism that was also anti-Christian yet culminated in the mass annihilation of European Jewry. Several distinguished theologians have wrestled with the religious implications of the mass annihilation of European Jewry asking: "... does the affirmation that the task of the Church is to bring

[42] "Information and Views Communicated by the Holy See on 18 September 1972," *Study 1975*, p. 74. Similar trends are being developed among Protestants, part of them as a result of the decisions made by the Uppsala Assembly of the WCC in 1968 and the subsequent meeting of the Central Committee in Canterbury in 1969. These are but a few examples of a growing attempt in the Church at reconciling the traditional theology of salvation with current ethnopolitical reality. Not all circles and movements in the Church share these approaches, though Clyde W. Taylor, General Director of the National Association of Evangelicals, in his "Foreword" to Winger's report on the tribal warfare and genocidal violence in Burundi and Rwanda emphasizes that "... amid the facts and circumstances related in this book we are reminded that only through the penetration of the Gospel ... can this terrible hatred and lust of power be removed;" see Norman A. Winger, *No Place to Stop Killing*, Moody Bible Institute, Chicago, 1974, p. 117 and Chapter 12 "The Christian Church in Burundi," p. 90 ff.

the world into the Covenant through Jesus the Jew, contribute in and through itself to a perpetuation of the anti-Semitism?"[43]

B. *Genocidal Policy and the Holocaust*

The history of the spread of Nazism throughout Europe, and within it of the genocidal policy, reveals numerous and varied motives.[44] They were on the one hand economic and imperialistic, and on the other ideological, irrational,mythic and even apocalyptic in political dress, with the slogan "Space-Reich-Race" (*Raum-Reich-Rasse*) expressing their essence. Influenced by the spirit of the times in his youth, Heinrich Himmler wrote in his diary on November 22, 1921 that he felt the West was doomed to decline, and East Europe was the source of vitality and promise for the future, hence "... in the East we must fight and settle..."[45] Some of the youth movements such as *Artamanen* and the *Artram Bund* whose members included men destined to play leading roles in the Third Reich, Heinrich Himmler among them,[46] turned the racial theory of the socio-political Darwinism founded by

43 Roy A. Eckardt, *Your People, My People—The Meeting of Jews and Christians,* Quadrangle, New York & Toronto, 1974, pp. 248–249. The relationship between Christianity and anti-Judaism, anti-Judaism and modern anti-Semitism, and finally the Holocaust, has been of growing concern to a number of well known theologians, philosophers, historians, writers, poets and community leaders, and will be dealt with by us in a separate study.

44 On universal aspects of the anthropological crisis in Europe, as reflected in "the emancipation of power" and in the "in-humanity," cf. Helmuth Plessner, *Diesseits der Utopie,* Eugen Diederichs Verlag, Düsseldorf, Köln, 1966, pp. 190–229.

45 See the brilliant study by Josef Ackermann, *Himmler als Ideologe,* Musterschmidt-Göttingen, Zürich, Frankfurt, 1970, p. 196, (hereafter—Ackermann); the book review, Uriel Tal, "Heinrich Himmler als Ideologe," *Freiburger Rundbrief,* Vol. XXVII, No. 101/104, 1975, p. 27 ff.

46 Ackermann, *op. cit.*, p. 196 ff.

Ernst Haeckel and his disciple Willibald Hentschel[47] into an ideology that justified and reinforced the pull toward the East. Supported by racial theory, the romantic yearning towards the magical and primordial source of power developed a political expression. That was the spirit which in the 1920's also inspired other youth movements which were close to the *völkisch* stream and which influenced Nazism such as the *Bund Nibelungen,* the *Deutschwandervogel* and groups which evolved around the periodical *Die Kommenden,* as well as small groups of *Ostlandscharen* who in the spring of 1924 already sought to have workers from Poland sent back.[48] The motives, feelings and dreams involved were summed up in the phrase "Bonds to Blood and Soil" (*Bindungen an Blut und Boden*). A parallel concept that developed at the same time in these circles, and which was also absorbed in Nazism, was that of the need for space (*Raumnot*), the essence of which was a sense of strain, of enclosure, a fear of confined spaces, a yearning for expansion, for further horizons, for renewal. According to that mood, industrialization, life in a metropolis, the petty bourgeois atmosphere of the home, the Weimar Republic's political and economic ineptitude following the Versailles peace treaty, all these, it was felt, brought the Germans to a state of alienation, of loss of identity, of detachment from the normal healthy

[47] Daniel Gasman, *The Scientific Origins of National-Socialism,* Macdonald London & American Elsevier, New York, 1971, p. 152 ff. When analyzing Social Darwinism in Germany, especially in connection with racism, anti-Semitism and later Nazism, the term "socio-political" would define that particular trend of Social Darwinism quite accurately. Ever since Ludwig Woltmann's "politische Anthropologie," the term "political" acquired a semi-sacral significance. On the other hand the term "social" seems to fit better the Anglo-American brand of Darwinism, cf. Richard Hofstadter, *Social Darwinism in American Thought,* rev. ed., Beacon Press, Boston, 1960, especially chapters 8, 9, p. 143 ff.

[48] Harry Pross, *Jugend, Eros, Politik—Die Geschichte der deutschen Jugendverbände,* Büchergilde Gutenberg, Frankfurt a/M Wien, Zürich, 1964. (hereafter—Pross), p. 305 ff.

base of life; in other words, to uprootedness (*Entwurzelung*). The yearning for geo-political expansion fed on the psychological stress suffered by the youth after the defeat in World War I, and on a sense of helplessness in the face of the Weimar Republic's bureaucracy and political fragmentation. The depression of the inflation years, and the identification with its victims by intellectuals, students and young people, and along with it a feeling that there was no solution, no leadership, no future, strengthened the desire to escape to new-old territory, to the East.

In addition, many other ideological and mythical concepts of the Nazis' genocidal policy evolved within these circles, among them the notion of a struggle out of desperation (*Verzweiflungskampf*). The main point of this notion was that a fateful war for survival had been forced on the Germans by the victors in World War I, by the existential and social alienation of the individual in modern society in general and in the Weimar Republic regime in particular, and by the Jews who symbolized and epitomized all those disrupting forces. During those same 1920's other concepts appeared which were likewise to form part of the Nazi genocidal policy, among them the idea of "poisons for the people" (*Volksgifte*), which were poisons produced by the Jew or in his spirit in the rotten decadent modern Western civilization to contaminate the German individual, nation, state and race.[49] Another notion that was also to play an important role in the application of the genocidal policy was that of the un-German alien powers (*fremdvölkische Mächte*); these were not the international powers (*überstaatliche Mächte*) like Rome or Moscow in the real, political sense, but rather the alien, tribal-

[49] Adolf Hitler, *Mein Kampf,* München, 1943 (815–820 ed.), p. 316, 449. On the students' *Zeitgeist* see Hans Peter Bleuel and Ernst Klinnert, *Deutsche Studenten auf dem Weg ins Dritte Reich,* Sigbert Mohn Verlag, Gütersloh, 1967, "Student und Republik," p. 79 ff., "Der Antisemitismus," p. 130 ff.; Anselm Faust, *Der Nationalsozialistische Studentenbund,* Vol. 1, Pädagogischer Verlag, Düsseldorf, 1973, "Die Gedankenwelt der studentischen Verbände," p. 128 ff.

biological, mythic elements operating like microbes, infections, parasites and destroying Germany from within, destroying the body of the German people, the blood of the Germans, the soul of the Nordic or Aryan race, ruining natural, healthy instinctive morality which originates in the blood, and thus doing away with the German capacity to cope with the struggle for existence and win it. The figure that symbolizes and personifies these cursed forces is the Jew, who must consequently be removed entirely,[50] while one of the military solutions to that danger is the thrust to Eastern Europe.

Control of that expanse will pump natural healthy blood into the diseased body of the German people. This added energy will give rise to a new peasantry (*ein neues Bauernvolk*) who will produce an elite group of young Germans, healthy, sound and even perfect in body and spirit. For the sake of these sources of vitality, Germany must embark upon a sacred war, as a result of which the pure, superior Aryan race will attain control of Europe and perhaps the world.

Even in those days, still unrelated to Hitler's own criticism of exaggeratedly romantic dreams, these young people warned themselves against unrealistic romanticism. Modern cities, heavy industry, and advanced technology would all be needed by the

50 These ideas were articulated in the Nazi literature already in the early 1920's and were consistently maintained until the end of World War II; cf. *Völkischer Beobachter*, Vol. XXXIV, Nos. 32, 52, 85, 1920; among the last expressions see *Die Rassenfrage ist der Schlüssel zur Weltgeschichte*, published by the heardquarters of the SS 1945, Bundesarchiv, Koblenz, (hereafter—BA), NS 19/456; Saul Friedländer, *L'antisémitisme nazi—histoire d'une psychose collective*. Editions du Seuil, Paris, 1971, p. 173 ff. The psycho-historical methodology developed and applied by Friedländer is most helpful for a better insight into the complicated interrelationship of irrational motivations and pragmatical, down to earth policy in Nazi history; cf. the excellent theoretical study by Saul Friedländer, *Histoire et psychanalyse — essai sur les possibilités et les limites de la psychohistoire*, Editions du Seuil, Paris, 1975, p. 85 ff.

German people in order to win the battle for survival in modern society and achieve a position of leadership in it. However, the push to the East and the seizure of the sources of natural power would contribute to balancing the forces. They would provide the root soil (*Wurzelgrund*). A new covenant with blood and soil, it was said, embodied the solution "to all spiritual questions . . . the bondage to the soil commits us to the creed of peoplehood determined by blood. . ." (*Zu allen geistigen Fragen . . . die Erdgebundenheit verpflichtet uns zum Bekenntnis eines blutmässig bestimmten Volkstums . . .*)[51] In this context considerable response was elicited also by Hans Grimm's call for renewing the image of the German, returning to a healthy productive way of life, reviving the German breed (*deutschen Menschenzuwachs*), producing a thoroughbred human being who was handsome, strong and authoritative, who found his own identity through overcoming his enemies, especially his polar opposite, the Jew.

Another notion which evolved in the 1920's as a political term and was likewise to serve the genocidal policy was that of living space (*Lebensraum*). Under the influence of Hans Grimm's expanse ideology and R. Walther Darré's blood and soil ideology,[52] and first and foremost following the conception of Hitler

[51] Pross, *op. cit.*, p. 347. Similarly in *Nationalsozialistische Briefe,* Halbmonatsschrift für NS Weltanschauung, Nos. 25, 26, Elberfeld, October 1926.

[52] Hans Grimm, one of the influential authors of "Nordic thinking" did not join the Nazi party. The "Lippoldsberg poets' meetings" held under Grimm's auspices since 1934 in which writers such as Rudolf G. Binding, Friedrich Bischoff, Ernst v. Salomon and E.G. Kolbenheyer participated, greatly contributed to the growth of Germanic poetry and the romantic yearning for space, expansion and return to primordial forms of life-experience. R. Walther Darré, one of the founders of the Blood and Soil mythology lost much of his impact after 1941–1942; his teachings, however, especially about *Menschenzüchtung,* i.e. breeding selected Nordic or Aryan Germans, were accepted and taught by various SS departments, especially the main

himself, the heads of the SS persuaded their rank and file that the need for *Lebensraum* was the moral justification for the conquest of as much East European land as needed, "in order to generate harmony between the ethnic body and its geo-political space" (*. . . um zwischen Volkskörper und geopolitischem Raume einen Einklang hervorzustellen . . .*)[53]

Hitler himself reacted to these trends in Nazism in a pragmatic and equivocal manner. He opposed irrationality, warned against it and ridiculed it, and at the same time fostered and institutionalized it in ideology and in practical policy. Cautioning against sentimentality and flight from the reality of modern industrial society, he nurtured mythic forces and even built on them. Within this two-directional policy, the ideology of race occupied a significant place, and this was true also of foreign policy to the extent that it involved an aspiration for control of Central and Eastern Europe. In the second volume of *Mein Kampf* Hitler noted:

> . . . The foreign policy of a People's State must first of all bear in mind the duty of securing the existence of the race which is incorporated in this State. . . Our Movement must seek to abolish the present disastrous proportion between our population and the area of our national territory . . . it must bear in mind the fact that we are members of the highest species of humanity on this earth . . . We put an end to the perpetual Germanic march towards the South and West of Europe and turn our eyes towards the lands of the East . . . we must principally think of Russia and

office for "Race and Settlement." Cf. Hans Grimm, *Volk ohne Raum,* Vol. I, Langen, München, 1929, p. 129 ff.; "Amerikanische Rede," *Das Innere Reich,* Vol. II, 1935, p. 924 ff.; Richard Walther Darré, *Das Bauerntum als Lebensquell der nordischen Rasse,* München, 1929, 9th ed., 1942; *idem, Neuadel aus Blut und Boden,* München, 1930, 5th ed., 1943; *idem, Um Blut und Boden—Reden und Aufsätze,* Hans Deetjen und Wolfgang Clauss, eds., München, 3rd ed., 1941.

53 Karl Haushofer, *Raumordnung,* pamphlet issued by the German Academy, 1936, YIVO Archives, New York, Goebbels' Papers and Clippings, Box 2.

> the border States subject to her... Just as it is impossible for the Russian to shake off the Jewish... by exerting his own powers, so too it is impossible for the Jew to keep this formidable State in existence... He himself is by no means an organizing element, but rather a ferment of decomposition. This colossal Empire in the East is ripe for dissolution. And the end of the Jewish domination in Russia will also be the end of Russia as a State. We are chosen by Destiny to be the witness of a catastrophe which will afford the strongest confirmation of the nationalist theory of race...[54]

Later, in a conference with some of his most important military and diplomatic assistants, held in the Reich Chancellery, Berlin, on November 5, 1937, Hitler repeated the same ideas, and applied them to his socio-economic strategy. Among other things, it was stated that "...the aim of German policy was to make secure and to preserve the racial community (*Volksmasse*) and to enlarge it. It was, therefore, a question of space..."[55]

With the outbreak of the war, and especially as the invasion of Soviet Russia approached, even greater emphasis was placed on the ideological racist motives in Nazi policy. In the course of the war, the mythic aspiration toward the domination of the conquered areas by the pure race became one of the decisive factors in the policy of Heinrich Himmler and Hitler himself, who stated in his speech of March 30, 1941 that the war against Russia was a "struggle of two creeds" (*Kampf zweier Weltanschauungen gegeneinander*).[56]

54 Hitler, *op. cit.*, p. 523 ff.

55 Jeremy Noakes and Geoffrey Pridham, eds., *Documents on Nazism, 1919–1945,* The Viking Press, New York, 1975. Critical remarks on the "Minutes" of that conference, see pp. 521–529.

56 Hans-Adolf Jacobsen, ed., *Generaloberst Halder—Kriegstagebuch,* Vol. II, (1.VII.1940–21.VI.1941), W. Kohlhammer Verlag, Stuttgart, 1963 (hereafter—Halder), p. 336. At the same time Hitler often gave expression to what were supposed to appear as rational, pragmatic calculations, such as his remark to Reichsecretary Dr. Todt on

HOLOCAUST AND GENOCIDE

On instruction from Hitler on October 7, 1939, Heinrich Himmler was appointed Reich Commissioner for the Strengthening of German Nationhood (*Reichskommissar für die Festung deutschen Volkstums*). Among the main duties listed were the following: repatriating persons of German race and nationality now resident abroad who are considered suitable for permanent return to the Reich; eliminating the harmful influence of those alien parts of the population, which constitute a danger to the Reich and the German community; forming new German settlements by the transfer of populations and in particular by settling the German citizens and racial Germans returning from abroad.[57]

In the course of the next few weeks, basic premises and practical directives were evolved with regard to the policy in conquered Poland and especially the General Government, and among other things it was declared that the war was to be viewed as "a hard racial struggle which will not permit any legal restrictions. The methods will be incompatible with the principles which we otherwise adhere to..." In addition the chief goals of the occupying regime were set, goals which were defined as genocidal after World War II. They included a provision, for example, that "...the Polish intelligentsia must be prevented from forming itself into a ruling class. The standard of living in the country is to remain low; it is of use to us only as a reservoir of labor...the formation of national political groups will not be permitted..."[58] The program for the General Government outlined by Hitler on October 2, 1940, as recorded by Martin Bormann, emphasized that "...there must be no Polish masters; where there are Polish masters, they would have

June 20, 1941, against illusions about an economic autarchy in Germany: "...that which one needs yet does not own one has to conquer," cf. Hans-Adolf Jacobsen, *1939–1945: Der Zweite Weltkrieg in Chronik und Dokumenten,* Wehr und Wissen Verlagsgesellschaft, Darmstadt, 1959, p. 230.

57 *Blue Series,* Vol. XXVI, Document 686–PS, p. 225.

58 *Blue Series,* Vol. XXXIX, Document 172–USSR, pp. 426–429.

to be killed off (*umgebracht*), however cruel that may sound . . ."[59]

It was in that spirit that Heinrich Himmler on March 15, 1940 addressed the camp commanders of occupied Poland, announcing that it was Nazi policy to see to it that ". . . all Poles disappear from the world," simply through "the extirpation (*Ausrottung*) of 'Polishdom'; hence the aim of the war is "to destroy (*zu vernichten*) all the Poles. . ."[60]

At this point the notion of re-Germanization (*Wiedereindeutschung*) emerges as one of the central concepts in the Nazi genocidal policy, insofar as it served the occupation policy in Central and Eastern Europe. That notion was described by one of the American prosecutors in the trial of Ulrich Greifelt and others at Nuremberg as an expression of the Nazi historic and mythic credo. The Nazi ideology held that due to wanderings of the ancient Germanic tribes all through Europe, the Poles and other Central and Eastern European nations included people with "Nordic blood" (*nordisches Blut*) in their veins. Thus, even if the genealogical trees of Polish families show no trace of Germanic ancestors, if people are found whose outward physical appearance (*körperliche Erscheinungsformen*) resembles that of the mythical master race (*mythische Herrenrasse*), they are to be restored to their origin, to the bosom of the German people.[61] In conjunction with scientists, the SS and the party made various plans for occupied territories such as Bohemia, Moravia, and even in more remote areas in Eastern Europe, to

59 *Ibid.;* Martin Broszat, *Nationalsozialistische Polenpolitik 1939–1945,* Deutsche Verlagsanstalt, Stuttgart, 1961, p. 25.

60 Jacob Robinson, *And the Crooked Shall Be Made Straight,* JPS, Philadelphia, 1965, (hereafter—Jacob Robinson), p. 93.

61 *Green Series,* Vol. IV, p. 599 ff.; "The RSHA Case," Case 8, Count One: Crimes against Humanity (pp. 609–617); Count Two: War Crimes (pp. 617 ff.); *Law Reports of Trials of War Criminals,* selected and prepared by UN War Crimes Commission. Vol. XIII, H.M. Stationery Office, London, 1949, p. 2 ff.

achieve what was referred to as "the recovery of lost German blood" (*Rückgewinnung verlorengegangenen deutschen Blutes*). In a document dated May 20, 1940 listing plans for handling the population of occupied zones in Eastern Europe,[62] Himmler stipulates that all the inhabitants who look Nordic (have a *nordisches Aussehen*) can be absorbed into the ranks of the *Herrenvolk*, while the rest of the people, even if they are of the same nationality, will be subject to a regime of conquest or even slavery. If those chosen to be annexed and grafted on to the German people refuse to abandon their erstwhile nationality (*ihrem bisherigen Volkstum*) they may expect to be imprisoned in concentration camps or even executed by the *Liquidationskommandos*. Later, the special decree (*Erlass*) concerning the supervision (*Überprüfung*) and selection (*Aussonderung*) and separation of the population in the conquered territories in Eastern Europe issued by Heinrich Himmler in his capacity of Commissioner for the Strengthening of German Nationhood, outlined additional plans for accomplishing the re-Germanization of residents of the occupied territories.[63] Thus, even if they are of alien ethnic origin (*Fremdvölkische*) from the point of view of their citizenship, education or heritage, such people can be considered of German descent (*deutschstämmig*) from the point of view of their blood and body, or as Hitler put it, they are needed because of their usefulness for the racial strengthening of the Third Reich.[64] Here, too, Himmler

62 "Reflections on the Treatment of Peoples of Alien Races in the East," *Blue Series*, Vol. XIII, Document NO–1880. The text of the document was approved by Hitler and submitted to Lammers on May 28, 1940, cf. *Green Series*, Vol. XIII, Documents NO–1880, NO–1881, pp. 147–151. The document erroneously dated May 20, 1940 instead of May 25, has been reproduced in Ackermann, *op. cit.*, pp. 298–300.

63 Quoted in Ackermann, *op. cit.*, p. 207. For additional aspects of that policy of the Nazis particularly relating to the Jews see also *Red Series*, Vol. V, p. 581 ff.

64 "Top Secret Report" of October 20, 1939, on the conference between

planned strict administrative arrangements which obliged the local police to see to it that the suitable candidates among the people of German descent (*Deutschstämmigen*) in the occupied zones should be listed in the "Registry of the German people" (*deutsche Volksliste*), and those who despite prior warning refused to be so listed were subject to imprisonment in concentration camps.[65]

Similar plans were made by Otto Hoffman, head of the SS Race and Settlement Department (*Rasse- und Siedlungshauptamt*) and by Freiherr von Neurath, between August and October 1940, in regard to what was termed "the solution of the Czech question in the Protectorate of Bohemia and Moravia." One of the primary aims of the various plans was "... assimilating the *Tschechentum,* i.e., absorbing about half of the Czech peoplehood into Germandom, in so far as they are of blood—or otherwise valuable significance ... the other half of the Czech peoplehood must in various ways be rendered powerless, excluded and deported. This applies especially to the racial Mongol parts and to the major part of the class of intellectuals ..."[66] To achieve these ends the SS heads planned to sift (*sieben*), pick out (*herauszuholen*) and assimilate toddlers, schoolchildren and even young adults who in their physical features resembled the ideal

Hitler and Keitel concerning the future of Poland, held October 17, 1939, in *Blue Series,* Vol. XXVI, Document 864–PS, p. 377. Accordingly Poland is to be considered as a source of labor and possibly a military deployment area for Germany; a bare minimum of existence is to be allowed and the policy of exploitation and degradation should not be hampered by legal considerations.

65 Decree by Himmler in his capacity as Reich Commissioner for the Enhancement of Germanism (*Festigung deutschen Volkstums*), issued on September 12, 1940, in *Blue Series,* Vol. XXXI, Document 2916–PS, pp. 283–294.

66 "Report of the Army Plenipotentiary with the Reichprotector in Böhmen and Mähren, Lieutenant General Friderici," of October 15, 1940, in *Blue Series,* Vol. XXVI, Document 862–PS, p. 376, quoted in Ackermann, *op. cit.,* p. 209.

image of the "good blood" or "German blood" as to color of hair and eyes, body structure, general appearance and the like. It was necessary to remove these people from the masses of Slavs, or as Himmler put it, from the "ethnic hash of millions of subhumans" (*Völkerbrei von Millionen Untermenschen*) and through them strengthen, fertilize and enrich the German people of Nordic blood.[67]

A secret report of the administration of the General Government dated March 30, 1942 sums up a speech Himmler made in Cracow about two weeks earlier in which he again stressed that if the physical appearance of Slav children accords with the ideal of the Nordic race, it is an indication of racial filiation, and anybody in this category is eligible for better living conditions which would enable him to acquire the German language and familiarize himself with the German intellectual treasury (*sich mit dem deutschen Gedankengut vertraut zu machen*).[68]

[67] Ackermann, *op. cit.*, p. 206. Also see the recommendations by Erhard Wetzel of the Ministry of Occupied Eastern Territories and the Department of Racial Policy of the NSDAP, for the solution of the "Czech Question" (*zur Tschechenfrage*); while the Czechs are less violent than the Poles, the hatred of the Germans by the Czech intellectuals is particularly dangerous. Plans that have been made to simply remove (*abzuschieben*) the Czechs who were undesired from a racial point of view, Wetzel noted, were out of the question as far as intellectuals were concerned. Therefore, just like the Polish intellectuals at that stage, they are to be forced to emigrate; see reproduction of the original document in *VJZG*, No. 3, 1958, p. 319. Wetzel was also involved in the "Final Solution" conferences held on March 6, 1942, and October 27, 1942, in *Green Series*, Vol. XIII, Document NG–2586 H(8), pp. 209–210, and Document NG–2586 M(18), pp. 222–225.

[68] *Blue Series*, Vol. XXVI, Document 910–PS, pp. 409–410. Martin Broszat, in his aforementioned study *Nationalsozialistische Polenpolitik* describes the purpose of this policy as follows: "... Verminderung eines zweiten Zuwachses zur polnischen Intellektuellenschicht aus germanisch bestimmten, wenn auch polanisierten Sippen ... die Vermehrung des rassisch erwünschten Bevölkerungszuwachses für das

These goals were the concern of the Nazi ideological leadership with regard to the population in the occupied zones of Soviet Russia as well. Here, too, the racist ideology was defined as a motive and justification for a genocidal policy. In an ideological speech on March 30, 1941, explaining the necessity of destroying the communist intelligentsia and the Bolshevik political commissars of the Red Army, Hitler described the war itself as "a war of extermination" because it was a struggle between two world views.[69] Also the spatial-political foundations (*raumpolitische Grundlagen*) of the *Generalplan Ost* as worked out by Professor Konrad Meyer Hartling of the SS, Heinrich Himmler's speech to SS and police officers on September 16, 1942, and Hitler's September 30, 1942 address at the *Berliner Sportpalast*, all indicated clearly the racial goals of the Nazi war in East Europe. According to Hitler, the war was aimed not only at the expansion of space (*Raumerweiterung*) but also "to fill this space with a consolidated nation..." Consequently, Himmler told his people, "whenever you happen to find good blood, you must obtain it for Germany or you have to make sure that it will no longer exist" (*Wo Sie ein gutes Blut finden, haben Sie es für Deutschland zu gewinnen, oder Sie haben dafür zu sorgen, dass es nicht mehr existiert . . .*)[70]

Again, in the autumn of 1943, and even later, in fact to the end of the war, Himmler continued to reiterate the aims of the racial policy in respect of the population of Eastern Europe. Thus the Slavs were actually subhumans but those of them who looked Aryan were to be counted as belonging to the master

deutsche Volk," cf. p. 131 and chapter V, "Völkisch nationalsozialistische Neuordnung in den eingegliederten Ostgebieten," pp. 118–137.

69 Halder, *op. cit.*, p. 336; Hans-Adolf Jacobsen, "Kommissarbefehl und Massenexekutionen Sowjetischer Kriegsgefangener," in Hans Buchheim *et al.*, *Anatomie des SS-Staates*, Gutachten des Instituts für Zeitgeschichte, Walter-Verlag, Olten und Freiburg i.Br., 1965 (hereafter—*Kommissarbefehl*), p. 173 ff.

70 Ackermann, *op. cit.*, p. 209.

race. Except for those, most of the peoples of the East (*Ostvölker*), and considerable sectors of the Balkan and Danube peoples, especially the leadership, were destined for extinction by a variety of methods, depending on circumstances; "forced to die out" through sterilization and extermination (*durch Sterilisierung und Vernichtung zum Aussterben gezwungen*)[71] was one of these means.

C. *The Holocaust**

Except for the annihilation of European Jewry, the various plans to implement the policy of genocide were carried out only in part. Some methods, among them euthanasia, were abandoned because of public opinion in and outside Germany including that of the churches.[72] Some were discontinued due to public

[71] Ackermann, *op. cit.*, p. 210. Similarly Ernst Kaltenbrunner, Chief of RSHA, stated that the eastern peoples must be forced to die out by means of sterilization and extermination of their higher classes, cf. *Blue Series,* Vol. XXXIII, Document 3462–PS, p. 295 ff. Also see the fundamental speech by Heinrich Himmler at the SS commanders' conference, Posen, October 4, 1943, on the non-German peoples who are to be looked upon as slaves in the service of German culture and destiny, and on the need to annihilate the Jew, in *Blue Series,* Vol. XXIX, Document 1919–PS, pp. 110–173. Cf. Alexander Dallin, *German Rule in Russia 1941–1945—A Study of Occupation Politics,* Macmillan, London & St. Martin Press, New York, 1957 (hereafter—*Dallin*), p. 444 ff.

* Cf. "Excursus on Hermeneutical Aspects of the Term "Shoah", see appendix, pp. 46–52.

[72] Reinhard Henkys, *Die nationalsozialistischen Gewaltverbrechen,* Kreuz Verlag, Stuttgart, Berlin, 1964, p. 61. On the struggle of the Church see the excellent study by John S. Conway (translated by Carsten Nicolaisen), *Die nationalsozialistische Kirchenpolitik 1933–1945,* Chr. Kaiser Verlag, München, 1969, p. 281 ff.; Martin Broszat, "Nationalsozialistische Konzentrationslager 1933–1935," *op. cit.*, p. 125 ff.; Jäger, *op. cit.*, p. 355 ff., and Walter Schulte, " 'Euthanasie' und 'Sterilisation' " in Andreas Filtner, ed., *Deutsches Geistesleben und Nationalsozialismus,* Rainer Wunderlich Verlag, Tübingen, 1965, p. 89 ff.

pressure, the objections of German army officers, or strategic considerations. That is what happened in connection with the "Commissar Order" of June 6, 1941, which laid down that captured Red Army political commissars be liquidated by the SS. Under the pressure of Russian resistance, Hitler, on May 6, 1942, ordered that as an experiment the commissars and politruks should be kept alive in order to encourage encircled Russians to desert or surrender.[73]

There were plans which were set aside until the war ended, such as the one Heinrich Himmler announced in his speech of September 7, 1940 to the officers of the "Adolf Hitler *Leibstandarte* SS" regarding the organization of selected units for the "struggle against sub-humanity..." (*Kampf mit dem Untermenschentum*). In order to train those units it would be necessary to establish concentration camps where it would be possible to provide "teaching about sub-humanity and lesser-racedom" (*Unterricht über Untermenschentum and über Minderrassentum*).[74] There were long-term goals that were deferred till the end of the war, such as genocidal plans for the Church, notably the Roman Catholic. In addition, in a March 15, 1940 speech to camp commanders, Heinrich Himmler declared that he foresaw "... the disappearance of the Poles from the world, the extirpation (*Ausrottung*) of 'Polishdom' and the destruction of all the Poles."[75] A few weeks later, on May 30, 1940, Governor Hans Frank explained that the policy of exterminating the intellectuals would have to be completed after the war was won,

[73] Halder, *op. cit.*, p. 243. On various ways in which the genocidal order about the commissars was received, carried out or opposed, cf. Kommissarbefehl, *op. cit.*, pp. 174–175, 193 ff.

[74] Ackermann, *op. cit.*, p. 154. Germans as "supermen" (*Übermenschen*) were ordered to avoid contact with the Slavic "submen" (*Untermenschen*), cf. Dallin, *op. cit.*, p. 445 ff.

[75] Jacob Robinson, *op. cit.*, p. 93; "Der Generalplan Ost—Dokumentation," in *VJZG*, No. 3, 1958, p. 281 ff.: Kommissarbefehl, *op. cit.*, p. 168.

for then, when the Third Reich had become a *Weltmacht* (world power) it would be possible to carry out *politischen Aktionen,* including the *Kolonisieren* of the occupied territories, more intensively. And toward the end of the war Frank again stated, "Once we have won the war, for my part all the Poles and Ukrainians and the rest that are roaming around here can be made mincemeat of..." (*Wenn wir den Krieg einmal gewonnen haben, dann kann meinetwegen aus den Polen und aus den Ukrainen und dem was sich hier herumtreibt, Hackfleisch gemacht werden*).[76]

The deferment in the implementation of the genocidal policy towards non-Jews in Poland and the other European countries, was explained by Erhard Wetzel, a high official in the Ministry of Occupied Eastern Territories. "...It goes without saying that one cannot resolve the Polish problem by liquidating the Poles as is being done with the Jews. Such a solution would brand the German people into the far future and would cost us sympathy on all sides..."[77]

In the same vein, Hans Frank noted in his diary that the liquidation of all the Poles unfit for work could not yet be carried out, for world opinion was still not ready to accept the extermination of millions of human creatures..."[78] This concept of "human creatures" (*menschlicher Wesen*) in Hans Frank's diary is important for an understanding of the special nature of the Holocaust. The Jews were excluded from the definition of

[76] Hermann Langbein, *Wir haben es getan—Selbstporträts in Tagebüchern und Briefen 1939–1945,* Europäische Perspektiven, Wien, 1964, p. 115, 124.

[77] Reproduced in *VJZG,* Vol. VI, 1958, p. 297 ff., also quoted in Jacob Robinson, *op. cit.,* p. 93. On earlier suggestions made by E. Wetzel about different treatment of Poles and Jews, cf. his "Memorandum" of October 20, 1939, in *Documenta Occupationis Teutonicae,* Posen, 1958, Vol. V, Document NO–3732 (documents in German), pp. 2–28.

[78] *Blue Series,* Vol. XXIX, Document 2233–PS, p. 565, excerpts from the Diary of December 14, 1942.

"human" as was stated years earlier by Walter Buch, supreme judge of the Nazi Party (NSDAP): "The National Socialist has recognized (that) the Jew is not a human..." (*Der Nationalsozialist hat erkannt: Der Jude ist kein Mensch*).[79] With the excision of the Jew from humankind and his transformation into a germ, a parasite, a bloodsucker, or, as Heinrich Himmler stated before the outbreak of the war into the "basic material of everything negative" (*Urstoff alles Negativen*),[80] the ontological status of the Jew was revolutionized; he evolved from a subject with natural rights into an object without natural rights. As such an object he could be used in any way for any purpose, and there was no longer any need to maintain any kind of factual or logical connection between the characteristics and deeds attributed to him and his empirical, factual or historical identity.

Thus the Jew was simultaneously described as the father of Marxism, Communism, Bolshevism, and international defilement (*Verseuchung*) and on the other hand, of exploitative capitalism, sterile capital, usury, big business, and the liberal republican or democratic system; the Jew was helpless, weak and uncreative on the one hand, and on the other the overt or mainly secret and deceitful master of the economy, the press, art or academic life; the Jew is the source of Christianity and thus bears primary responsibility for the inculcation of the slave morality that destroys the will to live and the ability to prevail in the struggle for survival, and on the other hand, it is he who crucified God

79 Walter Buch, "Die Ehre etc.," in *Deutsche Justiz, Amtliches Blatt der deutschen Rechtspflege*, ed. by Franz Günter, Reich Secretary of Law, 1938, p. 1660. This statement has been quoted in a number of studies, first by Max Weinreich, *Hitler's Professors*, YIVO, New York, 1964, p. 249 (cf. p. 89); later by Alexander Bein, "Der jüdische Parasit," in *VJZG*, No. 2, 1965, p. 140, and in Ackermann, *op. cit.*, p. 163.

80 Heinrich Himmler's speech on a conference of SS commanders ("Gruppenführer") on November 8, 1938, quoted in Ackermann, *op. cit.*, p. 160.

and spilled the blood of the redeemer; the Jew is a mixture of races, without character, form, or backbone, and on the other hand the perfect, explicit, obvious symbol of the anti-race (*Gegenrasse*).

This image of the Jew proved to be quite useful in Nazi policy. As early as the 1920's Hitler noted that all possible propaganda methods should be used to focus the attention of the general public, with all its varied groups, on one enemy.[81] Hitler's path was followed by most Nazi propagandists, and the Jew became the archtype of the enemy, while the plethora of contradictions in the image of the Jew made their propaganda more attractive. Adolf Wagner, Bavarian Minister of the Interior and Vice-Premier declared in 1933, for example, that "the constant and everlasting watchword of our movement is the fight against every force that would destroy our right to live . . . an unending fight against the Jews, and in this fight it makes no difference to us whether the eternal Jew runs about in the red rags of the Bolshevik or in the black clothes of the Ultramontane. . ."[82]

Thus it became possible to present the Jewish image as the diametric opposite of the Aryan; in this polar contrast many of the personal motives and desires of the Nazis themselves were projected. From then on the Jew was the one aspiring to world domination, to the extermination of all his enemies; it was the Jew who was Godless, conscienceless, and immoral or unrestrained in everything deriving from his base and perverse sexual instinct. Every evil, from the economic crises of the Weimar Republic, to personal or family problems, to the casualties of World War I, were the fault of the Jew, and thus a defence mechanism was evolved through which the Nazi regime could

81 Adolf Hitler, *Mein Kampf*, Vol. I, München, 1934, pp. 124–125.

82 Adolf Wagner's speech to the NSDAP in Munich, October 1936, has been cited in one of the earliest source collections on this topic, cf. *Catholic Church—The Persecution of the Catholic Church in the Third Reich—Facts and Documents*, Burnes Oates, London, 1940, p. 276.

attribute the blame for any failing, difficulty or suffering to the Jew.

The Jew was the epitome of everything hostile to the Nazis, the total enemy, and thus his extermination had to be total as well. In contrast to the policy on other peoples, including communists, no candidates for re-Germanization could be selected from among the Jews, even if their outward appearance fitted the Nordic ideal.[83] The Jew was not a foe because of any function he fulfilled, any position he represented; he was enmity personified. This total conception was systematically inculcated into the SS as indicated for example by an SS training pamphlet dated April 22, 1936, entitled "Why is Jewry Being Studied?" And the answer is "... because the Jew is the German people's most dangerous enemy."[84] The educators of the SS also stressed that history teaches that Jews have been a disruptive element at all times and places especially because of "planned destruction of the blood consciousness of the host people, by destroying their racial pride, ethnic way of thinking and feeling, morals, law and culture..." (*planmässige Zerstörung des Blutbewusstseins der Wirtsvölker, durch Zerstörung ihres Rassenstolzes, ihres arteigenen Denkens und Fühlens, ihrer Sittlichkeit, ihres Rechtes und ihrer Kultur*).[85]

[83] Gerd Rühle, *Das Dritte Reich—Dokumentarische Darstellung des Aufbaus der Nation*, Hummelverlag, Berlin, 1933, p. 47 ff. On the complexity of the term "enemy" especially in the framework of a culture as highly developed as that of the Western and European civilization, cf. August Nitschke, *Der Feind—Erlebnis, Theorie und Begegnung, Formen politischen Handelns im 20. Jahrhundert, W.* Kohlhammer Verlag, Stuttgart, 1964, p. 62 ff., 135 ff., and Part III, p. 194 ff.

[84] Ackermann, *op. cit.*, p. 159.

[85] *Ibid.* The interpretation of the Jew as embodiment of evil can be better understood if studied against the background of the historical consciousness as taught by the SS prior to war, cf. *Leitheft SS*, No. 2, (June 3, 1937), No. 3 (July 1, 1937), No. 5 (September 1, 1937), No. 6 (October 5, 1937), published by the Education Department

HOLOCAUST AND GENOCIDE

In view of this total concept of the Jew as the symbol and substance of the hostile as such, of the anti-Nazi, the Holocaust was not carried out as a means of achieving some definite aim, military or economic for instance, but as an end in itself. If it had any purpose, that purpose was beyond the realm of interhuman relations and, as Hans Buchheim said, it was not war, but combatting insects (*Schädlingsbekämpfung*) or *soziale Desinfektion.*[86]

In 1943, at the height of the Holocaust, Alfred Baeumler, one of the foremost scholars in the Nazi movement, pointed out that in Nazi ideology and practice, the Jew represented not only Judaism, but the forces against which Nazism was struggling—the legacy of Monotheism, Western civilization, critical rationalism and humanism. Therefore Judaism was "... the demon who became palpable and who is the archfiend of the German... hence this is a fight for life or death, it is either us or him [the Jew]... The nation requires the whole person and thus reaches into the religious domain."[87]

Indeed at this point there seems to have been full agreement between the various conflicting trends within the Nazi leadership. Moreover, this interpretation of anti-Judaism was perhaps one of the few consistencies in Nazi ideology and policy from the early twenties up to 1945. The Jewish question and its solution reflected a fundamental feature of Nazism, one that was structured in terms of transfiguration of reversing meanings. Forms of thought, feeling, expression and behavior rooted in historical tradition were transferred to the political domain. Theology and

(*Schulungsamt*) of the Main Office for Race and Settlement. At the same time different approaches to history and historical consciousness were maintained, cf. Karl Ferdinand Werner, *Das NS-Geschichtsbild und die deutsche Geschichtswissenschaft,* W. Kohlhammer Verlag, Stuttgart, 1967, p. 123 ff.

86 Hans Buchheim, *Totalitäre Herrschaft—Wesen und Merkmale,* Köselverlag, München, 1965, p. 52.

87 Alfred Baeumler, *Alfred Rosenberg und der Mythos des 20 Jahrhunderts,* Huheneichen Verlag, München, 1943, p. 19 ff.

religion were secularized while politics and state became sacred and served as an *ersatz* substitute religion.[88]

This process of reversing meanings assumed the form of a political myth which was expected to become a main instrument in the creation of a new image of man, a new type of society and a new Reich. Political myth was to contribute to the crystallization of a new consensus, new conventions and new taboos; it had to motivate the new Aryan to internalize civic commitment and political discipline. Political myth was to establish a system of values that would penetrate the realm of personal and family life, culture, education, art and the economy. In the individual's daily life political myth had to provide relief from tension and fear, from uncertainty and frustration, from feelings of existential alienation and civic powerlessness. Political myth had to encourage a historical consciousness, an awareness of mission to what was called the political cosmos. Political myth was to bring home to the Aryan citizen that the Reich was founded on law and order and on normative standards all of which were embodied in the Führer.

The framework in which political myth had to function was that of the race. The race, chosen and mighty, was to give the individual a sense of belonging to a higher, a transcendent entity. This entity was above rational criticism or scientific verification. Race was perceived, similar to the family, as an entity into which the person is born, to which he belongs by virtue of nature or fate. Man is one of the limbs of the organism called race, connected to it by blood and descent, as a son, father or mother might be. This blood pact between man and race, constitutionally affirmed in 1933, served as a cornerstone of Nazi anti-Jewish policy. The pact was stronger than any social contract or rational consensus; it was a given condition that could not be changed, and thus was expected to bring about stability, security, confidence

[88] Uriel Tal, *"Political Faith" of Nazism Prior to the Holocaust,* Annual Lecture of the Jacob M. and Shoshana Schreiber Chair of Contemporary Jewish History, Tel Aviv University, Tel Aviv, 1978.

and truth. Whoever did not belong to it was its enemy, since he was an alien body endangering the wholeness of the sacred organism.

In reality Nazism accomplished but few of its goals. In one area though, in the Jewish Question, political myth fully achieved its purpose. Here the regime met the least opposition from among those who in other matters of genocidal policy were hardly in accord with Nazism—be they intellectuals, the Church, or public opinion in the Reich or abroad. The Jew served as a focal point around which Nazism revolved and on which the structural process of value-transformation and reversal of meanings took place. Among the values and meanings that were transformed, the symbol itself was turned into substance; hence the negation of Judaism had to be transformed into the annihilation of the Jew, this time not spiritually but rather physically, not symbolically but in substance,[89]—it is here that the metahistorical uniqueness of the Holocaust emerges.

One of the difficult questions in the study of genocide and the Holocaust is what they have in common and how they differ and, indeed, the similarities and differences between particular instances of mass extermination of human groups, be they differentiated by their ethnic origin, tribe or nation, their socio-economic class, ideology or religion. Is not mass extermination a phenomenon that outweighs all the differences between various

89 Saul Friedländer, "The Historical Significance of the Holocaust," based on his lecture delivered at the International Scholars Conference on the Holocaust—A Generation After, held in New York, March 3–6, 1975, published in *The Jerusalem Quarterly,* Vol. I No. 1, Fall 1976, p. 40 ff., and from a methodological point of view see Yehuda Bauer, "Trends in Holocaust Research" in *Yad Vashem Studies,* Vol. XII, Jerusalem, 1977, pp. 7–63; and his recent book *The Holocaust in Historical Perspective,* University of Washington Press, Seattle, 1978, pp. 30–49; as to the psychohistorical background of the process of value transformation, see Friedländer, Histoire et psychanalyse, *op. cit.,* pp. 168–195.

URIEL TAL

human groups? Are not the phenomena accompanying mass extermination universal in nature, phenomena such as fear, pain, agony, death, manifestations of the absurd and of the alienation of the victim in the face of the forces affecting his fate, manifestations of prejudice, injustice, evil, cruelty, hate and violence? Is not the fact that genocide is happening in the twentieth century, that is, in the age of critical rationalism, of enlightenment and modern civilization, in the age in which man has at his disposal technology which could be a blessing if he could only control it according to the criteria of social morality; is not that fact an indication of the universal nature of genocide?

And on the other hand, is not particular differentiation in the study of the mass annihilation of human groups absolutely necessary, for the victimizers themselves practice genocide on particular groups precisely because of that particularity? Furthermore, is not the universality of genocide composed of particular instances, with every instance exemplifying a particular aspect of the general phenomenon? And in regard to the specific case of Holocaust, does it not demonstrate the need to differentiate among particular cases? The Nazis themselves, and especially those primarily responsible for the Holocaust, like Hitler and Himmler, viewed the Jew as both the symbol and substance of anti-Nazism as such. The triumph of Nazism over the Jew was the proof, but also a symbolic means of overcoming Monotheism and its legacy within civilization. Thus, the mass annihilation of the Jews was unique, different from other genocidal phenomena.

Appendix

Excursus on Hermeneutical Aspects of the Term *Sho'ah*

In Biblical tradition, the term "Holocaust" which originally indicated a sacrificial offering wholly consumed by fire, has been defined as a "burnt offering wholly" sacrificed "unto the Lord" (*Ola Kalil la-Shem,* I Samuel VII:9). Later the term "Holocaust" was applied to historical phenomena of massacre and other forms of destruction of large numbers of human beings.

Already by the end of 1940 the term *Sho'ah* was used to indicate the mass annihilation of Jews in Europe. The collection of reports and surveys on the persecution and killing of European Jews starting September 1939, submitted by eyewitnesses such as Apolinary Hartglass (then President of the Zionist Organization of Poland and former Member of the Polish Parliament) and Moshe (Sneh) Kleinbaum (then Chairman of the Central Committee of the Zionist Organization of Poland and one of the editors of the Warsaw *Haint*) was published in Hebrew by "The United Committee to Aid Polish Jewry," under the title *Sho'at Yehudei Polin*, Goldberg Press, Jerusalem, 1940. Then, until spring 1942, the term *Sho'ah* was but infrequently used, while nowadays its connotation is not only the destruction of the Jews of Europe, but genocidal policies by which additional human groups are wiped out as well. The mass annihilation of the Jews has become a prototype for different cases of genocide (cf. Gerd Korman "The Holocaust in American Historical Writing," *Societas*, Vol. II, No. 3, Summer 1972, pp. 251–270. On some aspects of the background cf. Alice and Roy Eckardt, "Christentum und Judentum—die theologische und moralische Problematik der Vernichtung des europäischen Judentums," *Evangelische Theologie*, Vol. XXXVI, No. 5, Chr. Kaiser Verlag, München, 1976, pp. 406–426; Ismar Schorsch, "Historical Reflections on the Holocaust," *Conservative Judaism*, Vol. XXXI, Nos. 1–2, New York, 1976–1977, pp. 26–33).

It seems that the term *Ḥurban* with its Jewish historical and Yiddish connotations, was one of the first, spontaneous, choices (similar to the term "catastrophe"). When leading members of the Zionist labor movement and Hebrew writers and thinkers in what was then called Palestine, started publicly to relate to the destruction of European Jewry, the Hebrew term *Sho'ah* appeared. (One of the earliest significant sources dates to April 1942, cf. Jacob Eshed, *Ḥeshbon shel Zehut*, Ha-Kibbutz ha-Me'uḥad, Ein-

URIEL TAL

Ḥarod. 1978, p. 37. The collection of essays is edited by Even Shoshan and Zerubabel Gilad.) On July 12–13, 1942, a significant conference of Hebrew writers and poets called "In Times of Distress to Jacob" was held in the Jewish Agency offices in Jerusalem. Shaul Tchernichovsky, an outstanding Hebrew neoromantic poet entitled his moving address "The Command of the Horrible *Sho'ah* that is Coming Over Us." The poet used the term *Sho'ah* in assonance with the Hebrew expression "The Command of the *Sha'ah*" (of this hour). Describing some of the horrors that European Jewry was undergoing, Tchernichovsky exhorted the writers not to remain silent. On that occasion, Rabbi Benjamin (pseudonym for J. Radler-Feldmann), one of the active members of the Brith-Shalom peace movement and one of the founders of the "Al Domi" group, in summarizing the conference stated that one of the events that made him and others more aware of the mass annihilation of European Jewry was the Lidice massacre. That event, Rabbi Benjamin continued, should be looked upon as "... part of the world *Sho'ah*" (cf. *Ha'aretz*, July 13, 1942, p. 4; and *Moznayim*, August 1942, p. 380, 396).

Afterwards, even following the official declaration on the Holocaust by the Jewish Agency of November 1942, use of the term *Sho'ah* was still limited. On November 30, 1942, a conference in Jerusalem, in which about four hundred rabbis participated, proclaimed that the *Sho'ah* that European Jewry was undergoing was without precedent in history. With Memorial Day to be observed on December 2, 1942, the Rabbis admonished the *Yishuv*, the Jewish community in Palestine, for not being sufficiently concerned about the fate that was befalling their brethren in Europe.

One of the first to use the term *Sho'ah* in historical perspective was Benzion Dinur (Dinaburg). In the spring of 1943 Dinur stated that the *Sho'ah* was a catastrophe that symbolized the uniqueness of the history of the Jewish people among the nations. Cf. two of the three speeches by Dinur reprinted in his *Remember! Addresses on the Holocaust and its Moral*, Yad Vashem,

Jerusalem, 1958, pp. 14–45 (Hebrew). Another source indicating the growing significance of the use of the term *Sho'ah* during the spring of 1943 and afterwards, is the collection of essays and studies by Fishl Shneerson entitled *Psycho-History of Sho'ah and Rebirth,* ed. by Eliezer Tur Shalom, Yezreel Publishing House, T.A., 1958 (Hebrew); (I am indebted to Dina Porath, Research Fellow, for this reference). Shneerson in his address to the writers' conference at Kibbutz Hulda in July 1943, pointed out that the term *Sho'ah* is sometimes used in connection with guilt-feelings, subconscious rejection of facts, escape into numbness and stunned paralysis or dramatic and artificial gestures of grief. Shneerson, citing historical and Talmudic traditions, urged not to give away to excessive and destructive mourning, as did Rabbi Yishmael ben Elisha and his sect of "Mourners of Zion and Jerusalem," nor to false Messianism as did Rabbi Akiba in his support of Bar Kochba, but rather to develop spiritual strength and moral integrity, as indeed one could learn from Rabbi Yochanan ben Zakai (*Baba Batra,* p. 60/b and Gittin, p. 58). Later, during 1944 the term *Sho'ah* was used for psychological studies of the reaction of children to the mass annihilation of European Jewry, carried out by the "Seminar on Psychology and Medical Social Pedagogy" under Shneerson's supervision (cf. *op. cit.* p. 104 ff).

Methodologically it might be useful to analyse the current use of the term *Sho'ah* in Hebrew scholarship and literature in the light of two different yet complementary hermeneutical approaches: critical semantical hermeneutics such as by Emilio Betti (cf. *Die Hermeneutik als allgemeine Methodik der Geisteswissenschaften,* J.B.C. Mohr, Tübingen, 1962), on the one hand, and existential hermeneutics such as by Hans-Georg Gadamer (*Wahrheit und Methode,* 2nd edition, J.B.C. Mohr, Tübingen, 1965, part II, pp. 162–360), on the other. Betti strongly objects to an excess of subjectivity in the hermeneutical interpretation of texts or concepts. Obviously the existential interpretation of traditional texts or of concepts derived from historical sources, must necessarily involve an application to the present. Moreover, following the analytical studies of Betti and Wolfhart Pannenberg, it would seem that the very structure of hermeneutics requires a constant renewal of the interpreted "meaning" (*Sinn*, or *Hora'at-Davar* and *Muvan* in Hebrew) through ever changing "explication" (*Deutung*, or *Perush* and *Be'ur* in Hebrew) of the text. Yet in contradistinction to what critically has been called the subjectivism of Martin Heidegger and, following him, Gadamer, Betti warns against blurring the original meaning (here in the sense of *Bedeutung* or in Jewish tradition *Ka Mashma Lan*). Accordingly the verbal meaning of the explicated text or concept should remain consistent with its original implications, though not necessarily identical, as E.D. Hirsch Jr. would have it. Hans-Georg Gadamer, on the other hand, emphasizes that contemporary motivations and forms of "understanding" (here similar to the term *Verstehen* in Dilthey's teachings) in the interpretation of historical texts are not only legitimate but rather necessary and unavoidable for the continuous development of tradition. Man's use of concepts and his interpretation of texts are necessarily structured by his own existential presuppositions (cf. also Rudolf Bultmann in *Existence and Faith,* ed. by Schubert M. Ogden, Hodder and Stoughton, London, 1961, pp. 289–296), while these presuppositions themselves are rooted in the past, in transmitted tradition (*Überlieferung*, or *Massoret* and *Morasha* in Hebrew), i.e. in history as experienced in semantic forms of expression.

It is in this analytical framework that the current use of the term *Sho'ah* can perhaps be better understood. Semantically the term *Sho'ah* has remained close to its verbals roots in biblical language and symbolism, while existentially its contemporary interpretations have added historical and personal dimensions to the theological meaning of the biblical sources (cf. the "neo-Midrashic" hermeneutics to Elie Wiesel's Sinai-Holocaust comparison by Emil L. Fackenheim, *God's Presence in History,* Harper Torchbook Edition, New York, 1972, p. 84 ff.). In the prophetic literature, such as Isaiah VI:11, X:3, XLVII:11, and Zephania I:15, the term *Sho'ah* is used in order to give expression to threatening danger stemming from the surrounding nations, from the Assyrian conqueror or the hordes of Scythian invaders; *Sho'ah* is also a key word in the ode on the humiliation of Babylon. Job XXX:14, Proverbs I:27, III:25 and Psalms XXXV: 8, LXIII:10 use the term *Sho'ah* in order to articulate distress, anguish, desolation, disaster, destruction, as reflected less in history and more in the realm of one's personal experience. Several of the major traditional exegetes, such as Rashi and Radak, have enriched the meaning of *Sho'ah* by interpreting it in terms of *Ḥurban* i.e. "catastrophic destruction," as indeed we can find in Hebrew and Yiddish writings before the concept *Sho'ah* became generally accepted. Also, traditional exegesis described *Sho'ah* as darkness, devastation or emptiness. All biblical meanings of the term *Sho'ah* clearly imply Divine judgement and retribution.

At this point, the rather authentic, i.e. symbolic or even literal use, of the Biblical term *Sho'ah* undergoes a structural transformation in modern Hebrew. While religious thought tries to preserve textual consistency (cf. Norman Lamm, "Teaching the Holocaust," *Forum*, No. 1 (24), Jerusalem, 1976, pp. 51–60, also Norman Lamm's lecture "Transmitting the Teaching of the Holocaust," Address to UOJCA Convention, November 30, 1974, Boca Raton, Fla.), existential and historical thought develops non-biblical and non-theological forms of interpretation. The biblical meaning of *Sho'ah* is rooted in strict theological structures of *Verstehen*, such as the causal relationship of sin and punishment, commandment and reward, divine revelation in history and divine providence in one's personal experience. The existential and historical meaning of *Sho'ah* implies metaphysical doubt, reconsideration of the validity of man's rational faculties, sometimes even personal indulgence in despair.

Thus, from an analytical point of view, the current use of the term *Sho'ah* represents a new phase in the methodological development of hermeneutics in the modern era. At this point, the beginnings of modern hermeneutics acquire new relevance. J.J. Rambach already in 1723 differentiated between three hermeneutical faculties: *Subtilitas Intelligendi* i.e. "Understanding" (*Verstehen, or Binah-Lehavin* in Hebrew); *Subtilitas Explicandi,* i.e. "Explication" (*Deutung, Auslegung* or *Perush, Be'ur* in Hebrew), and in the tradition of the Pietists, influenced by Friedrich Christoph Oetinger, *Subtilitas Applicandi,* i.e. "Application" (*Anwendung or Hanhagat-Adam* in Jewish tradition.

The semantic use of the term *Sho'ah* as we have seen, fulfills an additional interpretative function—that of transformation; it transforms an unexplicable historical event into a phenomenon relatable through the power of language.

The Place of the Holocaust in Contemporary History[1]

Yehuda Bauer
(HEBREW UNIVERSITY)

In recent discussions on the place of the Holocaust in the history of our century, there has been a clear tendency to find a way to reconcile the concept of its uniqueness with the idea of its universal importance. Most observers feel that both concepts are valid and indeed can hardly exist without each other. However, such attempts rarely link definitions with historical analyses of what the Holocaust actually was. It is therefore essential to devote attention first of all to questions of definition.

The Holocaust is the name now customarily used in English for the planned total annihilation of the Jewish people, and the actual murder of six million of them at the hands of the Nazis and their auxiliaries.[2] What sets the Holocaust apart from other crimes committed by Nazis, or by others, against many millions of other people, was neither the number of victims nor the way of their murder, nor the proportion of the murdered compared to the total number of the targeted victims. Many more Russians were murdered by the Nazis than Jews. In past history there have been cases in which a much higher proportion of a given community was annihilated than the thirty-five percent of the Jewish people that died in the Holocaust. And, while most of the victims of the gas chambers were Jews, some were not—Gypsies, Soviet POWs and others.

What made the Holocaust different from other cases of what is loosely termed "genocide" was the motivation behind it. It is perfectly clear that Nazi ideology saw in the Jew the non-human antithesis of what it considered to be the human ideal: the German Aryan. In the controversy regarding the problem of whether there was a Nazi ideology or not, it seems obvious that there were some tenets that were generally held by the Nazi elite, whether or not they constitute an ideology. Above all, there was the Manichean approach that saw in the world victory of the Germanic Aryans not only a geopolitical necessity for the survival of the Germanic race and its peoples, but a precondition for the continued existence of humankind. At the other pole stood the Jew, a Satanic element and a parasitic one, both weak and contemptible, and yet also immensely powerful and absolutely evil.

The Jew, though he looked human, was not. He controlled most of the world through his control of both capitalism and Russian Bolshevism; only Germany and, to an extent, England were still outside his grasp. His victory was imminent, and with it the destruction not only of Germany, but of all humanity. Germany's war against its enemies was therefore waged for two complementary reasons: the "positive" one of ensuring the victory of the Germanic peoples in Europe, and then in the entire world; and the "negative" one, of defeating the Jewish Satan and his world government. The former was unattainable except through the latter.[3]

An analysis of the events leading up to World War II and of the war itself shows that the expansionist policies of Nazi Germany were motivated primarily not by concrete German interests—political or strategic or economic—but rather by ideological considerations. These were expressed often enough in no unmistakable terms, but some historians tend to ignore documents that do not fit into their preconceived picture. Nazi Germany sought "Lebensraum" for the Germanic peoples (primarily, but by no means solely, for the Germans) so that they might control Europe and the world; in order to do so, war had to be waged against enemies, who were united by the arch-enemy that lurked behind all of them: the Jew. The anti-Jewish struggle was one of the two inextricably connected motivations which underlay the Nazi decision to wage World War II. The struggle against the Jews was a crucial part of the Nazi eschatology, an absolutely central pillar of their world-view, and not just one part of their program. The future of humanity depended on their "victory" over the Jew. This pseudo-religious motivation made their anti-Jewish actions unprecedented. There could be no exceptions to the murder of Jews, once that was decided upon, because Satan had to be extirpated completely, or else he would arise again. Anyone with three Jewish grandparents was sentenced to death, and the principle was that anyone with two Jewish grandparents should either be killed or sterilized. What was unique in the Holocaust was the totality of its ideology and of its translation of abstract thought into planned, logically implemented total murder. More than that—it became a central part of the rationale for a total war that caused some 35 million casualties[4] in the six-year long struggle. That is the uniqueness of the Holocaust.

What is the universality of that experience?

Mass murder of noncombatants in times of war or of quasi-peace has been with us since time immemorial. Massacres of civilian populations by conquering or marauding armies or police can be documented for most of human history. The very concept of mass murder, however, is highly problematical. When does murder become mass murder? With ten victims? Or a hundred? Or a thousand? When somebody causes mass starvation and epidemics—is that mass murder? When masses of prisoners are killed, is that on the same level as the murder of civilians? When, in the course of World War I, masses of soldiers were killed by gas, was that mass murder, or an acceptable taking of life in the course of armed action?

A detailed comparative analysis of such occurrences in past centuries is a task for the future. But, it may be argued, is not this all too scholastic? If a person was murdered at Verdun by German gas, at Dresden by British bombers, at Auschwitz by gassing, at Hiroshima by atomic fallout or at My Lai by an American bullet—or in the thirteenth century at Isfahan by a Mongol knife—it is all the same. Or is it? We do, after all, differentiate between different types of good. We know that there is a difference, however hard it may be to define, between helping an old lady across the street, and rescuing that same old lady from a burning building. We try to differentiate between different types of—in this case—socially commendable action which we call morally good, because we accept the Kantian approach which would see in such action an example to be, ideally, universally followed. In order that that may be so, we grade and differentiate. In effect, we usually do the same with actions that most of us would consider to be evil. In human history, judicial norms have clearly differentiated between crimes according to socially accepted criteria of what was seen as more serious or less so. The argument presented here is that the same consideration applies to different types of arbitrary life-taking. True, it makes, perhaps, no difference to the victim of My Lai or Auschwitz or Verdun, but it does make a great difference to the survivor.

Let us then try to differentiate. After a relatively civilized nineteenth century, in the course of which "only" tens of thousands of soldiers died in the many wars that took place between 1815 and the American Civil War, methods of more efficient mass killing brought about an increase in what one might call the level of brutalization. This process reached its apogee in World War I, with its hecatombs of soldier-victims. But, one might argue, they died in the course of war, when ordinary social norms do not apply to the armies which butcher armed men. The murder of civilians in large numbers was the exception rather than the rule in 1914–1918. The most obvious such case was of course the destruction of the Armenian people in Anatolia, and we will return to this case later.

Whether one considers the murder of millions of soldiers, by more and more sophisticated means, mass murder or an unfortunate act of war—and it is suggested here that the former seems to be the more appropriate—it is clear that George Mosse's analysis of the First World War as a catalyst of aggressions manifesting themselves in a general brutalization of modern civilization is very convincing.[5] Surely the major point is that while mass murder was not the norm in a society which prided itself on its 'progress,' the First World War constituted a watershed event after which mass murder first becomes acceptable, or perhaps acceptable once again. One can point to the events of the Russian Civil War, including the murder of perhaps a hundred thousand Jews, as an example; or to the frightful wars that rocked China in the twenties, even prior to the Japanese invasion of 1931. The Holocaust, surely, is unimaginable without this shift in attitudes to mass destruction of human life.

What, then, is the relation of mass murder to what we know as 'genocide'? Much has been written on the origin of the term and its meaning. The legal mind has, of course, no difficulty in defining a term that has received the sanction of the proposed United Nations Convention on Genocide. As approved on 9 December 1948, it reads as follows: "In the present Convention, genocide means any of the following acts committed with intent to destroy, in *whole* or in *part* (our emphasis added), a national, ethnical or religious group, as such:

(a) Killing members of the group; (b) Causing serious bodily or mental harm to members of the group; (c) Deliberately inflicting on the group conditions of life calculated to bring about its physical destruction in whole or in part; (d) Imposing measures intended to prevent births within the group; (e) Forcibly transferring children of the group to another group". The wording seems to indicate that genocide is meant, in the extreme case, to be an act designed to destroy a group totally. However, a group can be totally destroyed without killing all of its members, so that the planned total physical annihilation of a group would appear not to be necessarily included in this definition.

These definitions followed those offered by the inventor of the term, Raphael Lemkin. Lemkin, in early 1943, under the influence of the information received from Europe on the Holocaust as well as on the persecution of other nationalities, formulated a contradictory definition. On the one hand, he defined genocide as the total "extermination" of a people; on the other hand, he defined it as extreme deprivation, destruction of educational institutions, interference in religious life, general denationalization and even moral poisoning by the introduction (for example) of pornography. In effect, we have here two definitions, which are obviously mutually exclusive: one cannot interfere in the religious life or destroy the educational institutions of a people who has been exterminated. Nor does it make sense to see in these actions steps necessarily leading to extermination, because in the case of many of the peoples under Nazi rule this did not happen. The first definition fits the case of the Jews during the war, while the other is suited to the fate of the Slav nations, for instance, under the Nazis.[6] It is here suggested that Lemkin's second definition be called 'genocide'—whatever the United Nations have to say about the matter; while the first be called, for want of a better term, Holocaust, or more accurately *Shoah* (Catastrophe), using the Hebrew term, which is more appropriate.

Lemkin's secondary definition of his term does indeed fit the fate of the Czechs, the Poles, the Serbs and others. Their institutions of self-government were destroyed; the social cohesion of these nations was disrupted; their intelligentsia largely killed; their churches harassed; the masses reduced to near-starvation. But only one people was sentenced to total and absolute annihilation: the Jews.

Some historians reject this description and maintain that the Nazi intention was to destroy all the members of certain Slav nations, such as the Czech and the Polish. This was simply not so. Because of the importance of this issue of differentiating between evil and evil, it is important to examine this problem more closely.

As far as the Slavic nations were concerned, documentary evidence makes it clear that the intention of the Nazis was to kill the leadership, to deport a part of these peoples, and to enslave the rest. There never was a plan for the physical mass annihilation of any one of these nations. To argue that Nazi policies would logically have led to such total annihilation policies has no basis in fact, and is a hypothesis at best. It is illogical, too, because the Third Reich needed millions of slave laborers, and a policy seems to have been evolving to turn the Slav peoples into a permanent population of Helots to serve their German masters.

Basic to the way the Nazis saw these things was the need to reconcile the racial, the economic and the political-strategic aims of a future Germanic world empire. In the writings of Nazi officials and ideologists alike, however, the racial-ideological element clearly dominates.

The Nazis viewed the Slavic peoples as Aryans, albeit of a lower racial order.[7] The Czechs, Poles, Ukrainians, Byelorussians and the Russians fell into this category. In addition, the Nazis had to contend with the three non-Slavic peoples in the Baltic states: the Lithuanians, the Latvians and the Estonians.[8]

"Nordic" elements among these populations were to be identified—a racial survey, based largely on external characteristics, was to be conducted—and those found racially akin to Germans would be germanized, voluntarily or by force. This meant, among other things, the kidnaping of racially "valuable" children, to be raised in Germany. Nordic leadership elements among the Poles, the Czechs and the Russians would be eliminated, because they might provide rallying points for anti-German resistance movements. The rest of the population was to be divided, part to be exiled to the East and part to form the slave labor force needed to make life bearable for the master race.

In the period before the Barbarossa Plan took shape (the plan to invade the USSR), Nazi planning for the future had to contend with the fact that one could not evict the existing Slav populations—the Czechs and the Poles—who were now living in territories controlled by the Germans. In a discussion that took place on 17 October 1939, Hitler declared that in the General-gouvernement the Nazi officials were to ensure "a low standard of living. We want only to get labor from there."[9] He repeated this view on 2 October 1940, when he said that he wanted to establish the General-gouvernement as "a Polish reservation, a big Polish labor camp."[10]

Prior to the German invasion of the USSR, therefore, we find the main lines of Nazi policy towards the Slav peoples clearly defined. It was indeed a program of genocide—slavery, removal of leadership groups by murder and intimidation, germanization and deportation—a program intended to destroy these nations as nations; it was not a program of holocaust: a planned, total physical annihilation.

After the decision to invade the USSR was taken, a new situation arose. In the time span between early 1941 and the end of 1942, we find the development of plans dealing with the future treatment of East European populations after a German victory. These plans revolved around the so-called Generalplan Ost, a first draft of which was submitted to Himmler at the end of 1941.[11] Meyer-Hetling dealt mainly with the problem of resettling the eastern areas that Himmler wanted cleared of the Slavic populations. Of the forty-five million "foreigners" *(Fremdvölkische)* who were in these areas, which included the Baltic states, Poland and most of the western part of European Russia, all of White Russia and the Ukraine, thirty-one million were to be deported and the rest germanized. It did not, however, go into the details, as its attention was focused on the resettlement of Germans and other "Teutonics" in the areas to be cleared. If we want to follow Nazi plans regarding the indigenous populations, we have to turn to two main sources: the comments on the "Generalplan" submitted to Himmler by

Dr. Erhard Wetzel, and Heydrich's speeches on the "Czech question."[12]

Wetzel saw considerable difficulties in the plans for germanization *(Eindeutschung)*, mainly because of the lack of German manpower to settle areas from which other populations would be removed. He also foresaw grave political difficulties in separating the populations, giving favorable treatment to one part and deporting the other.

Regarding the Baltic peoples, Wetzel opposed deportation by force, lest those whom the Germans hoped to germanize realize "that such a forcible evacuation would probably bring with it the demise *(Untergang)* of their brothers and sisters." Wetzel therefore proposed a program of more or less voluntary removal of the "Ungermanizables," the motivation to be the opportunity for the evacuees to become the middle class in eastern areas ruled, but not settled, by Germans. If, says Wetzel, we can use these racially unsuitable people to save German manpower in the East, we would have gained a great advantage from both the 'racial-political' and also the political viewpoint."[13] In contrast to the plans for the Poles and the Czechs, this strategy envisaged the elimination of the Baltic nations as such and the use of their members for German power strategies.[14]

As for the Poles, he thought that most of them were not fit for germanization, and would have to be deported to western Siberia. Dispersed among the local population there, they would form an anti-Russian element. The transport of seven or eight hundred thousand people each year for the next thirty years would ensure the realization of this plan.

"It is obvious that the Polish question cannot be solved in such a way that one would liquidate the Poles in the same manner as the Jews. Such a solution of the Polish question would be a standing accusation against the German people into the far distant future and would deprive us of all sympathy, especially as the other neighboring nations would have to assume that they would be treated similarly when the time came."[15]

The Ukrainians would be concentrated in the northern and eastern parts of the Ukraine, and there be used for the Ukrainization of the considerable Russian minority. Wetzel opposed the deportation of the 'ungermanizable' *(nicht eindeutschungsfähige)* Ukrainians to Siberia. Those who were 'germanizable' would be treated in the same way as similar groups among the other peoples. As far as the Byelorussians were concerned, Wetzel believed they should mostly be left where they were, to be used as laborers. Many of the groups which were sound socially could be used as permanent slaves in Germany, and replace the South and Southeast Europeans who were then, in 1942, streaming to Germany and who were racially farther removed than the Slavs from the master race.

The main problem as he saw it was the Russian question. A leading German intellectual, Prof. Dr.phil. Wolfgang Abel, of the Kaiser Wilhelm Institute for Anthropology at Berlin-Dahlem, had suggested that either the Russians be exterminated *in toto* (the term used was '*Ausrottung*'), or that the Nordic part of the Russian people be selected for germanization (I could not find out what the professor intended to do with the non-germanized Russians, but it is not very difficult to guess what he thought). Wetzel rejected Abel's proposal: "The policy proposed by Abel, to liquidate the Russian people, is impossible, not only because it is hardly possible to implement it, but also for political and economic reasons." In other words, it would be technically difficult, and then of course Germany needed the Russians for labor. The political difficulties would be the same as with the Poles. Instead, Wetzel proposed the subdivision of the Russian area into administrative units independent of each other in order to foster separatism. He also suggested giving Finnic and Turkic groups autonomy within these areas, and he joined a number of others in the Nazi hierarchy who advocated a policy of discouragement of population growth by various quasi-medical and political-hygienic measures. He mentioned that the racial experts of Nazi Germany had discovered among the Russians a so-called 'primitive europide' race, which had not been taken into account by Hans Günther. There were also many Nordics among the Russians. These should be germanizable and/or should be used in the Reich for labor.

Himmler's response to these ideas was generally positive.[16] They fitted well into the conception which he shared with Hitler of a future Pax Germanica in Eastern Europe—apart of course from the general injunction that anyone in the least opposed to the Germans should be immediately shot.[17]

For our purpose the above considerations seem to be sufficient. They show that there was an explicit rejection of ideas of total mass annihilation—not, of course for moral reasons—and instead the older ideas of a destruction of nations as such, their enslavement, forced germanization and deportation, in different proportions for the different nations, was to be adopted.

As far as the Czechs are concerned, we have Heydrich's speeches to tell us what the Nazi plans were. We must use the Czechs as Helots, Heydrich said on 2 October 1941.[18] On 2 February 1942, Heydrich further suggested that the removal of non-germanizable elements should be camouflaged as labor outside the country, with those sent for labor being granted the right to bring their families.[19]

What emerges quite clearly from Heydrich's speeches is the same line of policy as that favored by Wetzel towards the Poles and others: genocide, not holocaust. There was not only no plan for the physical annihilation of all or some of these nations, but there was an explicit rejection of such ideas by those who had the decision-making power.

However, the case of the Gypsies was different again. Nobody really knows the precise number of Romany people living in Europe in 1939. Some estimates put the number of Romanies murdered by the Nazis at 810,000[20] and their number today at 6 million in Europe, and 10 million in the entire world.[21] The first figure can hardly be proved, and both are probably considerably higher than the facts would indicate. However, in sheer demonic, cold-blooded brutality, the tragedy of the Romanies is one of the most terrible indictments of the Nazis. The fact that their fate is hardly ever mentioned, and that the mutilated Romany nation continues to be vilified and persecuted to this day should put all their European host nations to shame.

Branded and persecuted as thieves, sorcerers and child-kidnapers, the Romanies (Gypsies) in Germany largely belonged to the Sinti and to the Lalleri in Austria. Their numbers were given in Himmler's *Runderlass* of 7 August 1941, as 28,607 in Germany, and 11,000 in Austria.[22] Of those in Germany, 2,652 were "persons wandering about in Gypsy manner."[23] The figures for those murdered are unclear, but we know that 13,080 were deported to Auschwitz (this does not include non-German Romanies), and 5,007 Austrian Lalleri were deported to Lodz, and murdered at Chelmno. Three thousand more Austrian Romanies were put into concentration camps, and two and a half thousand deported to Poland, mostly into Jewish ghettoes. Most of these probably perished. When we add up all these victims, we arrive at 23,587, of the 39,607 total indicated above, most of whom died. We shall see that 14,017 Sinti and Lalleri were exempted by Himmler. The figures seem to tally.

What was the principle according to which the Gypsies were treated? Romanies (Gypsies) were considered "*artfremd*" (radically alien). The 1935 Nuremberg Laws really applied to them as well, as the two Nazi experts, Wilhelm Stuckart and Hans Globke made clear.[24] As they were considered to be asocial, their fate was affected by Himmler's order of 14 December 1937, to arrest 'asocials', defined as persons "who, without being criminals, endanger the community by their asocial behavior."[25] Further explications of that decree (4 April 1938) mentioned "e.g., beggars, vagabonds (Gypsies), prostitutes, etc." As this seemed to be a bit too extreme, Himmler issued a clarification on 1 June 1938, which included among the "asocials" "Gypsies and persons wandering about in Gypsy manner, when they do not show any desire for regular work or when they are the subject of criminal proceedings."[26]

Himmler's own attitude to the Romanies was ambivalent. In his *Runderlass* of 8 December 1938, he stated that in accordance with experience gathered in fighting the "Gypsy scourge" *(Zigeunerplage)* and with the results of racial-biological research, the Gypsy problem would be solved in the light of the "inner characteristic of that race" *("aus dem Wesen dieser Rasse heraus").* "For the final solution *(endgültige Lösung der Zigeunerfrage)* of the Gypsy problem it is therefore evidently essential to treat the racially pure Gypsies and the mixed breeds [*Mischlinge*] separately." In his explanation of the correct attitude to the Gypsy question, Himmler stated quite clearly the obvious dilemma of the racialist struggling between theoretical racialism, which would accord an equal status to all pure human races, and the variety adopted by the Nazis, which, of course, established a hierarchy led by the Nordic Aryans: "It must be established as a basic thesis in the fight against the Gypsy scourge that the German *Volk* also respects every race that is alien to its *völkish* essence . . . [and advocates] the racial separation of Gypsydom from the German *Volk,* and thus the prevention of race mixing and finally the ordering of the lives of racially pure and mixed-breed Gypsies [becomes necessary]."[27] Himmler did indeed try to solve the Gypsy problem in this way. His "Regelung" of 13 October 1942, separated the "racially pure" Sinti from the rest, and assimilated to them "good *Mischlinge* in the Gypsy sense" *(im zigeunerischen Sinne gute Mischlinge)* who should be again led towards Gypsydom *(sollen einzelnen reinrassigen Sinte-Zigeunersippen wieder zugefürt werden).* In line with Nazi policies, nine Romanies were appointed, who would be responsible for the organization of the segregated "pure" and "assimilated" Sinti and Lalleri and lead them in a Nazi-approved non-sedentary Gypsy life. This indeed appears to have happened, and 14,017 Romanies were exempted.

The fate of the others was eventually sealed, in close connection with the other racial policies of the Nazis. On 6 December 1942, an SS order established that the non-protected Gypsies should be sent to Auschwitz, except for ex-Wehrmacht soldiers, socially adapted Gypsies, and armament workers. For these, sterilization was to be provided. Prior to that, Gypsy soldiers were to have been dismissed from the army.

The execution of the December order was harsher than the order itself. In a "Schnellbrief" of 29 January 1943, the SS provided for the sending of Gypsy *Mischlinge*, Gypsies of the Rom tribes (presumably those in the Reich area) and "members of Gypsy clans of Balkan origin who are not of German blood" into concentration camps.[28]

In effect, we have limited knowledge as yet of what exactly happened, beyond the fact that two-thirds of the German Romanies were murdered, many of them (2,897) gassed in Auschwitz, on 2 August 1944. We do know that many of the survivors were put into German uniforms in the last period of the war and deployed in punitive battalions, on dangerous missions and the like. Others were sent to be slaves in armament factories. We have even less knowledge of what happened to the large Gypsy populations in the Balkans and in Eastern Europe. But it is known that Einsatzgruppe D under Otto Ohlendorf murdered all the Romanies it could find in its area of operations. Many Polish Gypsies were killed where they were—in forests, on the roads, etc. At least fifty (and possibly ninety) thousand Romanies were killed in Yugoslavia. But despite pioneer efforts by some writers, we are still in quest of a detailed description of the fate of the Romany people in Europe as a whole.[29]

And yet, what stands out very clearly are both the parallels and the differences in the Nazi treatment of the Gypsies and the Jews. These two peoples shared certain characteristics in the Nazi period: they both lacked a national territory and basic cultural differences separated them (each people in its own way) from their European host nations. The Nazi technique of dealing with both was similar, not only bureaucratically (they were handled by the same SS organizations) but also ideologically (Himmler applied the same racialist theories to them). The difference is indeed of great significance—Gypsies who were racially "pure" in Nazi eyes, or could be re-assimilated to "gypsydom" were spared. This could be done because the Nazis could live with another, albeit inferior, race, provided there was no 'mixed breeding'. Therefore the '*Mischlinge*', but not the "pure" Gypsies, had to die. The murder even included 2,652 Germans who lived as Gypsies.

With the Jews, only quarter-Jews were relatively safe, because, contrary to the Gypsy case, Jews were not just another race, but the anti-race, Satan, bacteria, contaminators of culture, and mortal enemies of the Aryan peoples. Gypsies were just another inferior race, to be dealt with according to the rules of Nazi racial hygiene. The murder of innocent humans was the same; we are here interested in the motivation, and its implications, and these differed.

Let us now return to the discussion of genocide. The contradiction inherent in Lemkin's original definition became even clearer in the resolution passed by the U.N. General Assembly in December 1946. There, as we have seen, genocide is defined as "a denial of the right of existence of entire groups." There is an obvious difference between the denial of the right to exist and actual total murder.

In any case, the U.N. Convention is a purely arbitrary document, arrived at as a result of heated discussions between delegates of member states at the U.N.[30] There is actually no clear definition of genocide, because such a definition would have to emerge inductively, and not, as has in fact been the case, deductively—i.e., as a result of politically and ideologically motivated pressures. Lemkin did indeed try to define inductively: he was, naturally, affected and influenced by what he knew—in late 1942 and early 1943—of Nazi policies. He defined, as we have seen, what happened to Czechs, Poles and Serbs. When he came to discuss Jews, he seems to have been unable to comprehend fully what was happening to them. It seems that cognitively, he "knew" that they were being totally annihilated. But this was not something that could be accepted, or grasped. He therefore left his "first" definition—that of total "extermination"—in, and then went on to describe something else.

An argument evolved as to the correctness of including the destruction of political groups in the definition of genocide. One point to be remembered is, it seems, that political associations are voluntary, and the destruction of political groups is conditioned by the decision of the intended victims to stick to their convictions—with the exception, perhaps, of the leadership elites. Social Democrats and Communists were not killed in Germany, by and large. Millions of them recanted, or kept their views to themselves. Even leaders were—in the thirties—often arrested, and after a while, released from concentration camps. Many survived in the camps, having become part of the *Prominenz* in them. The other point is that in the destruction of political groups, the annihilation of their families is the exception rather than the rule. The destruction of political groups, whether by Nazis, Soviets, Chilean dictators, or Chinese Communists, while utterly to be condemned, is not genocide, though it is true that in their motivation, political and racial issues are at times intermingled. In some cases, such as that of the Communists in Indonesia—for the most part, ethnically Chinese—total mass murder, usually including the families, was aimed at.

Genocide should really be left where the etymology places it—the destruction of racial, tribal, national or ethnic groups. Even the destruction of religious groups poses problems, because there again, religious affiliation is a voluntary act. Admittedly, there are obvious cases where the element of choice is hardly there: the Druse are a religious community, but although they define themselves as ethnically Arab, persecution of the Druse has had a clearly religio-ethnic tinge about it. Persecution of the Jews in pre-modern times had that same quality about it. The mass murder of heretics in France in the Middle Ages was intended to be total, and included the total annihilation of whole towns (Beziers), without providing much choice to the hapless inhabitants whether or not to recant. But then, the concepts of ethnic, national or racial groups were much less clear in pre-modern times than they are today. Christians saw themselves as in some sense a "nation", as did the Muslims. In the industrial era, with the rise of nationalism, religion has become increasingly more voluntary, and the persecution of religious groups more and more parallels that of political ones. It would seem, therefore, that genocide ought to be defined so as to exclude religious persecution.

We thus arrive at a much narrower definition, and it seems that one ought to concentrate on the modern era, or the last one hundred years, because pre-modern genocide cannot really be subsumed under the same category as the modern variety. Bloody massacres there undoubtedly were. Entire cities were razed to the ground (Carthage by the Romans). But this was done for political power reasons. Those who ran away were not pursued, and there seems to have been little desire to eradicate ethnic groups or cultures as such, unless there were weighty power-political reasons to do so. Modern genocide, by contrast, has two decisive characteristics: it is ideological, and it is relentless, in that it desires the disappearance of a racial, national or ethnic group as such.

A limited, and therefore, it seems, more realistic definition of genocide would therefore run somewhat as follows: the planned destruction, since the mid-nineteenth century, of a racial, national, or ethnic group as such, by the following means: (a) selective mass murder of elites or parts of the population; (b) elimination of national (racial, ethnic) culture and religious life with the intent of "denationalization"; (c) enslavement, with the same intent; (d) destruction of national (racial, ethnic) economic life, with the same intent; (e) biological decimation through the kidnaping of children, or the prevention of normal family life, with the same intent.

Genocide, as thus defined, would include the Nazi policies towards Czechs, Poles, or Gypsies, for example, and Soviet policies towards the Chechens, Volga Germans, or Tatars. It would include the policies of American settlers towards many native American tribes (Seminoles, Blackfoot, Arapaho, Apache and others), though there are cases where policies went beyond what is here defined as genocide (Nez Percé, Lakotas). It would probably also include the cases of the Hutus, the Biharis and the Ibos.

Two cases are obviously outside the definition as offered here: one is that of so-called auto-genocide, when both the perpetrators and the victims of mass murder belong to the same national group—as in the case of Cambodia, or, earlier, Stalin's anti-kulak campaign. In all such cases, the mass murder is the result of tremendous internal upheavals, and should be seen as constituting a category of its own. Understanding such tragedies will not be made easier by lumping them together with cases of genocide as here defined. The other case is that of the use of nuclear weapons. Here warfare is escalated to the mass destruction of enemy populations, but there is no intention to "denationalize". In a sense, of course, the use of nuclear weapons indicates the danger of what might be called *urbicide*, i.e., the destruction of civilized life as such, going beyond both genocide and holocaust.

We are then left with a re-statement of Lemkin's "first" definition, namely, the planned physical annihilation, for ideological or pseudo-religious reasons, of all the members of a national, ethnic or racial group. That, indeed, seems to be the true meaning of holocaust. So defined, it becomes a general term, not limited to the Jewish experience in World War II, though that experience is the most thoroughgoing to date, the only case where "holocaust" (or *"Shoah"*, as previously suggested) would appear fully applicable.

We then arrive at a kind of continuum of evil that would lead from 'mass murder' in recent times through 'genocide' to 'holocaust' (*'shoah'*). Such a continuum does not imply a value judgment as to the degree of moral condemnation, so that one could argue that 'mass murder' is in some way less reprehensible than 'genocide' or 'holocaust'. Whatever it is called in the context of our definition, any particular event of the sort we are describing will have to be put somewhere on the continuum, and may not fit precisely the three orientation points.

We would suggest that some of the most tragic events that have occurred in this century have to be placed between the terms 'genocide' and 'holocaust'. The two outstanding examples are those of the Romanies and the Armenians. The fate of the Romanies has been discussed above. Outside of Germany, there was wanton and near-total, but not very precisely organized, murder. The motivation was social rather than political; in Germany, racism operated almost the other way: it tended to save a remnant (one-third) of the Romany people. Escape from the general fate was made possible either by settled status, or by disappearance into the crowd of non-Romanies. We do not know of any special hunts for individual Romanies—it was the wandering groups that were the hardest hit. The massive destruction went beyond selective mass murder and therefore beyond our definition of genocide, but paradoxically, in Germany itself no attempt was made to destroy the life-style of the protected 'racially pure' remnant. This, at least, was the case in theory; in practice, things were different. We would therefore argue that what befell the European Romanies under Nazi rule has to be placed on our continuum between genocide and holocaust.

The case of the Armenians is grimmer still. There had been massacres of Armenians in 1894–1896, including the murder of three thousand Armenians burnt in the Armenian cathedral at Urfa on 28/29 December 1895. The total number of victims at that time has been estimated at three hundred thousand. Although the Armenian nationalists were welcomed among the Young Turks who gained control over Turkey in 1908, the triumvirate of Talaat, Enver and Djamal which gained control in 1913, finally broke with the Armenians. Massacres took place in 1909 (Adana) and 1912.

The Armenians in Turkey numbered, according to some sources, 1,850,000 in 1914. They were a Christian nationality, mostly peasants, but with a strong middle class and a significant stratum of intellectuals who played an important role in Ottoman society. Ostensibly, the Young Turks wanted to eliminate the Armenians in order to create a Pan-Turkic empire extending into Central Asia. The Armenians were an important element in the population of eastern Anatolia, which was regarded by the Turks as part of the Ottoman heartland. Frustration over the loss of the Ottoman Empire in Europe, and a resulting extreme nationalism played their part. The instigators and organizers of the murder were intellectuals who had seized the government. They utilized a war situation, and used primitive tribesmen and criminals, driven by sadistic instincts, greed and lust, to aid in mass murder. Religious factors may have been part of the general background, and appear from testimonies to have partially motivated the execution of government policy. However, the Young Turks themselves were not only secularist, but anti-religious. Post factum, Turkish apologists argued that the massacres were the result of an Armenian rebellion, or a threat of a rebellion. This is clearly incorrect.

Starting on 24/25 April 1915, with the arrest of two hundred and thirty five top Armenian intellectuals and leaders, the massacres spread in Anatolia, and lasted until early 1916. Armenian soldiers in the Turkish army were first disarmed, then used for slave labor, and then murdered. Women, children and the aged were "evacuated" from their villages and towns. En route, a high proportion were murdered, in part by Kurdish and Circassian tribesmen. The rest were brought to the Syrian desert, and there most of them died.[31]

It is very difficult to arrive at an agreed figure of the number of victims. The German expert on the Armenian question, Johannes Lepsius, says that 1.4 million Armenians were deported. Others put the number of the victims at between eight hundred thousand and over a million. The massacres were committed by central planning and the use of modern technology (the telegraph, the rail transportation of troops, modern propaganda and disinformation techniques, modern bureaucratic procedures). No contradiction appears to exist between that and the use of the most primitive methods—killing with clubs and knives, mass rapes, the denial of water and food.

The decisive document appears to be a cable of the ruling Turkish group to the provincial governors of 28 February 1915: "Jemiyet has decided to free the fatherland from the covetousness of this accursed race and to bear upon their shoulder the stigma that might malign the Ottoman history. Unable to forget the disgrace and bitterness of the past, filled with vengeful episodes, Jemiyet, hopeful about its future, has decided to exterminate all Armenians living in Turkey, without allowing a single one to remain alive."[32] At the trial of the killer of Talaat in Berlin in 1921, another cable by Talaat to the prefect of Aleppo, of 9 September 1915, was quoted: "The right of the Armenians to live and work on Turkish territory is totally abrogated. The government, which assumes all responsibility in this respect, has ordered not to leave even children in their cribs. In several provinces the execution has been evidenced. Out of reasons unknown to us, exceptions were made with (sic) persons who were allowed to stay in Aleppo, instead of being sent to the place of exile, thus causing new difficulties for the government. Make women and children, whoever they may be, leave, without giving any reason, even those who cannot walk, and do not give the population any grounds for defending them . . . Wipe out every Armenian from the eastern province whom you can find on your territory" (text quoted as in the original).[33]

The parallels with the Holocaust are too obvious to require elucidation. Due to the corrupt and disorderly nature of the Young Turkish regime, some Armenians survived: women were taken to Turkish harems or carried off by tribesmen; children were kidnaped and brought up as Turks; some people were left in villages, and there were small numbers who survived the death marches to the Syrian desert. In Istanbul and Izmir relatively large numbers of Armenians were spared, largely because of the proximity of foreign representatives. But, clearly, the intention was the planned, total annihilation of the Armenian nation in Turkey. This is the closest parallel to the Holocaust.

However, there are differences. They become evident in the above quote from Talaat Bey of 28 February 1915. The perpetrators announced that they had decided "to bear upon their shoulders the stigma that might malign Ottoman history." In other words, they were part of a moral world that rejected their deed, but for political-ideological reasons they decided to persist in it nevertheless. They saw themselves, no doubt, as Turkish patriots, and saw the murder of the Armenians as in line with the interests of the Turkish people; but they also knew that the murder could not be justified by appealing to national interest, and they took the responsibility on themselves for something they had difficulty in justifying. Compare this to Himmler's well-known speech at Posen on 4 October 1943: speaking of the "extermination of the Jewish people," he called it "an unwritten and never-to-be-written page of glory in our history." Himmler accepted petit-bourgeois morality (in the same speech he insisted that SS murderers must not take any Jewish property); he prided himself on the SS having "stayed decent" and "suffered no harm to our inner being, our soul, our character."[34] At the same time, he literally turned accepted morality upside-down: instead of 'thou shalt not kill', he decreed—'thou shalt kill'. Killing the Jewish enemy was a moral command, not as in the Armenian case, a practical "necessity" known to be in contrast to standards accepted even by the initiators of the murder.

This consideration is linked to another, perhaps more obvious one: the Nazis saw the Jews as *the* central problem of world history. Upon its solution depended the future of mankind. Unless International Jewry was defeated, human civilization would not survive. The attitude towards the Jews had in it important elements of pseudo-religion. There was no such motivation present in the Armenian case; Armenians were to be annihilated for power-political reasons, and in Turkey only. No anti-Armenian ideology developed in the writings of the Turkish leadership, and the Armenians were not seen as a universal threat. The motivation, in other words, was different in the two cases.

The differences between the holocaust and the Armenian massacres are less important than the similarities—and even if the Armenian case is not seen as a holocaust in the extreme form which it took towards the Jews, it is certainly the nearest thing to it. On the continuum, the two events stand next to each other.

The two definitions of holocaust indicate the dialectical tension between the universal and the particularistic aspects of that watershed event: holocaust has to be seen as a general category, as the outermost pole on a continuum of evil; yet at the same time, as an event which has (so far) overtaken Jews alone—for reasons which have to be explained in part by reference to the specific nature of Jewish history and to the inter-relationship of Jew and gentile throughout the ages. Being general, as well as specific, the term holocaust carries with it the implication that, because it happened once, it may happen again—to any group if the conditions are right.

Unless both parts of this duality are borne in mind, one runs the risk of making misleading and false comparisons between the Holocaust and other events. Any serious attempt to determine the contemporary significance of the Holocaust must start from the awareness that historical analogies usually distort and that history does not repeat itself.

Indeed, because political leaders, in particular, have recently indulged so frequently in the kind of nonsense that equates every act of war, every isolated terror attack, with Auschwitz, Belsen and Dachau,[15] it is not out of place here to point out that there has not been a holocaust since World War II. Such equations are certainly misleading, and often dangerous.

Moreover, Jews are no less vulnerable to the trap of false analogy. Two different kinds of historical error frequently recur in Jewish thought on the Holocaust.

A number of Jewish religious authorities have said that the Holocaust is not essentially new, and represents a continuation of the persecution which has plagued the Jews for two thousand years. The need to integrate the Holocaust into the tradition of Jewish martyrology is understandable from a religious point of view, but it is historically erroneous. For one thing, never before was there a plan to annihilate the Jewish people everywhere. Persecutions were limited in area—Jews usually had the possibility of escaping elsewhere. The attacks and expulsions were the result of local social, religious, economic or political tensions. And the Jews had, as a rule, the option of abjuring their faith—sometimes only temporarily—and if they chose to do so, their lives were usually spared. There was never a persecution that saw in the total annihilation of the Jewish people a panacea for the ills of humanity. In that sense, Nazi anti-Semitism represented a new departure, because while the elements on which it built were familiar, their combination was qualitatively unprecedented, total and murderous. From a Jewish historical perspective, therefore, the Holocaust, while containing many elements familiar from the long history of Jewish martyrdom, is unique.

The second type of false analogy increasingly common among Jews involves references to the Holocaust in the attempt to draw "lessons" for application to topical political situations. For example, it is absurd to compare (as some have done) the plea of a democratic French government that acts of anti-Semitic terror be regarded as an internal French problem which it will confront resolutely, with the Nazi claim in the thirties that the "Jewish problem" was an internal German one.[16] The context is entirely different—French society in the eighties is not Germany of the thirties.

When Israeli politicians thus invoke the Holocaust, accuse foreign statesmen of anti-Semitism reminiscent of the Nazi period, or engage in similar analogies, they often do so because they are under the influence of a collective (sometimes personal) trauma, with which they do not know how to deal. The Holocaust remains an unhealed psychic wound.

Collective traumatization has also produced a type of Jewish backlash. Jewish people and Jewish leadership, especially in Israel, seem to be developing a stance which assumes that anyone who is critical of actions by Jews anywhere, especially in Israel, is anti-Jewish and that therefore the only possible reaction of Jews must be to regard all non-Jews as potential or actual enemies, and to respond to any incipient danger with the threat of force. This attitude seems to be based on two misinterpretations of the events of the Holocaust.

On the one hand there is the assumption that all gentiles as individuals, and all nations (save for the Danes and sometimes the Bulgarians) somehow joined forces with the Nazis. And on the other, it is assumed that the Jewish reaction to the Nazi threat was almost wholly passive, and that therefore the lesson to be learned is that Jews must never again be caught in passivity.

Both these arguments are wrong. I have discussed them elsewhere[37] and will not repeat myself at length here. Belgians, Italians, Serbs and other nations, as well as individuals and groups elsewhere, proved ready by and large to help Jews. True, the picture is dark indeed, especially in Eastern Europe; but were it not for those who helped, not even the small remnant would have survived.

The charge of passivity is uniquely Jewish—no other people has similarly accused itself (though some of them would have had good reason to do so). Czechs and Hungarians glorify almost non-existent undergrounds, and no Soviet writer has yet asked the question why there were no major rebellions among the millions of Soviet POWs who were starved to death or were tortured and murdered by the Nazis. In reality, unarmed active resistance to Nazi policies permeated Jewish life under the Nazis. In Europe in general, armed resistance was marginal, except in Yugoslavia and, debatably, in the USSR (especially in Byelorussia); nevertheless, Jewish armed resistance was relatively widespread.

Peculiarly, the very uniqueness of the Holocaust on which so many Jewish leaders insist—rightly so—contradicts facile analogies. Nonetheless, because the Holocaust was certainly unique but also has its place on a continuum, room has to be found for carefully controlled historical comparisons. The fact that there are no facile "lessons" to be learned does not mean that nothing can be learned, or that this event should be beheld simply in mute horror.

First of all, and probably most important of all, there is the sense of the continuity of Jewish history, in which the Holocaust was a watershed event. The sense of continuity obliges us to know the 'why' and 'how' of the Holocaust, both because we are the heirs to the civilization of the victims and because we or our parents were intended to be the victims no less than those who actually were.

Behavior of the victims ranged from one extreme to the other. In part, this behavior was conditioned by the Jewish environment, by Jewish education, Jewish religion, culture and civilization, or specifically Jewish family and social structures. We can learn what these influences were, and whether they resulted in patterns of behavior that were different from those of non-Jews persecuted by the Nazis. We may be able to understand better who we are, as a Jewish society, by analyzing the history of those who were like us and whose heritage we share. We may be able to empathize with them through our learning, and empathy may lead to a deeper feeling of identification with them and their lives. All this need not be limited to an understanding of Jews only—though there is no possible way to understand universal problems unless we also approach them through the discrete, particular instances of particular people at a particular time.

Beyond these basic issues, more immediate historical and political problems emerge, because the context of the Holocaust is that of our century and our era, and we cannot escape from it. One problem is that of retaining a sense of moral values opposite to that espoused by Himmler, in an increasingly violent, increasingly cynical world.

An analysis of Jewish policies, Jewish leadership reactions in Europe and in the free countries during the Holocaust is called for: not in order to accuse and "draw lessons," but in order to see what the dynamics are that operate on the leadership of a largely dispersed people in times of stress; whether certain historic patterns of Jewish behavior tend to repeat themselves; and whether, in the extreme case of the Holocaust, there were not beginnings of behavior patterns that were different from the traditional ones and that might indicate new developments. By 'old' patterns, we mean attempts by Jewish philanthropic groups (JDC, HIAS, ICA) to come to the aid of victims of persecution within the legal framework of, and in complete loyalty to, the host societies; squabbles between individuals and groups as to primacy in leadership; attempts to influence governments by 'quiet diplomacy,' etc. The abandonment of strictly legalistic attitudes, even by JDC leaders (in Europe); the growing awareness of the need for publicity and of the efficacy of grass-roots organization and democratic procedure; the relatively quick adjustment to the new conditions by some Jewish groups both inside and outside Nazi-occupied Europe—

all these appear to be new departures, or at least new emphases, influencing the post-Holocaust Jewish world.

Jewish contemporary consciousness of the Holocaust is troubled by the dialectical tension between the Holocaust as a traumatic caesura in Jewish history and the Holocaust as a part, albeit a tragic part, of the continuity of Jewish history. As such, the current argument about whether the Holocaust is over-emphasized, as some would have it, becomes rather irrelevant. It is a crucial, central event in general and Jewish history. It is set in this history. It has exerted and still exerts a vast impact on our objective situation and on our subjective reaction to events. It therefore has to be dealt with within the context of Jewish life in our era as the central event it is. Its interpretation is bound to have a vital influence, for good or for bad.

Notes

1. This article is based on a very fruitful discussion that took place on 4 August 1977, at the Hebrew University in Jerusalem. The participants should not be surprised if some of their input is being used here, though of course, the sole responsibility for the views expressed lies with the author. Those who participated, and to whom I wish to extend my thanks, are: Moshe Davis, Emil Fackenheim, Israel Gutman, Dov Otto Kulka, Seymour M. Lipset, Deborah Lipstadt, Malcolm Lowe, Avraham Margaliot, Michael Meyer, George Mosse, Leni Yahil. The symposium, and the research on which this article is based was made possible by the Philip M. Klutznick Fund in Contemporary Jewry. I am grateful to Mr.Philip M. Klutznick for his constant encouragement and great personal interest in these topics.

2. Cf. Uriel Tal, "On the Study of the Holocaust and Genocide," *Yad Vashem Studies* XIII (1973) pp. 7–52.

3. Cf. *Hitler's Secret Book* (New York, 1961); Joshua Trachtenberg, *The Devil and the Jews* (New Haven, 1944); Norman Cohn, *Warrant for Genocide* (New York, 1967); Andreas Hillgruber, "Die Endlösung und das deutsche Ostimperium," *Vierteljahreshefte für Zeitgeschichte* 1972, no. 2, pp. 133–53; Jacob Talmon, in: *The European Jewish Catastrophe* (Jerusalem, 1974); Uriel Tal, "Anti-Christian Anti-Semitism," *ibid.* Alice L. and A. Roy Eckardt, "The Holocaust and the Enigma of Uniqueness," in: *Reflections on the Holocaust, The Annals of the American Academy of Political and Social Science* (July 1980) pp. 165–78; Yehuda Bauer, "Genocide: Was It the Nazis' Original Plan?," *ibid.*, pp. 35–45.

4. Cf. Lucy S. Dawidowicz, *The Holocaust and the Historians* (Cambridge, Mass., 1981) pp. 5–11.

5. E.g., George L. Mosse, *Nazism: A Historical and Comparative Analysis of National Socialism* (New Brunswick, 1978) p. 55.

6. Raphael Lemkin, *Axis Rule in Occupied Europe* (New York, 1943) pp. xi–xii.

7. The Slavs were supposed to be a mixture of what the racial anthropologist Hans Günther had defined as "eastern" and "east Baltic" racial sub-groups, with additions from the Mongol and Finnic peoples, some Nordic influences, and even some Jewish influence.

8. In all the discussions on this matter there were two centers of power that had the most impact on policy-making: Alfred Rosenberg's *Ostministerium,* set up before the German invasion of the USSR to deal with the civilian administration of the territories to be conquered from the Soviets; and the various power structures controlled by Heinrich Himmler. Of these two, it was not the "Chaosministerium" (as it was known among Nazis in the know) but Himmler's empire that had the decisive voice. Himmler's general ideas on the subject were articulated in May 1940 in his memorandum on the treatment of foreign peoples, which he submitted to Hitler and which was approved by the Führer. (Printed in the original German in the *Vierteljahreshefte für Zeitgeschichte (VfZG)* 1957, no. 2, pp. 196–98; at Nüremberg this was Prosecutor's Exhibit 1314, NO-1880. For a partial English translation see my *A History of the Holocaust* [New York, 1982] p. 22).

9. PS-864; quoted in: Martin Broszat, *Nationalsozialistische Polenpolitik, 1939–1945* (Stuttgart, 1961) p. 22.

10. *Ibid.*, p. 24; USSR-172. It is hardly surprising to find the same basic attitude prevailing in the case of the Czechs. In a report on a speech of the state secretary to the German viceroy ('Protector') of Bohemia-Moravia, Karl H. Frank, of 9 October 1940, we read that Frank opposed "the most total solution, namely the deportation *(Aussiedlung)* of all the Czechs *(des Tschechentums)*. He proposed the dissolution *(Aufsaugen)* of about one half of the Czech people in the German Folkdom, insofar as they are of any value from the point of view of their blood and anything else. This will occur through increased labor by Czechs in the Reich area (not in the Sudeten border areas), that is, through the dispersion of the concentrated Czech people. The other half of the Czech people must be made powerless, must be removed *(ausgeschaltet)* and deported . . . Elements opposed to the germanizing tendency must be dealt with harshly and must be removed . . . The Führer has approved the assimilation solution." (PS-867. Report of 15 October 1940 by Friderici, Wehrmacht plenipotentiary with the Reichsprotektor, on Frank's speech of 9 October.)

11. See Helmut Heiber, "Der Generalplan Ost," VfZG 1958, no. 2, pp. 281–325; also Josef Ackerman, *Himmler als Ideologe* (Göttingen, 1970) pp. 222–31.

The author of the plan's final version, Dr. Konrad Meyer-Hetling was not just another Nazi official. He was responsible for population matters in another of Himmler's offices, the *"Reichskommissariat zur Festigung des deutschen Volkstums"* (Reich Office for Strengthening the German Volkdom), in charge of the planning of racial and population policies. Closely allied with Heydrich's *"Reichssicherheitshauptamt"* (Reich Main Security Office), the RKF proposed its policies—and that included Meyer-Hetling's plan—with Heydrich's approval.

12. Dr. Erhard Wetzel (he survived the war) was not an old Nazi, but a latecomer: he joined the Party on 1 May 1933. A servile and intelligent bureaucrat, he became a leading light in the office of Racial Policy of the Nazi Party *(Rassenpolitisches Amt der Reichsleitung)* in 1939. He then became involved with the RSHA, especially with its section III B dealing with racial problems, and in 1941 received a post in Rosenberg's Ostministerium.

13. *VfZG* 1958, no. 2, pp. 302–03.

14. Before Wetzel dealt with the problem of the Slav nations, he had some

interesting things to say about the Jews. Wetzel was not only informed of the mass murder by the Einzatsgruppen in the East, but actively supported it from his office. It was therefore very significant when he said this about the Jews: "A deportation *(Aussiedlung)* of the Jews as envisaged in the plan (i.e., Meyer-Hetling's plan—Y.B.) becomes redundant with the solution of the Jewish question. A possible removal *(Überführung)* after the end of this war of the still remaining Jews into forced labor camps in the area of northern Russia or Siberia is no 'removal.'" We have here a clear indication that the term *'Aussiedlung'* (removal, resettlement) as used towards the Jews has a different meaning in the language of German bureaucracy from the same term when used towards others. The context makes it clear that as far as the Jews are concerned, *'Aussiedlung'* means murder, rather than forcible deportation. (*VfZG* 1958, no. 2, p. 305)

15. *Ibid.*, p. 308.

16. *Ibid.*, p. 325.

17. *Ibid.*, p. 221–26.

18. Vaclav Kral, *Die Vergangenheit Warnt* (Praha, 1961) Doc. 19, pp. 122–23. "We have the following people: some are racially good and well disposed; this is very simple, we can germanize them. Then we have the others, that is, the other extreme: racially bad and ill-intentioned. These people I have to get out. There is plenty of room in the East. We then remain with the middle group, which I have to check out precisely. There are those who are racially bad but well-intentioned, and racially good but ill-intentioned. The racially bad and well-intentioned ones we will probably have to use for labor somewhere in the Reich and see to it that they do not have any more children . . . But we should not antagonize them . . . Then we are left with the racially good but ill-intentioned. Those are the most dangerous ones, because they are the racially good leadership group . . . only one thing will be left to do, namely . . . to settle them in the Reich, in a purely German environment, and educate them ideologically and germanize them, and if this does not work, to stand them up against the wall; because I cannot deport them, since they would form a leadership group over there in the East and would turn against us."

19. *Ibid.*, Doc. 22, pp. 145–48. For some of these people Heydrich foresaw the possibility of using them as labor stewards *(Vorarbeiter)* in the arctic area "where the concentration camps will, in the future, be the ideal homeland of the eleven million European Jews." Waxing enthusiastic about the possibilities of developing the arctic areas for utilization of their raw materials, Heydrich added that he did not want the non-germanizable Czechs to go there as enemies of the Reich, but to give them certain material advantages, so that they could serve as guardians of European culture. (*Ibid.*, Doc. 22, p.. 145–48.) Heydrich's speech took place about two weeks after the Wannsee conference (20 Jan. '42) the figure of eleven million Jews is that used by Heydrich at that conference. At Wannsee, the arctic concentration camps were not mentioned; but Wetzel alluded to them (see note 14).

20. Tilman Zülch (ed.), *In Auschwitz vergast, bis heute verfolgt* (Hamburg 1979) p. 382; Annegret Ehmann, "Gerechtigheit für Zigeuner," *Zeichen* no. 4 (Dec. 1970) p. 25; Ulrich Völklein, "Lästig ist das Zigeunerleben," *Die Zeit*, (7 March 1980) pp. 9ff.

21. *Ibid.*

22. *In Auschwitz vergast, bis heute verfolgt*, p. 315.

23. "Nach Zigeunerart umherziehende Personen."

24. *Kommentar zur Deutschen Rassengesetzgebung*, I (Munich, 1936).

25. *In Auschwitz vergast, bis heute verfolgt*, p. 76.

26. *Ibid.* In 1936, Dr. Robert Ritter was nominated to head a special research department for genetic science dealing specifically with Romanies (*"Erbwissenschaftliche Forschungsstelle"*). This became, in 1937, a research department on race hygiene and population biology (*"Rassenhygienische und bevölkerungsbiologische Forschungsstelle"*). Their researches into the racial purity of Gypsies resulted in a well-ordered card index, which was deposited with the health authorities. Just as those who decided on the murder of children and women in Auschwitz were medical doctors, so the fate of Gypsies was determined by pseudo-scientists attached to the Nazi health authorities. Does one have to mention that none of these Nazi women and men were ever punished?

27. Rd.Erl. des RFSS u ChdDtPol, 12/8/38, S-Kr. I., No. 557 VIII 38-2026-6; *In Auschwitz vergast, bis heute verfolgt*, p. 78.

28. The wording of the order is contradictory. Obviously, Gypsies were not of "German blood" so that what appears to have been meant is non-Sintis and non-Lalleri Romanies of Balkan origin. RSHA VA2 Nr. 59/43g; *In Auschwitz vergast, bis heute verfolgt*, pp. 327–28.

29. Cf. Donald Kenrich and Grattan Puxon, *The Destiny of Europe's Gypsies* (London, 1972); Siegfried Wölffling, "Zur Verfolgung und Vernichtung der Mitteldeutschen Zigeuner," *Wissensch. Zeitsch. der Martin-Luther Universität* 1965, H. 7.

30. Cf. Leo Kuper, *Genocide, Its Political Uses in the Twentieth Century* (New Haven, 1981) pp. 24–39.

31. The above has been culled from a number of sources: Richard G. Hovanissian, *Armenia on the Road to Independence* (Berkeley, 1967); Stanford J. Shaw and Ezel K. Shaw, *History of the Ottoman Empire and Modern Turkey* (Cambridge, Mass., 1976/77); Robert Melson, "A Theoretical Enquiry into the Armenian Massacres of 1894–1896," *Comparative Studies in Society and History* XXIV, no. 3 (1982) pp. 481–509; Johannes Lepsius, *Deutschland und Armenien, 1914–1918* (Potsdam, 1919); Tessa Hofmann, *Der Prozess Talaat Pascha* (Berlin, 1921/Göttingen, 1980); St. Stephanian, "Deutsche Armenien Politik," *Pogrom* X (1964) pp. 22–28.

32. Quoted from Helen Fein, *Accounting for Genocide* (New York, 1979) p. 15. Original document to be found in: *The Memoirs of Naim Bey* (Neuton Sq., Pa., 1966).

33. Stephanian, "Deutsche Armenien Politik;" cf. Hofmann, *Der Prozess* . . . , p. 133ff.

34. *Documents on the Holocaust* (Jerusalem, 1981) pp. 344–45.

35. In an Israel TV interview on 8/20/82, Lebanese Christian leader Dany Chamoun referred to Bashir Jemayel's responsibility for the murder of men, women and children as tantamount to being responsible for Belsen and Dachau.

36. Prime Minister Menachem Begin made that comparison in a Knesset speech on 12 August 1982.

37. Yehuda Bauer, *The Holocaust in Historical Perspective* (Seattle, 1978) and *idem, The Jewish Emergence From Powerlessness* (Toronto, 1979).

Part Two
Historical Writing on the Holocaust

Publications on the Holocaust

Henry Friedlander

The murder of millions of Jews is central to any discussion of Hitler's Germany, because for the Nazis the war against the Jews became the only objective to be pursued with single-minded determination and without any deviation. At times they might compromise with the churches, with the West, even with the Bolsheviks, but never with the Jews. The Nazis persecuted their political and ideological opponents—Marxists, liberals, or churchmen—for what they believed, said, or did; only Jews suffered for just existing. Against the Jews they applied administrative measures without regard for the age, sex, nationality, or politics of their victims; while governed by self-interest and reason, they employed against their actual opponents pseudo-judicial procedures which, however perverted, still granted to the accused a remnant of protection. Even in the camps, political opponents—including members of the resistance—had a chance to survive degradation and torture. Only Jews—and gypsies—were gassed as a matter of policy.[1]

Unfortunately, the papers and discussions have not yet faced fully the interdependence between the Church Struggle and the Holocaust. While Eberhard Bethge (chap. 10) and Beate Ruhm von Oppen (chap. 4) recognized the need to analyze the dilemma of the churches in the Nazi era by showing how they reacted to the fate of the Jews, Ferdinand F. Friedensburg (chap. 13) and the discussion that followed provided for us an example of the failure to understand the central importance of Antisemitism.

As most of the conference members[2] are theologians engaged in the practical work of teaching those not familiar with the Holocaust and are not historians undertaking to do research in it, I shall only attempt to present an analytical survey of the already available literature, concentrating on easily obtainable sources for my study of the Jewish Catastrophe.

I. The Textbook Treatment

That Germans killed Jews during World War II is widely known but, considering the importance of the Jewish fate in the Nazi scheme, the details of how the murderers killed and how the victims perished are, surprisingly, almost unknown.

In 1961 a study of American high school textbooks showed that their treatment of Nazism was brief, bland, superficial, and misleading. It found that racism and Antisemitism received only perfunctory coverage and that the Holocaust, if mentioned at all, was discussed in a few lines which usually transformed millions shot or gassed into thousands mistreated or killed, and organized mass murder into an excess of traditional Jew-hatred.[3]

There is no reason to believe that these textbooks have improved during the last decade. Moreover, even at the universities, coverage of the Holocaust in history textbooks used today is not substantially better than in those used at the high schools ten years ago. Thus, a survey of Western civilization widely used by college freshmen takes one hundred thirty-one lines to discuss the persecution of Jansenists and Huguenots in its chapter on Louis XIV, but only eight to discuss the persecution of Jews in its chapter on World War II. It mentions Dunkirk and Stalingrad but not Auschwitz and Treblinka. Discussing "conquered and intimidated peoples" it alludes to "mass extermination in the appalling concentration camps," but does not even mention Jews.[4]

Textbooks used in advanced university history courses are not much better. Time does not permit me to give a complete analysis. But perhaps by citing a few random examples I can illustrate their deficiency, and thus the failure of the articulate classes to face the Holocaust, showing how authors who should know better talk about the Jewish Catastrophe only in passing, if they mention it at all.

Thus, R. R. Palmer's survey of modern Europe, often considered the best of its kind, does mention the murder of six million Jews. It even gives the names of some of the extermination centers (but surprisingly they do not appear in an otherwise excellent index).

However, these short, though incisive, comments are submerged in other information and spread across a number of different pages. Nowhere do we find a detailed discussion of the Holocaust, which does not even get its own paragraph. The students, who learn nothing specific, will not remember anything.[5]

Although Palmer's coverage of the Holocaust is unsatisfactory, it is still far superior to that of other authors, who exhibit an ingenious ability to avoid the subject. Thus, Gordon Craig, an expert in German history, does not mention Jews at all. In his text, they only appear in his chapter on Germany as "non-Aryans" fired from the civil service. In his chapter on the war he lists its casualties without mentioning Jews. In his discussion of German behavior in the East he analyzes the mistreatment of civilians with the same omission. Only while talking about the recapture of Kiev does he mention—as an afterthought between parentheses—that the Germans had killed all Jews in that city. Apart from this, the students will not find anything on the Holocaust, not even the names of the extermination camps—except in a puzzling reference where Craig compares the brutality practiced in the camps run by Vichy France in North Africa for "foreigners who had volunteered for service in the Foreign Legion" to conditions in Auschwitz and Dachau.[6]

Craig's book is a rather crass example, but unfortunately it is not unique. Even textbooks concentrating on the twentieth century exhibit a similar blind spot; when they do touch on the Holocaust they are seldom more detailed than Palmer's survey. For example, Stuart Hughes's widely used text openly speaks of the Holocaust, but fails to treat it in detail as a separate subject. True, unlike Craig, Hughes does not submerge the fate of the Jews in that of all other peoples caught by the war. In his coverage of the Nazi regime he sets aside adequate space to describe the attack upon Germany's Jews before the war. He shows how the racist ideology led to the Nuremberg Laws, to the 1938 pogrom, to economic spoliation, and to the flight of the Jews. He correctly points out that "anti-Semitism and the concentration camp together created a demonic atmosphere of torture and frenzy which made Hitlerism unique in modern history," and shows that during the war most German Jews would die "in the holocaust of six million of their coreligionists that ranks as the greatest crime of modern times." It is therefore surprising that after this admirably forthright discussion Hughes only gives eight lines to the Holocaust in his chapter on the war. Students will not find any details about the "greatest crime."[7]

This hesitancy to discuss the Holocaust is not confined to traditional textbooks. We find the same story in the new type of history books—more essay than text—available at reasonable prices in paperback editions. They are well written, beautifully illustrated, and designed for the general public as well as for the college student. For our purposes two of these books on the twentieth century by specialists in German history are instructive.

Felix Gilbert's study in *The Norton History of Modern Europe* avoids mentioning the Holocaust. After the usual passing references to Hitler's Antisemitism and the anti-Jewish legislation of the 1930s, he discusses oppression and resistance in Europe under German rule. But in the two pages he gives to this subject, only eight lines cover the Jewish fate. Without even mentioning names or places he comments that "The number of those who were killed—about six million—is almost beyond imagination."[8] Obviously, with this kind of treatment the deed and the victims will remain an unimaginable abstraction for the reader.

A. J. P. Taylor's study in the British History of European Civilization Library is quite different. Although some historians have ranked him among the revisionists and accused him—unjustifiably, I believe—of downgrading Hitler's crimes, Taylor's treatment of the Holocaust stands out among the bland discussions we find in all other textbooks. True, he also does not provide the details needed for a thorough discussion in the classroom, but this is understandable in a provocative essay; still, though his book is substantially shorter than Gilbert's, he spends more space on the Jewish fate.

More important, Taylor treats the Jewish Catastrophe as an integral part of the Nazi era. With unusual candor he talks about Nazi barbarism without hiding the acquiescence of the churches and of the democracies which, even worse, closed their doors against the victims. Without mincing words, he tells how Jews were segregated, massacred, and finally killed in "gas-chambers of a most scientific type." Unlike all other textbook authors, Taylor sees the Holocaust as "an intrinsic part of the New Order," rejecting the interpretation that views it as "the aberration of a few Nazis or even solely of Hitler himself." Even more unusual, Taylor, concluding that "every civilization has its characteristic monuments. . . . The monument of German civilization was the death camp of Auschwitz," places alongside his text two photographs from the extermination centers.[9]

Some might disagree with Taylor's pedagogical methods. But after reading his essay teachers and students will not bypass the Holocaust. They might even study it further, something that is unlikely after reading the bland and evasive accounts in the other texts.[10]

It becomes clear how unique is Taylor's essay and how pervasive is bland evasion when we look at the college textbooks in German history. Here, if anywhere, the student should be able to learn about the Holocaust; unfortunately he does not. Thus, Marshall Dill's history of Germany in the University of Michigan series adequately covers the plight of the German Jews before the denouement, but, like all other texts, does not seriously treat the Holocaust during the war. In less than one paragraph Dill mentions the destruction of European Jewry. And, once again, an author finds himself unable to discuss the details of these "almost incredible" events.[11]

Coverage is not substantially better in the late Hajo Holborn's far more detailed work. In the last volume of his three-volume history Holborn adequately treats the anti-Jewish repression before 1939, but passes over, in one paragraph, the roundups and the killings during the war. More detailed than Dill, he does mention the specialists (*Einsatzgruppen*) and the extermination camps; he even talks about the Wannsee Conference called by Heydrich, but, hesitant to be more specific, uses the passive voice to tell us that there "agreement was reached on the final program"; he leaves the impression that Wansee was purely an SS affair, thus preventing his readers from discovering that many ministries—including Foreign Affairs, Justice, and Interior—sent representatives to and received memoranda about a conference assembled to coordinate mass murder.[12]

One exception to the usual treatment proves that authors of textbooks could give to the Holocaust as much space as they reserve for other, sometimes less important, topics. Thus, students will find the most thorough discussion in the late Koppel Pinson's scholarly history. In five paragraphs Pinson, a former editor of *Jewish Social Studies*, discusses the brutality, size, and geography of the Jewish Catastrophe; he outlines the development and organization of what the perpetrators called "the final solution," showing also how civil service and industry collaborated. Yet even here the treatment of the Holocaust, though adequate and better than anywhere else, remains skeletal, the minimum acceptable.[13]

The failure to reveal details about the Holocaust is not due to ignorance or ill-will; the authors we have discussed are knowledgeable and humane scholars. How then can we explain their reticence? The answer, it seems to me, is that scholars have been unwilling to recognize and to acknowledge the fact of genocide. Thus, even Stuart Hughes, who, as we have seen, clearly categorizes the murder of the Jews as an unprecedented crime, understandably prefers to see this crime as a macabre excess. He therefore argues, after discussing it, that "these demonic features, however, were not central to Fascism. The tendency of historians to focus attention on such horrifying aspects of the system has frequently obscured the less spectacular side of its relationship to the society and the economy which it dominated."[14]

But Hughes is wrong—and not only by failing to see that SS, camps, genocide were an essential part of the Nazi system—when he contends that most historians have concentrated on the criminality of the regime. To the contrary, a false delicacy seems to prevent most scholars from facing the history of the Holocaust. They seem to feel that it would be offensive to discuss details; here Taylor is a refreshing exception.

The anti-Nazi historian Golo Mann, scion of a famous family, exemplifies this false delicacy. His study of modern Germany, now available in English translation, shows us clearly why historians have been unable to confront the Holocaust.[15] While Mann gives a separate section of five pages to the story of the German resistance, he discusses the Holocaust in passing, when dealing with other matters, and fails altogether to treat the SS, the police, or the concentration camps.

Mann mentions the Jewish fate in a general section on the "Character and Course of the War."[16] There he briefly alludes to the murder of the Jews in Poland as he covers the Polish campaign, the murder of those in Russia as he covers the Russian war, and that "the Jews in France and in the Netherlands" suffered the same fate as he covers events in Western Europe. He makes the statement that "the worst" of all Nazi crimes were committed in "the gas chambers in the extermination camps in Poland where Europe's Jews, millions of them, were killed."

Surrounding Mann's short references are explanations and comments which, it seems to me, are even more representative of historians—and scholars in general—than the examples I have listed.

Mann does agree that "there can be no doubt about a crime which happened in our time and which will cast a shadow on the image of man and his story for ever." But he argues that "the worst" of all, the extermination by gas, "was then known only to a very small number of criminals." Of course, even if we accept this, it does not apply to Russia where, Mann acknowledges, officers and men of the army knew about the mass shootings. Citing Carl Goerdeler's lament: "What have they done to the proud army of the wars of Liberation and William I?" Mann blames the SS and objects to the idea "that the German Army as a whole behaved more brutally than other armies"; as if to prove this point he later discusses the "nightly mass murders" committed by the Allied air forces over German cities.[17]

Thus the deed remains, but the means and the culprits continue to elude us. All Mann tells us is that "the worst crimes were committed by units of the SS and the SD," adding only the curious proviso: "Let us not describe and list these things. But let us not think either that inhuman cruelty is a specifically German characteristic. The French under Napoleon did similar things in Spain—one need only look at Goya's drawings. If the leaders erect a system out of bestiality there will always be a minority willing to obey. This has been so everywhere at all times."[18]

How then does the historian explain the Holocaust? Again Mann gives us the clearest answer: "Just as the Army looked the other way and did not want to know about these things, the historian also does not like to speak of them. These are deeds and figures which the imagination can not grasp, which the mind refuses to believe, however clearly they can be proved by reason."[19] As to the Jewish victims, Mann asks, "Who can visualize four or six million human beings, men, women, and children, picked up at random, in the devilish gas chambers of Auschwitz and Maidanek?" And thus he concludes: "Darkness hides this vilest crime ever perpetrated by man against man."[20] We can only add that if we leave it to the historians and their textbooks, ignorance and distortion will not only hide but also bury it.[21]

II. Institutes, Bibliographies, Journals, and Readers

The failure of the general literature to treat the Holocaust cannot be explained by a lack of available materials. If anything, we are overwhelmed by the sources. This is of course a general phenomenon in our century; still, it is amazing how much has survived. The Jews in the ghettos and in the camps, driven by the compulsion to inform posterity, recorded everything. Afterwards, the survivors, determined to reveal all, wrote memoirs. The perpetrators who, unlike their victims, wished to hide their deeds, also left for us a complete account. Their documents remain, a tribute to modern bureaucracy and Teutonic thoroughness. Never in history has a crime been so well documented.

To help the student through this maze, a number of aids are now available.[22] The most valuable and detailed of these is the *Guide* published as part of their Joint Documentary Project by Jerusalem's Yad Vashem and New York's Yivo Institute.[23] Basically a guide to bibliographies and collections rather than to individual works, this volume is of inestimable value. With over thirty-five hundred entries (and with exemplary indices) it provides for the student a perfect introduction to any aspect of the Holocaust.

All important items in the *Guide*, which is divided into four sections, have explanatory notes and many entries are annotated with a reference to review articles, thus transforming a simple guide into an essay on the sources. The first section on "The Historical Perspective" lists comprehensive studies and general interpretations on the Holocaust and, as an appendix, on Nazism totalitarianism, and institutions of the Third Reich (party, army, Foreign Office, SS, camps). In addition, it lists as an "Excursus" studies on *The Protocols of the Elders of Zion* and on Arnold Toynbee's comments about the Jews. And as in all other sections, the *Guide* here lists works in any language, published as well as manuscript, mimeographed reports as well as articles and books, general treatments as well as specialized accounts grouped by regions.

The second section lists reference tools: bibliographies, chronologies, biographies, maps, and dictionaries. The third section deals with techniques of research such as the methodology of using eyewitness accounts. In addition, this section includes a valuable discussion of research institutes, archives, and libraries, listing their addresses, their holdings, and their publications.

Section four covers "Documentation." Here are included items on wartime anti-Jewish legislation, on postwar restitution, and on the reaction of non-Jewish organizations (allied, neutral, Christian, etc.). Other items deal with works on the resistance and still others list periodicals and newspapers, including the contemporaneous underground press. Most important, this section also provides the best available coverage of the history, procedures, records, and publications of the War Crimes Trials.

Anyone wishing to pursue the study of the Holocaust further will soon find that a number of institutes have done much of the preparatory work.[24] The earliest to collect and publish materials were organized by survivors soon after the war. Now defunct, the most active one was set up in Munich by Jewish D.P.'s as the Central Historical Commission attached to the Central Committee of Liberated Jews in the United States Zone of Germany. It collected records, now deposited at Yad Vashem, and published a Yiddish periodical.[25]

Of those institutes still functioning the most important is undoubtedly the Central Jewish Historical Commission of the Central Committee of Polish Jews, established in Lublin in 1944 and after 1947 known as the Jewish Historical Institute in Poland. It has the most important collections on the ghettos and the camps located—as were most—in Poland, including the famous Ringelblum Archives; it has published documents, Yiddish and Polish bulletins, and a Yiddish quarterly.[26]

The Yad Vashem Martyrs' and Heroes' Memorial Authority in Jerusalem probably has the most comprehensive holdings of any institute in the West concerned with the Holocaust. Hosting one of the largest documentary collections—both originals and microcopies—it also promotes Holocaust teaching and research in Israel; a number of Hebrew works, mostly documents and memoirs, have appeared under its auspices. In English Yad Vashem publishes a bulletin and a yearbook which, though they appear irregularly, are an important source for the student of the Holocaust.[27]

The Wiener Library in London is an equally useful and possibly more impressive institute. Specializing in the history of Nazi Germany and international fascism, it has accumulated an unusually rich collection of books, pamphlets, and reports. Expanding its original interest after the war, it now also covers neo-fascism, racial discrimination, right-wing extremism, and the state of Israel. Always concerned with Jewish matters, it is also a center for the study of Central European Jewry, Antisemitism and, of course, the Holocaust.

The Library's archives contain numerous eyewitness accounts and a unique collection of newspaper clippings. Its three published catalogues cover only a small part of its holdings, but they count among the most comprehensive bibliographies on recent German and Jewish history.[28] In addition the Library publishes a unique quarterly *Bulletin.*[29] In it the student will find short bibliographical and research notes; these cover a wide range of subjects, including Nazi policies, wartime collaboration, resistance activities, and Jewish emigration. Of special interest is the *Bulletin*'s survey of the press in Germany and elsewhere, including the neo-fascist papers. Covering Europe, the Americas, the Arab world, and southern Africa, this survey permits us to follow the trial of war criminals, the resurgence of Antisemitism, the activities of the Radical Right, and lately the growth of the militant Left.

Two other institutes are of special interest for Holocaust studies. One of these is the Parisian Centre de Documentation Juive Contemporaine. An important depository of Holocaust materials, particularly concerning France, it has published numerous monographs, catalogues, documentary collections, as well as its own journal.[30]

The other is the Yivo Institute for Jewish Research, the New York successor to the Yiddish Scientific Institute of Vilna. Particularly concerned with the history and culture of East European Jewry, its archives contain important documentary collections on Jewish history in the Nazi era and its library probably possesses the largest number of Holocaust publications available in this country. The Yivo publishes two journals—one in English and one in Yiddish—which contain articles on the Holocaust, and, together with Yad Vashem, the Holocaust Bibliographical Series.[31]

The work of a number of other institutes touches on the Holocaust. Of these we might mention The Leo Baeck Institute of Jews from Germany and the Institut für Zeitgeschichte. The former, with

Publications on the Holocaust

centers in Jerusalem, London, and New York, publishes a bulletin in German as well as monographs and memoirs, some in German and some in English, dealing with Central European Jewry since the Emancipation. Most important, it publishes a yearbook containing scholarly articles, mostly in English but also in German, and a very useful annual bibliography compiled by the Wiener Library.[32] The Institut für Zeitgeschichte, located in Munich, is one of the major centers for the study of the Third Reich. Its scholarly publications include a journal and specialized monographs.[33]

Finally, almost every European country has at least one institute charged with collecting documents and publishing research on the German occupation during World War II. Of these the most important are in The Netherlands and in France. The Rijksinstituut voor Oorlogsdocumentatie in Amsterdam has been most active in the study of the Holocaust, treating the fate of the Jews as an important and integral part of Dutch history under the occupation. All this has been reflected in its collections and its numerous scholarly publications. The Comité d'Histoire de la Deuxième Guerre Mondiale in Paris is primarily known as publisher of the most important journal dealing with Nazi domination and anti-Nazi resistance in occupied Europe.[34]

However, the overabundance of the sources on the Holocaust has not facilitated but inhibited research and its publication. The institutes have served admirably by collecting and preserving the sources; they have contributed much by publishing bibliographies, documents, diaries, and eyewitness accounts. But, with the notable exception of the Parisian Centre, institutes specializing in the Holocaust have so far failed to provide us with studies that approach the qualitative standards we expect in rigorous scholarship.

This is particularly true for Yad Vashem. Its *Studies*, a periodical dedicated exclusively to an investigation of the Holocaust, bears the mark of overly subjective dilettantism. Employing haphazard methods to investigate poorly conceived topics, its contributors seem to use *Studies* to publish their research notes without the disciplined labor of analysis. In addition, these articles, though published in English, usually read like poor translations of pedantic works in a Central or East European language.

Dawidowicz has argued that the reason Yad Vashem and similar institutes have performed so badly is that they are staffed by Holocaust survivors not trained as professional historians.[35] I have no personal knowledge to substantiate or to refute this contention. True or not, it can only be a partial answer.

Basically, Holocaust research has been monopolized by a group of older men and women who, though usually not survivors, have been involved in Jewish affairs most of their lives. Their vociferous attacks upon new and different viewpoints have probably kept many members of a younger generation from breaking into their preserve. Further, I suspect that professional historians as a group have often discouraged graduate students from undertaking Holocaust research. And, most important, neither "Establishment" has been eager to provide the essential support—foundation grants or university appointments—needed to attract young scholars. One has reserved the field for insiders and the other has considered it lacking in academic prestige.

Dawidowicz has also complained that "no American-born Jewish historian that I know of has undertaken any study of the Holocaust, though in the United States at least 1,500 Jews have doctoral degrees in history."[36] As we have seen, this is understandable. Her conclusion, however, that "native American Jews evade, suppress, deny, escape from the very thought or articulation of the Holocaust" applies primarily to the established leaders and older institutions of American Jewry. It does not apply to the next generation, although the evasion by their elders has not made it easy for the young to confront the Holocaust. Thus, I know of at least one young Jewish historian—American-born and Harvard-trained—engaged in research on an East European ghetto, who has, however, been unable to obtain financial support from any foundation, Jewish or non-Jewish.

Considering all this, it is not surprising that the Holocaust is not taught in the schools. Even in Israel, where the schools do attempt to teach it now, instruction before the Eichmann trial, if undertaken at all, was neither consistent, systematic, nor integrated into the curriculum.[37] In the United States, as we have seen, the history of the Holocaust is almost totally suppressed. No public or private school, college or university teaches it; Stern College in New York and Gratz College in Philadelphia are the notable exceptions. If we are to believe a recent catalogue, even New York's Jewish Theological Seminary does not offer a single course on the Jewish Catastrophe.

Publications on the Holocaust

As you can imagine, the status of Holocaust history is even more dismal in less prestigious educational institutions. Jewish schools—day, afternoon, and Sunday—have not made room for the Holocaust as a subject. In a number of cities, synagogues and, less frequently, Jewish centers have asked me to give a short course on it to advanced students or older adults. But this was always an *ad hoc* program, a sudden inspiration due to personal contact; although the students reacted with enthusiasm, there was never a follow-up and these courses always remained a one-shot affair. With the best intentions, the isolated educator concerned about offering a course on the Holocaust in the school he directs can do little when, without a budget, he must confront institutional indifference and public apathy.

Most striking is the lack of teaching materials. As Jewish history textbooks are not much better on the Holocaust than those used in the public schools, this has imposed a serious limitation on Jewish schools. For the students there are no textbooks; for the teachers there are no study guides. Teaching materials only recently produced by Jewish institutions to fill this gap are inadequate. Poorly conceived and badly executed, they combine the methods of the Sunday schools stressing heroism and martyrdom with the techniques of the "educationists" employing superficiality and gimmicks; the result is an invitation to mediocrity.

A particularly unfortunate example is Joseph Mersand's *Teachers' Study Guide*, a joint publication of the Anti-Defamation League and the Catholic Archdiocese of New York. Designed to accompany a film lecture on the "Writings of the Nazi Holocaust" by Ernst Pawel, the last in a series on "The Image of the Jew in Literature" produced by these two organizations, it illustrates perfectly the error of applying the usual techniques to the study of the Holocaust. Thus under "Classroom Activities and Discussion Topics" Mersand suggests: "A multi-media study of Anne Frank's Diary." As the diary appeared as book, play, and movie, he argues that "a comparison of the three treatments could make an interesting topic for a class report." Also in a "Model Instructional Unit" appended to this study guide, its author, Milton Silver, includes "required writing" which "should be creative in nature." Among his suggestions here are "Additional Entries in Anne Frank's Diary" and "A Series of Letters

Appealing for Help in a Holocaust Situation." This kind of effort, unfortunately not at all atypical, is not only meaningless but also in poor taste.

Other less objectionable examples are two recently published so-called Holocaust Readers. Appearing under semiofficial auspices, they are expensive, hardcover books designed to fill the gap created by the absence of textbooks on the Holocaust. But with inadequate introductions, confusing bibliographies, and almost no annotations, they are not very useful in the classroom; instead, these books have become prestigious items to grace the bookshelves of every Jewish library.

One of these, the better of the two, is frankly, though with hesitation, described by its authors as an "Anthology." True, their decision also to include rare materials, usually translated by them from Yiddish, is meritorious. But they defeat their purpose by printing selections that are far too short to convey real meaning. The student would do better to select an entire work from among the many now available in English. Also, without bibliographical and historical annotations these selections often seem torn out of context. Usually one can not even distinguish between eyewitness accounts and creative literature.[38]

The other reader, published under the auspices of the Union of American Hebrew Congregations, stresses the literary over the historical and the prestigious over the obscure. Most of its selections are from works of fiction long popular and widely distributed. Truly an anthology, this reader does not really treat the history of the Holocaust. Instead, it introduces a new, suddenly popular subject: Holocaust Literature with a capital L.[39]

Unfortunately this is all that is easily available for high school and college students. However, if the schools must use readers, I would prefer an older compilation published in 1949 to fill an obvious need because at that time almost nothing had yet appeared in English. Including eyewitness accounts, often unpublished, and not literary works, then still unknown, this collection still speaks to us with a compelling immediacy totally lacking in its glossy successors.[40]

Surprisingly, more is available for younger children. Of course I do not believe we should teach Holocaust history in elementary school. There are, however, books these children will find worthwhile. Hopefully without the intervention of study guides and anthologies, these original sources can convey to them something about the Jewish fate in general human terms on a level they can understand. One of these is the captivating and haunting *I Never Saw Another Butterfly*, already mentioned by Littell, in which the poems and drawings of Jewish children incarcerated in Theresienstadt tell the story of captivity.[41] At an early age poems like this one can have more meaning than long explanations:

I'd like to go away alone
Where there are other, nicer people,
Somewhere into the far unknown,
There, where no one kills another.

Maybe more of us,
A thousand strong,
Will reach this goal
Before too long.

Furthermore, younger children could read Anne Frank's *Diary*, which reflects through the experiences of a young girl the anxieties of Jews hiding under the German occupation. Her words, still imbued with hope and expectation, assume a special poignancy through our knowledge that she later perished at Belsen. Her *Diary* should be read together with the one by Charlotte Salomon, who, somewhat older than Anne, tells a similar story in the form of paintings and accompanying text. Drawn in Southern France before her deportation to Auschwitz, Charlotte's pictures, more morbid than the record left in Amsterdam, complement the widely known *Diary* of Anne Frank.[42]

III. Histories and Interpretations

The failure of our schools to teach the Holocaust is no longer due to a dearth of scholarly books. Enough works are now available for teachers and students to study the destruction of European Jewry in the Nazi era, and, while much remains to be written, the time has come to introduce legitimate courses treating the Jewish Catastrophe. Such courses should not only deal with the events between 1933 and 1945 but should also investigate the causes and origins of the Holocaust. This would obviously involve a history of Nazism, a study of the Jewish past, and an analysis of Antisemitism.

The first of these should pose no problem. The literature on the origins and history of Nazi Germany is large and well known. The second might prove a little more difficult. As a subject Jewish history is almost nonexistent in our colleges; American schools seldom mention the Jewish minority in the Christian world, just as they do not teach about other minorities, something which educated opinion has only recently discovered but which students from minorities—Jewish, black, or others—have always known. However, books on these subjects are easily obtainable; I do not have to mention them here.

The third, Antisemitism, is of course directly connected to the Holocaust, and should serve as an introduction to it. There is, however, some disagreement about its relevance to the Nazis' attack upon the Jews. While some see the hatred of Jews in our times as unrelated to that of earlier ages, almost as *sui generis*, others see it as only the latest, and most ferocious, expression of an old, traditional hostility.

Without trying to resolve this controversy, it might be sufficient for our purpose to state that possibly both viewpoints are partly correct. True, Antisemitism based on race differs substantially from that based on religion. In the Middle Ages Jews could escape persecution by conversion; under the Nazis even those born as Christians could not avoid death if they were descended from Jews. Medieval Antisemites, and most of their modern successors, killed Jews but did not attempt to extirpate Judaism. The Nazis, however, tried to kill every Jew and thus totally destroy Judaism. As Salo Baron has pointed out, the two cannot be separated:

> Judaism cannot exist, for any length of time, without Jews, nor Jews without Judaism. . . . The Jewish religion without the "chosen people" is unthinkable. Neither could it, like the other religions, be transplanted from the Jewish to another people. No matter how many adherents it might gain in the outside world, the physical extinction of the Jewish people would sound the death knell of Judaism.[43]

This made Nazi Antisemitism radical, and thus qualitatively different from the earlier variety.

Still, it would be an error to disregard the older history of

Antisemitism. Even if it did not guide the actions of the Nazis, the slogans and images made popular by traditional Jew-hatred were used. And, most important, religious Antisemitism influenced those populations—regardless of whether they were Germany's allies, subjects, or enemies—without whose cooperation, or at least acquiescence, the Nazis could not have carried out their anti-Jewish program.

Numerous studies of Antisemitism are available. An interesting survey by a Catholic historian, one my students have always found informative, might be the best introduction: Malcolm Hay's *The Foot of Pride* (1950).[44] For greater detail, I would suggest Poliakov's scholarly and provocative four-volume study, of which the first volume, most applicable for our purposes, has already been translated into English.[45]

In comparison, works dealing with Antisemitism in the modern period—the nineteenth and twentieth centuries—are surprisingly rare; thus we still lack a scholarly study of its Russian manifestation, essential because in the homeland of the pogroms Right and Left probably first used it for political ends. On Antisemitism's modern uses Hannah Arendt's chapter on the Dreyfus Affair and Koppel Pinson's collection of essays are probably still the best introduction.[46]

More is available on Antisemitism in the lands inhabited by Germans. Several good studies treat it as part of the rise of the "Germanic ideology" in the nineteenth century.[47] A number cover it as part of the fully developed Nazi ideology in the twentieth century. Of these, one shows how Germany's intellectual community in the Third Reich supported the anti-Jewish program of the Nazis.[48] Another, recently published in Germany, illustrates how a majority of university students in the Weimar Republic—and many of their teachers—had embraced racial Antisemitism.[49] But for the most detailed analysis we must turn to the work of scholars concentrating on German Antisemitism.

Paul Massing's history of Antisemitism before 1914 still provides us with the most thorough discussion of the Stöcker movement and of the band of racial Antisemites that appeared after the failure of the Christian Socials (*Evangelische Social Kongress*). He also discusses the reaction of parties and interest groups; of particular interest is his analysis of the Socialist stand. Although they too were

Introduction and Historical Background

not altogether immune, their resistance to Antisemitism retarded its growth before World War I.[50]

Peter Pulzer's more recent history covers, with less detail, the same material, but adds to it a comprehensive analysis of Antisemitism in German Austria. Considering the influence Schönerer and Lueger had on the development of Nazi racism, Antisemitism in Austria, more virulent than in Germany, is of central importance. Basically, Pulzer's valuable study is the only one we have.[51]

Eva Reichman's sociological investigation is an interesting attempt to explain Nazi Antisemitism. Rejecting the view that the Holocaust proves the failure of assimilation, she argues that in the twentieth century, at least in Germany, hatred of Jews no longer reflected an actual group conflict. Thus, a Subjective Jewish Question, based on older stereotypes more dangerous than actual conflict because they could not be corrected by reality, represented a projection on the Jews of German fears and insecurities.[52]

According to Reichman, the psychology of Germans, not their history, might provide an explanation. Several suggestive studies have attempted to do this. Most have analyzed the language of Nazism. Of these, by far the best is Klemperer's dissection of the *Lingua Tertii Imperii.*[53] Using his professional skills and his personal observations, Klemperer, who survived as a Jew inside Germany, shows how the Nazis subverted the outlook of the entire German people—even of anti-Nazis—by manipulating their language. Revealing the hidden techniques of Nazi mythology, his analysis illuminates an aspect of totalitarianism usually hidden from anyone except perhaps a perceptive novelist like Eugene Zamiatin. Another, more experimental attempt to probe the German psyche is a new work that looks for an answer in the nation's visual arts.[54]

Each of these studies proves how central to the Nazi scheme was the image of "the Jews." Thus, for example, Klemperer shows how for almost all Germans World War II became "the Jewish War," as "the Dwarf," usually for effect surrounded by all members of his family, served as an essential antithesis to the image of "the German," always sans relations, as "the Solitary Hero." Norman Cohn has delved deeply into this question of the Jewish image, and his *Warrant for Genocide* is therefore the best scholarly analysis of the mythology of modern Antisemitism.[55]

Cohn, well known for his work on the millennial movements of the Middle Ages, has studied the creation and dissemination of the forgery known as *The Protocols of the Elders of Zion* to illuminate the history of modern Antisemitism. Arguing that Nazi hatred of the Jews is only a modern variation of an older Christian theme, he sees, like Poliakov, the cause for Antisemitism in an earlier rivalry between Judaism and Christianity; in the popular mind the image of the Jews as communistic-plutocratic conspirators is thus a modification of the older image of them as the conspiratorial representatives of Satan. Cohn shows how in the nineteenth century "right-wing Christians, some Roman Catholic and some Greek Orthodox," secularized medieval demonological Antisemitism and how in the twentieth century the Nazis and their allies adopted it as an essential ingredient of their racialist doctrine.

Novelists writing about the Holocaust have basically seen its causes in a way similar to Cohn's. Thus, Schwarz-Bart depicts the recent Jewish Catastrophe as only the latest, though more destructive and more modern, of a long line of persecutions stretching from the Middle Ages, perhaps even from the Hellenistic and Roman world, to our times.[56] A similar thread runs through Wiesel's work. In his latest novel, set symbolically at Jerusalem's Wailing Wall, the experiences of the Holocaust blend—a link and an explanation—with stories of past and present Jewish travail.[57] And in an earlier one, who can escape the demonological interpretation after reading the tale about the survivor who, hiding from the fate of the Holocaust in an East European village, is beaten by the peasants while performing as Judas Iscariot in the local Passion play.[58]

Controversy, however, has centered on the events of the Holocaust, not on the causes. The literature has increased year by year, but few have been able to construct a synthesis. For example, Tenenbaum, writing on Nazi racialism in general, failed by trying to cover too much.[59] Only three scholars have so far successfully attempted a comprehensive history.

The oldest of these, Poliakov's *Bréviaire de la haine*, published in 1951, is still the best survey. Brief, concise, yet still comprehensive, it quotes extensively from original sources. Although unfortunately unavailable in paperback edition, the English translation, *Harvest of Hate*, is undoubtedly the best introductory text for students approaching the history of the Holocaust.[60] Reitlinger's work, published two years later, covers the same ground in more detail. In reviewing how the Nazis developed their plan of extermination, he also describes—country by country—how they implemented mass murder.[61]

These two comprehensive histories cover only one half of the Holocaust. Poliakov and Reitlinger picked as their subject the deed of genocide—the organized plan to kill all Jews. Obviously, they therefore concentrated on the perpetrators. And in their studies the Jewish victims appear only as objects. Still, read together with any of the documentary collections already published,[62] they provide a fairly complete picture of the Nazi deed.

Yet on this aspect of the Holocaust—the conception and execution of the Nazi plan—we now have Raul Hilberg's definitive history, superseding all previously published studies.[63] In his massive work (769 pages of double-column text and numerous charts) based on an exhaustive study of the documentary evidence, Hilberg describes in minute detail all aspects of this plan, adding a convincing and perceptive analysis. And he writes about this macabre subject in a dry and unemotional tone essential, it seems to me, for any scholar interested in retaining his sanity.

Hilberg for the first time presents a clear picture of the destruction process, which the Nazis euphemistically called "the final solution of the Jewish question." He describes the murder of Europe's Jews and shows also how a modern state can and did accomplish genocide. Describing how one step logically followed another, he argues that such deeds could only succeed if based on a plan. And most important, he proves that the Nazi leaders and their SS minions could not have accomplished their task without support from all segments of German society. As H. R. Trevor-Roper commented in his review of Hilberg's book: "The mere technical process [required] national involvement."[64]

Hilberg's impressive study suggests other topics that deserve further investigation. The most important one is the problem of those who acquiesced in the process of destruction by participating in it or by watching it. Undoubtedly, the Nazis could not have murdered the Jews of Europe without the cooperation of Germany's allies and of Germany's satellites. We know the outline of their behavior—the enthusiasm of the Rumanians, the hesitancy of the Italians, the resistance of the Danes—but we still lack the details. We need monographs on every country in Europe; only a few have so far appeared.[65]

Neutral countries and international organizations in the role of spectators had to perform a crucial role. They could have publicized the crimes and rescued the victims or, by abstaining, facilitated the slaughter. Here we still lack good monographic studies on the neutrals and on the central role of the International Red Cross.[66] On the role of the churches, however, we face a constantly expanding literature as the papers at this conference have shown.[67]

The behavior of Hitler's enemies—the United Nations—also deserves serious attention. The Western democracies did not actively intervene to save the Jews, and Russia, clinging to the provisions of the Nazi-Soviet pact, did not even warn its Jews about the mortal danger they faced from German troops. At the time the Allies excused their inaction by arguing that victory on the battlefield had to take precedence and that only the defeat of Germany could save the Jews. Critics have pointed out, however, that Great Britain and the United States did not treat the Jews as a national group deserving protection; in fact, they impeded rescue operations, refusing to bomb the tracks leading to the gas chambers of Auschwitz or even to open their doors to the victims later to be murdered there. But on all this, as well as on the political maneuvers of world Jewry, we still lack detailed accounts. Only one scholarly study has so far appeared; it treats the role of the United States, of special interest to us here. Illuminating the political machinations of the Roosevelt administration, it presents an appalling chronicle of Allied—and Jewish—failures to rescue the victims.[68]

IV. L'Universe Concentrationaire

The fate of European Jewry might have been sealed in chancelleries and embassies, but the ghettos and camps erected by the Nazi regime became the actual arena of the Catastrophe. Historians find it relatively easy to unravel and explain the deeds of diplomats and bureaucrats, while the denizens of the camp world remain shadowy figures difficult to comprehend. Yet no history of the Holocaust can be complete without insight into this world best described as *l'universe concentrationaire.*

Introduction and Historical Background

The executioners are undoubtedly the least difficult to understand. Still, we do not yet possess a truly adequate history of the SS as an institution or a satisfying analysis of the technicians of mass murder as individuals.[69] They have revealed themselves, however, in the documents they left behind and in the testimony they gave at their trials. The memoir of the Auschwitz commanding officer, written in a Polish jail before his execution, is a typical revelation which, available in English translation, is easily accessible to us.[70]

Nevertheless, in some ways we find these men incomprehensible; their banal personalities do not fit their evil deeds. The diary of the SS physician Kramer is a good example. In his entry of September 2, 1942, after his first direct contact with radical evil, he records his stilted and conventional impressions: "Went around three this morning to be present at a special Sonderaktion for the first time. In comparison Dante's Inferno seems almost a comedy. It's not for nothing that Auschwitz is called an annihilation camp!" But only four days later, in his entry of September 6, he reveals the shallow preoccupations typical of those callous technicians while performing their monstrous acts: "Today, an excellent midday meal: tomato soup, half a chicken with potatoes and red cabbage, *petits fours*, and wonderful vanilla ice cream. Around eight o'clock out again for another Sonderaktion, the fourth I have witnessed."[71]

The victims have been much harder to understand. Obviously we can not measure the reactions of those caught in the camp world of the Holocaust against the behavior of men in normal times. And attempts to use the psychoanalytical tools fashioned for the study of extreme situations in analyzing their behavior have, in my opinion, so far failed to provide fully satisfying results.[72] Social scientists tend to view the Holocaust as a single event, but, different from sudden, natural or man-made disasters like Hiroshima, it stretched over six years and covered a continent. In retrospect the Jewish victims might appear to have been an undifferentiated mass, but, unlike their executioners, they were millions of separate individuals. The Jews of Europe formed heterogeneous groupings divided by differences in language, custom, politics, and class; each group, facing the Holocaust at a different time and a different place, behaved in its own way in the polyglot world of the concentration camps.

It is therefore not surprising that controversy has centered on the behavior of the Jewish victims. Their decision to comply with and their failure to resist their own destruction have posed the most divisive questions. Thus Hilberg concluded that "the Jewish victims—caught in the straitjacket of their history—plunged themselves physically and psychologically into catastrophe."[73] But some of his critics, viewing all victims as martyrs, have denounced this interpretation as "defaming the dead and their culture."[74] Others have emphasized the few instances of resistance to prove the fallacy of any analysis stressing compliance.[75]

Discussion has tended to focus on the role of the Jewish leaders as reflected in the work of the Jewish Councils, the so-called *Judenräte.*[76] Unfortunately, the controversy surrounding Hannah Arendt's *Eichmann in Jerusalem* has obscured the essential points by turning the discussion into a debate.[77] Arendt's unfortunate choice of language tended to nullify her usually perceptive and often valid arguments.[78] The responses of her many critics—often shrill and vitriolic—have done little to illuminate this controversial issue.[79]

To evaluate these conflicting interpretations we must therefore turn to the sources. The documents are only of value to the specialists. But survivors have published enough accounts for our purposes. If we read them with care and discrimination, we can hope, in part, to understand the camp world.[80]

For the Jews of Europe, catastrophe began long before they entered the concentration camps of the Third Reich. In occupied Russia the Nazis usually dispensed with camps; there the SS in numerous mass executions performed by specialists (*Einsatzgruppen*) murdered the Jews on the spot. Knowledge about most of them has survived only through the statistical reports compiled by the SS commanders. But survivors and witnesses have left accounts about a few of them, such as the killings at Babi Yar near Kiev.[81] Similar massacres, though less organized, were carried out by local fascists and Antisemites in Poland, Rumania, and the Baltic states.

In West and South Europe the Nazis seized the Jews for deportation to the extermination centers of the East. The trains with their human cargo—often a hundred or more stuffed for days into a cattle car without bread or water—moved eastward across Europe, some from as far away as Greece.[82] Before boarding the trains they usually spent days, weeks, or months in transit camps like Westerbork in Holland or Drancy in France.[83]

Many Jews, however, went almost directly from home to train, because sudden and brutal roundups sometimes preceded the deportations. Thus, on July 16, 1942, the Nazis, with the cooperation of the French police, seized thirteen thousand Jews in Paris, confining them at the Vélodrome d'Hiver, in full view of the city's residents, until their deportation to Auschwitz; very young children, separated from their parents, faced these deportations alone—an act as horrible as any the Germans committed in East Europe.[84] A similar roundup took place in Rome on October 16, 1943. There German troops, with the help of the fascist police, plucked Jews from the streets of the city, some from beneath the windows of the Vatican.[85]

In the East the Nazis transformed old city neighborhoods into ghettos which only superficially appeared to resemble their medieval namesakes. Into these ghettos they crowded the Jews of the cities and villages, adding also deportees from Germany, Austria, and Czechoslovakia. Forced to work for the German war economy without the means of subsistence, thousands died of starvation and disease; the survivors were sent to the death camps. Under constant pressure from the German authorities, these ghettos, dressed up to resemble autonomous Jewish communities, became perverted societies whose only goal was the death of their members. Under these conditions self-government became a farce: the ghettos had a *Judenrat*, but no elected leaders; a Jewish police, but no Jewish schools.

These ghettos differed greatly in size and organization; for most of them, including important ones like Vilna, Kovno, and Riga, we still do not have adequate historical accounts.[86] In fact, only the atypical ghetto in Theresienstadt—designed, in part, as a camp for older and privileged Jews from Germany, Austria, and Bohemia—has been analyzed in a major scholarly account by a former inmate. Adler's work, unfortunately unavailable in English, is a model history not yet duplicated for other ghettos.[87]

The literature is most extensive about the two largest Polish ghettos—Warsaw and Lodz. Of these two the Warsaw ghetto, whose life and death has been described in numerous excellent memoirs,[88] remained a viable Jewish community even under extreme pressure and terrible deprivation. Its Jewish Council, selected by the Germans, had to share authority with an intellectual elite and an underground of political parties. Exhibiting an unusual pluralism, Warsaw's ghetto economy retained a private sector where groups organized self-help and where black marketeers became a political factor. The ghetto had illegal theaters, schools, lectures, and, most important, historians whose work, buried beneath its ruins, has survived the war.[89] It is therefore not surprising that when the Germans began their deportations, but not until most Jews had already been shipped with extreme brutality to Treblinka, a youthful political underground—Zionist and Bundist—seized power and organized revolt, an event almost unique in the annals of the Holocaust.[90]

In contrast, the Lodz ghetto community reacted to the imposed pressures and deprivations by transforming itself into a tightly regimented society, hoping to survive through labor for the German war machine. Without the opposition of an intellectual elite or a political underground, its appointed Elder and his cohorts constructed an authoritarian system that did not provide for economic or cultural diversity. As the last surviving ghetto in the East, not dissolved until the Fall of 1944, Lodz produced no historians, few memoirs, and no revolt; only its documents survive.[91]

Eventually all Jews, except those killed in Russia or starved in the ghettos, entered the concentration camps of the Third Reich. At first designed to hold the enemies of the regime, real or imagined, the number of camps expanded rapidly into a large system of central camps (*Stammlager*) and a vast network of subsidiary camps (*Nebenlager*) to hold prisoners from all conquered lands, especially the Jews. To the three original camps—Dachau, Buchenwald, Sachsenhausen—the Nazis added after 1938 eight new camps—Ravensbrück, Gross-Rosen, Mauthausen, Neuengamme, Flossenbürg, Stutthof, Natzweiler, and Bergen-Belsen. Compulsive regimentation, physical brutality, and sadistic torture characterized the camps and made these Teutonic institutions different from those of other totalitarian states. Holding about a million inmates at any one time, the concentration camps came to represent the essence of the Nazi system.

To understand this system, we must turn to books by former inmates. Eugen Kogon's account, originally composed for the United States army, is still the best introduction. Centered on but not confined to Buchenwald, Kogon's work, treating both SS and inmates, is an analytical description of the camp world's organization, structure, and function.[92] Kogon's clinical report alone, however, does not make it possible to comprehend this surrealistic world. For this we must turn to the accounts of other former inmates. Perhaps two of these can complement Kogon's book: Elie Cohen's medical study, originally a Dutch thesis in psychiatry, and David Rousset's impressionistic memoir, more a literary work than a journalistic report by a French academician.[93]

For the Jews of Europe the camp world included yet another, even more demonic, dimension: the death factories. Although the SS killed in all camps, they concentrated the mass extermination of the Jews in the killing centers of the East. There, in the "scientific" installations of Treblinka, Maydanek, Belzec, Sobibor, and Chelmno, they used gas chambers and crematoria to practice mass murder on the assembly line. Few escaped to tell about it, and those have found it difficult to talk about their experiences. For this reason Steiner's documentary novel is probably the best report we have about these camps.[94]

The SS established its largest killing operation in the Upper Silesian concentration camp Auschwitz. Comprising three camps, it became a giant complex. Camp number one, Auschwitz proper, served as the central camp, and camp number three, the I. G. Farben installation Monowitz, served as the industrial labor camp. Camp number two—Birkenau—served as the killing center. In its gas chambers the SS murdered millions; the flames belching from its crematoria chimneys turned night into day while the stench of burning human flesh pervaded the entire camp.

We now know a great deal about Auschwitz-Birkenau. There have been trials, plays, and a great number of memoirs.[95] The best of these is Primo Levi's eyewitness account. Levi, an Italian Jew, reports about his Auschwitz experiences in the dry tone and comprehensive detail of an observant scientist.[96] Different, but equally illuminating, are the short stories, terrible in their simplicity, about the Auschwitz experiences left to us by the Polish poet Borowski.[97]

In May 1945, the Third Reich collapsed. But against the Jews of Europe Hitler won his war. Still, some Jews survived; for them the gates of the camps opened in the spring of 1945. This is another story. Those who wish to follow it should start by reading Primo Levi's second book, the best available account of the days and months that followed the liberation of Auschwitz.[98]

Notes

1. The best analysis of the totalitarian nature of Nazism, showing how the innocent suffered more than the regime's opponents, is still Hannah Arendt's *The Origins of Totalitarianism*, 2d rev. ed (Cleveland and New York: World Publishing Co., 1958).

2. I would like to take this opportunity to thank the Center for International Studies of the University of Missouri, St. Louis, whose support made it possible for me to attend this conference.

Notes

3. Gerald Krefetz, "Nazism: The Textbook Treatment," *Congress Bi-Weekly: A Review of Jewish Interest,* Nov. 13, 1961, pp. 5-7.

4. Wallace K. Ferguson and Geoffrey Brunn, *A Survey of European Civilization* 4th ed. (New York: Houghton Mifflin, 1969), 2:839, 874.

5. R. R. Palmer and Joel Colton, *A History of the Modern World* 3d ed. (New York: Knopf, 1965), esp. pp. 810, 815, 829.

6. Gordon A. Craig, *Europe since 1815* (New York: Holt, Rinehart and Winston, 1961), pp. 638-39, 714, 726, 744-46.

7. H. Stuart Hughes, *Contemporary Europe: A History* (Englewood Cliffs, N.J.: Prentice-Hall, 1961), pp. 227, 331. The treatment did not change in the 2d ed. (1966).

8. Felix Gilbert, *The End of the European Era* (New York: W. W. Norton, 1970), pp. 224, 231-32, 299.

9. A. J. P. Taylor, *From Sarajevo to Potsdam* (New York: Harcourt, Brace & World, 1966), pp. 144, 169; first published (London: Thames and Hudson, 1964).

10. Not one of the many volumes in the widely used Problem Series published by Heath and Holt-Rinehart-Winston treats the Holocaust. Even texts concentrating only on World War II are of no help. Thus, though straightforward, the discussion of the Holocaust occupies only one paragraph in John L. Snell, *Illusion and Necessity: The Diplomacy of Global War, 1939-1945* (Boston: Houghton Mifflin, 1963), PB, pp. 101-2. The best treatment is probably Gordon Wright, *The Ordeal of Total War, 1939-1945* (New York: Harper & Row, 1968), pp. 126-28, the last volume of Rise of Modern Europe series.

11. Marshall Dill, Jr., *Germany: A Modern History* (Ann Arbor: University of Michigan Press, 1961), pp. 370-71, 412.

12. Hajo Holborn, *A History of Modern Germany.* Vol. 3: *1840-1945* (New York: Knopf, 1969), pp. 759-61, 810. On the involvement of the German ministries, see Nuremberg Military Tribunal, *Trials of War Criminals,* 15 vols. (Washington: GPO, 1949-53), case 11: U.S. vs. Ernst von Weizsaecker et al. (The Ministries case), 13:118 ff. On Wannsee and other such conferences, see esp. the various documents labeled NG-2586.

13. Koppel S. Pinson, *Modern Germany: Its History and Civilization* (New York: Macmillan, 1954), pp. 524-25. Perhaps the detail provided by Pinson is the best we can expect because the nature of textbooks imposes a limitation on depth. But Pinson takes an entire chapter to analyze the German Revolution of 1918/19, a subject skipped by all other texts. This kind of coverage, plus his citations from original sources, makes his text unusual and valuable. It is unfortunate that Pinson does not take a chapter, or part of one, to analyze the Holocaust, a subject which is as essential to an understanding of the Nazi era as the Revolution of 1918/19 is to that of the Weimar period.

14. Hughes, *Contemporary Europe,* p. 238. Referring to both the German and Italian variation of fascism, Hughes we must admit, argues in his text for the Italian one as typical.

15. Golo Mann, *The History of Germany since 1789,* trans. Marian Jackson (New York: Frederick A. Praeger, 1968).

16. Ibid., pp. 466-83.

Notes

17. Ibid., pp. 474-75, 489.
18. Ibid., p. 482.
19. Ibid., p. 474.
20. Ibid., p. 482.
21. A good example is *The American Historical Association's Guide to Historical Literature* (New York: Macmillan, 1961), a prestigious work with "20,000 items selected and annotated by more than 230 experts . . . according to a plan devised by a committee of the American Historial Association." But nowhere, not even in the chapters on "Recent History" or "The World Wars," does this plan provide us with a section on the Holocaust. On it the entire bibliography has only one lonely item: the chapter on "International Relations" lists a book published in 1943. Moreover, in the chapter on German history Hajo Holborn, its compiler, does not list a single book or article on the SS, the concentration camps, or, except for one work covering the Second Empire, on Jews and Antisemitism.
22. I am not including here the guides to the vast holdings of Nazi documents captured by the Allies.
23. Jacob Robinson and Philip Friedman, *Guide to Jewish History under Nazi Impact*, Bibliographical Series no. 1 (New York: Yivo, 1960).
24. For an early survey, see Philip Friedman, "Research and Literature on the Recent Jewish Tragedy," *Jewish Social Studies* 12 (1950): 17-26.
25. *Fun Letstn Khurbn* [About the final catastrophe], nos. 1-10 (Munich, 1946-48).
26. *Bleter far Geshikhte* (Warsaw, 1948-).
27. *Yad Vashem Bulletin* (Jerusalem, 1957-), *Yad Vashem News* (Jerusalem, 1969-); *Yad Vashem Studies on the European Jewish Catastrophe and Resistance.* Vols. 1-5 (Jerusalem, 1957-63); vols. 6-7 (Jerusalem, 1967-68).
28. Ilse R. Wolff, ed., *Books on Persecution, Terror and Resistance in Nazi Germany*, Wiener Library Catalogue Series, no. 1, 2d rev. ed. (London, 1960). Also Catalogue Series, no. 2: *From Weimar to Hitler Germany, 1918-1933* (London, 1951), and Catalogue Series, no. 3: *German Jewry: Its History, Life and Culture* (London, 1958).
29. *Wiener Library Bulletin* (London, 1946-).
30. *Le Monde Juive* (Paris, 1946-). See also the Center's Catalogue no. 1: *La France: De l'Affaire Dreyfus à nos jours* (Paris, 1964); and Catalogue no. 2: *La France, Le Troisième Reich, Israël* (Paris, 1968).
31. The Yivo journals: *Yivo Annual of Jewish Social Science* (New York, 1946-) and *Yivo Bleter* (Vilna and New York, 1931-). The Yivo-Yad Vashem bibliographies, in addition to no. 1 (see above, note 23): Philip Friedman, ed., *Bibliography of Books in Hebrew on the Jewish Catastrophe and Heroism in Europe*, no. 2 (Jerusalem, 1960); P. Friedman and J. Gar, eds., *Bibliography of Yiddish Books on the Catastrophe and Heroism*, no. 3 (New York, 1962); Randolph L. Braham, ed., *The Hungarian Jewish Catastrophe: A Selected and Annotated Bibliography*, no. 4 (New York, 1962); nos. 5-8 cover the Hebrew press and nos. 9-11 the Yiddish press; no. 12, for books published in various European languages including English, is due to appear soon. For published works on the Holocaust we might use the excellent collection available

Notes

in the Judaica Room of the New York Public Library (42nd Street Research Branch).

32. *Bulletin für die Mitglieder der Gesellschaft der Freunde des Leo Baeck Institut* (Tel Aviv: Bitaon, 1957-); *Year Book of the Leo Baeck Society* (London: East and West Library, 1956-).

33. *Vierteljahrshefte für Zeitgeschichte* (Stuttgart, 1953-).

34. For the work of the Dutch institute, see its *Nederland in Oorlogstijd* (1946-50) and *Jaarverslag van het Rijksinstituut voor Oorlogsdocumentatie* (1945-). For the French institute, see its *Revue d'historie de la deuxième guerre mondiale* (Paris, 1950-).

35. Lucy S. Dawidowicz, "Toward a History of the Holocaust," *Commentary* 47 (1969): 51-56.

36. Ibid., p. 56.

37. Yaakov Shilhav, "A Turning Point in the Teaching of the Heroism and the Holocaust," *Yad Vashem Bulletin*, no. 12 (Dec. 1962): pp. 57 ff.

38. Jacob Gladstein et al., eds., *Anthology of Holocaust Literature* (Philadelphia: Jewish Publication Society of America, 1969).

39. Albert H. Friedlander, ed., *Out of the Whirlwind: A Reader of Holocaust Literature* (Garden City, N.Y.: Doubleday, 1968).

40. Leo W. Schwarz, ed., *The Root and the Bough: The Epic of an Enduring People* (New York: Rinehart, 1949).

41. Hana Volavkova, ed., *I Never Saw Another Butterfly . . . Children's Drawings and Poems from Terezin Concentration Camp 1942-1944* (New York: McGraw-Hill, 1962).

42. Charlotte Salomon, *Charlotte: A Diary in Pictures* (New York: Harcourt, Brace and World, 1963).

43. Salo Wittmayer Baron, *A Social and Religious History of the Jews: Ancient Times*, 2 vols, 2d rev. ed. (Philadelphia: Jewish Publication Society of America, 1952), 1: 3. It does not matter here whether we consider Judaism in religious or in cultural terms.

44. Malcolm Hay, *The Foot of Pride: The Pressure of Christendom on the People of Israel for 1900 Years* (Boston: Beacon Press, 1950); PB as *Europe and the Jews* (Boston: Beacon Press, 1960).

45. Leon Poliakov, *A History of Anti-Semitism*. Vol. 1: *From the Time of Christ to the Court Jews*, trans. Richard Howard (New York: Vanguard, 1964).

46. Hannah Arendt, *Origins of Totalitarianism*, chap. 4; Koppel Pinson, ed., *Essays on Anti-Semitism*, 2d rev. ed.; (New York: Conference on Jewish Relations, 1946).

47. See, for example, Peter Viereck, *Metapolitics: The Roots of the Nazi Mind* (New York: Putnam, 1961); Fritz Stern, *The Politics of Cultural Despair: A Study in the Rise of the Germanic Ideology* (Garden City, N.Y.: Doubleday, 1965); George L. Mosse, *The Crisis of German Ideology: Intellectual Origins of the Third Reich* (New York: Grosset and Dunlap, 1964).

48. Max Weinreich, *Hitler's Professors* (New York: Yivo, 1946).

49. Hans Peter Blauel and Ernst Klinnert, *Deutsche Studenten auf dem Weg ins Dritte Reich: Ideologien, Programme, Aktionen, 1918-1935* (Gütersloh: Sigbert Mohn, 1967). It is interesting but not unexpected that German students

Notes

outside the borders of the Reich tended to be the most radical. Thus, at Prague's German language university they even occupied buildings to force the ousting of a newly elected rector because he was Jewish.

50. Paul R. Massing, *Rehearsal for Destruction: A Study of Political Anti-Semitism in Imperial Germany* (New York: Harper, 1949).

51. Peter G. J. Pulzer, *The Rise of Political Anti-Semitism in Germany and Austria* (New York: John Wiley, 1964).

52. Eva Reichman, *Hostages of Civilization: The Social Sources of National Socialist Anti-Semitism* (Boston: Beacon Press, 1951).

53. Victor Klemperer, *LTI. Notizbuch eines Philologen* (Berlin: Aufbau Verlag, 1946). See also Dolf Sternberger/Gerhard Storz/W. E. Süskind, *Aus dem Wörterbuch des Unmenschen* (Munich: Deutscher Taschenbuch Verlag, 1962). A number of articles, more compilation than analysis, have studied this language as it applies to the Holocaust: Shaul Esch, "Words and Their Meanings: Twenty-five Examples on Nazi-Idiom," *Yad Vashem Studies* 5 (1963): 133-67; and two articles by Nacham Blumenthal: "On the Nazi Vocabulary," *Yad Vashem Studies 1* (1957): 49-66; "From the Nazi Vocabulary," *Yad Vashem Studies 6* (1967): 69-82.

54. Bill Kinser and Neil Kleinman, *The Dream That Was No More a Dream.A Search for Aesthetic Reality in Germany, 1890-1945* (New York: Harper & Row, 1969).

55. Norman Cohn, *Warrant for Genocide: The Myth of the Jewish World-Conspiracy and the Protocols of the Elders of Zion* (New York: Harper & Row, 1969).

56. André Schwarz-Bart, *The Last of the Just*, trans. Stephen Becker (New York: Atheneum, 1961).

57. Elie Wiesel, *A Beggar in Jerusalem*, trans. Lily Edelman (New York: Random House, 1970).

58. Elie Wiesel, *The Gates of the Forest*, trans. Frances Frenaye (New York: Avon Books, 1967).

59. Joseph Tenenbaum, *Race and Reich: The Story of an Epoch* (New York: Twayne, 1956).

60. Leon Poliakov, *Harvest of Hate: The Nazi Program for the Destruction of the Jews of Europe*, trans. from the French (Syracuse, N.Y.: Syracuse University Press, 1954).

61. Gerald Reitlinger, *The Final Solution: The Attempt to Exterminate the Jews of Europe, 1939-1945* (New York: A.S. Barnes, 1961); American hard-cover edition (Beechhurst Press, 1953).

62. For example, Leon Poliakov and Josef Wulf, *Das Dritte Reich und die Juden: Dokumente und Aufsätze* (Berlin: Arani, 1955), or the collection *Dokumenty i materialy*, 3 vols. (Warsaw, Lodz, Cracow: The Central Jewish Historical Commission, 1946).

63. Raul Hilberg, *The Destruction of the European Jews* (Chicago: Quadrangle, 1961).

64. "Nazi Bureaucrats and Jewish Leaders," *Commentary* 23 (1962): 352.

65. See, for example, Jacob Presser, *The Destruction of the Dutch Jews,*

Notes

trans. Arnold Pomerantz (New York: Dutton, 1969). Few other studies are, unfortunately, available in English.

66. For an interesting early memoir about neutral and Red Cross efforts during the last days of the war, see Count Folke Bernadotte, *The Curtain Falls. Last Days of the Third Reich*, trans. Eric Lewenhaupt (New York: Knopf, 1945).

67. The most applicable monograph is still Guenter Lewy, *The Catholic Church and Nazi Germany* (New York: McGraw-Hill, 1964).

68. Henry L. Feingold, *The Politics of Rescue. The Roosevelt Administration and the Holocaust, 1938-1945* (New Brunswick, N.J.: Rutgers University Press, 1970). For an earlier popular account, see Arthur D. Morse, *While Six Million Died: A Chronicle of American Apathy* (New York: Random House, 1967); for a recent account, see Saul S. Friedman, *No Haven for the Oppressed* (Detroit: Wayne State University Press, 1973).

69. Apart from the details provided by Hilberg, the best history is Gerald Reitlinger's *The SS. Alibi of a Nation, 1922-1945* (New York: Viking, 1957); for two recent German studies, see Hans Buchheim/Martin Broszat/Hans-Adolf Jacobsen, *Anatomy of the SS State*, trans. R. Barry and others (London: Collins, 1968); and Herbert Jäger, *Verbrechen unter totalitärer Herrschaft. Studien zur nationalsozialistischen Gewaltkriminalität* (Olten: Walter-Verlag, 1967).

70. Rudolf Hoess, *Commandant of Auschwitz. The Autobiography of Rudolf Hoess*, trans. Constantine FitzGibbon (New York: Popular Library, 1961).

71. Cited in Leon Poliakov, "The Mind of the Mass Murderer," *Commentary* 12 (1951): 452.

72. For two such attempts, see Bruno Bettelheim, *The Informed Heart: Anatomy in a Mass Age* (Glencoe, Ill.: The Free Press, 1960); and Robert Jay Lifton, *History and Human Survival* (New York: Random House, 1970).

73. Hilberg, *The Destruction of the European Jews*, p. 669.

74. Oscar Handlin, "Jewish Resistance to the Nazis," *Commentary* 24 (Nov. 1962): 399. But Handlin's position becomes inconsistent when he also argues that "if there is a lesson to be salvaged from the Nazi period, it is that all of us are potential victims and all of us potential executioners."

75. The work of Yad Vashem reflects this emphasis; in fact, the Israeli Knesset wrote it into the constitution of the Memorial Authority. See Benzion Dinur, "Problems Confronting 'Yad Vashem' in Its Work of Research," *Yad Vashem Studies* 1 (1957): 7-30. For a serious attempt to analyze the problem of resistance, see Philip Friedman, "Jewish Resistance," ibid., 2: (1958): 113-31.

76. See Philip Friedman, "Problems of Research in Jewish 'Self-Government' (Judenrat) in the Nazi Period," *Yad Vashem Studies* 2 (1958): 95-113.

77. *Die Kontroverse: Hannah Arendt, Eichmann und die Juden* (Munich: Nymphenburger Verlagshandlung, 1964).

78. Hannah Arendt, *Eichmann in Jerusalem. A Report on the Banality of Evil*, rev. ed.; (New York: Viking, 1964). Thus her use of the term "Jewish Führer" as applied to Baeck. Rabbi Leo Baeck made impossible a judicious evaluation of his decision to conceal the facts of extermination from those

Notes

deported to the East. (Citation in original Arendt articles in *The New Yorker,* March 2, 1963, p. 42, but omitted in rev. ed. of the book, p. 119).

79. A good example is Jacob Robinson's book, which tries to refute Arendt page by page. His notes provide a good bibliography, but his interpretation, attempting even to exonerate Rumkowski of Lodz, does not contribute to our understanding. See *And the Crooked Shall Be Made Straight: The Eichmann Trial, the Jewish Catastrophe, and Hannah Arendt's Narrative* (New York: Macmillan, 1965). For the Eichmann trial itself, see Gideon Hausner, *Justice in Jerusalem* (New York: Schocken, 1968).

80. See H. G. Adler, "Ideas toward a Sociology of the Concentration Camp," *American Journal of Sociology* 63 (1958): 513-22; Hannah Arendt, "Social Science Techniques and the Study of Concentration Camps," *Jewish Social Studies* 12 (1950): 49-64; Samuel Gringanz, "Some Methodological Problems in the Study of the Ghetto," ibid. 12 (1950): 65-72.

81. See Anatol Kusnetsov, *Babi Yar,* trans. from the Russian (New York: Dial Press, 1967).

82. See Cecil Roth, "The Last Days of Jewish Salonica," *Commentary* 10 (1950): 49-55.

83. See Georges Wellers, *De Drancy à Auschwitz* (Paris: Editions du Centre, 1946).

84. Claud Lévy and Paul Tillard, *Betrayal at the Vel d'Hiv,* trans. Inea Bushnaq (New York: Hill and Wang, 1969).

85. Robert Katz, *Black Sabbath: A Journey through a Crime against Humanity* (New York: Macmillan, 1969).

86. However, we do possess a number of Yiddish works. See, for example, Mark Dworzecki, *Yerushelayim d'lite in kamf un umkum. Zikhroynes fun vilner geto* (Paris: Yidisher Folksverband, 1948); Joseph Gar, *Umkum fun der yidisher kovne* (Munich: Farband fun Litvishe Yidn, 1948).

87. H. G. Adler, *Theresienstadt 1941-1945: Das Anlitz einer Zwangsgemeinschaft* 2d ed. (Tübingen: J.C.B. Mohr, 1960). See also his *Die verheimlichte Wahrheit. Theresienstädter Dokumente* (Tübingen: J.C.B. Mohr, 1958).

88. The best memoir available in English translation is the Socialist Bund leader Bernard Goldstein's *The Stars Bear Witness,* trans. Leonard Shatzkin (New York: Viking, 1949); PB as *Five Years in the Warsaw Ghetto* (Dolphin Books, 1961); see also Philip Friedman, ed., *Martyrs and Fighters. The Epic of the Warsaw Ghetto* (New York: Lancer Books, 1954).

89. Emanuel Ringelblum, *Notes from the Warsaw Ghetto,* ed. and trans. Jacob Sloan (New York: McGraw-Hill, 1958); Chaim Aron Kaplan, *Scroll of Agony,* ed. and trans. A. I. Katsh (New York: Macmillan, 1965).

90. All authors and sources discuss the uprising (see above, notes 86 and 87). Also see the Yiddish works: Tovye Bozykowski, *Tsvishn falendike vent* (Warsaw: Hechalutz, 1949); Melekh Neustadt, *Khurben un oyfshtand fun di yidn in varshe,* 2 vols. (Tel Aviv: Histadrut, 1948); Jonas Turkow, *Azoy is es geven. Khurbn varshe,* 2 vols. (Buenos Aires: Zentral Farband fun Poylishe Yidn, 1948-50). For the German view, see the text and pictures of the macabre report presented to Hitler by the SS commander: The Stroop Report (PS-1061: "Es gibt keinen jüdischen Wohnbesitz in Warschau mehr!"), International Military Tribunal,

Notes

Trial of the Major War Criminals, 42 vols. (Nuremberg, 1947), 26: 628 ff.; English trans. in Office of United States Chief of Counsel for Prosecution of Axis Criminality, *Nazi Conspiracy and Aggression*, 8 vols. and 2 supp. vols. (Washington: G.P.O., 1946-48) 3: 718 ff.

91. We now have two monographs—one in German and one in Yiddish—on the ghetto in Lodz, officially known as "Ghetto Litzmannstadt." Josef Wulf, *Lodz. Das letzte Ghetto auf polnischem Boden*, Schriftenreihe der Bundeszentrale für Heimatdienst, vol. 59 (Bonn, 1962); Isaiah Trunk, *Lodzer geto* (New York: Yivo, 1962). See also Solomon F. Bloom, "Dictator of the Lodz Ghetto. The Strange History of Mordechai Chaim Rumkowski," *Commentary* 7 (1949): 111-22.

92. Eugen Kogon, *Der SS-Staat: Das System der deutschen Konzentrationslager* (Frankfurt: Verlag der Frankfurter Hefte, 1946). English PB as *The Theory and Practice of Hell* (New York: Berkley Publ. Corp., 1950). See also *Le Système concentrationaire allemande*, 1940-1944, in *Revue d'histoire de la deuxième guerre mondiale*, nos. 15-16 (July-Sept. 1954). For a monographic study of one camp, see Eberhard Kolb, *Bergen-Belsen* (Hanover: Verlag für Literatur und Zeitgeschehen, 1962).

93. Elie A. Cohn, *Human Behavior in the Concentration Camp*, trans. M. H. Braaksma (New York: Grosset and Dunlap [Universal Lib.], n.d.); David Rousset, *The Other Kingdom*, trans. Ramon Guthrie (New York: Reynal and Hitchcock, 1947).

94. Jean-Francois Steiner, *Treblinka*, trans. Helen Weaver (New York: Simon and Schuster, 1967; Signet PB, 1968). For one of the best memoirs about the killing centers, covering the Warsaw ghetto, Maydanek, Auschwitz, and other camps, see Alexander Donat, *The Holocaust Kingdom* (New York: Holt, Rinehart and Winston, 1963).

95. Elie Wiesel's report is, due to its stark and direct language, the most effective of these: *Night*, trans. Stella Rodway (New York: Avon Books, 1969). For two rather typical accounts that, unable to translate the horror into the language of normality, appear sensational, see Olga Lengyel, *I Survived Hitler's Ovens (Five Chimneys): The Story of Auschwitz* (Boston: Ballantine Books, 1954); Miklos Nyiszli, *Auschwitz: A Doctor's Eyewitness Account*, trans. S. Becker (New York: Avon Books, 1969).

96. Primo Levi, *If This Is a Man*, trans. Stuart Woolf (New York: Orion Press, 1959), PB as *Survival in Auschwitz: The Nazi Assault on Humanity* (Collier Books, 1961).

97. Tadeucz Borowski, *This Way for the Gas, Ladies and Gentlemen and Other Stories*, trans. Barbara Vedder (London: Jonathan Cape, 1967).

98. Primo Levi, *The Reawakening (La Tregua). A Liberated Prisoner's Long March Home Through East Europe*, trans. Stuart Woolf (Boston: Little, Brown, 1965); pub. in England as *The Truce*.

The Holocaust in American Historical Writing

GERD KORMAN

I

PERMIT me, an ordinary historian and teacher, presumptuously poking around in other scholars' domains, to clarify some of my passions and fundamental convictions by using for a moment the works of Vladimir Jabotinsky, Alfred Kazin, Albert Speer, and Moses Herzog.

In 1940, Jabotinsky, leader of militant revisionist Zionism, told the world that Hitler's war against all of Europe's Jews would end in their annihilation if the Allies failed to respond constructively to recent events in Europe. As early as 1943, Kazin, subway rider out of Brooklyn's Brownsville Ghetto, literary historian, and writer put it, the pieces of his world, all together: Shmuel Zygelbojm, Warsaw Ghetto, annihilation of European Jewry, and the silence of the many: "all our silent complicity in the massacre of Jews . . . [whose] deaths were so peculiarly hopeless . . . means that men are not ashamed of what they have been in this time, and are therefore not prepared for the further outbreaks of fascism which are so deep in all of us." After the war, Speer, Hitler's genius of industrial organization, claimed to have learned in defeat and the distance of time that he could not absolve himself from crimes of omission and acquiescence even though he had understood then that "will alone" could not halt "the automatism of progress" which may well "depersonalize man further and withdraw more and more of his self-responsibility." In the "final analysis I myself determined the degree of my isolation, the extremity of my evasions, and the extent of my ignorance. . . ." For "one who wanted to listen," he wrote years later, Hitler never "concealed his intention to exterminate the Jewish people." Saul Bellow's American Jew was a survivor, shocked and on the verge of tears at "the realization of such election. . . . As the dead go their way, you want to call to them but they depart in a black cloud of faces, souls. They flew out in smoke from the extermination chimneys, and leave you in the clear light of historical success—the technical success of the West. Then you know with a crash of the blood that mankind is making it—making it in glory though deafened by the explosions of blood." And so, in Poland, where he visited, the stones still smelled of war-time murders. "He thought he scented blood."[1]

At bottom, these thoughts making a place for the disaster of European Jewry are not different from the counterrevolutionary interpretive frameworks suggested by some historians in America conscious of the fascism of the mind, and of the impact of a seemingly self-driven accelerating technology. Within these kinds of frameworks the historian considers himself free to do what he will with the Jew. Usually he does it this way, without explicitly involving the Jewish component. "The Dreyfus affair might have awakened in [Marc] Bloch awareness and concern for a problem which at this time some of the greatest of his contemporaries . . . began to investigate and which has remained in the center of the study of the social sciences: the limitation of reason and rationality, the strength of the unconscious, the irrational basis of our structured world." Or this way: "*Counterrevolutions* should be taken in the broadest sense to mean those movements that arose to oppose, divest, absorb, or check the familiar 'isms' that have molded the progressive conception of history. Obviously, what we have here is the obverse side of concern for lost progressive causes."[2]

I am trying to say something else as well. In Herzog and Speer the destruction of Jews is not consuming; it had consumed Zygelbojm and Jabotinsky. In *Herzog* and *Inside the Third Reich* it appears as an explicit subject five to ten times.[3] Both men lived in mental and physical worlds where the Jew in disaster emerged but occasionally: in Herzog's case barely long enough for expressing a fleeting, seering thought. Like Speer, Herzog had many, many other things on his mind.

Historians make explicit and conscious decisions in deciding the importance of Jews in the subject they explore. So did Speer. Thus he writes that in the summer of 1944, his friend Karl Hanke "advised me never to accept an invitation to inspect a concentration camp in Upper Silesia. Never, under any circumstances. . . . I did not query him. I did not query Himmler, I did not query Hitler. I did not speak with personal

---

[1] Vladimir Jabotinsky, *The Jewish War Front* (London, 1940), *passim*, but see pp. 9, 15, 19, 22, for comparison with the Armenian disaster and for passages demanding recognition of the war being waged against the Jewish people; Alfred Kazin, "In Every Voice, in Every Ban," *The New Republic*, CX (January 10, 1944), 46; Albert Speer, *Inside the Third Reich* (London, 1971), pp. 697-698, 171; Saul Bellow, *Herzog* (Harmondsworth, 1965), pp. 81, 31-32.

[2] Felix Gilbert, "Three Twentieth Century Historians," in John Higham, *et al.*, *History* (Englewood Cliffs, N.J., 1965), pp. 367-368; Leonard Krieger, "European History in America," *ibid.*, p. 307.

[3] Bellow, *Herzog*, pp. 31-32, 60, 80-81, 297. For Speer it is easy enough to consult his index although the one in my paperback edition is inaccurate.

friends. I did not investigate—for I did not want to know what was happening there."[4]

II

Within ten years after the public discussion of the destruction of European Jewry began in the United States, the Holocaust became a complex problem of contemporary history. So many dogmatic judgments were being made about the people in the disaster that Clio's most devoted disciples were bound to find it difficult to retain their position of detached fair-mindedness. Yet, where historians working in the United States would place the Holocaust in their writings was not quite clear.

William Shirer, of *Berlin Diary* fame, in 1943 inadvertently identified many of the cross-currents that would help to determine the historiographical status of the Holocaust. From the beginning of the war civilian slaughters, he wrote, left all Germans "completely cold." "From all reports . . . Hitler is believed to have slaughtered two million Jews. . . ." But it was wrong for Americans to confuse "the greatest moral problem of our times." "Our inhumanity." The harsh truth is that all our efforts are dependent on Hitler alone. "And even if the five million Jews are saved, what about the twenty million Poles, the fifty million Russians . . . ." Even in war these remarks prompted Shirer's editor, the famed Paul Kellogg of the magazine *Survey*, to respond in an editorial comment against so many sweeping generalizations. Kellogg could "only lean on my faith in Germans I have known abroad no less than here" but "my faith is not without support from fugitives who have cleared the border, from the testimony of refugees, from the glimpses of rebel daring that leak out through the underground. These support," he preached, "the living wisdom from Burke to Madame Chiang Kai-sheck [*sic*]—that you cannot indict a whole people."[5]

Many others contributed to the swirling currents. The Institute of Jewish Affairs, for example, established in 1940, primarily in response to the Hitler years, and through which Jacob Robinson, its director, made himself known, published a number of important studies under the title *Starvation Over Europe* (1943) and such other titles as *Hitler's Ten Year War on the Jews* (1943), *The Racial State* (1944), and *The Jewish Catastrophe* (1944). In the pages of the labor Zionist *Jewish Frontier* and in the scholarly *Jewish Social Studies* appeared a steady stream of explanation, analyses, and judgments from the powerful and provocative pen of Hannah Arendt.

[4] Speer, *Inside the Third Reich*, pp. 506-507.
[5] William L. Shirer, "The Nazi Reign of Terror," *Survey Graphic*, XXXII (April, 1943), 121-122. Kellogg's editorial comment is on p. 122.

One of these, from 1944, deserves extended quotation, in part because it turned out to be a prophecy about her relationship to the literature on the Holocaust. Thinking especially of Bernard Lazare, Heinrich Heine, and Franz Kafka, but surely as applicable to herself ("bold spirits who tried to make the emancipation of Jews that which it really should have been—an admission of Jews *as Jews* to the ranks of humanity. . . .") she wrote:

> That the status of the Jews in Europe has been not only that of an oppressed people but also of what Max Weber has called a 'pariah people' is a fact most clearly appreciated by those who had practical experience of just how ambiguous is the freedom which emancipation has ensured, and how treacherous the promise of equality which assimilation has held out. In their own position as social outcasts such men reflect the political status of their entire people. It is, therefore, not surprising that out of their personal experience Jewish poets, writers, and artists should have been able to evolve the concept of the pariah as a human type—a concept of supreme importance for the evaluation of mankind in our day and one which has exerted upon the gentile world an influence in strange contrast to the spiritual and political ineffectiveness which has been the fate of these men among their own brethren.[6]

In 1949, in the very months when a Jewish state was being developed in Palestine, these kinds of positions were advanced from the same plat-

---

[6] Hannah Arendt, "The Jew as Pariah: A Hidden Tradition," *Jewish Social Studies*, VI (April, 1944), 100. The Institute of Jewish Affairs was a creation of the American Jewish Congress and of the World Jewish Congress. After World War II, YIVO, established in Vilna in 1925, but moved to New York City in 1939, continued the work of the Institute on the subject of the Holocaust. In 1947, the *YIVO Bleter* was devoted to the subject, and also published Max Weinreich's *Hitler's Professors* (New York, 1946). After 1953, YIVO continued to publish works on the Holocaust as, for example, Volumes VIII (1954) and XXI (1969) of the *Annual of Jewish Social Science*, or with Yad Vashem, as for example, the multi-volume bibliography in English, Yiddish, and Hebrew, *Guide to Jewish History Under Nazi Impact* (9 vols.; New York, 1960-1966). There were, of course, many other sources contributing to information and interpretations about the Holocaust in those years. One steady stream came from the United States Department of State through formal pronouncements from its officials to audiences of different kinds and through the Department's *Bulletin*. Another came from Jewish organizations and leaders, especially from various Zionists such as Ben Hecht and Rabbi Abba Silver. In addition to the newspaper reports about the Nuremberg Trial, see Seymour Krieger, *Nazi Germany's War Against the Jews* (New York, 1947); Eugene Davidson, *The Trial of the Germans* (New York, 1967); Raphael Lemkin, *Axis Rule in Occupied Europe* (Washington, 1944), with his invention of "genocide" and "ethnocide," p. 49; and Eugen Kogon's *Der SS Staat* (Frankfurt, 1946); Henry L. Feingold, *The Politics of Rescue: The Roosevelt Administration and the Holocaust* (New Brunswick, 1970), especially pages 168-177; Louis W. Holborn (ed.), *War and Peace Aims of the United Nations* (Boston, 1944), I, 14, 99, 129, 482-484; II, 216-218, 266; Samuel Halperin, *The Political World of American Zionism* (Detroit, 1961), pp. 29-44; Philip Friedman and Koppel S. Pinson, "Some Books on the Jewish Catastrophe," *Jewish Social Studies*, XII (January, 1950), 88-89.

Gerd Korman

form where Jewish historians tried to make a formal start for the study of the disaster. Under the auspices of the Conference on Jewish Relations, an organization founded in response to the rising tide of anti-Semitism in the 1930's, at the New York School for Social Research (an institution which especially helped to absorb refugee scholars from Germany), the "Problems of Research in the Study of the Jewish Catastrophe, 1939-1945" came under scrutiny.[7] Some of the scholars asked questions about the disaster in the context of Jewish history; some in the context of society.

Salo Baron and Philip Friedman spoke as rigorous historians of their people's past. We must make every effort to determine if the "lachrymose conception of Jewish history" is still valid; the primary task of the Jewish historian, proclaimed Baron, in the opening remarks to the Conference, was to identify and examine the "dissimilarities as well as the similarities between the great tragedy and the many lesser tragedies which preceded it." Friedman, one of a number of refugee scholars who had come from Central Europe to make their homes in the United States, made the destruction of European Jewry the focal point of his work. He bemoaned the quality of what he called "khurbn literature." To write, he said, "about the catastrophe or about personal experiences of this period has come to be a rather elemental passion, a popular movement which has its deep psychological and sociological roots. . . ." The flood of "inferior" work from amateurs overshadowed "the worthwhile material" endangering the standing of serious work about "our catastrophe."[8]

As a professional historian already at work on the Holocaust, Friedman distinguished between the general history of the war and the history of the Jewish people during the conflict. To the first, he assigned subjects of military campaigns, economic warfare, governments in exile, puppet governments in occupied countries, diplomacy, and resistance move-

---

[7] On the New York School for Social Research, see Alvin Johnson, *Pioneer's Progress* (New York, 1952). On the early history of the Conference, see Morris R. Cohen, *A Dreamer's Journey* (Glencoe, Ill., 1949), pp. 241-257.

[8] Salo Baron, "Opening Remarks" to the Conference, *Jewish Social Studies*, XII (January, 1950), 14; Friedman, "Research and Literature on the Recent Jewish Tragedy," *ibid.*, 25, 26. Twenty years later Lucy S. Dawidowicz, another Jewish historian who made the Holocaust an area of special interest, said much the same thing in a review of Nora Levin's *The Holocaust: The Destruction of European Jewry, 1933-1945* (New York, 1968), in *Jewish Social Studies*, XXXII (July, 1970), 176-177. It is possible that the charge of amateurism is not always used in its proper sense: Jacob Robinson of YIVO does not consider Hannah Arendt a professional historian. Miss Arendt does not consider Robinson a professional historian: "The Formidable Dr. Robinson: A Reply," *The New York Review of Books*, V (January 20, 1966), 27. For examples of Miss Dawidowicz's work see "The Epic of the Warsaw Ghetto," *Menorah Journal*, XXXVIII (Winter, 1950), 88-103, and her long introduction to an anthology she called *The Golden Tradition* (New York, 1967).

ments. "Of a secondary character only are the German terror and persecution of the civilian population, forced labor, population movements, the reactions of the civilian populations, the concentration camps . . . and similar factors." Research on the Jewish question had to be governed by the principal difference existing between Allied countries and European Jewry: the Allies fought for a democratic victory; European Jewry also fought, but for survival. Thus, for the Jewish historian "a different gamut of topics, subjects, and emphasis" presented themselves. "Most relevant are the suffering of the Jewish civilian population and until the final catastrophe of extermination, the struggle for life." Guarding himself against unimaginative and unrealistic compartmentalization he made the obvious plea: "just as the Jewish catastrophe in the Nazi era can be studied only in the broader context of the general events so the general European history of the period cannot be adequately interpreted without full understanding of the German war against the Jewish people."[9]

Too much has happened and too much had been said for the Holocaust to remain in such seemingly modest parameters. The late Solomon Bloom, a student of European intellectual history, asked the sort of questions which in later years continued to arouse storms of controversy.[10] After examining the careers of the Jewish police chief in Vilna and of Mordechai Rumkowski, a man he called the dictator of Lodz, Bloom insisted that "the moral position of the dictator must be recognized as a datum for study. In accepting it, the student has the example of older, but not inferior social scientists, like Thucydides . . . who did not shrink from judgments of religion, taste and morality. . . ." For "Jewish social scientists, there is another obligation still." It is possible, Bloom thought, that the Jew who made life and death decisions for other Jews derived "his ideas from folklore rather than from the more self-conscious and sophisticated culture." Consequently, and, he might have added, in line with the ideas of Jewish secularists and anti-clerics, and even some devoutly religious Jews caught up in the destruction, the student of Judaism is obliged to raise the question about "the sense . . . of mission; the hope or conviction that the Jews are an indestructible

[9] Actually, these comments were made later, first in 1950, at the International Conference on World War II in the West held in Amsterdam, and then 1951, in *Jewish Social Studies*, XIII (July, 1951), 235, 250. In 1950, he also published *Oświecim* in Yiddish (Buenos Aires); in 1954, he edited *Martyrs and Fighters* (New York).

[10] I am assuming that the particular intensity of the controversy over *Eichmann in Jerusalem* (New York, 1964) is in part, but only in part, explained by the way readers responded to Bloom's kind of thinking. On the controversy, see Jacob Robinson, *And the Crooked Shall be made Straight: The Eichmann Trial, The Jewish Catastrophe, and Hannah Arendt's Narrative* (Philadelphia, 1965); Arendt, "Dr. Robinson," *The New York Review of Books*. The Leo Baeck Institute in New York has catalogued articles in the controversy under Miss Arendt's name.

and eternal people, that 'The Lord will leave a remnant.'" For all of "these and other such turn up in the thinking and self-justification of the dictator. . . ." Bloom dared the Jewish social scientists not to judge Jewish folklore, tradition, and ideology.[11]

Hannah Arendt pushed beyond him. For her, Hitler "was not like Jenghis Khan and not worse than some other great criminal but entirely different. The unprecedented is neither the murder itself nor the number of victims and not even 'the number of persons who united to perpetrate them.'" It was much rather, she said in 1949, "the ideological nonsense which caused them, the mechanization of the execution and the central and calculated establishment of a world of the dying in which nothing any longer made sense." Concentration camps were "the laboratories in the experiment of total domination" in which the "human person" was "transformed into a completely conditioned being whose reactions can be calculated even when he is led to certain death. . . ." Her evidence told her that "SS men in charge were completely normal; their selection was achieved according to all kinds of fantastic principles, none of which could possibly assure the selection of especially cruel or sadistic men." She could only "guess in what forms human life is being lived as though it took place on another planet," but it appeared "to be beyond doubt that within this whole system the prisoners did not fail to fulfill the same 'duties' as the guards themselves"; it also appeared that those inmates who had "not done anything," in comparison with criminals and political prisoners, "were the first to disintegrate." Bruno Bettelheim, she knew, had argued in 1943, that the speed of disintegration resulted from "the middle-class origins of the 'innocents'—at his time mostly Jews." But he was wrong. "We know from other reports, especially also from the Soviet Union, that 'lower-class innocents' disintegrate just as quickly."[12]

Obviously, Miss Arendt was after something big and frightfully im-

---

[11] Solomon F. Bloom, "Toward the Ghetto Dictator," *Jewish Social Studies*, XII (January, 1950), 77, 78. See also his "Dictator of the Lodz Ghetto: The Strange History of Mordechai Rumkowski," *Commentary*, VII (February, 1949), 111-122. In addition to the remarks in Emanuel Ringelblum's *Notes from the Warsaw Ghetto*, ed. Jacob Sloan (New York, 1958), pp. 291, 336-337, see the following: *Scroll of Agony: The Warsaw Diary of Chaim A. Kaplan*, translated by Abraham I. Katsh (New York, 1965), pp. 323-340; Joseph Kermish, "First Stirrings," *Yad Vashem Bulletin* (October, 1963), pp. 12-19; (August, 1964), pp. 22-23. Elie Wiesel has told about rabbis in a concentration camp putting God on trial and finding Him guilty of charges officially leveled against Him. All of the charges had to do with the fate that had befallen Jews under the Nazis. Wiesel, "The Holocaust of European Jewry: One Generation Later," a lecture given at the National Hillel Summer Institute, Starlight, New York, Summer, 1965.

[12] Hannah Arendt, "Social Science Techniques and the Study of Concentration Camps," *Jewish Social Studies*, XII (January, 1950), 64, 60, 61, 59, 63, 62; Bruno Bettelheim, "Behavior in Extreme Situations," *The Journal of Abnormal and Social Psychology*, XXXVIII (October, 1943), 417-452.

portant. Her context was society; her searchlights philosophy, history, sociology, and psychology. When Baron tried to identify the "unprecedented aspects of the Nazi attack on Jews, quite apart from its magnitude," he identified these points of difference within Jewish history: the geographic area was much larger; there had occurred a much greater loss of the world's Jewish population; there had existed a "considered plan to eliminate all Jews"; there had been a "finality and immutability of the fate of Nazi victims"; all the other disasters in Jewish history "almost invariably [were] mass reactions unsupported by, indeed often directed against, state organs." When Miss Arendt tried to identify the unique and unprecedented in the camps, she insisted it was only to be found in the absence of utilitarian criteria, as these had usually been understood in the past. (She had in mind aggressive wars, massacres of enemy populations, massacres of a "hostile people," extermination of natives in the "process of colonization," slavery, driving forced labor gangs, or striving for world rule.)[13]

These questions, generalizations, and judgments helped to determine the place of the Holocaust in American historical writing. In no time at all, Miss Arendt's words of 1944, seemed applicable to the kinds of thinking that engaged her, Bloom, and Bettelheim. In no time at all, too, historians in the United States seemed content to ignore the works of colleagues in America and elsewhere especially concerned with "the suffering of the Jewish population and . . . its struggle for life," and with the efforts to find a place for the Holocaust in Jewish history.[14]

The publication and reception of Raul Hilberg's book in 1961 made that vantage point only too apparent for anyone who also knew the works of Gerald Reitlinger and Robert Koehl, and the English-language publications from the Wiener Library in London, Yad Vashem in Jerusalem, the Leo Baeck Institute, and YIVO Institute for Jewish Research in New York City.[15] Hilberg's astounding study, preoccupied with

---

[13] Baron, "Opening Remarks," p. 15; Arendt, "Social Science Techniques," p. 51.

[14] Historians in the United States ignorant of the work of Jewish historians usually are also unaware that Jewish historians had problems similar to those of German scholars who were trying to find a place for the Hitler period in German history. For a summary of the problem of Jewish historiography, see Leni Yahil, "The Holocaust in Jewish Historiography," *Yad Vashem Studies*, VII (1968), 57-71. For comment on the problem in German historiography see Hans Herzfeld, "Germany: After the Catastrophe," in Walter Laqueur and George L. Mosse (eds.), *The New History: Trends in Historical Research and Writing Since World War II* (New York, 1967), pp. 77-89, and Hans Mommsen, "Historical Scholarship in Transition: The Situation in the Federal Republic of Germany," *Daedalus*, C (Spring, 1971), 475-508.

[15] Raul Hilberg, *The Destruction of the European Jews* (Chicago, 1961); Gerald Reitlinger, *The Final Solution* (London, 1953); Robert L. Koehl, *RKFDV: German Resettlement and Population Policy, 1939-1945* (Cambridge, 1957); *Wiener Library Bulletin; Yad Vashem Bulletin; Yad Vashem Studies; Leo Baeck Institute Yearbook;*

Gerd Korman

the problems of bureaucracy and administration in modern totalitarian states, could only evoke admiration from anyone with respect for an approach which had been first used so successfully in the 1950's on Prussia by Hans Rosenberg, then a colleague of Bloom's at Brooklyn College.[16] Even though Hilberg stated explicitly that his book was about Germans and the ways in which they hunted and killed Jews, his loose comments about Jewish behavior made his work generally known and talked about.[17] It was clear enough that his study was based largely on German sources, but an American scholar thought his section explaining Jewish passiveness was one of the finest in the book. By itself such praise would not be so startling, even in *The Journal of Modern History*, but the same reviewer thought that Hilberg had gone "too far in his wholesale condemnation of the German bureaucracy. There were courageous officials who did what they could to alleviate the lot of the Jews. . . ."[18] He saw no reason to criticize Hilberg for his "wholesale" judgments about Jews during hundreds of years of European history.[19]

III

I believe now that the indifference to the Jewish side of the war may have been aggravated by a strange transformation in the vocabulary people used when they spoke and wrote about the catastrophe. I have used "Holocaust" in this article, but in 1949, there was no "Holocaust" in the English language in the sense that word is used today. Scholars and writers had used "permanent pogrom"—this term of Jacob Lestschinsky in 1941, meant that the pogrom had "no passing or limited political and economic aims but the extirpation, the physical elimination of its Jewish citizens"—or the "recent catastrophe," or the "recent Jewish catastrophe," or the "great catastrophe," or "disaster," or "the disaster." Sometimes writers spoke about annihilation and destruction without use of any of these terms. All of them, by intent or accident, translated accurately the Hebrew words *shoa* and *khurban* because like them they carried only secular freight. (Yiddish, the other language so

---

YIVO *Annual*, VIII (1954) and XXI (1969). The Leo Baeck Institute has offices in New York, London, and Jerusalem.

[16] Hans Rosenberg, *Bureaucracy, Aristocracy, and Autocracy: The Prussian Experience, 1660-1815* (Cambridge, 1958). The connection is direct and personal. See Hilberg's expression of gratitude to Rosenberg in *Destruction*, preface.

[17] For examples of these kinds of comments see Hilberg, *Destruction*, pp. 662-669, 675, 676.

[18] Andreas Dorpalen, in *The Journal of Modern History*, XXXIV (June, 1962), 226-227. See also Gerhard L. Weinberg, in *The American Historical Review*, LXVII (April, 1962), 694-695.

[19] If one takes him literally, Hilberg ranges over 2,000 years, covering the entire Diaspora. See his comment in *Destruction* on p. 666.

profoundly involved with the disaster and with the literature about it, contributed besides *khurbn*, the word *umkummen.*)[20]

In 1953, the state of Israel formally injected itself into the study of the destruction of European Jewry, and so became involved in the transformation. In the anguish of mourning the dead of Europe and the dead who fell in Israel's lonely fight for nationhood, the Knesset gave posthumous citizenship to the 6,000,000 and established, in controversy, Yad Vashem as a "Martyrs' and Heroes' Remembrance Authority" in language not especially encouraging to the spirit of objective scholarship. "May every person in Israel, every Jew wherever he may be, know that our People has its own reckoning, the reckoning of the generations of the Eternal People—a reckoning of an Eternal People, whose entire history is proof and evidence of the prophetic promise: And I said unto you in your blood, 'Live' [Ezekiel, 16-6]." Two years later Yad Vashem translated *shoa* into "Disaster" and announced for itself and YIVO in New York that henceforth the study of the catastrophe would be divided this way: "The approach of the Disaster, 1920-1933"; "The beginnings of the Disaster, 1933-1939"; and "The Disaster, 1939-1945."[21]

But then the change occurred quickly. When catastrophe had lived side by side with disaster the word holocaust had appeared now and then. In 1951, for example, Jacob Shatzky of YIVO spoke of "the Nazi holocaust," but apparently he did not mean to apply the phrase specifically to the destruction of European Jewry. Between 1957 and 1959, however, "Holocaust" took on such a specific meaning. It was used at the Second World Congress of Jewish Studies held in Jerusalem, and when Yad Vashem published its third yearbook, one of the articles dealt

---

[20] Jacob Lestschinsky, *Erev Churbn* (On the Eve of Destruction) (Buenos Aires, 1951); Samuel Gringanz, in *Jewish Social Studies*, XIV (October, 1952), 326-327; Leo Schwartz, *ibid.*, 378-379; Theodor Abel, *ibid.*, V (January, 1943), 79; Werner J. Cahnman, "A Regional Approach to German Jewish History," *ibid.*, (July, 1943), 211-224; Oscar Karbach, "The Founder of Political Antisemitism," *ibid.*, VII (January, 1945), 3-4; Adolf Kober, "Jewish Communities in Germany from the Age of Enlightenment to Their Destruction by the Nazis," *ibid.*, IX (July, 1947), 230-238; Lestschinsky, "The Anti-Jewish Program: Tsarist Russia, The Third Reich and Independent Poland," *ibid.*, III (April, 1941), 147-148; Yad Vashem, *Aims and Activities* (Jerusalem, 1955); Friedman, "Research and Literature," used most of these terms interchangeably. For examples of the use of *shoa* in Biblical writings see Ps. 35-8, 63-10, 35-17; Job, 30-3, 14, 38-27; Ez. 38-9.

[21] Yad Vashem, *Martyrs' and Heroes' Remembrance Authority* (Jerusalem, 1955), pp. 7, 9, 17, 19; *Jerusalem Post*, August 20, 1953. The Zionist Congress discussed such an authority in August, 1945. The *Va'ad Leumi* of Palestine Jewry kept the idea alive. After the establishment of Israel, Ben Zion Dinur, historian and Minister for Education and Culture, was instrumental in the Knesset's passage of the bill establishing Yad Vashem; Professor Dinur became its first head. Controversy in the Knesset involved the opposition of *Herut* to Moshe Sharet's government over the Reparations Agreement with Germany, and the Knesset's left-wing members, some of whom wanted to mention by name in the law specific groups of fighters.

Gerd Korman

with "Problems Relating to a Questionnaire on the Holocaust." Afterwards Yad Vashem switched from "Disaster" to "Holocaust" although it retained the title of its yearbooks *Yad Vashem Studies of the Jewish Catastrophe and Resistance.*[22]

In other words, conversion of the destruction of European Jewry into "Holocaust" began before the publication of Hilberg's book and before Eichmann's capture. There were those who refused to use the word so exclusively, preferring to apply it to the Civil War, World War II or III (a nuclear holocaust), but there appeared no formal effective opposition. Within the Jewish world the word became commonplace, in part because Elie Wiesel and other gifted writers and speakers, in public meetings or in articles for *Commentary* and journals such as *Judaism* and *Midstream* made it coin of the realm. By 1968, even the Library of Congress had no choice. As Jewish scholars in various parts of the world and in various languages revealed with Jewish sources the details of the suffering of the Jewish population and its struggle for spiritual and physical survival, the international serial and monographic literature using "Holocaust" became so significant, said the Library's Catalogue Division, committed to a policy of following usage, that it felt compelled to create a major entry card: "Holocaust—Jewish, 1939-1945."[23]

---

[22] *Jewish Social Studies*, XIII (April, 1951), 175-176. Bernard Mark, "Problems Related to the Study of the Jewish Resistance Movement in the Second World War," *Yad Vashem Studies*, III (1959) 41-65; Zvi Bar-Or and Dov Levin, "Problems Relating to a Questionnaire on the Holocaust," *ibid.*, 91-117. These papers and a number of others, such as Friedman's "Problems of Research on the European Jewish Catastrophe," pp. 25-40, published in this volume were read at the Second World Congress of Jewish Studies held in Jerusalem in 1957. The *Yad Vashem Bulletin* (April, 1957), p. 35, has a reference to "Research on the Holocaust Period." Of course, there had been writers who spoke of the Nazi holocaust even before 1951, but their use of the phrase was applied to the general destructive impact of Nazism. Morris Cohen used the phrase in that way as early as 1945. Cohen, *A Dreamer's Journey*, pp. 256-257.

[23] Higham, *History*, pp. 200, 201; Robert E. Osgood, *Ideals and Self-Interest in America's Foreign Relations* (Chicago, 1964), p. 415; Louis L. Snyder, *The War: A Concise History 1939-1945* (New York, 1960), preface, and the caption underneath a picture of Hiroshima after the bomb—this picture is opposite a page showing "Ghastly scenes in a Nazi extermination camp." *Holocaust!* by Paul Benzaquin (New York, 1959) was a novel about the Coconut Grove fire, but increasingly the word was used in titles of anthologies, memoirs, and surveys of the destruction of European Jewry: Alexander Donat, *The Holocaust Kingdom: A Memoir* (New York, 1965); Sam E. Bloch (ed.), *Holocaust and Rebirth* (New York, 1965); Jack Kuper, *Child of the Holocaust* (London, 1967); Levin, *Holocaust;* Albert H. Friedlander, *Out of the Whirlwind: A Reader of Holocaust Literature* (New York, 1968); Jacob Glatstein, *Anthology of Holocaust Literature* (New York, 1969); Irving Halperin, *Messengers from the Dead: Literature of the Holocaust* (Philadelphia, 1970). My information about the Library of Congress comes from Charles Bead and Theodore Wiener via telephone on August 10, 1971. The Catalog Division has some correspondence from individuals who tried to find out why the new category was being used. Before 1968, the Library catalogued "Holocaust" books under various subcategories of World War II—Personal Narrative, Jewish, is one example—or under the history of Jews by communities.

Thus it was that a word brought into the English language by Christian writers centuries ago—they took the Greek word used in the Septuagint exclusively for translating words in the *Torah* meaning sacrifices consumed by fire—came to be the noun symbolizing a new phenomenon in Western civilization: the destruction of European Jewry. It was also, I believe, that a change in word usage in the English language helped to shift concern from the particularity of the disaster within Jewish history to an emphasis on its uniqueness in modern history. In turn, that shift made it easier to level the charge of parochialism against Holocaust advocates, who, like myself, usually cannot conceive of Auschwitz without the Nazis' anti-Semitism. After all, Miss Arendt had all along insisted that the uniqueness of Auschwitz lay elsewhere! "Antisemitism by itself," she declared, "has such a long and bloody history that the very fact that these death factories were chiefly fed with Jewish 'material' has somewhat obliterated the uniqueness of this operation. . . . Antisemitism only prepared the ground to make it easier to start the extermination with the Jewish people."

However, that difference between Holocaust advocates and those who share Miss Arendt's views on the place of anti-Semitism in the development of Nazi Germany's particular methods of domination and annihilation must not obscure the more fundamental agreement between them. In its totality, she also said in 1949, the German way "must cause social scientists and historical scholars to reconsider their hitherto unquestioned fundamental preconceptions regarding the course of the world and human behavior."[24]

IV

For most historians in America World War II cast so narrow a shadow that they almost missed the destruction of European Jewry. After 1945, they wrote textbooks about modern Europe, the twentieth century, or about the history of the United States without any concern for the kind of appreciation a Friedman or a Miss Arendt had for the actual past, or as it had been told by some colleagues here, in Europe, and Israel.[25] Moreover, the Holocaust did not usually reverberate in the consciousness of historians in the United States when they wrote the secondary litera-

---

[24] Roland de Vaux, O. P., *Ancient Israel Its Life and Institutions* (New York, 1961), p. 415; Arendt, "Social Science Techniques," pp. 49, 53; in the original these passages appear in a different sequence. Of course, from the very beginning, many people said or implied the sort of things Justice Robert H. Jackson declared in 1945: "History . . . does not record a crime ever perpetrated against so many victims or one ever carried out with such calculated cruelty. . . ." See Weinreich, *Hitler's Professors*, p. 6. See also Holborn, *War and Peace Aims*, II, 216-218, 266.

[25] On textbooks, see Gerd Korman, "Silence in American History Textbooks," *Yad Vashem Studies*, VIII (1970), 183-202.

ture of their profession. Admittedly, that literature is vast, but it would appear that the generalization applies to most colleagues writing about recent German and American history, or about World War II in particular. Leaving aside the historians whose primary professional preoccupation is Jewish history, after one adds to scholars already mentioned George Mosse, Fritz Stern, and Gunther Lewy, one soon runs out of names of historians working in the United States who have moved the Holocaust toward the center of their historical consciousness.[26]

No doubt there is many a historian whose work does not touch either subject, but who, in strange places, reveals the presence of each in his historical imagination. Richard B. Morris, for example, known especially for his work on colonial America and the early national period, felt compelled to write in a review that *A Dual Heritage* "is a serious contribution not only to an understanding of the role of American Jewry in the generation before the Holocaust but also to the development of the movement for political reform in America." Peter Gay, whose pagan hero in the enlightenment was David Hume, in his first venture into American history, wrote a beautiful dedication to "the many thousands of pilgrims, Jewish and not Jewish . . . whom Hitler compelled to discover America . . . to the D.P.'s who came out of the camps without families and who, with the indelible numbers on their arms and their indelible memories . . . started new families. . . ." All of these, he said, "were in their own ways heroes . . . in danger of being forgotten and deserve to be remembered."[27]

---

[26] I base this generalization primarily on an examination of a number of professional journals, especially the reviews of books on subjects related to the Holocaust. The journals I looked at most carefully were *The American Historical Review, The Journal of American History,* and *The Journal of Modern History*. See also the periodical guide, *America: History and Life,* I-VII. There are also historians like Arthur Hertzberg, Rudolf Glanz, and Zosa Szajkowski, who have made important contributions to the complex history of the background of the Holocaust, but, in comparison to those listed, their primary preoccupation was Jewish history. Hertzberg, *The French Enlightenment and the Jews* (New York, 1968), pp. 5-6, says his book is an effort to explain Auschwitz: "The era of Western history that began with the French Revolution ended in Auschwitz." Szajkowski has published important articles, some in *American Jewish Historical Quarterly:* "A Note on the American-Jewish Struggles Against Nazism and Communism in the 1930's," LIX (March, 1970), 277-281 is an example for American history; for French history, see *Jews and the French Revolutions* (New York, 1970). For Glanz, see *Studies in Judaica Americana* (New York, 1970), and "The Jewish Execution in Medieval Germany," *Jewish Social Studies,* V (January, 1943), 3-26. George Mosse has written *The Crisis of German Ideology* (New York, 1964), and *Germans and Jews* (New York, 1970); Fritz Stern, *The Politics of Cultural Despair* (Berkeley, 1961); Gunther Lewy, *The Catholic Church and Nazi Germany* (New York, 1964). See also Robert F. Byrnes, *Antisemitism in Modern France* (New Brunswick, 1950), and Michael A. Meyer, *The Origins of the Modern Jew* (Detroit, 1967).

[27] Richard B. Morris' review of Naomi W. Cohen's *A Dual Heritage: The Public Career of Oscar S. Strauss* (Philadelphia, 1969), in *Jewish Social Studies,* XXXII (July, 1970), 227; Peter Gay, *A Loss of Mastery* (Berkeley, 1966), p. vi.

In general, however, I believe, the place of the Holocaust in the secondary literature is like its place in histories of World War II written by Louis Snyder and Gordon Wright. Snyder's was a popularized account based on his vast knowledge of modern European history. From his own preface, where he speaks of the "devastating man-made holocaust of World War II," and from Eric Sevareid's remarks in the introduction ("in World War II . . . we shivered in the cold stench of medieval mania loosed from the catacombs of the Dark Ages, for this time men saw in the Germanic insanity mass butchering following from deliberate purpose, . . .") there is no doubt Snyder understood what happened, but in the work itself he makes about as much room for the Holocaust as a good survey of Western civilization since Columbus.[28]

Wright's account is different.[29] Even though in much of this book the destruction of European Jewry is at the periphery of his consciousness, he does stop for a moment and devotes two, long, tightly written paragraphs to the Nazi racial policy which "reached its epitome . . . when applied to the Jews." He does not attend to the special set of circumstances in which Jews found themselves and seems overly concerned to make sure his reader understands that Jews "were not the only victims of the extermination camps." But, by leaning heavily on Hans Buchheim and his German colleagues, and on Koehl's monograph he is able to convey an impression about the execution of the Final Solution with which scholars steeped in Jewish sources could find little fault.[30] The problem with Wright lies elsewhere.

For Wright there is no Jewish community, and perhaps for that reason no Jewish resistance. In and of itself his silence on the subject of resistance among Jews would not be so startling. However, Wright has an especially good discussion of the entire resistance movement in Europe in which he seeks to explain why patterns of resistance were different in character and timing from one country to the next. Thus, he lauds the

---

[28] Snyder, *World War II*. Some historians may have a methodological principle which prevents them from asking "why" if their evidence is silent about Jews, or reveals decisive indifference to them. I do not pretend to understand such a principle, but see Osgood, *Ideals*, pp. 400, 415, and William E. Leuchtenburg, *Franklin D. Roosevelt and the New Deal 1932-1940* (New York, 1963), p. 286. On World War II literature, see also Louis Morton, "World War II: A Survey of Recent Writings," *The American Historical Review*, LXXV (December, 1970), 1987-2008.

[29] The quotations come from *The Ordeal of Total War 1939-1945* (New York, 1968), pp. 35, 74, 75, 93-94, 101, 112, 126-127, 156, 158-159, 162.

[30] Koehl, *RKFDV*, pp. 198, 199. See also his sensitive remarks in a review of Eberhard Kolb's *Bergen Belsen: Geschichte des "Aufenthaltslagers" 1943-1945* (Hanover, 1962), in *The Journal of Modern History*, XXXV (September, 1963), 327-328. A comparison of Gordon Craig's *The Politics of the Prussian Army 1640-1945* (New York, 1964) with Karl Demeter's *The German Officer Corps in Society and State 1650-1945* (London, 1965) is also instructive.

Poles: "Hitler's policy, to be sure, left Poles virtually no choice: not to resist meant ruthless exploitation and national degradation. To a people as proud and stiffnecked as the Poles their duty was clear: they gradually organized an elaborate network of institutions that some Poles described as a 'secret state'." Their uprising in 1944, in Warsaw, was one of the "most heroic chapters in the history of the European resistance." In the text there is not a whisper about that other uprising in Warsaw a year before when a tiny group of descendants from the Bible's stiff-necked people rose against the Germans.[31]

By comparison, and only by comparison, Wright spends an inordinate amount of space probing the particularity of the admittedly complex and poignant positions in which anti-Nazi Germans found themselves. He wrote:

> More than 200,000 Germans were imprisoned or interned during the prewar years, and many others went into voluntary exile. The flow into the concentration camps continued after 1939, though at a slower rate. This preventive action destroyed much of the potential resistance leadership. Furthermore, the Nazi regime's police state techniques made underground plotting exceptionally hazardous, for no one could be sure whom to trust. An additional handicap was Allied suspicion. Efforts by resistance leaders to make contact with Allied officials were usually viewed skeptically by the latter; the German underground failed to get the kind of aid and encouragement that buoyed up the spirits of resisters elsewhere. All in all, it is perhaps astonishing that active resistance ever developed in war-time Germany.

Word for word, Hannah Arendt and Oscar Handlin have used almost identical language about Jewish resistance.[32]

A recent issue of *The American Historical Review* illustrates the ways the Holocaust reverberates in the minds of European historians working in the United States on subjects other than the war. Fritz Stern, Gerald D. Feldman, and Henry Ashby Turner each examined the subject of economics and politics in the period between Bismarck's time and the rise of Hitler. To be sure, writing about the friendship between Gerson Bleichröder and Bismarck all but forced Stern to say something about the Jewish component of the relationship, but Stern demonstrates that he has worked through the conceptual problem of the place of Gentile-Jewish relations in nineteenth-century German history, and knows what

---

[31] This comment does not apply to the bibliography where there are references to the uprising in 1943, but under the section "Nazi Persecution of 'Racial' and Political Enemies." There are no entries under "Resistance Movements."

[32] Arendt, "Formidable Dr. Robinson"; Oscar Handlin, "Jewish Resistance to the Nazis," *Commentary*, XXXIV (November, 1962), 398-405.

is demanded of him as a European historian by virtue of the destruction of European Jewry. "What was it that linked the Jew—hedged in by apprehensions and uncertainties, a partial stranger in the land he loved too well, and the Junker. . . ." He remarks that Bleichröder's visit to Versailles in 1871 "inflamed the already surprisingly fierce anti-Semitism in those all-Gentile surroundings." Finally, he takes the long view:

> Bleichröder's spectacular rise marked an important stage in the history of German Jewry. . . . In their rise and fall the Bleichröders describe a kind of Jewish Buddenbrooks. The social and psychological precariousness of their position, always present beneath the glittering surface, became desperately clear after the rise of the Nazis. Bleichröder's descendants appealed to Adolph Eichmann to be exempted from deportation. It was a poignant, futile end to the story of the Bleichröders in Germany.

There is nothing like this at all in the articles by Feldman and Turner, who are interested in the relationship of big business to the Weimar Republic and the Nazi Party. Turner includes the following passage, which is the only reference in both pieces to Jews and anti-Semitism in Germany: "[Emil] Kirdorf did not withdraw because the Nazis were anti-democratic, aggressively chauvinistic, or anti-Semitic (even though he, like most business leaders, was himself not an anti-Semite). What drove him out of the party was the social and economic radicalism of the Left-wing Nazis." Fortunately, for readers of *The American Historical Review*, Ernst Nolte, a German scholar from Marburg, admittedly associated by some with a monolithic and "totalitarian" interpretation of National Socialism, identified an important issue which simply was excluded by Feldman and Turner. Hitler seemed to share the "passionate thinking" of most businessmen, together with officers, professors, clergymen, civil servants, and even functionaries of the Social Democratic Party, and therefore gained their support. "The guilt of the German industrialists lies not in the fact that they were children of their time. . . . It lies in their failure to recognize that the fundamental nature and ultimate consequences of National Socialism—the self-sufficient racial state, withdrawing from all disturbing communication with the world. . . ."[33]

I have left to the last historians working in the field of American history because the phenomenon of the Holocaust at the moment directly

---

[33] Fritz Stern, "Gold and Iron: The Collaboration and Friendship of Gerson Bleichröder and Otto von Bismarck"; Gerald D. Feldman, "The Social and Economic Policies of German Big Business, 1918-1929"; Henry Ashby Turner, Jr., "Big Business and the Rise of Hitler"; Ernst Nolte, "Big Business and German Politics: A Comment"; all of which are to be found in *The American Historical Review*, LXXV (October, 1969), 38, 40, 46, 78; Mommsen, "Transition," p. 489.

Gerd Korman

affects only the years since 1933. Until 1962, only Handlin ventured into print specifically examining aspects of the Holocaust in Europe, but in the last few years a number of book-length studies have looked at the Jewish refugee crisis of the 1930's and American policies towards Jews seeking to leave Europe then and during the war itself. All these works address themselves to the question Leon Poliakov raised in 1949, two years after Henry Morgenthau, Jr. had published his dramatic article in *Collier's*. Are Morgenthau's charges well-founded, he asked? "Is it true that another attitude in 1942, 1943, and 1944 would have made it possible to save the lives of hundreds of thousands of Jews?" He knew only the historians of the future could provide the answer.[34]

In 1971, in that future, after a number of articles and after three books on the subject—Henry Feingold uses the word "Holocaust" in his subtitle—the question remains as open-ended as it was in the midst of World War II. In conjunction with other studies about Roosevelt and his administrations, these works are helping us to know what decisions were in fact made about European Jewry by men in government and all other elements of the American population.[35] As that knowledge is be-

---

[34] Handlin, "Resistance"; Leon Poliakov, "Mussolini and the Extermination of the Jews," *Jewish Social Studies*, XI (January, 1949), 1; Arthur D. Morse, *While Six Million Died: A Chronicle of American Apathy* (New York, 1968); David S. Wyman, *Paper Walls: America and the Refugee Crisis* (Amherst, 1968); Feingold, *Politics of Rescue;* Edward N. Saveth, "Franklin D. Roosevelt and the Jewish Crisis 1933-1945," *American Jewish Yearbook*, XLVII (1945-1946), 37-50; David Brody, "American Jewry, The Refugees and Immigration Restriction (1932-1942)," *Publications of the American Jewish Historical Society*, XLV (June, 1956), 219-247; Sheldon Spears, "The United States and the Persecution of the Jews in Germany, 1933-1945," *Jewish Social Studies*, XXX (October, 1968), 215-242. I am aware that American historians can *use* the Holocaust as one of the ways for showing FDR's clay feet and for making the argument that American society became increasingly dehumanized after World War I. James R. Leutzer, for example, knows that Roosevelt could have "done something, had he tried," that "Long was a sticking cog in the machinery," and "that human lives were the subject of the paperwork routinely shuffled from in-box to pigeon hole." See *The Journal of American History*, LVIII (June, 1971), 216-217. James T. Patterson adds Roosevelt's "reluctance to admit Jewish refugees" to the president's "timid support" of the Fair Employment Practices Commission during the war and to his "dealing with Japanese Americans." Patterson's sum of such evidence enables him to say that James MacGregor Burns in his *Roosevelt: The Soldier of Freedom* (New York, 1970) shows FDR to have been a "better Jeffersonian in principle than in practice." *Ibid.*, p. 218. Robert A. Divine, on the other hand, makes no reference at all to the Jewish refugee crisis in a review of Burns' second volume of his study of Roosevelt in *Political Science Quarterly*, LXXXVI (June, 1971), 289. See also Robert H. Ferrel's review of Divine's *Roosevelt and World War II* (Baltimore, 1969) in *The American Historical Review*, LXXV (December, 1969), 613-614.

[35] In addition to the books already cited see also Arnold A. Offner, *American Appeasement: United States Foreign Policy and Germany, 1933-1938* (Cambridge, 1969); Selig Adler, *The Isolationist Impulse: Its Twentieth Century Reaction* (Glencoe, Ill., 1966); Robert A. Divine, *American Immigration Policy, 1924-1952* (New Haven, 1957); John M. Blum (ed.), *From the Morgenthau Diaries* (3 vols.; Boston, 1959-1967); Allan Nevins, *Herbert Lehman and His Era* (New York, 1963); Robert Dallek, *Democrat and Diplomat: The Life of William E. Dodd* (New York, 1968).

coming grounded in reliable evidence, the written history of the United States since World War I is being drawn into the entire question of the destruction of European Jewry. In time, no doubt, some scholars examining American history since 1914 will also wonder if America's responses to the Armenian disaster in the first year of the war were symptomatic of fundamental changes in American society which led to the institutionalization of racism and nationalism in the quota principle of immigration legislation.[36]

One other area in American history has involved the Holocaust. Stanley Elkins has used Bruno Bettelheim and other students of personality disintegration in the concentration camp to probe the effects of slavery on personality. Coming at a time when many historians were especially attracted to the behavioral sciences, his concern with personality changes prompted much informal and formal discussion about Jewish behavior in concentration camps and the use of each without the other in the study of adult personality changes under slavery or in modern industrial society.[37]

These discussions have probably expanded the reverberative distance of the Holocaust in the time consciousness of American historians, but they seem not to have made them more aware of the substantial histori-

---

[36] John Higham in his *Strangers in the Land* (New Brunswick, 1955) makes some suggestions along this line at the very end of the book. Charles A. Beard, *The Open Door at Home* (New York, 1934), pp. 179-209. In 1935, the quota concept was being applied by the Works Project Administration in Chicago for assuring blacks at least five percent of the jobs in the construction industry. Correspondence in the files of Lawrence Oxley: National Archives. I am grateful to Professor James Gross, New York State School of Industrial and Labor Relations, Cornell, for this reference.

[37] Stanley M. Elkins, *Slavery: A Problem in American Institutional and Intellectual Life* (Chicago, 1963). As well as Bettelheim, Elkins refers to Eli Cohen's *Human Behavior in the Concentration Camp*, translated by M. H. Braaksman (New York, 1953). Although he does not refer to him, it is important to know that Erik H. Erikson, always conscious of the historical context in which a person develops, had written on a related phenomenon in "Hitler's Imagery and German Youth," *Psychiatry*, V (November, 1942), 475-493. This essay was reprinted in Clyde Kluckhohn and Henry A. Murray (eds.), *Personality in Nature, Society, and Culture* (New York, 1948), pp. 485-510; he also published "Wholeness and Totality," in Carl J. Friedrich (ed.), *Totalitarianism* (Cambridge, 1954). The latest use of psychiatry is made by Peter Lowenberg in "The Unsuccessful Adolescence of Heinrich Himmler," *The American Historical Review*, LXXVI (June, 1971), 612-641. For historians' discussion of slavery and concentration camps see "The Question of 'Sambo,'" *Newberry Library Bulletin*, V (December, 1958), 14-40; Earle E. Thorpe, "Chattel Slavery and Concentration Camps," *Negro History Bulletin*, XXV (May, 1962), 173-175; Eugene Genovese, "Rebelliousness and Docility in the Negro Slave: A Critique of the Elkins Thesis," *Civil War History*, XIII (December, 1967), 308-309, 312-313; George M. Frederickson and Christopher Lasch, "Resistance to Slavery," *ibid.*, 315-329; Kenneth Stampp, "Rebels and Sambos: The Search for the Negro's Personality in Slavery," *The Journal of Southern History*, XXXVII (August, 1971), 376-392. To me it is extraordinary that such knowledgeable students of slavery as Genovese, Stampp, and Thorpe can remain satisfied with evidence from Bettelheim (1943), Kogon (1946), and Miss Arendt (1953).

Gerd Korman

cal literature available from their colleagues especially involved with the Jewish side of the Holocaust. Why not? (1) Amateurs continue to flood the market, overshadowing the good work available in English, and perhaps leaving unsoiled only Hilberg and Miss Arendt, just because their work is not steeped in Jewish sources and has been severely attacked by the other side.[38] (2) Historians in the United States, sensitive to our closeness to the events, may consider the combined efforts of Reitlinger and Hilberg and of Miss Arendt as the best obtainable for the time being. (3) From the very beginning, perhaps, historians here assumed the subject was the special domain of colleagues in Europe, particularly in Germany. (4) Efforts among social scientists to identify the fundamental components of human behavior make the particularity of detailed European history about Jews, Jews and Gentiles, and about Jewish behavior under German rule all but unnecessary for even the historian engaged in analogical analysis. (5) The other millions who died in World War II, and since then, the outrageous suffering and killing of millions in Africa and Asia make it difficult to treat the destruction of European Jewry as another unique experience of the peculiar Jewish people. (6) Finally, it is also possible that historians in the United States may well consider the Holocaust as a subject whose primary significance lies in Jewish history and as such is parochial in nature.

There are three cogent reasons for suspecting that this last answer is closest to the mark of an admittedly fascinating but difficult problem whose roots are deep and entangled. (1) As a breed, historians are not especially heroic. They know that their work will be scrutinized for the tell-tale marks of anti-Semitism or self-hate. (2) The Jew has not been an indigenous element in the literary imagination of Americans as he has been in the imagination of Europeans. Leslie Fiedler once claimed that when the Jew did appear in American letters, as in the 1920's, he was usually an importation from medieval Europe's storehouse of stereotypes.[39] (3) Most working historians are so overwhelmed by nationalism that they forget in practice what they know in theory. David Potter ten years ago reminded his colleagues that they do not treat nationalism as one of many sets of competing devotions within one person or group of persons residing in a political territory. Thus, they often assume as legitimate only one set without considering the legitimacy of

---

[38] Dawidowicz, *Jewish Social Studies*, XXXII (July, 1970). Miss Arendt provides evidence of the animosities between herself, Hilberg, and other Jewish commentators in "Formidable Dr. Robinson."

[39] Leslie A. Fiedler, "Negro and Jew—Encounter in America," *Midstream*, II (Summer, 1956), 6-8.

any of the competitors.[40] The Jew in any nation-state in the hands of that kind of historian is always at a competitive disadvantage. Hence, to Samuel Eliot Morrison and Henry Steele Commager, Anne Frank was a little "German" girl even when writing her diary.[41] In 1969, however, Anne became a "Jewish" girl.[42]

Evidence abounds that Americans are becoming more sensitive about the complexity of their nationality. "Southern novelists, Jewish writers, Negro authors, and Beat pundits," we are told by the *Literary History of the United States* evaluating postwar fiction in America, "had emerged from the tragic underground of culture as the true spokesmen of mid-century America."[43] No doubt in response to them and in response to the events of their times, historians in the United States struggled to make room for Blacks and Indians as they never had before, and for the first time appeared to find new room for Jews and other ethnic groups whose devotions American historians, beclouded by nationalism or material environmentalism, sometimes attributed to the slow rate of Americanization or disparagingly considered as distractive delusions of romantic nationalism.[44]

But for the present, it is fair enough to say that there is no Holocaust phenomenon in the historical writing of Clio's disciples in the United States, except among practitioners of Jewish history and Jewish intellectuals.

---

[40] David A. Potter, "The Historian's Use of Nationalism and Vice Versa," *The American Historical Review*, LXVII (July, 1962), 924-950.

[41] *The Growth of the American Republic* (2 vols.; New York, 1962), II, 605-606.

[42] *Ibid.*, (6th rev. ed., 1969), pp. 609-610. See also p. 536 of the same work.

[43] Robert E. Spiller, *et al.*, *Literary History of the United States* (2 vols.; New York, 1963), I, 1420. There are some other indications of this trend. In 1971, for the first time in its history, the American Historical Association at its annual convention devoted one session to the "Holocaust" (co-sponsored by the YIVO Institute for Jewish Research and the Conference Group for Social and Administrative History) and another to "The Prussian Government and the Jews in the Wilhelmian Era." American Historical Association, *Program of the Eighty-Sixth Annual Meeting, December 28, 29, 30* (Washington, D.C., 1971), pp. 53, 59. The following titles were also published during that year: Michael R. Marrus, *The Politics of Assimilation: A Study of the French Jewish Community at the Time of the Dreyfus Affair* (New York, 1971), and Donald L. Niewyk, *Socialist, Anti-Semite, and Jew: German Social Democracy and the Problem of Anti-Semitism, 1919-1933* (Baton Rouge, 1971).

[44] In addition to the work of Charles A. Beard, see, for example, Sam B. Warner, *Streetcar Suburbs* (Cambridge, 1962), pp. 11-12; Caroline F. Ware (ed.), *The Cultural Approach to History* (New York, 1940), pp. 1, 72; Christopher Lasch, "The Trouble with Black Power," *The New York Review of Books*, X (February 29, 1968), 4-14.

The Soviet Treatment of the Holocaust

ERICH GOLDHAGEN

The guiding star of Soviet historiography has been the maxim enounced by the first doyen of Soviet historians, Pokrovsky, "history is politics projected into the past." The historian must depict the past in accordance with the prescriptions of the supreme political authority. He is to serve the state as "an engineer of human souls," as a propagandist wearing the toga of scholarship, as a workman who contributes to the unending task of keeping the minds of the citizens within the fetters of orthodoxy. "Objectivity" is not an ideal to be aspired to, but a "bourgeois" heresy to be guarded against.

To the Soviet leaders historiography is anything but bunk. When guided by the firm hand of the party the historian is an invaluable auxiliary in its perpetual struggles, but when allowed to pursue the uncontrolled course of his own mind, he may succumb to the blandishments of objectivity and become a source of infectiously seditious thought. "Historians are dangerous people. They must be controlled," said a Soviet leader. What Western leader would pay such tribute to any branch of Western historiography?

These prescriptions have found one of their most glaring fulfillments in the Soviet treatment of the Holocaust.

From the very beginning of the extermination of the Jews, Soviet historians and Soviet organs of opinion would not recognize the systematic extermination of the Jews as a singular event of the Second World War, let

---

ERICH GOLDHAGEN *teaches at Harvard University. This article was originally delivered at the annual meeting of the American Historical Association held in San Francisco on December 29, 1978.*

alone as an event almost without parallel in history; and the extermination itself was shrouded in a blanket of generalities. In mentioning the mass slaughter, Soviet writers would not call the victims "Jews" but Soviet citizens. For example, Soviet historians performed the remarkable feat of describing the Ghetto of Minsk without mentioning that Jews, and only Jews, were confined to it. An unpublicized prohibition has tended to bar the word Jew from the Soviet annals of Nazi atrocities.

This attitude is conspicuous in a diary of the Vilno Ghetto written by a young woman, M. Rol'nikaite, and published in an edition of 200,000 copies in 1965 under the title *I Must Recount (Ia Dolzhna Rasskazat)*. The book has been likened to the diary of Anne Frank, but unlike Anne Frank's diary Rol'nikaite's is in a fundamental respect manifestly inauthentic. It is an un-Jewish book, made so on purpose to accord with the party's political precepts. The book portrays the Ghetto inmates not as Jews bearing the stamp of the singular fate to which the Nazis had condemned them, giving voice to their anguish in the particular idiom of their people, expressing their hatred of the Lithuanian collaborators with the Germans, but as Soviet citizens pure and simple, imbued with the standardized sentiments of Soviet patriotism and speaking, or rather declaiming, official Soviet cliches. Indeed, the name Jew appears in the book only sporadically. Such are the falsifying effects of Soviet censorship.

A Yiddish writer, who spent the Second World War in Moscow in the circle of Soviet Yiddish literati there, observes that in the Soviet Union the road between the writer's desk and the printing press is long, so long that on the way a writer's thought "may lose its original essence and become utterly transformed."[1] It may well be, however, that the misrepresentation of the Vilno Ghetto offered by the book is not the direct work of the censor, who had ruthlessly plucked out its original Jewish spirit, but of the author's self-censorship. Many a Soviet writer, eager to publish his work, anticipates the censor by tailoring his manuscript to conform to the canons of orthodoxy. In committing his thought to paper the writer cuts it, trims it, adds to it ideas alien or even repugnant to his mind, so that it will pass the vigilant scrutiny of the guardians of mental rectitude. The writer's pen turns into an implement of intellectual self-mutilation.

The suppression of nearly all public commemoration of the Holocaust appears particularly striking when compared with the freedom the Soviet government has granted the Armenians to memorialize their Holocaust. On a hill near the capital of Soviet Armenia a shrine was erected in memory of the Armenians slaughtered by the Turks. It is an unmistakable national shrine to which Armenians openly make pilgrimages to mourn their collective national tragedy. By contrast, at the grave-site of Babi Yar, where some 30,000 Jews are buried, the Soviet government, after many years of neglect, grudgingly erected a monument from which it omitted as much as a hint that the buried victims were all Jewish — killed because they were Jews. Soviet Jews who come there to commemorate the massacre do so fearfully and furtively, as though engaged in a subversive conspiracy.

Originally the chief motive for this falsifying reticence was the fear of the Soviet government that by dwelling upon the fate of the Jews it would draw upon itself the displeasure of its subjects whose anti-Semitism had greatly increased during the War. After the War, another motive joined the first one to perpetuate the veil of silence that the regime had cast over the Holocaust, namely the determination to deny the renascent Jewish ethnic and religious consciousness a public source upon which to feed, for the collective recollection of the Holocaust is a powerful stimulus to Jewish identity.

In the late 60s Soviet writers began to mention the Holocaust, but only as the basis for a new propagandistic myth, according to which Zionism had been an accomplice of Nazism in its design against the Jews, had rejoiced in the expulsion of the Jews from Europe, had aided the Nazis, and even looked with favor upon the murder of Jews, for Zionists are so unscrupulous that they would not shrink from causing the death of countless Jews so that the survivors would flee to Palestine and thus bring about the fulfillment of the Zionist ambition to establish a state over which they would lord. During the last two years this fantasy has been elaborated into a phantasmagoric demonology by a small corps of eager pseudo-historical hacks.

This demonology has not been confined to "learned" journals and books meant for scholars and ideologues; it has been set forth prominently in the most popular organs of opinion. It was printed in *Ogonek*, a weekly whose circulation of 2½ million makes it the rough equivalent of the American magazine *Life* when it was a weekly; and in April of 1978, twice on Moscow television, Yurii Zhukov, the most distinguished and authoritative foreign policy commentator in the Soviet Union, expounded on the Nazi-Zionist alliance. Excerpts from the two articles in *Ogonek* appearing over the signature of one L. Korneev may serve as examples of how the Soviets represent the performance of Zionism during the Holocaust:

> The Zionists have aided the Nazis in murdering the Jews — the women, the old, and the children. By 1939, the youthful contingent of European Jewry had been in the main exhausted by the Zionists. Already at that time the Zionists needed above all working hands and "cannon fodder" for the struggle against the Arabs of Palestine.

The women, the old, and the children, being useless, were then left to be annihilated by the Nazis. It was not mere opportunism, but ideological kinship that induced the Zionists to enter with the Nazis into a partnership to murder their own brethren. "The logical foundation of this rapprochement was the definite ideological community of fascism and Zionism — their expansionism, their racism, the religious mysticism, and of course, their anti-communism and anti-Sovietism."[2]

In pondering this fantastic concoction two questions inescapably arise. What are the motives of the Soviets? And, do the Soviets believe in their own propaganda, or are they cynical forgers of a Big Lie? Or to put the question in the terms of Hegelian-Marxian philosophy, does the Soviet theme of the Nazi-Zionist kinship and collaboration express a consciousness of falsehood or a false consciousness in its authors?

I discern three motives for this ideological campaign. First, the tale of Zionist complicity in the Holocaust is meant to denigrate Zionism in the eyes of Soviet Jews, to fill Soviet Jews with revulsion against it, a revulsion that would render them immune to its blandishments, for Soviet Jews would recoil from a movement which had fallen to the utmost depth of depravity by collaborating with the Nazi murderers of the Jewish people. Second, it is meant as music to Arab ears. It merges harmoniously with the Arab chorus of vituperation against Zionism and thereby fortifies the bonds that unite Arab extremists and the Soviets in common enmity to Israel. Third, it is the sheer, uncalculating expression of the bitter hatred that the Soviet leaders bear towards the organized Jewish world. It is a world that seems to the Soviets to be possessed of enormous global power. For the most part invisible, it reaches into every country. Its minions have been ceaselessly attacking the Soviet Union, and by affixing the stigma of anti-Semitism to its name, have denigrated it in the eyes of the world. Moreover, by artful propaganda the Zionists have stirred nationalistic feelings in Soviet Jews, inducing in them a desire to emigrate; it then forced the Soviet Union to open its gates to an exodus of tens of thousands of its citizens. The hatred the Soviet leaders harbor towards the organized Jewish world is intense; and in the manner of men who hate fiercely they vent their hatred in clamorous denunciations and defamations.

But do they believe what they say about Zionism? This question, like most questions about whether people do indeed hold the beliefs they profess, cannot be answered with certainty. But after probing the present Soviet harebrained propaganda confections in the light of the communist esoteric doctrine that permits the faithful to lie for the sake of the Cause, the conclusion appears warranted that in this case, as in so many other cases, the Soviets intermix sincere belief with conscious lying.

That Zionism is an evil, a species of fascism, has long been an article of faith in Soviet ideology, an axiom-like truth sustained by self-hypnotizing constant repetition. This belief seemed to find confirmation in documents discovered in Nazi archives telling of contacts, negotiations, and deals between Nazi officials and Zionist emissaries — the *Haavarah* agreement providing for the transfer of Jewish funds from Germany to Palestine, the parleys between Zionist agents and Nazi officials for the purpose of securing the emigration of German Jews, and kindred contacts. This intermittent commerce between Zionists and Nazis, long known to Western scholars, attests to no more than the desperate endeavor of the Zionists to extricate from Nazi hands as many human lives as possible. But the same facts are unconsciously misconstrued by the Soviets in the manner of men who, in their hatred, are ready to believe anything about their enemies. The Soviet ideologue in this instance is like a surrealistic painter in whose vision the objects of his hatred lose their authentic shape and become riotously deformed. To this unconsciously deformed picture the propagandist adds details which he has consciously invented. These purposefully invented lies are designed to lend color to the picture, to present Zionism in a particularly lurid, arresting light that would intensify the revulsion from it. Such lying the propagandists justify to themselves in the manner of Plato, as a noble lying, ennobled by the lofty purpose it serves. Their inventions are to them not lies, strictly speaking, not utterly baseless untruths, but embellishments of the truth, popular renditions of it. "To convey the truth it may sometimes be necessary to exaggerate it," said the prominent American Marxist Paul Sweezy in reviewing a Chinese diatribe against the Soviet Union that contained manifest falsehoods.[3]

The distinguished communist intellectual, Ernst Fischer, who, before he detached himself from communism, was a leader of the Austrian Communist party, explains brilliantly in his book, *Kunst und Koexistenz* (*Art and Coexistence*), Rowohlt 1966, pp. 110ff., how deception and self-deception become intermixed in the communist mind and how beliefs are engendered and maintained in it by the incantatory repetition of ritual phrases. To illustrate communist justifications of "noble lying" he tells the following story: "A Soviet miner in the 1930's, in reply to the question of a British workers' delegation what his wages were, named a very high sum. The interpreter was taken aback and later returned to ask the miner 'do you indeed earn so much?' 'Of course not,' answered the miner, 'I tripled my wages.' 'Why did you lie to your British comrades?' asked the interpreter. 'So that they would at last make The Revolution.'"

The above-described flights of Soviet propagandists into what the structural anthropologists call "wild thinking" are not characteristic of the dominant tone and temper of contemporary Soviet historiography. On the contrary, they run counter to it. Ever since the death of Stalin the canons of orthodoxy have grown more relaxed, allowing Soviet historians to observe the rules of reason and to honor factual evidence in a far greater measure than previously; their tone has grown less strident and abusive. But in regard to the Holocaust and the Jews a regression has occurred — a flight into venomous fantasies.

It is a measure of the mental and moral perversion of which Soviet propaganda is capable that it tells the story of the greatest slaughter in Jewish history in a manner meant to incite hatred of the contemporary Jewish world.[4] ■

Notes

1. L. Yanasovich, *Mit Yidishe Shraiber in Rusland*, Buenos Aires, 1959, p. 111.
2. Lev Korneev, "Zloveshchie Taĭny Sionizma," *Ogonek*, Nos. 34, 35, 1977.
3. P. Sweezy, "Czechoslovakia Capitalism and Socialism," *Monthly Review*, 1968, p. 16.
4. Two other groups have been peddling the tale of the willful complicity of the Zionist movement in the Nazi slaughter of Jews: the Jewish ultra-Orthodox, anti-Zionist religious sect Neturei-Karta and the German Neo-Nazis. Both these groups juggle some of the same "evidence" exhibited by Soviets in proof of the Zionists' guilt. In the U.S. the Neturei Karta has been disseminating their indictment chiefly by means of the pamphlet of Reb Moshe Shonfeld, *The Holocaust Victims Accuse*, New York, 1977. The most conspicuous of the Neo-Nazi publications purporting to demonstrate how the Zionists profited by the Nazi extermination of Jews is a tract by one Hannecke Kardel titled *Hitler-Begruender Israels (Hitler – The Founder of Israel)* published in Geneva in 1975. L. Korneev, in *Ogonek*, (No. 34, 1977, p. 29) mentioned the Neo-Nazi book approvingly and chose its title for one of the subtitles of his own article.

Historians of the German Democratic Republic on Antisemitism and Persecution

BY KONRAD KWIET

The Marxist–Leninist historiography of the German Democratic Republic, which for many years had remained outside the purview of Western scholarship – studiously disregarded or made the subject of polemics only – has for some time now engaged the serious attention of West German historians.[1] Even so, one specific group of topics is still awaiting critical treatment:[2] it is the question of the study and interpretation of German antisemitism, of the role of the German Jews in German society and of their persecution; and that of the destruction of European Jewry. The present study sets out to give a picture of the development and current state of GDR research in this field, and in so doing takes up some points raised by Ismar Schorsch in his paper in this Year Book, in which he discussed the most important tentative propositions and interpretative models evolved by non-Marxist – or to be more precise: by Jewish and contemporary Western and West German historians.[3]

We propose to present the various contributions from GDR historians against the backdrop of the several stages traversed by the GDR in the course of its development.[4] One point of our findings may be anticipated at the outset: antisemitism, the history of the German Jews and their persecution are not themes considered worthy of study for their own sake within the terms of reference of GDR historiography. The literature on the subject is modest in volume. First attempts at a serious scholarly approach appear to have been made in the early 1960s but it was only very recently that a marked upsurge occurred, reflected both in the quantity and quality of the output. It can be shown that the aims as well as the results of such studies never fail to fit into a specific obligatory

[1]To mention only a few publications: D. Riesenberger, *Geschichte und Geschichtsunterricht in der DDR*, Göttingen 1973; F. Reuter, *Geschichtsbewußtsein in der DDR*, Cologne 1973; A. Dorpalen, 'Die Geschichtswissenschaft in der DDR', in *Geschichtswissenschaft in Deutschland*, ed. B. Faulenbach, Munich 1974, pp. 121–137; B. Blanke/R. Reiche/J. Wirth, 'Die Faschismus-Theorie der DDR', *Das Argument* 33 (1965), H.-D. Kittsteiner, 'Bewußtseinsbildung, Parteilichkeit, dialektischer und historischer Materialismus. Zu einigen Kategorien der marxistisch-leninistischen Geschichtsmethodologie', *Internationale wissenschaftliche Korrespondenz zur Geschichte der deutschen Arbeiterbewegung* 10 (1974), pp. 408–430; J. Kocka, 'Zur jüngeren marxistischen Sozialgeschichte', *Soziologie und Sozialgeschichte. Kölner Zeitschrift für Soziologie und Sozialpsychologie*, Special Issue 16/1972, pp. 491–514.

[2]An exception is Reinhard Rürup's encyclopaedic contribution, 'Die kommunistische Wissenschaft und der Antisemitismus', in *Sowjetsystem und Demokratische Gesellschaft*, vol. 3, cols. 401–403, Freiburg/Breisgau 1968, now republished and expanded in Rürup's *Emanzipation und Antisemitismus. Studien zur "Judenfrage" der bürgerlichen Gesellschaft* ('Zur Entwicklung der modernen Antisemitismusforschung'), Göttingen 1975, pp. 115 ff.

[3]Ismar Schorsch, 'German Antisemitism in the Light of Post-War Historiography", in *LBI Year Book XIX* (1974), pp. 257–271.

[4]According to the official interpretation; see for instance *DDR. Werden und Wachsen. Zur Geschichte der Deutschen Demokratischen Republik*, [2]Berlin 1975.

frame of reference designed by the Party and handed down to the historians. The underlying party directives, it will be found, invariably point back to the methodological–theoretical and ideological–political "fundamental truths", which must be seen to be vindicated and confirmed by the study and interpretation of antisemitism and the holocaust as of any other subject.

These mandatory points of reference are characterised by the dogmatic acceptance of the basic positions adopted by the Marxist "classics" on the "Jewish Question", and by the endorsement of the Soviet-Marxist doctrine on the nature of fascism and the correlated concept of anti-fascism. These in turn lead to an analysis in class terms of imperialism, capitalism and Zionism, with the Federal Republic of Germany and Israel being singled out – next to the USA – for the role of protagonists.

PHASE I: 1945–1949

The first post-war years in the Soviet Occupation Zone were dominated by the slogan of the "anti-fascist–democratic transformation". (Today they are being interpreted as the "first victorious democratic revolution in the history of the German people".)[5] Denazification and reforms of schools, universities and administration were speedily carried through and measures were taken in hand in an attempt to re-educate a population whose consciousness had been largely determined by fascism and by earlier bourgeois notions and values, and which was now faced with the task of coming to terms with the catastrophic effects of the war followed by collapse.

It turned out that during those first agitated debates on the question of "overcoming the recent past" the issue of the annihilation of the Jews played only a minor part. When in 1945 the full extent of the Nazi policy of genocide became known, no spontaneous cry of anguish was forthcoming from the German population, and that was equally the case in all occupation zones. It was left to isolated individuals to raise their voices in horror, to lament and to accuse in the aftermath of the "Jewish catastrophe".[6]

It was the opponents of the Nazi régime – Jews as well as non-Jews – who had been cast out of German society who, on returning from emigration or concentration camps, were the first to speak up and present the facts of persecution and terror.[7]

[5]Cf. the official research and bibliographical report by G. Benser on historical publications concerning the period 1945–1949, *Zeitschrift für Geschichtswissenschaft* (=*ZfG*), Special vol. XVIII (1970), p. 591.

[6]Cf. Eva G. Reichmann, *Flucht in den Haß. Die Ursachen der deutschen Judenkatastrophe*, Frankfurt a.M. [7]1969, pp. 9 f.

[7]W. A. Beckert, *Die Wahrheit über das Konzentrationslager Buchenwald*, Weimar 1945; *Konzentrationslager Buchenwald*, eds. W. Bartel, S. Heyman, J. Hennings, vol. 1: *Bericht des Internationalen Lagerkommites*, Weimar 1945; W. Bukofzer, *Judengesetzgebung und Judenverfolgung unter den Nazis*, Berlin 1946; S. Heyman, *Marxismus und Rassenfrage*, Berlin 1948; B. Baum, *Widerstand in Auschwitz. Bericht der Internationalen Antifaschistischen Lagerleitung*, Berlin 1949; J. Wolff, *Sadismus und Wahnsinn. Erlebnisse in den deutschen Konzentrationslagern im Osten*, Greiz 1947; *KZ-Sachsenhausen* ed. L. Grosser, Berlin 1948; *Todeslager Sachsenhausen. Ein Dokumentarbericht vom Sachsenhausen-Prozeß*, ed. F. Sigl, Berlin–Leipzig 1948.

The persecution of the Jews also featured in the programmatic political writings of leading Communist Party officials.[8]

These writings were of considerable significance at the time, serving as they did both the political indoctrination of the Party members and the ideological re-education of the public, serving moreoever as a substitute for a – still non-existent – academic Marxist–Leninist historiography. In pursuit of their two-fold aim, the authors sought to marshal the historical evidence in such a way as to prove that the "anti-fascist–democratic transformation" corresponded to the "lessons" of history. Later on, when an academic historiography had come into being in the GDR, it glorified these early writings as great historical works.[9] Walter Ulbricht's *Die Legende vom deutschen Sozialismus* was singled out in particular as an authoritative book.

The interpretation of fascism put forward by Ulbricht in 1945 rested on two oddly contrasting hypotheses. Going back to the classical Comintern formula of 1935 (Dimitrov Doctrine), he defined Nazism as "the open terroristic rule of the most reactionary, most chauvinistic, most imperialist elements of German finance capital".[10] But at the same time he took over the explanation in terms of German national history – which at the time was the theory favoured in the West – and so he presented a long ancestral rogues' gallery of Hitler's "precursors" and characterised Hitlerite fascism as the "summation, development, intensification of all that is reactionary in German history".[11]

Ulbricht devoted only a few lines to a discussion of the function of the "anti-Jewish pogroms", which in his interpretation were nothing but a weapon used by the ruling class for the enslavement of the German working class and the destruction of other peoples. This explanation was followed by an expression of horror at the genocide for which frightfulness there could be no explanation, only the accusation against the "lowest pit of cultural decline", against the "bestiality" and "rottenness" of German imperialism.

What Ulbricht had cursorily dealt with in a few sentences in 1945 was treated at greater length three years later in another concise tract: Siegbert Kahn's *Antisemitismus und Rassenhetze*.[12] Together with other Communists of Jewish origin, Kahn had returned at the end of the war from emigration in the West.

Unlike the Ulbricht group in Moscow, the Communist emigrants in Western countries had perforce to engage in a dialogue with other groups and with associations of Jewish exiles, as they were out to canvass support for their Popular

[8]W. Ulbricht, *Die Legende vom deutschen Sozialismus*, Berlin 1945; the fourth edition of this book was published under the main title *Der faschistische deutsche Imperialismus 1933–1945*, Berlin 1956; A. Norden, *Lehren deutscher Geschichte. Zur politischen Rolle des Finanzkapitals und der Junker*, Berlin 1947; A. Abusch, *Der Irrweg einer Nation. Ein Beitrag zum Verständnis deutscher Geschichte*, Berlin 1949.

[9]Cf. J. Streisand, *Deutsche Geschichte von den Anfängen bis zur Gegenwart*, Cologne 1972, pp. 435 f.

[10]The "key document", i.e., Dimitrov's speech at the Seventh Comintern Congress was not published in the GDR until 1957: W. Pieck/G. Dimitroff/P. Togliatti, *Die Offensive des Faschismus und die Aufgaben der Kommunisten für die Volksfront gegen Krieg und Faschismus*, Berlin 1957.

[11]Ulbricht, *op. cit.*, pp. 99 f.

[12]S. Kahn, *Antisemitismus und Rassenhetze. Eine Übersicht über ihre Entwicklung in Deutschland*, Berlin 1948.

Front policy among the refugees.[13] Consequently they were not in a position to evade either the question of the future role and position of the Jews in Germany or the problem of material restitution. Moreoever, they were compelled to argue out their case also with the Zionist movement, which had made considerable headway in all sections of German Jewry as a result of the Nazi persecution. In these debates Kahn had played a leading part, and his demands and insights were still in harmony with the official Party line in 1948 when he was assigned the task of drawing the appropriate lessons from the history of antisemitism and the persecution of the Jews, seen from the angle of the "anti-fascist–democratic transformation".

Kahn shows periods of German history in succession, in order to uncover the "baleful" and "reactionary" tradition of German intellectual life, thus tracing the path that led logically to Auschwitz. The function of antisemitism as an instrument of manipulation and diversion in the arsenal of the ruling class is a recurrent theme.

Three separate functions are attributed to fascist antisemitism: the obfuscation of class antagonisms through the formation of the Nazi *Volksgemeinschaft*; the justification of expansion; and thirdly the economic function of enrichment and the quest for profits. Confronted with the crucial question as to what possible connotation there could be between mass murder and the profit interests of the ruling finance capital, Kahn is really at a loss to provide any satisfactory answer because he is himself forced to say that the Jews were wiped out "only because they were Jews".[14]

Writing in 1948, Kahn in his summing up conceded to the surviving Jews what in the GDR today is contested and regarded as a cue for anti-Zionist attacks: the right "to a national development of their own".[15] In 1948 the State of Israel had been founded, and the Soviet Union had not been slow in bestowing its approval. Those who do not wish to take the road to Israel, Kahn argued, are left with no other choice than that of unreserved and complete assimilation. Nevertheless one feature was to be preserved and safeguarded: the free unfolding of "Jewish cultural–religious life".

As Kahn saw it, that promise – for the fulfilment of which the surviving Jews in most countries of the Eastern bloc were to wait in vain – could only be translated into reality once every form of racial hatred had been overcome, thus establishing "the indispensable prerequisites for a genuine democratic regeneration". Indeed, according to Kahn, "*one of the yardsticks for assessing the true substance of a democracy is its attitude towards the Jews or other national or religious minorities*".[16] Here he anticipated an insight with which the bourgeois social sciences did

[13]H. Duhnke, *Die KPD von 1933 bis 1945*, Cologne 1972. For the political concept of the KPD, cf. A. Sywottek, *Deutsche Volksdemokratie. Studien zur politischen Konzeption der KPD 1935–1946*, Düsseldorf 1971.

[14]Kahn, *op. cit.*, p. 7.

[15]*Ibid.*, p. 88. For the then official point of view of the *Sozialistische Einheitspartei Deutschlands* cf. *SED Informationen. Sonder-Material. Erdöl-Krieg in Palästina*, published by the *ZK der SED*, 1948.

[16]*Ibid.*, p. 74 (my italics).

not catch up until years later, when it became the starting point for the systematic study of minorities.[17]

Kahn went on to list a number of measures he considered essential for the new "democratic order" in Germany. He demanded the outlawing of the dissemination of racial hatred. War and Nazi criminals should be brought to trial, punished and expropriated. Restitution was recognised as a moral duty which, however, should not be confined to a moral gesture but should include a material aspect "within the framework of actual economic conditions". And Kahn added: "Yet all that can still be done in order to make amends must today be done voluntarily and from deep inner conviction by the German people themselves."[18] Nothing more was heard of such statements later on.

These "lessons" fitted the "anti-fascist–democratic transformation" and propagated precisely those elements that were to be pressed home at that first preparatory stage in the advance to the "construction of socialism": the ousting of fascist "modes of thinking"; democratisation through de-Nazification; structural economic changes through the expropriation of landed estates and the property of war and Nazi criminals.

PHASE II: 1949–1955

Until the early 1960s Kahn's booklet remained the only publication on the history of antisemitism and the persecution of the Jews. Though some pamphlets and personal reminiscences were published in the years following the appearance of Kahn's study,[19] historians persisted in their silence on the subject. It was left to the departments of theology and German to bring Jewish themes in the widest sense within the ambit of university research.

According to the bibliographies compiled by Guido Kisch,[20] the total output of studies in this field consisted of seven, mainly theological, dissertations. When so little urgency was attached to the historical treatment of the subject, there was even less reason to expect any tentative explanations or interpretations to be forthcoming from the quarters of sociology or social psychology.

In the 1930s undogmatic socialists engaged in the struggle against fascism had forged links between Marxism and psychoanalysis, but later psychoanalysis

[17]This approach, manifested above all in the US social sciences, was taken up in the Federal Republic only in isolated cases since the middle of the 1960s. Cf. E. Becker, 'Soziale Vorurteile', in *Evangelisches Staatslexikon*, Stuttgart/Berlin 1966, cols. 2039–2042; Reinhard Rürup, 'Jewish Emancipation and Bourgeois Society', in *LBI Year Book XIV* (1969), pp. 67–91; S. Jersch-Wenzel, 'Die Lage von Minderheiten als Indiz für den Stand der Emanzipation in einer Gesellschaft', in *Sozialgeschichte Heute. Festschrift für H. Rosenberg zum 70. Geburtstag*, ed. H.-U. Wehler, Göttingen 1974, pp. 365–387.

[18]Kahn, *op. cit.*, p. 89.

[19]S. Hermlin, *Die erste Reihe*, Berlin 1951; R. Weinstock, "*Rolf, Kopf hoch!*". *Die Geschichte eines jungen Juden*, edited by A. Fischer, Berlin–Potsdam 1950; 'Vor 15 Jahren begann der Leidensweg der Juden in Deutschland', in *Dokumentation der Zeit* (November 1953), No. 57.

[20]G. Kisch/K. Roepke, *Schriften zur Geschichte der Juden. Eine Bibliographie der in Deutschland und der Schweiz 1922–1955 erschienenen Dissertationen* (Schriftenreihe wissenschaftlicher Abhandlungen des Leo Baeck Instituts 4), Tübingen 1959, and G. Kisch, *Judaistische Bibliographie. Ein Verzeichnis der in Deutschland und der Schweiz von 1956 bis 1970 erschienenen Dissertationen und Habilitationsschriften*, Basle–Stuttgart 1972.

was cast into outer darkness as "ideological bric-à-brac of the bourgeois superstructure".[21] No notice was taken in the GDR of the writings of Wilhelm Reich,[22] until his expulsion a member of the KPD, any more than of Erich Fromm's investigations,[23] or of the fundamental contributions made by Adorno and his associates.[24] However, GDR scholarship was able to field its own contribution, in Dietfried Müller-Hegemann's study *Zur Psychologie des deutschen Faschisten*.[25]

Müller-Hegemann also used the Dimitrov Doctrine as his point of departure. He began by confronting the "great problem"[26] of countless individuals having succumbed so readily to fascist ideology. Marx's theory of alienation provided the first approach towards an explanation. In addition, empirical material was evaluated, derived from "clinical experience" gained in the course of the investigation of "several hundreds of fascist individuals". A portrait of the "average fascist" and his antecedents emerged: an authoritarian, a physically violent education, aggression and *Angst* complexes, sexual impotence, sentimentality, orderliness and submissiveness. Yet the attempt to deduce these character traits from the "correlated social structures" turned out to be superficial and dilettantic.[27]

In the view of Müller-Hegemann, the "underdeveloped psychic structures" are simply the manifestation of a "mouldering social consciousness" that is attributed without distinction to all individuals "integrated into the capitalist economic system".[28] The destructive forces of capitalism oppress the individual. Oppression generates fear and "enhanced aggressiveness", and since these tendencies are not purposefully directed against the oppressor, they constitute material "readily open for abuse" by monopoly capital. "And so," the author concludes without further ado, "we have grasped the mechanism actuating all aggressive urges and pogrom moods inclusive of antisemitism".[29]

It must be noted that until the middle of the 1950s the science of history in the GDR was not exclusively dominated by Marxist orientation. When the history departments of the Universities resumed their activities in the winter term 1946–1947, they were staffed predominantly by bourgeois historians who during the first post-war years took charge of research and teaching under the supervision, in accordance with the directives, of the authorities. Later their overriding influence, their "monopoly of education" was gradually broken.[30]

It is not unreasonable to assume that this older generation of bourgeois

[21]K. Horn, 'Zur Sozialpsychologie des Faschismus', in *Psychoanalyse – Kritische Theorie des Subjekts*, Frankfurt a.M. 1972, p. 58.

[22]W. Reich, *Massenpsychologie des Faschismus*, Copenhagen–Zürich–Prague [2]1933.

[23]Erich Fromm, *Die Furcht vor der Freiheit*, Zürich 1945. It is also particularly noteworthy that Otto Heller's Marxist classic on the Jewish question with his advocacy of Birobidjan, written in the last years of the Weimar Republic, was not "resurrected" in the GDR. Otto Heller, *Der Untergang des Judentums. Die Judenfrage. Ihre Kritik. Ihre Lösung durch den Sozialismus*, Wien–Berlin 1931. True, Heller, who died in Mauthausen after the Gestapo had arrested him as a member of the French resistance, had fallen out with the Party during the emigration.

[24]Th. W. Adorno, E. Frenkel-Brunswik, D. J. Levinson, R. Nevitt, *The Authoritarian Personality*, ed. M. Horkheimer and S. H. Flowerman, New York 1950.

[25]Rudolstadt 1955. [26]*Ibid.*, p. 31. [27]*Ibid.*, p. 118. [28]*Ibid.*, p. 43 [29]*Ibid.*, p. 47.

[30]Cf. for instance, A. Fischer, 'Der Weg zur Gleichschaltung der sowjetzonalen Geschichtswissenschaft 1945–1949', *Vierteljahrshefte für Zeitgeschichte* (= *VJHZG*) 10 (1962), pp. 156 ff.; A. Timm *Das Fach Geschichte in Forschung und Lehre in der Sowjetischen Besatzungszone seit 1945*, Bonn [4]1965.

historians shared the most conspicuous weakness of established historiography in Western Germany: their incapacity in the aftermath of the stunning shock of the "German catastrophe" to search for a scholarly approach to the phenomena of antisemitism and the holocaust. Indeed, these themes were not dealt with either in the lecture room or in the research programmes. It was left to Ernst Niekisch – newly elevated to the rank of a Marxist University teacher – to introduce at his seminar (1948–1949) a topic from the period of the Third Reich: a lecture on the German resistance movement.[31]

The problem was further aggravated by a well-established tradition of bourgeois historiography: its persistent refusal to include subjects related to Judaism, Jewish history or antisemitism in its canon of themes worthy of study.[32] And so, unprepared and uncommitted, there was only too great a readiness to leave the exploration of the "Jewish catastrophe" once again to those directly affected, to the Jews themselves. Protected by a bland conviction that the matter concerned them only indirectly, the academics considered themselves relieved of responsibility to render account of a society that had made Auschwitz possible.

No more than its bourgeois competitor was Marxist historiography able or willing to include antisemitism and the destruction of the Jews in its teaching and research programmes. Only very few qualified historians were available after the end of the war, the survivors of persecution and illegality or exile. At that initial stage priority was given to the task of building up Marxist–Leninist historiography and securing for it equality of status with the rival bourgeois school. In the subsequent period of the "socialist refashioning" of society, however, the task was to eliminate the competition and enforce the claim to leadership asserted by historical materialism.

Success depended decisively on the training of a younger generation of Marxist specialists capable of taking over the key positions in research and teaching. A major effort was devoted to ideological education and theoretical training and the intense study of historical materialism and the history of the German workers' movement was bound to show that the "classics" of scientific socialism had given relatively little attention to the "Jewish question" and antisemitism, which they had never regarded as "autonomous phenomena".

Marx had come forward with his trail-blazing interpretation[33] in 1844, when he equated Jewry – based on "rapacity", "haggling" and "money" – with capitalism. In his eyes the emancipation of the Jews, as that of mankind at large, was bound up with the dissolution of class society. His famous dictum "The social emancipation of the Jews is the emancipation of society from Jewry" was to some extent in line with the emancipation demands of the contemporary bourgeoisie, which similarly aimed at the ultimate disappearance of Jewry and Judaism. Viewed from the angle of these fundamental positions, it is not difficult to understand the reluctance of both bourgeois and Marxist historians

[31]Cf. Fischer, *loc. cit.*, p. 168, n. 84.

[32]H. J. Bieber, 'Zur bürgerlichen Geschichtsschreibung und Publizistik über Antisemitismus, Zionismus und den Staat Israel', *Das Argument* 75 (1972), p. 253. Cf. also W. Schochow, *Deutsch-Jüdische Geschichtswissenschaft. Eine Geschichte ihrer Organisationsformen unter besonderer Berücksichtigung der Fachbibliographie*, Berlin 1969.

[33]'Zur Judenfrage', in Karl Marx–Friedrich Engels–Werke, Bd. I, Berlin (DDR) 1964, pp. 347–377.

to grapple with the problem of an autonomous Jewish history. This common national tradition undoubtedly continued to be effective for a long time in both German post-war states.[34]

One thing the German workers' movement is certainly entitled to claim: Unsure as it often was in its tactical attitude towards antisemitism, it was virtually united in rejecting and condemning the anti-Jewish campaigns. It also believed, with equal unanimity, that the "Jewish Question" and antisemitism were a problem of the bourgeoisie that would be automatically resolved through the overthrow of the capitalist order.*

When, after the defeat of fascism, the construction of socialism was taken in hand, there seemed to be no longer any need to face up to the problem of antisemitism, relic of a "backward culture". But, quite apart from this fundamental Marxist position, there was yet another barrier that is likely to have been decisive for the Marxist historians' silence.

No sooner had the German Democratic Republic been founded in 1949, with the SED now in the position of the state Party, than the vast post-war purges were launched. Following the model of the East European trials many party officials were called to account in the years 1950 to 1952. It was impossible not to hear the familiar strains of anti-Zionism and antisemitism in the attacks made on *émigrés* who had returned from Western countries and on Communists of Jewish descent who were now being denounced and penalised. With these events being enacted, any serious study or discussion of antisemitism and the destruction of the Jews was bound to appear ill-advised.

Even before the Second Party Conference of the SED proclaimed the "planned and systematic construction of the foundations of socialism", the Central Committee had issued the appropriate directives to the historians. Among these were: development of a socialist picture of history; establishment of new teaching and research institutions; publication of a textbook of German history for use at universities.

Then, following the events of 1952 and 1953, historiography came in for criticism, especially from Kurt Hager, the Politburo member and Central Committee Secretary, whose responsibility it was. In spring 1954 he complained that the two leading scientific journals – *Zeitschrift für Geschichtswissenschaft* and *Deutsche Zeitschrift für Philosophie* – had so far failed to publish any "serious contribution to the struggle against imperialist ideology".[35]

In 1955 the Federal Republic joined NATO, and thus gave sufficient cause for a campaign conjuring up the dangers of a resurgent West German militarism. Before the year was out a basic "decision on the improvement of research and teaching in the historical sciences of the GDR" was adopted.[36] The his-

*For a detailed discussion of the attitude of the German workers' movement to the Jewish Question until the First World War see the essay by Robert S. Wistrich, 'German Social Democracy and the Problem of Jewish Nationalism 1897–1917', in this volume of the Year Book – Ed.

[34]Cf. Werner Jochmann, 'The Jews and German Society in the Imperial Era', in *LBI Year Book XX* (1975), pp. 5–11.

[35]*Der 4. Parteitag der SED*, Berlin 1954, p. 278.

[36]*Dokumente der Sozialistischen Einheitspartei Deutchlands*, vol. V, Berlin 1956. See also *ZfG* 3 (1955), pp. 509 ff.

torians were assigned new tasks, including among others an intensified struggle against bourgeois falsifications of history and the preparation of studies depicting the anti-fascist resistance struggle.

It was then that "Marxist historical research in the GDR set out on its forward march on a widened front."[37] In 1956 Hager complained that the ideological showdown with the Federal Republic was not being pursued in a sufficiently "offensive spirit", and he noted critically that the study of contemporary history had "not advanced as rapidly as would have been necessary for the ideological-political education of the public".[38] The instruction for the study of contemporary history was worded accordingly: "We need publications of official documents and major works on the domestic and foreign policies and on the crimes of German imperialism."

PHASE III: 1955–1961

During the period ending in 1961, which witnessed the beginnings of an education in the spirit of "socialist patriotism", the output of books on contemporary history showed a sudden and dramatic increase. Interest centred on the anti-fascist resistance and the Second World War.[39] Yet antisemitism and the persecution of the Jews remained outside the range of subjects deemed worthy of study, although they were no longer ignored altogether. A number of books were published under licence: monographs and personal records, diaries and documentations of foreign authors and institutions, most of them devoted to Auschwitz and the destruction of Polish Jewry.[40]

The established historiography, however, confined itself to covering the persecution and destruction of European Jewry within the framework of the account it had been commissioned to produce of fascist crimes and the anti-fascist resistance.[41] Documentation was used in the first place to supply historical

[37] E. Engelberg/R. Rudolph, 'Zur Geschichtswissenschaft der Deutschen Demokratischen Republik', *ZfG Sonderband 8* (1960), *Historische Forschungen in der DDR. Analysen und Berichte. Zum XI. Internationalen Historikerkongreß in Stockholm, August 1960*, p. 18.

[38] *Protokolle der Verhandlungen der 3. Parteikonferenz der SED. 24.3. – 30.3.1956*, Berlin 1956, p. 350.

[39] These broad topics also provided the headings for the two bibliographical reports presented by GDR historiography to the Eleventh International Congress of Historians in Stockholm in 1960. Cf. H. Schumann/W. Wehling, 'Literatur über Probleme der deutschen antifaschistischen Widerstandsbewegung', and G. Förster, 'Der Stand der Erforschung der Geschichte des zweiten Weltkriegs in der DDR', in *ZfG Sonderband 8* (1960), pp. 381–402 and 403–425.

[40] For instance, Lord Russell of Liverpool, *Geißel der Menschheit*, Berlin 1955; O Kraus/E. Kulka, *Die Todesfabrik*, Berlin 1957; *Im Feuer vergangen. Tagebücher aus dem Ghetto. Mit einem Vorwort von A. Zweig*, Berlin 1958 (1960); B. Mark, *Der Aufstand im Warschauer Ghetto*, Berlin 1959; J. Hellwig/G. Deike, *Ein Tagebuch für Anne Frank*, Berlin 1959; *Faschismus–Getto–Massenmord. Dokumentation über Ausrottung und Widerstand der Juden in Polen während des zweiten Weltkrieges*, edited by the Jewish Historical Institute Warsaw, Berlin 1960 (1961).

[41] We here single out: *SS im Einsatz. Eine Dokumentation über die Verbrechen der SS*, published by the Committee of Antifascist Resistance Fighters in the GDR, Berlin 1957 (1964); F. Köhler, *Geheime Kommandosache. Aus den Dokumenten des Nürnberger Prozesses gegen die Hauptkriegsverbrecher*, Berlin 1956; *Zur Geschichte der deutschen antifaschistischen Widerstandsbewegung 1933–1945*, Berlin 1957; W. A. Schmidt, *Damit Deutschland lebe. Ein Quellenwerk über den deutschen antifaschistischen Widerstandskampf 1933–1945*, Berlin 1958; *Erkämpft das Menschenrecht. Lebensbilder und letzte Briefe antifaschistischer Widerstandskämpfer*, with an introduction by W. Pieck, Berlin 1958; W. Bartel, *Deutschland in der Zeit der faschistischen Diktatur 1933–1945*, Berlin 1956.

evidence of the "glorious", "sacrificial", yet ultimately "victorious" Communist resistance struggle. These books were published under the auspices of the Committee of Anti-fascist Resistance Fighters.

At almost the same time source books and pictorial reports on Buchenwald, Auschwitz, Ravensbrück and Sachsenhausen were published in large editions[42] and supplemented by a number of articles and documentations.[43] Nevertheless, in the judgment of the GDR historian Klaus Drobisch, the sum total of that literature still fell short of the requirements of a comprehensive scientific investigation of the "concentration camp complex".[44] Kühnrich's study *Der KZ-Staat*, a book for the general reader published in 1960, may be considered a typical example.[45]

The author lists three functions which the concentration camps had to perform under the fascist régime: isolation and annihilation of opponents; the creation of an anxiety psychosis; economic interests. This functional description is acceptable, and so is the author's chronological outline of the main facts, but his interpretations do not stand up to critical scrutiny. According to him it is no longer the Jews but the Communists as the most active anti-fascist force who were subjected "in the first place" to the Nazi terror. This is a notion common to the entire GDR literature on the subject, but Kühnrich asserts it with unusual vigour.[46]

We do not propose here to serve up numerical comparisons or macabre statistics, as the whole theory and practice of the Nazi régime point unequivocally to the conclusion that it was the Jews who were singled out as the legendary, omnipresent "world foe", against whom a universal racial–ideological campaign of annihilation was waged to compel the restoration of the political and national vigour of the German master race whose secure "biological" and economic existence was to rest on the foundation of Germany's envisioned position as a world power. The Manichaean interpretation of the world that went hand in hand with the hatred of the Jews, and the insane chiliastic visions of an end of time were by no means in contradiction to the second immutable "idea": the conquest of "living space" in the East and the extirpation of bolshevism. Antisemitism and anti-bolshevism, the two rallying and vindicating ideas were conveniently combined in the image of "Jewish bolshevism" as the enemy. It was the military invasion of the Soviet Union which brought in its train the practical execution of the programme of annihilation, the "Commissar's Order" for the

[42] *Mahn- und Gedenkstätte Buchenwald – Ein viersprachiges Bildwerk mit einem Vorwort von A. Zweig*, Berlin 1959; *Buchenwald. Mahnung und Verpflichtung*, Berlin 1960; B. Baum, *Widerstand in Auschwitz*, [a]Berlin 1959; E. Buchmann, *Frauen von Ravensbrück*, Berlin 1959; *Damals in Sachsenhausen. Solidarität und Widerstand im Konzentrationslager von Sachsenhausen*, Berlin 1961; *Buchenwald mahnt*, Weimar 1961.

[43] E. Greuner, 'Sklavenarbeit bei IG-Farben (Auschwitz-Buna 1941–1945)', in *Dokumentation der Zeit*, No. 143 (1957); H. Schumann/H. Kühnrich, 'Die Rolle und Bedeutung der Konzentrationslager des Nazi-Regimes', in *Internationale Hefte der Widerstandsbewegung*, No. 3 (1960).

[44] See, for instance, *ZfG* 10 (1962), p. 1701, for his review of E. Kolb, *Bergen-Belsen*, Hanover 1962.

[45] H. Kühnrich, *Der KZ-Staat. Rolle und Entwicklung der faschistischen Konzentrationslager.* (*Wahrheiten über den deutschen Imperialismus 1*), Berlin 1960.

[46] *Ibid.*, p. 10.

liquidation of the leading "Jewish-bolshevik" stratum and the order for the physical extermination of European Jewry.

This pattern of events – thrown into relief most clearly by recent West German work in the field of contemporary history[47] – was presented by Kühnrich with a peculiar shift of emphasis: "When the Führer talked about the peril posed by the Jews and the need to destroy them, what he meant was the repression of the revolutionary workers' movement and the destruction of the Soviet Union."[48] This proposition was the starting point for bringing in finance capital and for fitting antisemitism into the picture. Finance capital had made use of antisemitism to divert attention from those twin aims, the "real chief objectives". Moreoever, the oppportunity of profitable "Aryanisation" deals arose, and it became possible to harness an army of cheap labour to the production process.

Thus Hitler and the SS had been no more than the "menials", the "custodians of the interests of monopoly capital".[49] Nevertheless, Kühnrich admits that in the pursuit of the "final solution of the Jewish question" economic problems had been ignored.[50] Physical destruction had been given priority, an act of "unspeakable frightfulness" that called for an explanation. The author went on to offer an unfortunate attempt at an explanation in economic terms. He looked upon the ghastly by-products of the gigantic murder industry as evidence confirming the official doctrine on the nature of fascism. It is not purposed here to deny the fact that numerous industrial and other economic enterprises were participating in the enslavement and exploitation of hundreds of thousands of forced labourers and concentration camp prisoners. But there is up to date no evidence, not a single hard fact indicating that the genocide was initiated and engineered by finance capital itself.

Kühnrich's book was published at a time when antisemitism and the persecution of Jews were again attracting the attention of the world. The winter of 1959–1960 witnessed new outbreaks of antisemitism in the Federal Republic. Shortly afterwards, Adolf Eichmann was put on trial and the personalised reconstruction of the "Jewish catastrophe" was placed on record and disseminated by a world-wide media coverage.

The two events between them marked the beginning of a new chapter in both East and West. Prompted by dismay over the revival of antisemitism – which, one had imagined, had long been forgotten – and by the world-wide repercussions of the Jerusalem trial, a broad enlightenment campaign was launched in the Federal Republic, which before long reached saturation point and threatened to become counter-productive.

Repressed guilt complexes were jerked to the surface. People discovered their Jewish "fellow citizens" and "fellow human beings". Exhibitions were organised, debates were held at synods and church conferences, memorial publica-

[47]Cf. H. Krausnick, 'Judenverfolgung', in *Anatomie des SS-Staates*, vol. 2, Freiburg/Olten 1965, pp. 360 ff.; A. Hillgruber, *Hitlers Strategie. Politik und Kriegführung 1940–1941*, Frankfurt a.M. 1965; U. D. Adam, *Judenpolitik im Dritten Reich*, Düsseldorf 1972, pp. 303 ff.

[48]Kühnrich, *op. cit.*, p. 38.

[49]*Ibid.*, p. 52.

[50]*Ibid.*, p. 74.

tions on the fate of the Jewish population in certain West German towns were produced. Guidelines were issued for improving the teaching of history in the schools, and special research projects were started at a number of universities.

In the GDR, too, antisemitic daubings and the Eichmann trial provided a decisive impulse for giving more attention to a topic that had hitherto been treated somewhat casually. Political propaganda immediately construed a line of continuity linking the Federal Republic to the fascist past in order to "unmask" the "men behind Eichmann" to be found in leading state and economic positions.[51]

It was again Siegbert Kahn who took the lead, this time with the re-publication of four appeals issued by the KPD in 1938 to protest against the anti-Jewish pogroms and urging the population to display solidarity with the victims of persecution and to help them.[52] A brief introduction established the relevance of the documents to the current West German situation.[53]

In 1948 Kahn had still seen fit to criticise the attitude of the workers' movement, but now the glorification of the Communist resistance precluded any retrospective criticisms. The declarations and entreaties issued by the KPD were taken out of their historical context and presented as a "correct analysis", to pay tribute to the "many thousands of upright Germans", who had "shown solidarity with the persecuted Jews and helped them to the best of their ability".[54]

Reality presented a very different picture. The "many upright" Germans of "anti-fascist convictions" had been unmoved by the endeavours to mobilise them either for solidarity with the victims of persecution or for the Popular Front that had been proclaimed in order to bring about the overthrow of Nazism. This is not to detract from the credit that is undoubtedly due to the KPD for having been among the few who raised their voices against the persecution of the Jews, but the historical reputation of the anti-fascist resistance is not enhanced by wishful thinking.

The political propaganda effort was followed by the intervention of scholarship. In 1961 an international conference was held in East Berlin for the purpose of "taking the Eichmann trial in Jerusalem as a point of departure for bringing scientific proof of the anti-democratic and barbarous nature of Ger-

[51]Cf. *Globke – Bürokrat des Todes*, published by the Committee for German Unity, n.d.; *Globke und die Ausrottung der Juden*, Berlin 1960; *Die Wahrheit über Oberländer*, Berlin 1960; W. H. Krause, *Der Fall Eichmann u.a.*, Berlin 1960; H. Kühnrich, *Judenmörder Eichmann – Kein Fall der Vergangenheit*, Berlin 1961; F. K. Kaul, *Der Fall Eichmann*, Berlin 1963; *Antisemitismus in Westdeutschland. Tatsachen, Ursachen, Vollstrecker. Eine Dokumentation des Verbandes der Jüdischen Gemeinden in der DDR*, Berlin 1967.

[52]S. Kahn, 'Dokumente des Kampfes der revolutionären deutschen Arbeiterbewegung gegen Antisemitismus und Judenverfolgung', in *Beiträge zur Geschichte der deutschen Arbeiterbewegung* 2 (1960), pp. 252–264. In the same year the Berlin Rabbi M. Riesenburger published a booklet entitled *Das Licht verlöschte nicht. Dokumente aus der Zeit des Nazismus*, Berlin 1960. It is an impressive record, based on personal reminiscences, of the collapse and the new beginnings of the Berlin Jewish Congregation. The book was intended as a memento and as a reminder of the moral duty to fight antisemitism in any shape or form.

[53]Kahn, *Dokumente . . .*, *op. cit.*, p. 552.

[54]*Ibid.*, p. 554.

man imperialism".[55] The economic historian Jürgen Kuczynski read the main paper, on "Barbarity – the most extreme manifestation of monopoly rule in Germany."[56]

Antisemitism and the persecution of the Jews were dealt with by Kuczynski in a few sentences. By a simple process of reasoning by analogy he arrived at the identity of the "truly guilty", the initiators. Eichmann is appointed "manager" of "German monopoly capital as a whole", and in particular of the most influential IG-Farben combine. Kuczynski proceeded to sketch the policies of monopoly capital and to expound his theory of the rivalry and conflicting claims of the two leading industrial groups within the state monopoly system: on the one side coal, iron and steel, on the other the electrical and chemical industries.

However, Kuczynski refrained from fitting the "final solution" into this picture. Gas deliveries by IG-Farben, forced labour etc., figured in his account. "Barbarity" was noted and declared to be a characteristic of monopoly capitalist rule, which was rampant once again, preparing to employ its destructive powers in order to unleash a third, atomic war that would end in total destruction.

The other contributions to the discussion similarly centred on the "antihuman crimes" of German monopoly capital. One thing, however, emerged very clearly at this conference: the GDR had fallen far behind in the study of antisemitism and the holocaust. The gap was so conspicuous that even the official report placed on record that there were "promising *beginnings* of a lively discussion, e.g., on the role of antisemitism".[57] Furthermore, it was not so much the contributions of German participants but rather the remarks of Polish and Czechoslovak guests which "revealed wide-ranging knowledge of the field and gave fresh impulses to the discussion".

The insights and criticisms of the conference had a stimulating effect on historiography. Within a few weeks a concise article on the 'Development and role of antisemitism in Germany 1871–1914' was published in *Zeitschrift für Geschichtswissenschaft*. Its authors, H. Schleier and G. Seeber, had written it in some haste with the intention of "drawing the attention of Marxist historians again to a group of subjects that is still topical".[58] A critique of bourgeois historiography followed immediately. In the same issue of the *Zeitschrift* Klaus Drobisch reviewed a number of recent West German contributions to the history of Nazi persecution of the Jews and subjected them to criticism in a comparatively unbiased and friendly vein.[59]

Drobisch confined his review to the most recently published paperbacks on the Eichmann trial. This literature, he pointed out, was less concerned with a scientific study of the subject than with the identification of the guilty, the beneficiaries and the accessories in those crimes. The aim of this approach is clearly

[55]Quoted by H. Heitzer, 'Die Barbarei – extremster Ausdruck der Monopolherrschaft (Tagungsbericht)', *ZfG* 9 (1961), p. 1632.

[56]*Ibid.*, pp. 1484–1503. [57]*Ibid.*, p. 1637. My italics. [58]*Ibid.*, pp. 1592–1597.

[59]*Ibid.*, pp. 1680–1686. The books reviewed are W. Scheffler, *Judenverfolgung im Dritten Reich 1933–1945*, Berlin 1960; A. Wucher, *Eichmanns gab es viele*, München–Zürich 1961; G. Schoenberner, *Der gelbe Stern*, Hamburg 1960; S. Einstein, *Eichmann. Chefbuchhalter des Todes*, Frankfurt a.M., n.d. [1961].

to prove the unbroken continuity of fascist–capitalist rule in the Federal Republic. In contrast, the accuser can impressively point to his own contribution to "overcoming the past": the punishment of all war and Nazi criminals and the elimination of imperialism and militarism, which had cut the ground from under the feet of any variety of antisemitism. And that, it was explained – at variance, incidentally, with the argument used in 1948 – was the only "genuine" form of restitution. (This assertion was regarded by Drobisch at the time – and is still regarded by the GDR today – as a convincing refutation of any demands for restitution that other states, above all Israel, might put forward.) Another contribution came from Wolfgang Heise, and he, too, could see in the destruction of the Jews nothing but "the confirmation of the rule of German finance capital".[60] He granted that the practice of genocide could not be satisfactorily explained as a result either of demagogy or of economic causes. The crucial point, in Heise's view, is the fact that a régime capable of ensuring the country's total subjection to Germany's monopoly capital needed "a sphere of arbitrary destruction as an instrument of its rule". The "final solution" neatly fulfilled that need. It had served as a "model" for transferring the domestic terror to the relations with other peoples, so as to establish an order divided into members of the master race and subhumans.

The derivation from the supposed ineluctable laws of capitalist development fails to carry conviction, resting as it does entirely on the logical consequences of a doctrine the truth of which is taken as axiomatic and must not be called in question. Heise did not attempt to provide factual proof in support of his contention, but offered theoretical considerations instead. Like Kuczynski before him, he extended his argument to the current state of the Federal Republic. The framework remained unchanged: the continuity and "bestiality" of capitalism, which after the extermination of the Jews was no longer resorting to antisemitism, but using instead the ideology of anti-communism.

PHASE IV: 1961–1967

The construction of the Berlin Wall marked the beginning of a new stage devoted to the comprehensive "building of the socialist society on indigenous socialist foundations". Once again, a clear "guide-line" was assigned to historiography.[61] Demands were formulated for higher standards, higher productivity and "a unified direction and guidance of research so as to avoid fragmentation and the isolated treatment of important topics of research".[62]

In January 1963 Ulbricht acknowledged the Party's achievement in having

[60] W. Heise, 'Antisemitismus und Antikommunismus', *Deutsche Zeitschrift für Philosophie* 12 (1961), pp. 1423–1445. The thoughts and theses put forward in this paper are used again, though in an abridged form, in his fundamental work *Aufbruch in die Illusion. Zur Kritik der bürgerlichen Philosophie in Deutschland*, Berlin 1964, pp. 289 f. and 323 ff.

[61] M. Einhorn/H. Habedank, 'Das Programm des Sozialismus und die Aufgaben der Historiker in der DDR', *ZfG* 11 (1963), p. 251, and H. Bartel/E. Diehl/E. Engelberg, 'Die Geschichtswissenschaft in der DDR 1960–1970', in *ZfG Sonderband XVIII* (1970), p. 22.

[62] *Neues Deutschland*, 25th January 1963, quoted in Timm, *op. cit.*, p. 74.

driven out "the evil fascist mentality and the reactionary ideologies of the capitalist past from the heads of most people". Now historians were set a new task: the study of the German workers' movement was to be further intensified and a comprehensive history of the German people was to be compiled.[63]

Work on the interpretation of antisemitism and the persecution of the Jews was now undertaken within the terms of reference of these guide-lines. Both groups of topics figured in the authoritative standard works as well as in the publications on the Nazi régime and the concentration camp complex.[64] Compared with the total volume of this literature,[65] the output on the two Jewish topics was still very modest. Nevertheless, the progress is unmistakable.

GDR historiography had not yet produced a comprehensive account, but the gap was filled temporarily by a translation from the Czech.[66] An important contribution was also made by F. K. Kaul, a prominent barrister who had intervened as a private plaintiff in numerous West German trials of Nazis accused of the murder of Jews, and who was bent at the same time on an historical clarification of the fascist crimes.[67]

The first historian to deal with the subject was M. Unger, who in 1963 edited in the *Zeitschrift für Geschichtswissenschaft* a number of documents on the history of the persecution of the Jews in Leipzig.[68] This was the first, and has up till now remained the only regional documentation published in the GDR. In his introduction, invoking the Berne resolution of 1939, Unger extolled the "clear stand" of the KPD against the persecution of the Jews and its "glorious record" as the only organisation to have offered a consistent anti-fascist resistance.

The second contribution, Görschler's paper on 'The revolutionary workers' movement and its relationship to antisemitism'[69] displays all the characteristic elements. The general theoretical position is outlined, elucidated with reference to the texts of the Marxist "classics" and confirmed in a broad, historical–

[63] H. Hörning, 'Ein neuer Abschnitt in der Geschichtswissenschaft', *ZfG* 12 (1964), p. 383. See also M. Einhorn/H. Habedank, *loc. cit.*, p. 251.

[64] Basic a.o.: *Geschichte der deutschen Arbeiterbewegung*, vol. 5, Berlin 1966, pp. 56 f., 72 f., 322 and 509; L. Berthold, 'Das System des faschistischen Terrors in Deutschland und die Haltung der einzelnen Klassen und Volksschichten, *ZfG* 12 (1964), pp. 5 ff.; K. Drobisch, *Widerstand hinter Stacheldraht*, Berlin 1962; B. Baum, *Die letzten Tage von Mauthausen*, Berlin 1965; B. Puchert, 'Aus der Praxis der IG-Farben in Auschwitz-Monowitz', *JBWiG* T.2 (1963), pp. 203–211; K. H. Thieleke, 'Die "Arisierungen" des Flick-Konzerns', Appendix to *Fall 5. Anklageplädoyer, ausgewählte Dokumente, Urteile des Flick-Prozesses*, compiled by K. H. Thieleke with an introduction by K. Drobisch, Berlin 1965, pp. 353–551.

[65] For a bibliography, see G. Förster/B. Löwel/W. Schumann, 'Forschungen zur deutschen Geschichte 1933–1945', in *ZfG Sonderband XVIII* (1970), pp. 552–589.

[66] O. Kraus/E. Kulka, *Massenmord und Profit. Die faschistische Ausrottungspolitik und ihre ökonomischen Hintergründe*, Berlin 1963. The two Czech authors present a graphic account of the stages, methods and aims of Nazi policy towards the Jews. But here again, the attempt to present genocide as a manifestation of the moribund capitalist order is dubious and unconvincing: cf. pp. 423 f.

[67] See for instance his *Der Fall Eichmann*, Berlin 1963, *Der Fall des Herschel Grynszpan*, Berlin 1965; and *Ärzte in Auschwitz*, Berlin 1968.

[68] M. Unger, 'Die "Endlösung" in Leipzig. Dokumente zur Geschichte der Judenverfolgung 1933–1945', *ZfG* 11 (1963), pp. 941 ff.

[69] *Wissenschaftliche Zeitschrift der Karl-Marx-Universität Leipzig* (*Gesellschafts- und Sprachwissenschaftliche Reihe*) 14 (1965), No. 3, pp. 539–551.

chronological context. For Görschler the central question was the function of antisemitism in the class struggle. He raised a new point by stressing the need "to observe the historical continuity in the development of antisemitic theory and practice". Indeed, "throughout the nearly 2,000 years of its history, antisemitism was invariably exploited by the ruling classes, who, by pointing to the sinfulness of the Jews, contrived to divert attention from the social evils of an order based on exploitation, to obscure their true causes and put the blame on the Jews". With the same lucidity Görschler outlined the consistent campaign conducted by the workers' movement against antisemitism.

These "fundamental truths" provided the ground rules also for the treatment of the "Jewish" resistance. Margot Pikarski's paper on the German-Jewish resistance group led by Herbert Baum[70] is a striking example. Here, the most crucial aspect of that movement, the specific and tragic situation of the antifascist of Jewish origin – an aspect fully discussed by the Polish historian Bernhard Mark[71] – had to be suppressed or suitably re-interpreted. All the author is concerned with is to prove the decisive guidance exercised by the KPD leadership over the Baum Group.

The investigation of the problems of antisemitism and the persecution of the Jews initiated during that period was not confined to the subjects of the workers' movement and the resistance. Other branches of learning, too, tended to give more attention to Jewish themes from the early 1960s onward. By 1967 the number of theological dissertations had risen to nineteen and the philosophical faculties accepted seventeen dissertations, among them three on topics of contemporary history.[72] Another sign of the growing interest was the appearance of the first publications on the attitude of the Evangelical Church to antisemitism and the persecution of the Jews.[73]

Lastly, another gap was closed during this phase. In 1966 GDR historiography presented the first comprehensive documentation on the persecution and destruction of the German Jews. Edited by Helmut Eschwege, it was published under the title *Kennzeichen J.*[74] Arnold Zweig wrote the foreword. Klaus

[70]M. Pikarski, 'Über die führende Rolle der Parteiorganisation der KPD in der antifaschistischen Widerstandsgruppe Herbert Baum Berlin 1939 bis 1942', in *Beiträge zur Geschichte der deutschen Arbeiterbewegung* 8 (1966), pp. 867–881. Presented at greater length especially for members of the Free German Youth: *Sie bleiben unvergessen*, Berlin 1968.

[71]Bernhard Mark, 'Die Gruppe von Herbert Baum. Eine jüdische Widerstandsgruppe in den Jahren 1937–1942', in *Blätter für Geschichte*, Warsaw 1961, vol. XIV, pp. 34 ff. (Yiddish).

[72]H. Dohle, *Die Stellung der evangelischen Kirche in Deutschland zum Antisemitismus und zur Judenverfolgung zwischen 1933 und 1945*, p. 110, Berlin 1963; H. Eckert, *Die Beiträge der deutschen emigrierten Schriftsteller in der "Neuen Weltbühne" von 1934–1939. Ein Beitrag zur Untersuchung der Beziehungen zwischen Volksfrontpolitik und Literatur*, p. 88, Berlin 1962; D. Coburger, *Die Beziehungen zwischen der westdeutschen Bundesrepublik und Israel von 1949 bis 1961. Unter besonderer Berücksichtigung des sogenannten Wiedergutmachungsabkommens*, p. 429, Leipzig 1964. All these are unpublished dissertations.

[73]K. Meier, 'Kristallnacht und Kirche', *Wissenschaftliche Zeitschrift Leipzig* (1964), No. 1; *idem*, *Kirche und Judentum. Die Haltung der evangelischen Kirche zur Judenpolitik des Dritten Reiches*, Halle 1968; H. Fink (ed.), *Stärker als die Angst. Die sechs Millionen, die keinen Retter fanden*, with a foreword by E. Fuchs, Berlin 1968.

[74]H. Eschwege (ed.), *Kennzeichen J. Bilder, Dokumente, Berichte zur Geschichte der Verbrechen des Hitlerfaschismus an den deutschen Juden*, Berlin 1966.

Drobisch compiled a framework of dates and facts. Rudi Goguel supplied the introduction. This collective effort put before a broad public a comprehensive, carefully chosen collection of source material and pictorial documents. Moreover, Goguel's introductory remarks constituted the first attempt to modify the doctrine on the nature of fascism, in order to explain the "final solution".

Goguel followed his predecessors in that he saw his "principal task" in exposing the "responsibility of the ruling class . . . for the most frightful crime in human history". Even if "one or another representative of the big bourgeoisie" might "possibly" have disapproved of the anti-Jewish outrages, that could not alter the fact that finance capital had benefited from the persecution through the plunder of Jewish property and the exploitation of Jewish labour. Yet, since the Nazi State had "knowingly decided to do without that urgently needed manpower", it must be concluded that "murder was given priority over exploitation".[75] In other words, the "purely ideologically motivated" extermination of the Jews was deemed more important than all the political, economic and military requirements of the war.

To explain these facts, Goguel – in contrast to Kühnrich, Kuczynski or Heise – resorted to the "autonomy thesis". He argued that the close links between the monopoly bourgeoisie and the state apparatus had not ruled out a "measure of autonomy of the state sphere", and he went on: "To maintain its power and mobilise the masses for its goals, the ruling class needed an ideology offering some fascinating symbol calculated to divert attention from the class struggle. Adolf Hitler's demagogy offered such an ideology, and – no less importantly – he offered in addition a mass party, tautly organised on military lines. *In return he demanded a free hand for the execution of his antisemitic fighting programme.*"[76]

This interpretation represents an obvious modification of Dimitrov's fascism doctrine, and it is worth noting that the new departure met with the tacit approval of Kühnrich, who reviewed the work in *Zeitschrift für Geschichtswissenschaft.*[77] He regretted however that, in spite of its large section on the anti-fascist resistance, the work should have omitted the "trail-blazing documents of the KPD".

Just how far Goguel had gone in his lone advance can be gauged in the light of a controversy conducted at the same time between the British historian Tim Mason and the leading GDR contemporary historians Czichon, Eichholtz and Gossweiler.[78] Mason asserted the "primacy of politics", which he sought to explain by his thesis of the "autonomous evolution of the Nazi state apparatus" irrespective of the economic interests of the ruling class. And he adduced precisely the destruction of the Jews as proof of the "self-destructive measures" and the "irrationality" of Nazism.[79] The GDR historians were unable to come up

[75] *Ibid.*, pp. 18 f. [76] My italics. [77] *ZfG* 16 (1968), p. 648.

[78] T. Mason, 'Der Primat der Politik – Politik und Wirtschaft im Nationalsozialismus', *Das Argument* 41 (1966), *(1968), pp. 473–494; E. Czichon, 'Der Primat der Industrie im Kartell der nationalsozialistischen Macht', *Das Argument* 47 (1968), pp. 168–192; T. Mason, 'Primat der Industrie? Eine Erwiderung', *ibid.*, pp. 193–209; D. Eichholtz/K. Gossweiler, 'Noch einmal: Politik und Wirtschaft 1933–1945', *ibid.*, pp. 210–227.

[79] In support of his thesis Mason instances the gassing of thousands of skilled Polish engineering workers; the unavailing intervention of the Wehrmacht in an attempt to preserve irreplaceable

with an effective answer to Mason's arguments. References to the Jews, persecution of the Jews, destruction of the Jews did not figure in their rebuttals. Czichon objected that Mason had reduced "the category of self-destruction somewhat arbitrarily and without any discernible reason to individual instances of the National Socialist rule",[80] while Eichholtz and Gossweiler simply reaffirmed the role of the state monopoly régime, which had transformed its productive into destructive forces, "into means of destruction and mass annihilation".[81]

PHASE V: 1967–1971

In 1967 Walter Ulbricht issued the watchword of the fashioning of the "developed social system of socialism". Accordingly a new frame of reference was handed down, within which historiography was to discharge its function as an academic discipline dedicated to moulding consciousness. Historiography thus was called upon to make an effective contribution "to the further development in depth of socialist modes of thought and behaviour . . ."[82] In order to substantiate that claim to historical legitimacy of the GDR which served the dual purpose of countering the Federal Republic's claim to the sole representation of Germany as a whole and instilling civic pride in the GDR citizens, historiography was to investigate and disseminate "in general . . . all the great revolutionary, democratic and humanistic traditions and achievements of the German people". Historians were requested to supply investigations which should rest on a broad basis of source material, and which should reveal the "large historical patterns" and "manifestations of the laws of history".

Beginning in 1966–1967, comprehensive accounts, textbooks, handbooks, documentations and reference works on the history of the German workers' movement as well as on German history in general were published. And all these standard works contained material on antisemitism and the persecution of the Jews.[83] In respect of both method and subject matter, the new material did not go beyond the ground already covered, apart from one exception.

The exception was the new work of D. Fricke and W. Menke who, in connec-

---

manpower for the German war economy, resulting in the dismissal from his command of the general who raised the issue; the diversion of rolling stock from military supplies to the transport of Jews to the destruction camps. Cf. T. Mason, 'Der Primat der Politik . . .', *loc. cit.*, p. 492. These examples have been lifted almost verbatim in the West German literature on fascism inspired by the "New Left". Cf. R. Kühnl, *Formen bürgerlicher Herrschaft*, Reinbek (Hamburg) 1971, p. 150.

[80]E. Czichon, 'Der Primat der Industrie . . .' *loc. cit.*, pp. 190 f.

[81]Eichholtz/Gossweiler, *loc. cit.*, pp. 217 f.

[82]Quoted by H. Bartel/E. Engelberg, *loc. cit.*, p. 29.

[83]*Geschichte der deutschen Arbeiterbewegung*, vol. 5, Berlin 1966; E. Paterna (*et al.*), *Deutschland von 1933 bis 1939*, Berlin 1969; W. Bleyer (*et al.*), *Deutschland von 1939 bis 1945*, Berlin 1969; Streisand, *op. cit.*; *Sachwörterbuch der Geschichte Deutschlands und der deutschen Arbeiterbewegung*, vol. 1, Berlin 1969, articles on: Antisemitismus/Faschistischer Terror/Endlösung/Judenverfolgung/Arisierung der Wirtschaft/Nürnberger Gesetze/Konzentrationslager; *Kleines politisches Wörterbuch*, Berlin 1967 (new edition 1973).

tion with the study of the history of the bourgeois parties then in progress, were the first to focus attention on the antisemitic parties of the Wilhelminian Empire and the Weimar Republic as well as on the *Centralverein deutscher Staatsbürger jüdischen Glaubens* and the *Verein zur Abwehr des Antisemitismus*. Their findings were published in the form of concise and informative handbook articles.[84]

As regards Menke's contribution on the *Centralverein*, it is worth noting that it was based on a state of research that was largely outdated by the time of its publication. Menke virtually ignored the latest findings of bourgeois (Jewish) historiography, notably the fact – well documented in work published in the 1960s – that during the Weimar period the bourgeois Jewish organisations had conducted a massive camouflaged anti-fascist propaganda. Thus, certain "reproaches" levelled in the handbook article against the C.V. were invalidated in advance.[85]

In the portrayal of the Nazi régime, the main weight continued to rest on the two mandatory corner-stones of communist resistance and the rule of finance capital. While endeavours to elaborate the doctrine on the nature of fascism by empirical research were attended by a measure of success,[86] the problem of fitting the holocaust into the officially sanctioned explanatory model was evaded. Not a single study published in this period attempted to deal with the subject.

Lack of interest also characterised the attitude to another topic, the treatment of which was no longer compatible with the "fundamental convictions" and political aims of the Party. At the end of the 1960s Helmut Eschwege completed his study on the Resistance of German Jews against Nazism. By that time, however, the GDR had intensified its anti-Zionist course. In these circumstances the publication of a book dedicated to the appraisal and appreciation of a "Jewish" anti-fascism and outlining the particular difficulties encountered by the German-Jewish community was clearly inopportune. So the supervisory authorities lodged a veto, and the manuscript found no publisher. Eschwege responded by passing the manuscript to the Leo Baeck Institute in London with the request to publish an abridged version in the Year Book.[87]

PHASE VI: 1971–1975

It was the finding of the Eighth Party Congress of the SED in 1971 that the GDR had in the meantime developed into a "socialist nation". Accordingly

[84]D. Fricke, 'Antisemitische Parteien', in D. Fricke (ed.), *Die bürgerlichen Parteien in Deutschland. Handbuch der Geschichte der bürgerlichen Parteien*, vol. 1, Leipzig 1968, pp. 36–40; W. Menke, 'Centralverein deutscher Staatsbürger jüdischen Glaubens (CV)', *ibid.*, vol. 1, pp. 236–240, and 'Verein zur Abwehr des Antisemitismus', *ibid.*, vol. 2, Leipzig 1970, pp. 784 f.

[85]Cf. in particular the literature quoted in notes 91 and 92 below.

[86]Notably: D. Eichholtz, *Geschichte der deutschen Kriegswirtschaft 1939–1945*, vol. 1, *1939–1941*, Berlin 1969; D. Eichholtz/W. Schumann (eds.), *Anatomie des Krieges*, Berlin 1969; W. Bleyer, *Staat und Monopole im totalen Staat. Der staatsmonopolistische Machtapparat und die totale Mobilmachung im ersten Halbjahr 1943*, Berlin 1970.

[87]Helmut Eschwege, 'Resistance of German Jews against the Nazi Régime', in *LBI Year Book XV* (1970), pp. 143–180. See also Arnold Paucker, 'Some Notes on Resistance', in *LBI Year Book XVI* (1971), pp. 239–247.

Kurt Hager confirmed previous instructions by telling the historians: "History must be written in such a way as to highlight the fact that the GDR is the socialist state where all the great progressive and revolutionary traditions of our people are in safe keeping."[88]

The importance currently attributed to the role of anti-fascism and the official doctrine on fascism in tackling the problems of antisemitism and the persecution of the Jews, and the preoccupation of GDR historiography with the discovery of the "large historical patterns" and "manifestations of the laws of history" can be inferred from the most recent work published in this field. This comprises three publications, which reflect a serious endeavour to catch up and gradually to close the gaps in the state of GDR research in the field of antisemitism and the persecution of the Jews, while at the same time broadening the topic to include patterns of Jewish behaviour and tracing inner-Jewish developments from the foundation of the *Reich* to the final deportations in 1943.

Mohrmann's book on the development and function of antisemitism in the Wilhelminian Empire and the Weimar Republic was published in 1972.[89] Much space is given to a description of the "consistent campaign" waged by the workers' movement against antisemitism, racism and imperialism. Mohrmann also seeks to include the attitudes and reactions of the Jewish community in his narrative. He finds no difficulty in showing that the Jewish section of the population was subject to inhibitions that rendered it incapable of waging a successful "defensive struggle". His proof is simple: belonging, as they did, to the bourgeoisie, the overwhelming majority of the Jews were prevented by their own class interests from seeing through the "true" class character of antisemitism and joining the ranks of the struggling revolutionary workers' movement. Hence the *Centralverein* had only "philosemitic" arguments to offer in its efforts to win the favour of the ruling apparatus of the capitalist régime (philosemitism being, of course, only the reverse side of antisemitism, its so to say reactionary twin). Furthermore, in mobilising its supporters in 1914 for the war, the C.V. had committed itself to the aggressive power drive of German imperialism. (The truly ironic implications of these strictures are dealt with by Arnold Paucker in the sources given further below.)

Like his predecessors, Mohrmann does not hesitate to establish the mandatory lines of continuity leading to the contemporary scene, and to come out with broad generalisations about Jewish political behaviour, going far beyond the scope of a study which after all is dedicated to the subjects of German antisemitism and German Jewry.

It is of some interest to note, however, that unlike his predecessors, Mohrmann, as well as the other authors whose works are discussed below, is beginning to engage in a serious dialogue with "Jewish-bourgeois" historiography. All three books refer to and criticise above all the two collective volumes published by the Leo Baeck Institute, *Entscheidungsjahr 1932* and *Deutsches*

[88]K. Hager, *Die entwickelte sozialistische Gesellschaft. Aufgaben der Gesellschaftswissenschaften nach dem VIII. Parteitag der SED*, Berlin 1971, pp. 48 f.

[89]W. Mohrmann, *Antisemitismus. Ideologie und Geschichte im Kaiserreich und in der Weimarer Republik*, Berlin 1972.

Judentum in Krieg und Revolution,[90] and Arnold Paucker's monograph *Der jüdische Abwehrkampf*.[91] That these "Jewish-bourgeois" authors, though commended for their scholarship, are found wanting in their grasp of the true class basis of antisemitism goes without saying. That much of the "evaluation" is based on their well-documented findings is equally obvious. "Jewish-bourgeois" historiography for its part has not ignored these recent GDR contributions either. With regard to the Jewish defence against antisemitism they are summed up in a contribution to a third collective volume just issued by the Leo Baeck Institute.[92] Here Arnold Paucker counters with the thesis of a Jewish community and its defence organisations as a "progressive" factor in the context of German history since 1890, and argues convincingly for the superiority of the more differentiated and sophisticated "Jewish-bourgeois" approach over one-sided "Marxist" interpretations.[93]

The Marxist historian Mohrmann of course voices the conviction that all instances of the persecution of Jews are readily explained by the formula defining antisemitism as "one of the most brutal weapons used by the exploiting classes for the stabilisation and extension of their position of power".[94] Since this statement is considered "generally valid for all periods of history", it naturally leads up to the accepted doctrine on the nature of fascism, and the author arrives at the conclusion that "again, the methodical destruction of all persons of Jewish origin initiated by Hitlerite fascism . . . was carried out at the

[90] *Entscheidungsjahr 1932. Zur Judenfrage in der Endphase der Weimarer Republik.* Ein Sammelband herausgegeben von Werner E. Mosse unter Mitwirkung von Arnold Paucker, Tübingen 1965, [2]1966; *Deutsches Judentum in Krieg und Revolution 1916–1923.* Ein Sammelband herausgegeben von Werner E. Mosse unter Mitwirkung von Arnold Paucker, Tübingen 1971 (Schriftenreihe wissenschaftlicher Abhandlungen des Leo Baeck Instituts 13 and 25).

[91] *Der jüdische Abwehrkampf gegen Antisemitismus und Nationalsozialismus in den letzten Jahren der Weimarer Republik*, 2nd edn., Hamburg 1969 (Hamburger Beiträge zur Zeitgeschichte IV).

[92] Arnold Paucker, 'Zur Problematik einer jüdischen Abwehrstrategie in der deutschen Gesellschaft', in *Juden im Wilhelminischen Deutschland 1890–1914.* Ein Sammelband herausgegeben von Werner E. Mosse unter Mitwirkung von Arnold Paucker, Tübingen 1976 (Schriftenreihe wissenschaftlicher Abhandlungen des Leo Baeck Instituts 33), pp. 479–548. See in particular the author's emphasis on the anti-imperialist stance of the Centralverein deutscher Staatsbürger jüdischen Glaubens (*loc. cit.*, pp. 527 ff.); the C.V.'s role as a democratising factor in Wilhelminian society (*loc. cit.*, p. 530); his remarks on the futility of a more left-wing strategy of the Jewish organisations, as advocated in retrospect by the adversaries of the bourgeois-Jewish defence (*loc. cit.*, p. 540 f.); on the crude "Marxist" recommendation that the German Jews *should* have stabbed Germany in the back in the First World War (*loc. cit.*, p. 547) etc. etc. Arnold Paucker also counters some of the allegations of the New Left and of GDR historiography in three further essays: 'Jewish Defence against Nazism in the Weimar Republic', in *The Wiener Library Bulletin*, vol. XXVI, Nos. 1 and 2, New Series, Nos. 26 and 27 (1972), pp. 21–31; 'Documents on the Fight of Jewish Organizations against Right-Wing Extremism', in *Michael.* The Diaspora Research Institute, Tel-Aviv University, vol. II (1973), pp. 216–246; 'La Posizione degli Ebrei e loro Autodifesa in Germania dal 1890 all' Avvento del Nazismo', in *Atti della Societa Leonardo da Vinci*, Serie III, vol. VI (1975), pp. 65–81. See also the Introduction of Cécile Lowenthal-Hensel and Arnold Paucker to Ernst Feder, *Heute sprach ich mit . . . Tagebücher eines Berliner Publizisten 1926–1932*, Veröffentlichung des Leo Baeck Instituts, Stuttgart 1971, especially pp. 19–21.

[93] Arnold Paucker, 'Zur Problematik einer jüdischen Abwehrstrategie in der deutschen Gesellschaft', *loc. cit.*, pp. 539–541.

[94] Mohrmann, *op. cit.*, pp. 11 f.

behest of the ruling class and represented the most savage expression of the pursuit of their economic and political interests".[95]

Not surprisingly Mohrmann fails to supply any historical evidence for his assertion. He emphasises himself that it is not his intention to embark on a "detailed analysis" of Nazi racial policy; he only wishes to discuss its beginnings. He breaks off his investigation in 1923, with the remark that the fascist threats were not directed against the Jews alone, but "in the first place" against all "forces of democracy and socialism which resolutely opposed the rise of fascism as well as its class basis".[96] So we are coming round full circle: the doctrine on fascism is confirmed; West German finance capital and its imperialist ally Israel stand condemned – here the inclusion of Israel is a novel feature, the first appearance of the anti-Zionist propaganda line in a work of historiography – and finally, due praise is given to the "one and only historically real" anti-fascist concept of the KPD, a concept that prior to 1923, in 1933 and in the years from 1933 to 1945 served as the "guiding principle in the heroic resistance struggle". That concept, the author says in the closing passage of his book "formed the foundation for the creation and development of the German Democratic Republic into a stable socialist state within whose frontiers antisemitism, racism and all other reactionary manifestations of the exploiters' society have for the first time been eliminated with their class-conditioned roots".[97]

The historical self-image reflected in this passage is characteristic of the GDR. It vindicates the political and moral claim that through the construction of socialism the "Jewish Question" has been solved in the Marxian sense, that thus the fascist past has been mastered,[98] and restitution has been rendered in the only true and valid sense of the term.

This particular contribution of the GDR – invoked by the Party and state leadership in justification of its refusal to accept Israeli restitution demands – is also prominently treated in the second recent publication, entitled *Juden unterm Hakenkreuz*.[99]

This collective work, published in 1973, is the first comprehensive account of the persecution and destruction of the German Jews produced by GDR historiography. The authors were spared the effort of first-hand research in the relevant archives. The book was compiled at the suggestion of Eschwege, who was still in a position to do the preparatory work. In content it is based almost entirely on the evaluation of previously published material from Western-bourgeois, Jewish and Marxist sources, both academic and journalistic. The fact that no use is made of any material in GDR archives must arouse the suspicion that the so-called "Jew files" have for some time been barred not only to bourgeois historians.

The retrospective review begins with Imperial Germany. The authors then present an effective account of the various phases of the persecution of the

[95] *Ibid.*, pp. 11 f. [96] *Ibid.*, p. 189. [97] *Ibid.*, pp. 204 f.

[98] S. Eichhöfer, 'Der 8. Mai 1945 und die geistige Bewältigung der Vergangenheit', *ZfG* 18 (1970), pp. 480–496.

[99] K. Drobisch/R. Goguel/W. Müller (unter Mitwirkung von H. Dohle), *Juden unterm Hakenkreuz. Verfolgung und Ausrottung der deutschen Juden 1933–1945*, Berlin 1973.

Jews. The authors' attempts to interpret and explain events are not particularly remarkable: they stress the class character of antisemitism and the glorious role of the KPD; they point out that the persecution of the Jews is a predominantly ideological phenomenon; they confirm that mass murder is "immanent in the imperialist system", and thus in accordance with the inexorable laws of history.

More remarkable is the authors' ambivalent assessment of Jewish modes of behaviour. On the one hand the reactions of the Jewish organisations in 1933 are pilloried as undignified attempts to curry favour, as "pro-Nazi proclamations", calculated to "misdirect the Jewish citizens", and which had "militated against the timely organisation of political resistance within the ranks of the Jewish minority".[100] Once again, the bourgeois class status and class interest of the Jews are invoked in explanation of their "false political orientation", for which "they had to pay in subsequent years with bitter experiences and heavy sacrifices".[101]

Wittingly or unwittingly, this thesis in fact assigns part of the blame for their destruction to the Jews themselves, giving the impression that attempts to help them would have been hopeless in any case. Yet the authors themselves arrive at conclusions which are difficult to reconcile with their fundamental thesis.

They concede that "in the light of current knowledge, it appears more than dubious whether the adoption of a different policy by the *Reichsvertretung*, the national representative body of Jewry, could have altered the fate of the German Jews as a whole".[102] In the same vein the authors argue that ". . . even if those whom it concerned had succeeded in fully grasping the aims and essential character of fascism, not enough Jews would have opted for open organised rebellion."[103] All these would seem contradictions in terms as almost in the same breath they stress the virtually total isolation of the Jewish population from the German people which makes this dwelling on the possibilities of such "organised" or even "armed" resistance a purely academic exercise.

On the other hand, the authors express appreciation of Jewish activities, especially in the fields of emigration and culture. The attempt at Jewish self-assertion and regeneration is appraised as a form of spiritual resistance against fascism, the foundation of the *Jüdische Kulturbund* is assessed as the creation of an oasis of Weimar humanism in a desert of inhumanity. And it is particularly noteworthy that the *Reichsvereinigung*, formed in 1939 on the orders of the Nazi

[100]*Ibid.*, p. 89. As regards the *Reichsbund jüdischer Frontsoldaten* it is even castigated as having weakened by its reactionary policy antifascist resistance to the Nazi régime. Such strictures barely deserve serious consideration by historians familiar with the activity of that organisation; which prior to 1933 had cooperated with the *Reichsbanner* and the *Eiserne Front*.

[101]*Ibid.*, p. 89. This is, of course, a good example of one-sided reliance on material published under the nose of a dictatorship. It is common knowledge, well attested by documentation, that Jewish emissaries were meanwhile despatched to England and America explaining that no credence was to be given to such "official" declarations, while themselves providing information on the true situation pertaining then in Germany and the steps obligatory for Jewish representatives. Quite apart from this the semantics of the Jewish press in Nazi Germany deserve a study in themselves. It is futile and totally misleading to cite Jewish press statements as examples of undignified collaboration.

[102]*Ibid.*, p. 117.

[103]*Ibid.*, p. 261.

régime, is here strongly defended against the charge of "collaboration" which has so frequently been put forward elsewhere.

Questions relating to the reaction of the Jewish minority and the role of the anti-fascist resistance movement are also touched upon in a dissertation submitted in 1973 and published in 1975 under the title *Faschismus. Rassenwahn. Judenverfolgung*. Kurt Pätzold's important study closes a further gap.[104]

He introduces his work as "a study on the political strategy and tactics of German fascist imperialism". The investigation is confined to the years 1933 to 1935. To emphasise the relevance of that first phase of the persecution of the Jews, Pätzold uses a methodological approach hitherto severely avoided by GDR historiography. Its novelty lies not so much in his "general postulate" that history should be judged "by its causes rather than by its results" as in his "firm conviction" that the observation of historical sequence of events "cannot be divorced from the problem of the *alternative* in history".[105] Thus the author denies the inevitability of the "final solution", and points out alternatives, "crossroads" which could have given a different direction to German history in 1941.

Another aspect that marks out this publication is its rich documentation. Exhaustive use is made of important material in the Koblenz Federal Archives and the GDR State Archives, notably files of the *Reich* Chancellery, the Foreign Office, the Ministries of Justice, Economic Affairs and the Interior, the German *Reich* Bank, as well as of the *Stimmungs- und Lageberichte* issued regularly by Prussia's Regional and Provincial Governors and the Main Offices of the State Police, records almost completely preserved for the years 1933–1935.

Thanks to this documentary basis, Pätzold is in a position to present in minute detail an empirically sound reconstruction of the beginnings of the Nazi policy on the Jews. (No comparably authentic account has been published by students of contemporary history in the Federal Republic.) Pätzold's main concern is the question of the relationship between the ideological justification and the practice of the persecution. He answers the question by placing it in the context of the general political and economic development and by spotlighting the strategic and tactical links which relate antisemitism and the persecution of the Jews to the "overall policy" of the party leadership and the ruling monopoly bourgeoisie.

His conclusion is that antisemitism and the persecution of the Jews, serving as instruments of manipulation and mobilisation, were assigned a twofold function. From the tactical angle, their role was to transform the class struggle into a race struggle. From the angle of strategy, their purpose was to prepare and justify the expansion of German imperialism.

Soundly based as these findings are, on one crucial point Pätzold's reasoning fails to carry conviction. The problem of tracing the decisive influence of finance capital in initiating the persecution of the Jews can be equated to all intents and purposes with the investigation of the role and the activities of Hjalmar Schacht.

[104] K. Pätzold, *Faschismus. Rassenwahn. Judenverfolgung. Eine Studie zur politischen Strategie und Taktik des faschistischen deutschen Imperialismus (1933–1935)*, Berlin 1975.

[105] *Ibid.*, p. 11.

He is rightly characterised as a "cultured", soft-spoken antisemite, who sought to settle the "Jewish Question" by means of traditional discriminating legislation or by expulsion. Yet it is on record that in 1935 – prompted by the need to ensure Germany's rapid and undisturbed economic rearmament and to promote exports in the face of critical foreign opinion – Schacht attempted to change the policy towards the Jews and the Churches and to direct the activities of the Gestapo against the Communists alone, and that he failed in his attempt.

Surely, the unavailing interventions of this so-called "economic dictator" can be taken as proof that the ultimate decision rested after all in the hands of Hitler and the SS. In thus pinpointing the seat of ultimate authority, however, we do not seek to diminish the part played by the other leading groups and their share of responsibility. Indeed, Pätzold must be given credit for having established the respective roles of the bureaucracy, the *Wehrmacht*, the Churches and the population in the process of persecuting and expelling the Jewish minority.

Positive as Pätzold's contribution is, he cannot, any more than his colleagues, evade the obligation of responding to the demands of anti-Zionist propaganda. This starts at the precise point where the anti-fascist resistance is introduced into the narrative. The author emphasises that the Jewish sections of the population had no chance whatever of finding protection or security within the fascist dictatorship, and after rejecting the concept of "a separate line of defence for the Jewish Germans" as unhistorical and reactionary, goes on to argue on the tenuous ground of the "objective logic of the class struggle" that "their only chance of salvation lay in the anti-fascist resistance",[106] because the revolutionary workers' movement had "moved into the centre of the historical arena, and while engaged in the struggle for the communist future of mankind, was at the same time preserving and continuing the progressive achievements and ideas of earlier periods".

Pätzold argues that, unable to perceive these facts, the Jews held aloof from "these interrelationships" and thus contributed to a weakening of "the ranks of the objectively anti-imperialist forces". This is followed by the abstruse though obligatory statement that it is the ideological and practical-political course of Zionism which must also be held responsible for the failure of the "international anti-fascist defence". Zionist leaders "though certainly not they alone" had helped to prevent an anti-fascist world front from taking shape. Its absence "opened the road to war for the fascist power bloc, without which the extinction of millions of Jews and Slavs would have been inconceivable".[107]

Obviously this picture leaves out or distorts a great many "objective facts" that had also "helped to prevent an anti-fascist world front from taking shape", such as the effects of the theory of social fascism; the KPD's dependence on the Soviet Union; the Stalinist purges (in the course of which, in one of the cruellest exchanges of political prisoners on record in modern times, Communists of Jewish origin were handed over to the Gestapo to be liquidated) and, finally, the German-Soviet non-agression pact of 1939 – which eased the way for Germany to embark on the invasion of Poland – a tactical alliance, which was to

[106] *Ibid.*, p. 78. [107] *Ibid.*, p. 277.

last two years, with the "principal enemy" of the workers' movement and of the Jews. (The resulting dilemma and soul searchings for Jewish Socialists and Communists who had been constantly exhorted by the KPD to take part in anti-fascist sabotage and resistance should perhaps only be mentioned here in passing.)

Lastly, there is no room in this picture for the fact that in 1936–1937 anti-fascists of Jewish origin were withdrawn from the German underground movement on orders from the KPD, to avoid exposing the illegal cadres to the greatly increased risks involved. The active Jewish anti-fascists, then, were either gathered in specific Jewish groups – like that of Herbert Baum – which drove them yet deeper into hopeless isolation, or they were instructed to emigrate. Such were some of the barriers erected by the KPD itself, obstacles which made it anyway very hard for German Jews to join the Communist anti-fascist resistance.

Undoubtedly, some of the more recent works which have emanated from the German Democratic Republic have done much to trace in detail the path which was to lead to the destruction of Jewry and have certainly added to our factual knowledge of the period. Yet no major contribution to our real understanding of German-Jewish history has hitherto come out of the GDR. The treatment of antisemitism and the persecution of the Jews continue to occupy only a subordinate position in Marxist–Leninist historiography. Working within strict methodological rules and inhibited by ideology GDR historians are precluded from arriving at independent assessments. Not one of the authors here discussed has really come to grips with the complex problem of German-Jewish co-existence. There is little indication that we shall see any improvement in the near future.

Major Trends and Tendencies in German Historiography on National Socialism and the "Jewish Question" (1924–1984)

BY OTTO D. KULKA

The historiography of the Holocaust period no longer settles for one-dimensional descriptive accounts of prejudice against the Jews, their persecution and destruction, as had been presented in the first comprehensive works on the "Final Solution" in the fifties.[1] Today, it is more diversified and deals not only with the political and ideological role of the Jewish Question, but also with the attitude of the German population toward the regime's anti-Jewish policy as well as with the communal life of Jewish society in the Third *Reich*, and its organisation and leadership. Furthermore, a characteristic of the historiography of the last twenty years has been the development of diverse and opposing methodological approaches, currents and schools. Yet, systematic research of the subject reveals that basic methodological approaches, and even seemingly new currents and schools, can be traced back to contemporaries of National Socialism and their attempts to comprehend the nature of the movement, from its emergence in the twenties and its establishment as a political system in the thirties.*

With respect to its salient features and the various stages of its development, German historiography can be divided into three main periods:

1. From the first half of the twenties till close to the collapse of the Third *Reich* (1924–1944); the political struggle is predominant in the literature of this period.
2. From the collapse of the Third *Reich* until the beginning of the sixties (1945–1960). The historiography of this period is characterised by almost total silence on the Jewish Question. It concentrates on assessing the "guilt" or responsibility for the fall of Weimar and the rise of Hitler, and passes gradually to discussion of the question of "totalitarianism or Hitlerism".
3. From the beginning of the sixties to the beginning of the eighties. This period

[1] Léon Poliakov, *Bréviaire de la haine. Le IIIe Reich et les Juifs*, Paris 1951; Gerald Reitlinger, *The Final Solution. The Attempt to Exterminate the Jews of Europe 1939–1945*, London 1953; Artur Eisenbach, *Hitlerowska Polityka Eksterminacji Żydów w Latach 1939–1945* (Hitler's Policy of Extermination of the Jews 1939–1945), Warsaw 1953; Raul Hilberg, *The Destruction of the European Jews*, Chicago 1961, (based on his 1955 dissertation, Columbia 1955).

* For the purposes of this paper, the term "German historiography" denotes publications written in Germany, especially before 1933 and after 1945, as well as publications by émigrés, which were written outside Germany from 1933 onwards.

is characterised by a critical re-examination of the conclusions of the earlier stages. On the basis of the historical perspective that has developed and the wider range of sources that have become available, this historiography seeks to arrive at an examination of the subject through categories and methods of historical research.

I. THE PERIOD OF POLITICAL STRUGGLE

Let us now look more closely at the first stage, the years 1924–1944. The dominant feature of this stage is the literature describing the political struggle against the growing influence of the National Socialist movement in the twenties, and after 1933 against Hitler's regime. Although this literature was based on limited sources and its purpose was not research *per se*, in several cases it produced achievements of lasting research value.[2] Most of this literature in the twenties and thirties regarded Hitler, and Fascism generally, as an instrument devised to serve the needs of German capitalism in its struggle with Communism, and as a kind of continuation of Prussian militarism and of the frustrated colonial imperialism of the Second *Reich*. This view was especially characteristic of the anti-Fascist interpretation common to both the left and liberal sectors in Germany; by contrast, in the interpretations of the conservative trends and part of the liberal camp, Hitler appears as a vulgar demagogue devoid of all ideology and principles other than a lust for power. The anti-Jewish aspect is generally overlooked or seen as marginal in both of these interpretations. To the extent that Nazi antisemitism is dealt with, it is presented as a demagogical ploy aimed at diverting the masses from their real problems, an instrument to incite passions, or a kind of antinomian irrational outburst. The publications that were devoted especially to the subject of the Jews are for the most part descriptive accounts of anti-Jewish incitement, persecution and stigmatisation. As typical examples, we may note here the so-called *Braunbuch* published in 1933, in which there is a special chapter on this subject, called 'Juda Verrecke!',[3] *Das Schwarzbuch*,[4] *Der gelbe Fleck. Die Ausrottung von 500.000 deutschen Juden*,[5] or *Der Pogrom. Dokumente der braunen Barbarei*.[6]

Nevertheless, even before 1933 we find important assessments of the essentially modern character of Fascism, and especially of National Socialism. Such assessments point to these movements as a potentially powerful historical factor, uniting the politicised masses of the era following the First World War by means of radical ideas, including radical antisemitism. A significant example of this type of analysis are the two brilliant essays by the Jewish Marxist

[2]Concerning the problem of historiographical assessment of contemporary interpretations of National Socialism and the Third *Reich* see for example Ernst Nolte, *Der Faschismus in seiner Epoche*, 2nd edn., Munich 1965, pp. 23–35, 42–47; Klaus Hildebrand, *Das Dritte Reich*, Munich–Oldenburg 1980, pp. 123–131.

[3]*Das Braunbuch über Reichstagsbrand und Hitler-Terror*, Basle 1933, pp. 222–269.

[4]*Das Schwarzbuch. Tatsachen und Dokumente. Die Lage der Juden in Deutschland 1933*, Paris 1934.

[5]Paris 1936.

[6]Zürich 1939.

philosopher, Ernst Bloch: 'Erinnerung: Hitlers Gewalt' of 1924, and 'Ungleichzeitigkeit und Pflicht zu ihrer Dialektik' of 1932.[7] As opposed to the schematic Marxist theory of the time, Bloch does not view Fascism simply as a higher stage of capitalism, whose end is foreordained, and as the representative of the disintegrating forces of counter-revolutionary reaction; he also sees it as a force with a modern message and with a decidedly modern praxis. To be sure, he also identifies it with a manifestation of an ancient force, much older than the bourgeoisie and capitalism, and that identification is what gives rise to the new perspective on the nature and power of the movement and its potential to spread and leave its mark on the era. Its revolutionary message appears in the form of the political messianism which is a feature of revolutionary movements of the Left. Even though, in the end, fascist messianism must lead to destruction and death, on the ascent, its allure is greater than that of the Marxist revolutionary movement, which has become institutionalised and has lost its messianic momentum. Bloch was also one of the first to view Germany, and not Italy, as the most important country with respect to Fascism's possibilities, even before National Socialism came to power.[8]

As Uriel Tal has had the occasion to note,[9] similar assessments and analyses were presented, but from a theological point of view, by the Catholic Erhard Schlund, in his *Neugermanisches Heidentum im heutigen Deutschland* of 1924 and by the Protestant, Richard Karwehl, in *Politisches Messiastum* of 1931. From the Jewish side, this view was given a profoundly pessimistic expression in the apocalyptic presentiments of the German Zionist leader, Kurt Blumenfeld, in 1932.[10]

A different analysis, which attempts to explain the sources of National Socialism's power and its influence on the masses in Weimar Germany in terms of sociological processes, was published that same year by a representative of the *Centralverein deutscher Staatsbürger jüdischen Glaubens*, Eva Reichmann-Jungmann, in her article 'Flucht vor der Vernunft'.[11] The most important study on our subject published that year in Germany, the first volume of Konrad Heiden's *Geschichte des Nationalsozialismus. Die Karriere einer Idee*,[12] also attributes a certain role to antisemitism and its use as a revolutionary ideology in the new social quality of the post-war nationalism that was sustained by the activation and politicisation of the masses. It was his prognosis that whether or not National Socialism would come to power, it would henceforth leave its mark on all areas of public life in Germany and in German society.

[7]The first article, which has so far been unnoticed in research literature, appeared in *Das Tagebuch*, No. 15 (April 1924). The second one was reprinted in Ernst Nolte (ed.), *Theorien über den Faschismus*, 3rd edn., Cologne 1972, pp. 182–204.

[8]Nolte, *Theorien* . . . , p. 38.

[9]Uriel Tal, *"Political Faith" of Nazism Prior to the Holocaust*, Tel-Aviv 1978.

[10]*Jüdische Rundschau*, 16th September 1932.

[11]Eva G. Reichmann-Jungmann, 'Flucht vor der Vernunft. Kritische Bemerkungen zu neuer Literatur über Soziologie des Nationalsozialismus', in *Der Morgen*, VIII, No. 2 (June 1932), pp. 116–121.

[12]Konrad Heiden, *Geschichte des Nationalsozialismus. Die Karriere einer Idee*, Berlin 1933 (copyright 1932 by Rowohlt Verlag).

After Hitler's rise to power we find one of the most profound analyses in the literature of the political struggle in the frightful prognosis, written in exile, by Leopold Schwarzschild. Here National Socialist antisemitism is given a central place in a process of universal significance. After stressing the unique role given to the deterministic principle of race by the new regime in Germany, which set it apart from all other authoritarian or totalitarian regimes, Schwarzschild concludes his article by declaring that:

> "... die Verteidigung gegen den Nationalsozialismus eine Aufgabe ist, die in einer völlig anderen und unendlich wichtigeren Zone liegt als irgend eine andere politische Auseinandersetzung ... was da heranstürmt, nicht etwa nur Politik ist, sondern das Ungeheuerste: eben der Urwald".[13]

A similar recognition of the epochal significance of the processes contributing to the National Socialist regime's rise to power was published in 1933 in Germany by Martin Buber. His call to come to grips with the new situation is addressed to the Jew *qua* individual and to the Jewish community:

> "Die Situation kann etwa dahin ausgesprochen werden, dass die Geschichte der Erdbevölkerung wieder 'labil' geworden ist, und anscheinend labiler als je. Die 'festen Verhältnisse', die vor zwei Jahrzehnten noch den einigermassen gleichbleibenden Hintergrund all der wechselnden Ereignisse, Entwicklungen, Konflikte und Krisen abgaben, sind allsamt mit ins Gleiten geraten. Die 'Sicherheit der Voraussetzungen', das Werk der von der französischen Revolution emporgetragenen bürgerlichen Gesellschaft, ist entschwunden. Der Mensch ist *exponiert*. Die exponierteste Menschensippe aber sind die Juden ... Hier wird der Kampf des Menschen exemplarisch ausgefochten."[14]

Similarly, three years later he writes of the far-reaching significance of the stance assumed by the Jews *qua* community in a situation unprecedented in its severity:

> "Wird ein Stundenschlag der alten Turmuhr so vernehmbar, als hätte sie noch nie geschlagen, dann ist es an der Zeit, ihn und die Uhr zu deuten. Man braucht die Deutung nicht zu erdenken, man darf sie nicht erdenken, man muss nur die wahrnehmen, die von je da ist, wie eben die Wahrheit da ist, und sie aussprechen. Warum sie aussprechen? Damit die Schar, die vernommen hat, im Schicksal der Stunde und ihrer Erkenntnis beisammenbleibe, wie auch im Raum sie zersprengt wird. Ob sie Gemeinschaft bleibt — nein, ob sie es wird, ob sie es jetzt wieder wird, davon hängt geheimnisvoll auch der nächste Stundenschlag mit ab. Zerfällt sie in unverbundene Einzelne, dann ist sie, dann ist vielleicht mehr als sie verloren."[15]

However important the analyses we have so far mentioned are, it was only at the end of the thirties and the beginning of the forties that a number of comprehensive studies of National Socialism and of the Third *Reich* were published in which an attempt was made to examine the whole phenomenon with the help of historical categories and tools. Among them mention should be made of the works of Ernst Fraenkel,[16] Franz Neumann,[17] and additional books

[13]Leopold Schwarzschild, 'Rückbildung der Gattung Mensch', in *Das Neue Tagebuch*, Paris, 19th July 1933, pp. 61–64.

[14]Martin Buber, 'Unser Bildungsziel', in *Jüdische Rundschau*, 7th July 1933 (republished in the collection of his articles from the years 1933–1935: *Die Stunde und die Erkenntnis*, Berlin 1936, pp. 88–94).

[15]Buber, *op. cit.*, preface, p. 7.

[16]Ernst Fraenkel, *The Dual State. A Contribution to the Theory of Dictatorship*, London–New York–Toronto 1941. The book was originally written while Fraenkel was still in Germany, before 1938. Three years later it was published as an English translation. Only later was it translated

by Konrad Heiden[18] on the nature of the regime and its practice; and on Hitler of the intimate report, with important analytical assessments, by Hermann Rauschning,[19] and the first systematic monograph on the Third *Reich* and the Jews by Gustav Warburg.[20]

It appears that these authors, precisely because of their position as a combatant and persecuted party, imposed on themselves an exceptional degree of methodological objectivity – perhaps possible only at that stage, which preceded knowledge of the concrete horrors of the Holocaust. Indeed, such knowledge eliminated any possibility of dealing with the subject in categories that require distance and abstraction to which research could return only after the passing of a generation.

Fraenkel's book, *The Dual State*, using administrative sources and internal publications, examines the heterogeneous structure of the regime and the internal contradications in its functioning, which he takes to be characteristic of the essence of the Third *Reich*. Although the Jewish Question has only an incidental place in his schematic description and explanations of diversionary class struggle propaganda, there is no doubt that even today his approach can be a very useful methodological tool for the study of the developments in the policy of the "solution of the Jewish problem".

Within the conservative school, Rauschning's work stands out as the most important research achievement of the period. Rauschning perceived the connection between National Socialist antisemitism and the struggle against western cultural heritage and its principles, as well as distinguishing the centrality of the Jews even in Hitler's foreign political concepts:

> "Für Hitler ist der Jude das schlechthin Böse. Er hat ihn zu dem Herrn seiner Gegenwelt emporgesteigert . . . Mag man dafür Erklärungen in seinem persönlichen Erleben suchen, mag man Hitler selbst als nach den Nürnberger Rassengesetzen nicht arisch bezeichnen, die Nachhaltigkeit seines Antisemitismus wird erst durch die mythische Übersteigerung des Juden zu einem ewigen Prototyp des Menschen verständlich. Streng genommen irrt Hitler damit sogar nicht einmal . . . Und ging nicht das ganze, verhasste Christentum, der Erlösserglaube, die Moral, das Gewissen, der Begriff der Sünde auf das Judentum zurück? War nicht im politischen Leben der Jude immer auf der Seite der zersetzenden, kritischen Tätigkeit? . . .
>
> Nur von hier aus versteht man den Antisemitismus Hitlers. Der Jude ist ein Prinzip . . .
>
> Sie werden sehen, in wie kurzer Zeit wir die Begriffe, und Massstäbe der ganzen Welt einzig und allein mit dem Kampf gegen das Judentum umstürzen werden . . . Aber damit dürften wir uns nicht beruhigen. Das sei alles erst der Anfang eines erbarmungslosen Kampfes um die Weltherrschaft . . ."

back to German and published under the title *Der Doppelstaat*, Frankfurt a.Main–Cologne 1974.

[17]Franz Neumann, *Behemoth. The Structure and Practice of National Socialism*, London–New York–Toronto 1942, (2nd. rev. edn., 1944).

[18]Konrad Heiden, *Geburt des Dritten Reiches. Die Geschichte des Nationalsozialismus bis Herbst 1933*, Zürich 1934; *idem, Adolf Hitler. Das Zeitalter der Verantwortungslosigkeit*, Zürich 1936; *idem, Ein Mann gegen Europa*, Zürich 1937; *idem, Der Führer. Hitler's Rise to Power*, London 1944.

[19]Hermann Rauschning, *Gespräche mit Hitler*, Zürich 1940. Even before the publication of the first German edition, two French editions had appeared in 1939, *Hitler m'a dit*, one English edition, *Hitler Speaks*, as well as one Dutch and one Swedish edition. For the significance of this work, see Theodor Schieder, *Hermann Rauschnings Gespräche mit Hitler als Geschichtsquelle*, Cologne-Opladen 1972. Another well-known book by Rauschning, *Revolution des Nihilismus. Kulisse und Wirklichkeit im Dritten Reich*, Zürich–New York 1938, is less relevant to this topic.

[20]Gustav Warburg, *Six Years of Hitler. The Jews under the Nazi Regime*, London 1939.

In this context Hitler points to the role of the Jews as controlling hostile regimes in Europe and the United States and adds:

> "Auch wenn wir den Juden aus Deutschland vertrieben haben, bleibt er immer noch unser Weltfeind."[21]

In the light of these views on the meaning of antisemitism in Hitler's *Weltanschauung*, the studies of the sixties in this field, such as those of Nolte, Hillgruber and Jäckel, appear to be a direct continuation of Rauschning's analysis; similarly, the "structuralist" studies of the regime of the Third *Reich* clearly continue the course laid out by Ernst Fraenkel.

Gustav Warburg's volume, *Six Years of Hitler*, published in 1939, should be regarded as the most important study of this period relating to the Jews in the Third *Reich*. This work was one of the first in the field to be based on the systematic study of official, ideological, administrative and judicial publications. One of his most important achievements is his emphasis on the centrality of the antisemitic ideology in National Socialism, not merely as an instrument of propaganda but as a central issue for the movement, and especially for its leadership. On the basis of a variety of sources, Warburg also pointed out the lack of uniformity in the attitude of the population to the anti-Jewish policy of the regime and the different factors involved in the government's anti-Jewish policy. These analyses may be seen as the beginnings of new trends in research, which, however, did not have direct successors in the following stages.

In Neville Laski's preface to the book, the major theses of the work are spelled out with unmistakable clarity:

> "Antisemitism is not a side-issue of Nazism. It is the very root of the Nazi creed, particularly in the mind of the Leader, the very essence of his doctrine."[22]

This aspect is specially highlighted in the book's first chapter, 'The Creed of Antisemitism', which concludes with the statement:

> ". . . the racial question, and that is in the main the Jewish question, is one of the fundamental principles, nay, the fundamental principle, of the Nazi creed".[23]

A special contribution here is the presentation of the internal dynamics of the Third *Reich* in the search for a practical interpretation of the ideology and its translation into action along the way to the "Final Solution".

> "It is typical, too, that at about the same time when Minister Frank declared in Rome that the Nuremberg Laws had solved the Jewish question finally, the organ of the Nazi Storm Troopers demanded: 'The Jew must be made innocuous for our people. How this is done, whether we establish a concentration colony for the Jews, whether we send them to Moscow, or whether we send them one day to the moon, does not matter very much at the moment.' If this statement, made over two years ago, is considered in the light of recent decrees driving the Jews into a new ghetto, and of some sinister hints in the *Schwarze Korps*, the organ of the Secret Police, threatening to kill off all the Jews remaining in Germany (probably an alternative expression for 'sending them to the moon'), the article in the *S.A. Mann* can hardly be regarded merely as an idle boast."[24]

[21]Hermann Rauschning, *Gespräche . . .*, pp. 220–223.
[22]Gustav Warburg, *Six Years of Hitler . . .*, p. 7.
[23]*Ibid.*, 'The Creed of Anti-Semitism', p. 26.
[24]*Ibid.*, p. 24.

In this context it is impossible not to cite a similar, even more far-reaching assertion, from another book by Konrad Heiden, also published in 1939, which for some reason has been entirely forgotten by researchers and which is the only one of his books devoted exclusively to the subject of the Jews. In this book, entitled *The New Inquisition*,[25] we find a chapter in which he deals with the most extreme depersonalisation of technocratic thinking with regard to the practical possibilities of the "solution of the Jewish question": the possibility of the physical annihilation of the Jews in Germany:

> "Men high up in the regime are fond of using the term 'to push the button', though their listeners are never quite sure whether the mocking tone should be taken seriously. Often they add the explanation – still in jocular vein; to assemble all Jews in a large hall and then to release the gas by pressing a button."[26]

Absent from all of these studies is an important dimension of the historical situation of the Jews in Germany in this period, namely, the internal life, culture and organisation of Jewish society under the regime of the Third *Reich*. As we have already seen from Buber's articles, he regarded the continuation of Jewish communal life and its non-disintegration in the face of historically unprecedented ideology and terror of the racist totalitarian state, as being of critical significance. A number of publications of basic importance, including works of Jewish historians such as Koppel S. Pinson's 'The Jewish Spirit in Nazi Germany'[27] and Yitzchak F. Baer's *Galut*[28] – both published in 1936 – and another article by Buber, 'Das Ende der Symbiose',[29] which appeared on the eve of the Second World War, can be seen as laying the methodological foundations for historical examination and research in this field, both as a *sui generis* phenomenon and as an inseparable part of the processes that characterise Jewish history in its various periods. These, however, do not belong to the same category of systematic research as the above-mentioned studies of National Socialist ideology and government during the late thirties and beginning of the forties. It should however be mentioned that all these interpretative attempts to understand the situation in the perspectives of historical causality, by Jews and non-Jews, came to a halt when, towards the end of the war, the full meaning of the Holocaust came to be known. They were resumed only after a long period of time had elapsed.

II. THE POST-WAR PERIOD AND THE FIFTIES

In the fifteen years that followed the fall of the Third *Reich*, during which the first comprehensive studies on the destruction of the Jews of Europe were published in non-German historiography, the history being written in Germany

[25]Konrad Heiden, *The New Inquisition*, New York 1939. The manuscript had been written in Paris following the events of the *Reichskristallnacht*, but it only appeared in book-form in its English version.

[26]Heiden, *The New Inquisition*, pp. 148–149.

[27]In *Menorah Journal*, 24 (1936), pp. 228–254.

[28]Berlin 1936, especially the last chapter 'Vom alten Glauben zu einem neuen Geschichtsbewusstsein'.

[29]In *Jüdische Weltrundschau*, Paris, March 1939.

was characterised by almost total abstention from anything dealing with the subject of the Jews. In surveying this astonishing fact one is tempted to believe that here Himmler's notorious dictum of 1943 hovers over the historiography of Germany or is engraved in writing on the wall of the study of every German historian. I am referring, of course, to his pronouncement: "This is a page of glory in our history which has never been written and which is never to be written."[30] That, of course, despite, or perhaps just because, of the very different meaning that the words "a page of glory" had here.

The special studies on National Socialism and the Third *Reich* that appeared regularly under the aegis of the Munich *Institut für Zeitgeschichte* deal with the circumstances and the "guilt" or responsibility for Hitler's rise, or seek to explain the processes of the decline and disintegration of the Weimar democracy. To the extent that the subject of the Jews does nevertheless appear here, it is in the form of documentary testimony, primarily documents from the Nuremberg trials, witnessing the last stage of the "Final Solution". It is in this way that the testimony of S.S. officer Kurt Gerstein on the mass gassings in Treblinka appears in the *Dokumentation* section.[31] Another volume published in the fifties presents documents on *Gauleiter* Kube, the *Einsatzgruppen* and the mass murder of Jews in the Soviet Union.[32] Even in the case of the publication of a secret memorandum of Hitler's,[33] which we may now regard as a key document for understanding the relationship between ideological assumptions, the war aims and the decisive role of the Jewish Question in that context, the Jewish aspect merits only an incidental comment in the interpretation supplied by the editor. In spite of the secret and operative nature of the document, in his view there is nothing more here than a reiteration of the vulgar phraseology of antisemitic propaganda, which of course he regarded as totally irrelevant to the document's actual political and military content.[34]

Similarly, Gerhard Ritter, the eminent historian of the post-war period, in the introduction to his edition of another fundamental source for the study of Hitler's antisemitism, treats the subject in an equally dismissive way.[35] The first

[30]From Himmler's speech to *SS-Gruppenführer* in Poznań on 4th October 1943, *Documents of the International Nuremberg Military Tribunal (IMT)*, PS-1919.

[31]'Augenzeugenberichte zu den Massenvergasungen', in *Vierteljahrshefte für Zeitgeschichte (VJHZ)*, 1 (1953), Dokumentation, pp. 177–194.

[32]'Aus den Akten des Gauleiters Kube', in *VJHZ*, 4 (1956), Dokumentation, pp. 67–92.

[33]Wilhelm Treue, 'Hitlers Denkschrift zum Vierjahresplan 1936', in *VJHZ*, 3 (1955), Dokumentation, pp. 184–210.

[34]Cf. for example the basic statement on the first pages of Hitler's memorandum, *loc. cit.*, pp. 204–205. For the crucial significance of this part as an ideological starting point for the memorandum and the central role played in Hitler's ideology by the historical conflict of the nations with Jewry, and the consequences for the "Final Solution", see Otto D. Kulka, 'The Jewish Problem as a Factor in Hitler's Policy toward the Soviet Union. Its Place in his Ideological Conceptions and Political Decisions', in *The Sixth World Congress of Jewish Studies*, Jerusalem 1973, Abstracts, pp. B–75 ff.; *idem*, *The "Jewish Question" in the Third Reich*, Jerusalem 1975 (in Hebrew), vol. 1, pp. 209–210; in this context see also Jacob L. Talmon, *The Myth of the Nation and the Vision of Revolution. The Origins of Ideological Polarisation in the Twentieth Century*, London 1981, pp. 530–531, and Yehuda Bauer, 'Genocide: Was it the Nazis' Original Plan?', in *Annals of the American Academy*, 450 (July 1980), pp. 35–45.

[35]Dr. Henry Picker, *Hitlers Tischgespräche im Führerhauptquartier 1941–1942* . . . , introduced and edited

systematic collections of selected documents on the Third *Reich* and the Final Solution were published in the mid-fifties by the Swiss historian Walther Hofer[36] and the two Jewish authors, Léon Poliakov and Joseph Wulf.[37] The fate of the Jews in the concentration and extermination camps had been dealt with by the Austrian Eugen Kogon in his *Der SS-Staat*,[38] written immediately after his liberation from Buchenwald. The only significant contemporary study published in Germany on the life and fate of the Jews during the period of the deportations, ghettos and annihilation was that of the Jewish scholar, H. G. Adler.[39]

The attempt undertaken immediately after the war by the venerable historian, Friedrich Meinecke, to deal with the meaning of the "German Catastrophe",[40] using historical categories and applying a broad perspective, does take up the Jewish issue. However, the marginal mention of this problem is but a repetition of conceptions current from the last third of the nineteenth century, which define the "Jewish problem" in Germany as a worrisome phenomenon that requires a "reasonable" solution; but the "shameful" National Socialist solution has besmirched the name of the German nation and all of German history with an indelible blot.

German historiography's attempts to cope with the National Socialist period and the Jewish problem in specific studies are confined to the works of emigrés who settled in the West, many of whom were Jews. Most outstanding among these are the books of Eva Reichmann, *Hostages of Civilisation. The Social Sources of National Socialist Anti-Semitism*;[41] Hannah Arendt, *Origins of Totalitarianism*;[42] Eleonore Sterling, *Er ist wie Du. Aus der Frühgeschichte des Antisemitismus in Deutschland (1815–1850)*;[43] Paul Massing, *Rehearsal for Destruction* (about the development of political antisemitism in the Second German Empire);[44] Waldemar Gurian, *Antisemitism in Modern Germany*;[45] Fritz R. Stern, *The Politics of Cultural Despair. A Study in the Rise of the Germanic Ideology*;[46] and George L. Mosse, *The Crisis of German Ideology. Intellectual Origins of the Third Reich*.[47] It should be noted that the common denominator of all these studies is the attempt

---

by Gerhard Ritter, Bonn 1951. The central significance of antisemitism in this very source is later proved impressively in Andreas Hillgruber's introduction to his revised edition of the *Tischgespräche*, published in 1968. Likewise in Ernst Nolte, 'Eine frühe Quelle zu Hitlers Antisemitismus' (see note 61).

[36]Walther Hofer (ed.), *Der Nationalsozialismus. Dokumente 1933–1945*, Frankfurt a.Main 1957.

[37]Léon Poliakov and Joseph Wulf, *Das Dritte Reich und die Juden*, Berlin 1955.

[38]Eugen Kogon, *Der SS-Staat. Das System der deutschen Konzentrationslager*, Frankfurt a.Main 1946.

[39]H. G. Adler, *Theresienstadt 1941–1945. Das Antlitz einer Zwangsgemeinschaft*, Tübingen 1955; *idem*, *Die verheimlichte Wahrheit. Theresienstädter Dokumente*, Tübingen 1958.

[40]Friedrich Meinecke, *Die deutsche Katastrophe. Betrachtungen und Erinnerungen*, Wiesbaden 1946.

[41]London 1950; The title of the German edition, *Flucht in den Hass. Die Ursachen der deutschen Judenkatastrophe*, Frankfurt a.Main 1956, seems to be a variation of 'Flucht vor der Vernunft' from the year 1932 (see note 11).

[42]New York 1951, 2nd. edn. 1958.

[43]Munich 1956; rev. edn. under the title *Judenhass*, Frankfurt a.Main 1969.

[44]New York 1949.

[45]In Koppel S. Pinson (ed.), *Essays on Antisemitism*, New York 1946, pp. 218–265.

[46]London 1961 (based on his Columbia University dissertation, 1954).

[47]New York 1964.

to investigate the background process, or the early history of National Socialist antisemitism.[48]

Similarly, only Jews who had emigrated broached the internal aspect of Jewish history under the Third *Reich* and in the Holocaust in the historiography, at this stage mostly in the form of publishing personal testimonies and recollections of central figures in the public life of that period (most of these were printed in the *Leo Baeck Institute Year Book* in London).[49] Publications on this subject in Germany itself, except for the dissertation by Hans Lamm,[50] were introduced indirectly only in the wake of Hannah Arendt's controversial book, *Eichmann in Jerusalem*,[51] and these German publications did not extend beyond the polemic about the Jewish leadership's purported "guilt", "responsibility" or "collaboration" in the destruction.[52]

It was only towards the end of this period in 1960, that Wolfgang Scheffler published a concise general work on the Jews in the Third *Reich*, which in its overall conception resembles the general descriptive accounts of the "Final Solution" that were published outside Germany in the fifties. It differs from them in that it includes a first rudimentary attempt to deal with the response of the Jewish population in Germany and the way it organised itself internally in the thirties.[53]

During that same period an attempt was made to examine the nature of the National Socialist ideology and regime from another aspect by Martin Broszat, who subsequently raised the suggestion that Hitler's antisemitism appeared to be the only invariable and constant element in the whole structure; were the idea itself not absurd, in his view, it could be regarded as a key that solves the contradictions and lack of consistency in all the other spheres, and even serves as the bridge between them.[54]

[48]Cf. Ismar Schorsch's illuminating historiographical study 'German Antisemitism in the Light of Post-War Historiography', in *LBI Year Book XIX* (1974), pp. 257–271.

[49]The summary reports of the most important spheres of internal life published in the first volume of the Year Book (1956) are of fundamental importance, for example; Robert Weltsch's introduction, pp. XIX–XXXI; Max Gruenewald, 'The Beginning of the "Reichsvertretung"', pp. 57–67; Ernst Simon, 'Jewish Adult Education in Nazi Germany as Spiritual Resistance', pp. 68–104; Herbert Freeden, 'A Jewish Theatre under the Swastika', pp. 142–162; Margaret T. Edelheim-Muehsam, 'The Jewish Press in Germany', pp. 163–176 (and its continuation in vol. V (1960), pp. 308–329); Werner Rosenstock, 'Exodus 1933–1939. A Survey of Jewish Emigration from Germany', pp. 373–390. Similar contributions have appeared in the Hebrew-English Yad Vashem Studies that have been published in Jerusalem since 1957. Finally, see also the first attempt to summarise this topic by Max Gruenewald, 'Education and Culture of the German Jews under Nazi Rule', in *The Jewish Review*, V, New York (1948), pp. 56–83, as well as the anthology published by Robert Weltsch, *Deutsches Judentum, Aufstieg und Krise. Gestalten, Ideen, Werke*, Stuttgart 1963, Veröffentlichung des Leo Baeck Instituts. (Most of the monographs mentioned here were written in the fifties.)

[50]Hans Lamm, *Über die innere und äussere Entwicklung des deutschen Judentums im Dritten Reich*, Erlangen 1951.

[51]*A Report on the Banality of Evil*, New York 1963; in German, *Eichmann in Jerusalem. Ein Bericht von der Banalität des Bösen*, Munich 1964.

[52]The most important opinions on this topic are included in A. Krummacher (ed.), *Die Kontroverse. Hannah Arendt, Eichmann und die Juden*, Munich 1964; also in German, Council of Jews from Germany, *Nach dem Eichmann Prozess. Zu einer Kontroverse über die Haltung der Juden*, Tel-Aviv 1963.

[53]Wolfgang Scheffler, *Judenverfolgung im Dritten Reich*, Berlin 1960.

[54]Martin Broszat, *Der Nationalsozialismus. Weltanschauung, Programm und Wirklichkeit*, Hanover 1960, 2nd. edn., Stuttgart 1960.

A year later, Broszat offers a view in this spirit, but without the reservations, with respect to Hitler's views as they are expressed in the publication of the German original text of *Hitlers zweites Buch* of 1928.[55] It should be noted that the main thesis here, the presentation of the concept "Jew as a principle" in Hitler's *Weltanschauung*, is actually a return to the definitions that appeared in 1939 in Rauschning's *Conversations with Hitler*. Nevertheless, despite the hesitant hypotheses proposed by Broszat, the prevailing view in the interpretation of Hitler and of National Socialism in Germany during this period still reflects the influence of Bullock's authoritative book on Hitler, which presents the German dictator as an unprincipled tyrannical figure, whose only motives are lust for power for its own sake, and whose antisemitism is anything but a "principle".[56]

III. THE TURNING POINT OF THE SIXTIES

(a) *National Socialism as Ideology and Political System*

A distinctly new stage appears at the beginning of the sixties and its major tendencies seem to have persisted into the present day. Casting aside several of the tenets of the previous research, this new trend has two major characteristics:

(1) A resumption of research of the ideological aspects of National Socialism, placing them within the general historical perspective – an approach which had already been taken in the thirties, e.g., by Rauschning. Incentive for this research stemmed from the discovery, or re-discovery of ideological sources from the beginning of Hitler's political career, as well as documents from his last years that had not been intended for publication.[57] As a result of these findings, and even more as a result of the changing historical perspective, a re-investigation and re-interpretation of the whole phenomenon of National Socialism began.

(2) The second feature is the use of the vast archival material which became available for fresh research into the governmental structure and practice of the Third *Reich*.[58] Here too we notice a kind of return to a basic conception already developed in the late thirties, mainly by Ernst Fraenkel.

[55] *Idem*, 'Betrachtung zu "Hitlers zweitem Buch"', in *VJHZ*, 9 (1961), pp. 417–429.

[56] Alan Bullock, *Hitler. A Study in Tyranny*, London 1952. See also the critical discussion of this view in Hugh R. Trevor-Roper (see note 59). In the revised edition of 1962, Bullock re-interprets some significant points, especially key parts of chapter 7, 'The Dictator', in the light of new and additional sources.

[57] Ernst Deuerlein, 'Hitlers Eintritt in die Politik und die Reichswehr. Dokumentation', in *VJHZ*, 7 (1959), pp. 177–227; Reginald H. Phelps, 'Hitler als Parteiredner im Jahre 1920', in *VJHZ*, 11 (1963), pp. 274–330; *idem*, 'Hitlers "grundlegende" Rede über den Antisemitismus', in *VJHZ*, 16 (1968), pp. 390–420; Dietrich Eckart, *Der Bolschewismus von Moses bis Lenin. Zwiegespräch zwischen Adolf Hitler und mir*, Munich 1925, (see Nolte, 'Eine frühe Quelle . . .' note 61); and the various versions of Hitler's *Tischgespräche* from the war years and his diplomatic talks edited by Andreas Hillgruber, *Staatsmänner und Diplomaten bei Hitler . . .*, vols. 1–2, 1939–1944, Frankfurt a.Main 1967/1970.

[58] Cf. Josef Henke, 'Das Schicksal deutscher zeitgeschichtlicher Quellen in Kriegs- und Nachkriegszeit. Beschlagnahme – Rückführung – Verbleib', in *VJHZ*, 30 (1982), pp. 557–620.

Obviously notwithstanding the importance of identifying these lines of methodological continuity, it is no less important to note the difference in the historical sense of the research. For, what in the late thirties and early forties had appeared as research into, and struggle against, the ideology and governmental structure of a totalitarian, racist, terror state establishing itself as a front-rank power, which apart from being a possible model for the establishment of similar regimes also sought to attain far-reaching political hegemony – appears from the perspective of the sixties as research into the genealogy of the Holocaust.

For this reason it is not surprising perhaps that within these two trends, which gradually develop into opposing schools, the treatment of the Jewish aspect also gradually increases and there is growing awareness of the fundamental or functional link between it and other central issues in the study of the Third *Reich*. These include, above all, foreign policy, war aims and the internal structure and functioning of state and party bureaucracy as well as the struggle against the churches (*Kirchenkampf*). In the following section we will review the development of these two trends from the sixties onwards.

The radical shift in the assessment of Hitler's views and of National Socialism as an ideology possessing an inner logic and an historical conception, and which as such, is a prime factor in the determination of long-range policy goals, came with the publication of a German-language article by the British historian, Hugh Trevor-Roper in 1960. His essay became the point of departure for many new studies in this field in German historiography.[59] Trevor-Roper pointed out that Hitler's ideas fused his consciousness of personal messianism with the *raison d'être* of National Socialism, that is, the destruction of Bolshevism and the creation of the Empire in the East. "Sein Krieg sei, betonte er immer wieder, nicht etwa ein konventioneller Krieg gegen den Westen, sondern ein revolutionärer Krieg gegen Russland."[60] However, Trevor-Roper failed to recognise the central role of "Judaism" within this world view. It was Ernst Nolte, in his study on Hitler's conversations with Dietrich Eckart,[61] published in 1961 in the *Historische Zeitschrift*, who recognised the far-reaching significance of this centrality and saw its connection with other aspects of Hitler's thought and political goals. He presented "Judaism" as a focal point and as a key to what I may call the bipolar unity of Hitler's anti-Christian and anti-democratic view: Judaism is the total enemy and destroyer of the natural state of society – its victory would result in the destruction of Germany and apocalyptic decline. "Erst ein unerhörter Sieg kann das Naturgewollte, die Existenz der Völker, endgültig sichern vor dem Ansturm der verderblichen Zwiegestalt, deren Leib

[59]Hugh R. Trevor-Roper, 'Hitlers Kriegsziele', in *VJHZ*, 8 (1960), pp. 121–133 (based on a lecture given in 1959). Of the essays in its wake cf. for example, Nolte, 'Eine frühe Quelle . . .' (see note 61), p. 584, note 2; Hillgruber, *Hitlers Strategie*, (see note 73), p. 564, note 2; Bracher, *Die Deutsche Diktatur* (see note 70), p. 218, note 14; Jäckel, *Hitlers Weltanschauung*, (see note 69), 1st. edn., p. 30, note 2; Adam, *Judenpolitik*, (see note 82), p. 16, note 4.

[60]Trevor-Roper, 'Hitlers Kriegsziele', p. 125.

[61]Ernst Nolte, 'Eine frühe Quelle zu Hitlers Antisemitismus', in *Historische Zeitschrift (HZ)*, 192 (1981), pp. 584–606.

aus minderwertigen Massen besteht und deren Kopf der jüdische Intellekt ist."[62]

Nolte's major work, *Der Faschismus in seiner Epoche*,[63] which appeared in 1963, is outstanding in that he comes to an overall understanding of Fascism as a two-fold revolution whose universal message is the redemption of the world from the religious-conservative (Judeo-Christian) and materialistic-secular (Judeo-Marxist) messianic creeds, denoted by him as the "theoretical" and "practical transcendency".

> "Damit ist zugleich evident geworden, was der Faschismus ist. Er ist nicht schon jenes Widerstreben gegen praktische Transzendenz, das allen konservativen Richtungen mehr oder weniger gemeinsam ist. Erst wenn die theoretische Transzendenz aus der jener Widerstand ursprünglich erwächst, ebenfalls verneint wird, ist der Faschismus an den Tag gekommen. Der Faschismus ist also Widerstand gegen die praktische Transzendenz und Kampf gegen die theoretische Transzendenz in einem . . . im klaren Bewusstsein eines Kampfes um die Erdherrschaft. Das ist der tranzendentale Ausdruck der soziologischen Tatsache, dass er über Kräfte verfügt, die aus dem Emanzipationsprozess geboren sind und sich dann gegen ihren eigenen Ursprung kehren."[64]

In this context Nolte declares:

> "Nichts wäre in der Tat falscher, als den Nationalsozialismus für eine Weltheilungslehre in dem Sinne zu halten, dass alle Menschen um ihrer selbst willen von einer Not, Gefahr oder Verschuldung befreit werden sollten. Geheilt werden soll die Welt gerade *von* der jüdisch-christlich-marxistischen Welterlösungslehre und *zu* jenem absoluten Herrenrecht, dass die Sklaven für immer in ihr Sklavenlos zwingt. Er kann nur als der Ausdruck einer Partikularität verstanden werden, die sich als solche für gefährdet hält und deshalb unter Abstreifung ihrer *geschichtlichen* Eigenart mit stärkster Betonung die naturhaft-urtümlichen Züge ihrer Existenz hervorkehrt und für immer zu sichern versucht."[65]

According to Nolte, Hitler carries forward the anti-Jewish trends inherent in most great ideologies of the nineteenth century, but lacking their inherent restraints, he consistently strives to realise their ultimate logical consequences.[66] "Auschwitz steckt in den Prinzipien der nationalsozialistischen Rassenlehre so sicher wie die Frucht im Keim. . . ."[67] Nolte demonstrated that the antisemitic idea occupied a central and unchanging position in Hitler's mind from 1919 until his will of 1945, and pointed out in this context the uniqueness of the National Socialist extermination of the Jews, "[die sich] ihrer Intention nach wesentlich von allen anderen Vernichtungsaktionen unterschied . . . für Hitler und Himmler ebenso wie für die Nachwelt".[68]

[62] *Ibid.*, p. 597.
[63] Munich 1963. This quotation from 2nd. edn., 1965.
[64] *Ibid.*, p. 544.
[65] *Ibid.*, pp. 504 f.
[66] *Ibid.*, pp. 408–409. This view of antisemitism has been exhaustively researched during the last decades. Cf. for example Shmuel Ettinger, 'The Origins of Modern Anti-Semitism', in Y. Gutman and L. Rothkirchen (eds.), *The Catastrophe of European Jewry*, Jerusalem 1976, pp. 3–39; *idem*, 'The Young Hegelians – A Source of Modern Anti-Semitism?', in *The Jerusalem Quarterly*, 28 (Summer 1983), pp. 73–83; Léon Poliakov, *Histoire de l'Antisémitisme*, vol. 3: 'De Voltaire à Wagner', Paris 1968; Hermann Greive, *Geschichte des modernen Antisemitismus in Deutschland*, Darmstadt 1983. The epochal though distorted meaning of the historical backdrop to antisemitism stressed here by Nolte seems to refer back to Rauschning's conversations with Hitler (see note 19), pp. 6–7.
[67] Ernst Nolte, *Der Faschismus* . . . , p. 438.
[68] *Ibid.*, p. 482.

The Jewish Question as a major issue in National Socialism and the Third *Reich*, with political significance, is taken up by other works of the sixties as well. We find a similar approach in the late sixties in Eberhard Jäckel's book on *Hitlers Weltanschauung*, based mainly on the analysis of *Mein Kampf*.[69] Karl D. Bracher's *Die deutsche Diktatur* presents the centrality of antisemitism in a broader context as a constitutive element in National Socialist ideology and politics:

> "Den Kern aber, die wohl zeit seines Lebens einzige 'echte', fanatisch festgehaltene und verwirklichte Überzeugung, bildeten schon jetzt Antisemitismus und Rassenwahn: das grandios vereinfachende Schema von Gut und Böse, verlegt ins Biologisch-Rassische, diente als übergreifendes Erklärungsprinzip der gesamten Weltgeschichte und Weltpolitik . . . Dass ihm auch darin ein ganzes Volk dann weitgehend zu folgen und eine Schar von Mordhelfern zu stellen fähig war, beweist freilich, dass man es hier nicht einfach mit einem unergründbaren persönlichen Rätsel zu tun hat, sondern mit einer furchtbaren Anfälligkeit des modernen Nationalismus, dessen Ausschliesslichkeits- und Zerstörungsbedürfnis gegenüber allem 'Fremden' zu den Grundkräften des Antisemitismus gehört."[70]

This approach is further developed in the framework of a monumental, though much disputed biography on Hitler by Joachim Fest in the seventies.[71]

One of the first to perceive the decisive role played by Hitler's antisemitic ideas in shaping his conceptions in foreign policy from the early twenties was Günter Schubert, in his dissertation on the *Anfänge nationalsozialistischer Aussenpolitik*.[72] In the monumental work of Andreas Hillgruber, *Hitlers Strategie, Politik und Kriegführung 1940–1941*[73] and his brilliant and concise study, *Deutschlands Rolle in den beiden Weltkriegen*,[74] both of which are based on administrative, diplomatic and military sources, predominance is given to the central and decisive role of the struggle with Judaism as a factor in Hitler's crucial decisions. In his list of the four main motives in Hitler's *Ostkriegskonzeption* he puts as number one: "1. die Ausrottung der 'jüdisch-bolschewistischen' Führungsschicht (einschliesslich ihrer biologischen Wurzel, der Millionen Juden in Ostmitteleuropa)".[75] In this connection he states in the concluding chapter dealing with the research situation in the mid-sixties:

> "Von noch grösserer, zentraler Bedeutung ist schliesslich die in der Forschung wohl mitunter schon angedeutete, aber nicht mit der nötigen Klarheit ausgesprochene Einsicht in die enge Verbindung von 'Judentum' und 'Bolschewismus' in den mythischen Vorstellungen Hitlers und den daraus erwachsenden Zusammenhang von Ostkrieg und 'Endlösung' . . . 'Antibolschewismus' war für Hitler weit mehr als nur ein propagandistisches 'Feigenblatt' zur Verdeckung der eigenen Eroberungsabsichten. Da 'Bolschewismus' für ihn die

[69]Tübingen 1969; 2nd. rev. edn. Stuttgart 1981.

[70]Karl Dietrich Bracher, *Die deutsche Diktatur. Entstehung, Struktur, Folgen des Nationalsozialismus*, Cologne–Berlin 1969, p. 67.

[71]Joachim Fest, *Hitler. Eine Biographie*, Frankfurt a.Main–Berlin–Vienna 1973. For a critical discussion of the book see, Hermann Graml, 'Probleme einer Hitler-Biographie', in *VJHZ*, 22 (1974), pp. 76–92. (Not to be confused with the discussion on the extremely irresponsibly produced film; for this see *idem*, *Geschichte in Wissenschaft und Unterricht*, XXVIII, 11 (Nov. 1977), pp. 669 ff.).

[72]Freie Universität Berlin 1961; published as a book, Cologne 1963.

[73]Frankfurt a.Main 1965.

[74]Göttingen 1967.

[75]*Deutschlands Rolle . . .*, *loc. cit.*, p. 115.

vollendete Herrschaftsform des 'Judentums' war (während 'Demokratie' die Vorstufe hierfür darstellte), richtete sich der am 22.6.1941 beginnende Vernichtungskrieg gegen 'Bolschewismus' und 'Judentum' in gleicher Weise. Er stellte gleichsam die letzte Steigerungsstufe seines (aus taktischen Gründen etappenweise geführten) 'Kampfes' seit den zwanziger Jahren dar."[76]

Hillgruber stressed this aspect especially strongly in his examination of Hitler's attitude to the invasion of the Soviet Union and the decision to initiate the "Final Solution of the Jewish Question". It has been further elaborated in a special article on 'Die "Endlösung" und das deutsche Ostimperium als Kernstück des rassenideologischen Programms des Nationalsozialismus'.[77] Later, in his article 'England in Hitlers aussenpolitischer Konzeption',[78] he emphasises the consistency of Hitler's view within the framework of his global aspirations, and points out the centrality of the factor of antisemitism as a criterion of his decisions.

Now let us take a look at the developments in the other "school". Parallel to the changes in the direction of research into the ideological aspects of National Socialism and their relevance to foreign policy, which took place in the sixties, a change occurred in research into the internal structure, development and practices of the Third *Reich*'s governmental system.[79] These changes took place mainly as a result of the impact of the abundant archival material that became available.[80] As I have already pointed out, in most of the works of this kind the authors were led back to general conceptions found in the basic studies of the late thirties and early forties. In contrast to the monolithic image of the regime in previous years, the picture that now emerges is of "polycracy"[81] or "authoritarian anarchy",[82] i.e., a war of all against all in state and party leadership and bureaucracy. The irrelevance or marginality of ideology is reflected in dealing with the major decisions, which are presented as being predominantly pragmatic. Dozens of publications appeared in the sixties and seventies describing the structure of the regime, detailing the administrative background of the persecution of the Jews, and dwelling on the contradictions between various groups in the State and the Party.[83]

These studies reveal a new conception of internal dynamics, or cumulative developments, leading to successive radicalisation of anti-Jewish policy and culminating in the "Final Solution".

[76]*Hitler's Strategie*, pp. 593–594 (see note 73).

[77]In *VJHZ*, 20 (1972), pp. 133–153.

[78]In *HZ*, 218 (1974), pp. 65–84. Cf. also the summary of his research report from 1982: *Endlich genug über Nationalsozialismus und Zweiten Weltkrieg? Forschungsstand und Literatur*, Düsseldorf 1982, and references there to further studies of his on this topic.

[79]Cf. Martin Broszat in the preface to his *Der Staat Hitlers. Grundlegung und Entwicklung seiner inneren Verfassung*, Munich 1969, p. 9.

[80]Cf. Henke (note 58).

[81]Already in 1969 in Broszat, *Der Staat* . . . in the title of chapter 9; historiographical discussion of the term in Peter Hüttenberger, 'Nationalsozialistische Polykratie', in *Geschichte und Gesellschaft*, 2 (1976), pp. 417 ff.

[82]Uwe D. Adam, *Judenpolitik im Dritten Reich*, Düsseldorf 1972, pp. 15 and 360.

[83]The following examples should be mentioned: Hans Mommsen, *Beamtentum im Dritten Reich*, Stuttgart 1966; Hans-Adolf Jacobsen, *Nationalsozialistische Aussenpolitik 1933–1938*, Frankfurt a.Main–Berlin 1968; Reinhard Bollmus, *Das Amt Rosenberg und seine Gegner. Studien zum Machtkampf im nationalsozialistischen Herrschaftssystem*, Stuttgart 1970.

The first attempt at this approach was Hans Mommsen's 'Der nationalsozialistische Polizeistaat und die Judenverfolgung vor 1938', published in 1962.[84] In contrast to the previous studies on the "Final Solution" outside Germany – for example, Reitlinger's or Hilberg's, which are based on isolated documents brought together for the Nuremberg Trials – here for the first time a systematic reconstruction of the developments has been drawn up from original integral files of archival sources.[85] Heinz Höhne's endeavours in this direction to reconstruct the history of the SS and its peculiar views on the policy of the "Solution of the Jewish Question",[86] led to an attempt at a reassessment by Mommsen, implied in the question mark of his article 'Entteufelung des Dritten Reiches?'[87]

The most impressive contribution in this direction in the sixties is the collective work based on the *Gutachten* of the *Institut für Zeitgeschichte* by Buchheim, Broszat, Jacobsen and Krausnick, *Anatomie des SS-Staates*.[88] The analytical structuralist tendency seems clearly demonstrated by the choice of the term *Anatomie* in the title of this work, although the two most important contributions for our subject, Krausnick's 'Judenverfolgung' and Buchheim's 'Die SS – das Herrschaftsinstrument', do not represent an orthodox view of this trend. Concerning the economic aspect of the anti-Jewish policy of the Third *Reich*, an outstanding work by Helmut Genschel appeared in 1966,[89] while a comprehensive attempt at a systematic reconstruction of the *Judenpolitik* of the Third *Reich* was undertaken by Uwe Adam at the beginning of the seventies. This study, orientated almost exclusively on the legal aspect, presents the whole policy of the "solution of the Jewish Question" as a quasi-autonomous process of the administration in which no place is left for ideological factors.[90]

At the same time, there also appeared in the German Democratic Republic the first overall description of the persecution and annihilation of the Jews in the Third *Reich* in the form of a team work study by Klaus Drobisch, Rudi Goguel, Werner Müller and Horst Dohle.[91] In contrast to Adam, it is not a work of primary research but rather a compilation of the results of the Western research literature in this field, presented from a Marxist viewpoint.[92] On the other

[84]In *VJHZ*, 10 (1962), pp. 68–87.

[85]See note 1, as well as Henke (note 58). Although filed material from the Bavarian archives was used, these documents reflect the Jewish policy of the *Reich* as a whole.

[86]Heinz Höhne, *Der Orden unter dem Totenkopf. Die Geschichte der SS*, Gütersloh 1967. This study, in many respects a problematic one, was published first in *Der Spiegel* (1966–1967).

[87]Hans Mommsen, 'Entteufelung des Dritten Reiches? Ein Nachwort zur SS-Serie', in *Der Spiegel*, 11 (6th March 1967), pp. 71–74.

[88]Hans Buchheim, Martin Broszat, Hans-Adolf Jacobsen, Helmut Krausnick, *Anatomie des SS-Staates*, vol. 1, *Die SS – das Herrschaftsinstrument. Befehl und Gehorsam*, vol. 2, *Nationalsozialistische Konzentrationslager 1933–1945; Kommissarbefehl und Massenexekutionen sowjetischer Kriegsgefangener; Judenverfolgung*, Olten–Freiburg 1965.

[89]Helmut Genschel, *Die Verdrängung der Juden aus der Wirtschaft im Dritten Reich*, Göttingen 1966.

[90]Uwe Adam (see note 82 and the terminology he used in this context for the "autoritäre Anarchie").

[91]*Juden unterm Hakenkreuz. Verfolgung und Ausrottung der deutschen Juden 1933–1945*, Berlin 1973.

[92]Cf. also Konrad Kwiet, 'Historians of the German Democratic Republic on Antisemitism and Persecution', in *LBI Year Book XXI* (1976), pp. 194 ff.

hand, Kurt Pätzold's book[93] which concentrates on the first years of the Third *Reich*, seems to be the only original research carried out so far in the GDR on this topic. Moreover, it is written on the sound basis of archival sources from both parts of Germany. Compared to the works of Adam or Genschel, the ideological aspect of the National Socialist anti-Jewish policy is taken into consideration here, but in an almost exclusively instrumental interpretation. In domestic affairs antisemitism is seen as a means of diverting the broad masses from class hatred to racial hatred, whereas in the domain of foreign political war objectives it is rather a hardening preparation of the German people for the imperialistic war of terror and annihilation against other nations.[94]

Much more complex are the views developed during the last fifteen years in several works by Broszat – *Der Staat Hitlers*;[95] 'Soziale Motivation und Führer-Bindung des Nationalsozialismus';[96] 'Hitler und die Genesis der Endlösung'[97] – which seems to me to strive towards a synthesis between the two methodologically and conceptually opposing approaches. Although the predominance of the ideological background, stressed in his early works (1960–61) receded behind the thick walls of administrative and social structures, it nevertheless seems always present, if only in the form of "metaphorical" sign posts which at the end mark the almost predestined road to the ultimate reality of the "Final Solution".[98] It appears that in certain points a similar

[93]Kurt Pätzold, *Faschismus, Rassenwahn, Judenverfolgung. Eine Studie zur politischen Strategie und Taktik des faschistischen deutschen Imperialismus (1933–1935)*, Berlin (GDR) 1975.

[94]Cf. also Kwiet, *loc. cit.*, pp. 196–198. It is interesting to note that in the seventies in other countries as well several general studies on the Jewish policy of the Third *Reich* and the "Final Solution" were published, for example: Karl A. Schleunes, *The Twisted Road to Auschwitz. Nazi Policy towards German Jews 1933–1939*, Urbana–Chicago–London 1970; Nora Lewin, *The Holocaust. The Destruction of European Jewry 1933–1945*, New York 1973; Lucy Dawidowicz, *The War against the Jews 1933–1945*, New York 1975; Otto D. Kulka, *The "Jewish Question" in the Third Reich. Its Significance in National Socialist Ideology and Politics and its Role in Determining the Status and Activities of the Jews*, Jerusalem 1975 (in Hebrew with English summary; vol. 2 Documents in German) and the study by the British author Gerald Fleming, *Hitler und die Endlösung*, Wiesbaden–Munich 1982, first published in German translation. As opposed to the first basic publications of the fifties, many of the differentiated studies from the sixties on the ideological and structural-political aspects of the topic could have been used in these works.

[95]*Der Staat Hitlers. Grundlegung und Entwicklung seiner inneren Verfassung*, Munich 1969.

[96]In *VJHZ*, 18 (1970), pp. 393–409.

[97]In response to David Irving's theory, in *VJHZ*, 25 (1977), pp. 739–775; see also Christopher Browning, 'Eine Antwort auf Martin Broszats Thesen zur Genesis der "Endlösung"', in *VJHZ*, 29 (1981), pp. 97–109.

[98]Cf. for example *Der Staat Hitlers* – summary, pp. 423–442; 'Soziale Motivation', ch. 2: 'Hitlers Führertum und die nationalsozialistische Weltanschauung', pp. 398–409; 'Genesis', ch. 2: 'Das Problem der Genesis der nationalsozialistischen Judenvernichtung', pp. 746–759 and ch. 3: 'David Irvings "Beweise"', pp. 759–775. Some examples from his theories: "Man müsse die Juden 'irgendwie ausrotten', diese fatale Äusserung tritt in Dokumenten unterschiedlicher Herkunft in dieser Phase (Herbst 1941) immer wieder zutage, ein enthüllendes Zeugnis für die 'Improvisation' der Vernichtung als der schliesslich 'einfachsten' Lösung, die dann, mit der Einrichtung weiterer Vernichtungslager im besetzten Polen schliesslich ein massives institutionelles und Erfahrungs-Potential der Tötung schuf, das man dann auch im weiteren Verlauf der Deportation aus Deutschland und den besetzten oder verbündeten europäischen Ländern nutzen konnte." (pp. 755–756); but also the following "non-revisionist" statement: "... dass zwischen dem militärischen Krieg, vor allem dem Krieg gegen die Sowjetunion, und dem Weltanschauungskampf gegen die Juden in Hitlers Denken und Wollen ein vielfältig motivierter

development, although in converse order, can be traced in the methodological and conceptual approach of Hillgruber. He started his monumental work with a study of massive military and administrative source material and subsequently attained an overall historical construction of the strategy and praxis of Hitler's Empire, in which the racial-ideological war of annihilation marks the decisive road toward the strategic goal of world hegemony.[99]

Nonetheless, the two basically opposed approaches in German historiography on National Socialism and the Holocaust still seem to prevail. The most clear-cut example of the conflicting views between the ideological-programmatic conception and the structuralist (in the heat of the controversy frequently dubbed "revisionist")[100] approach is demonstrated in two papers by Klaus Hildebrand and Hans Mommsen, both bearing – when first read and subsequently published – the same title: 'Nationalsozialismus und Hitlerismus'.[101] It is characteristic of the present stage of research that in spite of the almost diametrically opposed views, both Hildebrand and Mommsen converge in treating the problem of National Socialist policy regarding the "Jewish Question" as the central issue. This assessment is also borne out in their most recent major studies on the topic of the "Final Solution", in Mommsen's extensive article 'Die Realisierung des Utopischen. Die "Endlösung der Judenfrage" im Dritten Reich',[102] and in the central sections of Hildebrand's book, *Das Dritte Reich*,[103] which authoritatively summarises the

intensiver Zusammenhang bestand. Gerade dieser so evidente Zusammenhang entzieht ja Irvings revisionistischen Thesen alle innere Überzeugungskraft, zumal ohne diese ideologisch-pathologische Verknüpfung von Krieg und Judenvernichtung (in Hitlers Vorstellungswelt) letztere gar nicht erklärt werden könnte ... Die später immer wieder aufgegriffene Hitler-Prophezeiung der Judenvernichtung für den Fall eines neuen Weltkrieges vom 30.1.1939 war psychologisch gesehen nicht nur 'Warnung', sondern selbst ein Stück Kriegsmotivation." (pp. 769–771).

[99] See text relevant to note 76. The important study of Helmut Krausnick and Hans-Heinrich Wilhelm, *Die Truppe des Weltanschauungskrieges. Die Einsatzgruppen der Sicherheitspolizei und des SD 1938–1942*, Stuttgart, 1980, offers another valuable example for these methodological possibilities.

[100] Cf. also Andreas Hillgruber, 'Tendenzen, Ergebnisse und Perspektiven der gegenwärtigen Hitler-Forschung', in *HZ*, 226 (1978), p. 603.

[101] In Michael Bosch (ed.), *Persönlichkeit und Struktur in der Geschichte*, Düsseldorf 1977: Hildebrand, pp. 55–61; Mommsen, pp. 62–71.

[102] In *Geschichte und Gesellschaft*, 9 (1983), pp. 381–420. It seems that Mommsen is more keen here than in his other works to apply Hannah Arendt's thesis about the "Banality of Evil" and the universal character of the danger of totalitarian temptations in modern industrial societies. The last paragraph is particularly noteworthy: "Dass der Holocaust Realität werden konnte, ist mit ideologischen Faktoren – der Einwirkung der antisemitischen Propaganda wie der autoritären Färbung der tradierten deutschen politischen Kultur – nur unzureichend zu erklären ... Die Entstehung des Holocaust ist ein abschreckendes Exempel für die Verführbarkeit sonst normaler Individuen, sofern sie unter Bedingungen des permanenten Ausnahmezustandes der Auflösung der rechtlichen und institutionellen Strukturen und der öffentlichen Rechtfertigung verbrecherischen Handelns als nationaler Tat existieren. Der Holocaust ist daher nicht nur ein Menetekel gegenüber rassischen Phobien und sozialen Ressentiments gegen Minderheiten; er weist zugleich auf die anhaltende Gefährdung auch vorgeschrittener Industriegesellschaften hin, die in manipulativer Verformung der öffentlichen und privaten Moral besteht". (p. 420).

[103] *Grundriss der Geschichte*, vol. 17, Munich–Oldenburg 1979, especially ch. I, C2, 'Innere Entwicklung, Besatzungs- und Rassenpolitik', pp. 72–86; 'Conclusion', pp. 86–88: ch. II, 5, 'Die Aussen- und Rassenpolitik des Dritten Reiches', pp. 168–180. Cf. also the two contributions of

study of National Socialism as an ideology and a political system. Indeed, the conclusion that antisemitism constitutes "the very core" or "the dominant component" of National Socialist *Weltanschauung* established itself in the last decade even in the professional handbooks of German history. We can find it in the assessments of Karl Dietrich Erdmann in Gebhardt's *Handbuch der deutschen Geschichte*,[104] and similarly even in those of Kinder and Hilgemann in the paperback edition of *Pipers Weltgeschichte in Karten, Daten, Bildern*:

> "Der Nationalsozialismus entsteht nach 1918 als Gegenbewegung gegen die Revolution und das parlamentar-demokratische System. Seine geistigen Wurzeln sind uneinheitlich und zum Teil verfälscht . . . Dominierend wird Antisemitismus."[105]

In a broader context, this conclusion is presented in Bracher's authoritative volume of the *Propyläen Geschichte Europas*[106] as well as in Hermann Greive's attempt from a different angle. The latter is the first study in German historiography to depict National Socialist antisemitism in the overall framework of a history of modern antisemitism in Germany, from the enlightenment to the post-war period.[107]

These results of Western German historiography have been summarised in an impressive way, though from a polemical position, by Kurt Pätzold in his latest study on the Holocaust:[108]

> "Innerhalb der bürgerlichen Historiographie setzt sich jene Betrachtungsweise immer mehr durch, die Rassismus und Antisemitismus zum Ausgangs- und Endpunkt jeglicher Faschismusforschung erklärt. Die gesamte faschistische Politik und der Zweite Weltkrieg sollen einzig aus der vermeintlich zentralen und höchsten Zielsetzung des Hitlerfaschismus begriffen werden, die 'Juden' zu vernichten; alle Entscheidungen und Massnahmen des Regimes seien dem zu- und untergeordnet gewesen. Rassismus und Antisemitismus werden schlechthin als Wesen und Hauptcharakteristikum des deutschen *Faschismus* ausgegeben."

Significantly (and in my opinion, quite justifiably), Pätzold includes in this category authors who are considered in the Western German historiographical controversy as representatives of opposite trends, such as Hillgruber, Broszat, and Bracher.[109] However, in spite of this introductory statement, it seems that

---

Mommsen and Hildebrand, in Gerhard Hirschfeld and Lothar Kettenacker (eds.), *"Der Führerstaat": Mythos und Realität. Studien zur Struktur und Politik des Dritten Reiches*, Stuttgart 1981: Mommsen, 'Hitlers Stellung im nationalsozialistischen Herrschaftssystem', pp. 43–70; Hildebrand, 'Monokratie oder Polykratie? Hitlers Herrschaft und das Dritte Reich', pp. 73–96.

[104]Gebhardt, *Handbuch der deutschen Geschichte*, Stuttgart 1976, vol. 20, ch. 1: 'Hitler und sein Programm', pp. 24–36; and in a slightly different version, ch. 9, 'Judenvernichtung und "Ausmerzung lebensunwerten Lebens"', pp. 106–115. Though the National Socialist annihilation programme is not denoted here as comparable "with any other form of Jew-hatred" from other nations and other eras, the only explanation for annihilation given is that of "racial inferiority" while other ideological aspects of National Socialist antisemitism are not here taken into consideration.

[105]H. Kinder and W. Hilgemann, *Pipers Weltgeschichte* . . . , Munich 1970, p. 539.

[106]Vol. 6, Karl Dietrich Bracher, *Die Krise Europas 1917–1975*, Berlin 1980, especially the chapter, 'Vom Europäischen Konflikt zum globalen Krieg', pp. 199 ff., 215 ff.

[107]See note 66.

[108]Kurt Pätzold, 'Von der Vertreibung zum Genozid. Zu den Ursachen und Bedingungen der antijüdischen Politik des faschistischen deutschen Imperialismus', in Dietrich Eichholz und Kurt Gossweiler (eds.), *Faschismus-Forschung. Positionen, Probleme, Polemik*, Berlin (GDR) and Cologne 2nd. edn., 1980, pp. 181–208; quote p. 181.

[109]*Ibid.*, p. 181, note 3; p. 182, note 4; p. 191, note 19.

this noteworthy study – unique in the historiography of the GDR – is closer to Broszat's as well as Hillgruber's views than the author himself admits,[110] and apparently more so than any other publication emanating from the Socialist countries.[111]

This leads us to the ultimate question in this problematic complex: the historical meaning of defining the centrality of antisemitism in the National Socialist ideology and politics. Clearly, it is not that the Jews in their factual historical proportions gain such a central importance here. On this factual level they were but a small minority among the Germans and other European peoples. The matter at issue is the significance attributed in the conceptual world of National Socialism to the ideo-historical concept of Judaism and its promoter – the Jew. It seems that only from this point of view is it possible to make an attempt at "explaining the inexplainable". In other words, this centrality is the only possible key to a historical understanding of the significance of the Holocaust and of the assault that the National Socialist "revolution" made on the very roots of Western civilisation, its basic values and moral foundations. For on different levels of the ruling system in the Third *Reich*, the essence of the National Socialist counter-revolution was understood as a revolt against the all-embracing idea of the unity of the human race, which was fundamentally opposed to its own value system. In this context Judaism was conceived as the historical source and the continuous driving force of this idea, which was then expanded in the course of universal history through Christianity and later in the democratic and socialist systems.

Any attempt to explain the Holocaust without taking into account such a significant fact inevitably leads to explanations long-refuted and proven indefensible concerning the causes of the "Final Solution", whether these define it as being based on allegedly economic reasons, or as deceptive political manipulation of the masses, or an experiment in terror against one group as preparation for an imperialistic war of conquest and annihilation against other peoples throughout the world.

Undoubtedly, the two dominant trends in German historiography have contributed considerably to clarifying the ideological and political aspects of the National Socialist anti-Jewish policy. The research into the ideological concepts of National Socialism and its antisemitism has elaborated the historical-political framework of the events, but without analysing concrete developments in the political, bureaucratic, economic and social spheres connected with the ideological motivation. As a result this methodological approach easily leads to an inacceptable spiritualisation of the history of the Third *Reich*. On the other hand, the school of structure analysis has contributed enormously to the

[110]As to Broszat: see for example his critique on the "Programmologen", p. 190. Concerning Hillgruber cf. his view of the close connection between the "Final Solution" and the "war aims", mainly the imperialistic war of annihilation in the East, pp. 205 ff.

[111]Compare also Pätzold's article 'Der historische Platz des antijüdischen Pogroms von 1938. Zu einer Kontroverse', in *Jahrbuch für Geschichte*, 26 (1982), pp. 193–216 and the introduction to his collection of documents *Verfolgung, Vertreibung, Vernichtung. Dokumente des faschistischen Antisemitismus 1933–1942*, Leipzig 1983, which, however, I saw only after completing this article.

documentation and reconstruction of the administrative processes, possibly leading to important political decisions. But this approach seems to come dangerously close to creating a new quasi-mystical view, in which out of the "Programmlosigkeit" of the totalitarian chaos, the "Final Solution" ultimately has to emerge as a kind of *deus ex machina* solution.

Moreover, the formation of rival camps of "Intentionalists" versus "Functionalists", or "Programmologen" versus "Revisionisten",[112] within German historiography seems at the end to lead to deviation from the search for the essential contents and significance of an unparalleled historical complex, and to run into tiresome quarrels over dates, signatures and fragmentary statements.

(b) *The Social History of the Third Reich*

The relatively late start to intensive research in German social history[113] contributed also to the first systematic attempts to understand the Third *Reich* from a socio-historical point of view. The problem of National Socialist antisemitism and the attitude of the German population towards it, are treated in general terms, or partial aspects of these, in the works of Ralf Dahrendorf, William Allen, David Schoenbaum and Richard Grunberger. However, the conclusions reached by these authors do not go beyond hypotheses.[114]

Other scholars continue to follow Eva Reichmann's view that the year 1933 has to be considered as the ultimate chronological limit for a differentiated socio-historical examination of this topic.[115] In her argumentation she says:

> ". . . a strict line is to be drawn between Nazism during the so-called period of struggle, before accession to power and Nazism after this accession . . . No single word was spoken or written after the 30th of January 1933 which gives any direct indication of the feeling of the masses . . . The Nazi Party had then ceased to be a people's movement marshalling the whole nation for or against itself; . . . none of its utterances any longer expressed the natural reactions of the masses."[116]

This view now appears outdated, due to the changed situation regarding the

[112]About this controversy and its peculiar terminology, cf. Tim Mason, 'Intention and Explanation: A Current Controversy about the Interpretation of National Socialism', in *Der "Führerstaat"* (see note 103), pp. 23–40.

[113]Cf. Georg G. Iggers, *Neue Geschichtswissenschaft. Vom Historismus zur Historischen Sozialwissenschaft. Ein internationaler Vergleich*, Munich 1978, especially ch. 3, 'Vom Historismus zur "Historischen Sozialwissenschaft": Die bundesdeutsche Geschichtsschreibung seit der Fischer-Kontroverse', pp. 97–156, as well as the preface to the German first edition; and particularly the 1983 revised edition of his *German Conception of History. The National Tradition of Historical Thought from Herder to the Present*, Middletown, Connecticut 1983, ch. VIII, . . . 'The Impact of two World Wars and Totalitarianism on German Historical Thought', ch. IX, 'Epilogue', and the preface to this revised edition, pp. IX–XI.

[114]Ralf Dahrendorf, *Gesellschaft und Demokratie in Deutschland*, Munich 1965; William S. Allen, *The Nazi Seizure of Power. The Experience of a Single German Town 1930–1935*, Chicago 1965; David Schoenbaum, *Hitler's Social Revolution. Class and Status in Nazi Germany 1933–1939*, London 1967; and Richard Grunberger, *The 12-Year Reich. A Social History of Nazi Germany 1933–1945*, New York 1972.

[115]Eva G. Reichmann, *Hostages of Civilisation. The Social Sources of National Socialist Anti-Semitism*, London 1950.

[116]*Ibid.*, pp. 190–191.

sources, since rich archival material in the form of collections of secret reports of the *Gestapo* and the *SD*, as well as other governmental and Party authorities concerning the popular opinion in the Third *Reich* is now available for research.

From these reports emerges, *inter alia*, a differentiated picture of the attitudes of various sections of the population toward the anti-Jewish policy of the regime from the accession to power to the "Final Solution".[117]

As in the case of the above-mentioned more general attempts to understand the Third *Reich* from a socio-historical point of view, the analysis of this source material regarding the Jewish Question has also been almost exclusively pursued by non-German scholars. Some of these studies deal with the Third *Reich* as a chronological and geographical entirety;[118] others limit themselves to a certain area[119] or period.[120]

However, in some recent comprehensive studies, an attempt has been made in German historiography to integrate the results of the research into the total

[117]A systematic edition comprising several volumes of these sources, insofar as they pertain to the Jewish topic, is presently being prepared jointly by my colleague at the Hebrew University in Jerusalem, David Bankier, and myself in cooperation with Heinz Boberach and the Bundesarchiv Koblenz. This edition will appear in the *Schriften des Bundesarchivs* series. On the methodological problems of analysing these sources and findings see, in addition to the publications listed below, the two articles, A. L. Unger, 'The Public Opinion Reports of the Nazi Party', in *The Public Opinion Quarterly*, XXIX (1965), pp. 565–582 and A. L. Smith Jr., 'Life in Wartime Germany: Colonel Ohlendorf's Opinion Service', *The Public* . . . , XXXVI (1972), pp. 1–7.

[118]Otto D. Kulka, '"Public Opinion" in National Socialist Germany and the "Jewish Question"', in *Zion. Quarterly for Research in Jewish History*, XL (1975), pp. 186–290 (in Hebrew with English summary, documentation in German, pp. 260–290); additional material in revised condensed English version in *The Jerusalem Quarterly*, 25 (1982), pp. 121–144 and 26 (1982), pp. 34–45. For a similar conception, though based on limited primary sources (mainly the *Deutschland Berichte der Sopade* published in exile between 1934–1940, press clippings from newspapers of the Third *Reich*, and the Wiener Library collection of "eye-witness reports"), as well as extensive use of published secondary sources – see the still useful meticulous work of Aron Rodrigue, *German Popular Opinion and the Jews under the Nazi Dictatorship*, BA Thesis, University of Manchester 1978 (unpublished manuscript in the Wiener Library, London, and Yad Vashem, Jerusalem).

[119]Falk Wiesemann, 'Judenverfolgung und nichtjüdische Bevölkerung', in Martin Broszat *et al.* (eds.), *Bayern in der NS-Zeit*, vol. 1: *Soziale Lage und politisches Verhalten der Bevölkerung im Spiegel vertraulicher Berichte*, Munich-Vienna 1977, pp. 427–486; *idem*, 'Juden auf dem Lande: Die wirtschaftliche Ausgrenzung der jüdischen Viehhändler in Bayern', in Detlev Peukert and Jürgen Reulecke (eds.), *Alltag im Nationalsozialismus*, Wuppertal 1981, pp. 381–396; Sarah A. Gordon, *German Opposition to Nazi Anti-Semitic Measures between 1933 and 1945, with Particular Reference to the Rhine-Ruhr Area*, Buffalo University Diss. 1979 (substantial parts included in her recent book *Hitler, Germans, and the "Jewish Question"*, Princeton 1984, chapters 5–10); Ian Kershaw, 'Antisemitismus und Volksmeinung. Reaktion auf die Judenverfolgung', in Broszat *et al.*, *op. cit.*, vol. 2, Munich 1979, pp. 281–384 (English version in *idem*, *Popular Opinion and Political Dissent in the Third Reich: Bavaria 1933–1945*, Oxford 1983, pp. 224–277 and 358–372); as well as his *LBI Year Book* article in vol. XXVI (1981), pp. 261–289, where additional material relating to other parts of Germany has been used, particularly from the exile periodical *Deutschland Berichte der Sopade* and the "eye-witness reports" of Jewish refugees in England.

[120]Marlis G. Steinert, *Hitlers Krieg und die Deutschen. Stimmung und Haltung der deutschen Bevölkerung im Zweiten Weltkrieg*, Düsseldorf–Vienna 1970, pp. 236–263; L. D. Stokes, 'The German People and the Destruction of the European Jews', in *Central European History*, 6 (1973), pp. 167–191; William S. Allen, 'Die deutsche Öffentlichkeit und die "Reichskristallnacht" – Konflikte zwischen Werthierarchie und Propaganda im Dritten Reich', in Detlev Peukert (see note 119), pp. 397–411 (based in part on Gordon's work referred to in note 119); David Bankier, *German Society and National Socialist Antisemitism 1933–1938*, Jerusalem University Diss. 1983 (in Hebrew with English summary).

historical picture; here the contributions of Hans Mommsen,[121] Hermann Greive[122] and Konrad Repgen[123] are particularly noteworthy. One can sense though, that the authors are not quite familiar yet with this methodological approach. In applying it they sometimes lack the differentations made possible today by the present state of research. Thus for example, they do not distinguish between different assessments and consequences relating to concrete historical issues such as the promulgation of the Nuremberg laws, the excesses of 1938 and especially the deportations and mass extermination.[124]

A special chapter in religious and social history is provided by the research on the struggle between the Church and the State (*Kirchenkampf*)[125*] and on other aspects of resistance.[126] There the Jewish Question is usually not dealt with in the course of systematic historical research, but rather appears in controversies, as an argument against one side or the other. Here too, the material found in the secret reports not only makes it possible to examine the attitude of individual personalities of the church leadership, but also to observe the behaviour of broad social strata within the different denominations in their attitude towards the National Socialist *Judenpolitik*, be it in the framework of the *Kirchenkampf* or as part of their adjustment to the regime. The same applies to the possibility of studying the attitude of other groups of the population toward opposition and resistance against National Socialism, whether on the part of conservative or leftist circles.

[121]'Realisierung des Utopischen' (see note 102), p. 351, note 13, p. 402, notes 80–81, p. 404, note 91, p. 420 and note 160.

[122]*Geschichte des modernen Antisemitismus in Deutschland*, Darmstadt 1983, p. 149.

[123]'Der deutsche Katholizismus und die Juden 1933–1945', in *Judaism and Christianity under the Impact of National Socialism (1919–1945)*, International Symposium of the Historical Society of Israel, Jerusalem 1982.

[124]Cf. the in part rather different basis of sources and conclusions in the works of Kershaw and Wiesemann on the one hand and Kulka and Bankier on the other (notes 117–120). Where Mommsen refers, for example, to both approaches, without taking these differences into consideration (see note 121), all these studies can be easily understood as contributions of a "revisionist" character. Concerning the use of the term "revisionist" for Kershaw's methodological approach, see Andreas Hillgruber, *Endlich genug über Nationalsozialismus und Zweiten Weltkrieg? Forschungsstand und Literatur*, Düsseldorf 1982, p. 19. Hillgruber points particularly to Kershaw's *Der Hitler Mythos. Volksmeinung und Propaganda*, Munich 1980, and it seems that here the differences concerning the Jewish aspect are indeed the most conspicuous. Cf. for example the different views on Hitler's most outspoken public speech on the "Final Solution" of 30th January 1942 and the SD-report of 2nd February on the reaction as reflected (i.e. not in fact reflected) in Kershaw's *Hitler Mythos*, pp. 132–133, and the underlying thesis on this issue on p. 158, as against Kulka, 'Public Opinion', *Zion* (see note 118), pp. 246–247; *idem*, *Jerusalem Quarterly* (*ibid.*), 26, p. 36. See also Otto D. Kulka and Aron Rodrigue, 'The German Population and the Jews in the Third Reich. Recent Publications and Trends of Research on German Society and the "Jewish Question"', in *Yad Vashem Studies*, XVI (1985), pp. 421–435, with detailed reference to the work of Ian Kershaw, its importance and limitations.

[125]Cf. Otto D. Kulka, 'Popular Christian Attitudes in the Third Reich to National Socialist Policies towards the Jews', in *Judaism and Christianity* (see note 123), p. 244, note 1; for further publications stressing particularly the post-war repercussions, see J. S. Conway, 'Antisemitism and the Conflict in the Churches since 1945', in *Christian Jewish Relations*, 16 (1983), pp. 21–37.

* On the *Bekennende Kirche* see the preceding essay by the late Uriel Tal, 'On Modern Lutheranism and the Jews', in the current volume of the Year Book – (Ed.).

[126]Cf. Christof Dipper, 'Der deutsche Widerstand und die Juden', in *Geschichte und Gesellschaft*, 9, No. 3 (1983), pp. 349–380.

No doubt, a broad field of research has thus been opened, which will perhaps provide more concrete answers to some of the most pressing questions concerning the moral responsibility of German society for the actions of the regime. It will be necessary to trace the extent of common knowledge, an area which until today has been concealed by a haze of apologetic argumentation. Finally, it will be necessary to consider what influence the reactions of the population, as recorded in those reports and presented to the political leadership, had or could have had, on the shaping of anti-Jewish policy and its implementation.[127] The question is most acute with regard to the last, most horrifying phase of the "solution of the Jewish Question" – the complete isolation and ostracism of German-Jewish citizens, their stigmatisation, their mass deportations, and finally, the million-fold extermination of the European Jews in the East European areas under German domination.[128]

(c) *The Internal Jewish Aspect*

The recently deceased Nestor of historical research in Israel, the German-Jewish historian Fritz Baer, concluded his reflections in his above-mentioned work, published in Germany in 1936, with the following words:

> "Um das Schicksal eines Volkes zu verstehen, muss man zuerst wissen, wie das Volk selber sein Schicksal, sein Verhältnis zu Gott und zur Geschichte verstanden hat."[129]

Whether we regard the internal history of the German Jews in the modern era as a continuity, as did the eminent Jewish historian of the nineteenth century, Heinrich Graetz[130] (an opinion rejected as unpatriotic by his German contemporaries Heinrich Treitschke and even Theodor Mommsen,[131] but maintained by representatives of the *Wissenschaft des Judentums* during the Weimar Republic and the Third *Reich*, such as Franz Rosenzweig, Martin Buber and Leo Baeck), or whether we consider the Jewish community under the Nazi regime to be a compulsory community (*Zwangsgemeinschaft*),[132] the

[127]For a more detailed examination of this problem, with respect to the preparation and decision-making process behind the decree of the Nuremberg Laws, see Otto D. Kulka, 'Die Nürnberger Gesetze und die deutsche Bevölkerung im Lichte geheimer NS-Lage- und Stimmungsberichte', in *VJHZ*, 33 (1985).

[128]One should note here especially the differing reactions of the population to the so-called "Euthanasia", or the removal of crucifixes from schools on the one hand, and the simultaneously executed mass deportations and extermination of the Jews on the other. Cf. Kulka, *Jerusalem Quarterly* (see note 118), 26 pp. 36–45; *idem*, 'The Churches in the Third Reich and the "Jewish Question" in light of Secret Nazi Reports on German "Public Opinion"', in *Bibliothèque de la Revue d'Histoire Ecclésiastique, Miscellanea historiae ecclesiasticae*, t. VI, section IV, Louvain 1984, pp. 490–505.

[129]Y. Fritz Baer, *Galut* (see note 28), p. 106.

[130]*Die Konstruktion der jüdischen Geschichte*, Breslau 1846 (new edition Berlin 1936) and especially his *Geschichte der Juden*, vol. 11, Leipzig 1870.

[131]Heinrich von Treitschke, 'Herr Graetz und sein Judenthum', *Preussische Jahrbücher*, December 1879, (reprinted in Walter Boehlich (ed.), *Der Berliner Antisemitismusstreit*, Frankfurt a.Main 1965, pp. 31–45); Graetz's replies, *ibid.*, pp. 45–52; Theodor Mommsen, *Auch ein Wort über unser Judenthum*, Berlin 1880, pp. 210–225.

[132]H. G. Adler (see note 39), *Theresienstadt 1941–1945. Das Antlitz einer Zwangsgemeinschaft.*

existence of an independently defined spiritual and social life among German Jews after 1933 remains an undeniable fact. One can even point here to a paradoxical phenomenon. In contrast to the National Socialist *Gleichschaltung* of German society in all spheres of life, Jewish society maintained almost all of its own religious and ideological trends and organisations under the racial-totalitarian regime. Furthermore, the Jews were even able to deepen and develop activities in their own sphere, since they were excluded from the general process of *Gleichschaltung* of Germany's "Aryan" population. So we find in 1933 various major religious and ideological groups united to form a central federative organisation. At the same time, there was an unprecedented expansion of the German-Jewish press, in which the different religious and ideological polemics between liberals and Orthodox, "assimilationists" and Zionists could be continued, and even various Jewish-Marxist and anti-Marxist views could and did polemicise with each other. In a similar vein, we note the foundation of new organisations and associations, the largest and most important of which was the *Kulturbund*, numbering 80,000 members, as well as an extensive development of the Jewish social welfare, school and adult education systems.

All this took place, however, under conditions of continuous physical terror against Jews as individuals and under collective discrimination and persecution, conditions which led in the most extreme cases to suicides both within Germany and even among emigrés.[133] We are thus dealing here with a pluralistic-democratic[134] society operating within a totalitarian terror state. Contrary to assumptions expressed in testimonies from the fifties,[135] this paradoxical phenomenon in the history of the German Jews did not come to an end with the general destruction of the *Reichskristallnacht* in November 1938. The archival material at our disposal today reveals that there was an intrinsic continuity in the basic modes of communal life and the organisation of the Jews during the war years up to the time of the mass deportations and exterminations.[136] We even find such traditional features of Jewish life as education and social welfare in the ghetto[137] and in the extermination camp.[138]

Studying the internal Jewish aspect of the National Socialist "Final Solution", we are thus confronted with the phenomenon of a certain "freedom"

[133] See one of the most devastating documents on this, a letter by Kurt Tucholsky written a few days before his suicide in exile in December 1935, in *Exil-Literatur 1933–1945*, 2nd. edn., Frankfurt a.Main, 1966, pp. 43–44. On the topic of Jewish suicide within Germany see now Konrad Kwiet, 'The Ultimate Refuge. Suicide in the Jewish Community', in *LBI Year Book XXIX* (1984), pp. 135–167.

[134] The description of Jewish society in the Third *Reich* as an organisation conducted on democratic principles ("demokratisches Verwaltungsprinzip") was even put forward by the Security Service of the SS in a secret report for the year 1938. See Kulka (note 34) vol. 2, doc. no. 35; expounded in vol. 1, pp. 248 ff.

[135] See publications of the fifties, notes 49–52.

[136] See the below-mentioned studies of recent years. Kulka (note 142), Hildesheimer (note 143).

[137] *Patterns of Jewish Leadership in Nazi Europe 1933–1945*, Yad Vashem, Jerusalem 1979.

[138] Otto D. Kulka, 'Ghetto in an Annihilation Camp. Jewish Social History in the Holocaust Period and its Ultimate Limits', in *The Nazi Concentration Camps. Structure and Aims. The Image of the Prisoners. The Jews in the Camps*, Yad Vashem, Jerusalem 1984, pp. 315–332.

of thought and action. It is, however, a "freedom" of the outlawed or rather, a freedom of the doomed.

While the ideological-strategical and structural-political aspects of the Third *Reich* and the Holocaust have been extensively examined and the research of the socio-political field has started to expand, the internal aspect of the history of the Jews has remained largely ignored in the present phase of German historiography as well. Compared with the current publications of the Leo Baeck Institute on this topic, mostly written by authors living outside Germany,[139] and to the first studies of fundamental importance on the central organisations and on Jewish internal life in the Third *Reich* carried out in Israel, England and the United States, German scholars have written only sporadically on this aspect and on less central issues.

Of the first group, the following studies should be mentioned particularly. In Israel: Abraham Margaliot on the political reactions of the Jewish organisations in Nazi Germany until 1938;[140] Joseph Walk on Jewish education;[141] Otto D. Kulka on the *Reichsvereinigung der Juden in Deutschland* during the war years;[142] and Esriel Hildesheimer's recently completed research on the two successive central organisations of the German Jews in the Third *Reich*, the *Reichsvertretung der deutschen Juden* and the *Reichsvereinigung* (1933–1945).[143] In England: Arnold Paucker's study on the largest political organisation of German Jewry, the *Centralverein deutscher Staatsbürger jüdischen Glaubens*, and its struggle against National Socialism;[144] and H. G. Adler's *magnum opus* on the German Jews faced with expulsion and annihilation.[145] In the United States: Jacob Boas's study on German Jewry's self-perception as reflected in the German-Jewish press

[139]In addition to the articles published in the *LBI Year Book* and in the *Bulletin des Leo Baeck Instituts*, see also some contributions that have appeared under the aegis of the *Schriftenreihe wissenschaftlicher Abhandlungen* of the Institute, especially the articles by Kurt Loewenstein, Eva G. Reichmann and Robert Weltsch in *Entscheidungsjahr 1932. Zur Judenfrage in der Endphase der Weimarer Republik*. Ein Sammelband herausgegeben von Werner E. Mosse unter Mitwirkung von Arnold Paucker, Tübingen 1965 (Schriftenreihe . . . 13).

[140]Abraham Margaliot, *The Political Reaction of German Jewish Organizations and Institutions to the Anti-Jewish Policy of the National-Socialists 1932–1935*, Jerusalem 1971 (in Hebrew with English summary); *idem*, 'The Dispute over the Leadership of German Jewry (1933–1938)', in *Yad Vashem Studies*, X (1974), pp. 129–148.

[141]Joseph Walk, *The Education of the Jewish Child in Nazi Germany*, Jerusalem 1975 (in Hebrew).

[142]Otto D. Kulka, *The "Jewish Question"* . . . (see note 94), vol. 1, pp. 77–98 and 231–268; *idem*, 'The Reichsvereinigung of the Jews in Germany (1938/9–1943). Problems of Continuity in the Organizations and Leadership of German Jewry under the National Socialist Regime', in *Patterns* . . . (see note 137), pp. 45–58.

[143]Esriel Hildesheimer, *The Central Organization of the German Jews in the Years 1933–1945. Its Legal and Political Status and its Position in the Jewish Community*, Jerusalem 1982 (in Hebrew with English summary).

[144]Arnold Paucker, *Der jüdische Abwehrkampf gegen Antisemitismus und Nationalsozialismus in den letzten Jahren der Weimarer Republik*, 2nd edn., Hamburg 1969. See also his various essays including 'Jewish Defence against Nazism in the Weimar Republic', in *The Wiener Library Bulletin*, XXVI, Nos. 1/2 (1972), pp. 21–31; and for a critical bibliography of the entire post-war historiography on the Jewish defence against antisemitism and Nazism, *idem*, 'Die Abwehr des Antisemitismus in den Jahren 1893–1933', in Norbert Kampe and Herbert A. Strauss (eds.), *Antisemitismus. Von der Judenfeindschaft zum Holocaust*, Bonn 1984 (Schriftenreihe der Bundeszentrale für politische Bildung 213), pp. 143–171.

[145]H. G. Adler, *Der verwaltete Mensch. Studien zur Deportation der Juden aus Deutschland*, Tübingen 1964.

between 1933–1938 and Jehuda Reinharz's unique documentation on German Zionism in its confrontation with National Socialist and other antisemitic trends and movements up to 1933.[146*]

In the second group, that of German authors, mention should be made of the following studies: Ulrich Dunker on the organisation and activity of the former Jewish front-line soldiers;[147] the contributions of Margot Pikarski,[148] Helmut Eschwege[149] and Konrad Kwiet[150] on the subject of the Jewish resistance under the Third *Reich*; and Volker Dahm on the Jewish publishing house, Schocken, until 1939;[151] as well as Monika Richarz's model edition of collected memoirs of German-Jewish life under the Weimar Republic and the Third *Reich*.[152]

Two additional smaller studies touch upon decisive aspects of internal Jewish history – one of them refers to the *Reichsvereinigung der Juden in Deutschland* during the war, the other deals with the Zionist organisation during the Third *Reich* – but it is precisely in these studies that the flaws of current German research in this field are exposed. In Ino Arndt's account of the *Reichsvereinigung* of the Jews in Germany (1939–1943),[153] the results of research carried out abroad, although available to the author, have apparently been ignored. Even though Ino Arndt usually distinguishes herself by her careful scholarly treatment of the questions concerning the persecution of the Jews in the Third *Reich*, the *Reichsvereinigung* is shown here once again as an "executive agent of the *Gestapo*" (*Ausführungsorgan der Gestapo*).[154] In Alexander Schölch's depiction of the relationship between National Socialism, Zionism and the Arab-Palestinian national movement,[155] the author seems to be influenced rather by current

[146]Jacob Boas, *The Jews of Germany: Self Perception in the Nazi Era as Reflected in the German-Jewish Press*, University of California, Diss. 1977, and his essays in *LBI Year Books XXVII* (1982) and *XXIX* (1984); Jehuda Reinharz (ed.), *Dokumente zur Geschichte des deutschen Zionismus 1882–1933*, Tübingen 1981 (Schriftenreihe wissenschaftlicher Abhandlungen des Leo Baeck Instituts 37).

* See now also the essay by Jehuda Reinharz 'The Zionist Response to Antisemitism in Germany', in this volume of the Year Book – (Ed.).

[147]Ulrich Dunker, *Der Reichsbund jüdischer Frontsoldaten 1919–1938. Geschichte eines jüdischen Abwehrvereins*, Düsseldorf 1977.

[148]Margot Pikarski, 'Über die führende Rolle der Parteiorganisation der KPD in der antifaschistischen Widerstandsgruppe Herbert Baum', in *Beiträge zur Geschichte der deutschen Arbeiterbewegung*, 8 (1966), pp. 867–881; *idem, Jugend im Berliner Widerstand. Herbert Baum und seine Kampfgefährten*, Berlin (GDR) 1978.

[149]Helmut Eschwege, 'Resistance of German Jews against the Nazi Regime', in *LBI Year Book XV* (1970), pp. 143–180; and now the first comprehensive study of all forms of German-Jewish resistance to Nazism: Konrad Kwiet and Helmut Eschwege, *Selbstbehauptung und Widerstand. Deutsche Juden im Kampf um Existenz und Menschenwürde 1933–1945*, Hamburg 1984.

[150]Konrad Kwiet, 'Problems of Jewish Resistance Historiography', in *LBI Year Book XXIV* (1977), pp. 37–57.

[151]Volker Dahm, *Das jüdische Buch im Dritten Reich*, part 2, *Salman Schocken und sein Verlag*, Frankfurt a.Main 1982.

[152]Monika Richarz (ed.), *Jüdisches Leben in Deutschland*, vol. 3, *Selbstzeugnisse zur Sozialgeschichte 1918–1945*, Stuttgart 1982, Veröffentlichung des Leo Baeck Instituts.

[153]Ino Arndt, 'Antisemitismus und Judenverfolgung', in M. Broszat and H. Möller (eds.), *Das Dritte Reich. Herrschaftsstruktur und Geschichte – Vorträge aus dem Institut für Zeitgeschichte*, Munich 1983, pp. 209–230.

[154]*Ibid.*, p. 216.

[155]Alexander Schölch, 'Das Dritte Reich. Die zionistische Bewegung und der Palästina-Konflikt', *VJHZ*, 30 (1982), pp. 646–674.

events and political literature of the Near East than by a genuine attempt to interpret the historical reality *per se*.[156]

In addition, many compilations illustrating the history of Jewish communities up to their destruction in the Third *Reich* have been published in the Federal Republic of Germany since the sixties. Some of these collections, especially those on the Jews of Frankfurt, Baden-Württemberg or Hessen,[157] also offer an insight into the intense internal life led there within the communal and regional frameworks. In the GDR we can note no similar publication trend,[158] except for the two general selections of documents by Helmut Eschwege[159] and Kurt Pätzold.[160]

IV. CONCLUSION

It seems impossible to close an attempt to deal with the main trends and tendencies in six decades of German historiography on National Socialism and on the last chapter in the history of German Jewry under its impact without pointing out the main, and unsolved, problems of its present stage. It appears that research in this field not only suffers from a lack of synthesis between opposing methodological approaches, but more than that, reveals a highly unbalanced engagement in the study of the three basic aspects of this historical complex. Perhaps it is due to this fact that so far there have not been even modest attempts to provide an overall description of the Jews in National Socialist Germany, which would take into account not only Hitler's *Weltanschauung* and the *Judenpolitik* of the regime, but also the social situation of the Jews and the history of their community within the totalitarian-racial power system. The methodological and conceptual framework presented here should make such an enterprise feasible, particularly since important conditions such as the developing historical perspective and a broad basis of available source material have by now been established.

[156]In addition to the fact that he is familiar with Arabic, but not with the Hebrew language, Schölch for some reason also completely ignored contemporary German source material of primary importance written by such eminent leaders of German Zionism as Martin Buber and Kurt Blumenfeld, who represent the humanist, even pacifist character peculiar to the German brand of Zionism.

[157]Dietrich Andernacht, Eleonore Sterling *et al.* (eds.), *Dokumente zur Geschichte der Frankfurter Juden 1933–1945*, Frankfurt a. Main 1963; Paul Sauer (ed.), *Die Schicksale der jüdischen Bürger Baden-Württembergs während der nationalsozialistischen Verfolgungszeit 1933–1945*, Stuttgart 1969; and *idem, Dokumente über die Verfolgung der jüdischen Bürger in Baden-Württemberg durch das Nationalsozialistische Regime 1933–1945*, 2 vols., Stuttgart 1966; Paul Arnsberg (ed.), *Die jüdischen Gemeinden in Hessen*, vol. 1–2, Darmstadt 1971–1972.

[158]Cf. Konrad Kwiet, 'Historians of the German Democratic Republic on Antisemitism and Persecution', *loc. cit.*, (see note 92), p. 187.

[159]Helmut Eschwege (ed.), *Kennzeichen J. Bilder, Dokumente, Berichte zur Geschichte der Verbrechen des Hitlerfaschismus an den deutschen Juden 1933–1945*, Berlin (GDR) 1966.

[160]Kurt Pätzold (ed.), *Verfolgung, Vertreibung, Vernichtung* (see note 111).

Review Article

The History of the Holocaust: A Survey of Recent Literature*

Michael R. Marrus
University of Toronto

Historians have often approached the history of the Holocaust—the systematic mass murder of European Jewry by the Nazis—with a kind of awe seldom found in professional historical writing.[1] "The Holocaust refuses to go the way of most history," writes Nora Levin, author of a survey of the subject, "not only because of the magnitude of the destruction—the murder of six million Jews—but because the events surrounding it are still in a very real sense humanly incomprehensible. No one altogether understands how mass murder on such a scale could have happened or could have been allowed to happen. The accumulation of more facts does not yield this understanding; indeed, comprehensibility may never be possible."[2] Even terminology has prompted the removal of this subject from normal scholarly discourse. During the late 1950s and 1960s, "Holocaust"

*I want to thank my colleagues at the Institute for Advanced Studies of the Hebrew University of Jerusalem in the academic year 1984–85, with whom I discussed many of the ideas in this paper: Shmuel Almog, Yehuda Bauer, Christopher Browning, Richard Cohen, Saul Friedländer, Yisrael Gutman, Otto Dov Kulka, Dina Porat, and Bernard Wasserstein.

[1] Of necessity I have had to exclude from this article any discussion of work from the Soviet Union or eastern Europe. On this theme, see Erich Goldhagen, "Der Holocaust in der Sowjetischen Propaganda und Geschichtsschreibung," *Vierteljahrshefte für Zeitgeschichte* 28 (1980): 502–7, and "The Soviet Treatment of the Holocaust," *Midstream* 25 (December 1979): 5–7. See also Konrad Kweit, "Historians of the German Democratic Republic on Antisemitism and Persecution," *Leo Baeck Institute Year Book* 21 (1976): 173–98. There is some useful background to Soviet and east European writing in Lucy Dawidowicz, *The Holocaust and the Historians* (Cambridge, Mass., 1981), chaps. 3 and 4. The most recent scholarly compilation of books on the Holocaust is Vera Laska, *Nazism, Resistance, and Holocaust in World War II: A Bibliography* (Metuchen, N.J., 1985), which has close to two thousand book entries in many languages. See also Henry Friedlander, "Publications on the Holocaust," in *The German Church Struggle and the Holocaust*, ed. Franklin H. Littell and Hubert G. Locke (Detroit, 1974), pp. 69–94. For works in English see Jacob Robinson, ed., *The Holocaust and After: Sources and Literature in English* (Jerusalem, 1973); and David M. Szoni, *The Holocaust: An Annotated Bibliography and Resource Guide* (New York, 1985).

[2] Nora Levin, *The Holocaust: The Destruction of European Jewry, 1933–1945* (New York, 1973), p. xi. In a similar vein, the relinquishment of customary modes of historical analysis is sometimes seen as commendable for the study of the Holocaust. Thus, in his appreciation of the work of the German historian Karl Dietrich Bracher, the philosopher

[*Journal of Modern History* 59 (March 1987): 114–160]

became the widely used term for the massacre of European Jews, setting this particular instance of mass murder apart from other episodes of genocide.[3] "Holocaust," the *Oxford English Dictionary* tells us, is "a sacrifice totally consumed by fire, a burnt offering." The widespread adoption of this specific designation reflected, I think, an urge not only to distinguish this massacre from all others but also to register the ethereal quality of this terrible episode, its removal from customary historical discourse. "Teaching about the Holocaust," writes Lawrence Langer, a distinguished authority on Holocaust literature, "is unlike teaching about any other subject. . . . The main problem, the one that differentiates this topic from virtually every other historical moment, is its *unimaginability.*"[4] Apparently novelists have a similar difficulty. According to Michael Brown, "Holocaust writing has generally sought to overwhelm rather than to interpret. Writers have been reluctant to transform the Holocaust experience creatively in order to understand; they have been even more reluctant to distance themselves from the Holocaust by writing about it in metaphor, preferring, instead, to write diaries or fiction in memoir form. They have, for the most part, refrained from universalizing the experience, as good writers do, by making connections between the Holocaust and other events in human history."[5]

To professional historians, however, this approach is a counsel of despair in a field that has in the past suffered too much from scholarly neglect.[6]

Emil Fackenheim writes: "Bracher is able to confront the trauma of the Holocaust authentically, that is, to relate it honestly without pretending to explain it." (Fackenheim, "The Nazi Holocaust as a Persisting Trauma for the Non-Jewish Mind," *Journal of the History of Ideas* 36 [1975]: 371).

[3] See Gerd Korman, "The Holocaust in American Historical Writing," *Societas* 2 (1972): 251–70. On the term "holocaust," see Paul R. Mendes-Flohr and Jehuda Reinharz, eds., *The Jew in the Modern World: A Documentary History* (New York, 1980), p. 482. For probing examinations of some terminological and methodological issues, see Uriel Tal, "On the Study of the Holocaust and Genocide," *Yad Vashem Studies* 13 (1979): 7–52; and Yehuda Bauer, "The Place of the Holocaust in Contemporary History," *Studies in Contemporary Jewry* 1 (1984): 201–24. Covering much the same ground, from a sociologist's viewpoint, is Leo Kuper, *Genocide: Its Political Uses in the Twentieth Century* (Harmondsworth, 1981). For an unusual view of the Holocaust in historical perspective, also see Eugen Weber, "Jews, Antisemitism, and the Origins of the Holocaust," *Historical Reflections* 5 (1978): 1–17. See also Alex Grobman and Daniel Landes, eds., *Genocide: Critical Issues of the Holocaust* (Los Angeles, 1983); and Israel W. Charney, *How Can We Commit the Unthinkable? Genocide: The Human Cancer* (Boulder, Colo., 1982).

[4] Lawrence Langer, "Langer Discusses Teaching about the Holocaust," *Facing History and Ourselves News* (Fall 1985), p. 8. Compare Elie Wiesel, "Trivializing the Holocaust: Semi-fact and Semi-fiction," *New York Times* (April 16, 1978): "Auschwitz cannot be explained . . . because the Holocaust transcends history."

[5] Michael Brown, "Metaphor for Holocaust and Holocaust as Metaphor: *The Assistant* and *The Fixer* of Bernard Malamud Reexamined," *Judaism* 29 (1980): 479.

[6] Dawidowicz's *Holocaust and the Historians,* published in 1981, is a survey of historical writing on the destruction process, but it is strikingly thin on German and Israeli scholarship, especially the work of the past two decades. Notably, Dawidowicz down-

Marrus

Some years ago, Dan Magurshak introduced some much-needed clarification of this issue when he pointed out how the Holocaust is no more "beyond the bounds of human imagination, unworthy of epistemic belief, or unintelligible in principle" than many other events.[7] From the standpoint of theology, or even more humble ruminations on human nature, the systematic massacre of so many innocent people doubtless in some profound sense escapes understanding. But so also do countless episodes of cruelty and destruction, however small or large their scale. Historians are used to tramping over their fields while suspending judgments on the fundamental human issues that are ultimately at stake. Once pointed in a scholarly direction, most of us simply forge ahead, hoping to navigate as best we can, using the customary tools of the trade.

With the passage of time, historians seem less reluctant to follow their professional instincts on these matters and more disposed to bring the study of the Holocaust within their customary purview. That is why recent writing on this subject frequently engages most of the important historiographical issues of the Third Reich. The place of ideology, the role of Hitler, the strategy of continental domination, and the functioning of the regime itself—all these questions must be pursued in order to explain the genocidal project that so powerfully engaged the energies of Nazi Germany.

A striking instance of interpretative discussions of the Third Reich informing our understanding of the Holocaust arose several years ago in a series of analyses of the origins of the Final Solution. What set the ball rolling was the mischievous contention of the British writer David Irving, to the effect that Hitler had nothing to do with launching the murder of European Jews, that he was largely uninterested in them, and that he had no knowledge of their terrible fate—at least until 1943.[8] Not for the last

---

grades Raul Hilberg's pioneering *The Destruction of the European Jews* (3 vols., rev. and definitive ed. [New York, 1985]), first issued in 1961 and probably the single most important book ever written on the subject, apparently because of a sharp disagreement with Hilberg on Jewish resistance—a subject only marginally, if provocatively, a part of that work. For a thoughtful, recent overview of German scholarship, see Otto D. Kulka, "Die Deutsche Geschichtsschreibung über den Nationalsozialismus und die 'Endlösung,' " *Historische Zeitschrift* 240 (1985): 599–640, published in English as "Major Trends and Tendencies in German Historiography on National Socialism and the 'Jewish Question' (1924–1984)," *Leo Baeck Institute Year Book*, pp. 215–42.

[7] Dan Magurshak, "The 'Incomprehensibility' of the Holocaust: Tightening up Some Loose Usage," *Judaism* 29 (1980): 233–42. Compare Alan Rosenberg, "The Problematic Character of Understanding the Holocaust," *European Judaism* 17 (Winter 1983–84): 16–20. See also Geoff Eley, "Holocaust History," *London Review of Books* (March 3–17, 1982), pp. 6–9; and John P. Fox, "The Holocaust and Today's Generation," *Patterns of Prejudice* 17 (1983): 3–24, for two historians' discussions of related issues.

[8] David Irving, *Hitler's War* (New York, 1977), pp. xiv, 330–32, 392–93, 503–5, 575–76, 601–2, 851, and passim. See the vigorous critiques by Alan Bullock, "The Schicklgruber Story," *New York Review of Books* (May 26, 1977), pp. 10–15; Geoffrey Cocks, "The Hitler Controversy," *Political Psychology* 1 (1979): 67–81; and the devastating review essay by Charles W. Sydnor, Jr., "The Selling of Adolf Hitler:

time in his controversial career, Irving blended a few undisputed facts into the most outrageous of hypotheses. Central to his argument, of course, was the Führer's universally acknowledged preference for oral instructions to his subordinates—particularly in the execution of his most brutal and secret policies. In contrast to the mountains of paper produced by his British counterpart Winston Churchill, Hitler left only dictated fragments, reports of conversations, and secondhand accounts of monologues to historians reconstructing his decision making. With the Final Solution it is hardly remarkable, therefore, that we have no explicit order, signed by Hitler, instructing Himmler, for example, that all the European Jews were to be killed.

What is one to make of this? One might contemptuously dismiss Irving's hypothesis by pointing out his egregious misuse of the documentation that *is* available—his removal of material from its context, his suppression of contrary indications, and in some cases his misconstruing or mistranslation of evidence that Hitler knew precisely what was happening to the Jews.[9] A recent book by Gerald Fleming, a student of German literature, builds an opposite case: not only was Hitler central to the Final Solution, but there is also an "unbroken continuity" in the Nazi leader's thinking on the subject of Jews, a direct line that leads from the earliest manifestation of anti-Jewish feeling by the young Hitler in Linz, Austria, when he was fifteen or sixteen, "to the liquidation orders that Hitler personally issued during the war."[10]

Fleming's discussion wanders through a variety of subjects related to his theme—and through some, such as the mass shootings outside Riga in December 1941, that are revealing but only marginally related—stringing together quotations that highlight the importance of the Jews to the Führer and his involvement in their murder. Notably, those who passed on instructions regarding the Jews repeated with monotonous regularity that such was "the Führer's wish," "the Führer's order," or some similar phrase. Even at the top of the Nazis' pyramid of terror, Reichsführer SS Heinrich Himmler told a group of Gauleiters and Reichsleiters in 1943 that the extermination of Jewish men, women, and children was "the most difficult [mission] that we have received to date."[11] Moreover, the evidence suggests that the Nazis placed a high priority on the concealment of their

---

David Irving's *Hitler's War,*" *Central European History* 12 (1979): 169–99. Martin Broszat's critique, "Hitler und die Genesis der 'Endlösung': Aus Anlass der Thesen von David Irving" (*Vierteljahrshefte für Zeitgeschichte* 25 [1977]: 739–75), is discussed below.

[9] See Sydnor, pp. 181–90, for examples.

[10] Gerald Fleming, *Hitler and the Final Solution* (Berkeley and Los Angeles, 1984), p. 2. Fleming's book was first published as *Hitler und die Endlösung: "Es ist des Führers Wunsch . . ."* (Wiesbaden and Munich, 1982). The title and some of the argument of a popular essay make this point about Hitler well: see Milton Himmelfarb, "No Hitler, No Holocaust," *Commentary* 77 (March 1984): 37–43.

[11] Fleming, p. 57.

Marrus

murderous enterprise: they draped their language in camouflage, spoke even to each other in *Sprachregelung* (semantic conventions), and wherever possible avoided open discussions of killing. Beginning with the "euthanasia" campaign of 1939 and extending to the massacre of Jews and communists during the invasion of the Soviet Union, the Germans became remarkably adept at speaking in code to one another.[12] The alternative was to remain silent. As Himmler told his senior officers in Posen in 1943, "We shall not speak of it. . . . This is an unwritten and never-to-be-written page of glory in our history."[13] It takes a particularly perverse commitment to historical revision to build reinterpretations on such linguistic formulas or deliberate lapses—intended at the time precisely to provide an alibi for mass murder. And it requires a particularly obstinate selectivity to ignore Hitler's ceaseless, murderous ravings about Jews, whom he persistently put behind every hostile force facing the Reich. Irving is, of course, not alone in these propensities.[14]

Beyond this, there is reason to doubt whether, in the Nazi frame of reference, explicit, written orders were really necessary at all to begin the killing process. Authority in the Third Reich flowed not from decrees and laws, issued by carefully delimited agencies, but from expressions of the Führer's will. Channels of government were frequently circumvented in favor of proclamations that such was "the Führer's wish." This is what Raul Hilberg, dean of Holocaust historians, refers to as "government by announcement." In Hilberg's view, it is quite possible that a signed order to kill the Jews may never have been issued. What counted was a "man-

[12] On the "euthanasia" campaign, see Ernst Klee, *"Euthanasie" im NS-Staat: Der "Vernichtung lebensunwerten Lebens"* (Frankfurt am Main, 1983) and Robert Jay Lifton, *The Nazi Doctors: Medical Killing and the Psychology of Genocide* (New York, 1986), which appeared too late for discussion in this essay.

[13] Cited in Yitzhak Arad, Yisrael Gutman, and Abraham Margaliot, eds., *Documents on the Holocaust: Selected Sources on the Destruction of the Jews of Germany and Austria, Poland and the Soviet Union* (Jerusalem, 1981), p. 344.

[14] I am referring here to the "Revisionist" school—the work of historical cranks who deny the facts of the Holocaust altogether. Best known among these is A. R. Butz, *The Hoax of the Twentieth Century* (Los Angeles, 1977). For a more recent venture see Walter N. Sanning, *The Dissolution of Eastern European Jewry* (Torrance, Calif., 1983). Compare an assessment of a German variant by Ino Arndt and Wolfgang Scheffler, "Organisierter Massenmord an Juden in Nationalsozialistischen Vernichtungslagern: Ein Beitrag zur Richtigstellung apologestischer Literatur," *Vierteljahrshefte für Zeitgeschichte* 24 (1976): 105–35. Excellent discussions of this genre, focusing mainly on the French practitioners, may be found in Nadine Fresco, "Les redresseurs de morts. Chambres à gaz: La bonne nouvelle. Comment on revise l'histoire," *Les temps modernes* 35 (1980): 2150–211; Pierre Vidal-Naquet, "Un Eichmann de papier," *Esprit* 45 (1980): 8–52; and Georges Wellers, "Réponse aux falsifications d'histoire," *Le monde juif* 89 (January–March 1978): 4–19, and *Les chambres à gaz ont existé: Des documents, des témoignages, des chiffres* (Paris, 1981). For the latest chapter in the French falsifications, see Georges Wellers, "A propos d'une thèse de doctorat 'explosive' sur le 'Rapport Gerstein,' " *Le monde juif* 121 (January–March 1986): 1–18.

date" from Hitler to proceed. Hitler frequently issued such mandates, and there is plenty of evidence that others understood just what the Nazi leader meant. Those in charge did not trouble with documentary niceties when the Führer expressed himself. "What he actually meant, or whether he really meant it, might have been a matter of tone as well as of language. When he spoke 'coldly' and in a 'low voice' about 'horrifying' decisions 'also at the dinner table,' then his audience knew that he was 'serious.' "[15] From one to another, Nazi leaders transmitted the latest impulse. Adolf Eichmann, the Gestapo expert on Jewish matters, was only one of those who reported Hitler's verbal instructions for the Final Solution. Eichmann claimed that he learned of the Führer's order from Reinhard Heydrich, Himmler's deputy, at the end of the summer of 1941. When he reported this to his boss at the Gestapo, he realized from his nod that Heinrich Müller already "knew."[16]

Quite apart from the role of Hitler, however, is the issue of coherence and consistency in the anti-Jewish program of which he was the principal inspiration. On this important point historians differ sharply, and their debate echoes similar controversies over other aspects of the Third Reich. Fleming, as we have seen, posits an "unbroken continuity" of Hitler's views on the Jews and consequently sees a straight path from his early anti-Semitism to the gas chambers of Poland. Borrowing from the British historian Tim Mason, Christopher Browning was the first to dub this the "intentionalist" viewpoint—accenting the role of Hitler in initiating the murder of European Jewry and, at the same time, seeing a high degree of logic, consistency, and orderly sequence in Nazi anti-Jewish policy, directed from a very early time to the goal of mass murder. Critics of this view, referred to as "functionalists," are rather impressed with the *evo-*

[15] Raul Hilberg, 3:996. Hilberg's citation is from an affidavit by Albert Speer, July 31, 1977. A facsimile is in Arthur Suzman and Denis Diamond, *Six Million Did Die* (Johannesburg, 1977), pp. 109–12. Compare Uwe Dietrich Adam, *Judenpolitik im Dritten Reich* (Düsseldorf, 1972), pp. 241–46. On the role of Hitler, see esp. J. P. Stern, *Hitler: The Führer and the People* (Berkeley, 1975); Martin Broszat, *The Hitler State: The Foundation and Development of the Internal Structure of the Third Reich,* trans. John W. Hiden (London, 1981), and "Soziale Motivation und Führer-Bindung des Nationalsozialismus," *Vierteljahrshefte für Zeitgeschichte* 18 (1970): 392–409. In a recent book, Eberhard Jäckel again makes the case that "Hitler ordered the Final Solution" (Jäckel, *Hitler in History* [Hanover, N.H., 1984], chap. 3).

[16] Adolf Eichmann, *Ich, Adolf Eichmann: Ein historischer Zeugenbericht,* ed. Rudolf Aschenauer (Leoni am Starnberger See, 1980), pp. 178–79, 229–30. Researchers who have compared this source with other documentary materials have expressed some doubts about its editor's reliability. See Christopher R. Browning, *Fateful Months: Essays on the Emergence of the Final Solution* (New York, 1985), pp. 24–25. For additional Eichmann testimony, see "Eichmann Tells His Own Damning Story," *Life Magazine* (November 28, 1960), pp. 19–25. See also Jochen von Lang, ed., *Eichmann Interrogated: Transcripts from the Archives of the Israeli Police,* trans. Ralph Manheim (New York, 1984), p. 75; Hilberg, 2:402.

Marrus

lution of Nazi goals, with the sometimes haphazard course of German policies, and with the way in which these are related to the internal mechanisms of the Third Reich.[17]

"Intentionalism," it may be supposed, was born in Nuremberg in 1945 when American prosecutors first presented Nazi war crimes as a carefully orchestrated conspiracy, launched together with the war itself. American legal experts hoped to prove that there had been a deliberate *plan* to commit horrendous atrocities as well as other breaches of international law; in this way they expected to designate certain German organizations and institutions as part of a criminal conspiracy, vastly simplifying the work of future prosecutions.[18] Years later, after much historical analysis, many historians continue to argue the case for a fixed plan. Broadly speaking, their method consists of adducing incriminating quotations. Eberhard Jäckel, the leading expert on Hitler's speeches and writings, assembled a fair sampling of these in a book that first appeared in German in 1969, arguing that as early as 1924, with the publication of *Mein Kampf,* the Führer's course was set for extermination rather than some other means of eliminating the Jews.[19] As a register of Hitler's ultimate objectives, such citations cannot easily be dismissed, particularly in the context of a brutally escalating persecution of Jews in the Third Reich. Hitler took himself desperately seriously on the matter and, by all indications, wanted others to take

[17] Tim Mason, "Intention and Explanation: A Current Controversy about the Interpretation of National Socialism," in *Der Führerstaat: Mythòs und Realität,* ed. Gerhard Hirschfeld and Lothar Kettenacker (Stuttgart, 1981), pp. 21–40; Christopher R. Browning, "La décision concernant la solution finale," in *L'Allemagne nazie et le génocide juif,* Colloque des hautes études en sciences sociales (Paris, 1985), pp. 190–91. On "functionalists" and "intentionalists," see also Ian Kershaw, *The Nazi Dictatorship: Problems and Perspectives of Interpretation* (London, 1985), esp. chap. 5 on "Hitler and the Holocaust"; and John Hiden and John Farquharson, *Explaining Hitler's Germany* (London, 1983), pp. 46 ff. Browning's excellent summary of this controversy also appears in his *Fateful Months,* chap. 1. For additional background material, see Erich Goldhagen, "Weltanschauung und Endlösung: Zum Antisemitismus der nationalsozialistischen Führungsschicht," *Vierteljahrshefte für Zeitgeschichte* 24 (1976): 379–405; Saul Friedländer, "From Anti-Semitism to Extermination: A Historiographical Study of the Nazi Policies toward the Jews and an Essay in Interpretation," *Yad Vashem Studies* 16 (1984): 1–50, and his introduction to Fleming. Compare Wolfgang Scheffler, "Zur Entstehungsgeschichte der Endlösung," *Aus Politik und Zeitgeschichte: Beilage zur Wochenzeitung "Das Parlament"* (October 30, 1982), pp. 3–10.

[18] For a discussion of the American legal strategy and its concern to demonstrate that a conspiracy existed, see Bradley Smith, *The Road to Nuremberg* (New York, 1981); cf. his *Reaching Judgment at Nuremberg* (New York, 1977).

[19] Eberhard Jäckel, *Hitlers Weltanschauung: Entwurf einer Herrschaft* (1969; 2d ed., Stuttgart, 1971), published in English as *Hitler's Weltanschauung: A Blueprint for Power,* trans. Herbert Arnold (n.d.; reprint, Cambridge, Mass., 1981). A recent entry in the "intentionalist" list is Simon Taylor, *Prelude to Genocide: Nazi Ideology and the Struggle for Power* (London, 1985), which argues that as early as 1927 the Nazi leadership "intended to carry out a systematic annihilation of the Jews once they had attained power" (pp. 217–18).

him seriously as well. In his famous address to the Reichstag on January 30, 1939, to which both he and others drew attention several years later, the Führer sounded a remarkably "intentionalist" note: "One thing I should like to say on this day which may be memorable for others as well as for us Germans: In the course of my life I have very often been a prophet, and have usually been ridiculed for it. During the time of my struggle for power it was in the first instance the Jewish race which only received my prophesies with laughter when I said that I would one day take over the leadership of the State, and with it that of the whole nation, and that I would then among many other things settle the Jewish problem. Their laughter was uproarious, but I think that for some time now they have been laughing on the other side of their face. Today I will once more be a prophet: If the international Jewish financiers in and outside Europe should succeed in plunging the nations once more into a world war, then the result will not be the bolshevization of the earth, and thus the victory of Jewry, but the annihilation of the Jewish race in Europe!"[20]

Even Hitler's statements require interpretation, however. Delivered in the wake of the Munich conference, Hitler's speech of January 30 lasted several hours but included only a few sentences on the Jews. It was seen as relatively conciliatory by the British ambassador and was judged to be mainly concerned with economic matters. The context was certainly a troubled international scene, and a primary purpose was probably to sow confusion and division among the Western powers. Hitler did envisage war in Europe—likely not a world war, however, but a conflict with Poland. Whether this was truly a "prophecy" in the sense of forecasting European-wide extermination is therefore very much in doubt.[21] Even more dubious is to see in his words a preview of Auschwitz and the other death factories. In addition, there is a difficulty with Hitler's use of language. The Nazi leader always spoke in cataclysmic terms, was forever calling for the most drastic action, the most ruthless stroke, the most complete annihilation. In retrospect, one can identify those instances in which the Nazi leader's words proved more than simply bluster; but there are others in which the "prophecies" were not fulfilled. Hitler undoubtedly was determined to settle his score with the Jews and certainly meant it when he demanded that the Jewish problem be "solved" one way or another—*so oder so*. His predilection was also to do so in the most brutal and devastating way. As Uwe Dietrich Adam points out, he and the other Nazi leaders certainly

[20] N. H. Baynes, ed., *The Speeches of Adolf Hitler* (London, 1942), 1:735–41; Arad, Gutman, and Margaliot, eds., pp. 132–35.

[21] The full, authorized English version of the January 30 speech, published by Müller & Sohn, Berlin, extends through sixty-four pages of closely printed text. On the speech, see also Adam, pp. 235–36; Shlomo Aronsen, "Die Dreichfache Falle: Hitlers Judenpolitik, die Alliierten und die Juden," *Vierteljahrshefte für Zeitgeschichte* 32 (1984): 49; and Telford Taylor, *Munich: The Price of Peace* (New York, 1980), p. 946.

Marrus

looked to a ruthless crackdown on Jews in the event of war.[22] But did this mean mass murder? And if so, when?

For Lucy Dawidowicz, likely the most widely read author on the subject, the outbreak of war in 1939 signaled the beginning: "War and the annihilation of the Jews were interdependent. The disorder of war would provide Hitler with the cover for the unchecked commission of murder." The war, in this view, had a double purpose: one was the conquest of empire—Hitler's oft-declared goal of Lebensraum, or living space in the East—and the other was the "war against the Jews," their complete, physical destruction. Yet Dawidowicz does not explain the troublesome fact that systematic mass murder on a European-wide scale did not begin until considerably after the attack on the Soviet Union, two years later. If one accepts her view, asks Browning, why the thirty-month "stay of execution"?[23] For Andreas Hillgruber, a historian also committed to the intentionalist view, the key lies instead in the Barbarossa campaign. The Final Solution derived from Hitler's ideological fixation on Bolshevism and the East being inseparable from "international Judaism." Killing on a mass scale emerged from the mobilization for the onslaught on the Soviet Union that began on June 22, 1941.[24]

In the absence of reliable guides to Hitler's plans for the Jews, apart from his murky "prophecies," intentionalists differ among themselves as to when, precisely, Hitler's intentions became fixed. The weight of opinion seems to rest on the Barbarossa campaign. According to Helmut Krausnick, there was a wartime decision of the Führer, but its timing remains obscure. "What is certain is that the nearer Hitler's plan to overthrow Russia as the last possible enemy on the continent of Europe approached maturity, the more he became obsessed with the idea—with which he had been toying as "a final solution" for a long time—of wiping out the Jews in the territories under his control. It cannot have been later than March 1941, when he openly declared his intention of having the political commissars of the Red Army shot, that he issued his secret decree—which never appeared in writing though it was mentioned verbally on several occasions—that the Jews should be eliminated."[25] Together with a col-

[22] Adam, p. 236.

[23] Lucy Dawidowicz, *The War against the Jews, 1933–1945* (New York, 1975), p. 111; Browning, p. 15. On the link with war, see Jäckel's comments in *Hitler's Weltanschauung*, pp. 60–61.

[24] Andreas Hillgruber, "Die 'Endlösung' und das Deutsche Ostimperium als Kernstück des rassenideologischen Programs des Nationalsozialismus," *Vierteljahrshefte für Zeitgeschichte* 20 (1972): 133–53, and "Die ideologisch-dogmatische Grundlage der Nationalsozialistischen Politik der Ausrottung der Juden in den besitzten Gebieten der Sowjetunion und ihre Durchführung, 1941–1944," *German Studies Review* 2 (1979): 263–96. Compare his *Hitlers Strategie, Politik, und Kriegführung, 1940–1941* (Frankfurt am Main, 1965), pp. 593–94.

[25] Helmut Krausnick and Martin Broszat, *Anatomy of the SS State*, trans. Dorothy Long and Marian Jackson (London, 1968), p. 77. Compare Helmut Krausnick, "Kommisarbefehl und 'Gerichtsbarkeitserlass Barbarossa' in neuer Sicht," *Vierteljahrshefte für Zeitgeschichte* 25 (1977): 682–738.

league, Hans-Heinrich Wilhelm, Krausnick has pored over the activities of the murderous *Einsatzgruppen*—the killing units of motorized SS troops who followed in the vanguard of the Wehrmacht when they swept into the Soviet Union in the summer of 1941. As many as 2.2 million died at the hands of these and related teams. Krausnick and Wilhelm have documented the genocidal character of the campaign, which Hitler referred to as a *Vernichtungskrieg*, a war of destruction, and they have incidently demonstrated the extensive support and assistance given to their slaughters by the regular army.[26] In their view, the extermination of the Jews was included in the planning process of the campaign. This assessment has been contested, however, and another authority instead argues that killing evolved into genocidal proportions during the early course of the campaign itself.[27]

Reference to a murderous program that *evolved* rather than being launched under particular "cover" brings us to the "functionalist" approach mentioned above. One of the first coherent expressions of this viewpoint was by German historian Martin Broszat in his highly critical review of Irving's work in 1977.[28] Broszat attacked what he called Irving's "normalization" of Hitler, reasserting "the fanatical, destructive will to annihilate" that for traditional historiography had always been at the core of the Führer's personality. He sharply criticized Irving's apologetic drift, stressing Hitler's "totally irresponsible, self-deceiving, destructive and evilly misanthropic egocentricity and his lunatic fanaticism." For the author of *Der Staat Hitlers* there was no doubt about who was in charge and what kind

[26] Helmut Krausnick and Hans-Heinrich Wilhelm, *Die Truppe des Weltanschauungskrieges: Die Einsatzgruppen der Sicherheitspolizei und des SD, 1938–1942* (Stuttgart, 1981), pp. 150–72 and passim. Wilhelm's section of this massive work is a detailed study of *Einsatzgruppe A*. On the activities of the Wehrmacht see Krausnick; Jürgen Forster, "The Wehrmacht and the War of Extermination against the Soviet Union," *Yad Vashem Studies* 14 (1981): 7–34, and *Das Deutsche Reich und der Zweite Weltkrieg*, vol. 4, *Der Angriff auf der Sowjetunion* (Stuttgart, 1983), pp. 413–47, 1030–78. See also Norman Rich, *Hitler's War Aims*, vol. 1, *Ideology, the Nazi State, and the Course of Expansion* (New York, 1973), chap. 18, and vol. 2, *The Establishment of the New Order* (New York, 1974), chap. 1. Our understanding of the *Einsatzgruppen* may be shifting because of the dissertation work of Yehoshua Büchler, presented in part in "*Kommandostab Reichsführer-SS:* Himmler's Personal Murder Brigades in 1941," *Holocaust and Genocide Studies* 1 (1986): 11–25. Büchler discusses the activities of the *Kommandostab*, a large SS force of about twenty-five thousand men under Himmler's personal command, which conducted extensive murder operations in 1941–43 together with the *Einsatzgruppen*, the police (Orpo), and the Waffen-SS.

[27] Alfred Streim, *Die Behandlung sowjetischer Kriegsgefangenen im "Fall Barbarossa"* (Heidelberg and Karlsruhe, 1981), pp. 74–93. Compare Christian Streit, *Keine Kamaraden: Die Wehrmacht und die sowjetischen Kriegsgefangenen, 1941–1942* (Stuttgart, 1978), p. 127.

[28] Broszat, "Hitler und die Genesis der 'Erlösung' " (n. 8 above). His critique was later published in English as "Hitler and the Genesis of the 'Final Solution': An Assessment of David Irving's Theses," *Yad Vashem Studies* 13 (1979): 73–125. Compare the critique of this paper by Christopher Browning, "Zur Genesis der Endlösung: Eine Antwort an Martin Broszat," *Vierteljahrshefte für Zeitgeschichte* 29 (1980): 97–109.

Marrus

of person he was. But perhaps more important, Broszat disputed the notion that Hitler issued concrete orders for comprehensive, European-wide mass murder at some particular point. In his judgment, murder escalated to a genocidal level during the course of the campaign in Russia. Hitler and the Nazis, in this view, were utterly committed to getting rid of the Jews but hoped for some time, in a vague way, to see them pushed off "to the East." Some of the early deportations and ghettoization were part of the means to this end. Then, as the campaign in the Soviet Union slowed, as problems accumulated in the teeming ghettos of Poland, and as local Nazi satraps protested the congestion of even more Jews in their domains, killing initiatives began on a local level. In Broszat's view, Hitler drove the apparatus forward by setting a priority of getting rid of the Jews and by charging officials with his murderous fanaticism. But it was the particular circumstance of a frustrated Nazi war machine that led to the Final Solution. The path, moreover, was not straight, and policy moved by fits and starts. A full-fledged program for massacre was only set in place in the spring of 1942, after the construction of the death camps in Poland. And even then it continued to evolve. "As the military struggle appeared to become hopeless, the 'war of fate' against Jewry was promoted as the real war (which would be won). The death of hundreds of thousands of German soldiers had to be expiated and biologically revenged through the liquidation of an even greater number of Jews."[29]

This approach appeals to historians who view the Third Reich as a "polycentric dictatorship" run by an erratic autocrat who intervened only spasmodically in domestic and administrative matters. To those who have come to see the Nazi state as lacking clear, consistent policy direction—as indeed Broszat described it in his 1969 volume—it is difficult to accept that in one area, Jewish policy, there existed a Hitlerian blueprint. Hans Mommsen is one of those who has pursued this line of argument, but unlike Broszat he does not see Hitler's central importance in the evolution of the Final Solution. Mommsen believes that Hitler thought about the Jews mainly in propagandistic terms, without bothering to specify policy. Hitler was, nevertheless, the "ideological and political author of the Final Solution," but only in the sense of stimulating others to realize his "utopian" ravings. In the Third Reich, Mommsen observes, office was piled upon office, and underlings were left to find their way in a bureaucratic and administrative jungle. The only guide to success and a compelling one, was fidelity to the Hitlerian vision: underlings competed for the favor of this ideologically obsessed but essentially lazy leader. Given the Führer's

[29] Broszat, "Hitler and the Genesis of the Final Solution," p. 120. For an East German view in a similar vein, see Kurt Pätzold, "Von der Vertreibung zum Genozid: Zu dem Ursachen, Triebkräften und Bedingungen der antijudischen Politik der faschistischen deutschen Imperialismus," in *Faschismusforschung: Positionen, Probleme, Polemik*, ed. Dietrich Eichholtz and Kurt Grossweiller (Berlin, 1980), pp. 181–208.

mad compulsions, this programmed the regime for "cumulative radicalization"—a process that led ultimately, of course, to its self-destruction.[30]

Those who have directed their attention to particular aspects of what Hilberg has called the Nazis' "machinery of destruction" have often come away with an appreciation of the evolutionary or improvised character of anti-Jewish policy in the Third Reich. This has certainly been my own impression from the vantage point of France and from a study of Jewish refugees from Nazism. In both of these instances, the Nazis' policy objectives appear to have undergone important shifts in the second half of 1941, signifying a completely new direction that ultimately pointed toward mass murder in Eastern European camps.

Nazi goals for the Jews, as we know, were formally set on emigration in the 1930s, when this seemed to afford the most reasonable prospect of ridding the Reich of those held to be its most deadly enemies. The first emigration project was the *Ha'avara,* or Transfer Agreement, worked out with Jewish authorities in Palestine in 1933, enabling some Jews to migrate to Palestine and take a fraction of their property with them.[31] Emigration, however, competed with robbery, random harassment, and violence as a Jewish policy, and it lacked a clear priority. That came in 1938, when there was a new drive to liquidate Jewish assets and a new urgency given to solving the "Jewish problem." With the *Anschluss* that year, the Reich absorbed two hundred thousand Austrian Jews, acquiring at a stroke more Jews within its new, expanded frontiers than it had contained when Hitler took power. The prospective incorporation of Czechoslovakia promised to include many more. After the riots of *Kristallnacht* in November 1938, SS police boss Heydrich was ordered to accelerate emigration, and Jews were

[30] Hans Mommsen, "Die Realisierung des Utopischen: Die 'Endlösung der Judenfrage' im 'Dritten Reich,' " *Geschichte und Gesellschaft* 9 (1983): 397, and "National Socialism: Continuity and Change," in *Fascism: A Reader's Guide,* ed. Walter Laqueur (Harmondsworth, 1979), p. 180. For a critique of Mommsen, see S. Friedländer (n. 17 above), pp. 30–32. Ian Kershaw has a similar assessment of Hitler's responsibility: "His major role consisted of setting the vicious tone within which the persecution took place and providing the sanction and legitimation of initiatives which came mainly from others." An important explanation of the Holocaust is thus "the nature of the 'charismatic' rule in the Third Reich and the way it functioned in sustaining the momentum of escalating radicalization around 'heroic,' chimeric goals. . . . This was the essential framework within which Hitler's lunacy could be translated into practical politics" (Kershaw [n. 17 above], pp. 104–5).

[31] On the *Ha'avara,* see Francis R. Nicosia, *The Third Reich and the Palestine Question* (Austin, Tex., 1985); David Yisraeli, "The Third Reich and the Transfer Agreement," *Journal of Contemporary History* 6 (1971):129–48; Gerhard Weinberg, *The Foreign Policy of Hitler's Germany,* vol. 2, *Starting World War II, 1937–1939* (Chicago, 1980), p. 246; and Edwin Black, *The Transfer Agreement: The Untold Story of the Secret Pact between the Third Reich and Jewish Palestine* (New York, 1984). On the last, a book that has been sharply criticized, see the review by Richard S. Levy, "Dealing with the Devil," *Commentary* 78 (September 1984): 68–71.

Marrus

literally driven out of the country. The problem was, of course, that there was practically no place for them to go.[32]

Emigration remained, however, the Nazis' officially declared objective. Historians differ on the degree to which they accept this as the Nazis' "ultimate" goal for the Jews and on the extent to which the Nazis were committed to it as a serious project, particularly after the outbreak of war.[33] My own sense is that the Nazis were indeed serious about emigration. This is certainly the impression one receives from the very extensive German negotiations on the subject of Jews pursued by their emissaries in London in 1939 and charted by Eliahu Ben Elissar in a book first published in 1969.[34] Their objective in these talks was to negotiate agreements with Western countries patterned on the *Ha'avara* model, which would facilitate the removal of Jews from the Reich. Unfortunately, the Western countries were not interested.

Thereafter, the Nazis continued to support emigration and did so with an earnestness that suggests commitment. Yehuda Bauer reckons that between the outbreak of war in 1939 and the end of 1941 a total of 71,500 Jews left the expanded German Reich, many of them managing to escape to western Europe.[35] These Jews left openly and with the full knowledge of Nazi officialdom. Given the compulsive quality that ultimately characterized the Final Solution, in which the Nazis strained not to permit a single man, woman, child, or even a tiny infant to escape, this is certainly impressive testimony. In western Europe, Nazi occupation policies in the period immediately after the French defeat give a striking indication that emigration was genuinely intended. The Germans not only permitted Jews to leave—to travel to the West—they also periodically dumped them across the demarcation line that separated the occupied from the unoccupied zones of France.[36] The Nazis' priority was to facilitate departures from the

[32] On Nazi policy and its evolution, see Karl A. Schleunes, *The Twisted Road to Auschwitz: Nazi Policy toward German Jews, 1933–1939* (Urbana, Ill., 1970); and Helmut Genschel, *Die Verdrängung der Juden aus der Wirtschaft im Dritten Reich* (Göttingen, 1966).

[33] See Yehuda Bauer, "Genocide: Was It the Nazis' Original Plan?" *Annals of the American Academy of Political and Social Science* 450 (1980): 35–45.

[34] Eliahu Ben Elissar, *La diplomatie du IIIe Reich et les juifs* (Paris, 1981).

[35] Yehuda Bauer, *American Jewry and the Holocaust: The American Jewish Joint Distribution Committee, 1939–1945* (Detroit, 1981), p. 66. I have surveyed this and other aspects of Jewish refugee movements in *The Unwanted: European Refugees in the Twentieth Century* (New York, 1985). See also Abraham Margaliot, "The Problem of the Rescue of German Jewry during the Years 1933–1939: The Reasons for the Delay in Their Emigration from the Reich," in *Rescue Attempts during the Holocaust: Proceedings of the Second Yad Vashem International Historical Conference*, ed. Yisrael Gutman and Efraim Zuroff (Jerusalem, 1977), pp. 247–65; and Herbert A. Strauss, "Jewish Emigration from Germany: Nazi Policies and Jewish Response," *Leo Baeck Institute Year Book* 25 (1980): 313–61, and 26 (1981): 343–409.

[36] See Michael R. Marrus and Robert O. Paxton, *Vichy France and the Jews* (New York, 1981), and "The Nazis and the Jews in Occupied Western Europe," *Journal of Modern History* 54 (1982): 687–714.

History of the Holocaust

Reich, and only then from other territory. Naturally enough, few Jews managed to flee under wartime conditions, when entry visas were practically impossible to obtain and transport was scarce. German authorities repeated to one another that the "problem" would be solved with the end of the war, by which they undoubtedly meant the peace settlement that was widely expected after the defeat of France. From time to time the Nazis also committed themselves to "colonization" schemes—first, the Nisko or Lublin Plan to settle Jews near the demarcation line separating German-occupied Poland from that held by the Soviet Union; and later, the Madagascar Plan, a proposal to ship Jews off to the island in the Indian Ocean belonging to France. Those who have looked into these schemes certainly give the impression that such proposals were seriously intended.[37]

In his 1978 book on the Jewish section of the German Foreign Office, Browning pictured a group of Nazi bureaucrats eagerly pursuing the emigration line that came from their superiors. Martin Luther, chief of this section, was an archcareerist with a talent for organization but no pressing anti-Jewish vocation. Luther "was not a doctrinaire racist like Heinrich Himmler, dreaming of fantasies of a future Aryan heaven on earth. Nor was he an *Altkämpfer* like Goebbels, wallowing in nostalgia and ready to stick by Hitler to the end. . . . Primarily, Luther was an amoral technician of power."[38] Strikingly, with the shift toward the Final Solution in the latter part of 1941, these officials sensed a new direction and acted on it. Browning notes: "When zealous administrators like Luther were desperately trying to anticipate the will of the Führer in the Jewish question . . . a chain of command requiring obedience to the Führer's orders was superfluous. Initiative from below obviated the necessity for orders from above."[39]

In the most recent scholarly analysis of this turning point, Browning settles on a position that he terms "moderate functionalist."[40] He finds it implausible that Hitler was merely "awaiting the opportune moment" to realize his murderous intentions since he allowed nearly three years to pass between the conquest of Poland in 1939 and the onset of systematic, Europe-wide mass murder in 1942. During this time there was no "blueprint" for mass destruction but, rather, an ideological imperative that called for some sort of ultimate reckoning with the Jews in a manner that would

[37] Seev Goshen, "Eichmann und die Nisko-Aktion im October 1939: Eine Fallstudie zur NS-Judenpolitik in der letzten Etappe vor der 'Endlösung,' " *Vierteljahrshefte für Zeitgeschichte* 29 (1981): 74–96; Christopher R. Browning, *The Final Solution and the German Foreign Office: A Study of Referat D III of Abteilung Deutschland, 1940–1943* (New York, 1978), pp. 35–43; Ben Elissar, p. 407; Marrus, pp. 186–87, 229–30. Compare Philip Friedman, "The Lublin Reservation and the Madagascar Plan: Two Aspects of Nazi Jewish Policy during the Second World War," in *Studies in Modern Jewish History*, ed. Joshua A. Fishman (New York, 1972), pp. 354–80, for an earlier argument to the effect that the plan was a subterfuge.

[38] Browning, *The Final Solution and the German Foreign Office*, p. 28.

[39] Ibid., p. 184.

[40] Browning, *Fateful Months* (n. 16 above), chap. 1, passim.

Marrus

satisfy Nazi racial preoccupations. Competing Nazi agencies put forward one proposal after the next, schemes that continually shattered against practical obstacles. Nazi activists appealed to a Führer whose thoughts were sometimes elsewhere, who was worried about tactical issues of many sorts, and who often delayed making up his mind about important matters. The crisis came with Barbarossa, not only because of the apocalyptic character of the campaign but also because it promised to bring hundreds of thousands more Jews within the hegemony of the Reich. What were the Germans to do with them? During the early course of the campaign, Hitler tipped the scale for mass murder. The decision to massacre the Soviet Jews was probably taken in March as part of the Barbarossa planning process. That summer, before the end of July, Hitler likely issued his order for European-wide mass murder, buoyed up by the spectacular successes of the Wehrmacht in the early part of the Russian campaign. At that point, the Führer probably felt, everything was possible. On July 31, Göring authorized Heydrich to prepare a "total solution" (*Gesamtlösung*) of the Jewish question in territories under the Nazis' control. Before long, work began on the first two death camps—at Belzec and Chelmno, where construction started in the autumn. On October 31, Himmler issued a fateful order that passed along the Nazi chain of command throughout Europe: henceforth there would be no Jewish emigration permitted anywhere from German-held territory. Deportations of Reich Jews to Eastern Europe had started a few weeks before. On November 29, invitations went out to the Wannsee Conference, intended to coordinate deportations from all across Europe. The Final Solution was about to begin.

It is evident from this short summation that, in the absence of an explicit order from the Führer, there is plenty of room for surmise about the precise origins of the Final Solution. That is why other writers, such as Adam or Sebastian Haffner, have argued that a Hitlerian decision came somewhat later in the course of 1941, when the tide of battle was turning against the German forces in the Soviet Union. In their view, it was not the euphoria of victory but, rather, the distressing setbacks of the Russian campaign that prompted a decision from the Führer: Adam sees the Nazis depressed by the prospect of having to spend yet another winter with the Jews; and Haffner imagines, less plausibly, that Hitler saw as early as the end of 1941 that the European war could not be won and that the other contest, "the war against the Jews," could at least be pursued to its final completion.[41] As the controversy plays itself out in print, outsiders may be struck by the strong elements of agreement, rather than by the disagreement. In particular, there seems to be a clear consensus that there was *some* Hitler-

[41] Adam (n. 15 above), pp. 303–16, "An Overall Plan for Anti-Jewish Legislation in the Third Reich?" *Yad Vashem Studies* 11 (1976): 33–55, "Persecution of the Jews, Bureaucracy, and Authority in the Totalitarian State," *Leo Baeck Institute Year Book* 23 (1978): 139–48; and Sebastian Haffner, *The Meaning of Hitler*, trans. Ewald Osers (London, 1979), pp. 142–45. Compare Marrus, pp. 227–33.

ian decision to initiate European-wide killing. Opinion thus runs against Broszat's notion of local initiatives. Further, the range of difference over timing extends only across a few months, with "intentionalists" positing a Führer order some time in March 1941, with Browning and others opting for the summer, and with a few, such as Adam, looking to the early autumn. To nonspecialists, the difference may not seem particularly significant.

Where in this debate, one might ask, is Hilberg? Those looking in the "revised and definitive" edition of *The Destruction of the European Jews* for some pronouncement on the question will certainly be disappointed. First published twenty-five years ago, Hilberg's massive work was of breathtaking scope: its range extending across the European continent, the book provided the first detailed and systematic combing of German materials on the Holocaust. The product of painstaking and wide-ranging research, Hilberg's book offered a magisterial synthesis on a scale that no one has matched before or since. Wide-ranging though it is, however, Hilberg's analysis has a particular focus, more narrow than that of most historians. As he made clear in the first edition in 1961, and as he repeats now, a quarter century later, Hilberg is committed to exploring the "how" of Nazi genocide. "I wanted to explore the sheer mechanism of destruction, and as I delved into the problem, I saw that I was studying an administrative process carried out by bureaucrats in a network of offices spanning a continent. Understanding the components of this apparatus, with all the facets of its activities, became the principal task of my life."[42] Probing the "how" of Nazi genocide, Hilberg, a political scientist, developed the notion of "the machinery of destruction" grinding on to its ultimate end—the murder of over five million people. The machine had its own logic of destruction, moving through successive phases: first the definition of Jews, then their expropriation, concentration, deportation, and finally their murder. The machine remains Hilberg's controlling image, and his leitmotif is the gigantic scale of its work. In hundreds of pages he recounts officialdom across Europe working together in mechanized fashion. Hilberg ultimately sees the system itself, and not individual decision makers or their central plan, as the driving force. "With an unfailing sense of direction and with an uncanny pathfinding ability, the German bureaucracy found the shortest path to the final goal." This human machine generated its own momentum, "operating with accelerating speed and an ever-widening destructive effect." It is as though, at a certain point, this machine needed no operator. "In the final analysis, the destruction of the Jews was not so much a product of laws and commands as it was a matter of spirit, of shared comprehension, of consonance and synchronization."[43]

As with most of the historians I have discussed, Hilberg sees Hitler's role in the Final Solution as "salient," but he goes little beyond implying

[42] Hilberg (n. 6 above), 1:ix.
[43] Ibid., pp. 9, 28, 55.

Marrus

that the Führer nudged forward the machinery already programmed for murder in 1941. "For years, the administrative machine had taken its initiatives and engaged in its forays one step at a time. In the course of that evolution, a direction had been charted and a course established. By the middle of 1941 the dividing line had been reached, and beyond it lay a field of unprecedented actions unhindered by the limits of the past." While there can be no doubt about the Nazi leader's inspiration of mass murder, he seems an even more distant figure in the new edition than in the first. Passages that considered or speculated about his decisions have sometimes been removed, and the role of the machine and its destructive logic is thereby heightened. At the bottom of a footnote reference to the evidence of Adolf Eichmann and Rudolf Höss, commandant of Auschwitz, we find Hilberg's sole comment on an issue that has been so widely debated: "Chronology and circumstances point to a Hitler decision before the summer [of 1941] ended."[44]

Nothing could be further from Hilberg's intention than to relieve German society from the responsibility for having created this destructive machine. But he does not explore the ways in which German political traditions, social structure, or popular culture may have predisposed this particular society for the anti-Jewish paroxysm of 1933–45. There is, of course, a rich (if dated) literature on this subject, much of it at such a high level of generalization as to defy serious comparison with other societies, at other times and places.[45] Without comparative analysis, however, it is hard to know what to make of such general contentions. At every point, it is reasonable to ask, Was Germany any more murderously anti-Jewish than other societies?[46] and, Were Germans any more disposed to seek murderous comprehensive "solutions" than other peoples? Of course, no one knows.

[44] Ibid., 2:401–2, and n. 30.

[45] Raul Hilberg undertook a short analysis of this problem more than twenty years ago, but he has not returned to the subject. See his "German Motivations for the Destruction of the Jews," *Midstream* 11 (June 1965): 23–40. The most recent attempt to grapple with this question is to be found in George M. Kren and Leon Rappoport, *The Holocaust and the Crisis of Human Behavior* (New York, 1980), chap. 2, entitled "Why Germany?" Their conclusions do not go beyond familiar treatments of the problem: "Ultimately, then, the answer to the question 'Why Germany?' can be schematized very simply as a three factor sequence. First, Germany was culturally vulnerable to authoritarian and romantically anti-intellectual leadership. Second, Germany was pushed into profound political, economic, and social confusion by the consequences of World War I. And third, these conditions nurtured the rise of a fanatic leader who ended by using Germany to actualize his murderous racial hatreds" (Kren and Rappoport, pp. 36–37). See also Helen Fein, *Accounting for Genocide: National Responses and Jewish Victimization during the Holocaust* (New York, 1979), chap. 1.

[46] And, one should add, "Was Austria?" Until the Waldheim affair, there has been relatively little investigation of the important role of Austrian Nazis in the course of the Final Solution. Yet the activism and strong anti-Semitism of Austrian Nazis has been noted by more than one observer. See the useful comments in Peter R. Black, *Ernst Kaltenbrunner: Ideological Soldier of the Third Reich* (Princeton, N.J., 1984), pp. 82–83,

Nevertheless, several interesting recent explorations of German opinion in the Nazi years enable us to peer beyond the Führer's orders and the "machinery of destruction" and to evaluate the German public's attitudes to persecution and mass murder. With the aid of such studies we are able to get far closer than ever before to the German national mood, so often spoken about by writers of the last generation.

The first systematic investigations of such attitudes drew inconclusively on national summaries of the Nazi security service (Sicherheitsdienst or SD) reports for the war years, along with a great many memoirs, diaries, and other descriptive material. In his 1973 article, Lawrence Stokes considered the extent to which ordinary Germans grasped the essence of the Final Solution and concluded that "much, although not all, of the terror and destruction inflicted upon the Jews of Europe by the Nazis was generally known among the German people."[47] Going over the wider ground of German public opinion in the Third Reich, Marliss Steinert contended rather the opposite—that "only a few people knew about the monstrous scope of the crimes."[48] While able to elucidate a great deal, notably the wide diversity of opinion among Germans, neither author spoke with the authority of those who have combed materials that are available in particular localities. For it is on this scale that historians have best been able to grasp the popular mood on the subject of the Jews. Studies of Nazism on the local level have for some time proven useful in this respect. Looking at Lower Saxony during the *Kampfzeit*, Jeremy Noakes observed the very limited appeal of anti-Semitism among a population that was far more interested in economic and political matters; studying Bavaria in the same period, Geoffrey Pridham felt that aggressive and "ideological" anti-

---

which seems to put the matter nicely into perspective. Besides Kaltenbrunner, who succeeded Heydrich in 1943 as head of the SS police apparatus (the *Reichsicherheitshauptamt*), prominent Nazis born or raised in Austria who were involved in the administration of the Final Solution included Adolf Eichmann, Franz Stangl, Odilo Globocnik, Alois Brunner, and Hanns Albin Rauter. According to Black, Austrians constituted "nearly a third of the members of the Eichmann commando, four times the percentage of Austrians in the Reich (8.5 percent)" (Black, p. 283).

[47] Lawrence Stokes, "The German People and the Destruction of the European Jews," *Central European History* 6 (1973): 167–91. On the German sources, see Aryeh L. Unger, "The Public Opinion Reports of the Nazi Party," *Public Opinion Quarterly* 29 (1965): 565–82. For a useful survey of the historiography of this question, see Otto Dov Kulka and Aron Rodrigue, "The German Population and the Jews in the Third Reich: Recent Publication and Trends in Research on German Society and the 'Jewish Question,' " *Yad Vashem Studies* 16 (1984): 421–35. See also Otto Dov Kulka, " 'Public Opinion' in Nazi Germany and the Jewish Question," *Jerusalem Quarterly* 25 (1982): 121–44, and 26 (1983): 34–45.

[48] Marliss Steinert, *Hitler's War and the Germans: Public Mood and Attitude during the Second World War*, ed. and trans. Thomas E. J. de Witt (Athens, Ohio, 1977), p. 145. On the issue of what was known about the murder of Jews, see also Hans-Heinrich Wilhelm, "The Holocaust in National Socialist Rhetoric and Writings: Some Evidence against the Thesis That before 1945 Nothing Was Known about the 'Final Solution,' " *Yad Vashem Studies* 16 (1984): 95–127.

Marrus

Semitism was much stronger among party activists than among voters.[49] Both would agree, I think, with William Sheridan Allen, who concluded in an examination of a town in Lower Saxony that residents "were drawn to antisemitism because they were drawn to Nazism, not the other way around."[50] Summarizing the conclusions of his wide-ranging electoral analysis, Richard Hamilton emphasized regional differences in anti-Semitism: in places where it was strong, the Nazis played it up; where it was weak, they could ignore it altogether.[51]

Historians are increasingly casting their research nets more widely in their search for "public opinion." In one of the most recent and fruitful efforts, by the British historian Ian Kershaw, we see a rich panorama of Bavarian popular attitudes gleaned from many sources—including both the Nazi authorities themselves and, for the prewar period, the Social Democratic Party underground.[52] Kershaw is aware of pitfalls with both kinds of evidence, but he attempts to skirt these whenever possible by recourse

[49] Jeremy Noakes, *The Nazi Party in Lower Saxony, 1921–1933* (Oxford, 1971), pp. 206–10; and Geoffrey Pridham, *Hitler's Rise to Power: The Nazi Movement in Bavaria, 1923–1933* (New York, 1973), pp. 237–44.

[50] William Sheridan Allen, *The Nazi Seizure of Power: The Experience of a Single German Town, 1930–1935* (Chicago, 1965), p. 77. Further evidence for this proposition comes from the investigation done by Peter Merkl on the 581 biographies of early Nazis solicited by sociologist Theodore Abel in 1932. Merkl was struck by "how little the Nazi movement was motivated by shared, constructive goals of any kind. Instead, the movement owed its solidarity and dynamic drive to the skillful manipulation of fears and hatreds." But fear and hatred of Jews do not seem to have figured prominently among these. The party "was dominated by political antisemites," and the bulk of the Nazis in this sample seem simply to have followed their lead. About a third of the sample gave no evidence of anti-Semitism, 13 percent were extremely anti-Semitic, and the rest were somewhat in between (Merkl, *Political Violence under the Swastika: 581 Early Nazis* [Princeton, N.J., 1975], pp. 498–99, 505, and passim). For a concrete illustration, see Peter Merkl, *The Making of a Stormtrooper* (Princeton, N.J., 1980), p. 222.

[51] Richard Hamilton, *Who Voted for Hitler?* (Princeton, N.J., 1982), pp. 606–7, and passim. Broszat had described the process of *Salonfähigmachung* of the Nazi Party in 1930, when Nazi strategy made an effort to bid for mass support throughout the country. This could, under some circumstances, lead to a muting of the Party's anti-Jewish message. See Martin Broszat, "Zur Struktur der NS-Massenbewegung," *Vierteljahrshefte für Zeitgeschichte* 31 (1983): 52–76; Noakes, p. 209. According to Henry Ashby Turner, the captains of German industry, whom Hitler attempted to court at the time, "failed to take Nazi anti-Semitism seriously, dismissing it, as did so many Germans, as mere demagogic phrase-mongering" (Turner, *German Big Business and the Rise of Hitler* [New York, 1985], p. 337).

[52] Ian Kershaw, *Popular Opinion and Political Dissent in the Third Reich: Bavaria, 1933–1945* (Oxford, 1983), which draws on his "Antisemitismus und Volksmeinung: Reaktion auf die Judenverfolgung," in *Bayern in der NS-Zeit*, ed. Martin Broszat et al., 6 vols. (Munich, 1977–83), 2 (1979): 281–300. Bavaria is apparently the only part of Germany from which we have continuous Nazi reports on the local level (the *Lage-* and *Stimmungsberichte*) spanning the entire period of the Third Reich. See also Ian Kershaw, *Der Hitler-Mythos: Volksmeinung und Propaganda im Dritten Reich* (Stuttgart, 1980), and "The Persecution of the Jews and German Popular Opinion in the Third Reich," *Leo Baeck Institute Year Book* 26 (1981): 261–89.

to other materials, good judgment, and a close knowledge of the local scene. His quarry is "ordinary Germans": "the muddled majority, neither full-hearted Nazis nor outright opponents, whose attitudes at one time betray signs of Nazi ideological penetration and yet show the clear limits of propaganda manipulation."

Bavaria, of course, may not be "representative": largely Catholic, the cradle of Nazism, and for years the base of the movement, the province was by no means solidly pro-Nazi. Between fifteen thousand and twenty thousand Bavarians—mainly Socialist and Communist workers—were interned in 1933 alone, and the danger of being sent to Dachau increased following Goebbels's declaration of total war in 1943. Thousands paid for their grumblings in concentration camps or even worse; but others were either ignored, intimidated into silence, or bought off by Nazi functionaries. Generally, discontent did not produce active *opposition*. There were relatively few Jews in Bavaria—about forty-two thousand or 0.55 percent of the total population in 1933, roughly half the proportion in the Reich as a whole. Anti-Semitism, as we know, can easily exist without Jews. Yet it is the indifference of this population to the Jewish question that Kershaw finds so striking. There were some centers of anti-Semitism—notably Protestant Middle Franconia—under the influence of the rabble-rousing Julius Streicher.[53] But activity against Jews—arson, violence, boycotts, discrimination—was overwhelmingly the work of zealous party men and their agents rather than the general population. The culmination of a violent anti-Jewish campaign, the riots of *Kristallnacht* were widely disapproved of, mainly because of their hooligan, lawless character, with such wasteful destruction of private property. No one believed Goebbels's boast that the German people had risen "spontaneously" against the Jews, and Nazi leaders were plainly disappointed with the lack of enthusiasm for the pogrom.[54]

Thereafter, they attempted to shield their murderous policy from popular scrutiny in Germany. But, although very few Bavarians knew details of the Final Solution, and solid information about extermination camps was virtually nonexistent, there were certainly rumors about mass shootings and other atrocities, not to mention the physical disappearance of the Jews

[53] On Streicher, see the recent works by Dennis E. Showalter, *Little Man, What Now? "Der Stürmer" in the Weimar Republic* (Hamden, Conn., 1982) and Randall L. Bytwerk, *Julius Streicher* (New York, 1983). On the situation in Bremen, where apparently there was considerable local anti-Semitism, see Regina Bruss, *Die Bremer Juden unter dem Nationalsozialismus* (Bremen, 1983).

[54] On German reactions to *Kristallnacht*, see William Sheridan Allen, "Die deutsche Öffentlichkeit und die 'Reichskristallnacht'—Konflikte zwischen Werthierarchie und Propaganda im Dritten Reich," in *Die Reihen fast geschlossen: Beiträge zur Geschichte des Alltags unterm Nationalsozialismus*, ed. D. Peukert and J. Reulecke (Wuppertal, 1981), pp. 397–411, based on underground Social Democratic Party reports. But cf. Kulka, " 'Public Opinion' in Nazi Germany," pp. 138–42, for another view drawing on a wider range of sources.

from many localities. Remarkable as it may seem, public opinion does not seem to have concerned itself with the Jews. Far more important were the worsening conditions of life at home, the gloomy news from the front, and the fear of Allied retribution should the Reich be defeated. Occasionally, Bavarians worried that Allied air attacks were linked to German anti-Jewish persecutions. Churchmen were generally silent, reflecting the widespread lack of concern about the issue. Sometimes anti-Semitism showed up in reports on local attitudes to Nazi policies, suggesting that latent hostility toward Jews was widespread and that Nazi propaganda had had some effect at home. But these were exceptions. So although the Nazis succeeded in murdering the Jews largely without German resistance, they failed significantly to mobilize the population on behalf of anti-Semitism. "The road to Auschwitz," Kershaw notes in a memorable phrase, "was built by hate, but paved with indifference."[55]

Several historians have come away from this material, however, with much harsher views of German opinion. Notably, they remind us how durable the Reich proved to be despite the great trials of the latter part of the war, when allied bombs rained down on Germany and the achievements of Nazism lay in ruins. One cannot help but be impressed by "the stoic endurance of the German people . . . and the way in which their continued belief in Hitler apparently remained unshaken to the very end."[56] One aspect of this remarkable cohesion was the intense and continued opposition to Jews in Germany, constituting at times a genuine popular force that may have assisted the Nazis in their genocidal program. Anti-Semitism was hardly limited to hard-core Nazis. In 1932, as George Mosse pointed out many years ago, a seizure of power by non-Nazi elements of the German right—the *Stahlhelm* and the German National People's Party (DNVP), for example—would still have meant an anti-Jewish persecution.[57] Michael

[55] Kershaw, *Popular Opinion and Political Dissent in the Third Reich*, p. 277. Jeremy Noakes also concludes that the Nazi party had little success "in imposing its racist and Social Darwinist ideals on the German people," in "Nazism and Revolution," in *Revolutionary Theory and Political Reality*, ed. Noel O'Sullivan (Brighton, 1983), p. 90. This seems to conform with the conclusions of Sarah Gordon in *Hitler, Germans, and the "Jewish Question"* (Princeton, N.J., 1984), who surveys the literature on this question and who has examined Gestapo files on the Düsseldorf region in the Rhineland. Gordon's work seems to me insufficiently rooted in a specific locality to cast new light on the problem. She draws on small samples based on Nazi accusations of *Rassenschande* and *Judenfreundlichkeit* in order to detect "opponents of persecution." She finds certain classes of people "overrepresented" among "opponents" by this measure, but it turns out that these are the groups into which Jews were disproportionately integrated—older Germans, independents, and white-collar workers. We are not told how intermarriage affects these statistics.

[56] Hiden and Farquharson (n. 17 above), p. 57.

[57] George L. Mosse, "Die deutsche Rechte und die Juden," in *Endscheidungsjahr 1932: Zur Judenfrage in der Endphase der Weimarer Republik*, ed. Werner E. Mosse (Tübingen, 1966), pp. 183–246. Compare Donald L. Niewyk, *The Jews in Weimar Germany* (Baton Rouge, La., 1980), chap. 3 and passim.

Kater, author of an important work on the Nazi Party, has argued that historians like Kershaw have underplayed the genuinely spontaneous expressions of anti-Semitism that periodically erupted in prewar Germany.[58] "After January 30, 1933," he writes, "Nazi policy against the Jews came to resemble a pattern of interactions between private or personal initiative, semilegal activities . . . and, finally, government legislation." Immediately after Hitler took power the Sturmabteilung (SA) comprised about two million men over the age of seventeen, about 10 percent of the entire German population in corresponding age groups. Together with other Nazi formations, this certainly constituted a popular mass disposed to active anti-Jewish campaigning.[59] Moreover, anti-Semitism seems even to have had its place in the German opposition to Hitler within the Reich. Christof Dipper has gone over this ground and offers some sobering conclusions.[60] Among most of the conservative opponents of Nazism, "the bureaucratic, pseudo-legal deprivation of the Jews practiced until 1938 was still considered acceptable." To be sure, no one within the resistance movement supported massacre. But the conspirators linked to Leipzig mayor Carl Goerdeler, for example—probably the most important group within the resistance—apparently favored a special, diminished status for Jews, segregating them as outsiders in German society. Drawing on this evidence, Dipper concludes that "a large part of the German people . . . believed that a 'Jewish Question' existed and had to be solved."[61]

In a similar vein, Otto Dov Kulka contends that before the outbreak of war one clearly sees a tendency to "depersonalize" Jews, effectively isolating them in German society. Kulka has also looked in detail at anti-Jewish opinion at the time of the Nuremberg Laws, noting that, while the range of opinion varied considerably, there was substantial popular initiative for action against the Jews. According to Kulka, the "indifference"

[58] Michael Kater, "Everyday Anti-Semitism in Prewar Nazi Germany: The Popular Bases," *Yad Vashem Studies* 16 (1984): 129–59.

[59] Ibid., pp. 138, 142.

[60] Christof Dipper, "Der deutsche Widerstand und die Juden," *Geschichte und Gesellschaft* 9 (1983): 349–80, and "The German Resistance and the Jews," *Yad Vashem Studies* 16 (1984): 51–93.

[61] Goerdeler's 1941 memorandum, *"Das Ziel,"* declared that the Jewish people belonged to a different race from the Germans and were aliens in Germany. His plan was to limit their activity in Germany but to support their settlement elsewhere and the establishment of a Jewish state. See Dipper, "German Resistance and the Jews," pp. 71–73. For a much more positive evaluation of Goerdeler, see Peter Hoffman, *The History of the German Resistance, 1933–1945,* trans. Richard Barry (Cambridge, Mass., 1977), pp. 189–90: "He wrote in the belief that Jews living amongst other peoples in great numbers would always, again and again, become victims of persecution. It can be debated whether special discriminatory laws and the resulting separation were the best method. It is a fact, however, that even the most liberal and democratic nations, such as the Swiss or the British, have not found it possible in the twentieth century to do without special legislation aimed at certain groups of foreigners." It is pertinent to observe at this point that about 80 percent of the Jews in Germany in 1933 were German citizens.

Marrus

that lies at the heart of Kershaw's argument may not be an accurate representation of German views. In particular, the concept is misleading if it suggests a lack of interest in the Jews; certainly it does not convey what he feels is the widespread conviction that "something, one way or another, had to be done to 'solve the Jewish Question.'" Kulka contends "that the population of Germany was generally aware of what became of the Jews deported to the East," and he judges German reaction to be "a kind of national conspiracy of silence." "Indifference," he argues with a colleague in a recent review, might better be characterized as "passive complicity."[62]

"Complicity," however, has a legalistic ring that some may find bothersome as a term of historical explanation, suggesting as it does a determination of guilt rather than a basis for historical understanding. In the end, the examination of public opinion still leaves unclear the role of German anti-Semitism in the catastrophe. Shulamit Volkov, among others, makes an important distinction between traditional German anti-Semitism and the murderous enterprise of Adolf Hitler and the Third Reich, thereby drawing attention away from the "anti-Semitic background" to the Holocaust.[63] After all, one can easily trace the importance of anti-Semitism in other European countries, east and west; and it is highly unlikely, by any scale of judgment, that Germany would be deemed the most anti-Semitic country in Europe. For Volkov, therefore, Nazism must be understood as a dynamic force, and its genocidal project must be seen in the context of its own evolving qualities rather than through its "origins."[64]

Reference to "complicity" and "indifference" calls to mind an important area of Holocaust study—the investigation of the roles of conquered peoples, collaborationist states, countries allied to the Reich, and the Jews themselves. On each of these topics there has been considerable writing in recent years, shedding light, in turn, on Nazi policy and the course of

[62] Otto Dov Kulka, "Die Nürnberger Rassengesetze und die deutsche Bevölkerung im Lichte geheimer NS-Lage- und Stimmungsberichte," *Vierteljahrshefte für Zeitgeschichte* 32 (1984): 582–624, and " 'Public Opinion' in Nazi Germany" (n. 47 above); and Kulka and Rodrigue, "The German Population and the Jews," pp. 434–35. Pursuing their criticism of Kershaw, Kulka and Rodrigue conclude, "The degree to which the population agreed with 'the basic principles behind the persecution' while 'criticising the methods' will probably never be known. . . . What is known is that the composite picture that the regime obtained from popular-opinion reports pointed toward the general passivity of the population in the face of the persecution of the Jews."

[63] Shulamit Volkov, "Le texte et la parole: De l'antisémitisme d'avant 1914 à l'antisémitisme nazi," in *L'Allemagne nazie et le génocide juif* (n. 17 above), pp. 76–98, and "Kontinuität und Diskontinuität im deutschen Antisemitismus," *Vierteljahrshefte für Zeitgeschichte* 33 (1985): 221–43. Compare Michael R. Marrus, "The Theory and Practice of Antisemitism," *Commentary* 74 (August 1982): 38–42.

[64] Gordon, p. 48, also makes this point. Compare Fred E. Katz, "Implementation of the Holocaust: The Behavior of Nazi Officials," *Comparative Studies in Society and History* 24 (1982): 510–29: "The theme of this study is that one can account for a great deal of extremely violent anti-Semitic behavior without a basis in personal hatred for the Jews."

the Final Solution. For reasons of space, I will concentrate on how this literature elucidates the Holocaust as a whole.

Hilberg made the obvious link between European-wide involvement and Nazi policy many years ago when he pointed out that the apparatus of destruction was thinly spread across the European continent. Relatively few German officials engaged in anti-Jewish operations full-time. Instead, a handful of bureaucrats, the "experts" on Jewish affairs, enlisted legions of helpers inside Germany and outside, in the military, in ministries, in private industry, in the railways—virtually everywhere, in short. To achieve the task of comprehensive mass murder, the machine called on not only the cold-blooded killers of the SS but also remote officials of the postal ministry, tax and insurance adjustors, bankers and clergymen, mechanics and accountants, municipal officials and stenographers. The clear implication is that the work of murder on such a colossal scale involved the entire organized society in the Reich to one degree or another and depended heavily also on support from the outside. We tend, naturally enough, to think of the hideous moment of killing. But Hilberg's work reminds us, as no other has done, how much effort was necessary to reach that point and how much assistance the Nazis needed and obtained in practically every quarter in carrying out their Final Solution.[65]

One way of viewing the Holocaust on its European-wide scale is to examine the extent of Jewish victimization across the continent. This was the focus of a 1979 study by Helen Fein, who set out, with the aid of a computer, to ascertain the reasons for the wide variations in the proportions of Jews murdered in the European countries.[66] Fein assembled and coded such diverse variables as the extent of SS control, the amount of warning time permitted the Jews, the character of native government response, the prewar size and visibility of the Jewish community, the accessibility of havens, the intensity of prewar anti-Semitism, and the kinds of Jewish defense strategy adopted. In my own view, this effort was misguided, despite the suggestive material and analysis contained in the book, because the author did not take sufficient account of Nazi *policy*—the power and the inclination of the Germans to carry mass murder to such different places as, for example, Poland, with over three million Jews, or Finland, with two thousand. For the crucial issue was always the extent to which the

[65] Hilberg, *Destruction of the European Jews* (n. 6 above), 3:994, 1003. Reflecting on a related point, Robert Koehl considers the SS to have become "the alibi of a nation." Their task, he says, "was a task thrust on the men in the black coats, wholly consistent with their cultivated image at least since 1933 within the party and German society. The mask of evil which the SS donned at this time was desired for them by all who were in the know." See Koehl, *The Black Corps: The Structure and Power Struggles of the Nazi SS* (Madison, Wis., 1983), p. 245.

[66] Fein, *Accounting for Genocide* (n. 45 above), chap. 2, and passim. For a different critique than the one offered here, see Aharon Weiss, "Quantitative Measurement of Features of the Holocaust: Notes on the Book by Helen Fein," *Yad Vashem Studies* 14 (1981): 319–34.

Marrus

Nazis determined to do the job. In Poland, the heart of European Jewry, they were indeed determined; in Finland, an ally reluctant to deport its own Jews, and with a mere handful at stake, the Germans felt their victims could wait. Beyond this, we must realize that the decisive influence on the extent of the killing was the course of war. In the end, the Nazis failed to murder all the Jews because their empire crumbled in ruins in 1945. Had the war ended a year earlier, for example, the Jews of Hungary would have been saved; had it continued for yet another year or so, there would have been too few Jews left alive in Europe to constitute significant "national differences."

This said, it makes sense to look at the different experiences of Jews in various European countries in order to round out our sense of Nazi policy. In western Europe, where the Nazis worried in the first year or so of occupation about local sensibilities, one is struck by the caution exercised by occupation authorities in implementing anti-Jewish decrees and preparing the way for some ultimate "final solution." Browning's work on the Jewish section of the German Foreign Office is replete with evidence of how slow-moving the Germans were in setting up the apparatus of persecution in the West and how tentative were their first moves to enumerate the Jews, to isolate them from their countrymen, and to confiscate their property.[67] In *Vichy France and the Jews,* Robert Paxton and I argued that the Germans placed a low priority on Jewish policy for several months after their victory in the West in the summer of 1940, encouraging the French, at the same time, to do the work themselves. As the evidence abundantly shows, the French needed little encouragement. Drawing on a widespread antipathy toward foreigners in general and Jews in particular, plus a powerful backlash against the liberalism of the Third Republic, the Vichy government enthusiastically implemented its own anti-Jewish program. Official France had no murderous objective, to be sure, but it nevertheless launched a deliberate campaign to punish all Jews, particularly foreigners, to reduce their role in France, and to confiscate their property for the benefit of the rest of French society.[68]

Nazi policy in the West began a significant shift in the latter part of 1941, with the end of emigration formally decreed throughout Nazi-held territory. But the real change came only after the Wannsee Conference of January 1942, which decreed that Europe was to be combed of its Jews "from West to East."[69] The Wannsee meeting set occupation officials on notice that the time had come for the long-announced "Final Solution of the Jewish Question in Europe." Preparations went on everywhere with the SS now in charge. Once the deportation convoys started to roll in the summer of

[67] Browning, *The Final Solution and the German Foreign Office* (n. 37 above), chap. 4, passim.

[68] Marrus and Paxton, *Vichy France and the Jews* (n. 36 above), chaps. 1–3.

[69] Marrus and Paxton, "The Nazis and the Jews in Occupied Western Europe" (n. 36 above), provides an overview of German policy.

History of the Holocaust

1942, the Germans required substantial help from local officials, whether provided by collaborationist governments such as Vichy, local administrators working under Nazi authority such as in the Netherlands, or puppet regimes such as in Norway. With some exceptions, the literature on this subject recounts a depressingly high degree of local assistance provided to the Nazis' destruction machinery. In France, French police rounded up the Jews and placed them in camps pending their dispatch to the East; French municipal officials searched census files and processed the necessary documents; and French railwaymen took charge of conveying the Jews to the French frontiers. Throughout western Europe, the pattern was more or less the same.[70]

We have relatively few studies of popular reactions to anti-Jewish persecutions and deportations in the West. Paxton and I drew on French prefectoral reports to make a case for widespread indifference to the Jews' fate until the latter half of 1942. Broadly speaking, Vichy's anti-Jewish program left most Frenchmen unmoved, and their protests against the campaign were few and far between. The widespread (and quite mistaken) assumption was that persecution affected mainly foreign Jews and that, to some degree at least, this was justified, given the "preponderant influence" Jews were supposed to have had in French society.[71] In a recent investigation of the region about Clermont Ferrand, John Sweets provides evidence for a contrary interpretation, suggesting that Vichy had much more difficulty than has been assumed in selling its anti-Jewish policy.[72] In time

[70] See Marrus and Paxton, *Vichy France and the Jews,* chaps. 6 and 7; Georges Wellers, André Kaspi, and Serge Klarsfeld, eds., *La France et la question juive: Actes du colloque du Centre de Documentation Juive Contemporaine (10 au 12 mars 1979)* (Paris, 1981); Serge Klarsfeld, *Vichy-Auschwitz: Le rôle de Vichy dans la solution finale de la question juive en France, 1942* (Paris, 1983); Dan Erdmann-Degenhardt, "La déportation des juifs de Belgique," *Le monde juif,* no. 109 (January–March 1983), pp. 1–24; Louis de Jong, "Jews and Non-Jews in Occupied Holland," in *On the Track of Tyranny,* ed. Max Beloff (London, 1960), pp. 139–55; Jacob Presser, *The Destruction of the Dutch Jews,* trans. Arnold Pomerans (New York, 1969); B. A. Sijes, "Several Observations concerning the Position of the Jews in Occupied Holland during World War II," in Gutman and Zuroff, eds. (n. 35 above), pp. 527–53, and "The Position of the Jews during the German Occupation of the Netherlands: Some Observations," *Acta historiae Neerlandicae: Studies on the History of the Netherlands* 9 (1976): 170–92; Werner Warmbrunn, *The Dutch under German Occupation, 1940–1945* (Stanford, Calif., 1963); Leni Yahil, "Methods of Persecution: A Comparison of the 'Final Solution' in Holland and Denmark," *Scripta Hierosolymita* 23 (1972): 279–300; Paul M. Hayes, *Quisling: The Career and Political Ideas of Vidkun Quisling, 1887–1945* (Newton Abbot, England, 1971). Compare Alan Mitchell, "Nazi Occupation Policies and the Response of Polish, Dutch, and French Elites," *Wiener Library Bulletin,* n.s. 32, nos. 49/50 (1979): 34–39.

[71] Marrus and Paxton, *Vichy France and the Jews,* chap. 5; and Michael R. Marrus, "Die französischen Kirchen und die Verfolgung der Juden in Frankreich, 1940–1944," *Vierteljahrshefte für Zeitgeschichte* 31 (1983): 483–505. For a good assessment of the North African situation, see Michel Abitbol, *Les juifs d'Afrique du nord sous Vichy* (Paris, 1983).

[72] John Sweets, *Choices in Vichy France: The French under Nazi Occupation* (New York, 1986), pp. 118–36.

Marrus

we may know if this is more than an aberration. It is important to trace the shifts in opinion once deportations were under way, and there is no doubt that increased sympathy for the Jews could accompany the growth of opposition to the occupier. Throughout the West, the first months of 1943 marked an important drift toward resistance as the impact of the great German defeat at Stalingrad registered in occupied Europe and as German labor boss Fritz Sauckel intensified his drive to bring foreign workers to the Reich. The conscription of young men for this purpose prompted many to break openly with collaboration. Yet it is unclear whether the universal detestation of what was commonly known as "deportation" to work in German factories was accompanied by a significant wave of public sympathy for the Jews, who were facing a quite different kind of deportation. Paxton and I expressed some doubts in the case of France.[73]

It is certainly true that pockets of pro-Jewish feeling existed practically everywhere and that many thousands took risks to feed, hide, shelter, and provide cover or passage to Jews. In one outstanding case in France, the entire village of Chambon-sur-Lignon, a relatively isolated Protestant commune in the department of the Haute Loire, under the influence of two charismatic pastors, constituted itself as a kind of underground railway to assist hunted Jews and others to escape the Nazi and Vichy police.[74] Recently, the study of rescue activity by threatened populations inside Nazi Europe has become more systematic, with several researchers attempting to identify patterns that explain the presence of altruism amid cruelty, hatred, and indifference.[75] Preliminary results for Holland, where 80 percent of the country's one hundred forty thousand Jews were murdered, suggest that support for Jews was widespread among Dutch Calvinists, in whose tradition is a pronounced philo-Semitism.[76] Yet the Dutch case is instructive in demonstrating the strategic limits for resistance. Holland saw

[73] Marrus and Paxton, *Vichy France and the Jews*, pp. 278–79, 321–22, 352. Serge Klarsfeld apparently disagrees strenuously with us on this point but does not discuss the evidence we presented. See Klarsfeld, *Vichy-Auschwitz*, p. 9.

[74] Philip Hallie, *Lest Innocent Blood Be Shed: The Story of Le Chambon and How Goodness Happened There* (New York, 1979); Pierre Sauvage, "A Most Persistent Haven: Le Chambon-sur-Lignon," *Moment* (October 1983), pp. 30–35. Compare Leonard Gross, *The Last Jews of Berlin* (New York, 1982), for some German case studies.

[75] Samuel P. Olner, "The Need to Recognize the Heroes of the Nazi Era," *Reconstructionist* 48 (June 1982): 7–14. See also Moshe Bejski, "The Righteous among the Nations and Their Part in the Rescue of Jews," in *The Catastrophe of European Jewry: Antecedents—History—Reflections*, ed. Yisrael Gutman and Livia Rothkirchen (Jerusalem, 1976), pp. 582–607; Kazimierz Iranek-Osmecki, *He Who Saves One Life* (New York, 1971); Peter Hellman, *Avenue of the Righteous* (New York, 1980); and the fictionalized account in Thomas Keneally, *Schindler's List* (New York, 1982).

[76] Lawrence Baron, "The Dynamics of Decency: Dutch Rescuers of Jews during the Holocaust" (Frank P. Piskor Faculty Lecture presented at Saint Lawrence University, Canton, N.Y., May 2, 1985). Compare Henry L. Mason, "Testing Human Bonds within Nations: Jews in the Occupied Netherlands," *Political Science Quarterly* 99 (1984): 315–45; and Louis de Jong, "Help to People in Hiding," *Delta: A Review of Arts, Life, and Thought in the Netherlands* 8 (1965): 37–79.

the first public protest against Nazi Jewish policies anywhere—a two-day general strike in Amsterdam in February 1941, originally called by communists after widespread arrests of Jews and riotous outbursts against them by local Nazis. Not only did the Nazis succeed in crushing this demonstration of solidarity, but they also smothered the local resistance in retaliation, setting back its development for two years, and took other measures dramatically worsening the situation of Jews throughout the Netherlands.[77]

Catholic Italy and Protestant Denmark provide the two cases in which Nazi Jewish policy ran into significant obstacles. Interestingly, religious factors do not seem to have been significantly at play. Lutheran theologians in Denmark may well have been in the forefront of opposition to the persecutions in their country, but this was decidedly not the case with their coreligionists in Germany. The Italian people, on the other hand, seem to have exhibited a spontaneous distrust of anti-Semitism without any religious lead and certainly without instruction from the Vatican, which remained notably silent on the specific issue of anti-Jewish persecutions. Much of the explanation of the rescue activity in both countries is best understood in the context of Nazi policy. In Denmark, a country that surrendered to the Germans in 1940 practically without firing a shot, the implementation of the Final Solution coincided with a broad crackdown on the entire Danish nation in the second half of 1943—a time when resistance everywhere was taking heart from the repeated blows delivered against the Reich by the Allied military forces.[78] In Italy, as a recent book by Meir Michaelis argues, anti-Semitism struck a dissonant cultural note from the start because the emancipation of Italian Jewry had been remarkably successful, and the Jews were relatively few and fully integrated. Add to this the Italians' detestation of the Germans, their distrust of Nazi-style racism that only thinly disguised German feelings of superiority, and finally the Italian war weariness in 1942, and one has a good basis to understand the repeated obstruction of persecution and deportations by Italians everywhere in Europe—in Italy, of course, but in Italian-occupied France, Croatia, and Greece as well.[79]

[77] De Jong, "Jews and Non-Jews in Occupied Holland," pp. 145–46; Gerhard Hirschfield, "Collaboration and Attentism in the Netherlands, 1940–41," *Journal of Contemporary History* 16 (1981): 467–86; Fein (n. 45 above), pp. 269–70.

[78] On the Danish rescue, see Leni Yahil, *The Rescue of Danish Jewry: Test of a Democracy,* trans. Morris Gradel (Philadelphia, 1969), "The Uniqueness of the Rescue of Danish Jewry," in Gutman and Zuroff, eds. (n. 35 above), pp. 617–25, and "Methods of Persecution"; Harold Flender, *Rescue in Denmark* (New York, 1963); Hugo Valentin, "Rescue and Relief Activities on Behalf of Jewish Victims of Nazism in Scandinavia," *YIVO Annual of Jewish Social Science* 8 (1953): 224–51. For German policy, see Erich Thomsen, *Deutsche Besatzungspolitik in Dänemark, 1940–1945* (Düsseldorf, 1971).

[79] Meir Michaelis, *Mussolini and the Jews: German-Italian Relations and the Jewish Question in Italy, 1922–1945* (Oxford, 1978), and "The 'Duce' and the Jews: An Assessment of the Literature on Italian Jewry under Fascism (1922–1945)," *Yad Vashem Studies* 11 (1976): 7–32. See also Daniel Carpi, "Il problema ebraico nella politica italiana

Marrus

In eastern and east central Europe, of course, there was much more popular opposition to the Jews, whose steady if uneven acculturation throughout the region did not improve their troubled relations with their non-Jewish neighbors.[80] West of the Soviet Union the interwar period saw an erosion of the slender structures of liberalism and democracy and a rise of the extreme right. The various alternatives that Jews occasionally sought—national autonomy, Zionism, or emigration—all proved impossible. As a result, the arrival of the Wehrmacht in 1939 or after was often seen by the local population as an opportunity to settle a score with the Jews. Yet it is important to note that the Nazis did not count on such opinion in 1939, and, indeed, their attack on Poland seems hardly to have been affected by their animus against the Jews. *Fall Weiss*, as the campaign against Poland was known, curiously omitted Jews from the purposes of the war; there were no elaborate preparations to deal with them in a special way and no careful planning of anti-Jewish policy. If this was indeed a "war against the Jews," it was an odd way to begin. Rather, the Nazis seem to have assumed that their previously determined Jewish policy would remain the rule: it was and remained their object to rid the Reich of the Jews and then to force a European-wide solution once the fighting had ceased and a peace settlement had been determined. Details would be worked out eventually.

Nazi Jewish policy therefore evolved as a part of the wider demographic objectives of the Reich, as Robert Koehl implied in a useful volume pub-

---

fra le due guerre mondiali," *Rivista di studi politici internazionali* 23 (1961): 46–50, "The Rescue of Jews in the Italian Zone of Occupied Croatia," in Gutman and Zuroff, eds. (n. 35 above), pp. 465–525, "Notes on the History of the Jews in Greece during the Holocaust Period: The Attitude of the Italians," in *Festschrift in Honor of Dr. George S. Wise* (Tel Aviv, 1981), pp. 25–62, and "Nuovi documenti per la storia dell'Olocausto in Grecia—l'atteggiamento degli Italiani (1941–1943)," *Michael* (Tel Aviv, 1981), 7:119–200; Renzo De Felice, *Storia degli ebrei italiani sotto il fascismo* (Turin, 1972); Gene Bernardini, "The Origins and Development of Racial Anti-Semitism in Fascist Italy," *Journal of Modern History* 49 (1977): 431–53; Marrus and Paxton, *Vichy France and the Jews* (n. 36 above), pp. 315–21; Michael Ledeen, "The Evolution of Italian Fascist Antisemitism," *Jewish Social Studies* 37 (1975): 3–17. See also the fascinating memoir by Dan Segrè, "My Jewish-Fascist Childhood," *Jerusalem Quarterly* 26 (Winter 1983): 3–21.

[80] Ezra Mendelsohn, *The Jews of East Central Europe between the World Wars* (Bloomington, Ind., 1983) provides an excellent survey. See also Stanislav Andreski, "An Economic Interpretation of Antisemitism in Eastern Europe," *Jewish Journal of Sociology* 5 (1963): 201–13; Hugh Seton-Watson, "Government Policies towards the Jews in Pre-Communist Eastern Europe," *Soviet Jewish Affairs*, no. 4 (December 1969), pp. 20–25; and Yeshayahu Jelinek, "The Holocaust and the Internal Policies of the Nazi Satellites in Eastern Europe: A Comparative Study," *Proceedings of the Eighth World Congress of Jewish Studies, Division B* (Jerusalem, 1982), pp. 173–77. On Poland, see Celia S. Heller, *On the Edge of Destruction: Jews of Poland between the Two World Wars* (New York, 1977); Pawel Korzec, *Juifs en Pologne: La question juive pendant l'entre-deux-guerres* (Paris, 1980); and Edward Wynot, " 'A Cruel Necessity': The Emergence of Official Antisemitism in Poland, 1936–39," *American Historical Review* 76 (1971): 1035–58.

lished thirty years ago. In his study of the *Reichskommissariat für die Festigung deutschen Volkstums*, a gigantic bureaucracy set up under Himmler's auspices in 1939, Koehl described the Nazis' vast transfers of people throughout the region—moving ethnic Germans westward to settle newly incorporated parts of Germany and moving Poles, Jews, and other "undesirables" eastward, hoping eventually to achieve the racial reordering of the entire region.[81] The ghettoization of the Jews, a terrible process of upheaval and incarceration in the East, was a preliminary step taken to facilitate some ultimate dispatch of the Jews to their final destination. According to Hilberg, it cost the Jews a half million deaths in Poland, mainly through starvation, disease, and exposure.[82]

Polish-Jewish relations during the war were severely affected by the anti-Semitic climate of the time, the legacy of which persists to our own day. To a large degree, Polish and Jewish historians still conduct a *dialogue des sourdes* over the issue, with the former often denying any significant opposition to Jews among ordinary Poles. Jewish scholars tend to be more modulated in their judgment. Writing for the secret archives of Warsaw assembled in the ghetto before its liquidation and known by its code name *Oneg Shabbat*, the historian Emmanuel Ringelblum attempted to be objective, a remarkable exercise under the circumstances: "The attitude of the Polish population toward the Jews has not been uniform: the Polish Fascist camp has an entirely different attitude from that of the workers." Ringelblum claimed that at least ten thousand to fifteen thousand Polish families in Warsaw alone were helping to hide Jews—taking enormous risks in the process. Yet he felt that the helpers faced powerful Polish opposition. "Polish Fascism and its ally antisemitism," he felt, "have conquered the majority of the Polish people," making it even more dangerous for those

[81] Robert Koehl, *RKFDV: German Resettlement and Population Policy, 1939–1945: A History of the Reich Commissariat for the Strengthening of Germandom* (Cambridge, Mass., 1957), pp. 33, 250–51, and passim; Martin Broszat, *Nationalsozialistische Polenpolitik* (Frankfurt am Main, 1965); and Helmut Heiber, "Die Generalplan Ost," *Vierteljahrshefte für Zeitgeschichte* 6 (1958): 281–325. This is also the argument in Marrus, *The Unwanted* (n. 35 above), pp. 219–33.

[82] Hilberg, *Destruction of the European Jews* (n. 6 above), 3:1212. On one important ghetto, see the remarkable compilation of material in Lucjan Dobroszycki, ed., *The Chronicle of the Lodz Ghetto, 1941–1944*, trans. Richard Lourie et al. (New Haven, Conn. 1984). Leonard Tushnet, *The Uses of Adversity* (New York, 1966), draws on doctors' accounts of starvation in the Warsaw Ghetto. Classic diaries from Warsaw are *Notes from the Warsaw Ghetto: The Journal of Emmanuel Ringelblum*, ed. and trans. Jacob Sloan (New York, 1974); *The Warsaw Diary of Chaim A. Kaplan*, ed. and trans. Abraham I. Katsh (New York, 1973); Janusz Korczak, *Ghetto Diary* (New York, 1978); and Alexander Donat [pseud.], *The Holocaust Kingdom: A Memoir* (New York, 1978); but the genre is much too extensive to be discussed here. Among the most recent accounts are Joachim Schoenfeld, *Holocaust Memoirs: Jews in the Lwów Ghetto, the Janowski Concentration Camp, and as Deportees in Siberia* (Hoboken, N.J., 1985); and Janina Bauman, *Winter in the Morning: A Young Girl's Life in the Warsaw Ghetto and Beyond, 1939–1945* (New York, 1986).

Marrus

Poles who did attempt to rescue Jews.[83] There is ample indication of extensive aid provided to Jews by Poles on an individual level. And there is no question about the important help that the Polish Home Army, the *Armia Krajowa,* provided the Jews in transmitting to the West the news about massacres of Jews in Poland.[84] But there also seems little doubt that those who helped Jews swam against a powerful anti-Semitic current in the Polish population—generated by Nazism to some degree, of course, but also moved by long-standing Polish traditions. In her recent study of rescue of Polish Jews by non-Jews, Nechama Tec stresses the climate of hostility toward Jews among the Poles that compounded the dangers for those attempting to help. Interviewing rescuers many years later, she claims to have detected anti-Jewish stereotypes even among this group that had shown itself so favorable to Jews.[85]

In a new study of Poland under Nazi occupation, Richard Lukas forcefully argues the Polish case. At the center of his book is an account of the terrible trials faced by all Poles under German domination. But his work seems heavily preoccupied by the Jews. He contends—in my view unconvincingly—that Poles did not receive anti-Semitism sympathetically, were not generally hostile to Jews, and did their best to help them.[86] More usefully, he charts reasons other than anti-Semitism that help explain why Jewish and Polish interests were so divergent. Poles and Jews were cut off from one another with the Nazis' ghettoization program. Poles, he argues, believed that their situation was far worse than that of the Jews, that the latter were craven in their response to the Germans, and that they were pro-Russian or pro-Soviet. The Polish Home Army had understandable, if exaggerated, fears of communist influence within the Jewish resis-

[83] Emmanuel Ringelblum, *Polish-Jewish Relations during the Second World War,* ed. Joseph Kermish and Shmuel Krakowski, trans. Dafna Allon, Danuta Dabrowska, and Dana Deren (New York, 1976), pp. 246–47. On Ringelblum, see the introduction to this volume by Joseph Kermish.

[84] There is, however, substantial disagreement about whether the Poles conveyed this information as rapidly and as completely as they could. On this point see Walter Laqueur, *The Terrible Secret: An Investigation into the Suppression of Information about Hitler's 'Final Solution'* (London, 1980), pp. 106–7. See also the pertinent remarks by one of the Home Army emissaries to London (Jan Nowak, *Courier from Warsaw* [Detroit, 1982], pp. 274–76), who stresses the unwillingness of the Jews and non-Jews to believe the horrific messages from Poland. Compare Aviva Ravel, *Faithful unto Death: The Story of Arthur Zygielbaum* (Montreal, 1980), the biography of one of two wartime Jewish representatives on the Polish National Council in London.

[85] Nechama Tec, *When Light Pierced the Darkness: Christian Rescue of Jews in Nazi-occupied Poland* (New York, 1986), p. 59 and passim. See also the incriminating evidence in David Engel, "An Early Account of Polish Jewry under Nazi and Soviet Occupation Presented to the Polish Government-in-Exile, February 1940," *Jewish Social Studies* 45 (1983): 1–16, based on an assessment of Polish anti-Semitism by Jan Karski.

[86] Richard Lukas, *The Forgotten Holocaust: The Poles under German Occupation, 1939–1944* (Lexington, Ky., 1986) esp. chaps. 5 and 6. Compare the more balanced if more narrowly gauged study by Jan Tomasz Gross, *Polish Society under German Occupation: The Generalgouvernement, 1939–1944* (Princeton, N.J., 1979).

tance in Warsaw, and it had a completely different strategic objective from that of the Jews. On the one hand, the Home Army saw its task as the preservation of the Polish nation against Nazi depredations and the preparation for liberation under the most propitious circumstances; one of its important concerns, therefore, was to prevent "premature" uprisings that would cost the population dearly and would weaken resistance forces unnecessarily. The Jewish underground, on the other hand, increasingly realized that the Jews would not survive the war and finally decided to lash out at their tormentors, even at the cost of what remained of their communities. Despite their strategic differences, according to this view, the Home Army undertook diversionary attacks to help the Jewish fighters.

This kind of assessment has been strongly disputed by Yisrael Gutman, a participant in the ghetto uprising and the author of a solid monograph on the subject. There was much that the Poles could have done during the massive deportations of the summer of 1942, Gutman argues—from sabotaging the railway lines to Treblinka to supplying the ghetto with arms and equipment. In the course of those *Aktionen,* the great majority of Warsaw's Jews were taken from the city to be murdered. Gutman challenges the veracity of Home Army commander Tadeuz (Bor) Komorowski, who claimed the Poles were willing to help the Jews during that period.[87] Once the uprising began in 1943, the Jews received support from the communist resistance, the *Armia Ludowa,* and were brutally opposed by the Polish right. As for the Home Army, two attacks did take place in an effort to demonstrate solidarity with the Jewish fighters, but there was no serious military commitment to these efforts. And, in Gutman's view, Polish opinion "was permeated with deep-seated prejudice that surpassed even the sentiments of the various forces in the underground."[88]

Controversy of a quite different sort flares over the fate of the Jews of Hungary, discussed in Randolph Braham's massive two-volume work, which appeared in 1979. The Hungarian case is particularly dramatic because so many Jews survived for so long and because the final result was so catastrophic. Hungarian authorities counted some eight hundred twenty-five

[87] Yisrael Gutman, *The Jews of Warsaw, 1939–1943: Ghetto, Underground, Revolt,* trans. Ina Friedman (Bloomington, Ind., 1982), pp. 254–55, and "Polish Responses to the Liquidation of Polish Jewry," *Jerusalem Quarterly* 17 (Fall 1980): 40–55. See also the account of the Polish-Jewish Communist historian Ber Mark, *Uprising in the Warsaw Ghetto,* trans. Gershon Freidlin (New York, 1975), which refers to support for the Jews from "Polish democratic circles."

[88] Gutman, *Jews of Warsaw,* p. 414. Further evidence that reactions to the Holocaust involved serious differences within Polish opinion comes from Shmuel Krakowski, "Holocaust in the Polish Underground Press," *Yad Vashem Studies* 16 (1984): 241–70. Krakowski concludes that the split was largely along party lines and followed prewar divisions. See also Abraham Brumberg, "What Poland Forgot," *New Republic* (December 16, 1985), pp. 46–48; and Timothy Garton Ash, "The Life of Death," *New York Review of Books* (December 19, 1985), pp. 26–39, for some knowledgeable assessments written in response to the controversy on this issue raised by Claude Lanzmann's film *Shoah.*

thousand persons as Jews in 1941, including therein many who were in fact non-Jews. More than four hundred seventy thousand were deported, mainly to Auschwitz, beginning in the spring of 1944. Others were murdered on the spot, or sent elsewhere on transports or on forced marches, for a total mortality of over six hundred thousand.[89] Up to the last year of the war, Hungarian Jewry lived a tenuous existence, persecuted by the governments serving under the head of state Admiral Miklós Horthy but protected from repeated German requests for their deportation. Hungarian troops participated in massacres of Jews—notably at Novi Sad (Ujvidék) in January 1942, and possibly at Kamenets Podolsk in August 1941—and Jewish males suffered grievously in specially defined forced labor batallions that were responsible for tens of thousands of deaths.[90] But it seemed that the bulk of Hungarian Jewry might survive. Then, on March 19, 1944, the Germans swept into the country, fearing that the Hungarians were about to break away from the Axis and eager to implement the Final Solution in a previously untouched country heavily populated with Jews. While Horthy retained his position, a pro-German government led by General Dome Stójay was set in place, and a new round of persecutions began. In May, convoys of Jews started to roll toward Auschwitz, where the ovens incinerated as many as twelve thousand persons per day. After almost two months of this pitiless operation, punctuated by protests from around the world, Admiral Horthy finally suspended the deportations in July. For Horthy and his associates the end came a few months later, on October 15, when the Germans arrested the regent and helped set up a pro-Nazi government headed by Ferenc Szálasi and his Arrow Cross fanatics. The result was mayhem, more slaughter of Jews, and further deportations—many of them now on foot, to Mauthausen. The Soviets put an end to this grotesque regime with the advance of the Red Army in early 1945. The Russians captured Budapest in February and drove the last Germans out of the country a few weeks later.

Braham credits the government of Miklos Kállay, prime minister from March 1942 until the German occupation in 1944, with having prevented the imposition of the Final Solution in Hungary for two years through a policy of fence-sitting, verbal support of the Nazis, and a nominal anti-Jewish program. What collapsed this house of cards, in his view, was the provocative diplomatic effort to disengage the Hungarians from the German alliance in 1944.[91] Sympathetic though he may be to the government of

[89] Randolph Braham, *The Politics of Genocide: The Holocaust in Hungary*, 2 vols. (New York, 1981), 1:77; 2:1143–47. See also Mario D. Fenyo, *Hitler, Horthy, and Hungary* (New Haven, Conn., 1972), chap. 10; Andrew Handler, ed. and trans., *The Holocaust in Hungary: An Anthology of Jewish Response* (University, Ala., 1982).

[90] Braham, *The Politics of Genocide*, 1:199–215, *The Hungarian Labor Service System, 1939–1945* (New York, 1977); and Fenyo, pp. 69–70.

[91] Braham, *The Politics of Genocide*, 1:225–26, 229, and "The Jewish Question in German-Hungarian Relations during the Kallay Era," *Jewish Social Studies* 39 (1977):

History of the Holocaust

Kállay, however, Braham judges Horthy's role harshly, seeing the regent as preferring a Nazi takeover to a possible Russian invasion. With Germans swarming through his country, including Eichmann's two-hundred man commando, Horthy refused to abdicate, lent legitimacy to a viciously anti-Semitic regime, and helped thereby to mesh the Hungarian police and administration with the Final Solution. Braham extensively documents official Hungarian involvement in the deportations and massacres of 1944–both before and after the toppling of Horthy. He supports the postwar testimony of German officials, such as the Reich Plenipotentiary Edmund Veesenmayer, that the Hungarians bore a heavy responsibility for what followed. "The record clearly shows that the German demands could have been refused or sabotaged—they were in Bulgaria and Rumania as well as in the case of the Budapest Jews in July 1944—had Horthy and the Hungarian authorities really been concerned with their citizens of the Jewish faith. The Germans would have been quite helpless—as the post-July 1944 events demonstrated—without the wholehearted and effective cooperation of the Hungarian authorities."[92]

Even more controversial has been the debate about the role in these events of the organized Jewish community leadership. Ordered by the Nazis to form a Jewish council, or *Judenrat*, on the very day of the German invasion, the Jewish leaders in Budapest attempted throughout these horrors to negotiate with their German and Hungarian tormentors. In the view of many, Jewish leaders were seduced by this process, which included the possibility that some of their own number and their relatives would emerge

---

183–208. See the excellent review essay on Braham's work by Istvan Deak, "Could the Hungarian Jews Have Survived?" *New York Review of Books* (February 4, 1982), pp. 24–27, and the polemic "Genocide in Hungary: An Exchange," ibid. (May 27, 1982), pp. 54–55.

[92] Braham, *Politics of Genocide,* 1:374. Compare Zvi Erez, "The Jews of Budapest and the Plans of Admiral Horthy—August–October 1944," *Yad Vashem Studies* 16 (1984): 177–203. We lack an up-to-date survey of the Holocaust in Romania. See Martin Broszat, "Das dritte Reich und die Rumänische Judenpolitik," in *Gutachten des Instituts für Zeitgeschichte* (Munich, 1958), pp. 102–83; Stephen Fischer-Galati, "Fascism, Communism, and the Jewish Question in Rumania," in *Jews and Non-Jews in Eastern Europe,* ed. Bela Vago and George L. Mosse (New York, 1974); Nicholas M. Nagy-Talavera, *The Green Shirts and the Others: A History of Fascism in Hungary and Rumania* (Stanford, Calif., 1970); Jean Ancel, "Plans for Deportation of the Rumanian Jews and Their Discontinuation in the Light of Documentary Evidence (July–October 1942)," *Yad Vashem Studies* 16 (1984): 381–420. On Bulgaria there is an excellent survey by Frederick B. Chary, *The Bulgarian Jews and the Final Solution, 1940–1944* (Pittsburgh, 1972). Chary notes that there were more Jews living in Bulgaria after the war than before. Neither fascist nor anti-Semitic, the Bulgarians, on the one hand, managed to take advantage of their position as an ally of the Reich to prevent the deportation of their country's forty thousand Jews. On the other hand, Bulgarians facilitated the deportation of some eleven thousand foreign Jews from territories newly absorbed into Bulgaria—mainly Macedonia and Thrace. See also Nissan Oren, "The Bulgarian Exception: A Reassessment of the Salvation of the Jewish Community," *Yad Vashem Studies* 7 (1968): 83–106; and Vicki Tamir, *Bulgaria and Her Jews: The History of a Dubious Symbiosis* (New York, 1979).

Marrus

unscathed from the ordeal. The Jewish council slipped into its intended role of facilitating the gigantic bureaucratic and administrative operation required to deport hundreds of thousands of people. According to Hilberg, who is consistently critical of the Jewish leadership, council members were timid, hesitant, and failed to act. Only at the last moment did they even venture an appeal to Admiral Horthy. And according to Rudolf Vrba—a Slovak Jew who escaped from Auschwitz together with a comrade in April 1944, hoping to warn the Hungarian Jews—the council kept the dreadful facts of the death camp hidden from the Jewish masses. Hungarian Jewish leaders, he still feels, should have cried from the rooftops that the deportees were doomed; many would have perished if the leaders had undertaken such resistance, but the "resettlements" of Jews could never have proceeded as they did, destroying as many as twelve thousand a day in an orderly fashion. Instead, Vrba and others charge, the leaders continued to pursue their negotiations, maintained silence about Auschwitz, and worried about a breakdown of order within the ravaged Jewish community.[93]

Against these arguments others have responded more sympathetically to the Jewish leadership, noting that contemporary perceptions differed radically from those of the postwar era. Yehuda Bauer insists that information about Auschwitz hardly depended on a handful of Jewish leaders and that stories about mass killings were already widespread in Hungary by 1944. The great problem, in Hungary as elsewhere, was whether or not such stories would be *believed*. Beyond this, one can express serious doubts that much would in fact have changed in Hungary even if a few leaders had shouted from the rooftops.[94] There is no space here to discuss the substance of the Jewish negotiations with the Nazis—which were, in

[93] Hilberg, *Destruction of the European Jews* (n. 6 above), 2:842–47; Rudolf Vrba and Alan Bestic, *I Cannot Forgive* (New York, 1964); and Rudolf Vrba, "Footnote to Auschwitz Report," *Jewish Currents* (March 1966), pp. 22–28. See some recent amplifications of his views by Vrba in Martin Gilbert, *Auschwitz and the Allies* (New York, 1981), pp. 204–5. See also John Conway, "Frühe Augenzeugenberichte aus Auschwitz: Glaubwürdigkeit und Wirkungsgeschichte," *Vierteljahrshefte für Zeitgeschichte* 27 (1979): 260–84, and "Der Holocaust in Ungarn: Neue Kontroversen und Überlegungen," ibid., 32 (1984): 179–212, which follow Vrba's account closely, discussing important documentation. Compare the fictionalized account in Amos Elon, *Timetable* (Garden City, N.Y., 1980).

[94] Yehuda Bauer, *The Holocaust in Historical Perspective* (Seattle, 1978), p. 106. Compare his *The Jewish Emergence from Powerlessness* (Toronto, 1979), pp. 7–25, and "Jewish Foreign Policy during the Holocaust," *Midstream* 30 (December 1984): 22–25. Braham cites some important testimony that reinforces Bauer's view in *The Politics of Genocide*, 2:973. On "information" about the Holocaust and the failure to believe, see Bauer, "When Did They Know?" *Midstream* 14 (April 1968): 51–58. Compare Walter Laqueur, *Terrible Secret* (n. 84 above), "Hitler's Holocaust: Who Knew What, When, and How?" *Encounter* 55 (July 1980): 6–25, and "Jewish Denial and the Holocaust," *Commentary* 70 (December 1979): 44–55. On the American scene, see Alex Grobman, "What Did They Know? The American Jewish Press and the Holocaust," *American Jewish History* 68 (1979): 327–52; and Deborah Lipstadt's aptly titled *Beyond Belief: The American Press and the Coming of the Holocaust, 1933–1945* (New York, 1986).

retrospect, pathetic efforts to snatch Jews from the ovens of Auschwitz as the Third Reich was beginning its death agony. Yet it should be mentioned that, however pathetic, these efforts seemed sensible to some reasonable men caught in a desperate situation. Braham calls to mind the fog within which Hungarian Jewish leaders, like those of other countries, moved at the time. They did not, or would not, or could not, see clearly. But whatever they did, he implies, the machinery could not be stopped after the Germans arrived in force. "Their false optimism was based on the continued survival of the Hungarian Jewish community in the midst of the cataclysm that was engulfing the neighboring Jewish communities. When coupled with their inability to accept the worst, the result was ultimately a disaster. Although many of them continued to nurture the illusions of the past, many others awoke to the reality after the German occupation. But by that time it was too late: the fate of Hungarian Jewry had been sealed."[95]

This controversy over the role of the Hungarian Jewish council is part of a much wider dispute on the activity of Jewish leaders everywhere, both within and without occupied Europe, which one can trace to the Eichmann Trial in Jerusalem in 1961, when the Jewish response to Nazi persecutions had some part in the public proceedings and even more in the polemics that followed. Only European responses will concern us here. Writing about the trial for the *New Yorker,* the political philosopher Hannah Arendt made some startling claims about Jewish leaders that perhaps seem even more breathtaking in retrospect than they did at the time. "Wherever Jews lived," she claimed, "there were recognized Jewish leaders, and this leadership, almost without exception, cooperated with the Nazis." Whether in Amsterdam or in Warsaw, the Nazis counted on Jews to enumerate their fellow Jews, keep order in their communities, and assist in the confiscation of their property. In the end they provided the crucial administrative support the Nazis needed for their Final Solution. In Arendt's view, it must be said, this cooperation was not some special Jewish predilection—quite the reverse. It was rather, she contended, part of the "moral collapse the Nazis caused in respectable European society—not only in Germany but in almost all countries, not only among the persecutors but also among the victims." The Jewish failure in this respect was part of the ominous drift of Western society she had noted not long before in *The Origins of Totalitarianism.*[96] Notwithstanding this caveat, Arendt's book, *Eichmann in Jerusalem,* drew a firestorm of criticism from Jewish writers. And as the polemic unfolded, it became apparent how thin was the factual base on which she had made her judgments.[97]

[95] Braham, *The Politics of Genocide,* 2:724.

[96] Hannah Arendt, *Eichmann in Jerusalem: A Report on the Banality of Evil,* rev. ed. (New York, 1965), pp. 118–25, and *The Origins of Totalitarianism* (New York, 1973).

[97] Among the many critical works of *Eichmann in Jerusalem*, see esp. Jacob Robinson, *And the Crooked Shall Be Made Straight: The Eichmann Trial, the Jewish Catastrophe, and Hannah Arendt's Narrative* (New York, 1965), written by an assistant to Eichmann's

Marrus

Discussion moved to an entirely different plane ten years later, however, with the appearance of Isaiah Trunk's massive study of the Jewish councils set up by the Nazis in the ghettos of occupied Poland and the Baltic countries. Trunk's work was a painstakingly researched account, anchored in extensive archival sources, embracing every aspect of the activities of these *Judenräte*. Unlike Arendt, who was quick to generalize, Trunk overwhelmed the reader with detail, showing how many different paths were taken by Jewish leaders. At the very least, one must conclude that there were a variety of Jewish responses. Beyond this, Trunk emphasized that the Jews were *forced* to establish the councils, that individuals were *forced* to serve in them, and that the councils were *forced* to provide services for the Germans. While in retrospect it seems plain that the *Judenräte* did assist the Nazis, at the time most Jews felt they had no choice. Illustrating the difficulty of generalizing beyond a few basic issues, Trunk discussed the councils thematically, considering such issues as their organization, personnel, finance, public welfare, medical facilities, police, religion, and so forth. Seen this way, it became apparent that Berlin set few guidelines for the *Judenräte* and that, consequently, their circumstances differed enormously. "Utter lawlessness and virtual anarchy prevailed in the territories under German occupation during World War II."[98] This is the apt first sentence of Trunk's *Judenrat*, the constant backdrop of which is the terror, degradation, and spoliation that the Nazis wrought in eastern Europe. Trunk noted that some councils supported resistance activities—some violent, and some not—and that others opposed them; some ran corrupt and class-ridden ghettos, and others strove for equality. One might, of course, still make harsh judgments on the basis of this evidence; interestingly, Trunk's survey of the attitudes of survivors suggested that, with the passage of time, their own evaluations of the Jewish councils were increasingly positive.[99]

While aware of a wide variation in the responses of the Jewish leadership, Hilberg remains set in the idea that the *Judenräte* simply reflected, on an institutional level, the Jews' ingrained disposition to comply with their persecutors. Such, he claimed, was their two-thousand-year-old tradition.[100] However, this view seems increasingly difficult to sustain in view

---

prosecutor, Gideon Hausner; Friedrich A. Krumacher, ed., *Die Kontroverse Arendt, Eichmann, und die Juden* (Munich, 1964); Lionel Abel, "Aesthetics of Evil: Hannah Arendt on Eichmann and the Jews," *Partisan Review* 30 (Summer 1963): 211–30; Oscar Handlin, "Jewish Resistance to the Nazis," *Commentary* 34 (1962): 398–405; and Maurice Friedberg, "The Question of the Judenräte," *Commentary* 41 (July 1973): 61–63.

98 Isaiah Trunk, *Judenrat: The Jewish Councils in Eastern Europe under Nazi Occupation* (New York, 1972), p. 1. See also the collection of Trunk's essays, *Jewish Responses to Nazi Persecution: Collective and Individual Behavior in Extremis* (New York, 1982). Trunk's earlier work in Yiddish, as yet untranslated, is *Lodzher geto* (New York, 1962).

99 Trunk, *Judenrat*, app. 1.

100 Hilberg, *Destruction of the European Jews*, 3:1030–44, and "The Judenrat: Conscious or Unconscious 'Tool'?" in *Patterns of Jewish Leadership in Nazi Europe, 1933–1945: Proceedings of the Third Yad Vashem International Historical Conference, Jeru-*

History of the Holocaust

of accumulating evidence to the contrary, much of it compiled by Israeli scholars. Significantly, these historians have utilized Jewish sources instead of relying on German materials that tended to portray Jews according to their Nazi stereotype—cringing, acquiescent, and easily manipulated by crude appeals to individual self-interest. Working on the ghettos of Eastern Galicia, Aharon Weiss established that there was a spectrum of behavior from automatic compliance through suicide and resistance; he also reminds us how important it is to see phases of *Judenrat* activity, with a second tier of leaders having drastically less margin for maneuver than the first.[101] In Belorussia, an interesting case is the ghetto of Minsk, the fourth largest in Europe (after Warsaw, Lodz, and Lvov), where the head of the *Judenrat* Ilia Mishkin helped coordinate resistance activity.[102] Yitzhak Arad's study of the ghetto of Vilna, as well as work on Lodz and its Jewish dictator Chaim Rumkowski, enable us to see the rationale behind the "work to live strategy" in which ghetto leaders undertook to rescue the inmates by demonstrating their economic utility. While this stratagem seems utterly fanciful from our vantage point, it is important to envisage a quite different situation in which it was not. Yehuda Bauer points to a growing body of literature that suggests that such economic considerations were vitally important to the Germans, particularly as the war progressed. Under some circumstances, then, the Jews who took this desperate gamble reasoned correctly.[103] In the light of such work, Arendt's generalizations, and one must also say those of Hilberg, appear increasingly dated.

---

salem, April 4–7, 1977, ed. Yisrael Gutman and Cynthia J. Haft (Jerusalem, 1979), pp. 45–58, and "The Ghetto as a Form of Government: An Analysis of Isaiah Trunk's *Judenrat,*" in *The Holocaust as a Historical Experience,* ed. Yehuda Bauer and Nathan Rotenstreich (New York, 1981), pp. 155–71. Hilberg draws extensively on the important diary of the chairman of the Warsaw Ghetto *Judenrat,* Adam Czerniakow. See *The Warsaw Diary of Adam Czerniakow: Prelude to Doom,* ed. Raul Hilberg, Stanislaw Staron, and Josef Kermisz, trans. Stanislaw Staron et al. (New York, 1979). After heading the council for almost three years, Czerniakow killed himself on July 23, 1942, on the eve of a massive deportation of Jews from the ghetto to the Treblinka death camp.

[101] Aharon Weiss, "Jewish Leadership in Occupied Poland—Postures and Attitudes," *Yad Vashem Studies* 12 (1977): 335–65.

[102] Yehuda Bauer, *A History of the Holocaust* (New York, 1982), pp. 166–67; Shalom Cholawsky, "The Judenrat in Minsk," in Gutman and Haft, eds., pp. 113–32. Compare Erich Goldhagen, "The Mind and Spirit of East European Jewry during the Holocaust," *Midstream* 26 (March 1980): 10–14.

[103] See the articles by Yosef Kirmisz, Yitzhak Arad, Dov Levin, Yisrael Gutman, and Aharon Weiss in Gutman and Haft, eds.; Yitzhak Arad, *Ghetto in Flames: The Struggle and Destruction of the Jews in Vilna in the Holocaust* (Jerusalem, 1980); Lucjan Dobroszycki, "Jewish Elites under German Rule," in *The Holocaust: Ideology, Bureaucracy, and Genocide: The San José Papers,* ed. Henry Friedlander and Sybil Milton (Millwood, N.Y., 1980), pp. 221–30, and *Chronicle of the Lodz Ghetto* (n. 82 above); Shmuel Huppert, "King of the Ghetto—Mordechai Haim Rumkowski, the Elder of the Lodz Ghetto," *Yad Vashem Studies* 15 (1983): 125–57; Leonard Tushnet, *The Pavement of Hell* (New York, 1972); and Yehuda Bauer, "Jewish Leadership Reactions to Nazi Policies," in Bauer and Rotenstreich, eds., p. 180. On Rumkowski, see the fictionalized account by Leslie Epstein, *King of the Jews: A Novel of the Holocaust* (New York, 1979). But cf. some critical reactions in Huppert, pp. 125–27.

Marrus

In a similar vein, there has been significant revision of the "automatic compliance" view of the Jewish councils of central and western Europe. Kulka's writing on the *Reichsvereinigung der Juden in Deutschland* points in this direction, drawing on the archives of this umbrella organization for German Jews.[104] Sensitive to how careful one must be in evaluating the sources concerning *Judenrat* activity, Livia Rothkirchen refers to "the endless web of deception" enveloping the documents that historians use. For obvious reasons neither Jews nor Germans said what they meant in their correspondence with the other and even, sometimes, in their correspondence among themselves. In the case of Slovakia, which she has studied closely, the "Jewish Center" performed a "dual role," helping the implementation of the Final Solution on the one hand and attempting to safeguard Jewish interests on the other.[105] This pattern is common elsewhere. Writing on the Netherlands, where deportations devastated the Jewish population of one hundred forty thousand, carrying away 80 percent of their number, Joseph Michman raises the vital question, Was there any possibility for a different policy? His answer is extremely cautious, as is his assessment of the responsibility of Jewish leaders for what ultimately happened. To put the matter into perspective, Michman accents the extensive help the Germans received from the Dutch authorities "at all levels, from registration of the Jews to their removal to transit camps in trains guarded by Dutch policemen."[106] Seen in this light, the Jewish administration and its leaders appear more naive than criminal, more seduced than enticed into collaboration, and far down the chain of responsibility.

Studying the French equivalent, the Union Générale des Israélites de France (UGIF), Richard Cohen reaches similar conclusions.[107] The UGIF, it should be noted, never operated in a ghetto situation and was never responsible for preparing deportation lists. It did, however, coordinate a range of social services for the Jewish community, and it kept track of the whereabouts of many Jews; thus it helped facilitate the rounding up of Jews when the Final Solution in the West began in the summer of 1942. Some writers have charged the UGIF with flagrant negligence or even worse. "The Jews," writes Cynthia Haft, "showed themselves to be obe-

[104] Otto Dov Kulka, "The 'Reichsvereinigung of the Jews of Germany' (1938/9–1943)," in Gutman and Haft, eds., pp. 45–58. Compare Abraham Margaliot, "The Dispute over the Leadership of German Jewry, 1933–1938," *Yad Vashem Studies* 10 (1974): 129–48.

[105] Livia Rothkirchen, "The Dual Role of the 'Jewish Center' in Slovakia," in Gutman and Haft, eds., pp. 219–27.

[106] Joseph Michman, "The Controversy Surrounding the Jewish Council of Amsterdam," in Gutman and Haft, eds., pp. 255, 257.

[107] Yerachmiel (Richard) Cohen, "French Jewry's Dilemma on the Orientation of Its Leadership: From Polemics to Conciliation: 1942–1944," *Yad Vashem Studies* 14 (1981): 167–204, and "The Jewish Community of France in the Face of Vichy-German Persecution, 1940–1944," in *The Jews in Modern France,* ed. Frances Malino and Bernard Wasserstein (Hanover, N.H., 1985), pp. 180–203. Compare Leni Yahil, "The Jewish Leadership of France," in Gutman and Haft, eds., pp. 317–33.

History of the Holocaust

dient, unimaginative, and ingenuous."[108] But in editing the remarkable wartime diary of Raymond Raoul Lambert, arguably the most important French Jewish official in contact with the Vichy government and the Germans, Cohen has brought to public light a Jew who seems neither obedient, nor unimaginative, nor ingenuous.[109] He may indeed have been wrong to work with the French or German authorities, trying through official channels to ease the lot of indigent Jews or attempting to snatch individual Jews from camps or deportation trains; but he certainly had good reason for believing that he was right. Lambert, who was himself murdered in Auschwitz in 1943, was a complex personality, a highly assimilated Frenchman enamored throughout the occupation of the writings of Maurice Barrès. The evidence suggests that Lambert, like so many leaders of the Jewish councils, became involved in clandestine efforts to ease the lot of Jews and even in resistance activity—at the same time he was working through official channels. Like many other Jewish leaders, facing tremendous strain and moral pressure, he seems to have fallen victim to the tempting and self-serving illusion that he was indispensable to his Jewish charges. In retrospect, his actions are best understood in the light of a long history of assimilation, a tradition of paternalistic Jewish community leadership, the profound demoralization of French Jewry, and the extraordinarily difficult objective situation that he faced.

Reference to resistance by members of *Judenräte* brings us to one of the difficult questions faced by historians of the Jewish response to the Holocaust—the matter of defining "Jewish resistance." Definitions have ranged widely, from that of Hilberg, who seems to consider armed struggle as the only form coming under that rubric, to that of Bauer, who judges "keeping body and soul together" under circumstances of unimaginable privation and persecution to be a form of resistance.[110] As so often in our discipline, the definitions increasingly matter less than the information and explanations that historians bring to bear. And on this point we now have a substantial body of literature indicating a rich array of Jewish opposition to the Nazis.[111]

[108] Cynthia J. Haft, *The Bargain and the Bridle: The General Union of the Israelites of France* (Chicago, 1983), p. 38. Maurice Rajfus, *Des juifs dans la collaboration: L'UGIF (1941–1944)* (Paris, 1980), takes an even harsher line.

[109] Raymond Raoul Lambert, *Carnet d'un témoin, 1940–1943*, ed. Richard Cohen (Paris, 1985); and Richard Cohen, "A Jewish Leader in Vichy France, 1940–1943: The Diary of Raymond Raoul Lambert," *Jewish Social Studies* 43 (1981): 291–310.

[110] Yehuda Bauer, *They Chose Life: Jewish Resistance in the Holocaust* (New York, 1973), p. 33. Bauer formulates a definition as follows: "Any *group* action consciously taken in opposition to known or surmised laws, actions or intentions directed against the Jews by the Germans and their supporters" (emphasis in original; Bauer, *The Jewish Emergence from Powerlessness* [n. 94 above], p. 27). Compare Lionel Kochan, "Resistance—a Constant in Jewish Life," *Midstream* 22 (August–September 1976): 63–68; and Emil Fackenheim, "The Spectrum of Resistance during the Holocaust: An Essay in Description and Definition," *Modern Judaism* 2 (1982): 113–30.

[111] See Henri Michel, "Jewish Resistance and the European Resistance Movement," *Yad Vashem Studies* 7 (1968): 7–16; and Konrad Kweit, "Problems of Jewish Resistance Historiography," *Leo Baeck Institute Year Book* 24 (1979): 37–57.

Marrus

Conditions in the concentration and death camps, where a handful of revolts did occur, provide the most extreme illustration of how difficult it is to compare Jewish with non-Jewish resistance in occupied Europe.[112] In the camps the Jews were weakened by exhaustion, starvation, and disease and crushed by the most complete totalitarian structure devised by man. Help from the outside was nonexistent, and the Jews were utterly alone. The Nazis' most savage deterrent against opposition—called "collective responsibility"—was virtually unrestrained in the camps: not only were those responsible punished for any detected opposition, but usually all the others as well. In such circumstances, resistance was an immediate and mortal threat to every Jewish inmate. Opposition, therefore, was seemingly impossible. Yet even so, sabotage and individual attempts to escape were not uncommon. And in a few cases there were even substantial violent clashes. (In related circumstances, where hundreds of thousands of Soviet prisoners of war—mainly young men with military training—were being killed, we have no indication of collective uprisings, armed or unarmed.) Almost always the rebels had no chance, accounting for the frequent hesitation and delay of inmate strategists. Timing was crucial. A quite sophisticated resistance network existed in the Płaszów concentration camp, for example, but in the end its members failed to revolt. An uprising of the inmates in Treblinka led to a breakout of several score of prisoners, only twelve of whom survived; a few months later hundreds burst out of Sobibór, but most of them were immediately killed. In October 1944, when the death factory of Auschwitz was already being dismantled, there was a revolt of its Jewish *Sonderkommando*—men employed in grisly tasks by the Nazis before they were murdered themselves. The inmates succeeded in destroying one of the crematoria and killed a few guards. Almost all the rebels fell in the fighting or were captured soon afterward.[113] Elsewhere,

[112] See Yisrael Gutman and Avital Saf, eds., *The Nazi Concentration Camps: Structure and Aims, the Image of the Prisoner, the Jews in the Camps: Proceedings of the Fourth Yad Vashem International Conference, Jerusalem, January 1980* (Jerusalem, 1984), for the most up-to-date survey. A recent account by a Polish inmate is Anna Pawelczynska, *Values and Violence in Auschwitz*, trans. Catherine S. Leach (Berkeley, 1979). Konnilyn G. Feig, *Hitler's Death Camps: The Sanity of Madness* (New York, 1981), is a recent overview drawing unevenly on sources of uneven quality and apparently avoiding almost all material not in English. A highly influential analysis, arguing that the extreme situation of concentration camp existence produced passivity among the inmates, is that of Bruno Bettelheim, *The Informed Heart: Autonomy in a Mass Age* (New York, 1960). See also his "The Holocaust: Some Reflections a Generation Later," *Encounter* 51 (December 1978): 7–19. Bettelheim spent about a year in Dachau and Buchenwald in 1938. His analysis has been sharply disputed by Terrence Des Pres, *The Survivor: Anatomy of Life in the Camps* (New York, 1976), pp. 56–58, 79–80, 116–17, 155–63; and Eli Pfefferkorn, "The Case of Bruno Bettelheim and Lina Wertmüller's *Seven Beauties*," in Gutman and Saf, eds., pp. 663–81.

[113] See Bruno Baum, *Widerstand in Auschwitz* (Berlin, 1957); Hermann Langbein, *Menschen in Auschwitz* (Vienna, 1972), pt. 2, chap. 12; and Tzipora Hager Halivni, "The Birkenau Revolt: Poles Prevent a Timely Insurrection," *Jewish Social Studies* 41 (1979): 123–54. See the accounts by Yuri Suhl and Erich Kulka in *They Fought Back: The Story of the Jewish Resistance in Nazi Europe*, ed. Yuri Suhl (New York, 1975).

in smaller camps, collective uprisings also occurred, but here, too, the inmates were wiped out in almost every case.[114]

Reflecting on resistance in wartime Yugoslavia, Milovan Djilas speaks of a fundamental psychological requisite that was usually missing from the Jewish resistance groups—the "prospect of victory." According to Djilas, who monitored carefully what was necessary to keep Tito's partisans in the field, "victory must be worth the trouble and sacrifice. An insane form of human relations, war is nevertheless a highly motivated and extremely rational act."[115] In eastern Europe, at least, this expectation of victory was almost always missing, and the Jews fought, as the apt title of a recent work puts it, "the war of the doomed." In addition, the Jews lacked other important requirements for armed resistance usually found elsewhere: they had no link with or aid from the outside; they were encouraged and supported by no government in exile; and they frequently lacked the core of armed and trained former military personnel usually found in partisan groups. Quite often in eastern Europe, moreover, the Jews moved in a hostile environment without the support of non-Jewish elements of the population.[116]

Yet, despite these severe handicaps, there was significant Jewish resistance in eastern Europe outside the camps—in ghettos, in their own guerilla bands, and in non-Jewish partisan groups. Jewish fighters in camps, ghettos, and partisan units in Lithuania, for example, numbered close to ten thousand men and women—about 4 percent of Lithuanian Jewry when the Nazis invaded in 1941, or about 16 percent of the Jewish population still alive in early 1942. By any comparative measurement, this was an extraordinarily high proportion of the victimized population.[117] As with the *Judenräte,* the study of Jewish resistance, especially in eastern Europe, depends heavily on Jewish sources and is being undertaken mainly, though not exclusively, by Israeli scholars. Essential to an understanding of this phenomenon is the importance of politics in prewar Jewish community

[114] Jean-François Steiner, *Treblinka* (New York, 1967); Alexander Donat [pseud.], ed., *The Death Camp Treblinka: A Documentary* (New York, 1979); Yitzhak Arad, "Jewish Prisoner Uprisings in the Treblinka and Sobibor Extermination Camps," in Gutman and Saf, eds., pp. 357–99; Erich Kulka, "Escapes of Jewish Prisoners from Auschwitz-Birkenau and Their Attempts to Stop the Mass Extermination," in ibid., pp. 401–16; Richard Rashke, *Escape from Sobibor* (Boston, 1982); Miriam Novitch, ed., *Sobibor: Martyrdom and Revolt* (New York, 1980); and Shmuel Krakowski, *The War of the Doomed: Jewish Armed Resistance in Poland, 1942–1944,* trans. Orah Blaustein (New York, 1984), chap. 12.

[115] Milovan Djilas, *Wartime,* trans. Michael B. Petrovich (New York, 1977), p. 129.

[116] See Krakowski, *War of the Doomed,* passim; Philip Friedman, "Ukranian-Jewish Relations during the Nazi Occupation," *YIVO Annual of Jewish Social Science* 12 (1958–59): 259–96; and Reuben Ainsztein, *Jewish Resistance in Nazi Occupied Europe* (New York, 1974).

[117] Dov Levin, *Fighting Back: Lithuanian Jewry's Armed Resistance to the Nazis, 1941–1945,* trans. Moshe Kohn and Dina Cohen (New York, 1985), p. 227. Compare the useful material in John A. Armstrong, ed., *Soviet Partisans in World War II* (Madison, Wis., 1964).

Marrus

life. Resistance organizers moved within a dense network of preexisting organizations, and radical ideas flowed along channels used before 1939 to carry utopian political messages. Resistance seems to have sprung originally from the Bundist and Zionist youth groups, which were integral to the Jewish political landscape. Temperamentally disposed to make radical choices and to break out of accepted political norms, young people were often less burdened than their elders by family responsibilities and more able to sustain the arduous work of armed resistance.[118]

For ghetto revolts one obviously thinks of Warsaw, where the uprising of April 1943 was the first instance of collective violence in Nazi-dominated Europe by a civilian population. But there were plenty of other cases—several score, according to Bauer—although the statistics we have do not yet give a full sense of the scale of the hostilities involved.[119] Gutman's monograph on the Warsaw ghetto revolt puts this episode into the grisly perspective of Nazi-occupied Poland: the fighting began after more than 80 percent of the inmates had already been deported; of the forty thousand or so remaining, the ghetto fighters numbered under a thousand lightly armed youths. German losses possibly amounted to more than the SS commander, Jürgen Stroop, admitted, but they did not exceed a few score dead and wounded. After holding out remarkably for several weeks the Jews were overwhelmed. Afterward, the surviving inmates were massacred or deported, and the remains of the ghetto razed. There are few more eloquent indications of the unequal and utterly hopeless nature of the contest.[120]

Investigation of Jewish resistance bands in other ghettos permits comparative analysis and prompts generalizations. In Vilna, according to Arad, the first Jewish underground group anywhere in Europe arose; ghetto leader Jacob Gens counterposed a "work to live" strategy to that of the young fighters, however, winning over the majority of the ghetto population and preventing an uprising in 1943. Arad notes that the Jewish resistance there, unlike that in many other cities, had an alternative to armed revolt: the

[118] The best guide to the complexities of Jewish political life before 1939 is Mendelsohn (n. 80 above). For a critique of this theme as it appears in Dawidowicz (n. 23 above), see Yisrael Gutman, " 'The War against the Jews, 1939–1945,' " *Yad Vashem Studies* 11 (1976): 335–42. On the role of women, see Vera Lasker, ed., *Women in the Resistance and in the Holocaust: The Voices of Eyewitnesses* (Westport, Conn., 1983). For a picture of ideologically committed youth in one locality, see Zvi Yavetz, "Youth Movements in Czernowitz," in *Hunter and Hunted: Human History of the Holocaust*, ed. Gerd Korman (New York, 1974), pp. 135–45.

[119] Bauer, *A History of the Holocaust* (n. 102 above), p. 270.

[120] Gutman, *The Jews of Warsaw* (n. 87 above), pp. 348, 392–95. Jürgen Stroop acknowledged sixteen dead and eighty-five wounded on the German side. His official account has been recently published as *The Stroop Report: "The Jewish Quarter of Warsaw Is No More!"* trans. and annotated by Sybil Milton (New York, 1979). See also Yitzhak Zuckerman, "From the Warsaw Ghetto," *Commentary* 45 (December 1975): 62–69; Krakowski, *War of the Doomed*, chap. 10; and Reuben Ainsztein, *The Warsaw Ghetto Revolt* (New York, 1979).

History of the Holocaust

rebels could flee to the forests and form partisan units. In the end, as a result, a few hundred did manage to survive.[121] But such conditions were not available elsewhere: in western and central Poland, Bauer points out, there were no heavily forested regions to which Jews could escape. Armed clashes occurred in numerous ghettos, notably in Białystok where the ghetto fighters worked together with the head of the *Judenrat*, Ephraim Barash. But these clashes invariably came only after repeated deportations of the Jewish inmates, leaving them demoralized and decimated by ghetto conditions. In Lodz, where "work to live" also seemed to offer a plausible hope for survival, the ghetto was effectively sealed by the Germans, escape was cut off, and no weapons could enter. Largely left alone by the Nazis in 1943, when ghettos were being destroyed all around, the remnant of what had been the Jews of Lodz toiled for the Germans until August 1944; only then, as the Red Army drew close, did the Nazis deport them to their deaths. These are the essential elements—rather than a presumed Jewish passivity—that account for there being no armed resistance in the Lodz ghetto. A more general conclusion seems to be that as long as the Jews envisioned the possibility of survival, they were reluctant to risk a suicidal rebellion.[122]

Historians have been able to identify Jewish partisan units in Eastern Europe, numbering as many as fifteen thousand partisans in eastern Poland at the end of the war, for example. Conditions in eastern Belorussia seem to have particularly facilitated escape to the forests: between six thousand and ten thousand are estimated to have done so from the ghetto of Minsk alone.[123] It appears extremely difficult to establish a composite picture, given the many regions involved and the high mortality among the partisans during the two or three years such groups existed. One can say with some assurance that these bands were generally formed in the latter half of 1942, when the Final Solution was well under way throughout the Nazi-occupied East. A primary purpose was survival, but many also conducted a crude guerrilla warfare against the Nazis from time to time. Crucial to their fortunes was their relationship with the non-Jewish population, for without

[121] Arad, *Ghetto in Flames* (n. 103 above). See also Levin, *Fighting Back*, chap. 13.

[122] Bauer, *Jewish Emergence from Powerlessness* (n. 94 above), pp. 26–40; Isaiah Trunk, "Note: Why Was There No Armed Resistance against the Nazis in the Lódz Ghetto?" *Jewish Social Studies* 43 (1981): 329–34. Compare Trunk's *Jewish Responses to Nazi Persecution: Collective and Individual Behavior in Extremis* (New York, 1982), passim, for a wide-ranging analysis and discussion.

[123] Bauer, *History of the Holocaust*, p. 270. See Jack Nusan Porter, ed., *Jewish Partisans: A Documentary of Jewish Resistance in the Soviet Union during World War II*, 2 vols. (Washington, 1982), vol. 2, pt. 1; Zvi Bar-On, "The Jews in the Soviet Partisan Movement," *Yad Vashem Studies* 4 (1960): 167–90; Yitzhak Arad, "Jewish Armed Resistance in Eastern Europe," in Yisrael Gutman and Livia Rothkirchen, eds. (n. 75 above), pp. 490–517, and "Jewish Family Camps in the Forests—an Original Means of Rescue," in Gutman and Zuroff, eds. (n. 35 above), pp. 333–53. For an extraordinary fictionalized account see Primo Levi, *If Not Now, When?* trans. William Weaver (Harmondsworth, 1986).

Marrus

local support this kind of underground could scarcely exist. And on this point, generalization is difficult. In Poland, as we have seen, the Polish Home Army often opposed Jewish armed struggle as "premature"; the Soviet-backed communist *Armia Ludowa,* in contrast, did support the Jews on occasion but was a far weaker force and was in the field much later. Shmuel Krakowski concludes that the Jewish partisans were largely isolated in their struggle and, indeed, often worked within a hostile local environment.[124] Jews faced similar opposition in Lithuania, according to Dov Levin, because they viewed the Soviets as a "lesser evil" in the struggle against the Third Reich.[125]

Elsewhere in Europe there was significant Jewish involvement in armed resistance to Nazism, but historians have had difficulty attempting to move beyond the more traditional effort to record the "Jewish contribution" to the general struggle against Hitler. In each country the Nazi persecution created particular circumstances that shaped the Jews' role in resistance groups. In parts of Yugoslavia, for example, there were few Jews who could reach the partisans because they were immediately rounded up and placed behind barbed wire; the Nazis excepted doctors and pharmacists, however, and as a result, according to one testimony, "almost the entire medical corps of the Yugoslav partisans was made up of Jews."[126] In western Europe there was little resistance of any sort until 1943, and few underground networks existed from which the Jews could have received assistance, even assuming that Jews figured high on their agenda. About this there is at least some doubt.[127] Many Jews in western Europe, of course, claimed to have participated in resistance solely as citizens of their countries and not as Jews. But not all. From her work on France, Renée Poznanski has made a strong case that a distinctly Jewish resistance did indeed exist in that society. Many Jews constituted separate networks both for the purposes of assisting fellow Jews and to strike as Jews at the occupation forces.[128] Jacques Adler's book on the Jews of Paris reminds us how important the politics of the immigrant Jewish community in France were in preparing the ground for such resistance. East European immigrants, he argues, were more disposed to resistance, not only because they were so much more intensely victimized from an early point in the occu-

[124] Krakowski, *War of the Doomed* (n. 114 above), passim. However, Jews did participate in the Polish partisan movement, both as individuals and in groups that collaborated with the Polish underground. Jews were certainly present in the uprising of the city of Warsaw against the Nazis in 1944 (*War of the Doomed,* chap. 13).

[125] D. Levin, *Fighting Back,* p. 223.

[126] Trunk, *Jewish Responses to Nazi Persecution,* p. 301.

[127] Marrus and Paxton, *Vichy France and the Jews* (n. 36 above), pp. 189–91. Henri Michel noted that "on the day that the Warsaw Ghetto uprising broke out, not one partisan yet existed in France" (Michel [n. 111 above], p. 14).

[128] Renée Poznanski, "La résistance juive en France," *Revue d'histoire de la deuxième guerre mondiale,* no. 137 (1985), pp. 3–32.

pation but also because they were less inclined to defer to established authority in France. Jewish communists, he contends, were the first to grasp the Jews' predicament, and they established the first clandestine groups to offer help to their fellow Jews.[129] Other Jewish resistance groups drew mainly on prewar secular Jewish ideologies, as in eastern Europe, but one should not ignore mainstream Jewish community activists who worked together with immigrant groups to form the clandestine Conseil Représentatif des Juifs de France (CRIF) in 1943.[130]

Investigations of Jewish resistance, about which there has been considerable emotional fallout in the Jewish world, have managed to achieve a high degree of scholarly professionalism in recent years. But it would be wrong to omit reference to the cry of pain that is distinctly audible in the scholarly chorus, especially from survivors who have conducted serious academic research on the subject. For those who participated in Jewish resistance or otherwise experienced it directly, there remains a powerful commitment to disprove the legend that the Jews went to their deaths "like sheep to the slaughter"—a phrase first used by Jewish rebels to goad their demoralized compatriots to a suicidal revolt.[131] To historians like these, there is no more commanding injunction than that which was on the lips of more than one of Hitler's victims: Tell the story![132]

For this reason alone we are a long way from "detachment" from the history of the Holocaust, and the subject is not yet at the remove of, for example, the French Revolution or the First World War. We will continue to have important books, such as *The Holocaust* by Martin Gilbert, whose objective it is simply to chronicle the agony of the victims. And rightly so. Gilbert's work is a searing, eloquent compilation—perhaps far more so than any of the books considered here. But it ignores most of the issues discussed in the scholarly literature—questions of German policy, issues of Axis and collaborationist states and peoples, comparisons of the re-

[129] Jacques Adler, *Face à la persécution: Les organisations juives à Paris de 1940 à 1944* (Paris, 1980).

[130] See the special issue "La résistance juive en France: Où en est son histoire?" *Le monde juif*, no. 118 (April–June 1985); and Anne Grynberg, ed., *Les juifs dans la résistance et la libération: Histoire, témoignages, débats* (Paris, 1985).

[131] "Jewish masses, the hour is drawing near. You must be prepared to resist, not give yourselves up to slaughter like sheep" (proclamation of the Jewish Fighting Organization, January 1943); and from another manifesto of the same period, attributed to the Jewish Military Union: "Know that deliverance is not to be found in going to your death impassively, like sheep to the slaughter" (both quoted in Gutman, *The Jews of Warsaw* [n. 87 above], p. 305). See also Ringelblum, *Notes from the Warsaw Ghetto* (n. 82 above), p. 310; and Hilberg, *Destruction of the European Jews* (n. 6 above), 3:1037.

[132] Des Pres, *The Survivor* (n. 112 above), chap. 2. This theme also recurs in the extraordinary stories of the Polish writer Tadeusz Borowski, *This Way for the Gas, Ladies and Gentlemen*, trans. Barbara Vedder (Harmondsworth, 1976). Borowski recounts a nightmarish reflection of an inmate in Auschwitz: "If the Germans win the war, what will the world know about us?" (p. 132).

sponses of various states and societies, and problems of Jewish response.[133] Gradually, the study of the Holocaust is moving in this latter direction, raising questions such as those I have tried to discuss in this article. Scholars continue to write about the Holocaust; indeed, they are doing so more than ever. Their findings are gradually being integrated into the historical mainstream—to the enrichment, I believe, of the discipline as a whole.

[133] Martin Gilbert, *The Holocaust: A History of the Jews of Europe during the Second World War* (New York, 1986).

NORMALIZING THE HOLOCAUST? THE RECENT HISTORIANS' DEBATE IN THE FEDERAL REPUBLIC OF GERMANY*

NORBERT KAMPE

Centre for Research on Antisemitism, Technische Universitaet, Berlin

Abstract — For over a decade in the Federal Republic of Germany a process has been taking place — a process of the return of history into public awareness. In view of the obvious permanence of the division of Germany, along with the unbroken tradition of nationalism in the countries of the western world, as well as the profound doubt in the naïve belief in permanent technological progress, many people have been searching for the historical roots of the German present and ultimately their own place in the history of the world. Significant publications in German history have had wide reception in recent years. Indeed, there would be no reason to worry about the attempt (which has long been overdue) to redefine German 'identity', if the present government in Germany did not take it upon itself to make this trend into a political programme. The 'Achilles heel' of the German national identity — at the same time the cause of 'German amnesia' or, stated another way, the post-war 'collective silence' with respect to history — was and remains the responsibility for the crimes committed by Germans and in Germany's name during the Nazi era. An uncritical approach to German history, which up to recently was quite characteristic of the general consensus, is barred to us. Some renowned German historians now have earned the reputation — justly or unjustly — of repudiating this consensus and emerging as 'government historians' in a quasi-official capacity and suggesting the historical relativity of the Holocaust, with the intention of substituting a 'positive nationalism' for the previously 'negative' form. This article has been written mainly for a non-German audience. It is designed to provide information about the most important historiographical and political aspects of the intensely waged 'historians' debate' of the last year.

Since last summer a lively debate has been raging in the Federal Republic of Germany which has, in part, assumed the form of an 'intellectual civil war'. The centre of public interest focuses upon German professors of history, whose controversies, while generally very carefully conducted, have otherwise only been taken cognizance of by a specialized audience. The forum of the debate at first comprised two leading German newspapers: the liberal newspaper *Die Zeit* and the conservative newspaper *Frankfurter Allgemeine Zeitung*. The debate soon expanded to include almost the entire media landscape of the Federal Republic. The substance of this 'historians' debate' justifies this wide response. For the first time since 1945 internationally acclaimed German historians are demanding a new relationship which can best be defined as a lack of constraint on the part of Germans towards the Nazi era and especially towards the Holocaust, as well as towards the genocidal extermination of Poles, Russians and Gypsies. Contrary to those marginal voices which deny the Holocaust, these new 'revisionists' do not question the

*The author would like to thank Dr. Jerry Schuchalter for the English translation of this article.

irrefutable evidence. Instead, they are attempting with the aid of comparative historical analyses to trivialize the Holocaust — in short, to make it appear 'normal'. The core of the 'revisionist' questions and theses can be reduced to a brief formula:

> Is it necessary to revise the previously valid notion of the singularity and unparallelled monstrosity of state organized genocide? Is genocide rather not a universal, historical, anthropological constant? Was 'Auschwitz' merely the replication of the Bolshevist 'Gulag'? In fact, could one not argue that the 'Gulag' was the causal prerequisite of 'Auschwitz'? Did the Nazis not act in apparent or genuine self-defense? Was Hitler indeed not justified in deporting the Jews? Is it not necessary today for a German to identify with the courageous defensive struggle of the soldiers on the collapsing Eastern front in 1944/45 — even if it meant the continued operation of the death camps? Was the resistance of July 20, 1944, instead of being heroic, irresponsible? Is there cause more than forty years after the end of the war for Germany in its self-image and in its presentation of foreign policy to feel constraint? Hasn't this constraint up to now been exploited by the persecuted and their descendants for their own advantage, as well as abused by the left (since the days of student protest in 1968), in order to destabilize the Federal Republic? Isn't it time for the Federal Republic to free itself of historical ballast — in short, to conduct offensive policies which are commensurate with its position as an economic and military middle power?

The debate is, thus, highly political, not only because it attempts a revision of history, but also at the same time because of the political consequences derived from this revision. This point must be considered as a crucial aspect of this essay, even if the mode of argumentation of the 'revisionists' should be its central concern. A chronological presentation of the debate or of the polemic which borders on the slanderous — especially in the letters to the editor — is not the aim of this paper. The theses of the 'revisionists' have been presented in a highly abridged form in the international press.[1] By contrast, the 'revisionists' themselves will be given the word. The author assumes that this mode of argumentation from now on will be met with permanently on the political stage, since it has received a 'scholarly' sanction. However, in the more narrow confines of professional historiography, it still has to gain acceptance.

JÜRGEN HABERMAS'S CRITIQUE OF 'APOLOGIST' HISTORIANS

The debate was precipitated by Frankfurt philosopher Jürgen Habermas's severe critique of what he calls 'apologetic tendencies in contemporary German historiography'.[2] Taking as an example the publications of four historians,[3] Habermas shows that there is an attempt, at present, to politically transform the historical consciousness in Germany for the purpose of creating a neo-conservative, German-national political consensus. Because of the catastrophes already caused by German nationalism in the twentieth century, this is only possible by means of a new interpretation of German history. This process would consist, for example, of a kind of historical 'predating' of NATO. The anti-Bolshevist tradition of the German right, including the Nazis, according to this line of reasoning, ought to be redefined in a positive line of continuity, thus tempering its nightmarish aspect. However, since the word 'Auschwitz' renders the creation of a politically useful past impossible, it is then necessary to regard this part of German history in a relativizing light and at least attempt to make this chapter understandable by seeing it as a response to the Bolshevist menace which, by the way, is still present. Habermas posits, in contrast to the 'closed view of history established by government historians', a pluralistic approach to historical interpretation — what he terms 'the critical appropriation of multi-faceted traditions'. According to Habermas, what is deplored today often as a 'loss of history' should be regarded rather, in reality, as a repudiation of 'naïve identifications' with one's own national origin in favour of a post-nationalist, universal standard of values. The opportunity made available by this moral catastrophe has clearly not been completely lost:

> The unconditional opening of the Federal Republic to the political culture of the West is the great intellectual achievement of our post-war period — an achievement which especially my generation can be proud of. . . . The only mode of patriotism which does not alienate us from the West is constitutional patriotism. An attachment to constitutional principles, based on profound convictions, was unfortunately able to take shape only after and through Auschwitz. Those who attempt to expel the shame tied to this fact with empty phrases like 'guilt obsessed' (Stürmer and Oppenheimer) or those who induce the Germans to return to a conventional form of national identity will destroy the only reliable basis of our ties to the West.[4]

As Habermas stated in his reply to this debate,[5] this critique was levelled on the political–moral level without any claim to specialized historical competence. Habermas's central concern is the preservation of the hitherto underlying consensus of all political parties with respect to the necessity of a critical appropriation of the German past. This consensus is being 'dissolved by the right today'. Thus, Habermas would neither have objected to a debate among specialists nor become aware of its significance. The popularization of knowledge, he adds, always proceeds first through the mass media. The publication of the Nolte article in the *Frankfurter Allgemeine Zeitung* of 6 June marks 'an important turning point in the political culture and in the sense of identity of the Federal Republic. This is also how this article is being received abroad.'

ANDREAS HILLGRUBER — IDENTIFICATION WITH GERMAN SOLDIERS?

Anyone familiar with the previous work of the Cologne historian Hillgruber[6] knows that it presents without any apologetic undertone a relationship between German expansion to the East and genocide. But today there is some reason to ask for a reassessment of his view on the war. Habermas has accused Hillgruber of an apologetic bias on account of a little volume appealing to bibliophiles published by Siedler in Berlin.[7] In this work there is a new lengthy essay with the title 'The Collapse in the East 1944/45 as a Problem of German National History and European History', as well as the expanded version of the final lecture at the Stuttgart Conference of 1984 entitled 'Decision Making and Realization' of the Holocaust ('The Historical Place of the Destruction of Jewry').[8] The deficiencies of this book begin with the insensitive title, 'Dual Decline: The Destruction of the German Empire and the End of European Jewry'. The few supplementary pages on the Holocaust have been assessed by critics in part as an alibi for the preceding empathic description of the winter disaster on the German Eastern front in 1944/45.

In his introduction Hillgruber emphasizes his wish to add a 'profound dimension' to the Jewish and German catastrophe, namely, the dissolution of the 'European centre'. The destruction of the German Empire, according to Hillgruber, is not a result of crimes committed by Nazism; instead it arose from the genuine war aims of the Allies and their 'negatively stylized mythic image of Prussia' (p. 67). However, Hillgruber does not ask the question whether the allied war aims were still not legitimate in view of the two wars initiated by Prussia and Germany — even without 'Auschwitz'. Hillgruber's essay becomes altogether problematic when the question of identification arises.

NORBERT KAMPE

> Of course, the structural or functional problem presents itself that the stability of the fronts rendered possible the continuation of the crimes committed in the concentration camps. If one, however, wants to grasp what was happening in the German East during these winter months, one must also then consider the subjective assessment of the situation of those responsible and the actions which then ensued or the inability to act on the part of the military leadership.
>
> The observer also faces the dilemma of those who were involved at that time. On the one hand, the ethical code of the men of July 20th, who, realizing the futility of changing the situation by a new foreign policy, decided to assassinate Hitler in order to show the world that there was another Germany at the same time . . . that the way was being made free for the Red Army to invade East Prussia. On the other hand, the moral responsibility of the military leaders, district councilmen, and mayors, for whom it was absolutely essential to create at least a thin veil of security on the East Prussian border to prevent the worst from occurring: the threatening orgy of revenge of the Red Army against the German population in return for all the atrocities committed in those areas of the Soviet Union occupied by the German army, regardless by which organization or service.[9] . . .
>
> It was a hopeless situation. When one looks back, one is confronted with the problem of identification — a central problem which the historian cannot evade with general remarks about the ideal of objectivity which one can approach as closely as possible without ever, in fact, achieving it. Even the general principle of justice does not help us any further. It is easy to say which extremes cannot be considered. Even a partial identification with Hitler is not possible, but also an identification with the future victors — and that includes the Soviet Union and the Red Army on the Eastern front — was inconceivable. The concept 'liberation' implies such an identification with the victors, and, of course, this concept is completely valid for the liberated victims from the concentration camps and prisons of the National Socialist regime. However, in relation to the fate of the German nation as a whole, it is inappropriate. . . .
>
> When the historian looks at the catastrophe in the winter of 1944/45, only one position remains, even when it is difficult to defend in each case. The historian must identify with the actual fate of the German population in the East and with the desperate efforts and heavy sacrifices of the German army on the Eastern front and the German navy in the Baltic Sea area to protect the German populace in the East against the orgies of revenge of the Red Army, the mass rapes, the arbitrary murders and indiscriminate deportations, and, in the final phase, to keep the escape routes open to the West by land or by sea. (pp. 21–5)

The fact that the historian 'must' identify with one part of the power structure of the disintegrating Nazi regime seems not to dismay Hillgruber. He explained in this connection that he tried to introduce the perspective of those directly affected just as Hans Mommsen or Martin Broszat had done for other areas of the 'Third Reich'. He also did not have in mind the old concept of 'Central Europe' under German hegemony. This was, according to Hillgruber, historically settled as a result of World War II. He was thinking more of Germany's mediator role between East and West.[10]

Hillgruber's essay is obviously a late product of the daily political confrontations revolving around the form of the 40th anniversary celebration commemorating the end of the war. In this context the East-Prussian-born historian refers to a statement made by the Christian Democrat politician Norbert Blüm (today Minister of Labour in Bonn)

> who presented the thesis to a bemused and, at the same time, polarized public that the outrageous crimes in the concentration camps could go on unabated as long as the German fronts remained intact. Only one inference can be drawn from this thesis: it would have been desirable to allow the fronts to crumble — and that included the German Eastern front which protected the homeland against the inundation by the Red Army — in order to put an end to the horror in the concentration camps. (p. 18)

Unmentioned in this context is the open letter of the Chairman of the CDU/CSU faction Alfred Dregger, in Parliament to the 53 American senators who protested against President Reagan's visit to the military cemetery at Bitburg, which also contains SS graves.[11]

> On the last day of the war on May 8, 1945, I, who was at the time 24 years old, with my batallion, defended the Silesian city of Marklissa against the attacks by the Red Army. My only brother Wolfgang died in an encircling battle in 1944 on the Eastern front in the Kurland region under unknown circumstances. He was a decent young man like most of my fellow soldiers. If you demand that your president not perform the noble gesture planned at the military cemetery in Bitburg, then I must regard it as an insult to my brother and to the soldiers who fought with me. I ask you if you regard the German people, who were subjugated by a brown dictatorship for twelve years and who have been on the side of the West for forty years, as an ally?

In the light of these awakened 'dissonant perceptions', Hillgruber's essay appears as an attempt at mediation. He should have indicated that descriptive detail can hardly alter the total picture of senseless and criminal acts committed by the Germans during this time. However the charge that Hillgruber is a 'constitutional Nazi' who should be debarred from employment in his field,[12] cannot be taken seriously.

ERNST NOLTE — HOLOCAUST AS PUTATIVE SELF-DEFENCE

The Berlin historian, Ernst Nolte, in the aforementioned article of 6 June 1986 has criticized the mode of dealing with the National Socialist past.[13] This past 'is a past which does not want to go away', a past to which a historically detached relationship has not developed up to now. Instead, this past seems 'to be becoming more and more vivid and powerful'; 'hanging over the present like a vision of horror and an executioner's sword'. The 'Final Solution' has principally contributed to the inability of the past to go away, 'for the monstrousness of the industrialized liquidation of several million people has to appear more unfathomable, the more the Federal Republic joins the vanguard of humanitarian states through its legal system'.

The attention given to the 'Final Solution' diverts interest from the National Socialist euthanasia programme or 'the treatment of Russian prisoners of war, but, above all, concern with the decisive questions of the present', for example, the ethical problem of abortion 'or the case in question of "genocide" in Vietnam yesterday and today in Afghanistan'.[14]

Nolte sees two modes of argumentation, which are juxtaposed and unconnected in the attitude of the Germans to the National Socialist past: the so-called 'clean sweep' (*Schlußstrich*) and 'the demand to resolve, to overcome' (*Vergangenheitsbewältigung*). He asks whether only the ignorance of the 'neighbourhood pub' is calling for an end to the preoccupation with the past, or whether there is not 'a core of truth' in this demand. Nolte insinuates that the representatives of this 'demand to resolve and overcome the past' are serving their own interests, for example, in the case of the 'persecuted and their descendants' with their claim to a 'permanent status of the select and privileged'.[15] This juxtaposition of two series of argumentation, according to Nolte, leads to grotesque situations. Tasteless yet harmless comments, made by politicians, which can, in essence, be categorized as pre-Nazi, antisemitic remarks, are magnified into 'symptoms of antisemitism'[16] while, at the same time on television, 'the moving documentary "Shoah", made by a Jewish director', suggests that 'SS crews in the concentration camps could also be regarded as a kind of victim and that, on the other hand, there were also virulent antisemites among the Polish victims of National Socialism'. That Nolte — of all the possible lessons to be derived from 'Shoah' — favours the lesson of 'the clean sweep mentality' is puzzling, to say the least.

The emotional discussion surrounding the visit of the American president to the military cemetery at Bitburg 'with its fear of indictment and the settling of accounts with respect to crimes', prevented the simple question from being asked: what would have been the significance of the refusal of the German Chancellor to visit Arlington National Cemetery in 1953? The historian recognizes in this event 'the lamentable consequence of the inability of the past to go away'.

After this sketch of the present 'grotesque' relationship of the Germans to their past, Nolte announces that 'with the aid of some questions and key terms' he 'will suggest a perspective, in which this past ought to be regarded, if it is to receive that "equal treatment" which is an essential postulate of philosophy and historical scholarship'. Nolte begins his attempt at revision by discussing the genocide against the Armenians in 1915. The German consul in Turkey at the time, Max Erwin von Scheubner-Richter, attempted in vain, with support from Berlin, to protest against this crime which was unfolding in the not too distant future. His biographer described, in 1938, Scheubner-Richter's sense of helplessness towards 'the will to destruction of the Turkish government, towards the vulpine savagery of the incited Kurds, towards the unbelievably rapidly approaching catastrophe, in which one Asian people dealt with another Asian people in an Asian fashion far from European civilization'. Since Scheubner-Richter was Hitler's close adviser until his death in the Hitler Putsch of 1923, Nolte concludes, his rejection of genocide as a political means must have been identical to the attitude of Hitler, Himmler or Alfred Rosenberg. 'One must then ask the following question: How could men who came into close contact with genocide and experienced it as "Asiatic" be impelled to initiate a genocide of an even greater nature? There are illuminating key terms.'[17]

The only 'key term', which Nolte offers, is that of the 'rat cage'. Hitler used it at a conference on 1 February 1943 when he predicted some of the officers at Stalingrad who had just fallen into Soviet hands would collaborate. According to Nolte, Hitler meant by this a horrible method of torture with nearly starved rats, which is described by George Orwell in his novel *1984*. This Bolshevist method of torture had been widely known since the Russian Civil War.[18] That this has not been perceived is a 'conspicuous flaw' in the literature on National Socialism:

> Everything that the National Socialists later did with the single exception of the technical process of gassing had already been depicted in the literature of the early 1920's: mass deportations and executions, tortures, death camps, extermination of entire groups according to purely objective criteria, public demands with respect to the destruction of millions of innocent people who were considered 'hostile'. Probably many of these reports had been exaggerated. But nevertheless the following question has to seem acceptable, even inevitable: Did the National Socialists carry out — did Hitler perhaps carry out an 'Asiatic' act — only because Hitler and his party regarded themselves as potential or real victims of an 'Asiatic' act? Did not the 'Gulag Archipelago' serve as the model for Auschwitz? Was not the 'class murder' practiced by the Bolsheviks the logical and factual prototype of the 'racial murder' of the National Socialists? Can Hitler's most secret actions also be explained by his inability to forget the 'rat cage'? Did not Auschwitz perhaps in its origins emanate from a past which did not want to go away?

Nolte himself remarked that he had avoided posing such questions for a long time.

However, these questions touch on 'simple truths' which, if deliberately omitted, would violate the scholarly ethos. According to Nolte these questions have to be seen in the context of the last 200 years of European history and the frenetic search for 'guilty parties' or 'originators' of these criticized developments. The qualitative differences between Bolshevist and National Socialist genocide would only then become apparent. One form of genocide could not in any way justify another. However, according to Nolte, one is making a mistake by considering only the one form of mass murder, although between the two 'a causal nexus is probable'.

If the horrors of history are to have a meaning for future generations, this meaning must 'consist in freeing oneself from the tyranny of collective thinking'. A stigmatizing critique of 'the' Jews, 'the' Russians, 'the' Germans or 'the' *petite bourgeoisie* is, in Nolte's opinion, therefore inadmissible: 'The confrontation with National Socialism, moulded by this form of collective thinking, should be finally brought to a close.'

Even if the evidence could be regarded as methodologically acceptable, this would only explain at best the genocide against the Russians — and not the Holocaust. Does Nolte expect the reader himself to associate the term 'Bolshevist' with 'Jewish'? Or did the *Frankfurter Allgemeine Zeitung* undertake an unauthorized abridgement? It is thus necessary to refer to Nolte's essay, which the article in the *Frankfurter Allgemeine Zeitung* is apparently based upon.[19] In this essay Nolte establishes in detail the necessity of the historicization of the 'Third Reich' in the context of the history of collective phantasies and acts of extermination since the advent of modern society:[20]

> He who does not want to see Hitler's annihilation of the Jews in this context is possibly led by very noble motives, but he falsifies history. In his legitimate search for the direct causes he overlooks the main precondition without which all those causes would have remained without effect. Auschwitz is not primarily a result of traditional anti-Semitism. It was in its core not merely a 'genocide' but was above all a reaction born out of the anxiety of the annihilating occurrences of the Russian Revolution. This copy was far more irrational than the original because it was simply absurd to imagine that 'the Jews' had ever wanted to annihilate the German bourgeoisie or even the German people, and it is very hard to admit even a perverted ethos. It was more horrifying than the original because the annihilation of men was conducted in a quasi-industrial manner. It was more repulsive than the original because it was based on mere assumptions, and almost free from that mass hatred which, in the framework of horror, is nevertheless an understandable and as far as it goes a reconciling element. All this constitutes singularity but it does not alter the fact that the so-called [*sic*!] annihilation of the Jews during the Third Reich was a reaction or a distorted copy and not a first act or an original.

Nolte does not hesitate to borrow modes of argumentation of scholarly marginal importance from neo-Nazi literature if they support his theses. Thus, he rejects the principal theses of David Irving (Hitler's lack of knowledge of the Holocaust; possibility of a German military victory).[21] Nolte says:

> However, not all of Irving's theses and references can be set aside so easily. . . . But it can hardly be denied that Hitler had good reasons to be convinced of his enemies' determination to annihilate him much earlier than when the first information about Auschwitz came to the knowledge of the world. The 1940 pamphlet 'Germany Must Perish' by Theodore N. Kaufman has often been mentioned in the literature,[22] but I do not remember seeing it in any of the more important German books I have read about Chaim Weizmann's official declaration in the first days of September 1939,[23] according to which Jews in the whole world would fight on the side of England, . . . and it might justify the consequential thesis that Hitler was allowed to treat the German Jews as

prisoners of war and by this means to intern them. Equally Irving's a priori thesis that the bomb attack on Hamburg in July 1943 bore witness to the Allies' will to destroy the German civilian population, and that this could not have its origin in any knowledge of the 'Final Solution', cannot be refuted. Irving's tendency to place Auschwitz as well into a more comprehensive perspective would be remarkable even if the counter-thesis were acknowledged as convincing, namely that not even the President of the Jewish Agency had the right to pronounce something like a declaration of war, and that the attack on Coventry preceded the one on Hamburg by three years.[24]

In his newspaper reply[25] of 31 October, Nolte takes issue once more with the 'Weizmann Internment Argument'. It is infamous, he writes, to insinuate that a tendency to justify the 'Final Solution' can be inferred from this article. His concern in this article, he writes, is the central question of 'the passage to a new dimension which cannot be derived from what has gone before'. The Weizmann declaration anticipates, Nolte argues, despite all questions of international law, 'a future reality'. In the series of 'Jewish declarations of war', Nolte takes, in addition, a statement by the radical pacifist writer Kurt Tucholsky,[26] which he regards as 'far worse' than the malicious antisemitic and folkish commentary on the actual assassination of Foreign Minister Walter Rathenau. Otherwise, Nolte explicitly persists in defending his criticized theses.

NOLTE'S 'TRILOGY' — THE PHILOSOPHER OF HISTORY WHO TRIVIALIZES HIMSELF

Indeed, Nolte cannot be accused of conforming to the present 'spiritual change' in the Federal Republic of Germany. He emphasized this again and again in the debates surrounding his controversial article. In his 'trilogy', as Nolte calls his *grand œuvre*, all the elements of his recent article can already be found.[27] Nolte intends to present in this work the history of modernization in Europe during the industrial age. In this intellectual history (which Nolte denies is one), relationships are established at a very high level of abstraction between various ideologies and their political implementation. In order not to sink in this broad framework 'in the infinity of facts', Nolte introduces the method of empathy into history by means of 'abbreviated key terms'[28] (as, for example, the above-mentioned 'rat cage'). In his comprehensive (and scholarly) chain of argumentation he is able, for example, to define the National Socialist version of Fascism as a 'violent resistance against transcendence'. Further, he can establish a relationship beginning with the ideas of destruction of Maurras or even with the students of Malthus and then Lenin up to Hitler. Nolte also finds Hitler and Khomeini comparable in their 'struggle against the West'. At this level this may seem quite stimulating. However, this form of intellectual history runs a permanent risk of establishing relationships in world history which have a mythologizing quality. This occurs, for example, when he compares the wholesale murder of communists by the Indonesian dictator Sukarno with the Holocaust:[29]

> Fifty years after the Russian Revolution the principle of destruction was answered directly by the principle of counter-destruction. Thus, a light was cast from this unequivocal event on the ambiguous process of the extermination of the Jews in Germany which is couched in myth — proof of a new uniformity in the world which manifested itself in evil rather than in good.

Another example is Nolte's characterization of 'fear as a basic structure' of Hitler's personality — a fear which included a phobia towards microbes and the common cold. This fear, according to this reasoning, was directly transformed into hatred, the hatred of 'the Jews' as the cause of all these threats and against Bolshevism as the allegedly 'hitherto most radical form' of genocide committed by Jews.[30] These ideas of intellectual history perhaps merit discussion. However, what is not worthy of discussion is the superficial application of the '*fear* thesis' to maintain a causal relationship between civil war communism and the Holocaust at the level of a real historical process. All honours due to intellectual history *à la* Nolte, but also involved in the Holocaust besides the phobic Hitler were a few other people and genuinely pre-Nazi organizations.

Nolte defined the aim of his book on the 'Cold War' at the time as the 'de-demonization of National Socialism'. He added that there is no reason to escape into isolated formulations of questions, despite the danger that 'the most profound tendency in historical scholarship' will be denounced as an 'apology'.[31] Peter Gay criticized Nolte's aim and his method in 1978 as 'comparative trivialization'. Gay argues that Nolte's artifice consists in conceding the atrocities of the Nazis and yet 'humanizing' them and thus finding an apology.[32] Gay also rejects the bagatellization of the brutality of Nazi antisemitism, as it is intended in the following passage by Nolte. Considering the millionfold murder under Stalin between 1936 and 1938, confirmed at the 20th Communist Party Congress, 'the National Socialist state — with the exception of the Röhm affair — had to be characterized until 1939 very much as a state governed by the rule of law, as well as a liberal idyll'.[33] Nolte should have at least excluded from this alleged 'liberal idyll' the open terror from 1933 on, the murder of political prisoners, the concentration camps, or the so-called 'Crystal Night' of November 1938 and not only the power struggle within the National Socialist leadership. Owing to a lack of public demand, the discussion at the time remained confined to academia.

Nolte was supposedly inspired by the international Toynbee Debate in 1954/55.[34] Arnold Toynbee attempted in his mammoth work of 22 volumes — *A Study of History* — to write the rise and fall of cultures in world history. Throughout this work the term 'Judaic' appears with a mythologized and generally negative connotation. Finally Toynbee equates even the Holocaust with the fate of the Palestinian refugees and that of the African slaves in the New World.[35] Nolte and Toynbee appear to share a methodological approach in the sense that, with an ostensible empirical foundation, they both undertake a philosophical interpretation of history. Both have been received by the critics with correspondingly similar responses from 'original', 'speculative', to 'abstruse'. Nolte put together a little volume, in which he discusses for the most part unfavourable reviews of his 'trilogy'.[36] All further discussions of Nolte's theses should begin with this little volume. The term 'question interdict' (*Frageverbote*) (which has ostensibly been imposed upon German scholars) appears already, a term which Nolte's supporters use in the debate.[37]

To sum up clearly once more: eccentric thinkers are a necessary stimulus to scholarship. Anti-German 'question interdict' does not exist in scholarly discourse. Nolte the journalist has abridged in an adventurous reduction the philosophical and historical reflections of Nolte the historian to make it appear to be a conventional presentation of historical causality. He intends — as he himself says in several passages — to reassess in a positive light aspects of neo-Nazi constructs and to confirm the judgments of 'the neighbourhood pub'. Those who rushed to Nolte's side advocating the autonomy of scholarship, should also be reminded of another turning point in the political culture of Germany. Heinrich von Treitschke — the historian and journalist — who was highly regarded among the bourgeoisie, enabled the emerging antisemitism, which up until that time was an obscure phenomenon, to become acceptable. Treitschke supposedly wanted to hear in the most highly educated circles the call 'The Jews are our misfortune'. At the time, the famous historian of ancient history, Theodor Mommsen, berated Treitschke that he could not retreat to the autonomy of scholarship, but would have to accept the historical responsibility for the 'immeasurable harm' done by his articles on the Jews.

THE 'HISTORIANS' DEBATE' — AUTONOMY OR POLITICAL RESPONSIBILITY OF PROFESSORS OF HISTORY

Every German historian who is taken seriously believes that a historicization of the 'Third Reich' has to take place (and is already taking place). For only through scholarly detachment can we begin to understand what really happened. The 'dissonant perceptions', which are handed down to us by contemporaries of this period, will only become comprehensible when we become aware of the puzzling symbiosis between normality and outrage.[38] Similar to the question of 'historicization', the relationship between 'singularity' and 'comparability' does not present a genuine problem for the historian. Complex, historical processes are probably always 'singular'; however, this does not prevent the historian from searching for 'comparable' structures, motives of behaviour, causative factors, etc. On this level, the comparison of the Holocaust in the 'Third Reich' with other forms of genocide is methodologically valid and can definitely yield meaningful insights. Nolte cannot be indicted for merely making comparisons.

Further, it is important to remember that the term 'revisionists' in internationally common usage has already been bestowed upon another group in connection with Holocaust research. It characterizes the deniers of the Holocaust in the framework of a wide neo-Nazi literature and agitation, evoking such names as Faurisson, Butz, Stäglich, Rassinier, etc. The 'revisionists' who are the subject of discussion here, have absolutely nothing in common with the above-mentioned names. Even when Nolte employs snippets of arguments in an irritating fashion from the neo-Nazi camp, the fact is that the Holocaust itself is never called into question. Hence, the international context actually precludes the future use of the term 'revisionists', which is at present being introduced in the West German 'historians' debate'.

Of the allegedly more than 80 letters to the editor, which were received by the *Frankfurter Allgemeine Zeitung* after Nolte's article of 6 June 1986, the position of the Freiburg historian Heinrich A. Winkler was printed, which spoke of 'absurd contentions'.[39] Since, with this statement, the opinion of a section of the 'guild' was given a clear formulation, the Bonn historian Klaus Hildebrand and Joachim Fest, the Hitler biographer and co-editor of the *Frankfurter Allgemeine Zeitung*, responded to this by launching comprehensive counter-attacks against Habermas.[40] Divested of the polemical aspects, the principal statement of both historians is their repudiation of the 'question interdict' of scholarship. Eberhard Jäckel, the Stuttgart historian, characterized the mode of argumentation of Nolte, Hildebrand and Fest as a 'confusing game'.[41] Theses would be presented in question form but never substantiated. If proof is demanded, the following indignant response is given: it is still permitted to raise these questions. Jäckel counters that these historians do not indicate who has decreed the ostensible 'question interdict'. Concerning the question of the uniqueness of the Holocaust, Jäckel refers to his well-known thesis that 'never before had a state under the authority of its vested leader decided and proclaimed to murder a certain human group, including infants, and systematically realized this decision with the aid of all the means of state power available'.[42] The 'class murder' of the Tscheka was, by contrast, not basically directed against all the individual members of the bourgeoisie. Instead their aim was to eliminate the bourgeoisie as a class. Furthermore, a negation of the singularity of the Holocaust would not diminish its historical burden.

According to Jäckel, the proof of the assertion of a causal relationship is more crucial. In his erroneous interpretation of Hitler's 'rat cage' statement (which was, moreover, too late), Nolte, Jäckel maintains, has not succeeded in establishing a 'causal nexus'. The evidence is reduced to the logically highly disputable conclusion of *post hoc, ergo propter hoc.*[43] Hitler, in Jäckel's eyes, did not have any fear whatsoever of the 'sub-human' Slavs and Jews. Rather, he had early characterized 'Jew-ridden Russia' (for example, in *Mein Kampf* in 1926) as 'ripe for collapse' and intended to conquer the Soviet Union with a *Blitzkrieg* strategy in 1941 consistent with this erroneous assessment, based on racial and ideological considerations. On the other hand, Hitler was remarkably adept at exploiting the fears of Bolshevism on the part of the German bourgeoisie. In public Hitler was fond of speaking of the threat of 'Asian hordes', presenting the war of conquest as a preventive war. The thesis of a 'causal nexus' confuses Hitler's tactical statements and his actual motives: 'What is being implied here is the thesis of a preventive murder. But this thesis is as fallacious as the thesis of the preventive war, which, although it has been refuted hundreds of times, is always being fetched from Hitler's arsenal.' Martin Broszat, for many years director of the famous Institute of Contemporary History at Munich, in a comparatively speaking rigorous manner, rejects the 'Chaim Weizmann Declaration of War argument' as a point, in which 'objective apology' has achieved the form of stereotypical thinking found in right-wing pamphlet literature, which leaves him 'speechless'. It is incomprehensible, Broszat adds, that Fest and Hildebrand — against better judgment — make such arguments acceptable.[44] Hans Mommsen, the Bochum historian, does not share this 'dismay'. For he interprets the artificial attempts at present to create a new historical identity in connection with the ideological crises of West German neo-conservatism.[45] The ideological, political and historiographical caprioles of the German right since 1945 in its attempt to exculpate élites cannot be treated here. Hans Mommsen regards Nolte's 'approach in its one-sided presentation of the history of ideas' as unsuitable. Instead, the really significant question is how these phantasies of extermination (indigenous–*volk*ish) could be actually implemented. In an ominous way, Mommsen writes, Nolte's construct suggests:[46]

> that Hitler borrowed the idea of the 'holocaust' from Bolshevist writings and, at the same time, his actions were based on psychopathological compulsions, without at least asking the question: which social–psychological factors, political interests, and institutions enabled Hitler to make himself the executor of the resentments, not only of the 'masses', but also of the ruling élites, which could actually revere him in this role. . . . The psychological and institutional mechanisms which explain the passivity of the population must be studied carefully from the standpoint of doing everything possible to prevent a recurrence of a comparable phenomenon, even if the dimensions of the systematic extermination of European Jewry, especially its unflawed and perfect implementation, is unique. For the research on this question is in agreement that what has to be explained is the disparity between the unsuccessful attempt to maintain secrecy about genocide — perhaps with the exception of, for the most part, the unknown existence of the extermination camps — and the failure of protest especially among those people in authorized positions of power and less among the public. All comparisons with Stalinism do not help in this respect.

In two articles which complement one another, historians Jürgen Kocka and Wolfgang J. Mommsen (of Bielefeld and Düsseldorf respectively) analyse the development of public interest in history in the Federal Republic.[47] These articles inquire into political causes and historiographical schools. At present a wide public interest in history is enjoying a continuous boom, as evidenced by the success of the Prussian Exhibition of 1981 in Berlin and the best-seller status of various specialized monographs. Hence, it is hardly possible any more to speak of a 'people without history'. Historical consciousness has again become a factor of political orientation. Wolfgang Mommsen is disturbed, with respect to this indeed, positive development, by the attempt at neo-conservative exploitation, as exemplified by the work of Michael Stürmer. Mommsen believes that a historiographical Bitburg 'is incompatible with intellectual sincerity, and that, at any rate, evokes disbelief in other peoples'. In this context he refers back to Hillgruber's interpretation of the events on the Eastern front in 1944/45:

> We cannot escape the bitter truth that the defeat of National Socialist Germany was not only in the interest of those nations militarily overrun by Hitler and those groups singled out for extermination, oppression, or exploitation by Hitler's henchmen, but also the Germans themselves. Accordingly, at least aspects of this gigantic event of the Second World War have been, as far as we are directly concerned, simply meaningless, or, better yet, self-destructive. Ultimately, we cannot avoid this bitter truth by assigning responsibility — which is highly problematic — to other partners.

W. J. Mommsen sees the present 'revisionist' positions under discussion as a counter-movement to the social and structural approach to history oriented around the 'revisionism' of the 1960s and 1970s, which took as its model West European and American scholarship. Occasionally overemphasizing antidemocratic elements in the German tradition, this school of thought, Mommsen says, has come under fire, both in the German public, as well as in scholarly circles. In short, Mommsen adds, the established paradigm of the 'special German way' idealizes West European developments. Since this time, at both levels the call for a new, positive, national identity has been growing louder. The assessment of the role (the 'place') of Hitler in German history, according to Mommsen, will perforce become a central issue. For with this excessive personalization of history, the German élites and enduring state structures can be absolved of responsibility. Wolfgang Mommsen sees Nolte's present 'revisionism', which stands under the motto 'against the negative nationalism in historiographical writing', based on Nolte's own experience that his recognized concept of fascism has been instrumentalized by the 'New Left' since the 1960s as a critique of western societies. Nolte's latest attempt to divest the Holocaust of its singularity from the perspective of universal history is obviously a result of this experience. Mommsen assures us that it was not the comparison of the Holocaust with the depredations of the Bolsheviks which evoked protests, but Nolte's contention that the Holocaust was a response to the 'Asiatic act' of the Bolsheviks. Nolte's reply in which he transposes causality from the historical reality to Hitler's psyche, is unsatisfactory, especially in view of the mendacious propaganda and self-stylization of the Nazis as the saviours of Germany from Bolshevism: 'It is inappropriate to justify National Socialist policies of violence by pointing to comparable processes in the territory under Bolshevist rule or in any way to mitigate its immorality.'

The assumption that a broad 'revisionist' attempt is in process within historical scholarship is seen by W. J. Mommsen as confirmed by the revival of the old, anti-liberal 'geopolitical school' of German historiography with its primary tenet that the 'German position in the centre of Europe' and the threats resulting from this justify the powerful, authoritarian state. (Thus, the historian explicitly confirms a supposition made by the 'non-specialist' Habermas.) Klaus Hildebrand has taken up this mode of interpretation with the result that 'the special responsibility of German policies for unleashing the First World War' is no longer a serious issue.[48] W. J. Mommsen concludes with an appeal to the political successors of the first chancellor of the Federal Republic, Konrad Adenauer, to recognize his determined, successfully implemented breach 'with essential elements of the German historical tradition' and his 'voluntary adoption of Western European models'. The critical approach to dealing with one's own national history, Mommsen says, does not mean in any way the repudiation of the specific achievements of German culture.

Thomas Nipperdey, the Munich historian, regards the debate started by Habermas as a 'misfortune'.[49] In his article he makes an appeal for the autonomy of history and scholarship. By criticizing the debate at this abstract level, he avoids, however, the necessity of a concrete analysis of even one of the debated theses of the 'revisionists'. In such a highly sensitive field, Nipperdey argues, historical niceties tend to disappear in a polarized atmosphere. Further, colleagues of moral integrity would be accused of belonging to the camp of Nazi apologists. Habermas, Nipperdey writes, equates his own political bias with the truth. It is the old story, Nipperdey says, of using National Socialism as a weapon in political conflicts, to proclaim 'self-assured virtue and a monopoly over the truth'. Thus, it is important to speak about the charges of 'insinuation' and 'question interdict'. Moralizing history, according to Nipperdey, destroys history which exists beyond the plurality of perspectives and is accessible to solid findings:

> I am against the idea that scholarly statements and their achievement in providing knowledge are to be measured by their alleged political 'function'. Habermas's 'phantasy of the stereotyped enemy' who intends a national historical refurbishing of conventional identity does not exist. All German history is mediated by Hitler. It is also mediated by the Federal Republic. But it is also unmediated by something very different, namely, itself. Both belong to our identity, to our heritage. History disturbs our identity. But it also stabilizes it. And this forgotten truth should also be given its due respect.

CONCLUSION

The first widespread appearance of phantasies of destruction against Jews began in Imperial Germany around the 1890s. The phantasies were clearly of academic–intellectual origin, similar at first to the entire movement of '*volk*ish antisemitism'. In the course of the bloody trench warfare and the defeat and revolution in 1918–19, the radical *volk*ish antisemitism, which was popularized by intellectuals, spread to great numbers of people. In military circles definite plans to herd German Jews into concentration camps, along with summary executions were presented as a means of preventing the allied sanctions.[50] These hostage concepts appear again in the National Socialist movement. This aggressive potential was at first concentrated in the German 'Free Korps' troops with their barbaric acts of murder.[51] In fact, the projection of one's long-held wishes and intention towards the 'Jewish adversary', played, in general, an equally significant role since the emergence of antisemitism. The radical *volk*ish antisemitism arose under conditions rooted in German history. It needed its familiar political history in order for the Holocaust — for which no completed 'plans' ever existed, neither in 1933 nor in 1941 — to become reality. Neither did it require the model of Bolshevist 'class murder' nor fear, to which it could fall victim.

It is not necessary to agree with all of Habermas's theses to be grateful to him for making the public aware of the fact of a possible turning point in the political culture of the Federal Republic and the concomitant dangers associated with it. Granted, while the emotionalized debate is going on, there will be more damage than clarification. Yet the ensuing sensitizing process has been extremely necessary. It is inappropriate to assess in a positive light the self-trivialization and political instrumentalization of a colleague by referring to the necessity of a non-moralizing process of scholarly discussion, or by a distinguished retreat into the ivory tower. Christian Meier, who certainly is not a left-wing ideologue, but president of the Association of German Historians, in a brilliant lecture in Tel Aviv shortly before the eruption of the historians' debate, established the relationship between morality and historical presentation.[52] Even in his nearly too balanced commentary on the debate, Meier could not help observing that Michael Stürmer intends 'to enlist the services of history'.[53] But has not politics already enlisted the services of history?

At the end of 1986 Conservatives, expecting an almost certain election victory, began announcing the elimination of the liberal brakesmen within the coalition with regard to foreign policy and armament exports. Those who believed that they cannot do without the populistic effects of a campaign against liberal political asylum laws in the Federal Republic of Germany could also consider the 'salvation' of Germans from Auschwitz, especially if esteemed historians would provide the cues:[54]

> The 'grumbling' not only in the older generation, but also in the younger generation regarding the treatment of the Nazi period and the war period cannot be ignored. The Germans must not be portrayed 'continuously as the villains of world politics', the Christian Social Union chairman said. He added further that there must be an end to depicting German history 'solely as a chain of errors and crimes', at the same time that the war adversaries are portrayed as 'angels of light'. This could 'no longer be continued endlessly' forty years after the war. Strauss protested against 'humiliations as well as self-humiliations' of Germans in the speeches 'of certain politicians'.

In a determined continuation of these attitudes, the state of Bavaria refused to pay its contribution in December of 1986 for the newly built youth and conference centre at Auschwitz of 'Aktion Sühnezeichen' (well respected for its pioneering role in the reconciliation between Germans and Jews) with the explanation that the project is 'too focused on the past'. The Federal Minister of Health and Family Affairs, Rita Süssmuth, on the other hand, travelled to Auschwitz for the opening, representing in her speech still the line of the (obsolete) consensus.

In December 1986 the political scene was to raise some pessimism. The reality — not only of the 'neighbourhood pub' — had already hurried past the questions posed at the 'historians' debate'. The 'clean sweep mentality' was not only widespread, but had, at that time, taken an aggressive dynamic.[55] The worthy attempt by the president of the Federal Republic to interpret the 40th anniversary of the German surrender[56] was as much in danger of being marginalized ('self-humiliating') as the guild of history professors who are struggling at this time to find a scholarly and morally appropriate form of historicization with respect to the Third Reich. But the result of the 25 January election in the Federal Republic at least seems to have provided a temporary answer at the political level. Contrary to all predictions, the two Christian–Conservative parties achieved their worst result since 1953. On the other hand, the small liberal coalition partner was considerably strengthened. Independent observers assess the election result as a repudiation of nationalistic ambitions and as the desire for continuity in liberal foreign policy. Or, more carefully formulated: for the first time in the history of the Federal Republic right-wingers within the two Christian parties, with the aid of aggressive, nationalistic electioneering strategies, attempted to gain the absolute majority in the Bonn Parliament and were unsuccessful. The question remains open whether, in view of this experience, the attempt at other levels at 'normalizing the Holocaust' will also not give way to appropriate forms of treating the period of 'Nazi Germany'.

NOTES

1. Of the more elaborate analyses, compare for example: Judith Miller, 'Erasing The Past. Europe's Amnesia About the Holocaust', *The New York Times Magazine*, 16 November 1986, pp. 30–6, 40, 109f. and Saul Friedländer, 'The New German Nationalism: The Polemic Sharpens', *Haaretz*, 3 October 1986.

2. Jürgen Habermas, 'Eine Art Schadensabwicklung. Die apologetischen Tendenzen in der deutschen Zeitgeschichtsschreibung', *Die Zeit*, 11 July 1986, p. 40. According to tentative estimates, 37 German historians have commented on the 'revisionism debate' in articles and commentaries (by 1 December 1986). Less than five stood without reservations behind Habermas's judgment of the 'apologetic tendencies'.

3. The works of the historians Andreas Hillgruber and Ernst Nolte are discussed below. Klaus Hildebrand is cited in his role as a supporter of Nolte. The Erlangen historian Michael Stürmer, leading journalist of the *Frankfurter Allgemeine Zeitung* (*FAZ*), adviser and ghostwriter to Chancellor Helmut Kohl, is above all cited for the following sentence, which is seen as proof of the functionalistic grip on historiography: 'In a land without history those who fill in memory, coin the terms, and interpret the past, win the future' (*Das Parlament*, 17–24 May 1986). Compare also Stürmer, *Dissonanzen des Fortschritts* (Munich, 1986). In this work he sees historiography as 'treading the thin line between creating meaning and de-mythologization' (p. 12). With regard to the 'creation of meaning' through a deliberate appeal to nationalistic needs, Stürmer's position has changed remarkably. In his early publications up until the middle of the 1970s, he criticized the instrumentalization of nationalism as a central element to prevent modernization of German society. Compare Volker Berghahn, see note 50.

4. Franz Oppenheimer, 'Vorsicht vor falschen Schlüssen aus der deutschen Vergangenheit. Die Verführungen einer kollektiven Schuldbesessenheit', *FAZ*, 14 May 1986: the great majority of Germans share 'no greater guilt for Hitler's crimes' than others share for Stalin's and Gorbatschow's (crimes). Those obsessed by guilt cannot 'carry out the work of God'. Only the devil could have been amused by the Bitburg circus in the U.S. media. 'The devil wants the murdered victims of the past to make us forget the tortured slaves of an empire that continues into our present.'

5. Jürgen Habermas, 'Vom öffentlichen Gebrauch der Historie. Das offizielle Selbstverständnis der Bundesrepublik bricht auf', *Die Zeit*, 7 November 1986, pp. 12f.

6. To mention only one of his older publications: Andreas Hillgruber, 'Die "Endlösung" und das deutsche Ostimperium als Kernstück des rassenideologischen Programms des Nationalsozialismus', *Vierteljahreshefte für Zeitgeschichte* (*VfZ*) **20** (1972), 133–53.

7. Hillgruber, *Zweierlei Untergang. Die Zerschlagung des Deutschen Reiches und das Ende des europäischen Judentums* (Berlin, 1986).

8. See note 14, Jäckel and Rohwer.

9. Presented here is a remarkable revision of the previous evaluation of the resistance of the officers of 20 July 1944. After 1945 these officers were often seen as guilty of high treason and all the prerequisites for a construction of a new *Dolchstoßlegende* (stab in the back of the army) were present. Yet through the successful integration of the German nationalist élites in the Christian-Democratic republic the possibility developed for a positive integration of 20 July 1944 into the anti-fascist image of the Federal Republic. Concerning the question of re-evaluation of the officers' plot compare also the Hannover political scientist Joachim Perel's, 'Wer sich verweigerte, ließ das eigene Land im Stich. In der Historiker-Debatte wird auch der Widerstand umbewertet', *Frankfurter Rundschau* (*FR*), 27 December 1986. Compare also in this respect Kurt Pätzold, 'Von Verlorenem, Gewonnenem und Erstrebtem, oder: Wohin der "neue Revisionismus" steuert', *Blätter für deutsche und internationale Politik* (*Blätter*), December 1986, pp. 1452–63. The East German historian Pätzold sees in Hillgruber's book the attempt to separate the events on the Eastern front in 1944–5 from the

perspective of a fascist war of aggression by moulding it into a heroic, tragic defensive struggle. In fact, the cruelly enforced slogans of the National Socialist leadership to resist only served as a senseless postponement of the end of the war for the purpose of saving their own necks. Since Hillgruber also speaks of the genuine war aims of the allies, which did not stem from Nazi crimes and which conceal the responsibility of German capitalism for the enslavement of the peoples of Europe, he offers, with his suggestion of the 'reconstruction of the European center', a not hitherto completely disdained formula for the revision of the realities emerging in Central Europe since 1945.

10. Interview with A. Hillgruber, 'Für die Forschung gibt es kein Frageverbot', *Rheinischer Merkur/Christ und Welt*, 31 October 1986. See also A. Hillgruber 'Jürgen Habermas, Karl Heinz Janßen und die Aufklärung Anno 1986', *Geschichte in Wissenschaft und Unterricht* (*GWU*), **37** (1986), 725–38.

11. Heinrich Sprenger, '"Bitburg über alles". Versöhnung oder psychologische Nachrüstung?', *Vorgänge*, July 1985, pp. 31–44, here 36.

12. Rudolf Augstein, 'Die neue Auschwitz-Lüge', *Der Spiegel*, 6 October 1986, pp. 62f. See also the rejection of Augstein by Imanuel Geiss, 'Auschwitz, "asiatische Tat"', *Der Spiegel*, 20 October 1986, p. 10.

13. Ernst Nolte, 'Vergangenheit, die nicht vergehen will. Eine Rede, die geschrieben, aber nicht gehalten werden konnte', *FAZ*, 6 June 1986. The editorial comment introduces the article as a suppressed opinion. Nolte's invitation to participate in the Frankfurt *Römerberggespräch* (discussion forum), June 1986, held under the motto 'Political Culture — Today?', was withdrawn 'for unknown reasons'.

14. Apart from the questionable equations, the contention of 'diversion' does not hold. In the field of historiography the 'Euthanasia-action' and the '*Kommissarcommand*' are regarded as long-established cornerstones of the 'genocidal process' before 1941. See also Eberhard Jäckel and Jürgen Rohwer, eds., *Der Mord an den Juden im Zweiten Weltkrieg. Entschlußbildung und Verwirklichung* (Stuttgart, 1985). Remarkable progress has also been made in the last decade in the field of comparative and preventive genocide research and has become the editorial basis of this journal.

15. Anyone familiar with the Federal Republic knows that the *Verfolgten* (the persecuted) there do not enjoy any privileges and are, compared to, for instance, the refugee organizations from the former German territories, hardly represented in the public realm. Only the German Democratic Republic nurtures a group of quasi 'professionally persecuted' people, due to the claim to having its own, genuine anti-fascist roots.

16. Nolte seems to be referring to the following events in 1985 and early 1986: In connection with the sale of the Flick company, representatives of German-Jewish communities had demanded reparation payments to the former forced-labourers. In this connection, the *CSU Bundestags*-delegate Hermann Fellner, remarked "that Jews are quick to respond . . . to the sound of money jingling anywhere in Germany". During the budget-debate the mayor of Korschenbroich, Count von Spee, declared that "to balance the budget, a few rich Jews will have to be slain". The regional chairman of the *Junge Union* of Esslingen, Thaddäus Kunzmann, spoke "of the arrogance of Israel to hold our democratic constitutional state responsible for the murder of Jews in the Third Reich". At least the response of the press forced a retraction of the comments, and von Spee also resigned his post. Quoted from Robert Leicht, 'Das Tabu zerbricht. Antisemitismus meldet sich wieder zu Wort', *Die Zeit*, 14 February 1986.

17. In view of the many flaws in the argumentation it cannot be seriously considered acceptable in any way. Simultaneously the term 'Asiatic deed', introduced here, will play a special role in the debate to follow. What Hitler actually thought about the genocide of the Armenians is certainly well known. Before the attack on Poland, Hitler justified the intended extermination of selected groups of the Polish civilian population as a war aim in his speech before the Chief Commanders and Commanding Generals, 22 August 1939, as follows:

> Our strength lies in our quickness and in our brutality; Genghis Khan has sent millions of women and children into death knowingly and with a light heart. History sees in him only the great founder

of States. As to what the weak Western European civilisation asserts about me, that is of no account. I have given the command and I shall shoot everyone who utters one word of criticism, for the goal to be obtained in the war is not that of reaching certain lines but of physically demolishing the opponent. And so for the present only in the East I have put my death-head formations in place with the command relentlessly and without compassion to send into death many women and children of Polish origin and language. Only thus we can gain the living space that we need. Who after all is today speaking about the destruction of the Armenians?

(Documents on British Foreign Policy 1919–39, Third Series, Vol. 7, London, 1954, p. 258.)

18. Orwell's novel was first published four years after Hitler's death. The term 'gulag' was popularized by an Alexander Solzhenitzyn novel in 1973. Since Hitler began to demand an oath to a war of extermination from his aides and staff in his immediate surroundings with the planning of the Russian campaign in Spring 1941, one would have to be able to prove that his fears, which supposedly caused the Holocaust, existed before that time and to provide more than only one example. At the time of giving Göring the oral command to murder all of European Jewry, presumably in July 1941, Hitler found himself in the position of the victorious commander-in-chief of the war against Poland and France. He murdered out of the position of superiority — not out of fear!

19. Ernst Nolte, 'Between Myth and Revisionism? The Third Reich in the Perspective of the 1980s', H. W. Koch, ed., *Aspects of the Third Reich* (London, 1985), pp. 17–38: since this essay is easily accessible in the English version, it will not be elaborated on here fully.

20. *Ibid.*, pp. 35f.

21. David Irving, *Hitler's War* (London, 1977) (German, 1975).

22. Theodore N. Kaufman, *Germany Must Perish* (New Jersey, 1940). Reprinting of the 2nd edition together with German Translation (Bremen, without year, after 1981). In this book Kaufman suggests the complete division of Germany among its neighbouring states and the sterilization of all fertile Germans. Kaufman, embittered over Germany's war-mongering, was alone in his position and had no access to the U.S. administration. Yet German propaganda was thankful for his extremist view and assessed him as a 'leading and widely known Jewish personality' who also belonged to the 'Roosevelt brain trust'. See Wolfgang Dierwege, *Das Kriegsziel der Weltplutokratie. Dokumentarische Veröffentlichung zum Buch des Präsidenten der amerikanischen Friedensgesellschaft Theodore Nathan Kaufman* (Berlin, 1941), p. 5. The reference to the Kaufman pamphlet is part of the standard repertory of neo-Nazi apologetics. See: Wolfgang Benz, 'Judenvernichtung aus Notwehr? Die Legenden um Theodore N. Kaufman', *VfZ* **29** (1981), 615–30.

23. First published in *The Times*, 5 September 1939 and in *The Jewish Chronicle*, 8 September 1939.

24. Nolte, 'Between Myth', pp. 27f.

25. Nolte, 'Die Sache auf den Kopf gestellt. Gegen den negativen Nationalismus in der Geschichtsbetrachtung', *Die Zeit*, 31 October 1986, pp. 9f. Compare also Kurt Pätzold, 'Wo der Weg nach Auschwitz begann. Der deutsche Antisemitismus und der Massenmord an den europäischen Juden', *Blätter*, February 1987, pp. 110–72. Pätzold sharply rejects Nolte's attempt to attribute to the Jews at least partial guilt for their persecution. Outside of German-speaking countries it has hardly been noticed that in a series of publications by East German historians the special mercilessness of the persecution of the Jews in comparison with other groups, as well as the Jewish character of the Holocaust have been confirmed. Domestically, it has resulted in generous financial and moral support of the small Jewish community in East Germany.

26. Tucholsky's radical pacifist remark of 1927, which wishes the experience on the fronts (in World War I) of being gassed to death, on those 'burgher houses' which called for the re-armament (of Germany), serves as a 'classic' of revisionism as an 'antidote' to Hitler's well-known remark about the unfortunately not realized gassing of 15,000 *Hebräischen Volksverderbern* (Hebraic spoilers of the *Volk*), in order to preserve war morale (*Mein Kampf*, 1925). See: Wilhelm Stäglich, *Der Auschwitz-Mythos. Legende oder Wirklichkeit* (Tübingen, 1979), pp. 85f.

27. *Der Faschismus in seiner Epoche* (München, 1963). *Deutschland und der Kalte Krieg* (München and Zürich, 1974). *Marxismus und Industrielle Revolution* (Stuttgart, 1983).

NORBERT KAMPE

28. All citations are from the 2nd edn of *Deutschland und der Kalte Krieg* (Stuttgart, 1985), here p. 2.

29. *Kalte Krieg*, pp. 528f.

30. *Faschismus*, pp. 486–91.

31. *Kalte Krieg*, pp. 2f.

32. Peter Gay, *Freud, Jews and other Germans. Masters and Victims in Modernist Culture* (New York, 1978), pp. VII–XVI. Gay points out, for example, another thesis of the 'Cold War' (p. 111) on the annihilation of the European Jews, 'which — in the right perspective — was nothing else than the second and without the first unintelligible attempt (even much more irrational and nevertheless terribly modern) of solving problems raised through the industrialization by annihilating a numerous group of people'.

33. *Kalte Krieg*, p. 315.

34. For bibliography on the 'Toynbee debate' see Jacob Robinson and Philip Friedman, eds., *Guide to Jewish History under Nazi Impact* (New York, 1973), pp. 22–4.

35. Arnold J. Toynbee, *A Study of History*, Vol. 8. *The West and the Jews* (London, 1954), see esp. pp. 272–4, 288–92. For Nolte on Israel, see *Kalte Krieg*, pp. 285–94. Nolte points out the racial origins of Zionist ideology — as he sees it, Zionism was comparable to the Bolshevik revolution and Russian Civil War, when after 1945 and with the spread of the news about the 'Final Solution', directed terror was aimed at the English government and Arab citizens. The massacre of Deir Yassin is very well comparable with Oradour. Israel is a 'racial-' and 'ideology-state'. In Nolte's summary he emphasizes the primary, close relationship of Zionism, National Socialism and Marxism. However, Zionism, he continues, in its beginnings (Moses Hess, Leon Pinsker, Franz Oppenheim), shared basic assumptions with antisemitism. Therefore, all differences aside, Zionism and National Socialism are too close to regard them as total opposites. But a direct and propagandistic comparison of Israel with the 'Third Reich' cannot be maintained, because in Israel some degree of political opposition is allowed. See pp. 568f. Nolte only takes into account surface phenomena, not seeing a characteristic difference as apparent in the extremely aggressive character of Nazism and the mainly defensive character of Zionism.

36. Ernst Nolte, *Was ist bürgerlich? Und andere Artikel, Abhandlungen, Auseinandersetzungen* (Stuttgart, 1979), esp. pp. 88–113.

37. *Ibid.*, pp. 56–66.

38. See as platform: Martin Broszat, 'Plädoyer für eine Historisierung des Nationalsozialismus', *Merkur*, May 1985, pp. 373–85.

39. Heinrich August Winkler, 'Nationalapologetisches Bedürfnis', *FAZ*, 20 June 1986. A brilliant classification of the debate in respect to the changes in the field of domestic politics in the Federal Republic is to be found in Winkler, 'Auf ewig in Hitlers Schatten? Zum Streit über das Geschichtsbild der Deutschen', *FR*, 14 November 1986.

40. Klaus Hildebrand, 'Das Zeitalter der Tyrannen. Geschichte und Politik: Die Verwalter der Aufklärung, das Risiko der Wissenschaft und die Geborgenheit der Weltanschauung', *FAZ*, 31 July 1986. In a review in *Historische Zeitschrift* **242** (1986), 465f., Hildebrand says in reference to Nolte's essay 'Between Myth': 'This pioneering essay, which tries to project the seemingly unique elements in the history of the Third Reich onto the backdrop of global and European developments and thus explain them, will certainly occupy research and hopefully serve as stimulation.'

41. Eberhard Jäckel, 'Die elende Praxis der Untersteller. Das Einmalige der nationalsozialistischen Verbrechen läßt sich nicht leugnen', *Die Zeit*, 12 September 1986.

42. See Eberhard Jäckel, *Hitlers Weltanschauung. Entwurf einer Herrschaft* (Stuttgart, 1983). Eberhard Jäckel, *Hitlers Herrschaft. Vollzug einer Weltanschauung* (Stuttgart, 1986).

43. Nolte, 'Die Sache', insists nonetheless in his reply:

> The Gulag Archipelago is more original than Auschwitz for the reason that it stood before the eyes of the creator (singular — *sic*) of Auschwitz, and not Auschwitz before the eyes of the creators of the Gulag Archipelago. Yet at the same time a qualitative difference exists between the two. It is

impermissible to overlook the difference, but it is even more impermissible to deny the connection (between the two). Therefore, Auschwitz is not a direct reply to the Gulag Archipelago, but an answer mediated through interpretation.

44. Martin Broszat, 'Wo sich die Geister scheiden. Die Beschwörung der Geschichte taugt nicht als nationaler Religionsersatz', *Die Zeit*, 3 October 1986.

45. Hans Mommsen, 'Suche nach der "verlorenen Geschichte"? Bemerkungen zum historischen Selbstverständnis der Bundesrepublik', *Merkur*, September/October 1986, pp. 862–74. Hans Mommsen, 'Neues Geschichtsbewußtsein und Relativierung des Nationalsozialismus', *Blätter*, October 1986, pp. 1200–13.

46. H. Mommsen, 'Neues Geschichtsbewußtsein', pp. 1211, 1208.

47. Wolfgang J. Mommsen, 'Weder Leugnen noch Vergessen befreit von der Vergangenheit. Die "Harmonisierung" des Geschichtsbildes gefährdet die Freiheit', *FR*, 1 December 1986. Jürgen Kocka, 'Hitler sollte nicht durch Stalin und Pol Pot verdrängt werden. Über Versuche deutscher Historiker, die Ungeheuerlichkeit von NS-Verbrechen zu relativieren', *FR*, 23 September 1986. See in full length: Jürgen Kocka, 'Kritik und Identität. Nationalsozialismus, Alltag und Geographie', Neue Gesellschaft/Frankfurter Hefte, October 1986, pp. 890–7.

48. Kocka analyses in depth this old–new line of justification of the German *Sonderweg* (special path) which he sees as represented also by Michael Stürmer and Hagen Schultze.

49. Thomas Nipperdey, 'Unter der Herrschaft des Verdachts. Wissenschaftliche Aussagen dürfen nicht an ihrer politischen Funktion gemessen wenden', *Die Zeit*, 17 October 1986. See also the rejection of Habermas by the Berlin historian Hagen Schultze, 'Fragen, die wir stellen müssen. Keine historische Haftung ohne nationale Identität', *Die Zeit*, 26 September 1986. Also, the Erlangen historian Horst Möller, 'Es kann nicht sein, was nicht sein darf. Plädoyer für die Versachlichung der Kontroverse über Zeitgeschichte', *Beiträge zur Konfliktforschung*, No. 4 (1986), 146–51. Möller continues along the lines of making the non-historian Habermas seem ridiculous, owing to professional incompetence. With the emphasis on the important accomplishments of Nolte and Hillgruber, the questionable aspects of the recent publications are simply ignored. Are the above-quoted and recognized historians in their critique of Hillgruber and Nolte also simply incompetent and taking part 'in attempted slander' (Möller)?

50. See in this connection Herbert A. Strauss, 'Antisemitismus und Holocaust als Epochenproblem', *Aus Politik und Zeitgeschichte, Beilage zur Wochenzeitung Das Parlament*, 14 March 1987, pp. 15–23. The absurd idea of the extreme antisemitic right that the Jews could serve as hostages in order to exert pressure on the hostile 'international Jewry' found its counterpart (not only restricted to Jews) among the bourgeoisie. Strauss cites works by jurists of international law which regarded reprisals against civilians in occupied countries which even included their execution as legal. The two other essays in this magazine dedicated solely to the historians' debate — it can be obtained free of charge by the call number 'B 11/87' at the 'Bundeszentrale für politische Bildung', Berliner Freiheit 7, 5300 Bonn 1, Bundesrepublik Deutschland; as well as the book H. A. Strauss and N. Kampe, eds., *Antisemitismus. Von der Judenfeindschaft zum Holocaust* as Vol. 213 of the 'Schriftreihe (series) der Bundeszentrale' — are Karl Dietrich Bracher, 'Zeitgeschichtliche Erfahrung als aktuelles Problem', pp. 3–14 and Volker Berghahn, 'Geschichtswissenschaft und Große Politik', pp. 25–37.

51. See the well-documented psychoanalytic study of the literature of Free Corps members in Klaus Theweleit, *Männerphantasien*, 2 vols. (Frankfurt/M., 1977).

52. Christian Meier, 'Verurteilen und Verstehen. An einem Wendepunkt deutscher Geschichtserinnerung', *FAZ*, 28 June 1986. In retrospect, this lecture seems almost like an attempt to patch up the old consensus, that the self-image and politics of the Federal Republic are rooted in the acceptance of the moral responsibility for the NS-crimes. Armin Mohler, 'Nur ein negativer Nationalismus für die Deutschen?' (Letter to the Editor), *FAZ*, 19 July 1986, then also promptly criticizes the lack of 'precision of thought' of this 'quasi-officious' speech by Meier. His admission of 'responsibility' is only 'another name for "collective guilt"'. Meier makes fun of 'the words of the Chancellor which speak of the "grace of late(r) birth"'. According to Mohler those born after 1945 are

not permitted to enjoy the greatness and beauty of German history. Because of 'fundamentally unfulfillable demands' young people are being driven into 'foreign-nationalism' ('Nicaragua or Mandela') and becoming violent.

53. Christian Meier, 'Kein Schlußwort. Zum Streit um die NS-Vergangenheit', *FAZ*, 20 November 1986.

54. *FR*, 10 November 1986. Report from the conference of all Bavarian delegates of the C.S.U. in Munich.

55. See the public opinion poll of Renate Köcher, 'Der gefährliche Wunsch zu vergessen', *Stern*, No. 16 (1986), pp.33–5, 240.

56. Richard von Weizsäcker, *Zum 40. Jahrestag der Beendigung des Krieges in Europa und der nationalsozialistischen Gewaltherrschaft. Ansprache am 8. Mai 1985 in der Gedenkstunde im Plenarsaal des Deutschen Bundestages* (Bonn, 1985). This speech evoked an enormous echo in the German public, confused by polarization, in remembrance of the 40th anniversary of the end of the war. From the office of the *Bundespräsident* the text was ordered some 10,000 times.

Copyright Information

Salo W. Baron, "European Jewry Before and After Hitler," *American Jewish Yearbook*, 63 (1962), 3-49. © 1962, American Jewish Committee, New York, New York, USA.

Emil L. Fackenheim, "Concerning Authentic and Unauthentic Responses to the Holocaust," *Holocaust and Genocide Studies*, 1 (1986), 101-20. © 1986, Pergamon Press, Oxford, England.

Dan Magurshak, "The 'Incomprehensibility' of the Holocaust: Tightening Up Some Loose Usage," *Judaism*, 29 (1980), 233-42. © 1980, American Jewish Congress, New York, New York, USA.

Yehuda Bauer, "Against Mystification: The Holocaust as a Historical Phenomenon," in *The Holocaust in Historical Perspective*, (Seattle, 1978), 30-49 and notes, 159-161. © 1978, University of Washington Press, Seattle, Washington, USA.

Jacob Katz, "Was the Holocaust Predictable?" *Commentary*, May 1975, 41-48. © 1975, American Jewish Committee, New York, New York, USA, reprinted with the permission of the American Jewish Committee and the author.

Saul Friedländer, "Some Aspects of the Historical Significance of the Holocaust," *Jerusalem Quarterly*, (1976), 36-59. © 1976, Jerusalem Quarterly, Jerusalem, Israel.

Eugen Weber, "Jews, Antisemitism, and the Origins of the Holocaust," *Historical Reflections*, 5 (1978), 1-17. © 1978, University of Waterloo, Department of History, Historical Reflections Press, Waterloo, Ontario, Canada.

Uriel Tal, "On the Study of the Holocaust and Genocide," *Yad Vashem Studies*, XIII (1979), 7-52. © 1979, Yad Vashem, Jerusalem, Israel.

Yehuda Bauer, "The Place of the Holocaust in Contemporary History," *Studies in Contemporary Jewry*, 1 (1984), 210-24. © 1984, Yehuda Bauer, Institute of Contemporary Jewry, The Hebrew University of Jerusalem, Jerusalem, Israel.

Henry Friedlander, "Publications on the Holocaust," in *The German Church Struggle and the Holocaust*, edited by Franklin H. Littell and Hubert G. Locke, (Detroit, 1974), 69-94 (and notes at end). © 1974, Dr. Franklin Littell, Anne Frank Institute of Philadelphia, Philadelphia, Pennsylvania, USA.

Gerd Korman, "The Holocaust in American Historical Writing," *Societas*, 1 (1972), 251-270. © 1972, Gerd Korman, Cornell University, Ithaca, New York, USA.

Erich Goldhagen, "The Soviet Treatment of the Holocaust," *Midstream*, December 1979, 5-7. © 1979, Theodore Hertzl Foundation, Inc., New York, New York, USA, reprinted with permission of the Theodore Hertzl Foundation, Inc., and the author.

Konrad Kwiet, "Historians of the German Democratic Republic on Antisemitism

Index

Footnotes continued from "Against Mystification," by Yehuda Bauer, p. 117.

6. A. Roy Eckardt, "Is the Holocaust Unique," *Worldview*, Sept. 1974, pp. 21–35.

7. See, for instance, Uriel Tal, "On the Structure of Political Theology and Myth in Germany Prior to the Holocaust," lecture at "The Holocaust—A Generation After" conference, New York, March 1975.

8. Alex Bein, "The Jewish Parasite," in Leo Baeck Institute of Jews from Germany, *Leo Baeck Yearbook*, vol. 9 (London, 1964), pp. 3–39.

9. Norman Cohn, *Warrant for Genocide* (London: Eyre & Spottiswood, 1967).

10. See Elie Wiesel, "Talking and Writing and Keeping Silent," in *The German Church Struggle and the Holocaust*, ed. Franklin H. Littell and Hubert G. Locke (Detroit: Wayne State University Press, 1974), p. 272.

11. Cf. for instance Mark Arnold-Foster, *The World at War* (London: Collins, 1973), p. 293.

12. On the so-called "AB-Aktion" against the Polish intelligentsia and other such actions, see Martin Broszat, *Nationalsozialistische Polenpolitik* (Stuttgart, 1961), pp. 38–48, 182–87.

13. Reimund Schnabel, *Macht ohne Moral* (Frankfurt, 1957), p. 404.

14. Raphael Lemkin, *Axis Rule in Occupied Europe* (1943; reprint ed., New York: Howard Fertig, 1973), pp. xi–xii.

15. I. Caban and Z. Mańkowski, *Związek Walki Zbrojnej i Armia Krajowa w Okręgu Lubelskim,* 1939–1944, tom II, Dokumenty, Lublin, 1968, pp. 504–5.

16. Used at the Inter-University Seminar for the Study of Contemporary Jewry, August 1977, Jerusalem. Franklin H. Littell uses the term "alpine event" in much the same sense—see his *The Crucifixion of the Jews* (New York: Harper & Row, 1975), p. 2. Cf. also Fackenheim's *God's Presence in History* (New York: Harper & Row, 1972).

17. See also, Paul Rassinier, *Le Drame des Juifs Européens* (Paris, 1964).

18. Heinz Roth, *Why Are We Being Lied To* (Witten, 1975); Manfred Roeder, Introduction to Thies Christophersen, *Die Auschwitz-Luege* (Mohrkirch, 1970).

19. United Nations Security Council, S/PV, 1897, March 1976.

20. *New York Times,* 8 October 1977.

21. A. R. Butz, *The Hoax of the Twentieth Century* (Los Angeles: Noontide, 1977).

22. Jiří Bohátka, Třídní Význam Sionismu," two articles in *Tribuna, KSČ týdeník pro politiku a ideologii* (Prague, 1976).

23. See note 20 above.

24. See note 16 above.

25. David Irving, *Hitler's War* (New York: Viking, 1977).

26. Joachim C. Fest, "Revision des Hitlerbildes?" *Frankfurter Allgemeine Zeitung,* 29 July 1977.

27. Lucy S. Dawidowicz, *The War Against the Jews, 1933–1945* (New York: Holt, Rinehart and Winston, 1975).

28. Adolf Hitler, *Hitler's Zweites Buch* (Stuttgart, 1961), pp. 158–59, 220 [in English: *Hitler's Secret Book* (New York, 1962)].

29. Geoffrey Barraclough, *An Introduction to Contemporary History* (Harmondsworth, England: Penguin Books, 1968).

30. Testimony of Yehiel Dinur at the Eichmann trial, in Eduyot, *Mayoetz Hamishpati Lamemshalah neged Adolf Eichmann* (Jerusalem, 1963), pp. 122–23.

31. Cf. Abba Kovner's "Di Shlihes fun di Letzte," a speech delivered on 17 July 1945 at his first meeting with the Palestinian Jewish soldiers in the British army at Tarvisio, Italy. This has been published in a Hebrew translation in Yalkut Moreshet, no. 17 (April 1973), pp. 35–42. An English translation will appear in "The Holocaust—A Generation After," referred to in note 2 above.